aws

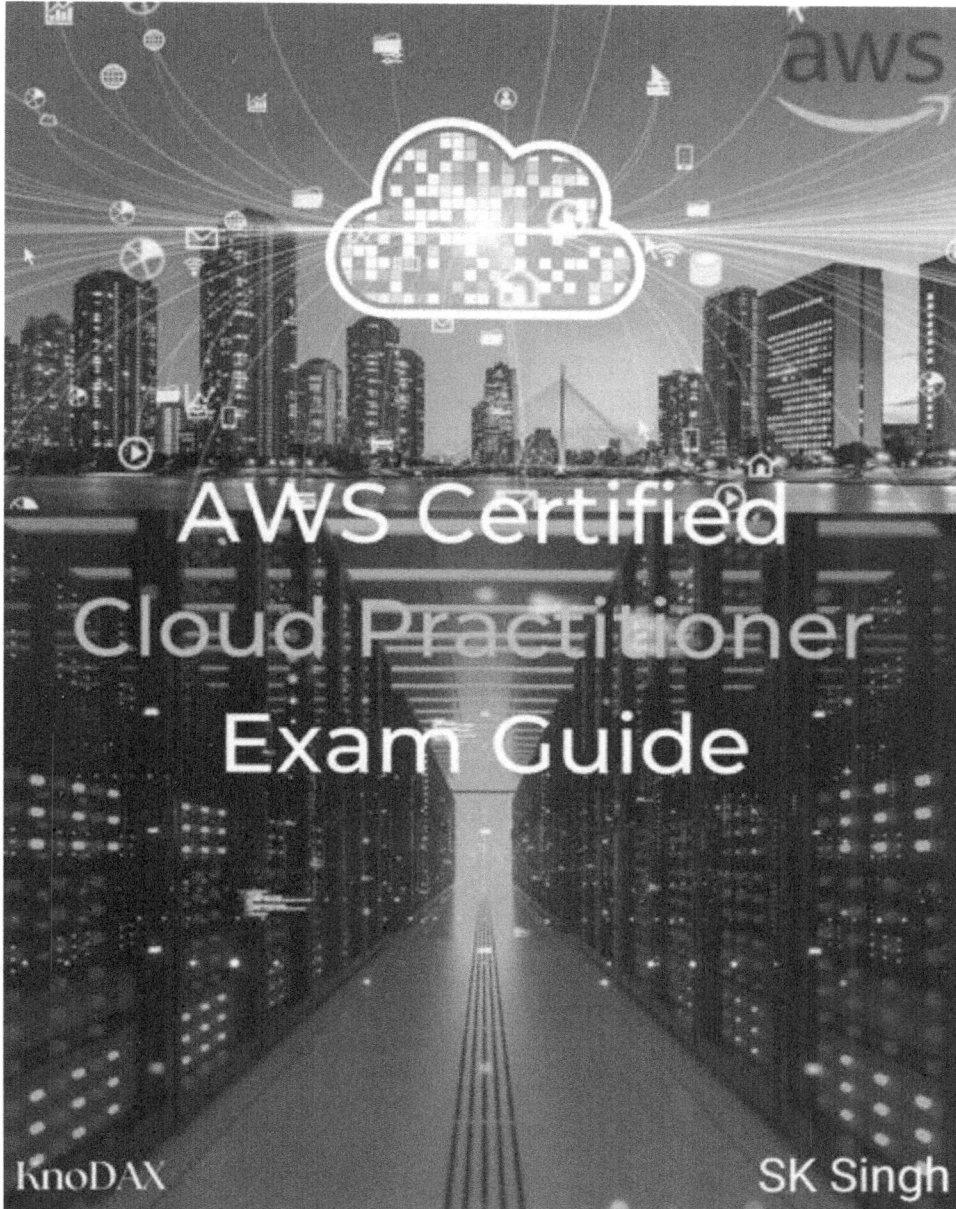

AWS Certified
Cloud Practitioner
Exam Guide

KnoDAX

SK Singh

Table of Contents

SECTION 6. CONTAINER & CI/CD   347

CHAPTER 26. CONTAINER   348

CHAPTER 27. AWS CI/CD SERVICES   362

Introduction

The purpose of the book is the help you pass the AWS Cloud Certified Practitioner exam. The book covers topics for all domains. Knowledge gained from this book will help you in other AWS certification exams as well.

To make understanding the subject a smoother experience, the book is divided into the following sections:
- Cloud Computing
- AWS Fundamentals
- AWS Advanced
- AWS RDS and Databases
- Serverless
- Containers & CI/CD
- Data & Analytics
- Machine Learning
- Security
- Networking
- Disaster Management
- Cloud Architecture
- Practice Tests

Please read the chapters in sequence. If you already know a chapter, at least go through the key points and diagrams/pictures (screenshots) in that chapter.

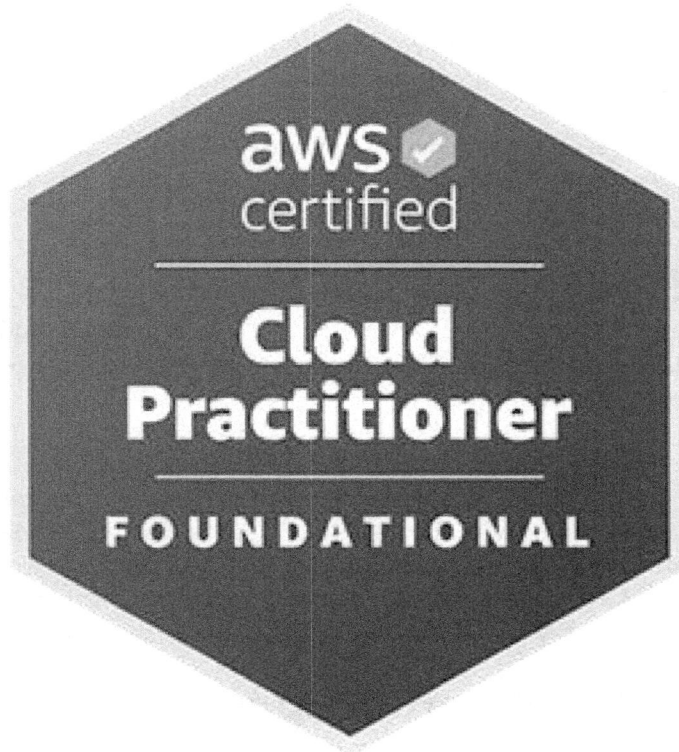

Chapter 1. Becoming an AWS Certified Cloud Practitioner

You will learn the following in this chapter:
- Why AWS Certified Cloud Practitioner (CCP) is a valuable cloud certification
- How to get AWS CCP certification
- High level overview of all domains covered in the exam

Whether we use Facebook, Twitter, Gmail, Zoom (for meetings), or Citrix server (to connect to the workplace remotely), cloud computing is everywhere around us. If we pay little attention, there are countless examples of cloud computing in our day-to-day life. The cloud computing has created titanic shift happening in how organizations used to have their IT infrastructure in 90s and compare to how the new trend which is: adoption to cloud.

The change in how cloud is being adopted in IT infrastructure, causing another type of change which is need for cloud applications of different types. In other words, now we need engineers who can build application that can be much easily deployed and managed on cloud. Developing cloud applications require different type of architect, design and programming skills than the skills needed for traditional classic client-server or monolithic applications.

Not only architecting, designing, and developing, new trend is occurring – it's already here -- how system administrator and technical operations engineers used to work – which is mainly dealt with

OS and network level operations and scripting. Now the new DevOps engineers not only have the role of developer but also of system admin operations which is build and deploy the application. What it means software industry needs now more DevOps engineers as well.

Based on the above discussion we can see that how software (also called by many "IT") industry needs cloud engineers of different types who can architect, design, build, deploy and manage cloud applications and cloud infrastructure.

Why Get Certified in AWS?

Though there are many cloud providers but AWS has been leader in the cloud computing industry based on the Gartner Magic Quadrant for Cloud Infrastructure & Platform Services AWS has over million customers in more that 200 countries.

As AWS is used by many types of organizations all over the world, this is creating more employment opportunities for people having AWS skills. The question is when hiring how employer can have some kind of proof that the engineer who they are interviewing has the AWS skills or not. In other words, having AWS certifications increases likelihood of not only getting interviews but also getting hired. In addition, because AWS exams are hard, having AWS certification, generates lots of self-confidence in making difference in your team and organizations with your AWS skills.

How to Get AWS CCP Certification?

Though there is no pre-condition for the certification exam, the target candidate should have 6 months of active engagement with AWS cloud platform with exposure of AWS Cloud design, implementation and/or operations. That's the reason, it is recommended or rather extremely important to have hands-on experience with AWS platform before taking the exam.

The candidate should have knowledge of AWS Cloud concepts, security and compliance with AWS Cloud, understanding of AWS core services, understanding of AWS economics of the AWS cloud.

The exam specifically mentions what are items are considered out of the scope for the exam. These are coding, designing cloud architecture, troubleshooting, implementation, migration, load and performance testing, and business application such as Amazon Arora, Amazon Chime, Amazon WorkMail.

The exam contains two types of questions: multiple choice in which there will be one correct answer, and multiple response in which there will be 2 or more correct answers. The unanswered questions are marked as incorrect and there is no negative marking for wrong answers. The exam contains 50 questions, which affects your score. In addition, there will be additional 15 questions that will not affect scores. AWS uses response of unanswered questions to make its quiz more better in future. Exam report is scaled and the minimum passing score is 700.

AWS CCP Exam Domains

The AWS CCP exam asks questions from the four domains and percentage of questions asked in each domain varies. The table below represents name of each domain and percentage of questions that are asked from each domain.

Domain	% of Exam
Domain 1: Cloud Concepts	26%

Domain 2: Security and Compliance	25%
Domain 3: Technology	33%
Domain 4: Billing and Pricing	16%
Total	100%

Let's see what the different topics are covered in each domain with respect to exam.

Domain 1: Cloud Concepts

This domain includes introduction to AWS and what value proposition AWS cloud provide to its customers which includes not only business value but also quality attributes such as security, reliability, high availability etc. to the deployed applications. Besides what value AWS provides, this domain also includes aspects of AWS cloud economics such as role of operational expenses (OpEx), role of capital expenses (CapEx), costs associated with on-premises data center operations, impact of cost of software licensing when moving to the cloud, and which operations costs will be reduced because of moving to cloud. Finally, this domain covers design and architecture aspect of cloud. It includes different design principles related to cloud architecture such as design for failure, decoupled vs monolithic architecture, implementation of elasticity, parallelism.

Domain 2: Security and Compliance

This domain includes AWS shared responsibility model which is about what the customer's responsibilities are and what the responsibilities are of AWS. For example, AWS provides virtual machine but who will be responsible for applying patches or who will be responsible for maintenance of launched virtual machine for example backup of data or maintenance of software installed. This domain also covers how AWS manages security of applications deployed on AWS cloud and what types of compliance certification AWS cloud has received. In addition, this domain also covers how users, and their identities are managed on the AWS platform. For example, how to manage users, groups and their permissions using Identity and Access Management (IAM), how to secure AWS account using concept called multi-factor authentication (MFA), what is AWS root account and protection of AWS root account. Additionally, this domain includes different documentation such as best practices, whitepapers, official documents, and such and how to find them. Finally, it covers how to secure resources using different network security capabilities (Network ACLs, AWS WAF) and 3rd party security products form the AWS Marketplace, and AWS Trusted Advisor.

Domain 3: Technology

This domain covers technology aspect of AWS platform such as different methods of deploying and operating in the AWS Cloud, understanding AWS global infrastructure, core AWS services, and resources for technology related support. With regards to deploying and operating in the AWS Cloud, it includes different deployment models, connectivity options; and different ways of provisioning and operating such as programmatic access, AWS API, AWS SDK, AWS Management Console, and AWS CLI. With regards to AWS cloud infrastructure, it includes understanding and how to use AWS regions, availability zones and other related concepts depending on the use cases. Finally, with regards to AWS core services, it includes compute (EC2, Lambda, ECS, Autoscaling), storage (S3, EBS, Glacier, Snowball, EFS, Storage Gateway), network (VPC, Route 53, VPN, Direct Connect), and database (RDS, RedShift, DynamoDB) related services.

Domain 4: Billing and Pricing

This domain includes compare and contrast of various pricing models for AWS, various account structure (consolidated and multiple accounts), and billing support related resources. With respect to pricing models, it includes On-Demand Instance pricing, Reserved-Instance pricing, and Spot Instance pricing. With respect to billing support, it includes different ways to get billing and support information such as Cost Explorer, AWS Cost and Usage Report, opening billing support case, and the role of the Concierge for AWS Enterprise Support Plan customers. It also includes where to find pricing information on AWS services such as AWS Simple Monthly Calculator, AWS Services product pages, AWS Pricing API. And finally, it includes alarms and alerts notification and how to use tags in cost allocation.

To summarize, this chapter we covered motivation and value of getting AWS CCP certification, and then we discussed about to how to get AWS CCP certification including number of questions and passing scores. Then we discussed different domains how much percentage of questions are asked from each domain. And then finally, we talked in detail about topics included in each domain. You can find detail further detail about the AWS CCP exam at https://d1.awsstatic.com/training-and-certification/docs-cloud-practitioner/AWS-Certified-Cloud-Practitioner_Exam-Guide.pdf.

References:

- https://d1.awsstatic.com/training-and-certification/docs-cloud-practitioner/AWS-Certified-Cloud-Practitioner_Exam-Guide.pdf
- https://www.zdnet.com/article/the-top-cloud-providers-of-2021-aws-microsoft-azure-google-cloud-hybrid-saas/
- https://aws.amazon.com/blogs/aws/aws-named-as-a-leader-for-the-11th-consecutive-year-in-2021-gartner-magic-quadrant-for-cloud-infrastructure-platform-services-cips/
- https://www.yahoo.com/video/15-biggest-companies-aws-011011152.html

Section 1. Cloud Computing

Chapter 2. Cloud Computing Introduction

You will learn the following in this chapter:
- Traditional IT infrastructure
- What is cloud computing
- Cloud computing related terms
- Cloud computing benefits / key features
- Software quality attributes in cloud computing

AWS is a leading cloud provider -- according to the 2021 Gartner Magic Quadrant for Cloud Infrastructure & Platform Services -- with over a million customers of different types in around 200 countries.

AWS or any cloud provider's underpinning architecture is based on cloud computing. Therefore, the first and most important learning is to build solid foundational and conceptual understanding of cloud computing as a cloud practitioner. But before starting cloud computing, we need to discuss some background, mainly traditional IT infrastructure, the reasoning, and motivation for the emergence of cloud computing.

Traditional IT infrastructure

In the late 90s, with the dot com boom, we saw so many startups. Some of them have become big names now, such as Amazon, Google. However, most of those startups have started from the so-called garage.

First, they started with a few servers. Then, as their user base started increasing, they needed more servers to scale up their business.

To handle the scalability issue, or in other words, to maintain system performance with the matching workload, they moved their server infrastructure from garage to office, where they set up their servers in a so-called computer room or server room. That helped them overcome network bandwidth, power supply, and AC challenges when running the business with more servers.

When the user base increased further, they needed to scale further again. To manage the scalability issue this time, they moved their servers or IT infrastructure to data centers. These data centers have more computing resources, power, air conditioning, security, and other related things that run 24x7 operations of 100s or 1000s servers.

But still, there are challenges and issues with data centers -- what are those? And is there a better solution for this? Let's talk about them.

Depending on how much space you require for your servers, it costs a lot. And there are reasons for the cost as data centers provide 24 x 7 power supply, AC, maintenance, and security. So, it's obvious there will be a cost to all these services.

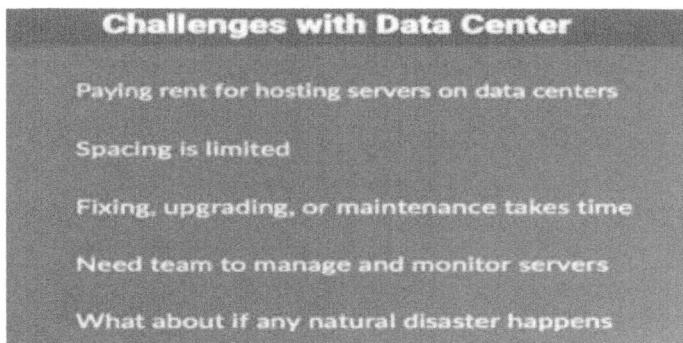

Challenges with Data Center

- Paying rent for hosting servers on data centers
- Spacing is limited
- Fixing, upgrading, or maintenance takes time
- Need team to manage and monitor servers
- What about if any natural disaster happens

There is limited space – each data centers have some limited capacity. Even though data centers have a vast area, the space is limited. If you need to upgrade servers or do some maintenance, you will have to go to the data center (in many cases) to replace the part or upgrade, etc. You also need to manage and maintain servers 24x7. There is a single point of failure. What if any natural disaster happens?

So, the bigger general question is -- do we have any solution for all these challenges? Is there any other solution besides leveraging data centers for IT infrastructure? And the answer is: Cloud Computing.

So, let's start with cloud computing.

What is Cloud Computing?

Whether we use Facebook, Twitter, Gmail, Zoom (for meetings), or Citrix server (to connect to the workplace remotely), cloud computing is everywhere around us. If we pay little attention, there are countless examples of cloud computing in our day-to-day life. That being the case, you might have an obvious question: what cloud computing is.

Before understanding the term **cloud computing**, it is important to know about the word **"cloud"** as this is an interesting word in this term. Interestingly, the word **"cloud"** in the term cloud computing is not related to the literal "cloud"-- at all. **Instead, the word "cloud" in cloud computing is a metaphor for the Internet.** Thus, cloud (as a metaphor for Internet) computing refers to Internet-based computing in which IT resources are delivered on-demand with pay-as-you-go pricing model.

Screenshot Reference: https://aws.amazon.com/what-is-cloud-computing/

Screenshot Reference: https://aws.amazon.com/what-is-cloud-computing/

Let's talk about a formal definition of cloud computing. According to Special Publication SP 800 – 145 [Sept 2011, Peter Mell (NIST), Tim Grance (NIST)] from The National Institute of Standards and Technology (NIST) of the United States.

Cloud computing is a model for enabling ubiquitous, convenient, on-demand network access to a shared pool of configurable computing resources (e.g., networks, servers, storage, applications, and services) that can be rapidly provisioned and released with minimal management effort or service provider interaction. This cloud model is composed of five essential characteristics, three service models, and four deployment models.

There are some keywords to notice in the NIST definition of cloud computing. These are: *on-demand network access, shared pool of configurable computing resources, rapidly provisioned and released.* On the other hand, in the traditional classic on-premises data center, the computing, storage, and network resources are bought, set up, and permanently configured by the customers in maximum capacity regardless of how much the actual need for help is.

Depending on the business season, this resource allocation may be less. In that case, resources are wasted. However, there is also a possibility that the resources cannot meet demand. In that case, there is the chance of reducing service quality and the risk of losing customers because of quality concerns. There is no demand concept, sharing of the resource pool, and rapid on-demand provision in a classic on-premises data center.

Another important point to keep in mind is that cloud computing is predicated upon the idea of purchasing "services" based on the needs of customers -- on-demand -- and stop, close the service, or terminate when you are done with the usage.

Using cloud computing, organizations (cloud computing providers) offer services such as virtual machines (compute resource that uses software instead of a physical computer), virtual storage (storage pool formed by combining multiple network storage devices), and many other types of software applications (or services) over the Internet.

For example, if you would like to set up a Linux virtual machine, and if you have an account with a cloud provider, you can launch it within a few minutes – just by using the web browser. And start using the Linux VM as you would use any regular physical Linux machine, such as setting up a web server, database, or any other regular use of Linux machine you do.

In addition to virtual servers, cloud computing providers can also offer virtual storage. For example, if you need extra storage to store large collection of media files, you can use cloud computing provider's storage service to store them – very fast. You just need an account with the cloud provider and a web browser -- no need to shop around to buy the storage and waste additional time to set up the device, such as installing a driver before using the storage. On the other hand, using cloud computing, cloud computing users such as organizations can develop and offer software applications (for example, Gmail, Office365, Facebook) or other related services.

In the above discussion, we learned about the term **cloud computing, cloud computing providers, and cloud computing users.**

Based on the above discussion, we can see that to launch a virtual machine or get virtual storage, we only need an account with the cloud provider and a web browser. In other words, cloud computing offerings (the common term is services) are provided over the Internet.

Talking about hardware in cloud computing,, in general, there is nothing special about hardware. Cloud computing's underpinning hardware is the same type of physical server, storage, and network used in on-prem datacenters.

Then, the question comes how cloud computing differs from classic (non-cloud) computing.

cloud architecture enables cloud providers to organize and consolidate massive hardware

The main difference is that cloud computing uses cloud architecture. The cloud architecture enables technology components to combine to help build a cloud that can perform resource pooling through virtualization – running virtual machines as an abstraction layer over a physical machine. In other words, cloud architecture helps organize and consolidate massive hardware such as computing resources, storage, and network -- to form resource pooling – and make it available over the Internet.

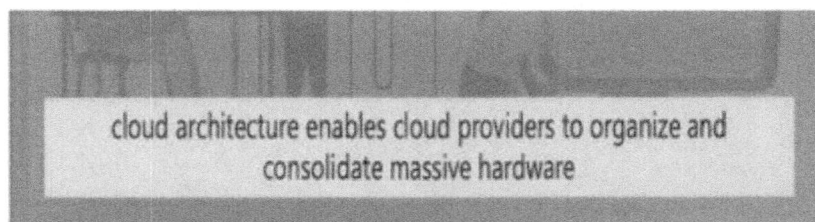

You may be thinking why there is so much talk about cloud computing. As you have noticed in the above discussion, cloud computing has many advantages. One aspect of the advantages is, though organizations have been developing, delivering, and managing software for many decades, cloud computing has made this process of developing, delivering, and managing software to end users -- globally --much faster and relatively cheaper (cheaper may not always be true).

The reason is that hardware infrastructure, software tools, and other whole hosts of things required for software development, testing, and deployment can be easily and quickly acquired and set up very fast. Additionally, it could be less expensive --- cloud providers nowadays offer various pricing models.

Though cloud computing has many advantages, it may not be appropriate for all use cases. Therefore, you will still need to do your cost-benefit analysis if cloud computing is fruitful for your use case or organization.

Cloud Computing Related Terms

Before talking about cloud computing features, service models, deployment models, let's talk about some other cloud computing terms and roles as these terms and roles may be used later. It's better to be equipped with the knowledge of these cloud computing terms and cloud computing roles as these terms are commonly used in cloud computing talks and books.

Cloud Computing Platform

The back-end system providing services is called a cloud computing platform.

Cloud Services (Web Services)

Services provided by the cloud computing platform are called cloud services, for example, Gmail, Office365.

Cloud Services definition which is based on ISO/IEC 17788, "Cloud Computing – Overview and Vocabulary":

One or more capabilities offered via **cloud computing** invoked using a defined interface.

Cloud Computing Platform Provider

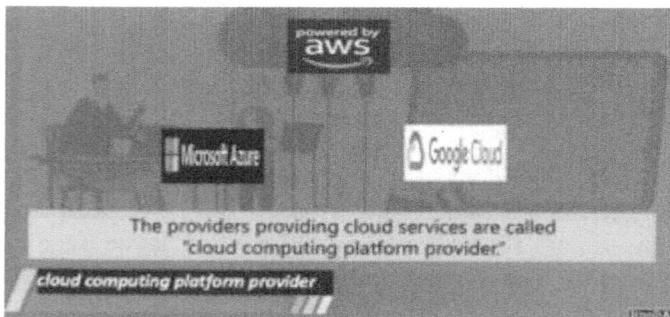

Another related term to know is cloud computing platform provider. Cloud providers such as AWS, Google, Microsoft, IBM, Oracle, Salesforce, SAP, and others that provide cloud services from their cloud computing platform are called cloud computing platform providers (also commonly called cloud services providers or cloud providers). AWS, Google, Microsoft are the leading cloud computing platform providers.

As a side note, sometimes you will notice that the word "computing" may be missing in some casual or informal discussion of cloud computing. For example, you might hear cloud service(s) as opposed to cloud computing service(s), cloud provider(s) as opposed to cloud computing provider(s), or cloud platform(s) as opposed to cloud computing platform(s). But that doesn't change their semantics.

Below some other cloud computing related terms and their definitions are given. These definitions are based on ISO/IEC 17788, "Cloud Computing – Overview and Vocabulary."

Availability

Property of being accessible and usable upon demand by an authorized entity.

Confidentiality

Property that information is not made available or disclosed to unauthorized individuals, entities, or processes

Integrity

Property of accuracy and completeness.

Information Security

Preservation of confidentiality, integrity, and availability of information. In addition, other properties, such as authenticity, accountability, non-repudiation, and reliability can also be involved.

Service Level Agreement (SLA)

Documented agreement between the service provider and customer that identifies services and service targets. A service level agreement can also be established between the service provider and a supplier, an internal group or a customer acting as a supplier. A service level agreement can be included in a contract or another type of documented agreement.

Cloud Application

An application that does not reside or run on a user's device, but rather is accessible via a network.

Cloud Service Provider

Party (Natural person or legal person, whether or not incorporated, or a group of either) which makes cloud services available.

Cloud Service Customer

Party (Natural person or legal person, whether or not incorporated, or a group of either) which is in a business relationship for the purpose of using cloud services

Cloud Service User

Natural person, or entity acting on their behalf, associated with a cloud service customer that uses cloud services. Examples of such entities include devices and applications.

Measured service

Metered delivery of cloud services such that usage can be monitored, controlled, reported and billed.

Tenant

One or more cloud customers sharing access to a pool of resources.

Multi-tenancy

Allocation of physical or virtual resources such that multiple tenants and their computations and data are isolated from and inaccessible to one another.

On-demand Self-service

Feature where a cloud service customer can provision computing capabilities, as needed, automatically or with minimal interaction with the cloud service provider.

Resource pooling

Aggregation of a cloud service provider's physical or virtual resources to serve one or more cloud service customers.

Cloud Computing Benefits / Key Features

Let's talk about key features of a cloud computing platform. Let's discuss each of these features in a little detail.

Agility

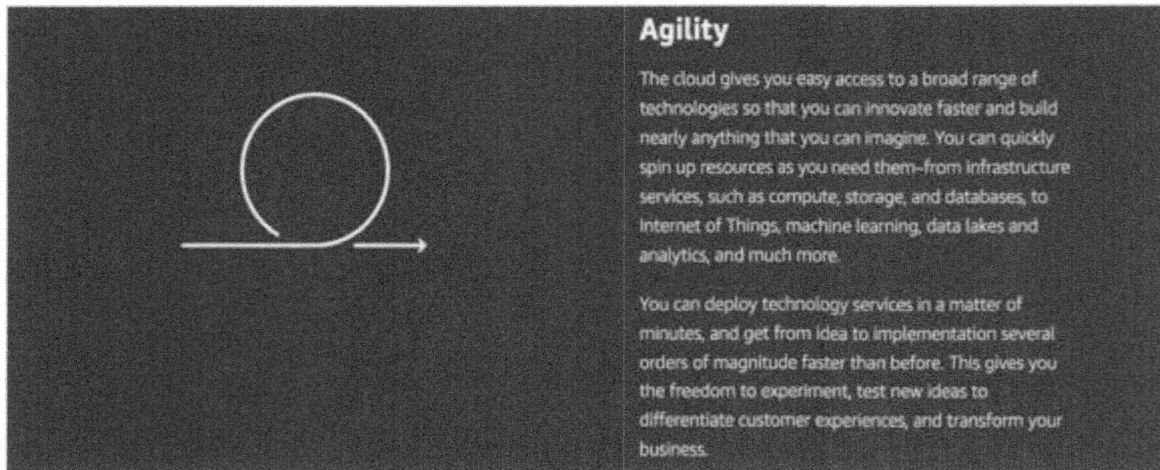

Screenshot Reference: https://aws.amazon.com/what-is-cloud-computing/

Offering a broad range of technologies on-demand by cloud providers to its customers is one of the key features of cloud computing. The most common mechanism to offer on-demand services is using Web UI. This is not the only way; the other ways are APIs, Command Line Interface (CLI), and the programmatic way, such as using SDK. If you take an example of AWS, AWS users can launch services from using Web UI, AWS API, AWS CLI, and AWS SDK.

Network Access

Network access, more specifically Internet access, is another key feature of cloud computing. In other words, a cloud provider must offer services over the Internet to be called a true cloud provider.

Resource Pooling

Another key feature of cloud computing is resource pooling. In fact, the main driver for cloud computing innovation was how to efficiently utilize a vast pool of idle resources and generate a business model for it. Cloud providers create a resource pool of compute, storage, and network resource of different types, shapes, and sizes and provide offerings from the resource pool based on what has been requested. The beauty of this is that when the resource is released from the customer, it goes back to the resource pool and is ready to be served to another customer.

Elasticity

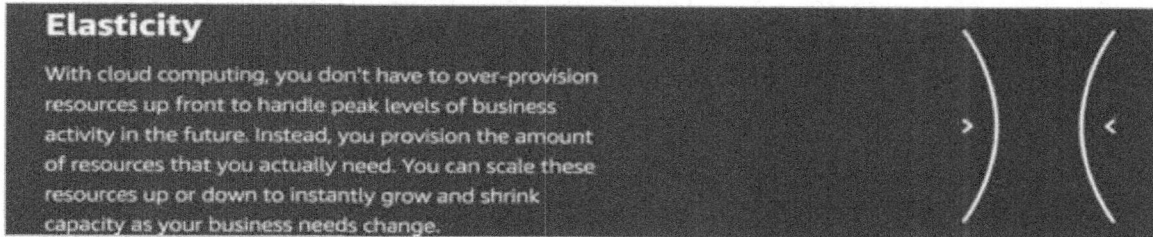

Screenshot Reference: https://aws.amazon.com/what-is-cloud-computing/

In cloud computing, you will come across the term *elastic* a lot. For example, AWS has many services that include the term *elastic* in its name, for example, Elastic Compute Cloud, Elastic Load Balancer, Elastic Block Storage, Elastic MapReduce.

The term *elastic* in cloud computing is sort of analogous to an elastic band. You can stretch an elastic band size beyond its rest state; when you let it go, it will return to its resting size. This elastic concept -- going back to its resting size when we let it go from its stretched state -- is extremely useful in cloud computing.

Let's take an example to understand the term *elastic* as it relates to cloud computing on AWS. The hypothetical use case is related to setting up a scalable web server. We set up the webserver with a minimum of 3, and a maximum of 6 EC2 instances. Each EC2 instance will be launched using a custom AMI to launch Apache webserver. We have also configured AWS Elastic Load Balancer to launch additional EC2 instances if CPU utilization for an EC2 instance reaches above 70% on AWS Cloud Watch – maximum up to six instances. And terminate the EC2 instance when the CPU utilization comes down to less than 70% -- minimum up to three instances. As you can see, we have set up a scalable and -- elastic -- web server.

Metered Service
Metered Service is very important feature of cloud computing. This concept is very similar to what we have already experienced such as paying for gas utility bill based on number of units of energy consumed or parking meter bill based on vehicle parking time.

There are many examples of metered service in our daily life. The metered service of cloud computing is one of key drivers that cloud computing is so popular today in technology – you pay what you use, how much you use.

Cost savings

The cloud allows you to trade fixed expenses (such as data centers and physical servers) for variable expenses, and only pay for IT as you consume it. Plus, the variable expenses are much lower than what you would pay to do it yourself because of the economies of scale.

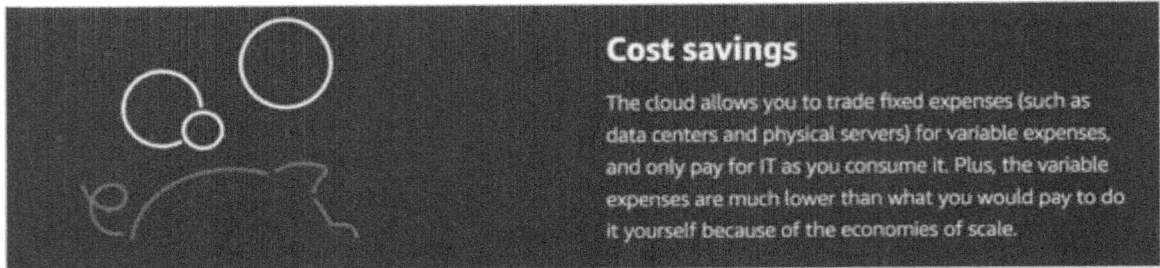

Screenshot Reference: https://aws.amazon.com/what-is-cloud-computing/

Let's try to understand with a concrete example of metered service in cloud computing. Say you need around 3TB storage to store some videos for a month – maybe to share with your friends or relatives or try out some new business model.

Let's first see how we can do without leveraging a cloud computing solution. We would try to find a machine with 3TB space available and then upload videos on this server, and then we also need to make sure to have this machine available on the Internet. Sounds easy, technically – right?

How much would it cost? It depends on how much your rate is and the billable hour. Of course, in real life, you will not calculate it – but there is a hidden cost to doing all this setup. In some cases, you may not have the hardware or have the hardware but not have the storage space. There is also the possibility that you may have an Internet connection issue. You get the idea that to get just 3TB storage space to share your videos with your friends and relatives sounds a bit of involved work technically.

Now let's see how easy to set up this use case on the cloud. We will consider AWS storage service S3 (you will learn later about S3). So, the question is how you would set up this use case. You register with AWS if you have. Once you have an account with AWS, you find an S3 service, create a bucket and upload all your videos on the bucket. You will get an URL that you can share with your friends. You pay based on how long you have videos on the S3, how much the storage usage is, and what AWS pricing is. Usually, it is per GB / month.

With the metered service feature, you pay for the cloud services based on your usage and pricing. This is a very attractive feature of the cloud as it saves lots of cost in many use cases for almost all organizations and individuals trying out or learning the cloud.

Deploy Globally in Minutes

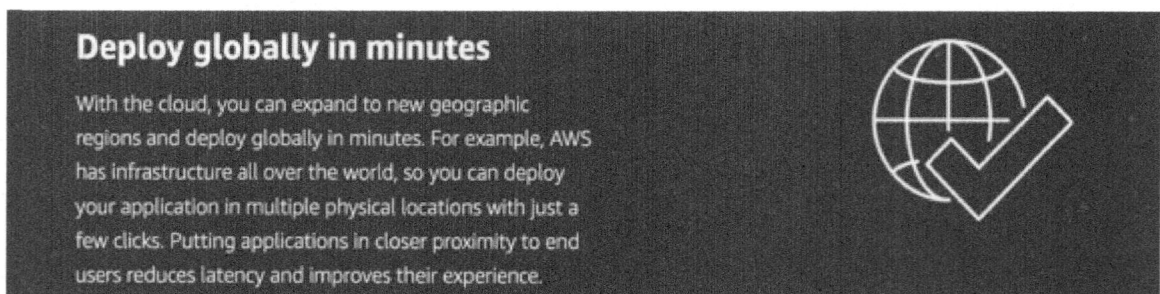

Deploy globally in minutes

With the cloud, you can expand to new geographic regions and deploy globally in minutes. For example, AWS has infrastructure all over the world, so you can deploy your application in multiple physical locations with just a few clicks. Putting applications in closer proximity to end users reduces latency and improves their experience.

Screenshot Reference: https://aws.amazon.com/what-is-cloud-computing/

Another advantage of cloud computing is the ability to make applications available worldwide within a few minutes.

Organizations can now quickly deploy their applications to multiple locations around the world with just a few clicks. This allows organizations to provide redundancy across the globe and reduce the application's latency.

Having redundant deployment across the globe helps increase applications availability. In addition, reducing network latency helps improve applications' network performance. The availability and reduced network latency translate applications' degree of usability and the organization's customers' footprint. And the critical point is that the organizations using cloud computing get these at a minimal cost and time.

There is one important point to bring to attention, which is the level playing field. Going global was very expensive in terms of cost and process. Only the organizations having deep pockets could afford to do. But cloud computing makes the deployment of applications globally – a level playing field. With cloud computing, any organization can deploy its applications globally at minimal cost and time.

Multitenancy

Multitenancy is another key feature of cloud computing. Let's understand this feature in a little detail.

What is Multitenancy? Multitenancy is a software architecture where multiple end-users or multiple distinct user groups can use an instance of a single software. SaaS software, such as Salesforce, Google Gmail, Microsoft Office 365, and TurboTax are typical examples of multi-tenancy.

Let's see what single tenancy is. This will further solidify understanding of multitenancy.

As the name suggests, it is the opposite of multitenancy. In a single tenant, each end-user or each group of users uses its software instance. There are plenty of examples. Let's take an example of tax software, for instance, TurboTax software has its SaaS version. They also have their old classic desktop version, which you can buy and install and use as a single user or single tenant. The typing software can be another example. There are many SaaS software to practice typing, but you can also purchase a single-tenant desktop version of typing software.

The multitenancy concept is not new. In the mainframe era, which was around the 1960s. At that time to share mainframe computing resources among multiple users, timeshare software was used. Cloud computing now uses the same multitenancy idea to allow sharing of computing resources – particularly in the public cloud computing deployment model. The pool of computing resources – processing power and memory – is divided among multiple users or multitenant in the public cloud. This multitenancy is at the server level.

Multitenancy saves costs and enables flexibility. With respect to saving cost advantage, the reason is apparent. Since the computing resources are consolidated and shared among multiple users or clients, this sharing helps lower costs for individual users in a multitenant environment.

For example, if you are using the TurboTax SaaS version instead of the TurboTax Desktop or single-tenant version, using the SaaS version software for tax filing is much cheaper than buying the TurboTax desktop single-tenant software.

Another advantage of multitenancy is that it enables flexibility. As we know, doing estimation is a challenging exercise. If you over-provision, the cost will go high. On the other hand, if you under-provision, then your output will suffer. But in a multitenant environment, you only pay for what you use. Also, you would be free to manage the resources, such as applying patches and securing them, as the provider takes care of resource management.

References:
https://www.zdnet.com/article/the-top-cloud-providers-of-2021-aws-microsoft-azure-google-cloud-hybrid-saas/
https://aws.amazon.com/what-is-cloud-computing/

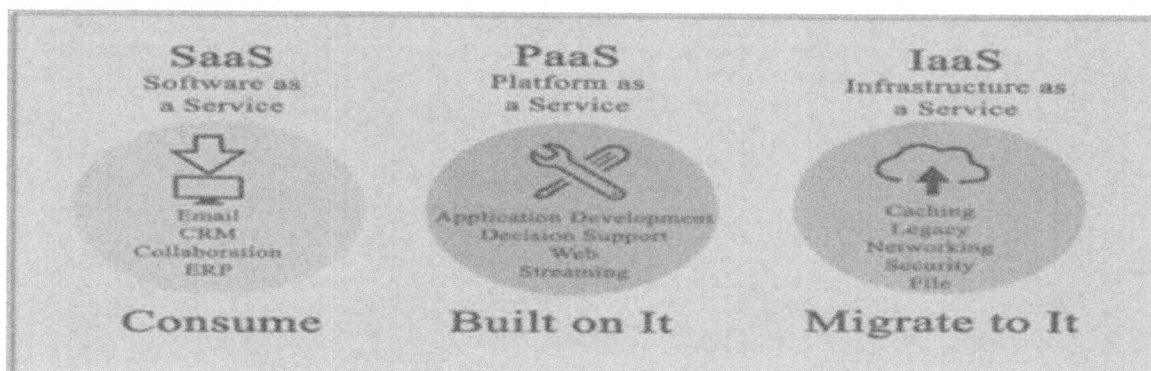

SaaS Software as a Service	PaaS Platform as a Service	IaaS Infrastructure as a Service
Email CRM Collaboration ERP	Application Development Decision Support Web Streaming	Caching Legacy Networking Security File
Consume	**Built on It**	**Migrate to It**

Chapter 3. Cloud Computing Types

You will learn the following in this chapter:
- Infrastructure-as-a-Service (IaaS)
- Platform-as-a-Service (PaaS)
- Software-as-a-Service (SaaS)
- Function-as-a-Service (FaaS)
- Scope of Responsibility – how the responsibilities are shared by the cloud provider and the customer in various cloud computing types

---

There are many names to this term -- cloud computing service categories, cloud service categories, cloud computing delivery models, cloud delivery models, cloud computing platform types, cloud platform types, cloud computing types -- and it's difficult to say which is more or most common. In this book, you may find any of these terms, but they all mean the same. With this note, let's start understanding about this topic.

A cloud computing platform is a back-end system that provides services over the Internet. The question is what kind of services the platform provides. For example, does the cloud computing platform provide Gmail, Office 365? Does it provide virtual servers, virtual storage? Or, does the cloud computing platform offer database services over the internet?

Depending on the cloud computing platform's kind of service, it has been categorized into a type. This categorization is called cloud computing platform types or cloud computing types.

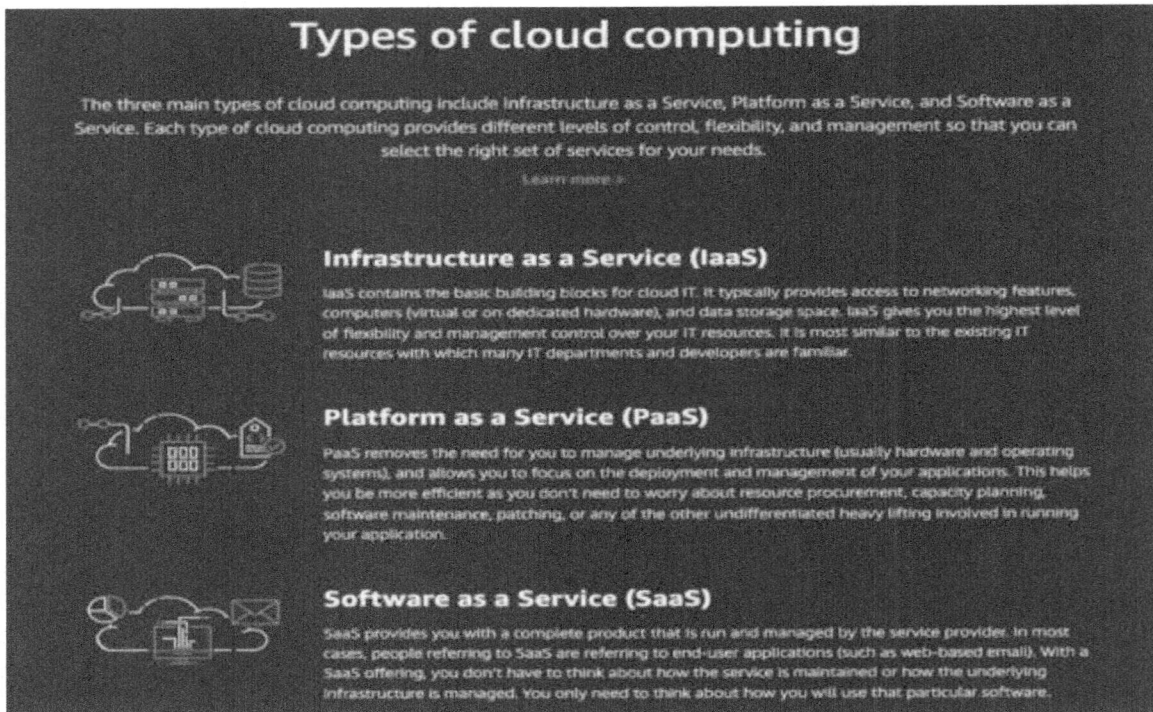

Screenshot reference: https://aws.amazon.com/what-is-cloud-computing/

Continuing further on our discussion about cloud computing platforms: cloud computing platform, the back-end system providing services, is a general term. To be more specific, there are three main types of cloud computing platforms: Infrastructure-as-a-Service (IaaS), Platform-as-a-Service (PaaS), and Software-as-a-Service (SaaS).

In addition to these main ones, other modern cloud computing platform types have emerged recently, such as Data-as-a-Service (DaaS), Desktop-as-a-Service, and Function-as-a-Service (FaaS). These modern cloud computing platform types, which provide more fine-grained kinds of services, are getting popular very fast.

Infrastructure-as-a-Service (IaaS)

One of the main types of cloud computing platforms is Infrastructure-as-a-Service, which is also called IaaS, in short. IaaS provides foundational types of services also called technology infrastructure that can be provisioned, managed, and maintained over the Internet. In other words, IaaS provides technology infrastructure components.

For example, IaaS offers virtual servers, virtual storage, and a virtual network as a service. As you can notice in the given picture, in the cloud computing pyramid diagram, IaaS is at the foundation. What it means is that IaaS acts as the foundation for the cloud computing platform.

The following is the definition of IaaS from the NIST:

The capability provided to the consumer is to provision processing, storage, networks, and other fundamental computing resources where the consumer is able to deploy and run arbitrary software, which can include operating systems and applications. The consumer does not manage or control the underlying cloud infrastructure but has control over operating systems, storage, and deployed applications; and possibly limited control of selected networking components (e.g., host firewalls).

Let's understand virtual servers in IaaS with a use case. Suppose we need three Linux machines to work on some proof-of-concept (POC) type of work, for example, to build your home-grown load balancer. And we know that once our POC is complete, we will not need those machines further, and we are students with a tight budget.

In this situation, IaaS is one of the best options. We could use the IaaS offering from a cloud provider to launch virtual servers and work on our POC. Once the POC is complete, we can terminate the servers and not be charged by the providers anymore.

Like virtual servers, we can also utilize the virtual storage feature of IaaS in situations where, for example, it would be a cheaper or more viable option to use virtual storage than buying physical storage.

Let's try to understand it with a use case. Suppose we need temporary storage of around 5TB to store some media files for about a month to share with our friends, and we don't want to use the other video hosting services because of our own decisions. In this situation, as you can realize, utilizing virtual storage from cloud providers would be a better feasible choice than buying physical storage. Once we decide that we don't need storage anymore, we can delete the media files, and the provider will not charge us.

As we discussed that IaaS provides technology infrastructure components. Some concrete examples of IaaS are AWS EC2 (Elastic Compute Cloud) for virtual servers, AWS EBS (Elastic Block Store) for virtual storage, and AWS Internet gateway for the virtual network.

For virtual servers, the AWS EC2 service is an example of an IaaS type of service. In other words, using the EC2 service, you can launch (AWS term of running virtual servers) Linux, Windows, or Mac virtual servers on AWS. For virtual storage, AWS EBS is an excellent example of an IaaS virtual storage service. EBS is an IaaS type of service as the service provides storage as a service.

We looked up virtual servers, and virtual storage examples. With regards to the virtual network, AWS Internet Gateway is an excellent example of a virtual network. AWS Internet Gateway manages Internet access for the servers launched on AWS.

Key Features and Advantages of IaaS

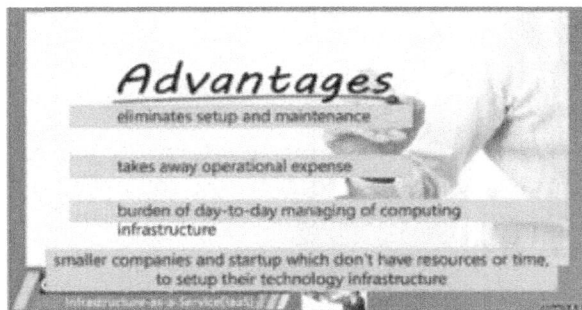

We got an understanding about what IaaS is. Let's try to understand IaaS fruitfulness. Some of the advantages listed here are common across all cloud computing delivery models.

Eliminate On-premises Data Center's Expense

One of the advantages of the IaaS type of cloud computing platform is that it could eliminate an on-premises data center's buying, setup, and maintenance expenses. It's an obvious advantage. When using IaaS -- to procure servers, storage, and network – depending on how much infrastructure you procure, you would be able to cut down huge on your on-premises data-center expenses.

Since IaaS helps reduce data-center expenses significantly, IaaS could be an excellent choice for smaller companies and startups that don't have the resources or time to set up their technology infrastructure. Not only does IaaS help reduce the setup cost of technology infrastructure, but IaaS also takes away the operational expense and the burden of day-to-day managing of computing infrastructure. For example, you can outsource day-to-day tasks such as taking backups, applying patches, and ensuring that the system is secured (not a security risk) to the IaaS provider.

Metered Billing

Customers get this common benefit in all cloud computing delivery models. In IaaS, cloud customers get bills based on what IaaS type of resources has been used and the duration of usage – this is very typical of how metered billing generally works.

There are many good practical advantages of metered billing, for example, there is no need to buy and maintain some special high-end servers only for some special needs for a day, or hour. If you need any servers, there is the likelihood that AWS will have that server available. You launch it and pay only for the usage duration.

Choice of Server Hardware

With IaaS it's much easier to get different types of servers. For example, AWS offers not only traditional Intel-based processors, but also offers AMD, GPU, and ARM processor options.

Scalability

IaaS helps in making systems scalable. IaaS systems can easily provision additional resources to meet unexpected or planned demands. The reason is IaaS utilizes a very large pool of resources.

High Availability

High availability is a general feature of the cloud irrespective of a delivery model. With respect to IaaS, since IaaS utilizes a very large pool of resources along with redundancy, it is easier to manage high availability by quickly provisioning additional resources or just failover to other available resources.

Security

Cloud providers take responsibility for the physical security of servers. In addition, there is network security -- in IaaS, by default, no inbound traffic is allowed. Additionally, there is security at the user level as well, for example, whether the user has access to the resource or not.

Platform-as-a-Service (PaaS)

Platform-as-a-Service (PaaS) is another primary type of cloud computing platform or cloud computing type. PaaS provides platform technology infrastructure-related services, for example, databases, web servers, and messaging, to build, test, and deploy software. In other words, PaaS offers complete development and deployment environment in the cloud.

The following is the definition of PaaS from the NIST:

The capability provided to the customer is to deploy onto the cloud infrastructure consumer-created or acquired applications created using programming languages, libraries, services, and tools supported by the provider. The customer does not manage or control the underlying cloud infrastructure including network, servers, operating systems, or storage, but has control over the deployed applications and possibly configuration settings for the application-hosting environment.

To understand how PaaS relates to IaaS, let's visit the cloud computing pyramid diagram as you can notice that PaaS is above IaaS. What it means is that PaaS can utilize IaaS for its infrastructure-related needs. In other words, PaaS can fulfill its virtual servers, storage, and network-related needs from IaaS.

Now we understand that PaaS offers development and deployment-related services on the cloud. Let's try to understand PaaS with a use-case example. Suppose you are the VP of engineering of a startup with a global team, and even for the local team members, you would like to have the flexibility of remote work. You have heard that platform-as-a-service is a cloud computing type where you can get complete development and deployment environment. So, the question is, what those tools, services, or platforms are that you could consider procuring for your team's software development needs using PaaS?

Depending on your needs, in PaaS computing type, you can find almost anything you require to set up a classic application software development environment. For example, PaaS can offer you IDE (Integrated Development Environment), source code management tools, and build tools. Moreover, in PaaS, you can also get databases, integration tools, web servers, ETL (Extract-Transform-Load) tools, analytic tools, and many more on the cloud platform like AWS. To summarize, PaaS can help you get complete development and deployment-related services on the cloud.

AWS has many PaaS services, such as AWS RDS (Relational Database Service), EMR (Elastic Map Reduce), to name a few. Google App Engine is also an excellent example of PaaS.

Let's discuss further PaaS examples, mainly what we can get on AWS. For IDE, AWS has Cloud9, an integrated development environment that lets you write, run, and debug your code with a browser. For the source code management system, you can use AWS CodeCommit, a secure, highly scalable, managed service that hosts private Git repositories.

To build a data pipeline and schedule ETL jobs, you can use AWS Glue. Finally, you can use AWS ECS to develop and manage your applications' Docker images. Elastic Beanstalk, an easy-to-service for deploying web applications, also qualifies as an AWS offering of PaaS.

Many services on AWS qualify for PaaS. The above ones are just examples to give you an overall understanding of PaaS.

Key Features and Advantages of PaaS

Following are the key features and advantages of PaaS. You may find that some of the features overlap with the cloud service models. That is because all cloud service models inherit general features of cloud computing, in addition to having specific features for the particular service model.

Multiple Environments

PaaS makes it easier to set up and test applications on multiple environments as it is much easier and quicker to provision different environments. For example, suppose you were testing an application on Windows, Linux, and macOS operating systems. In that case, you can launch these environments much more quickly, and you pay only based on metered billing.

You can also create a sandbox environment and provide access to a few developers to try out services to build a proof of concept. Sandbox environments are very good for testing applications built using AWS services in a separate environment before deploying to production.

Ease of upgrades

Since cloud providers take care of upgrades of PaaS, it becomes much easier for customers. Suppose that, for example, you are a data engineer on the AWS platform and use Jupyter Notebook or EMR (Elastic Map Reduce) to build an analytic data application. If any of these (Jupyter Notebook or EMR) need to be upgraded, it will be incumbent upon the cloud provider.

Cost effective

Since PaaS or any cloud service model used metered billing, customers only pay for the services they are using. For example, if you ran the EMR service to run some analytic job for two hours, you are only charged for using EMR for the duration you used the service.

Licensing

Licensing is another feature of PaaS. In a cloud environment, cloud providers are assumed to be handling and managing the licenses of operating systems and platforms, in addition to maintaining compliance and security of systems as opposed to the organization. Within the PaaS cloud service model, the licensing costs are assumed to be a part of the metered cost. What it means is that cloud providers -- not the customer -- are responsible for coordinating with vendors to manage the licensing aspect of PaaS.

To summarize, PaaS provides complete development and deployment-related tools and services in the cloud. Moreover, these services can be accessed anytime on-demand from anywhere over the Internet. Thus, it eliminates in-house buying and setup of databases, web servers, development, and deployment-related tools and services. PaaS can help in setting up multiple environments quickly. Upgrade and licensing of PaaS are incumbent upon the cloud provider, and it is cost-effective.

Software-as-a-Service (SaaS)

Have you used Gmail? Did you happen to watch movies on Netflix? Do you have a Facebook account? Does your workplace use Zoom for meetings? Have you used Microsoft Office 365? If your answer is "Yes" to any of these questions, essentially, you are using software-as-a-service (SaaS).

As IaaS and PaaS, SaaS is another main cloud computing platform or cloud computing type. If IaaS is about infrastructure, PaaS is about the platform – then SaaS is about software. In SaaS, essentially, software solutions are delivered as a service over the Internet. Therefore, SaaS software is mostly executed directly within a web browser. This feature of SaaS eliminates the need to install or download software to execute it.

For example, Gmail, Netflix, Facebook, Zoom, Microsoft Office 365 are some common examples of SaaS. There are countless examples of SaaS, but I'll limit it to a few to keep it simple. To illustrate further, to use Gmail, you don't need to install Gmail on your local computer. You just open a web browser, type the Gmail Web URL in the address bar, and start using Gmail. On the same token, to watch a movie on Netflix, since Netflix is a SaaS solution or SaaS software, you don't need to install

Netflix software on your local computer. Just open a web browser, type the Netflix web URL in the address bar, and you're ready to start watching movies on Netflix. As you can notice with these illustrations, that in SaaS, you don't need to install or download software to execute it.

The following is the definition of SaaS from NIST.

The capability provided to the customer is to use the provider's applications running on a cloud infrastructure. The applications are accessible from various client devices through either a thin client interface, such as a web browser (e.g., web-based email), or a program interface. The consumer does not manage or control the underlying cloud infrastructure including network, servers, operating systems, storage, or even individual application capabilities, with the possible exception of limited user-specific application settings.

SaaS is a very well-known type of cloud computing platform. The reason is SaaS is very visible to the common public usage wise. For example, as we know SaaS software such as Facebook, Netflix, Zoom, Microsoft Office 365 are very popular and have a global reach to millions of users. Additionally, with cloud computing, building SaaS applications have become relatively much faster, which further helps increase its popularity in the developer community.

Comparing SaaS with other main cloud computing types, if you look at the cloud computing pyramid diagram, SaaS is at the top. It means that if you are building SaaS solutions, you can use PaaS for platform-related needs and IaaS for infrastructure-related needs.

Key Features and Advantages of SaaS

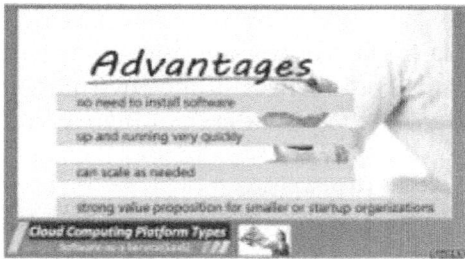

The following are the key features and advantages of SaaS. Similar to IaaS and PaaS, some general features are inherited from cloud computing. However, some of them are unique to SaaS.

Support Costs and Efforts

In SaaS, we do not need to install any special software. SaaS software can be up and running quickly and can scale as needed. There is a substantial cost benefit for smaller or startup organizations in using SaaS.

Licensing

With respect to cost, SaaS software is typically licensed on a subscription basis. SaaS providers manage all the aspects of software, such as delivery and management, ensuring that service level agreement (SLA) is maintained. Thus, the software is available whenever or wherever the customer needs it, and it performs as per the service level agreement (SLA).

Ease of Use

Since SaaS is delivered over the Internet, you don't need to deploy or install any software on your local computer -- you can start using SaaS software using a web URL as soon as the connection is established. In other words, it can be quickly up and running.

Scalability

Furthermore, SaaS software can be easily scaled as needed. What it means, we wouldn't notice any performance degradation if traffic or the number of users increases.

Standardization

This is a very important feature compared to the software of the 90s (software that is not of SaaS type). In the 90s or earlier, for large software, such as software in ERP, manufacturing, and financial domains, that needed to be installed on multiple locations, engineers would have to visit different geographical locations for the installation of new releases or a patch. If you compare it with SaaS, since the software is deployed centrally, all users get the same screen and same version; and new feature releases and patch management are much easier because of centralization. In other words, SaaS helps in having software more standardized in many key aspects.

In the late 90s, before cloud computing dominance, buying and setting up enterprise software such as ERP, CRM, and HR was very expensive. However, SaaS has significantly changed pricing, particularly for smaller or startup organizations, which could not afford to buy and set up expensive software such as ERP, CRM, HR, and many. In other words, the subscription-based pricing model of SaaS has made it much easier for smaller or startup organizations to use or subscribe to SaaS software to help grow their business.

Function-as-a-Service (FaaS)

Function-as-a-Service (FaaS), which is synonymous with serverless computing, is another type of modern cloud computing platform or cloud computing type.

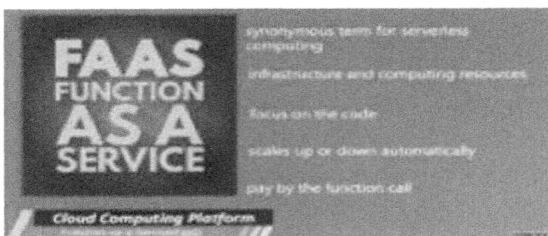

So what does FaaS do? Essentially, in FaaS, users only need to focus on the code (write a Java class, for example) – not on the infrastructure (no need to set up JVM, for example). Users deploy the code having a function (Java class, for example), and the FaaS provider executes the code. The runtime environment is not only provided by the providers but managed as well.

FaaS providers provide infrastructure and computing resources to functions without users setting up the infrastructure and computing resources to execute the process. Additionally, the execution environment scales up or down automatically. Because of the automatic theoretical unlimited scalability feature of FaaS, it is an excellent solution choice for method or function calls, which have a dynamic workload that fluctuates a lot.

One distinct advantage of FaaS is that we only pay for the computing resources used by function calls – essentially a pay-as-you-go-pricing model.

One of the main drawbacks of function-as-a-service is the execution time. Since process needs to have resource provisioned each time they run, there is a possibility of some performance lag.

One of the examples of function-as-a-service is AWS Lambda. For example, say we have an image processing function for generating thumbnail images. We can write the process in the language choices, such as Java, Python, and other supported languages by the cloud provider, and let AWS Lambda execute the function.

In this use case, we only need to write a function for image processing and configure the computing resource requirement on AWS Lambda. Then, AWS Lambda will take care of the allocation of computing resources and run the image processing function.

Scope of Responsibility

As we know, the software doesn't run in isolation – it needs a server, storage, operating system, virtualization (if virtual machines are used), networking, and database (if the application requires it). Software needs to be managed from its performance aspects, such as scalability. In addition, it needs to be secured as well – depending on the security needs of the application.

That being the case, the responsibilities of the different runtime aspects of the application: who will manage what (for example, what will be managed by IaaS, what will be managed by PaaS, or what will be managed by SaaS, what is the responsibility cloud provider, what is the responsibility of the application owner) -- depends.

In the on-premises data center deployment, the software owner takes responsibility for the entire application. The dependency of the application's runtime environment is managed and controlled by the software owner.

However, this responsibility changes in the case of a cloud deployment. The responsibility is shared between the cloud provider and the application owner. What aspect of the application's runtime environment is managed by the cloud provider and what aspects are to be managed by the application owner – depends on the cloud computing type leveraged by the application. Is the application using IaaS, is it using PaaS, or is the application a SaaS application?

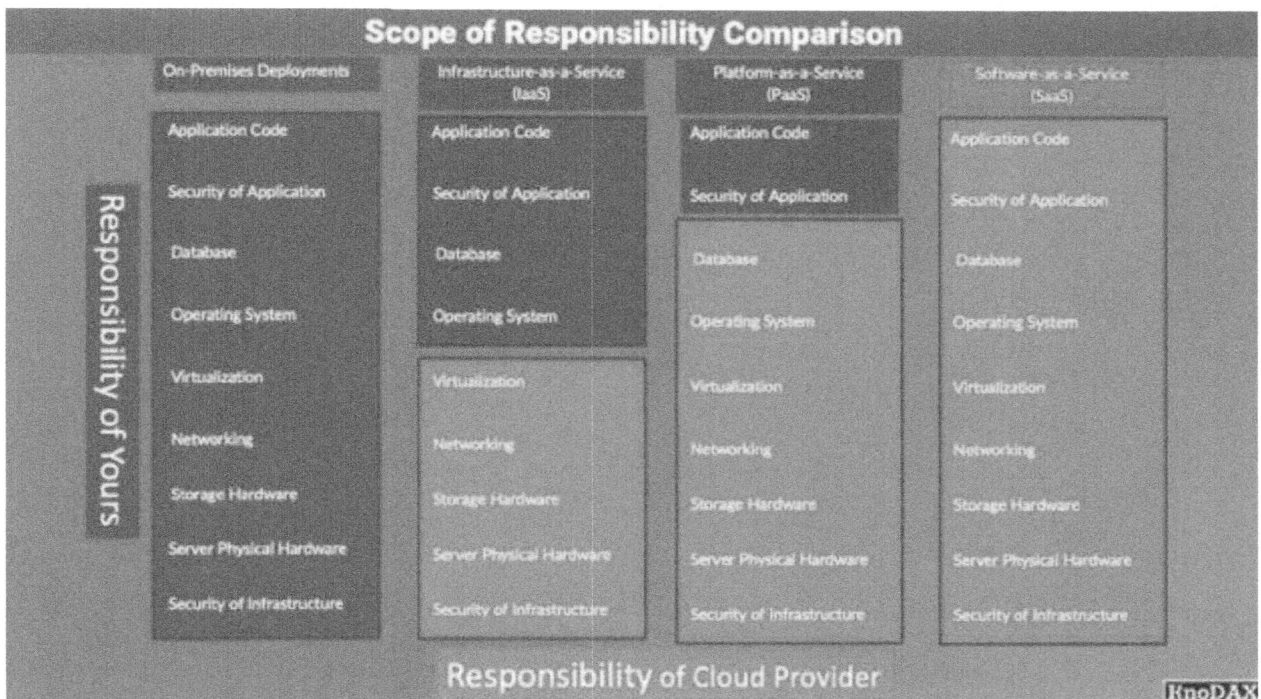

As you can notice in the diagram, in the case of on-premises deployments, each aspect, such as physical hardware, software, networking, and application security, needs to be managed and controlled by the software owner. On the other end -- in the case of SaaS applications -- all these aspects are managed and controlled by the cloud provider.

If the application uses IaaS and PaaS, the responsibilities are divided between the application owner and the cloud provider. In the case of IaaS, cloud providers are responsible for physical hardware, storage, networking, and virtualization. And the application owner is responsible for the operating system, database, application code, and security of the application. In the case of PaaS, only the application code and application's security fall on the application owner, and the rest of the other responsibilities are taken care of by the cloud provider.

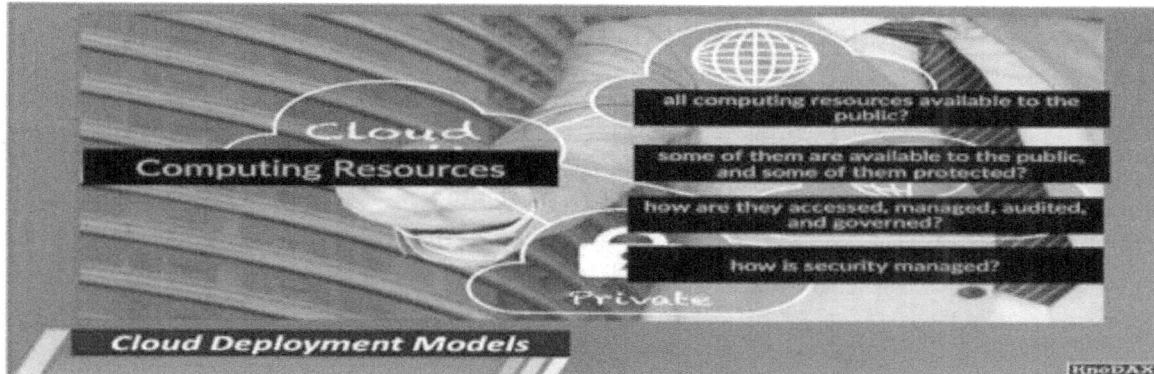

Cloud Deployment Models

Chapter 4: Cloud Deployment Models

You will learn the following in this chapter:
- What is cloud computing deployment model?
- Public cloud
- Private cloud
- Hybrid cloud
- Community cloud
- Multi Cloud

When we talk about cloud computing, it's critical to understand computing resources in terms of their accessibility, management, audit, governance, and security. Understanding computing resources in terms of these aspects of cloud computing comes under the term cloud deployment model. It's essential to understand about cloud deployment model because, as a cloud practitioner or solution architect, understanding this concept would help you choose appropriate architectural options regarding how to deploy applications on the cloud.

What is Cloud Deployment Model?
The cloud deployment model describes how a cloud computing platform is implemented and hosted and who has access to it. For instance, what is the accessibility of computing resources? Are all computing resources available to the public? Or not all -- only some are available to the public, and some computing resources are protected. How are computing resources accessed, managed, audited, or governed? How is the security of computing resources managed? Understanding computing resources in terms of cloud computing comes under the term cloud deployment model.

There are different types of cloud deployment models: public cloud, private cloud, hybrid cloud, community cloud, and multi-cloud.

Public Cloud

A public cloud deployment model (or public cloud) provides on-demand availability of all kinds (for example, IaaS, PaaS, SaaS) of cloud services worldwide. A public cloud, in general, has a massive amount of -- computing resources and storage -- easily available, and is easily scalable.

.

A public cloud has easy accessibility compared to any other type of cloud. This is because public clouds, by nature of the public, are generally available to everyone. So, for example, if you would like to launch a virtual server on AWS (a public cloud provider), you just need to have an account with AWS, and you can easily and quickly launch a virtual server on AWS. Similarly, you can quickly get storage on a public cloud, such as AWS.

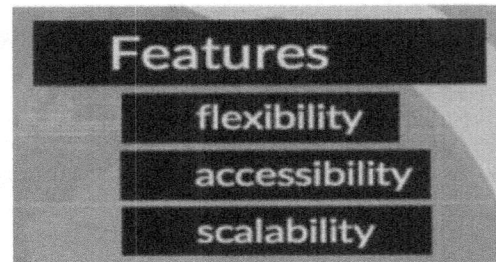

The main point to understand as it relates to accessibility is that getting cloud services from public cloud providers is relatively much more straightforward than getting cloud services in any other type of cloud deployment model (private, hybrid). The reason is that accessibility limits or permission issues are much lenient in the public cloud than in any other cloud deployment model.

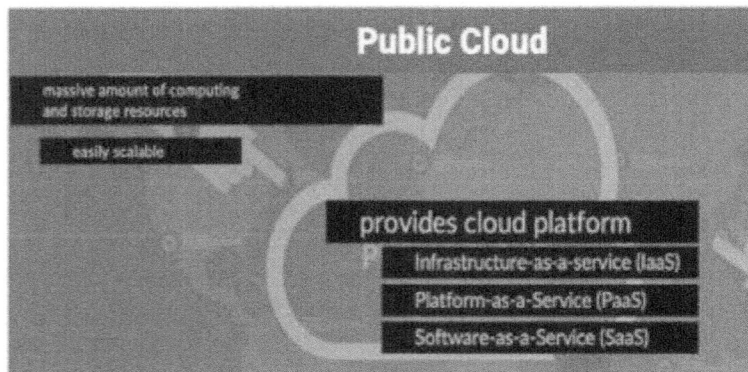

Public cloud providers generally provide cloud platforms for all main cloud computing types: Infrastructure-as-a-Service (IaaS), Platform-as-a-Service (PaaS), and Software-as-a-Service (SaaS).

For example, they provide infrastructure-as-a-service (IaaS), which means you can launch virtual servers on the cloud, such as Linux virtual servers, Windows virtual servers, or even macOS type of virtual servers on AWS. Furthermore, they provide platform-as-a-service (PaaS), which means, for example, you can get development and deployment software and tools on the cloud. Also, they provide software-as-a-service (SaaS), which means you can get application software solutions delivered over the Internet.

A public cloud is a recommended choice for developing cloud-based applications for globally distributed teams -- because the public cloud helps in team collaboration in terms of cloud resources. Moreover, once the application development is complete, if you would like to move the final application to a more secure private cloud, you can do that easily.

Examples of public cloud providers are AWS, Google, Microsoft, IBM, Oracle, Salesforce, SAP, AWS, Google, Microsoft are the leading cloud providers.

Pros & Cons of Public Cloud

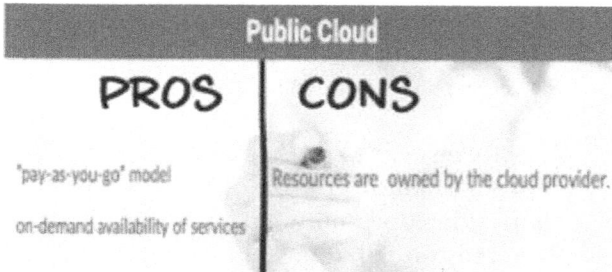

A public cloud provides most of the advantages of cloud computing, such as the pay-as-you-go pricing model and on-demand availability of all kinds of cloud services from across the world.

The one main drawback of a public cloud is that the cloud provider owns the computing resources. And in that sense, there is a single point of failure if something goes wrong at the provider's end, for example, if the provider goes out of business.

Private Cloud

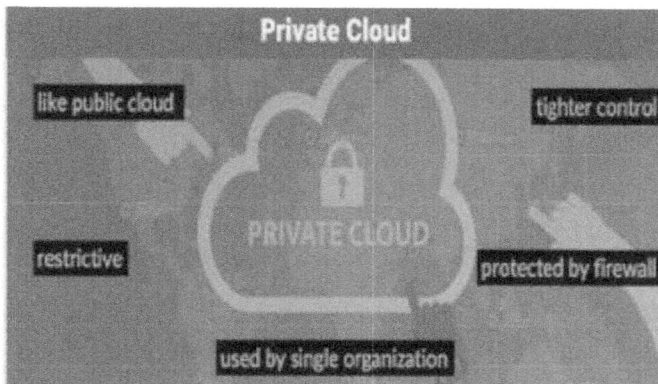

It is like a public cloud, but a private cloud is the most restrictive. A private cloud is sometimes also called an on-premises cloud solution if the cloud resources are within the organization's data center.

With respect to how a private cloud is like a public cloud, in a private cloud, you can get all the public cloud features, such as the on-demand availability of all kinds of cloud services from across the world. Like a public cloud, a private cloud also has massive computing resources and storage available, making it easily scalable -- but relatively lesser than a public cloud.

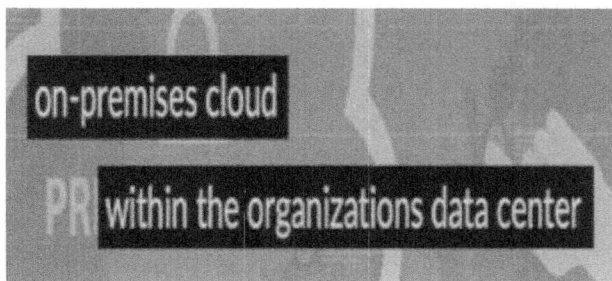

As we discussed, though a private cloud is like a public cloud, a private cloud is the most restrictive and has tighter controls -- typically protected by firewalls. Because of stricter control and firewall protection, usually, a single organization utilizes a private cloud. Organizations with solid security and regulatory requirements, such as banks, and healthcare providers prefer private cloud – particularly total on-premises cloud solutions.

There is an emerging trend of using colocation providers, in which the private cloud of an organization is set up inside a third-party data center. Thus, the organization, instead of having its own on-premises data center, is outsourcing to a third-party data center.

.

Pros & Cons of Private Cloud

Security and control are the main advantages of a private cloud. For example, since a private cloud is behind a firewall, the private cloud makes it easier to restrict access to valuable assets.

With respect to the control advantage of a private cloud, since an outside public cloud provider does not control a private cloud, there is no risk or a single point of failure if something goes wrong with the public cloud provider. This is a real plus, as in a private cloud, there is no dependency on public cloud providers -- the private cloud controls all computing resources. Another point about the controlling advantage of a private cloud is that a private cloud is recommended if regulatory needs are critical to controlling the environment.

Regarding its disadvantages, one of the disadvantages of the private cloud is cost. The company that owns a private cloud needs to bear the cost of the IT infrastructure of data centers and software. This cost factor makes private clouds less attractive compared to public clouds. Another disadvantage is that increasing scalability in the private cloud is not as quick as in the public cloud because, in the private cloud, resources are in a limited capacity.

Hybrid Cloud

In simple words, it combines both public and private clouds. The main point to keep in mind about a hybrid cloud is that it is a cloud solution that allows seamless interaction between public and private clouds. For example, a public cloud can access data and applications of a private cloud, and the converse is also possible.

Therefore, it is an excellent solution for organizations that need flexibility, cost-saving, quick scalability features of a public cloud, along with better security and control features of a private cloud.

Types of Hybrid Clouds

cloud bursting

when more resources are needed due to the increase of service needs, and if their private clouds infrastructure may not be sufficient

There are two types of hybrid clouds: cloud bursting hybrid cloud and the other one is classic hybrid cloud. In the bursting cloud type of hybrid cloud, organizations use private clouds to store their data and proprietary applications securely. However, when more resources are needed due to the increase in service needs, and if their private cloud infrastructure may not be sufficient, they look for public clouds and tap into public cloud resources to fulfill their increased service demands.

In a classic hybrid cloud, organizations store their data and proprietary applications on the private clouds. However, they outsource their non-critical applications to public clouds -- such as Microsoft Office 365, or CRM solutions such as Salesforce. Also, in a hybrid cloud, organizations can leverage multi-cloud architecture where organizations can use different cloud providers for their various cloud services' needs.

Pros & Cons of Hybrid Cloud

Hybrid Cloud

PROS | **CONS**

best of the both clouds

cost savings

potential performance and security risks

A hybrid cloud's main advantage is that we can leverage the best features of both types of clouds. For example, organizations can use private clouds to tightly secure and regulate their data. Furthermore, they can securely move them to public clouds such as AWS, for example, to leverage their analytical, machine learning services to build actionable insight solutions with cost and time efficiency.

Additionally, a hybrid cloud saves overall IT infrastructure costs because a public cloud can be used when scalability is needed. In addition to cost savings, many services are readily available on public cloud providers, which can be leveraged instead of developing your in-house solutions, for example, analytical services. With regards to cons, since there is integration involved between private and public clouds. This integration can cause potential performance issues because of -- network latency and security risks -- as data are shared between public and private clouds.

Community Cloud

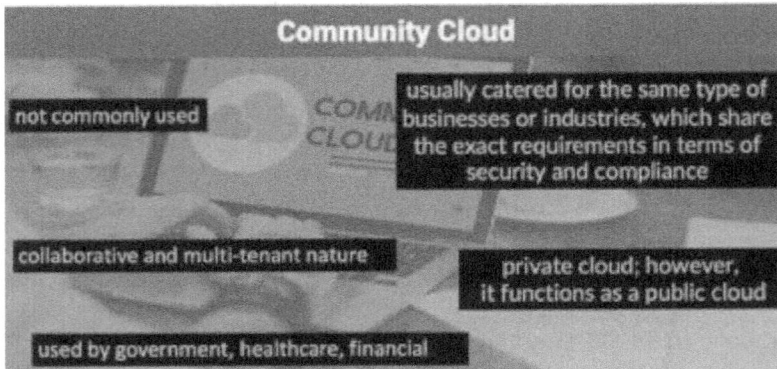

Essentially, a community cloud is a private cloud; however, it functions as a public cloud. Community clouds are collaborative and multi-tenant in nature and usually catered to the same type of businesses or industries, which share the exact requirements in terms of security and compliance.

Though community clouds are not commonly used, they are typically used by government, healthcare, financial and other types of organizations.

Pros & Cons of Community Cloud

The community cloud's advantages are scalability and cost. They are more scalable compared to private clouds. Also, costs could be shared among the organizations using community clouds. Besides advantages, community clouds have some significant drawbacks because of sharing nature of this type of cloud. These concerns are data security, bandwidth, resource utilization, and prioritizations.

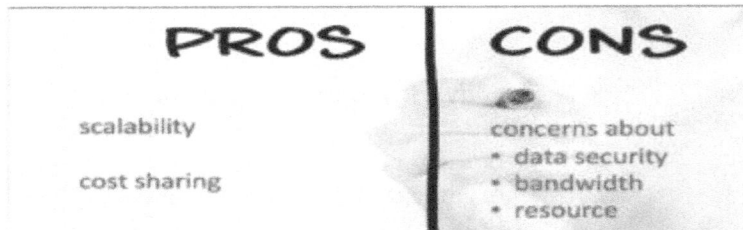

Multi-Cloud

In some cases, just one private, public, or hybrid doesn't fulfill all the cloud computing needs of organizations, and they resort to a multi-cloud model. The multi-cloud model involves private clouds and many public clouds. Though there are multi-clouds, all the clouds can be accessed from a single network.

A multi-cloud model use case generally fits into a larger organization, where one department cloud needs, and budgets may not be aligned with the other departments. For example, the engineering department needs cloud resources for their development and deployment needs. However, the marketing and HR departments cannot use the cloud setup or resources of the engineering department because marketing and HR departments may have additional requirements.

In these scenarios, organizations sometimes choose from the available public cloud providers that best fit their computing and budget needs rather than using the one-size-fits-all solution. Because of utilizations of multi-cloud providers, organizations not only avoid their dependency on a single provider, but multi-cloud also can help them decrease cost and increase flexibility in the long run.

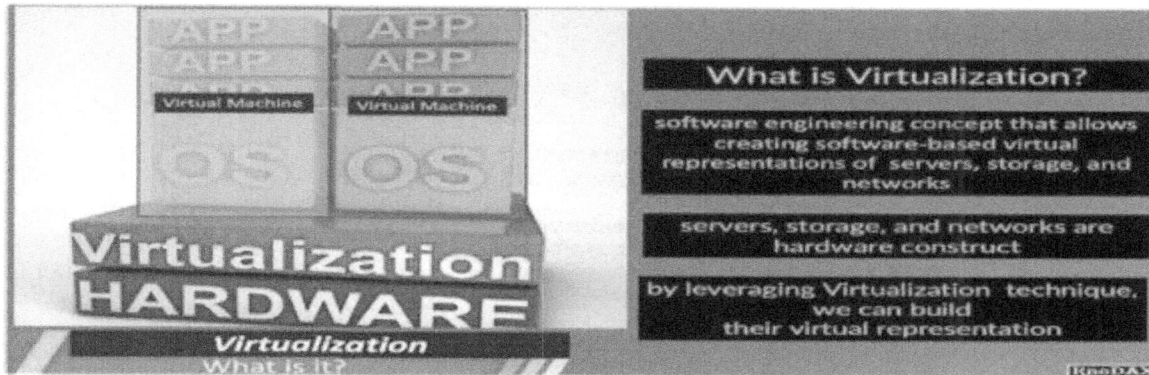

Chapter 5: Virtualization, Virtual Machine, and Hypervisor

You will learn the following in this chapter:
- Virtualization concepts
- Virtual Machine
- Hypervisor

There are many building blocks that make up cloud computing platform. Virtualization is the key technology building block of cloud computing. Another one is containerization (Docker) which you will learn in the Container chapter.

"Divide-and-Conquer" is one of the fundamental tenets of computer science, and we see examples of this principle in building many software solutions. That being said -- we can divide a single process into multiple execution paths, called multithreading. Likewise, we can run multiple processes on an operating system, which is called multiprocessing. In other words, we can run multiple execution paths on an operating system inside a single process and multiple processes.

On a similar token, the question is: can we run more than one operating system on single physical hardware? The answer is yes -- we can.

Virtualization is the software engineering mechanism that allows running multiple operating systems on a single physical hardware. In this chapter, you will learn about virtualization, virtual machines (instances of an operating system), and hypervisor, which is a go-to system between an operating system and physical hardware.

Virtualization

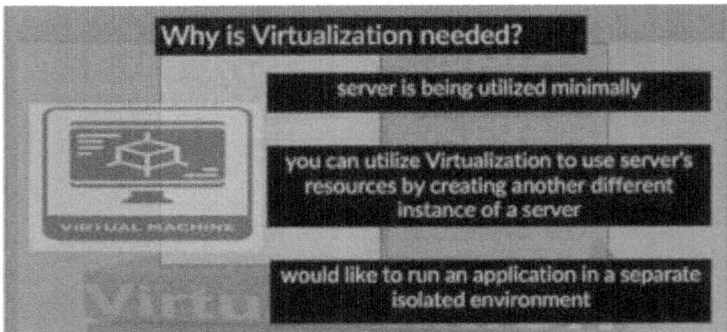

Virtualization creates virtual computer systems. Virtualization, or in practical terms, virtual computer systems, allows organizations to run more than one operating system on a single server. As a result, virtualization helps in reducing physical servers' needs.

As you can see, virtualization is a game-changer for saving costs in buying and maintaining physical servers. Typically, we run one operating system on one server. However, since more than one operating system can be run on a single physical hardware in virtualization, organizations can reduce their need to buy and maintain physical servers. This is because virtualization helps them consolidate their servers' needs into fewer servers.

Why is Virtualization Needed?

Let's continue our discussion about virtualization further, imagine a scenario, suppose we have a server that is being utilized minimally. Wouldn't it be better to utilize it in some way where we can use this server's resources to create another server inside that server? That's the basic idea behind virtualization.

Let's take another example. As we know, maintaining consistent SLA is very important in critical applications. How can we achieve consistent SLA when running multiple applications on the physical server? Maintaining consistent SLA would be a guessing game as each application would have to compete with other applications' processes for the resources.

One way to handle this is to run each application in a separate isolated environment on the same physical server. That way, the application would not compete with other resource processes. Thus, running applications in different environments would help provide consistent service level agreement (SLA). We can use the Virtualization technique to create a different independent running environment for each application on the same physical server.

What Can be Virtualized?

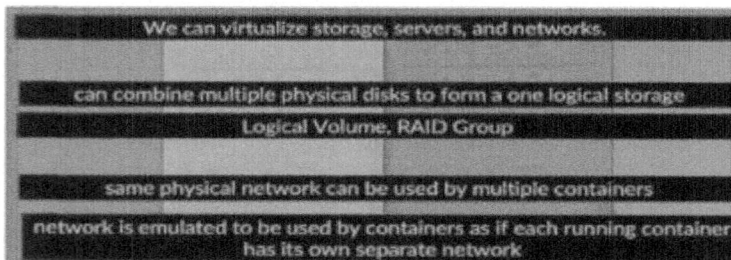

Let's talk about what we can virtualize. We can virtualize servers, storage, and networks. This means these hardware constructs can be created in software form using virtualization.

Using virtualization, we can run multiple servers on the same physical server. These virtual servers are called virtual machines or VMs. We will talk about virtual machines later in the chapter. For example, we can run Windows and Linux operating systems as virtual machines in two entirely different environments on a single physical machine. Each VM would have its own RAM, storage, and network.

Not only using virtualization can we run multiple separate operating systems on the same physical server, but also, using virtualization, we can run multiple applications in a completely separated isolated environment on the same physical machine. This type of virtualization is called containerization, for example, Docker container.

Besides server virtualization, storage can also be virtualized using the Virtualization technique. For example, multiple physical disks can be combined to form one logical storage (virtual storage), which can be assigned to a server. Examples are logical volume and the RAID (Redundant Array of Independent/Inexpensive Disks) group.

In addition to server and storage virtualization, the network can be virtualized using the Virtualization technique. Using network virtualization, a physical network can be used by multiple containers (separate runtime environments) running on the same physical server. The physical network is emulated so that it would be used by multiple containers as if each running container has its separate network.

Another type of virtualization is desktop virtualization. Desktop virtualization enables multiple desktop machines on a single physical server. This is also called desktop-as-a-server.

Virtualization Advantages
First, virtualization increases the efficiency of servers by allowing resource usage optimization instead of underutilized servers. Since we can run multiple OS instances on the same physical server, we can efficiently utilize underutilized resources on that physical server.

The next one is derived from the first one -- virtualization reduces capital expenditure on physical hardware. We can consolidate many physical servers underutilized into a few servers by using virtualization or virtual infrastructure. Thus, you save not only a physical server but also space, power, air conditioning requirements, maintenance, and other things that go with having more servers instead of fewer servers to get the same operating functionality.

Virtual Machine
Now we got an understanding of virtualization. As we talked about, one of the advantages of virtualization is that we can run multiple instances of operating systems -- also called virtual servers or VM – on single physical hardware. The virtualization technique used to create virtual servers, such as Windows or Linux servers, is called a virtual machine.

The virtual machine is also called virtual computer system, or VM, which is the more popular term for virtual machines. We can think of a virtual machine or VM as a separate isolated container having its own operating system and applications. VMs are discrete, separate, and isolated, self-contained, and completely independent.

Because they are self-contained and completely independent, we can launch multiple VMs on a single physical server. For example, we can have a Linux virtual machine and a Windows virtual machine, both of which can be run on a single physical server in their separate isolated environment. Not just two -- this is just an example. We can run many instances of operating systems on the same physical server.   Having multiple VMs on single physical servers enables various operating systems and applications to run on one physical server. This physical server is also called a host as it hosts multiple VMs.

Hypervisor

As we discussed, using virtualization, we can run multiple instances of operating systems on the same physical hardware. In other words, using virtualization, we can set up virtual machines. Now the question is: how do virtual machines -- as they run on the same physical hardware -- get the computing resources such as processors, memory, or storage?

There is a concept called Hypervisor or Virtual Machine Monitor, using which virtual machines get the computing resources such as processors, memory, or storage. The hypervisor is software that creates and manages virtual machines, and it also mediates communication between the host and virtual machines.

A hypervisor is a separate and decoupled layer between the host and VM. The hypervisor allocates and shares host resources with each VM. In other words, a hypervisor allows multiple guest VMs to share host resources such as processors, memory, and storage of the physical machine. For example, when we install hypervisor software and set up multiple guest VMs on it, hypervisor software will take care of sharing host resources with each VM.

Hypervisor Types

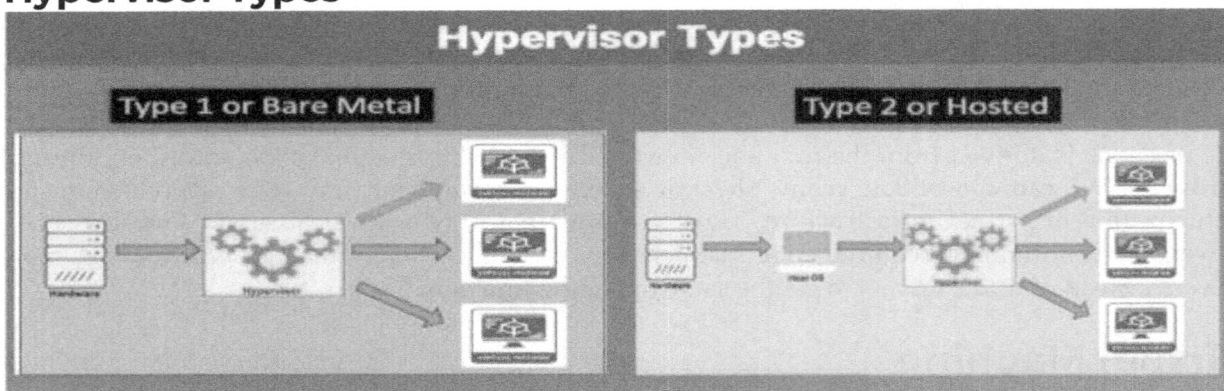

There are two main types of hypervisors: one is referred to as Type 1 or Bare Metal Hypervisor. The other one is referred to as Type 2 or Hosted Hypervisor.

A Type-1 hypervisor runs directly on top of bare metal hardware, acting as a lightweight OS. On the other hand, a Type-2 hypervisor runs on the OS. Since a Type-1 hypervisor runs straight on the hardware, it is also referred to as "Bare Metal," and a Type-2 hypervisor runs on the OS, that's why it is also called "Hosted."

Type-1 or Bare-Metal Hypervisor

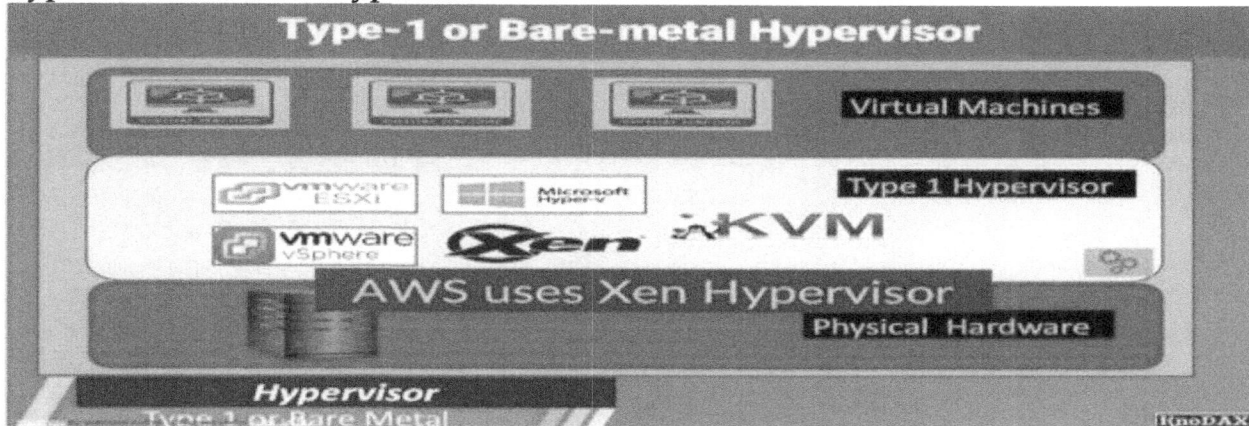

Let's talk further about Type-1 or Bare Metal hypervisor. It is installed directly on the hardware. In other words, Type-1 replaces the operating system. In place of the operating system, we install a Type-1 hypervisor.

Typically, a Type-1 or Bare Metal hypervisor is deployed most. There are some genuine reasons why this type of hypervisor is deployed most. Since it is directly installed on the hardware instead of on the OS, it is more secure than Type-2. And the other reason is that since no OS layer is involved, it performs better and more efficiently than Type-2 or hosted hypervisor. Because of security and performance reasons, Type-1 hypervisors are usually preferred for enterprises when deploying hypervisors on their data centers.

Type-2 or Hosted Hypervisor

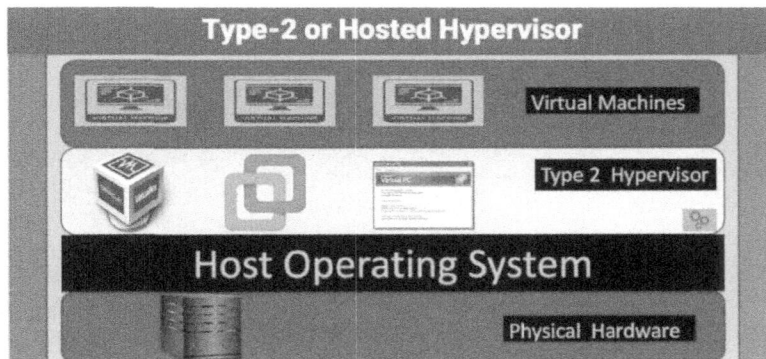

Type-2 or Hosted hypervisor runs on the host operating system. In the diagram as you can see that at the bottom layer, we have the physical hardware, then the OS is installed.

Since this is a Type-2 hypervisor diagram, first, a hypervisor is installed on the OS, then virtual machines are installed. Examples of Type-2 hypervisors that run on host operating systems are Oracle Virtual Box, VMware Workstation, and Microsoft Virtual PC.

The main difference between Type-1 and Type-2 is that Type-1 hypervisors are installed on bare metal, and Type-2 hypervisors are installed on an operating system.

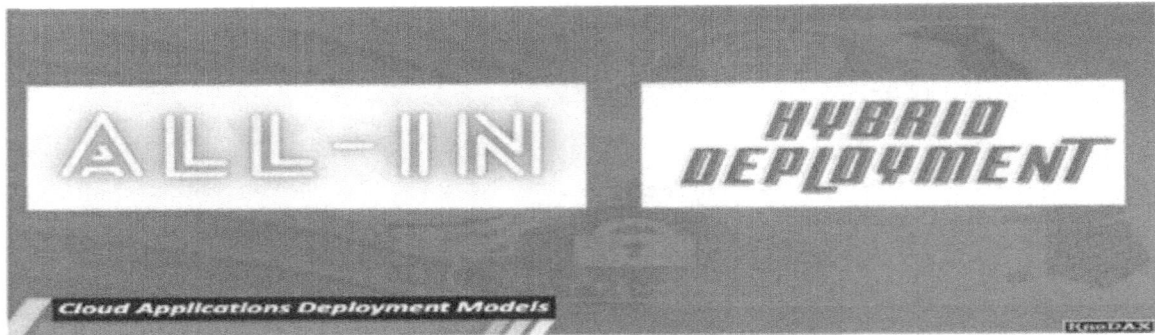

Chapter 6: Cloud Computing Deployment Models

You will learn the following in this chapter:
    Cloud computing deployment models: Cloud, Hybrid, and On-premises

Cloud Computing Deployment Models

Cloud

A cloud-based application is fully deployed in the cloud and all parts of the application run in the cloud. Applications in the cloud have either been created in the cloud or have been migrated from an existing infrastructure to take advantage of the benefits of cloud computing. Cloud-based applications can be built on low-level infrastructure pieces or can use higher level services that provide abstraction from the management, architecting, and scaling requirements of core infrastructure.

Hybrid

A hybrid deployment is a way to connect infrastructure and applications between cloud-based resources and existing resources that are not located in the cloud. The most common method of hybrid deployment is between the cloud and existing on-premises infrastructure to extend, and grow, an organization's infrastructure into the cloud while connecting cloud resources to internal system. For more information on how AWS can help you with your hybrid deployment, please visit our hybrid page.

On-premises

Deploying resources on-premises, using virtualization and resource management tools, is sometimes called "private cloud". On-premises deployment does not provide many of the benefits of cloud computing but is sometimes sought for its ability to provide dedicated resources. In most cases this deployment model is the same as legacy IT infrastructure while using application management and virtualization technologies to try and increase resource utilization.

Screenshot Reference: https://aws.amazon.com/types-of-cloud-computing/

Digital transformation or modernization is challenging, and for many organizations that already have their applications in a non-cloud environment, it could take more than a year or many years of effort to complete modernization. The success of modernization or cloud migration depends on many factors. The first is deciding which deployment model is the right choice for the applications.

When deploying applications on the cloud, we have mainly two approaches: one is All-in (Cloud), and the other is Hybrid. And there is another choice, which is On-premises, in which all IT infrastructure and IT assets are deployed on an on-premises data center as a private cloud.

Cloud or All-In Deployment Model

In Cloud or an all-in deployment model, all components of applications are deployed in the cloud. In this deployment model, either application is directly developed utilizing cloud components and deployed on the cloud – also can be called "cloud native" deployment. Or earlier deployed applications on the on-premises data center have been migrated entirely to the cloud – which is "all in with cloud" deployment.

Hybrid Deployment Model

In a hybrid deployment model (or hybrid model), as the name says in this deployment model, organizations still use on-premises data center for applications deployment and data needs, though partly – means applications are not entirely moved or migrated on the cloud.

In a hybrid model, cloud-based resources are connected with the existing on-prem data center resources. This is a standard method of the hybrid model where organizations grow their applications and infrastructure footprints on the cloud while connecting to their internal data centers for their core applications. Because of security or other related concerns, organizations in some domains always prefer a hybrid deployment model.

On-premises

Though cloud computing main advantages come from a public cloud, organizations in banking, finance, and health care domains have solid regulations and other strong security requirements compared to other business domains. Because of these and other reasons, such as if the cost-benefit analysis is not making a much difference to pivot to complete public or hybrid, they prefer complete on-premises private cloud deployment.

Section 2. AWS Fundamentals

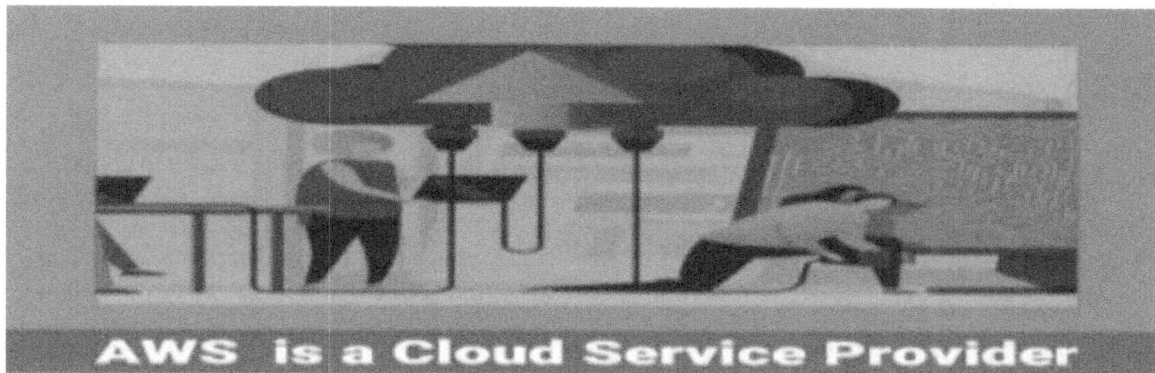

AWS is a Cloud Service Provider

Chapter 7. What is AWS?

You will learn the following in this chapter:
- A very high-level introduction to AWS
- AWS Cloud History

In the previous chapters, you have got an excellent understanding about cloud computing, which would help you answer cloud concepts domain questions. Now, we will start with an introduction to AWS, which will set up the momentum for the rest of the section with respect to preparing for the exam.

Cloud Services Provider

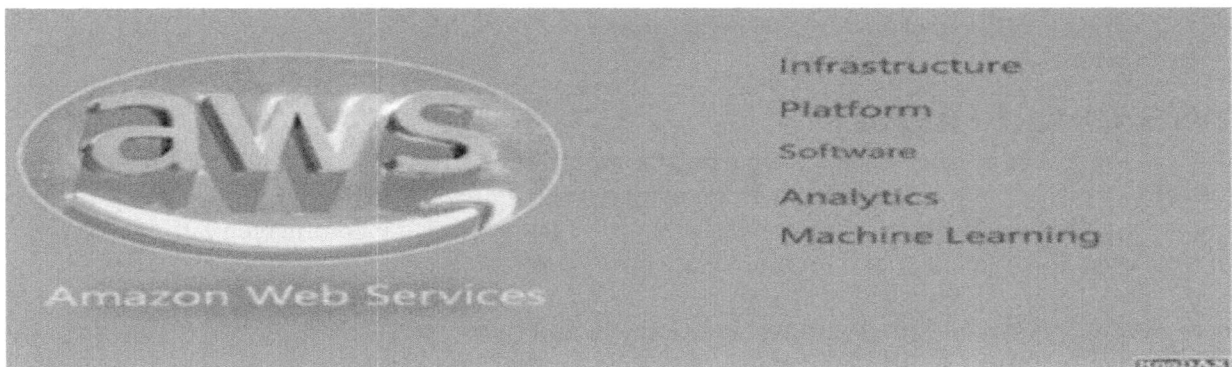

Infrastructure
Platform
Software
Analytics
Machine Learning

What is AWS? AWS is a public cloud service provider, and its architectural underpinning is based on cloud computing. AWS provides almost all kinds of cloud services such as infrastructure, platform, software, analytics, machine learning, and many other types of services over the Internet. These cloud services are highly reliable, scalable, and low-cost. AWS is an evolving cloud computing platform, and new services of different types are continuously getting added. It is a cloud computing platform to procure, deploy, and manage IT Infrastructure. Additionally, AWS is a secure modern platform to build, deploy, and run almost all kinds of software applications. Most importantly, it does it with time and cost-efficiency.

AWS Use Cases

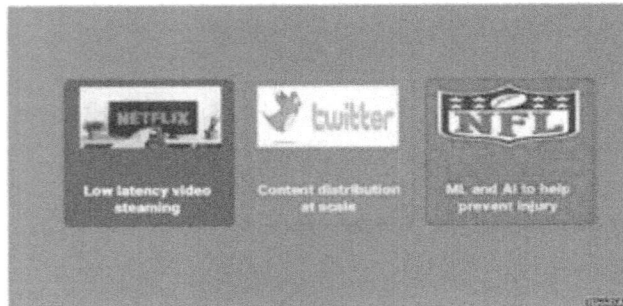

To understand further what AWS is, let's see some interesting use cases of AWS. Did you know how Netflix is streaming videos worldwide with low latency? Netflix uses AWS to achieve low latency performance. Have you ever wondered how Twitter can scale its distribution of content worldwide? Twitter uses the AWS platform to scale its distribution worldwide. Did you happen to know how NFL is leveraging AI and machine learning to predict and prevent injury in games? NFL is leveraging AWS machine learning and AI services to expect and to avoid damage in matches.

AWS Customers

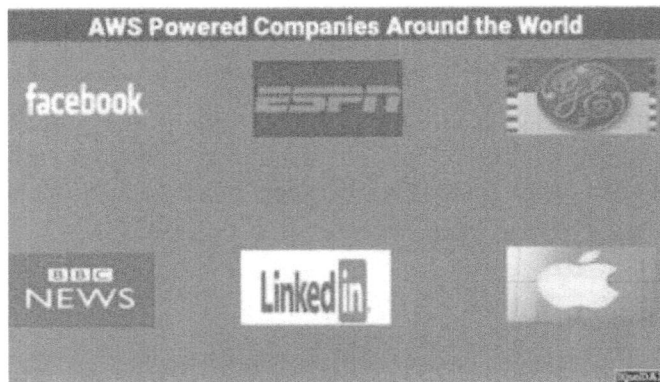

Now we have gone through a few use cases of AWS. Continuing further on what AWS is, let's try to understand AWS in terms of its customers. AWS has over a million customers in around 190 countries as of this writing. it has customers from organizations of all types, such as large, medium, and startups in various industries. Regarding companies that are using AWS, some well-known organizations that have big spending on AWS are Facebook, BBC News, ESPN, LinkedIn, GE, and Apple.

AWS Cloud History

AWS genesis came in early 2000 as Amazon started building SOA-based architecture to scale their platform. Around that time, Amazon was launching its e-commerce platform for third-party retailers to make a web store for their retail store. This effort of launching an e-commerce platform for third-party retailers led to the demand for a more scalable system.

Then in 2002, Amazon.com Web Services launched its first set of web services, opening the Amazon.com platform to all developers. The most exciting story is that Amazon was caught by surprise by its developers' unexpected interest in web service API.

Then in 2003, Andy Jassy, who is CEO now, put forth the idea of Internet OS made up of foundational infrastructure primitives. The first foundational infrastructure primitives -- compute, storage, and databases -- were identified. Based on this idea, Jeff Barr, Jassy, Bezos himself, and others formulated the concept of EC2 for compute, S3 for storage, and RDS for the database. These three are very famous AWS services now.

This [2003] was an essential year for AWS. In fact, according to Amazon Web Services Wiki, Jassy recalls brainstorming sessions about a week with ten of best technology minds and ten of best product management minds on about ten different internet applications, the most primitive blocks required to build them. That discussion and other related events paved the idea of AWS, where the mission was to expose all the atomic-level pieces of the Amazon.com platform.

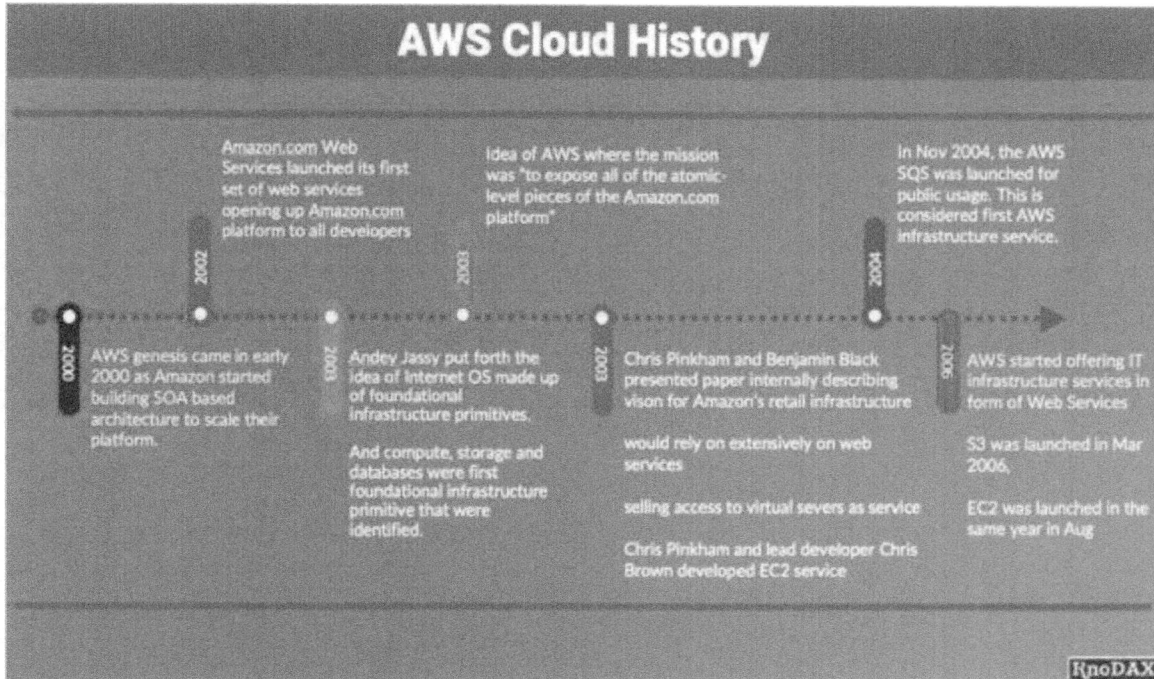

In 2003, Chris Pinkham and Benjamin Black presented a paper internally describing the vision for Amazon's retail infrastructure that was overhauling Amazon's retail infrastructure to be completely automated and would rely extensively on web services. The paper also mentioned the possibility of selling access to virtual servers as a service and proposed that the company generate revenue from the new infrastructure investment. And after that, Chris Pinkham and lead developer Chris Brown developed the EC2 Service.

In Nov 2004, the AWS SQS was launched for public usage. This is considered the first AWS infrastructure service.

After that, in 2006, AWS started offering IT infrastructure services in Web Services. S3 was launched in Mar 2006, EC2 was launched in the same year in Aug. Over the years, many more services have been added to the AWS platform. AWS is an evolving platform – more and more features and services are continuously added to its platform.

As of this writing, AWS has over 200 products and services in almost all possible categories where AWS can offer its services.

AWS Cloud Use Cases

With over 200 products and services, AWS enables you to build sophisticated and scalable applications in a diverse set of industries.

AWS Use cases include:
> Enterprise IT, Backup & Storage, Big Data analytics
> Website hosting, Mobile & Social Media Apps, and Gaming
> and more.

KEY POINTS

- In 2021, Amazon Web Services (AWS) generated revenues of 62.2 billion U.S. dollars with its cloud services. (Source: https://www.statista.com/statistics/233725/development-of-amazon-web-services-revenue/)

- AWS market share grew by more than a full percentage point during the second quarter of 2022, reaching nearly 34%. (Source: https://www.channelfutures.com/channel-research/aws-market-share-crept-up-a-full-percentage-point-in-q2)

- Over 1,000,000 active users

Summary

To summarize, AWS helps in cost savings, time savings. it is easy to use as well. Moreover, we don't need to buy any special hardware to use AWS. It has over a million active customers, and readily available all kinds of cloud services. AWS has a pay-for-what-you-use pricing model.

It is a cloud computing platform to build, deploy, and run almost all kinds of software applications. It is also a cloud computing platform to procure, deploy, and manage IT infrastructure with time and cost-efficiency. Today AWS provides highly reliable, scalable low-cost cloud services from its cloud computing platform.

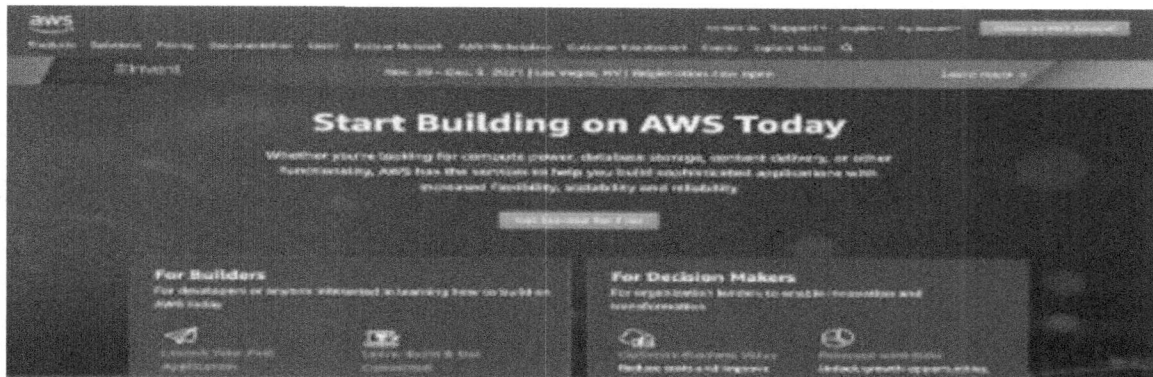

Chapter 8. AWS Account

You will learn the following in this chapter:
- Sign up for AWS Account
- AWS Root Account Best Practices
- Multi-Factor Authentication
- Access Keys
- Accessing AWS Platform

The theory is good to set up the conceptual understanding of AWS. However, the best way to learn AWS services is to know them by doing. In the chapter, we will learn many aspects of AWS account, such as signing up for an AWS account, and securing your AWS account.

Sign Up for AWS Account

Now you have got an understanding of what AWS is. Let's sign up for an AWS account so that you can learn AWS services. If you already have an AWS account, then you can skip this part of the chapter.

1. Go to https://aws.amazon.com/
2. Choose to Create an AWS account.

Note: If you signed into AWS recently, you might see this option. In that case, choose Sign into the Console. Then, if Create a new AWS account still isn't visible, select Sign in to a different account and then choose Create a new one.

3. Enter your account information, and then choose Continue. Ensure you enter your account information correctly, particularly your email address. If you didn't enter your email address correctly, you won't be able to access your AWS account.

Note: Because of the critical nature of the AWS account root user of the account, it is strongly recommended that you use an email address that can be accessed by a group rather than only an individual. That way, if the person who signed up for the AWS account leaves the company, the AWS account can still be accessed and used because the email address is associated with a group.

If you lose access to the email address associated with the AWS account, you can't get access if you ever lose the password.

4. Choose Personal or Professional.

Note: There aren't any feature differences between personal and professional accounts. Both of them have the same features and functions.

5. Enter your company or personal information.

Important
For professional AWS accounts, it's a best practice to enter a company phone number rather than a personal phone number. Creating professional AWS accounts using an individual email address or a personal phone number can make your account insecure.

6. Read and accept the AWS Customer Agreement.

7. Choose Create Account and Continue.

8. On the Payment Information page, enter the payment-related information and then choose to Verify and Add.

9. Next, you must verify your phone number.

10. Enter the code displayed in the CAPTCHA, and then submit.

11. When the automated system contacts you, enter the PIN you receive and then choose Continue. If the code is verified, it will take you to the "Select a Support Plan" page.

12. On the Select a Support Plan page, choose one of the available AWS Support plans. The "Select a Support Plan" page asks which support plans you want. Primarily for learning or trying out services for preparing for certification exams, the Basic Plan option is sufficient– as it is free. Essentially in the Basic Plan, you will leverage AWS documentation to get help if you get stuck. In my personal experience, Basic Plan is fine for learning or preparing certification exams. You will need the Developer Plan option if you need to contact someone in AWS to help solve your AWS issue. Essentially, you will create a support ticket in this option if you have any support-related questions, and the AWS support team will handle your support ticket. Finally, businesses using AWS typically use the Business Plan to get help on their AWS issue.

13. Once you select a support plan, wait for your new account to be activated. Next, you will get an email from AWS about your account setup. Then, you can log in to start using AWS. This usually takes a few minutes but can take up to 24 hours.

Check your email and spam folder for the confirmation message. After you receive this email message, you will have full access to all AWS services.

Reference: https://docs.aws.amazon.com/AWSCloudFormation/latest/UserGuide/cfn-sign-up-for-aws.html

AWS Root Account Best Practices

At the time of signing up to AWS, AWS creates a root user identity for your AWS account. The root user identity you can use to sign into AWS. You can sign into the AWS Management Console using this root user identity, which is the email address and password that provided when creating the account. Your email address and password combination are also called your root user credentials.

Some of the AWS account root user security best practices are as follows:

- Do not use the AWS account root user for any task where it's not required. Instead, create a new IAM user for each person that requires administrator access. Then make those users administrators by placing the users into an "Administrators" group to which you attach the AdministratorAccess managed policy.

- If you don't already have Access Key ID and Secret Access Key for your AWS account root user, don't create one unless you need to. If you have an access key for your AWS account root user, delete it.

- Do not share your root account and password with anyone. Instead, use a strong password to help protect account-level access to the AWS Management Console.

- Secure your root account by Multi-Factor Authentication (MFA). Enable AWS MFA on your AWS account root user account.

Multi-Factor Authentication (MFA)

What is MFA?

Multi-factor authentication, or in short, MFA, is an electronic authentication method in which a user is granted access to a website or application only after successfully presenting two or more pieces of evidence to an authentication mechanism: knowledge, possession, and inherence.
(Source: https://en.wikipedia.org/wiki/Multi-factor_authentication)

MFA for Security and Safety of Your AWS Account

Adding multi-factor authentication is a critical task with respect to the security and safety of your AWS account. Usually, in organizations, it is done by the system administrator. However, if you have a personal AWS account, you should make sure you have added MFA before using your AWS account. Therefore, it is highly recommended to add MFA to your AWS account before you start using the AWS account.

When using MFA, a password and additional validation mechanisms, such as a token number present on a security device you own, are used for logging in.

The main advantage of MFA is that if your password is stolen or hacked, your account is still not compromised, as you still have the security device.

Different Ways MFA Can be Added to Your AWS Account

In AWS, MFA can be added using three different mechanisms:
- Virtual MFA Device
- U2F Security Key
- Hardware MFA Device

Virtual MFA Device

MFA device is easy to set up. For example, you can install Authenticator App such as Google Authenticator, 1Password, Microsoft Authenticator on your mobile device. And use the code generated on the app to log in along with the password.

When using a virtual MFA (2FA) device, we can use Google Authenticator (an app that works on a mobile phone only) or Authy. Both Google Authenticator and Authy generate time-dependent six-digit codes, which you enter after you submit your username and password for the account.

In virtual MFA, you have support for multiple tokens on a single device.

Though Google Authenticator and Authy are very similar in terms of the functionalities they offer, Authy has multi-device support. In other words, when using Authy, your 2FA tokens are automatically synched to any device you authorize. And, if your device is lost, stolen, or retired, you can deauthorize it from any authorized device.

According to Authy, some people think having tokens on multiple devices is risky, so they have made the feature of having tokens on multiple devices optional.

If you are interested to learn more about the difference between Google Authenticator and Authy. You can find it at https://authy.com/blog/authy-vs-google-authenticator/.

Universal 2nd Factor (U2F) Security Key

U2F keys are often considered the strongest authentication method. Also, some described it as entirely resistant to phishing. U2F keys use public-key cryptography that protects users from phishing, session hijacking, man-in-the-middle attacks, and malware. U2F keys gained a good reputation after Google corporation introduced them to all its employees.

In addition to security, the most notable advantage of U2F keys over other authentication methods is their ease of use. U2F keys allow users to quickly, easily, and securely access any website. To authenticate, the user inserts the U2F key into a USB port and then confirms their identity by tapping a button on the key.

For example, FIDO (Fast Identity Online) U2F Security Key is a device that you plug into a USB port on your computer. Once you enable it using the instructions that follow, you just tap it on the device instead of manually entering a code when prompted to log in securely. Tapping helps make sure some human is logging – not a robot. FIDO2 is an open authentication standard hosted by the FIDO Alliance.

Hardware MFA Device

And the third option is to use hardware MFA devices. The concept is like the SecureID if you have used it. First, you register the device, and then, when prompted, enter the token generated on the device.

MFA for AWS GovCloud (US)

Multi-Factor Authentication (MFA) in AWS GovCloud (US)

AWS Multi-Factor Authentication (MFA) is a simple best practice that adds an extra layer of protection on top of your user name and password. With MFA enabled, when a user signs into the AWS GovCloud (US) region, they will be prompted for their user name and password (the first factor—what they know), as well as for an authentication code from their AWS MFA device (the second factor—what they have). Taken together, these multiple factors provide increased security for your GovCloud account settings and resources.

Enabling MFA in AWS GovCloud (US)

You can enable MFA for your GovCloud account and for individual IAM users you have created under your account. MFA can be also be used to control access to AWS GovCloud service APIs. After you've obtained a supported hardware or virtual MFA device, AWS does not charge any additional fees for using MFA.

For more information on Virtual MFA Devices, see the AWS MFA web page.

AWS GovCloud (US): MFA Options

Device	Virtual MFA Device	Hardware Key Fob Device
Physical Form Factor	Use your existing smartphone or tablet running any application that supports the open TOTP standard.	Tamper-evident hardware key fob device provided by SurePassID, a third-party provider.
Price	Free	$13.99
Features	Support for multiple tokens on a single device.	The same type of device used by many financial services and enterprise IT organizations.
Compatibility with Root Account	Yes	Yes
Compatibility with IAM User	Yes	Yes

Screenshot from: https://aws.amazon.com/govcloud-us/mfa/

Accessing AWS Platform

AWS Management Console is a common and popular choice to access AWS as it is a compelling UI. We can perform many AWS operations on the AWS platform without programming or knowing its low-level APIs. However, AWS can be accessed in other ways as well.

Different Ways to Access AWS
- AWS Management Console (protected by password + MFA)

- AWS CLI -- AWS Command Line Interface (protected by access keys)
- AWS SDK -- AWS Software Development Kit (for code: protected by access keys)
- Integrated Development Environment (IDE)

AWS Management Console

AWS Management Console, a more formal name for AWS UI, is a prevalent choice to access AWS. You don't need to know any programming language or scripting language to access AWS if you are using AWS its management console. You can access the AWS UI from mobile apps as well. For example, you can manage launched EC2 instances from mobile apps using AWS Management Console. It is protected by a password and optionally by MFA.

AWS CLI (Command Line Interface)

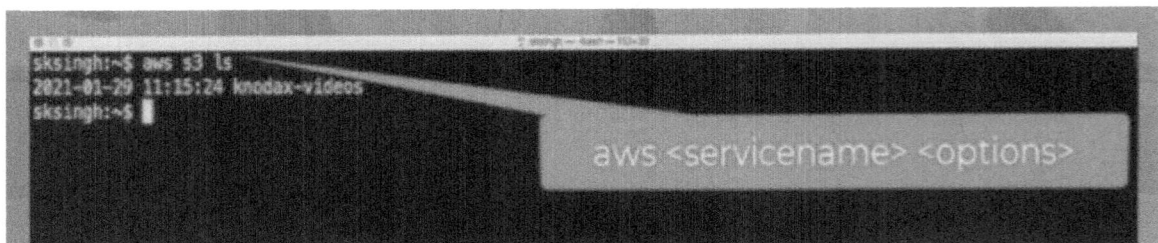

Another way to access AWS is using AWS CLI, which is AWS Command Line Interface. AWS CLI is handy for DevOps engineers who would like to access AWS from the command line to be more productive or to automate backend processes, such as launching or terminating AWS services without using its management console.

In other words, it is a tool that enables you to interact with AWS services using commands from the command-line shell. It provides direct access to the public APIs of AWS services. Using AWS CLI, you can write scripts to manage your AWS resources. It's open source: https://github.com/aws/aws-cli.

In order to access AWS Cloud using AWS CLI, you need to provide access keys.

AWS SDK (Software Development Kit)

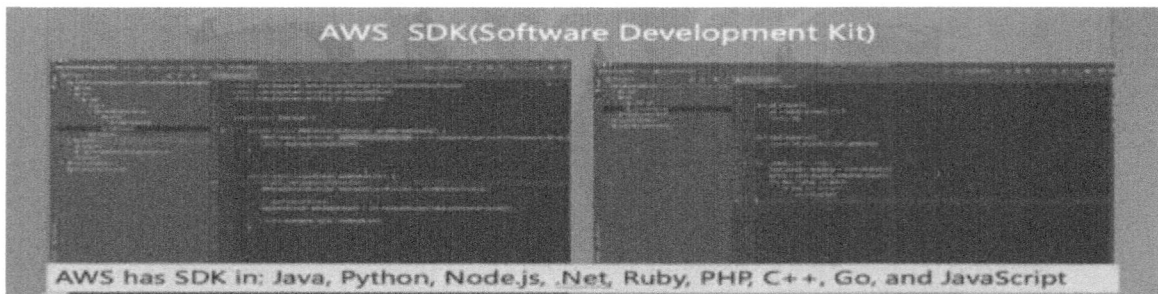

What if you want to perform actions on AWS directly from your application's code – without using SDK? You can use SDK -- Software Development Kit.

The AWS SDK is used mainly by AWS Developers. AWS SDK is handy for AWS developers who would like to develop programs on the AWS platform using AWS APIs. In other words, AWS Software Development Kit (AWS SDK) is a language-specific APIs (set of libraries). It enables you to access and manage AWS services programmatically. For example, if you would like to develop a chat application on AWS. You could leverage AWS SDK in that case.

- SDKs are available for the following programming languages: **Java, Python, Node.js, .Net, Ruby, PHP, C++, Go, and JavaScript.** There are mobile SDKs (Android, iOS) and IoT device SDKs (Embedded C, Arduino) are available as well.
- We have to use AWS SDK when coding for AWS services such as DynamoDB.
- **AWS CLI uses the Python SDK (boto3).**
- If you don't specify or configure a default Region, then **us-east-1 will be used by default**.
- When using AWS SDK, you need to provide access keys.

Integrated Development Environment (IDE)
You can also use IDE. An integrated development environment (IDE) provides a set of coding productivity tools such as a source code editor, a debugger, and build tools. Cloud9 IDE is an offering from AWS under IDEs.

Access Keys
You can generate access keys through the AWS Console. Users manage their own access keys. Access Keys are secret, like user id and password. Access Key ID is like user id, and Secret Access Key is like password -- don't share them.

Other ways to understand access Keys:
Access Key ID ~= username
Secret Access Key ~= password

Please don't share access keys, and make them inactive or delete them if you are not using them.

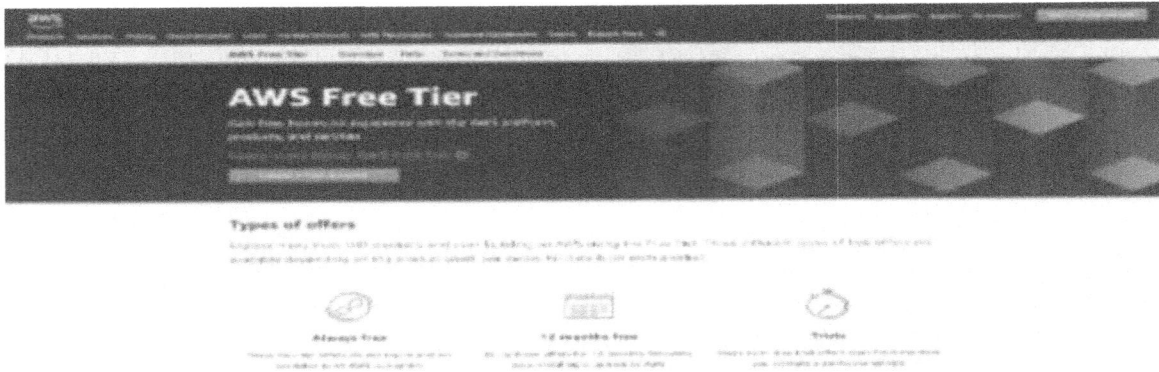

Chapter 9. AWS Free Tier

You will learn the following in this chapter:
- What is AWS Free Tier?
- Different type of offers in AWS Free Tier
- Free Tier related FAQ

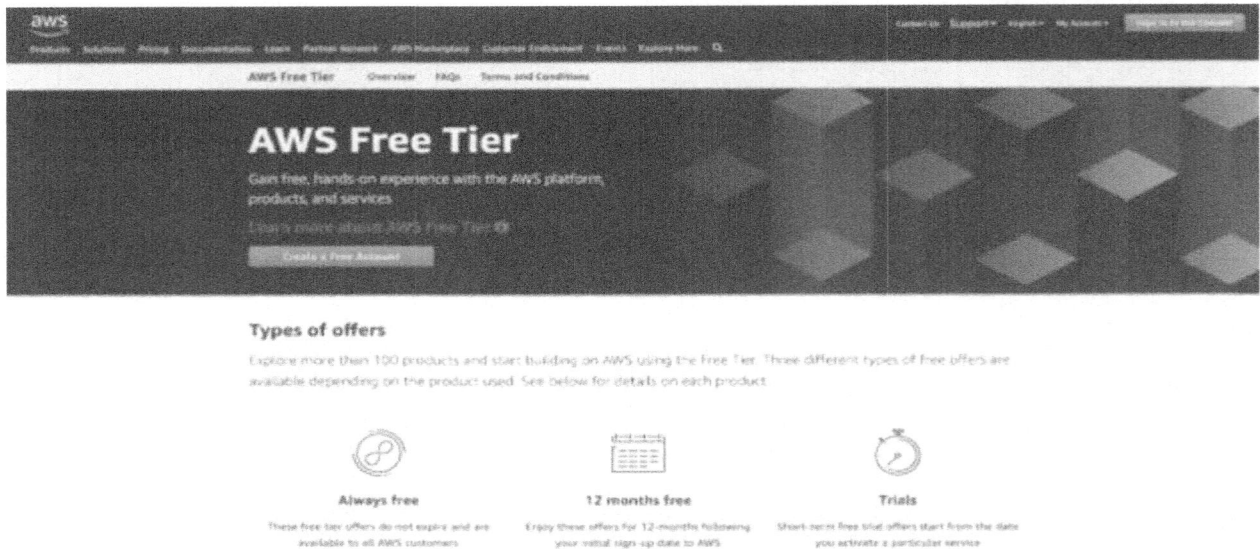

AWS Free Tier home page

AWS Free Tier (https://aws.amazon.com/free) is a feature provided by AWS to try out and learn AWS services free of charge within certain usage limits, for some time, typically for one year. The AWS Free Tier is automatically activated on each new AWS account.

AWS Free Tier Offers

AWS Free Tier provides three types of offers.

Always Free
Always Free offers do not expire at the end of your 12-month AWS Free Tier term and are available to all AWS customers.

12 Months Free
You will get 12-month free with limited usage after initial signup with AWS in this type of offer. After that, you pay standard rates after your 12 months free usage term expires, or your application use exceeds the free tier limits.

Short-Term Free Trials
In this type of offer, you will get short-term free trial, which starts from the date, you activate a particular service. Then, you pay standard rates after the trial period expires.

Free Tier Eligible label

One obvious question that comes to mind when you are new to AWS is how you would know if the service you are trying to use if it is in Free Tier or not. The next question is whether it is Always Free type, 12 Months Free type, or Trials type. Some other common questions related to AWS Free Tier are at the end of this chapter as FAQ.

In general, if you use AWS Management Console (other options are using AWS API and AWS CLI), AWS provides some label if it is in Free Tier.

For example, as you can see in the screenshot above, choosing instance type when launching an EC2 instance. There is a label "Free tier eligible" on the t2.micro instance with one vCPU and 1 GiB memory. So, if you launch an EC2 example using this instance type, it is Free Tier eligible.

AWS Free Tier Details Page

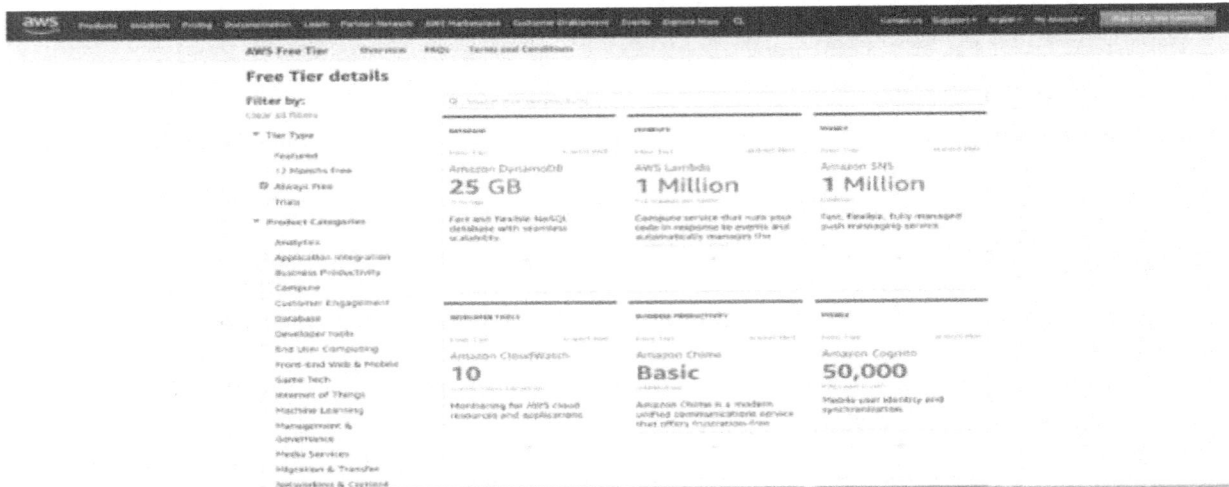

Another way is: on the AWS Free Tier page https://aws.amazon.com/free, on the left side, there is a Filter by option. Using this option, you can find detail such as which services are available as Always Free, which are available as 12 Months Free, which are on Trials. So, for example, in the screenshot above, Always Free is checked, displaying the services available as Always Free. You can also filter by Product Categories such as Analytics, Database.

Free Tier FAQ

These are some FAQs from the Google search (https://www.google.co/search)

How do I know if I have AWS free tier?

To get started, **simply navigate to the Billing and Cost Management Dashboard to view the "Free Tier Usage" data.** For details on Free Tier-eligible services and how to qualify as a Free Tier-eligible customer, please refer to the AWS Free Tier page. Aug 12, 2015

Is AWS free tier really free?

The AWS Free Tier is designed to give you hands-on **experience with a range of AWS services at no charge.** For example, you can explore AWS as a platform for your business by setting up a test website with a server, alarms, and database.

Which service is chargeable in the free tier?

Hourly usage in the AWS Free Tier. Some services, such as **Amazon EC2**, Amazon RDS, and Elastic Load Balancing, charge for usage on an hourly basis. The AWS Free Tier for these services provides you with a monthly allotment of hours for the first 12 months.

What happens after AWS free tier?

When your Free Tier period with AWS expires, **you can continue to use the same services**. However, all resources on your account are billed at On-Demand rates. ... If you don't want to incur charges, you must delete, stop, or terminate the resources on your account. If you want, you can then close your account. Nov 4, 2020

Does AWS free tier expire after 12 months?

12 Months Free – These tier offers include 12 months free usage following your initial sign-up date to AWS. ... Always Free – These **free tier offers do not expire** and are available to all AWS customers.

Why is AWS charging me for free tier?

When using AWS Free Tier, you might incur charges due to the following reasons: **You exceeded the monthly free tier usage limits of one or more services**. You're using an AWS service, such as Amazon Aurora, that doesn't offer free tier benefits. Your free tier period expired. Sep 25, 2020

Summary

- AWS Free Tier enables its customers to acquire practical knowledge about AWS platform and services by reducing the cost of learning.
- They of are three types: Always Free, Short-Term Free Trial, and 12 Months Free.
- http://aws.amazon.com/free page can be used to find more details about AWS Free Tier.

Chapter 10. AWS Cost and Billing Management

You will learn the following in this chapter:
- AWS Billing and Cost Management
- AWS Budgets
- AWS Budget Alarm Set up
- AWS Billing
- AWS Compute Optimizer

AWS Billing and Cost Management

AWS Billing and Cost Management is a central, go-to place service for all billing-related aspects. The AWS Billing and Cost Management allows you to pay your AWS bill, monitor your usage, and analyze and control your costs. You cannot use this service to create data-driven business cases for transitioning your business' on-premises IT infrastructure and applications to AWS Cloud.

AWS Budgets

AWS Budgets give the ability to set custom budgets that alert you when your costs or usage exceed your budgeted or forecasted amount. With AWS Budgets, you can be alerted by email or SNS notification when actual or forecasted cost and usage exceed your budgeted threshold or when your actual RI and Savings Plans' utilization or coverage drops below your desired threshold.

AWS Budgets can be created at different levels, for example, the monthly, quarterly, or yearly levels, and can customize the start and end dates as well. Additionally, you can further refine your budget to track costs associated with multiple dimensions, such as AWS service, linked account, tag, and others.

Budget Alarm Set Up

Before using AWS, one of the critical tasks is setting up a budget alarm to help keep your AWS bills within the check.

AWS has a Free Tier -- then why do I need to set up a budget alarm?

Typically for preparing AWS certification exam, it's good practice to use the services given in the AWS Free Tier. AWS Free Tier is a feature provided by AWS to try out and learn AWS services free of cost for some time, typically for one year. However, the free tier will not be sufficient to learn and try out the services if you are seriously preparing for the AWS Solutions Architect exam. For example, my AWS bill for preparing certification was around $15.

So, by setting up the budget alarm, you make sure to get some sort of notification such as email or text, depending on what you have configured if you're exceeding the budget threshold. The budget alarm will help in keeping your AWS bills within your budget.

That being said, let's go ahead to set up the budget alarm.

Step 1: Billing Dashboard
In the search bar, type billing to easily find the "Billing & Cost Management Dashboard" if you have previously visited this service, it will be shown on your home page once you logged in.

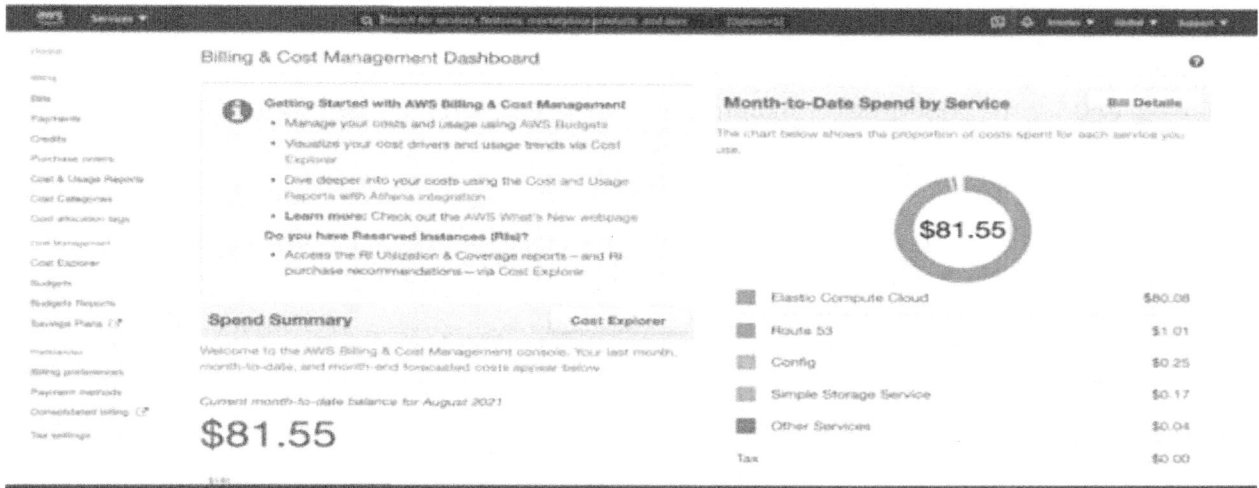

AWS billing dashboard

Step 2: Create Budget
Once you are on the "Billing & Cost Management Dashboard" page, here click on the Budget link on the left sidebar. You will get the Overview page. On the Overview page, click on the Create Budget button which is at the top right side.

It will take you to the "Choose budget type" page. Select a budget type, which is cost budget.

Step 3: Set your budget

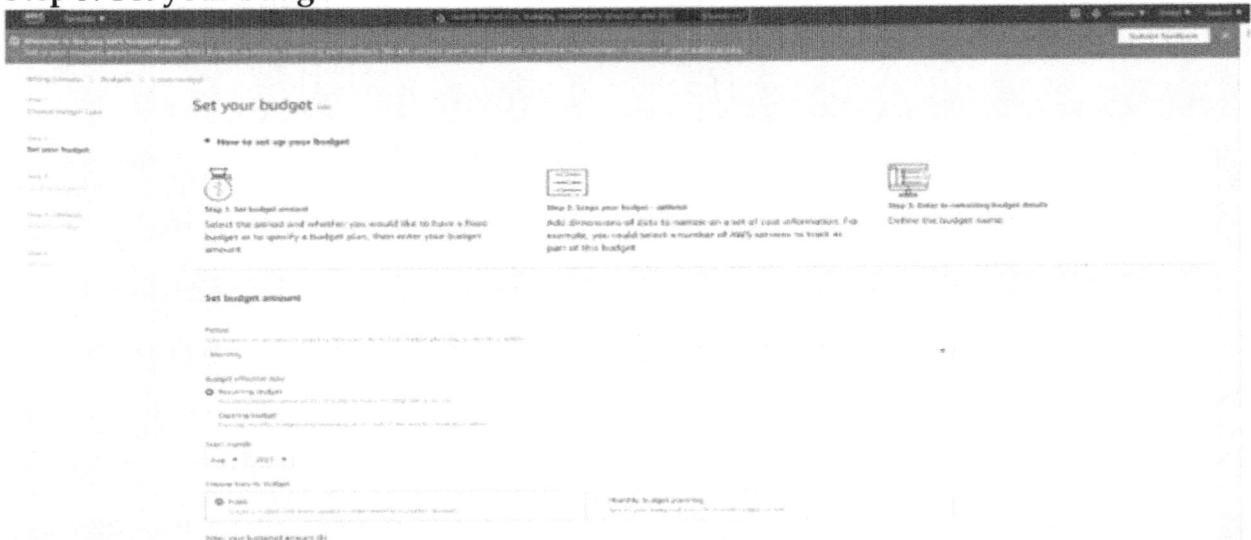

AWS billing & dashboard -- set your budget

Click next, and for the period, select monthly, and select recurring for the budget effective date. Set the starting month, and then enter the budget amount, for example, $1.00. Enter budget name, for example, "AWS Certification Preparation Budget," and then click Next.

On the next screen, enter threshold -- 80% is typical. Next, enter the email where you would like to get the notification. Please make sure you provide the correct email address.

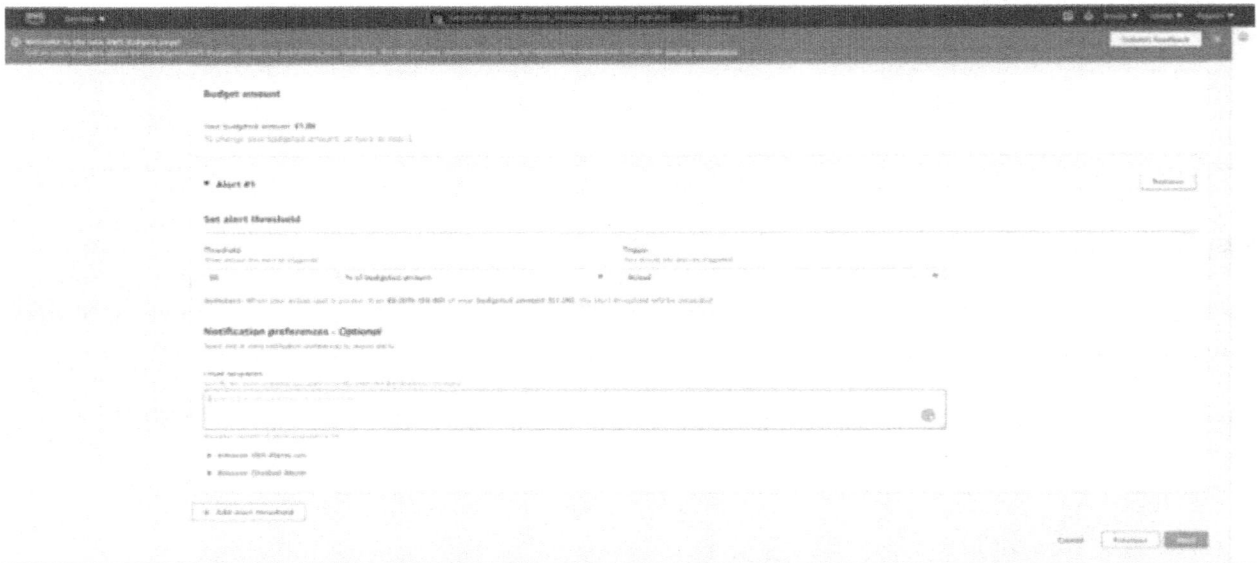

AWS billing & cost management -- budget amount

AWS Billing

Consolidated Billing

You can use the consolidated billing feature in AWS Organizations to consolidate billing and payment for multiple AWS accounts or multiple Amazon Internet Services Pvt. Ltd (AISPL) accounts. Every organization in AWS Organizations has a management account that pays the charges of all the member accounts. Consolidated billing has the following benefits: one bill, easy tracking, combined usage, and no extra fee.

Detailed Billing Report

AWS Detailed Billing Report (AWS DBR) contains similar information as AWS Cost and Usage Report (AWS CUR) regarding your charges but calculates the individual line items differently. If you've signed up for both the AWS DBR and AWS CUR, the line items will not match. However, when the reports are finalized at the end of the month, the total cost will align. The Detailed Billing Report feature is unavailable for new customers.

AWS Cost and Usage Report

AWS Cost and Usage Report contain the most comprehensive cost and usage data available. You can use Cost and Usage Report to publish your AWS billing reports to an Amazon Simple Storage Service (Amazon S3) bucket that you own. For example, you can receive reports that break down your costs by the hour or month, product or product resource, or tags that define yourself. AWS updates the report in your bucket once a day in comma-separated value (CSV) format.

Cost Allocation Report

AWS uses tags to organize resource costs on your cost allocation report. AWS provides two types of cost allocation tags: an AWS-generated tag -- AWS defines, creates, and applies this tag for you, User-defined tags -- you define, create, and apply these tags.

Cost Allocation Tag

Either you or AWS assigns Cost Allocation Tags to AWS resources. Each tag consists of a key and a value. For each resource, each tag key must be unique. Likewise, for each resource, each tag key can have only one value. On a detailed level, you can use tags to organize your resources; you can use cost allocation tags to track your AWS costs.

AWS provides two cost allocation tags: AWS *generated tags* and *user-defined tags*. AWS defines, creates, and applies the AWS-generated labels for you, and you define, create, and apply user-defined tags. You must activate both types of tags separately before they can appear in Cost Explorer or on a cost allocation report.

AWS Compute Optimizer

Overprovisioning resources can result in unnecessary infrastructure costs, and under-provisioning resources can lead to poor application performance. Analyzing historical utilization metrics by leveraging machine learning, AWS Compute Optimizer helps in reduce costs and improve performance by recommending optimal AWS resources for your workloads.

Compute Optimizer helps you choose optimal configurations for three types of AWS resources—Amazon Elastic Compute Cloud (EC2) instance types, Amazon Elastic Block Store (EBS) volumes, and AWS Lambda functions—based on your utilization data.

Compute Optimizer recommends optimal AWS resources by identifying workload patterns. It leverages the knowledge drawn from Amazon's own experience running diverse workloads in the cloud. Compute Optimizer analyzes your workload's configuration and resource utilization to identify dozens of defining characteristics, such as if it is CPU-intensive, if it exhibits a daily pattern, or if a workload accesses local storage frequently.

The Compute Optimizer service processes these characteristics and identifies the hardware resource required by the workload. Then, compute Optimizer infers how the workload would have performed on various hardware platforms or using different configurations to offer recommendations.

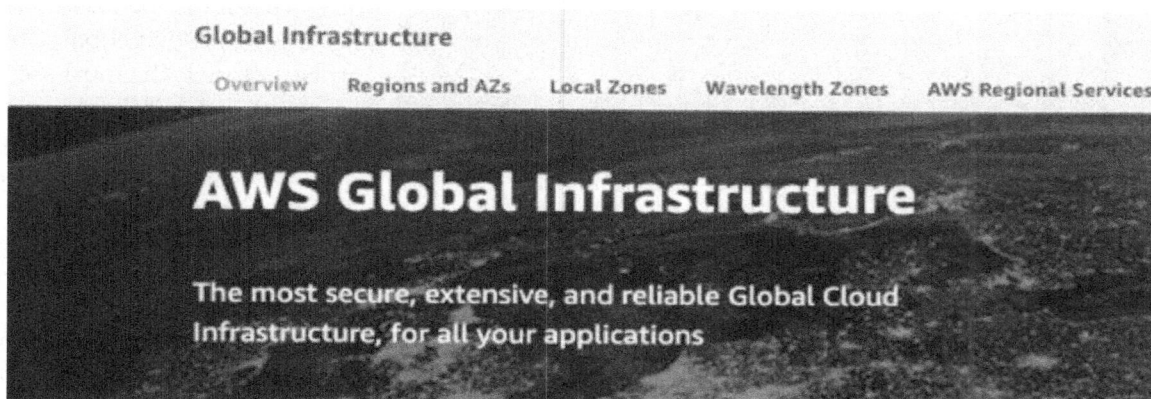

Chapter 11. AWS Global Cloud Infrastructure (Part I)

You will learn the following in this chapter:
- Introduction to AWS Global Infrastructure
- AWS Regions
- How to select an AWS Region
- AWS Availability Zones (AZs)
- AWS Local Zones
- AWS Wavelength
- AWS Edge Locations

The AWS Global Cloud Infrastructure is the most secure, extensive, and reliable cloud platform, offering over 200 fully featured services from data centers globally. Whether you need to deploy your application workloads across the globe in a single click, or you want to build and deploy specific applications closer to your end-users with single-digit millisecond latency, AWS provides you the cloud infrastructure where and when you need it.

We know that AWS is a public cloud service provider and provides on-demand availability of all kinds of cloud services from across the world. How is AWS able to provide on-demand availability of all types of cloud services from across the globe? Well, AWS has a massive amount of computing resources and storage available in data centers spread across all over the world. The AWS entire infrastructure setup of data centers across all over the globe is called AWS Global Cloud Infrastructure. In this chapter, we will learn about AWS Global Cloud Infrastructure and its related concepts, such as AWS Availability Zones and AWS Regions.

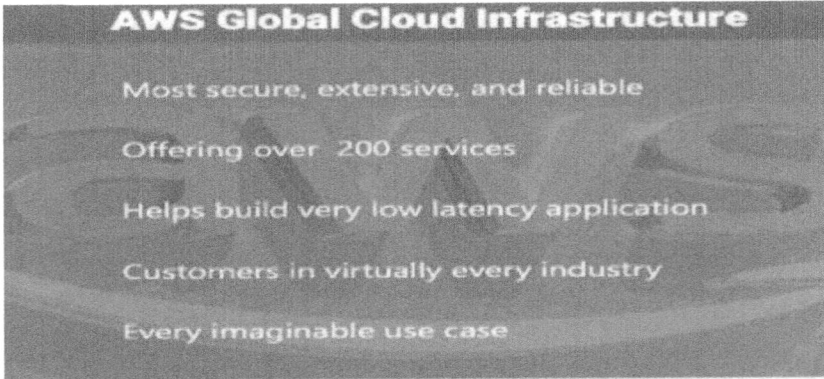

AWS Global Cloud Infrastructure

Most secure, extensive, and reliable

Offering over 200 services

Helps build very low latency application

Customers in virtually every industry

Every imaginable use case

AWS Global Cloud Infrastructure is the backbone of AWS. The AWS Global Cloud Infrastructure is the most secure, extensive, and reliable cloud platform, offering over 200 fully featured services from data centers globally. It not only allows you to deploy your application across the globe with a single click, but it also allows you to build and deploy specific applications closer to your end-users with single-digit millisecond latency. It helps millions of active customers from virtually every industry build and run every imaginable use case on AWS.

This was a high-level overview of AWS Global Cloud Infrastructure. Next, we will look into AWS Regions and AWS Availability Zones, which are other important concepts related to AWS Global Cloud Infrastructure.

AWS Regions

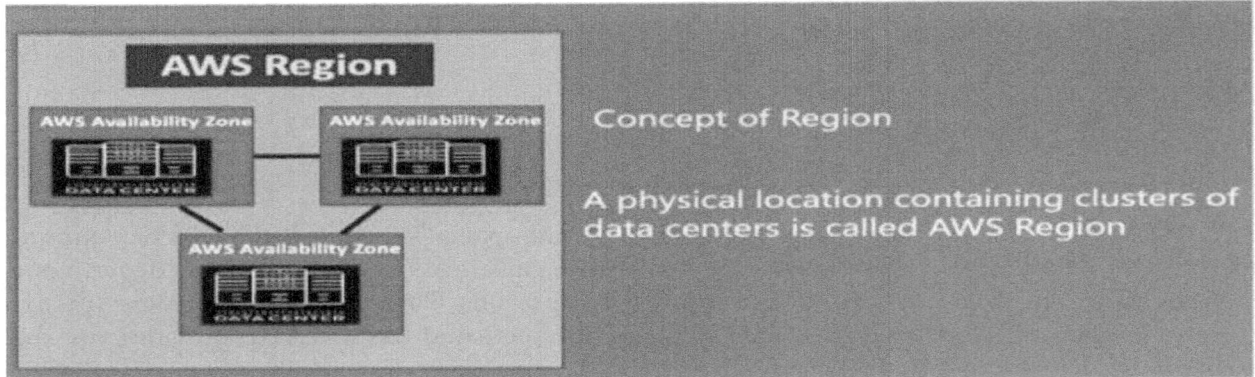

AWS Region

AWS Availability Zone

AWS Availability Zone

AWS Availability Zone

Concept of Region

A physical location containing clusters of data centers is called AWS Region

AWS has the concept of a Region, a physical location worldwide where AWS has clusters of data centers. AWS region is a physical location that has clusters of data centers. As you can see in the picture above, the AWS Region has 3 three clusters of data centers. And these clusters of data centers are connected. Each AWS region is a separate geographical region. Each AWS region is completely independent having its own internal private secured network and is isolated from the other AWS regions.

AWS Regions on the Management Console

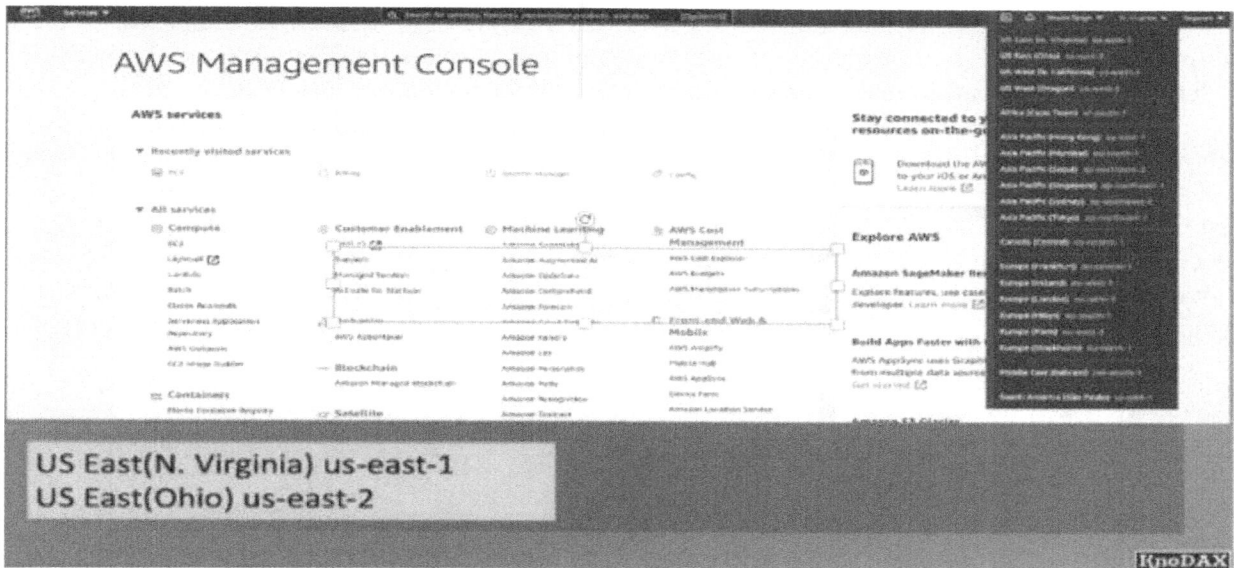

AWS region is displayed at the top right on the AWS Management Console. When you logged in to your AWS account, you will be assigned a default region. That way when you launch any AWS service, it will be served from that AWS region. Each AWS region is assigned a region code, which is used in various configuration when using AWS services and resources. For example, US East (N. Virginia) AWS Region has a region code us-east-1. If a particular service you are looking for is not available in your default AWS region, you can change it.

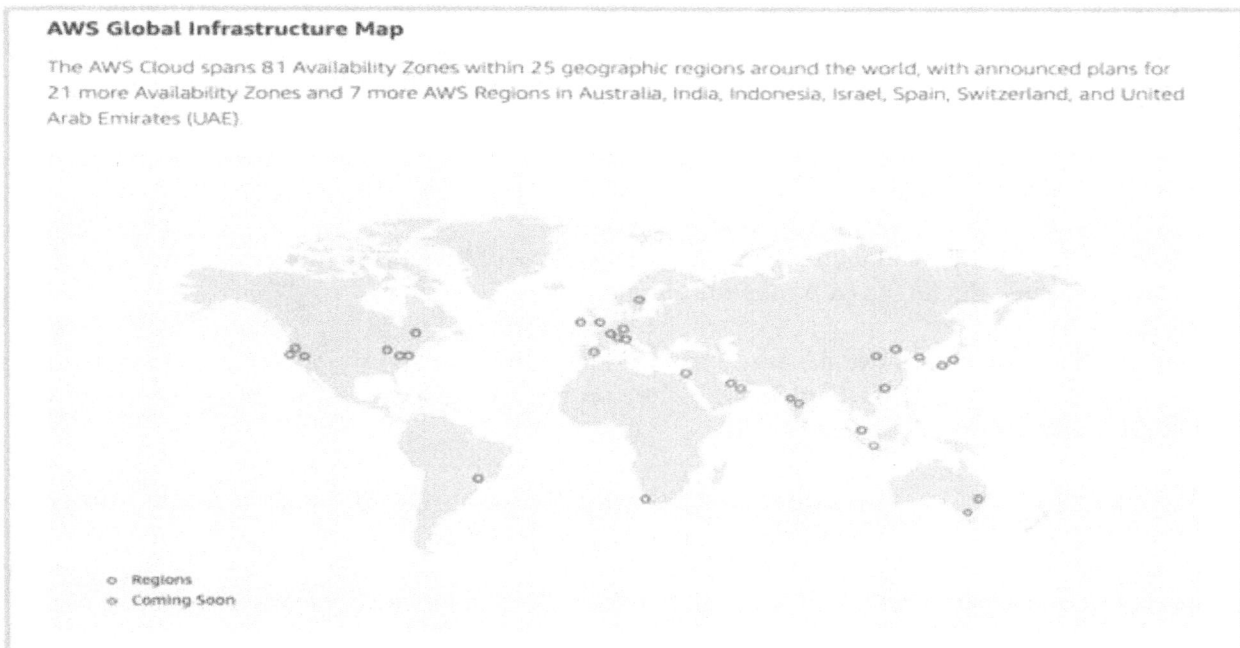

AWS Global Infrastructure Map

Let's try to understand AWS regions by looking at the AWS Global Infrastructure Map. On the AWS Global Infrastructure map above, AWS regions are represented with circles. The blue circle ones are the current AWS regions, and AWS Regions in red circles are coming soon.

As you can see, AWS has regions all over the world. The AWS Cloud spans 96 Availability Zones within 30 geographic regions around the world, with announced plans for 15 more Availability Zones and 5 more AWS Regions in Australia, Canada, Israel, New Zealand, and Thailand.

With regards to AWS regions in USA, there are 6 AWS regions in USA. Two AWS regions are on the US east coast: one is in Northern Virginia, and the other is in Ohio. Two AWS regions are on the US West Coast: one is in Oregon, and the other one is in Northern California. Additionally, there are 2 Gov cloud regions: one is on US East Coast, and other is on US West Coast. Some regions have more services than others. For example. US East (N. Virginia), US West (N. California) in America; Singapore, Sydney, Tokyo in Asia Pacific; Frankfurt, Ireland in EU offer more services in general.

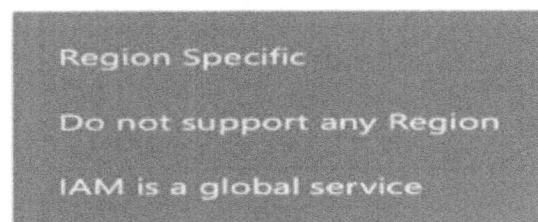

Region Specific

Do not support any Region

IAM is a global service

AWS Regions Features

AWS services are region specific. However, just to keep in mind there are some services which do not support any region. For example, AWS IAM is a global service and is not associated with any region.

KEY POINTS

- Each AWS Region is completely independent, having its own internal private secured network, and is isolated from the other AWS Regions.

- A group of availability zones within a geographic area forms an AWS Region. In other words, an AWS region consists of Availably Zones.

- An AWS Available Zone is a cluster of Data Centers connected with a low latency network.

- An AWS Region has 3 availability zones. However, some of them have more than 3; for example, Northern Virginia Region has 6 Availability Zones.

- Every AWS Region is assigned a Name and a Code. For example, N. Virginia Region has a Region code of us-east-1, and Ohio Region has a Region code of us-east-2, as you can see from the screenshot of AWS Management Console.

- AWS maintains regions in multiple geographic locations in North America, South America, Europe, China, Asia Pacific, South Africa, and the Middle East.

- Each region is a separate geographical region. For example, there are 6 regions in the US as of this recording. 2 regions are on the US east coast: one is in Northern Virginia, and the other is in Ohio. 2 regions are in the US West Coast: one is in Oregon, and the other one is in Northern California. Additionally, there are 2 Gov cloud regions: US-East and the other is US-West.

- Each AWS Region is completely independent, has its own internal private secured network, and is isolated from the other AWS Regions. However, Availability Zones in an AWS Region are connected with high bandwidth, low-latency networks.

- AWS services are region-specific; however, to keep in mind, some services do not support any Region; for example, AWS IAM is a global service and is not associated with any Region.

- Some regions have more services than others, for example. US East (N. Virginia), US West (N. California) in America; Singapore, Sydney, Tokyo in the Asia Pacific; Frankfurt, Ireland in EU offer more services in general.

How to Select an AWS Region

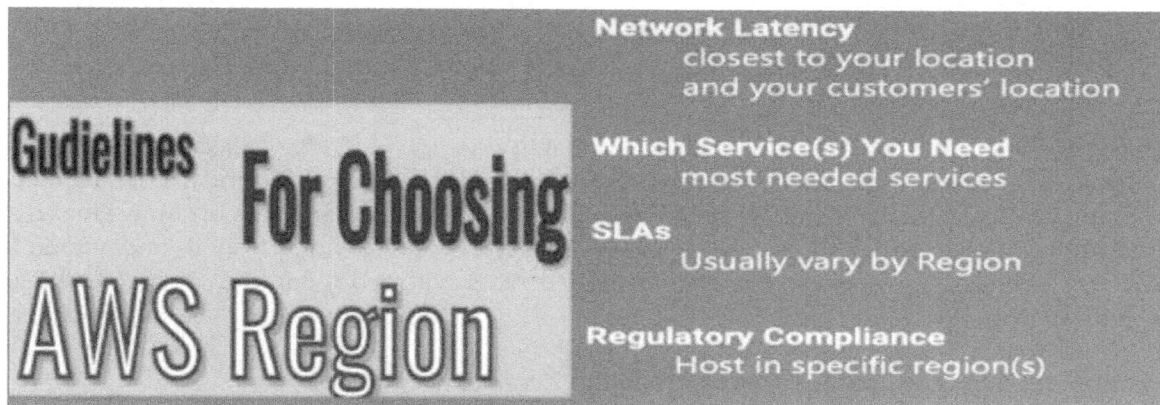

Selecting AWS Region

Following are the guidelines for choosing AWS regions to help ensure excellent performance and resilience:

- **Proximity to customers**: To get low latency performance, choose a region closest to your location and your customers' location to get low network latency.
- **Available services within a Region**: Find out what are your most needed services. Usually, the new services start on a few main regions such as regions on us-east and us-west before being available to other regions.
- **Pricing:** Some regions will cost more than others, so use built-in AWS calculator to do rough cost estimates to get idea about your choices. SLAs usually vary by region, so be sure to be aware of what your needs are and if they're being met.
- **Compliance with data governance and legal requirements**: You may need to meet regulatory compliance such as GDPR by hosting your deployment in a specific region or regions to be compliant.

AWS Availability Zones

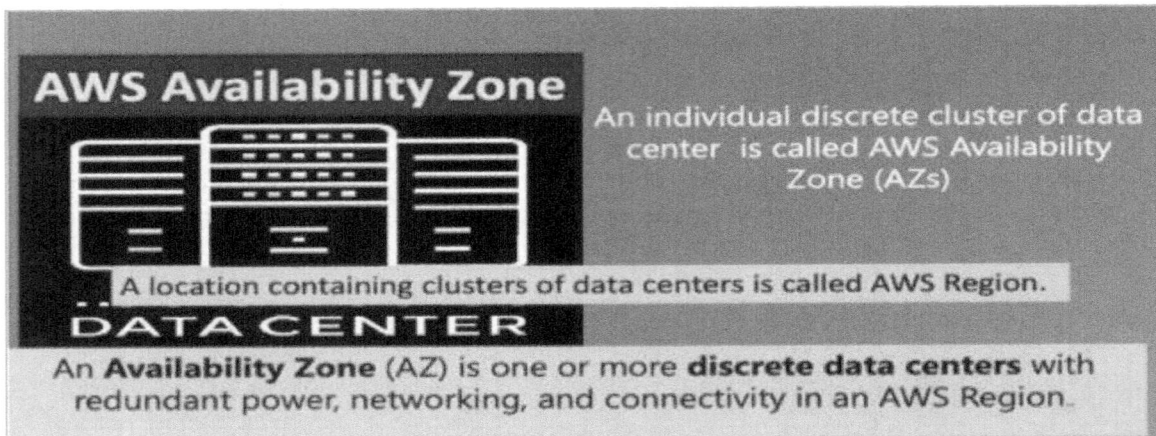

AWS Availability Zones

Another essential concept in AWS is AWS Availability Zone. It is also called AZ, in short. As I mentioned earlier, AWS has clusters of data centers on multiple locations worldwide, and a location containing clusters of data centers is called AWS Region. On the other hand, an individual discrete cluster of the data center is called AWS Availability Zone. Another way to way to understand is: An availability zone (AZ) is one or more discrete data centers with redundant power, networking, and connectivity in an AWS region.

Let's simplify AWS Regions and AWS Availability Zones concepts.

Let's simplify a bit. In an AWS region, there are clusters of data centers spread across the location. An individual discrete cluster of data center or a discrete data center is called AWS Availability Zone.

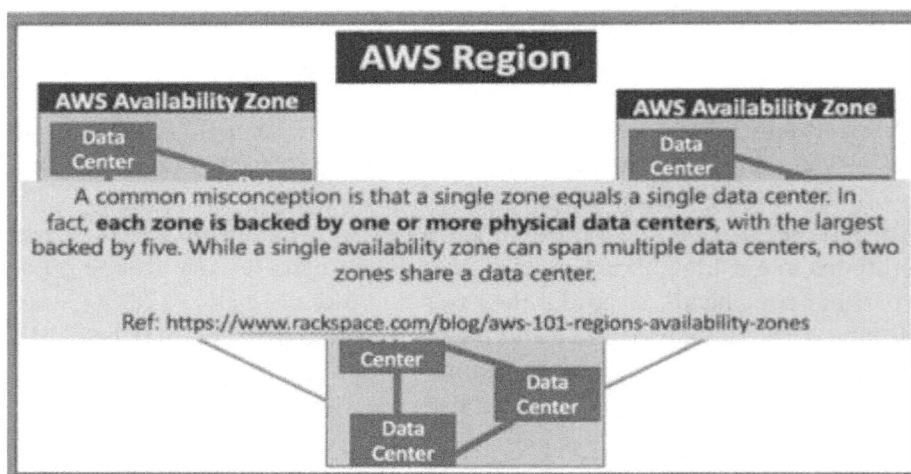

Understanding AWS Regions

AWS availability zones within a region have connectivity with one another. To strengthen the concept further, I would like to share this point:

More Details About AWS Availability Zones

Discrete data centers

Redundant power

Networking

Connectivity to AWS Region

Now you got a conceptual understanding of AWS Availability Zones. Let's go through some more details. Availability zones are separated in an AWS region. Availability zones are located away from the city and are in lower-risk flood areas to avoid the flood or any other kind of damage to the data centers. AZs are physically separated by a significant distance, many kilometers, from any other AZ.

An availability zone (AZ) is one or more discrete data centers with redundant power, networking, and connectivity in an AWS Region. All AZs in an AWS Region are interconnected with high-bandwidth and low-latency networking between AZs.

Each availability zone has its power supply and on-site backup generator. Furthermore, they are

Own power supply

Onsite backup generator

Connected via different grid

connected via different grids from independent utilities to avoid a single point of failure for any power outage.

Availability zones have code as well, like AWS regions. Availability zone code has region code + a letter added in the end. For instance, The US Ohio AWS region has region code us-east-2. And this AWS region has 3 availability zones with their code as us-east-2a, us-east-2b, and us-east-2c. If you notice, a letter has been added at the end of the region code (us-east-2+a = us-east-2a) to get the AZ code.

Availability Zones from Architectural Perspective

> **Replication of resources and data**
>
> **Helps avoid data loss and provide high availability to the deployed applications.**
>
> Redundancy and replication are architectural techniques to increase degree of high availability and fault tolerance of software applications.
>
> Replications across regions don't happen unless organizations explicitly would like to perform.
>
> The reason is AWS Regions are separate; and, they are not connected with the AWS private network unlike AWS AZs. AZs are connected with one another with AWS private network.

AWS Availability Zones – Architectural Perspective

Let's understand Availability Zones from the solution architecture perspective. Redundancy and replication are architectural techniques to increase the high availability and fault tolerance of software applications.

To provide redundancy, AWS allows replication of resources and data in multiple availability zones, which helps avoid data loss and offers high availability for the deployed applications. All traffic between AZs is encrypted. Furthermore, you can perform synchronous replication between AZs. However, replications across AWS regions don't happen unless organizations explicitly would like to do perform. The reason is AWS regions are separate, and they are not connected with the AWS private network, unlike AWS availability zones that are connected.

KEY POINTS

- AWS has data centers worldwide in multiple locations to help provide high availability and low latency services. These locations are divided into Regions and Availability Zones.

- Every AWS Region is divided into multiple isolated locations known as Availability Zones.

- Availability Zone is essentially an AWS Data Center with its own power supply, low-latency, and high bandwidth network setup.

- An Availability Zone (AZ) is a discrete data center with redundant power, networking, and connectivity in an AWS Region.

- Each Availability Zone has its own power supply and on-site backup generator. And, they are connected via different grids from independent utilities to avoid a single point of failure for any power outage.

- Typically, there are three Availability Zones in a Region. However, in some cases, there are more than 3. For example, N. Virginia Region has 6 Availability Zones.

- All AZs in an AWS Region are interconnected with high-bandwidth, low-latency networking between AZs.

- Availability Zones are separated in an AWS Region.

- Availability Zones are located away from the city and are in lower-risk flood areas to avoid the flood or any other damage to the data centers.

- AZ's are physically separated by a meaningful distance, many kilometers, from any other AZ.

- Availability Zones have codes as well, like Region. Availability Zone code has Region Code + a letter added in the end. For example. N. Virginia region has region code us-east-1. And this region has 6 Availability Zones with their code as us-east-1a, us-east-1b, and the rest AZs are coded in the same way.

- AWS customers focused on high availability can design their applications to run on multiple AZs to achieve even greater fault tolerance.

- AZs allow customers to operate production applications and databases that are more highly available, fault-tolerant, and scalable than would be possible from a single data center.

- AZs make partitioning applications for high availability easy. If an application is partitioned across AZs, the application is better isolated and protected from power outages, tornadoes, earthquakes, etc.

- To provide redundancy, AWS allows replication of resources and data in multiple Availability Zones. This helps avoid data loss and provides high availability to the deployed applications. However, these replications don't happen across regions unless organizations explicitly decide to do so.

- All traffic between AZs is encrypted. Therefore, the network performance is sufficient to accomplish synchronous replication between AZs.

- AWS Regions are separate, and they are not connected with the AWS private network, unlike AWS Availability Zones, which are connected.

AWS Local Zones

Another concept related to AWS Global Cloud Infrastructure is AWS Local Zones. As per the AWS Local Zones documentation (https://aws.amazon.com/about-aws/global-infrastructure/localzones/):

AWS Local Zones are a type of AWS infrastructure deployment that places AWS compute, storage, database, and other select services close to large population, industry, and IT centers. With AWS Local Zones, you can easily run applications that need single-digit millisecond latency closer to end-users in a specific geography. AWS Local Zones are ideal for use cases such as media & entertainment content creation, real-time gaming, live video streaming, and machine learning inference.

AWS Local Zones are infrastructure deployment that places compute, storage, database, and other select AWS services close to a large population and industrial centers. Thus, AWS Local Zones help deliver innovative applications requiring low latency closer to end-users and on-premises installations. Using AWS Local Zones, you could also leverage cloud services for edge computing with on-demand scaling, high availability, and pay-as-you-go pricing.

AWS Local Zones provide a high-bandwidth, secure connection to the AWS Region and allow you to seamlessly connect to the full range of services in the AWS Region.

Various AWS services such as Amazon EC2, Amazon VPC, Amazon EBS, Amazon RDS, Amazon Elastic Load Balancing, and Amazon ElastiCache are available locally in the AWS Local Zones. In addition, you can also use AWS services that orchestrate or work with local services such as Amazon EC2 Auto Scaling, Amazon EKS clusters, Amazon ECS clusters, Amazon CloudWatch, AWS CloudTrail, and AWS CloudFormation.

AWS Wavelength Zones

Build ultra-low latency applications to 5G

AWS Wavelength Zones

The other one is AWS Wavelength, an AWS infrastructure offering optimized for mobile edge computing applications. As per the AWS Wavelength Zones documentation (https://aws.amazon.com/wavelength/)

> *AWS Wavelength is an AWS Infrastructure offering optimized for mobile edge computing applications. Wavelength Zones are AWS infrastructure deployments that embed AWS compute and storage services within communications service providers' (CSP) data centers at the edge of the 5G network, so application traffic from 5G devices can reach application servers running in Wavelength Zones without leaving the telecommunications network. This avoids the latency that would result from application traffic having to traverse multiple hops across the Internet to reach their destination, enabling customers to take full advantage of the latency and bandwidth benefits offered by modern 5G networks.*

AWS Wavelength extends the AWS cloud to a global network of 5G edge. AWS Wavelength embeds AWS compute and storage services within 5G networks, thus providing mobile edge computing infrastructure for developing, deploying, and scaling ultra-low-latency applications. It enables developers to accelerate innovative 5G edge application development and build a whole new class of applications that require ultra-low latency by Leveraging proven AWS infrastructure and services.

Wavelength Zones provide a high-bandwidth, secure connection to the parent AWS Region. As a result, Wavelength Zones enable developers to also seamlessly connect to the full range of services in the AWS Region.

Edge locations

An AWS Edge location is a site that CloudFront service uses to cache copies of the content to reduce latency for faster delivery to users at any location. AWS Edge Locations are AWS data centers that are located in such a way to deliver services quick response with the lowest latency possible. They are often in major cities to provide the lowest latency response to city users. Edge Locations data centers are nearer than data centers in AZ a Region. Amazon has many of these types of data centers working as Edge Locations across the world. If you have global users for your web applications, it is not cost-effective and not always feasible to deploy your applications and replicate the infrastructure on different servers in many locations worldwide to overcome latency issues for your users.

A CDN, such as AWS CloudFront, allows you to utilize Edge Locations to deliver a cached copy of web content to your customers. To reduce response time, the CDN utilizes the nearest Edge Location to the customer or originating request location to reduce the latency.

AWS Points of Presence

(Edge locations and Regional Caches)

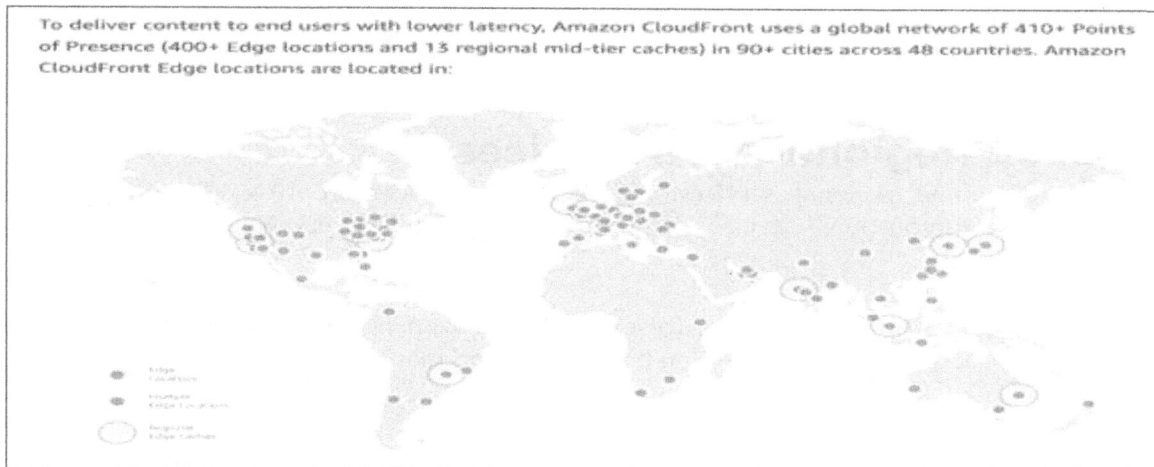

To deliver content to end users with lower latency, Amazon CloudFront uses a global network of 410+ Points of Presence (400+ Edge locations and 13 regional mid-tier caches) in 90+ cities across 48 countries. Amazon CloudFront Edge locations are located in:

AWS Outposts

AWS Outposts is a family of fully managed services providing a hybrid experience. It delivers AWS infrastructure and services to virtually any on-premises or edge location. AWS Outposts allows you to extend and run native AWS services on-premises. With AWS Outposts, you can run not only run AWS services locally but also can connect to the local AWS Region to access a broad range of available services.

You can run applications and workloads on-premises using familiar AWS services, tools, and APIs. AWS Outposts support workloads and devices requiring low latency access to on-premises systems. For example, workloads running on factory floors for automated operations in manufacturing, real-time patient diagnosis, medical imaging, or content and media streaming. You can use Outposts to securely store and process customer data that must remain on-premises or in countries with no AWS region. You can run data-intensive workloads on Outposts and process data locally when transmitting data to the cloud is expensive.

Use cases

Low latency compute

Deliver high-quality gaming experiences for interactive applications, like real-time multiplayer games, to players all over the world. When the nearest public cloud servers are not close enough to meet single-digit millisecond latency requirements, AWS Outposts can help run business applications where you need them for manufacturing execution systems (MES), high-frequency trading, or medical diagnostics.

Migration and modernization

Legacy on-premises applications often have latency-sensitive system dependencies, making them difficult to migrate. AWS Outposts allows you to segment migrations into smaller pieces on premises, maintaining latency sensitive connectivity between application components until you are ready to migrate.

Data residency

Data sometimes needs to remain in a particular country, state, or municipality for regulatory, contractual, or information security reasons. This is often the case with financial services, healthcare, oil and gas, and other highly regulated industries. With AWS Outposts, you can control where your workloads run and where your data resides, with low-friction movement between cloud and edge locations to easily adapt to regulatory changes.

Local data processing

Process data locally for use cases such as data lakes and machine learning (ML) model training, or set up a consistent hybrid architecture to process local, difficult-to-migrate data sets with cost, size, or bandwidth constraints and move data to the cloud for long-term archival.

Screenshot from:
https://aws.amazon.com/outposts/

Global vs. Regional AWS Services

AWS has global and regional services. AWS Global Services are IAM (Identity and Access Management), Route 53 (DNS service), CloudFront (Content Delivery Network), and WAF(Web Application Firewall).

Most AWS services are Region-scoped; for example, Amazon EC2 (IaaS), Elastic Beanstalk(PaaS), AWS Lambda (FaaS), Amazon Rekognition (SaaS type), and many more.

For further details about regional services, please visit: https://aws.amazon.com/about-aws/global-infrastructure/regional-product-services

AWS Identity and Access Management (IAM)
Apply fine-grained permissions to AWS services and resources

Chapter 12. Identity and Access Management (IAM)

You will learn the following in this chapter:
- Introduction of IAM
- Create IAM User
- IAM Group
- IAM Policy
- IAM Permissions
- IAM Password Policy
- IAM Role
- IAM Role for Services
- Using IAM Role on EC2 Instance
- IAM Use Cases
- IAM Access Keys
- Best Practices for IAM Service
- IAM Access Advisor
- IAM Credentials Report

IAM is a feature of your AWS account offered at no additional charge.

It is an essential chapter with regards to the AWS foundational concept. First, we will get the theoretical understanding of Identity and Access Management (IAM), IAM users and groups, IAM Policy, and then create an IAM user. Let's first start with what IAM is.

Introduction to IAM

IAM is the abbreviated form of Identity and Access Management. It is a global service, which means it is not associated with any AWS region -- most AWS services have a region scope. However, a handful of them has global scope -- IAM has global scope. It deals with the management of users, groups, and their permissions. In other words, using the IAM service, we can create users and groups and assign them permissions means what the users and groups can do on that AWS account.

You already used the IAM service when you signed up for AWS. When you sign up for AWS, an AWS root account is created. AWS root account is created default when you sign up for AWS. You should use your AWS root account in very rare situation. In fact, you should create another user, and use that user account instead of the root user account. And do not share your root user account user id, password, and access keys with anyone.

Amazon IAM service allows you to securely control access to AWS services and resources. You can create and manage AWS users and groups using IAM. You can set up permissions to allow and deny their access to AWS resources.

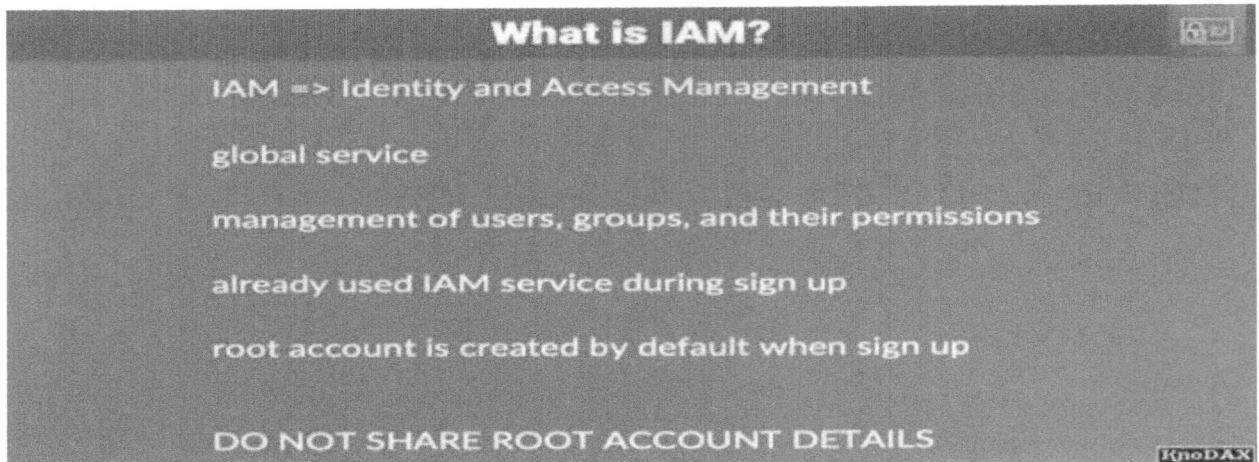

The IAM service provides fine-grained access control across your AWS account. With IAM, you can specify access permissions -- who can access what services and resources. With IAM policies, you manage access permissions to your workforce and systems to ensure the least privilege permissions. These features do IAM a critically important service for your account's overall security of AWS resources. IAM is secure by default; users cannot access AWS resources until permissions are explicitly granted. You also require strong password practices, such as complexity level, avoiding re-use, and enforcing multi-factor authentication (MFA).

For workloads that require systems to have access to AWS, you can enable secure access to IAM through roles, instance profiles, identity federation, and temporary credentials. You can use federation with your existing directory service.

Now we know that IAM is used for the management of users, groups. In other words, we can create users and groups using the IAM service.

IAM Users and Groups

Let's understand the IAM users and groups concept. Before going into details, I just wanted to clarify that you might hear both AWS and IAM users. Both are the same. Depending on the context, one is generally used over the other. AWS user is a more general term; however, we use the term IAM user when referring specifically to the context of IAM. Semantically both terms are the same.

You should create separate IAM users for each person in your organization. In other words, an AWS account/person in your organization. However, it's good practice to create a group for the users if they do similar operations. Why? Because that way, if you need to add additional permission, just add that permission to the group, and it will be assigned to all group users. On the same token, if you remove permission from the group, it will be removed for all group users.

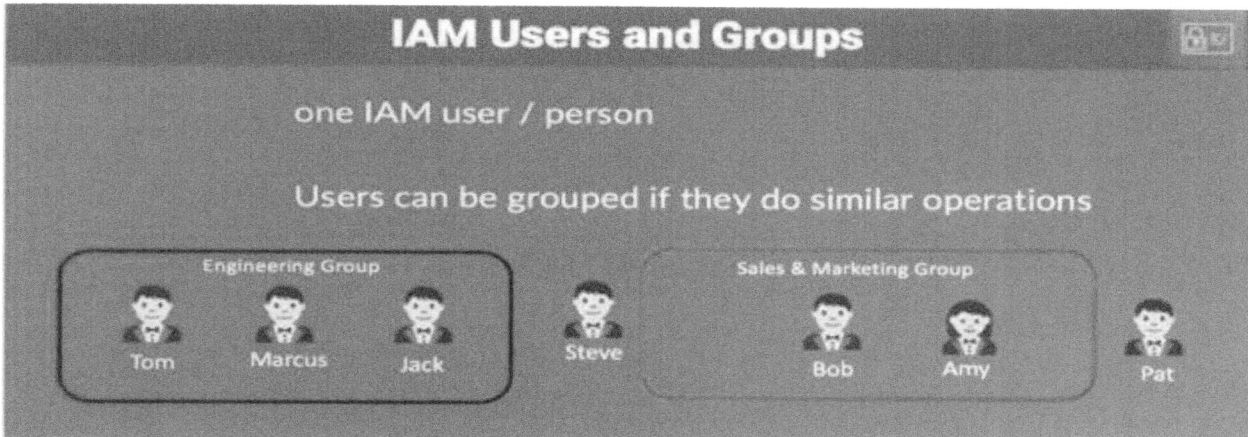

IAM Users and Groups

one IAM user / person

Users can be grouped if they do similar operations

Engineering Group: Tom, Marcus, Jack — Steve — Sales & Marketing Group: Bob, Amy — Pat

Let's try to understand the AWS users and groups concepts. Suppose we have a startup organization with seven employees. Tom, Marcus, and Jack are in the Engineering group; Bob and Amy are in the Sales & Marketing group; Pat is in Finance, and Steve is CEO.

In this scenario, we will have to create 7 IAM users -- one for each employee. Since Tom, Marcus, and Jack are in the engineer's group, we will need to create an Engineering group and add them to the engineering group.

Since Bob and Amy are in Sales & Marketing, we will create a Sales & Marketing group and add Bob and Amy to the Sales & Marketing. Now Steve is CEO. Being CEO, sometimes, he helps the Engineering group, and sometimes he allows the Sales & Marketing group. So, we will add Steve to both groups. Pat will be in no group as he takes care of the Finance department alone until he extends his fiancé group to add more employees.

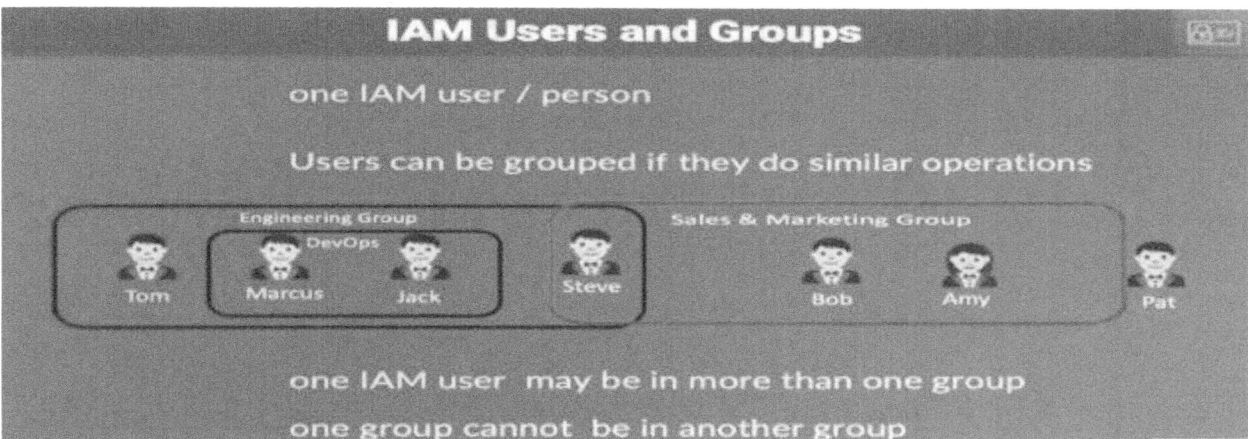

IAM Users and Groups

one IAM user / person

Users can be grouped if they do similar operations

Engineering Group: Tom, DevOps (Marcus, Jack) — Steve — Sales & Marketing Group: Bob, Amy — Pat

one IAM user may be in more than one group

one group cannot be in another group

As you can see, an AWS user could be in more than one group. For example, suppose you later created a DevOps group and if Marcus and Jack are part of the DevOps group. Then, you can add Marcus and Jack into the DevOps Group. So, we got the idea, we need one IAM user per person, and users could belong to a group if they perform similar operations. One IAM user may be in more than one group, which is generally good, making user management easier. You cannot have one group in another group.

IAM Group

IAM group is used to group the collection of IAM users. IAM group makes IAM users' permission management easier. If new permission needs to be added or revoked, just do it from the IAM group, and the change is applied to all users in the group immediately.

KEY POINTS

- IAM is a global service.
- The root account is created by default when you sign up for an AWS account.
- IAM users are people in an organization; they can be grouped.
- An IAM group can only contain IAM users – no other group.
- An IAM user can be associated with multiple IAM groups.

IAM Policy

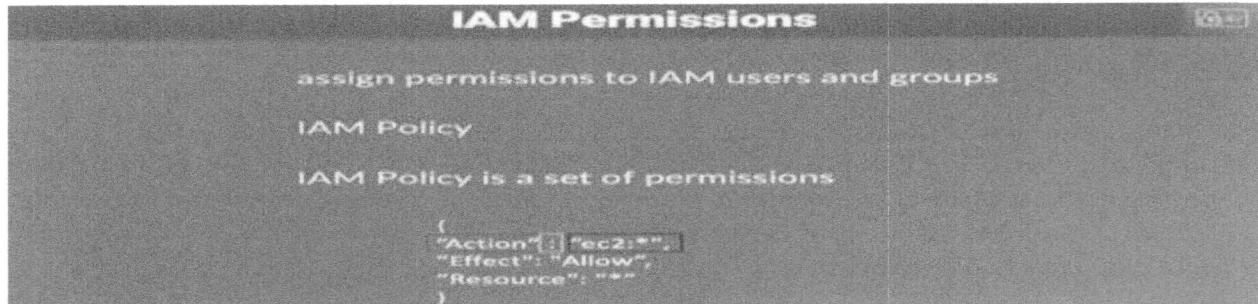

Now how will we allow AWS users and groups to use AWS? To enable users or groups, to do what they are allowed to do, we will have to assign permissions. How will we assign permissions? Well, there is a concept of IAM policy, which contains a set of permissions.

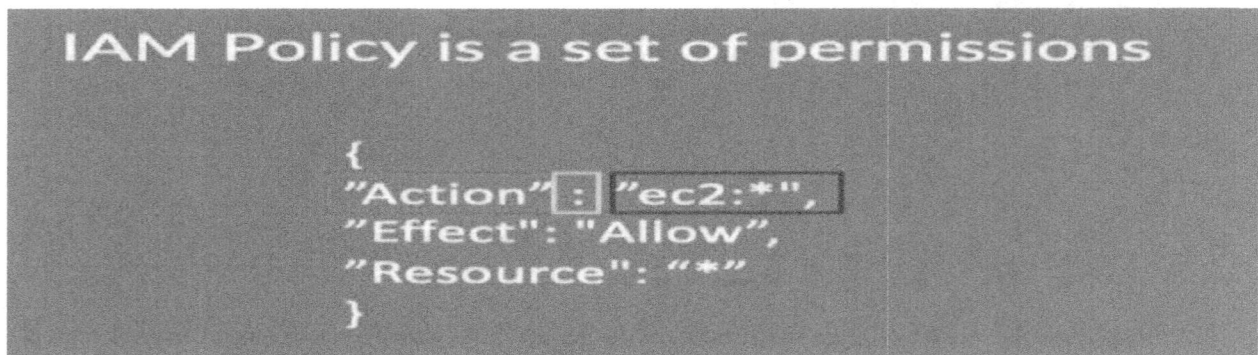

IAM policy is written in JSON as you can see in the screenshot. JSON is easy to understand. It is structured written in a key-value format separate as a colon. For example, the JSON statement in the picture says that all EC2 actions are allowed if any resource"*" represents any or all. If this permission is assigned to an IAM user or group, the user or group can perform any EC2 operation on any resource.

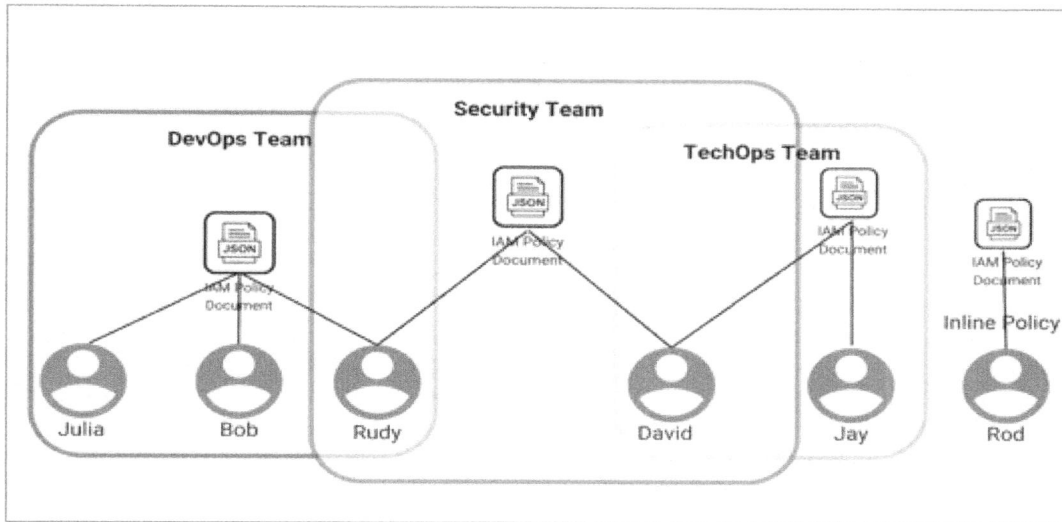

As shown in the diagram above, an IAM policy can be assigned to more than one user. In the diagram, Julia, Bob, and Rudy from the DevOps Team are assigned an IAM Policy. Rudy and David are on the Security Team; they have been assigned another IAM Policy. David and Jay are in the TechOps Team and have been assigned a different policy. And Rod has been given an Inline Policy, which is not a managed policy. What it means is that an Inline IAM Policy cannot be assigned to any other user. The important point is that Rudy has been assigned two policies since his roles overlap. On the same token, David has also been assigned two IAM policies.

The main point to understand here you assign permissions to an IAM user or a group using the IAM policy. IAM policy is a set of permissions, as you can see in the document. The individual lines, which are also called statements, are given within the curly brackets. So, for example, you have one set of permissions for EC2 and another set for elastic load balancing and so on. For each permission set, you provide action that you are considering, Effect which could Allow or Deny, and on which resource or resources you would want the defined action to be applied upon.

If we assign this policy to any user or group, then that user or group will perform operations based on the approach. An IAM user or group cannot do anything unless a policy is assigned. More than one policy can be assigned to a user or group.

You should not assign more permissions than a user needs it. The is called the principle of least privilege, which helps in your overall AWS account security. If you didn't follow this principle, you could have situations where users could be doing or trying out something, for example, launching hundreds of EC2 instances, and organizations would get surprised charges on the AWS bill. Additionally, there could be potential security-related issues as well.

KEY POINTS

- IAM Policy essentially is a JSON Document -- containing a set of permissions -- that can be assigned to IAM Users and IAM Groups.
- We apply the Least Privilege Principle, which means we don't assign more permissions than a user needs.

IAM Policy Document Structure

Mandatory Elements of an IAM Policy (Effect, Action)

Most policies are stored in AWS as JSON documents. Identity-based policies and policies used to set permissions boundaries are JSON policy documents that you attach to a user or role. Resource-based policies are JSON policy documents that you attach to a resource.

A JSON policy document includes the following elements:

- Optional policy-wide information at the top of the document. In this, we have "Version" which is the policy language version. And another is "Id" which is an identifier for the policy. -- the "Id" is optional.
- One or more individual statements, which is required.

```json
{
    "Version": "2012-10-17",
    "Id": "S3-bucket-permissions",
    "Statement": [
        {
            "Sid": "123",
            "Effect": "Allow",
            "Principal": {
                "AWS": ["arn:aws:iam::987654321013:root"],
            },
            "Action": [
                "s3:ListBucket",
                "s3:getObject",
                "s3:putObject",
            ],
            "Resource": ["arn:aws:s3:::mybucket/*"]
        }
    ]
}
```

Each statement includes information about single permission. The information in a statement is contained within a series of elements.

- Version – Specify the version of the policy language that you want to use. As a best practice, use the latest 2012-10-17 version.
- Statement – Use this main policy element as a container for the following elements. You can include more than one statement in a policy.
- Sid (Optional) – Include an optional statement ID to differentiate between your statements.
- Effect – Use Allow or Deny to indicate whether the policy allows or denies access.
- Principal (Required in only some circumstances) – If you create a resource-based policy, you must indicate the account, user, role, or federated user to which you would like to allow or deny access. If you are creating an IAM permissions policy to attach to a user or role, you cannot include this element. The principal is implied as that user or role.
- Action – Include a list of actions that the policy allows or denies.
- Resource (Required in only some circumstances) – If you create an IAM permissions policy, you must specify a list of resources to which the actions apply. If you create a resource-based policy, this element is optional. If you do not include this element, then the resource to which the action applies is the resource to which the policy is attached.
- Condition (Optional) – Specify the circumstances under which the policy grants permission.

Create IAM User

Let's log in to the AWS management console and search for IAM Service. A quick way to find the service is to type the service name in the Search area. Or you can find it from the recently visited services panel. Then, click on IAM. you will get the IAM service home page.

IAM Service Console

Whenever you need to create an AWS user, you will use the IAM service. In the beginning, some terms may be confusing, but as you do more learning of AWS, you will feel very comfortable with these terms.

IAM Users Page

For example, AWS user or AWS IAM user is the same thing. Click on Users; I already have a couple of users here.

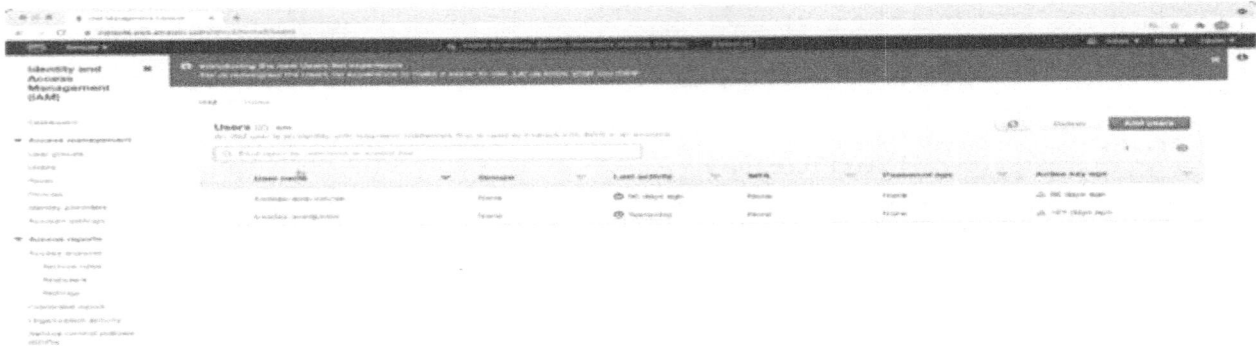

Click on Add Users button to add a new user.

Add User

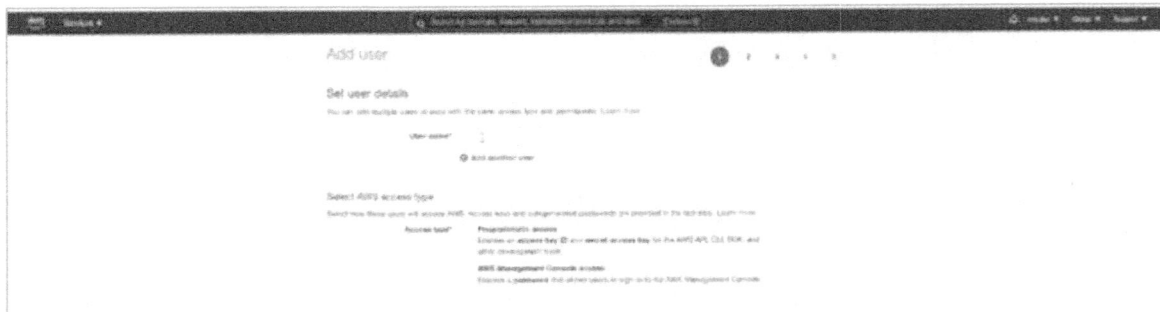

Enter username – I'll enter John Doe. This is just a demo user to show you how to add an IAM user to AWS. Next is the Select AWS Access type. I'll check both checkboxes.

The first one is for programmatic access. Checking this option will also generate and enable an access key ID and secret access key. These keys are needed to interact with AWS programmatically using AWS API, CLI, SDK, and other development tools. For example, you will need these keys if you use AWS CLI, AWS Command Line interface. AWS CLI is used mainly by AWS DevOps engineers.

These keys are also needed if you are using AWS SDK, which is AWS Software Development Kit. AWS SDK is used mainly by AWS developers who are building software using AWS APIs. The main point here is that if you are adding a new user and if this user will have an AWS Developer or DevOps type of role, have the programmatic access option checked.

And the other one is for the AWS Management Console Access. This is a typical and common way to access AWS, and most AWS users are comfortable with this option, so it is ok to have this option checked in most situations. So let me check this option.

The next option is about the console password, which will be used to log into the AWS Management Console. Please note, when using AWS API, you will be using your account access keys, which are AWS Access Key and AWS Secret Key. I'll have this option checked. If you are an admin and create a user for someone else, usually you will use an autogenerated password; and have this option checked. You can also add a custom password – it means not an auto-generated one.

Next is Require password reset check box. I'll leave it as it is -- it means checked. That way, AWS will force to create a new password at the next sign-in. Click on the Next button, which is about permission.

Attach Policy

Here click on "Attach existing policies directly" and select "AdministratorAccess" policy so that this new user will have admin privilege to this account.

AWS has many existing policies which you can directly attach to an IAM user.

Tag

IAM tags are just labels that are used when creating IAM users or roles.

Click on tags; I'm not creating any label for this user, as this is optional.

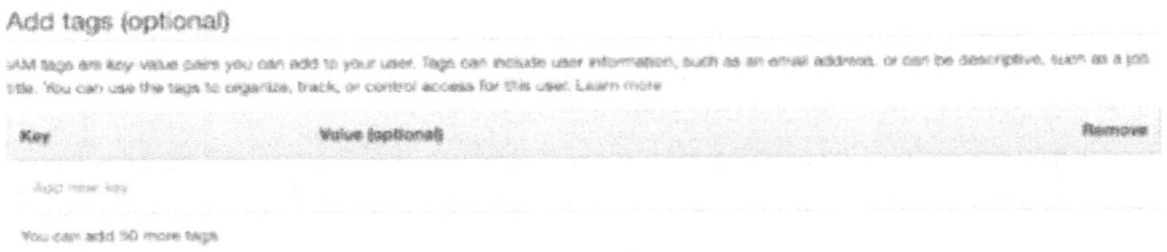

Add tags (optional)

IAM tags are key value pairs you can add to your user. Tags can include user information, such as an email address, or can be descriptive, such as a job title. You can use the tags to organize, track, or control access for this user. Learn more

Key	Value (optional)	Remove
Add new key		

You can add 50 more tags

However, you can add here user email address, job title as a tag.

Review

Next, click on the Review button. If you notice here, there are two policies attached to this user. One is AdministratorAccess, and the other one is IAMUserChangePassword.

Review

Review your choices. After you create the user, you can view and download the autogenerated password and access key.

User details

User name	JohnDoe
AWS access type	Programmatic access and AWS Management Console access
Console password type	Autogenerated
Require password reset	Yes
Permissions boundary	Permissions boundary is not set

Permissions summary

The following policies will be attached to the user shown above.

Type	Name
Managed policy	AdministratorAccess
Managed policy	IAMUserChangePassword

Tags

No tags were added.

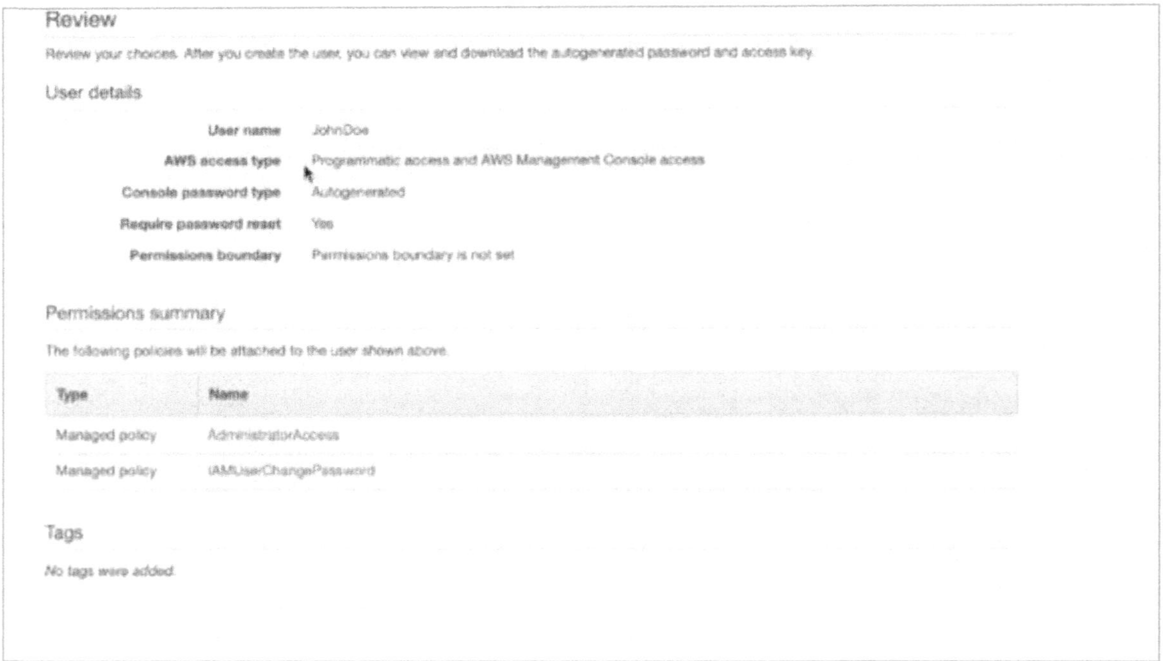

The IAMUserChangePassword policy is added as we chose the option for auto-generated passwords.

Create User

Next, click on Create User button. Now the user is created.

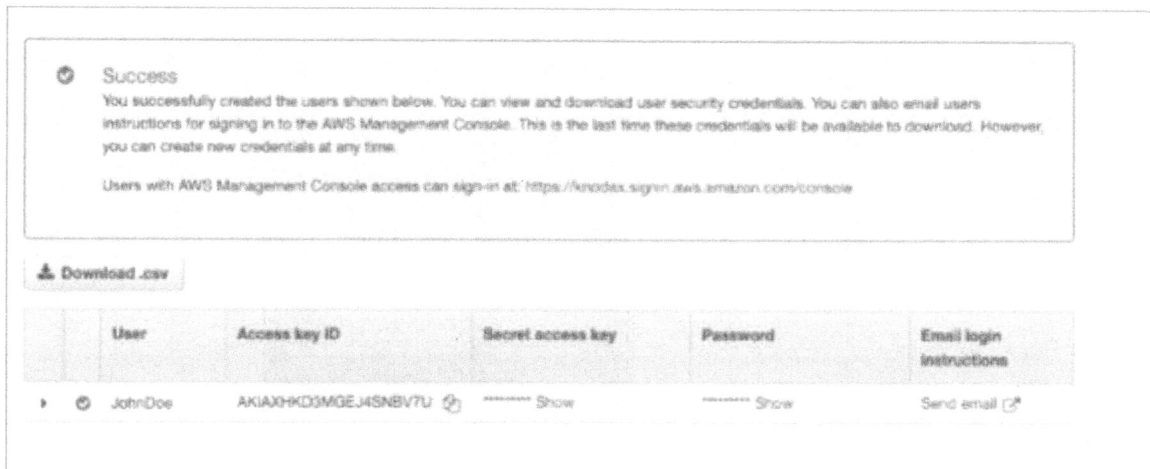

As you can see, since I have selected programmatic access, Access Key ID, Secret Access Key is generated. Furthermore, since I selected the option for the auto-generated password, the user Password is generated as well. I'll not note down the password and download access keys.

Since I selected AWS Management Console access, the newly created user will also get an AWS Management Console URL to log in to the AWS management console.

Test the Created User

Let's test if it works. First, I'll open a new window. Here enter the current password and new password.

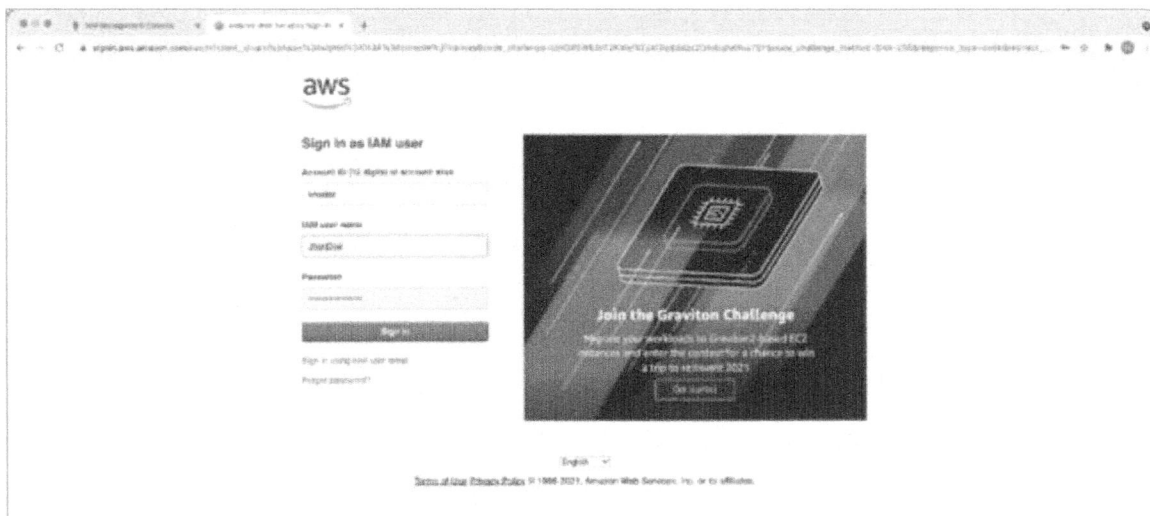

Since it was an auto-generated password, it is asking to change the password.

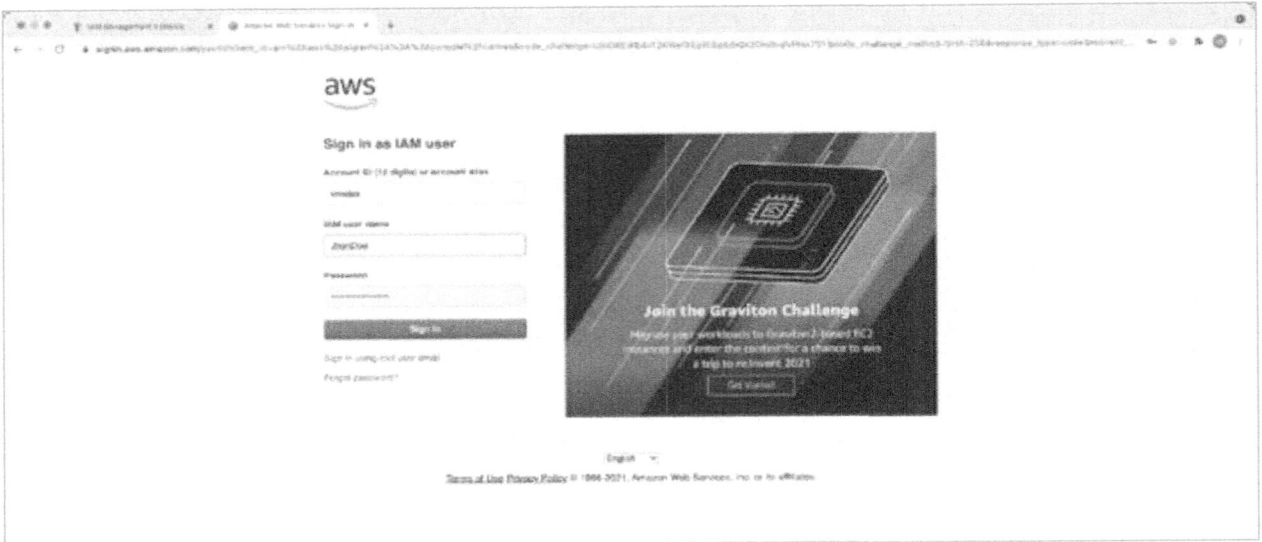

I'll create a new password and click on Confirm password change button. This will create an IAM user, which is JohnDoe.

Delete IAM User

If you would like to delete this user, go to the IAM Service home page. Then, click on the user and click Delete user. And the user is deleted.

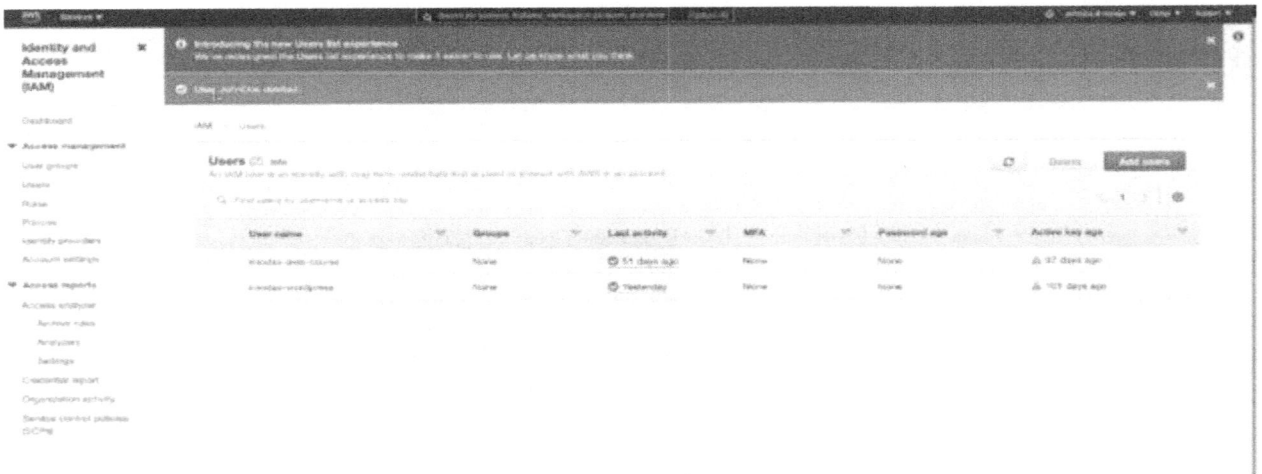

IAM Password Policy

Having a Strong password means higher security for your AWS account. In AWS, you can set up a password policy. Some important features to be considered in setting up the AWS password policy:

- Set a minimum password length
- Require specific character types, including uppercase letters, lowercase letters, numbers, and non-alphanumeric characters.
- Allow all IAM users to change their passwords.
- Enforce users to change their password after password expiration

- Prevent re-use of old passwords

IAM Role

An IAM user's credential is a long-term credential. An IAM role, however, is a short-term credential to which one or more than one IAM policy is assigned. An IAM *role* is an IAM identity that you can create in your AWS account having specific permissions. An IAM role is similar to an IAM user; however, instead of being uniquely associated with one user, a role is intended to be assumable by anyone who needs it. More importantly, a role does not have standard long-term credentials such as a password or access keys associated with it. Instead, when assuming an IAM role, it provides temporary security credentials for the session.

An IAM role, a short-term credential to which one or more than one IAM policy is assigned. Using an IAM is a best practice for accessing AWS resources from an EC2 instance. An EC2 instance can assume an IAM role when accessing AWS resources. When assuming rule to access a resource, a temporary credential is generated to access the AWS resource. You should use IAM roles to grant access to your AWS account by relying on short-term credentials, a security best practice. Authorized identities, AWS services, or users from your identity provider can assume roles to make AWS requests.

IAM Roles for Services

Sometimes you need an AWS service to perform some actions on your behalf, for example, an EC2 instance interacting with S3. In these situations, you will assign permissions to AWS services using IAM Roles.

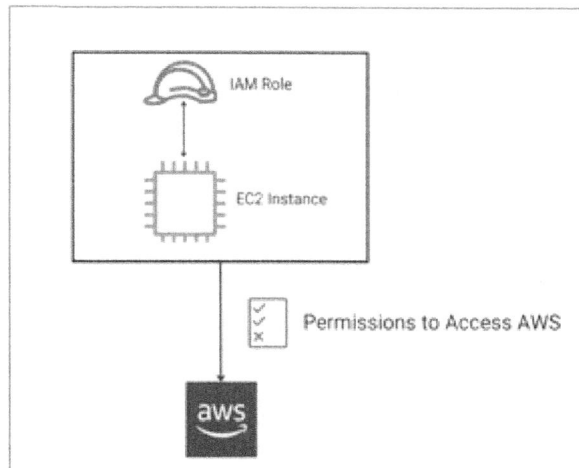

Using an IAM role is a best practice for accessing AWS resources from an EC2 instance. An EC2 instance can assume an IAM role when accessing AWS resources. When assuming the rule to access a resource, a temporary credential is generated to access the AWS resource. You should use IAM roles to grant access to your AWS account by relying on short-term credentials, a security best practice. Authorized identities, AWS services, or users from your identity provider can assume roles to make AWS requests.

Don't share security credentials between accounts to allow users from another AWS account to access resources in your AWS account -- instead, use IAM roles. You can define a role that specifies the IAM users' permissions in the other account. You can also designate which IAM users are allowed to assume the role.

Using IAM Role on EC2 Instance

Applications that run on an EC2 instance, and if they need to communicate with other services or resources, must include AWS credentials in the AWS API requests. One of the approaches is that developers could store AWS credentials directly within the EC2 instance and allow applications in that instance to use those credentials. But the issue with this approach is that developers would then have to manage the credentials and ensure that they securely pass the credentials to other instances or services. They will also have to update the credentials when it's time to rotate the credentials. That's a lot of additional work.

Instead, you should use an IAM role to manage *temporary* credentials for applications that run on an EC2 instance. When using a role, you don't have to distribute long-term credentials (username/password or access keys) to an EC2 instance. Instead, the role supplies temporary permissions that applications can use when making calls to other AWS resources. When you launch an EC2 instance, you specify an IAM role to associate with the instance. Applications that run on the instance can use the role-supplied temporary credentials to sign API requests.

IAM Use Cases

Use cases

With IAM, you can manage AWS permissions for workforce users and workloads. For workforce users, we recommend that you use AWS Single Sign-On (AWS SSO) to manage access to AWS accounts and permissions within those accounts. AWS SSO makes it easier to provision and manage IAM roles and policies across your AWS organization. For workload permissions, use IAM roles and policies, and grant only the required access for your workloads.

Apply fine-grained access control

Grant access to specific AWS service APIs and resources by using IAM policies. You also can define specific conditions in which access is granted, such as granting access to identities from a specific AWS organization or access through a specific AWS service.

Establish permissions guardrails and data perimeters across your AWS organization

With AWS Organizations, you can use service control policies (SCPs) to establish permissions guardrails that all IAM users and roles in an organization's accounts adhere to. You also can establish a data perimeter to help ensure that only your trusted identities are accessing trusted resources from expected networks. Whether you're just getting started with SCPs or have existing SCPs, you can use IAM access advisor to help you restrict permissions confidently.

Achieve least-privilege permissions with IAM Access Analyzer

Achieving least privilege is a continuous cycle to grant the right fine-grained permissions as your requirements evolve. IAM Access Analyzer helps you streamline permissions management as you set, verify, and refine permissions.

Automatically scale fine-grained permissions with ABAC

Attribute-based access control (ABAC) is an authorization strategy for creating fine-grained permissions based on user attributes, such as department, job role, and team name. With ABAC, you can reduce the number of distinct permissions you need for creating fine-grained controls in your AWS account.

Screenshot Reference: https://aws.amazon.com/iam/

IAM Access Keys

Access keys are long-term credentials for an IAM user or the AWS account root user. You can use access keys to sign programmatic requests to the AWS CLI or AWS API (directly or using the AWS SDK). Access keys consist of two parts: an access key ID (for example, AKIAIOSFODNN7EXAMPLE) and a secret access key (for example, wJalrXUtnFEMI/K7MDENG/bPxRfiCYEXAMPLEKEY). As a user name and password, you must use both the access key ID and secret access key together to authenticate your requests. Access Keys are secret, just like a password. You should never share them.

Use Access Key ID and Secret Access Key to access AWS resources programmatically

Access keys are long-term credentials for an IAM user or the AWS account root user. You can use access keys to sign programmatic requests to the AWS CLI or AWS API (directly or using the AWS SDK). Access keys consist of two parts: an access key ID and a secret access key. As a user name and password, you must use both the access key ID and secret access key together to authenticate your requests. When you create an access key pair, save the access key ID and secret access key in a secure location. The secret access key is available only at the time you create it. If you lose your secret access key, you must delete the access key and create a new one.

Use Multi Factor Authentication to access AWS resources programmatically - For increased security, AWS recommends that you configure multi-factor authentication (MFA) to help protect your AWS resources. You can enable MFA for IAM users or the AWS account root user. MFA adds extra security because it requires users to provide unique authentication from an AWS supported MFA mechanism in addition to their regular sign-in credentials when they access AWS websites or services. MFA cannot be used for programmatic access to AWS resources.

Use IAM Groups to access AWS resources programmatically - An IAM Group is a collection of IAM users. Groups let you specify permissions for multiple users, which can make it easier to manage the permissions for those users. IAM Group is for managing users and not for programmatic access to AWS resources.

Best Practices for IAM Service

Enable MFA for all users. AWS recommends that you require multi-factor authentication (MFA) for all users in your account. With MFA, users have a device that generates a response to an authentication challenge. Both the user's credentials and the device-generated response are required to complete the sign-in process.

Rotate credentials regularly. AWS recommends that you change your own passwords and access keys regularly, and make sure that all IAM users in your account do as well. That way, if a password or access key is compromised without your knowledge, you limit how long the credentials can be used to access your resources. You can apply a password policy to your account to require all your IAM users to rotate their passwords.

When you create IAM policies, grant the least privileges required to perform a task. When you create IAM policies, follow the standard security advice of granting the least privileges, or granting only the permissions required to perform a task. Determine what users (and roles) need to do and then craft policies that allow them to perform only those tasks.

Start with a minimum set of permissions and grant additional permissions as necessary. Doing so is more secure than starting with permissions that are too lenient and then trying to tighten them later.

Don't share security credentials between accounts, use IAM roles instead. Don't share security credentials between accounts to allow users from another AWS account to access resources in your AWS account. Instead, use IAM roles. You can define a role that specifies what permissions the IAM users in the other account are allowed. You can also designate which AWS accounts have the IAM users that are allowed to assume the role.

AWS IAM security best practices:

- Require human users to use federation with an identity provider to access AWS using temporary credentials
- Require workloads to use temporary credentials with IAM roles to access AWS
- Require multi-factor authentication (MFA)
- Rotate access keys regularly for use cases that require long-term credentials
- Safeguard your root user credentials and don't use them for everyday tasks
- Apply least-privilege permissions
- Get started with AWS managed policies and move toward least-privilege permissions
- Use IAM Access Analyzer to generate least-privilege policies based on access activity
- Regularly review and remove unused users, roles, permissions, policies, and credentials
- Use conditions in IAM policies to further restrict access
- Verify public and cross-account access to resources with IAM Access Analyzer
- Use IAM Access Analyzer to validate your IAM policies to ensure secure and functional permissions
- Establish permissions guardrails across multiple accounts
- Use permissions boundaries to delegate permissions management within an account

Reference: https://docs.aws.amazon.com/IAM/latest/UserGuide/best-practices.html

- AWS recommends that user account credentials should not be shared between users.
- AWS recommends granting the least privileges required to complete a certain job and avoid giving excessive privileges which can be misused.
- The access key for your AWS account root user gives full access to all your resources for all AWS services, including your billing information. You cannot reduce the permissions associated with your AWS account root user access key. You should never share these access keys with any other users, not even the administrators.

IAM Security Tools

To perform an IAM audit, they are two IAM security tools: AWS Access Advisor (user level) and IAM Credentials Report (account level).

IAM Access Advisor

This is a user-level IAM security tool for audit. IAM Access advisor provides information about the service permissions granted to a user and when those services were last accessed. You can use this provided information to revise your policies. This can be used to identify unnecessary permissions so that you can revise your IAM policies accordingly.

IAM Credentials Report

This is an account-level IAM security tool for audit. You can generate and download a credential report that lists all users, and the status of their various credentials such as passwords, access keys, and MFA devices in you AWS account. However, the report is not used to review permissions granted to a user.

Chapter 13. Elastic Compute Cloud (EC2)

You will learn the following in this chapter:
- Introduction of EC2
- EC2 User Data
- How to SSH to an EC2 instance
- EC2 Use Cases
- Amazon AMI
- Introduction to EC2 Security
- Elastic Network Interface (ENI)
- EC2 Security Group

Introduction

We know that AWS is a public cloud service provider and provides on-demand availability of all kinds of cloud services from across the world. Being a public cloud service provider, it offers different types of services, categorized into different types of cloud computing. For example, in the Cloud Computing Platform Types chapter, you learned that IaaS, PaaS, SaaS are the main cloud computing platform types. Virtual servers are one of the primary examples of IaaS cloud computing type, and EC2 (Elastic Compute Cloud) is AWS IaaS type of cloud computing type. In other words, using EC2, you can get the infrastructure as a service, such as virtual servers. Using EC2, we can launch Linux, Windows, macOS types of virtual servers. In this chapter, we will learn about Elastic Compute Cloud (EC2). First, we will understand EC2 theoretically, and later we will learn how to launch Ubuntu Linux virtual server using the EC2 service and understand various aspects of EC2. We will also learn about EC2 security, different EC2 instance types, EC2 pricing options, and placement groups.

Screenshot from: https://aws.amazon.com/ec2/

EC2 is a very old AWS service to launch virtual servers on AWS. Now, let's understand what EC2 does: "It is a web service that provides secure, resizable compute capacity in the cloud." In this statement, let's parse some keywords or phrases to understand EC2 better.

Web Service
The first is web service. What it means is that you can access an EC2 instance using an HTTP endpoint.

Secure
The other important word in this statement is secure. What it means is that you can control inbound and outbound traffic to an EC2 instance.

Resizable Compute Capacity
The other important phrase is resizable compute capacity. What it means is that EC2 instances have an auto-scaling feature. Using an auto-scaling feature, you can let EC2 instances scale up or down based on various metrics such as CPU utilization or I/O throughput.

Cloud
The last word is cloud. What it means is that EC2 instances are launched in AWS data centers. Or in AWS terms, we can say that EC2 instances are launched in AWS availability zones.

KEY POINTS

- EC2 = Elastic Compute Cloud = Infrastructure as a Service
- Its main features are renting virtual machines (EC2), storing data on virtual drives (EBS), distributing the load across machines (ELB), and scaling the services using an auto-scaling group (ASG).
- You can launch four hundred different types of EC2 instances.
- AWS is the only cloud provider that supports macOS.
- You can launch EC2 instances in 25 Regions and 80 Availability Zones globally.

- You have a choice of different types of processors.
- Knowledge of EC2 is fundamental to understanding how the Cloud works

EC2 Instance, Web Server, and SSH

We have got a high-level introduction of EC2. Let's understand how to launch an EC2 instance, set up an Apache Web Server on the EC2 instance. And finally, how to do SSH connection to a launched EC2 instance. This is a typical hands-on example of learning EC2.

Let's log in to the AWS management console. Go to EC2 service either by typing "EC2" on the search bar or selecting EC2 from recently visited services if it is shown.

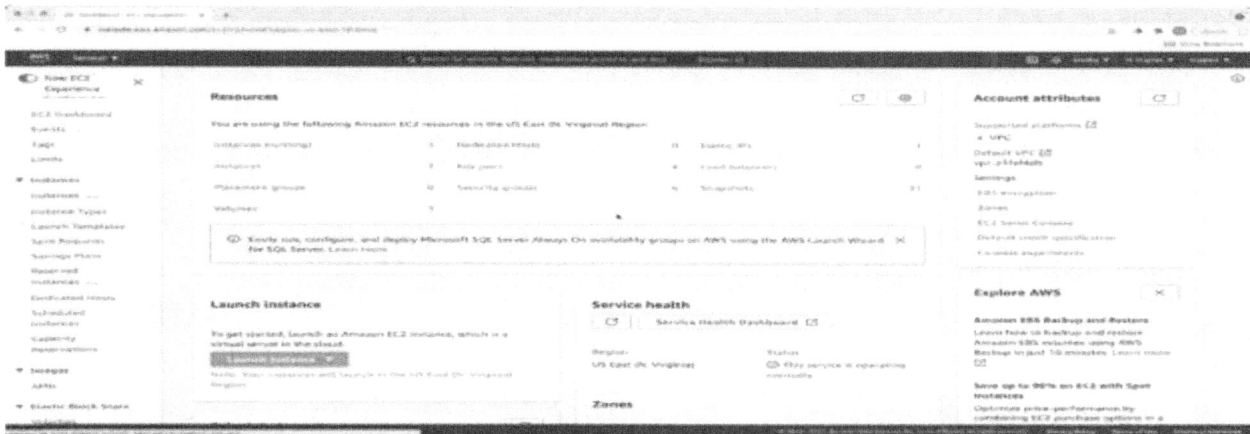

EC2 Dashboard

This is the EC2 Dashboard. As you can see in my account, one instance is already running. At the top right, you will see your account name. The next is your default AWS region. In my case, it is N. Virginia, which has AWS region code us-east-1. In your case, it could be different depending on your location.

Launching EC2 Instance

Since we will be launching an instance, click on the Launch Instance button.

Step 1: Choose Amazon Machine Image (AMI)

The next step is to choose AMI, which is Amazon Machine Image.

What is AMI or Amazon Machine Image?

Amazon Machine Image or AMI is a template of software configuration. So, for example, AMI of Red Hat Linux will have software configuration to the launched Red Hat Linux instance running as a virtual server in the cloud.

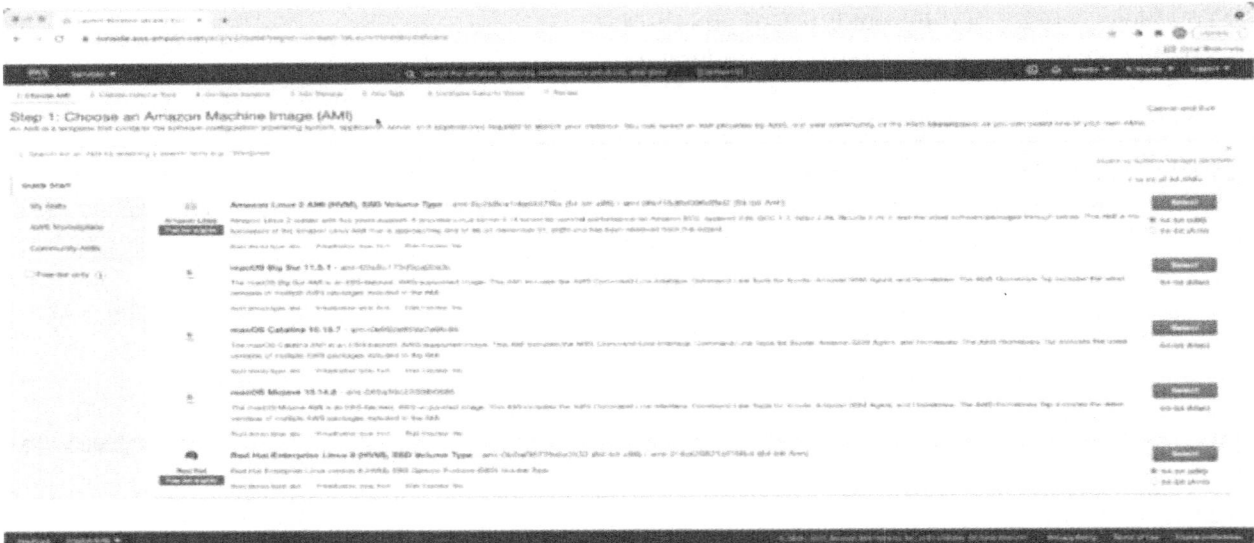

choose AMI

Default all AMIs are listed. You can search for Linux, Windows, Mac AMIs.

Windows AMIs

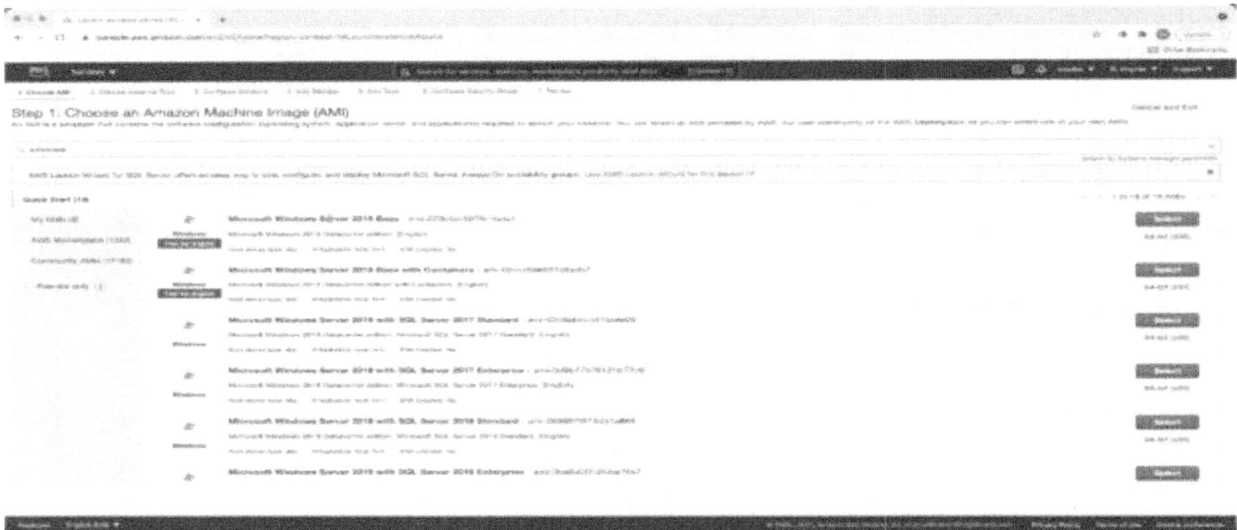

Search for Windows AMIs

Let's search for "Windows" to find out Windows AMIs. Here in the search results, you get all the Windows AMIs. So, if you are looking to launch Windows virtual machine on AWS, you can choose among these AMIs depending on what exactly you are looking for on Windows.

macOS AMIs

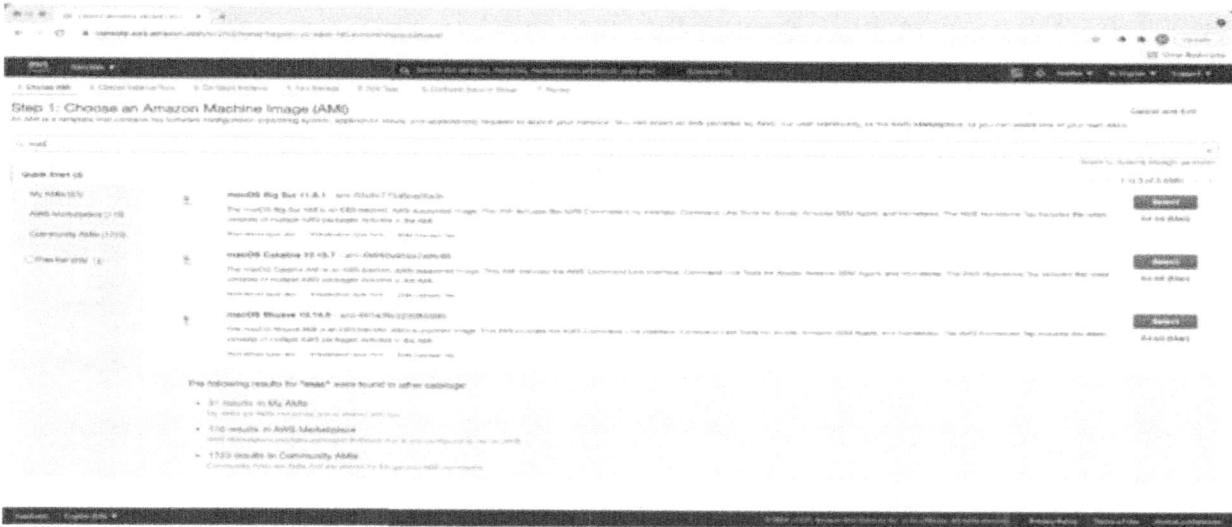

Search for macOS AMIs

You can launch macOS EC2 instance as well. Let's search for "mac" in the search area. You get three macOS AMIs.

Linux AMIs

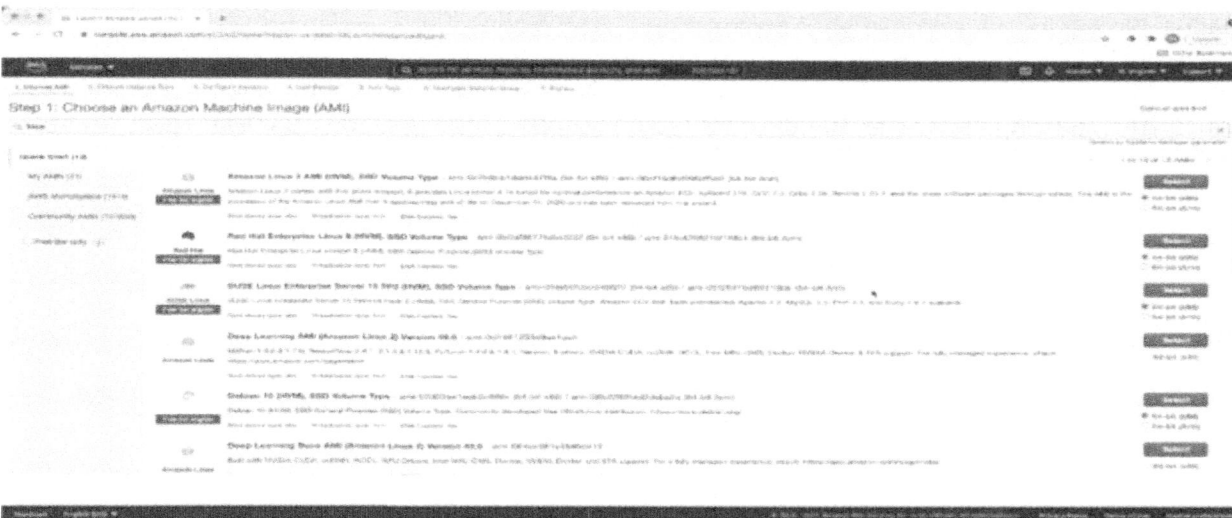

Search for Linux AMIs

Since we will be launching a web server on a Linux EC2 instance, let's search for Linux. We will get many choices in the result, which one should we select?

The first deciding factor is to look for an EC2 instance in the AWS Free Tier, as we are not looking for a high-end configuration. Just minimal RAM and Hard Disk are OK.

Amazon Linux AMI

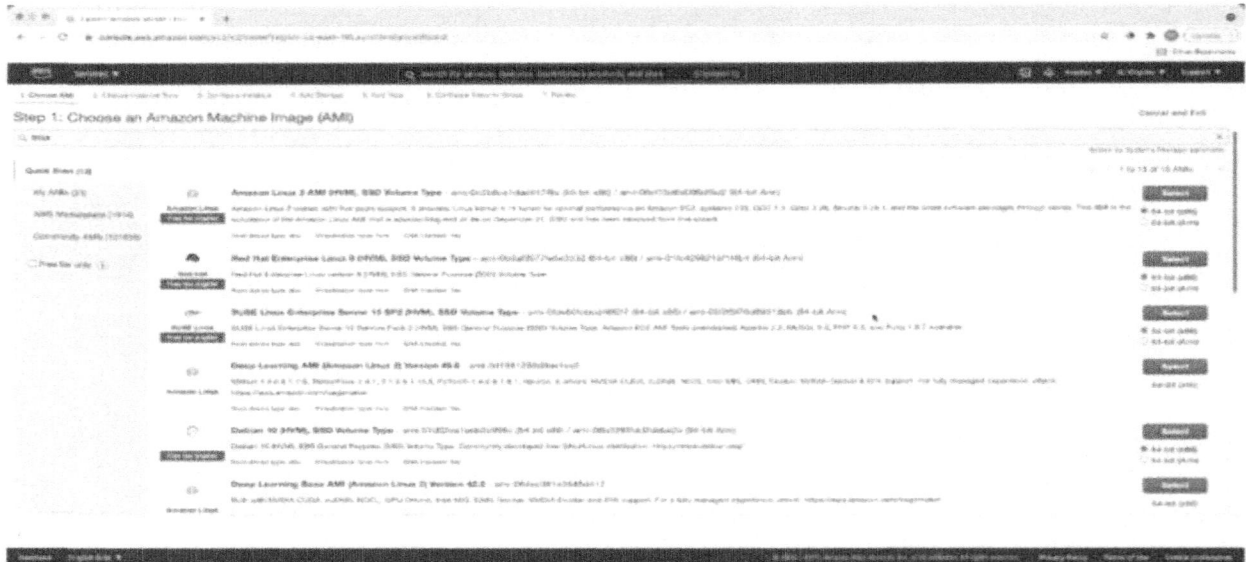

Search for Amazon Linux AMI

Since we are launching a Linux virtual machine on AWS, the next deciding factor is to look for an Amazon Linux AMI, which will have pre-installed AWS-related binaries.

Usually, it's a good idea to use an Amazon Linux AMI because you get some additional features related to AWS already set up. For instance, if you need to run AWS CLI commands on the launched EC2 instance, you don't need to install AWS CLI separately. That's the reason we will select Amazon Linux 2 AMI, which is Free Tier eligible, and the default 64-bit x86 is good. So, let's select Amazon Linux 2 AMI.

Step 2: Choose Instance Type
Here, select t2.micro as it is Free Tier eligible. The t2.micro is an instance type.

What is Instance Type?

AWS has EC2 instance categorization based on combinations of CPU, memory, storage, and networking capacity. The t2.micro is one of the instance types.

There are other instance types, such as t2.small, t2.medium, t2.large, and t2.xlarge. They all have a varying degree of memory, storage, and networking capacity. In other words, different instance types have different CPU, memory, storage, and networking capacity.

Step 3: Configure Instance Details

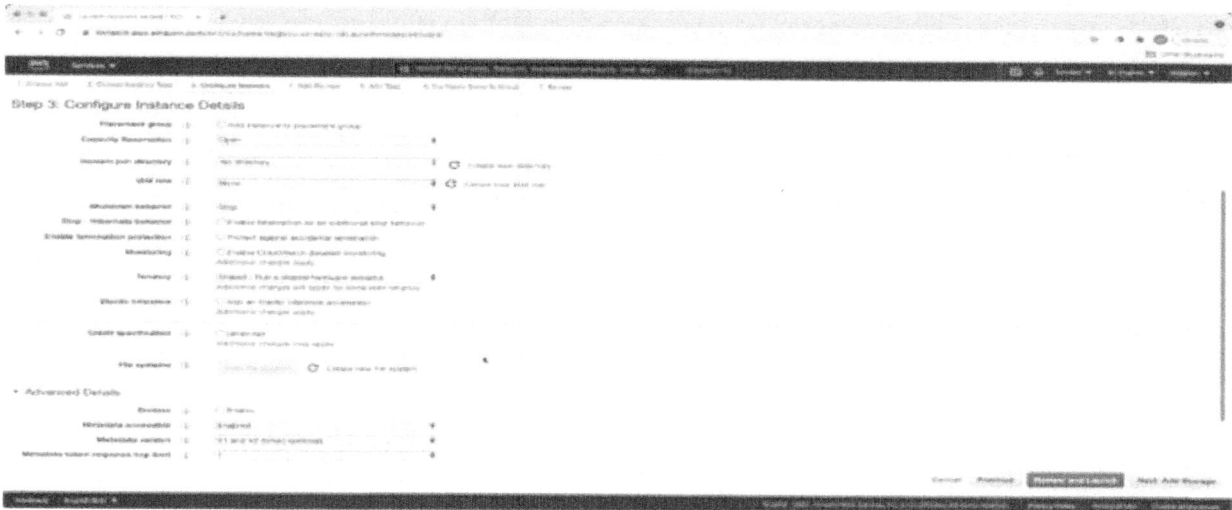

configure instance details

Here, default is OK. The only thing we will add here is we will add a couple of Linux shell commands in the User data section to install the webserver.

EC2 User data

It is used as bootstrap script to configure EC2 instance at launch. You can specify user data to configure an instance or run a configuration script during launch. The one advantage of User Data is if you launch more than one instance at a time, the user data is available to all the instances in that reservation.

The user data to set up a web server on the EC2 instance is given below:

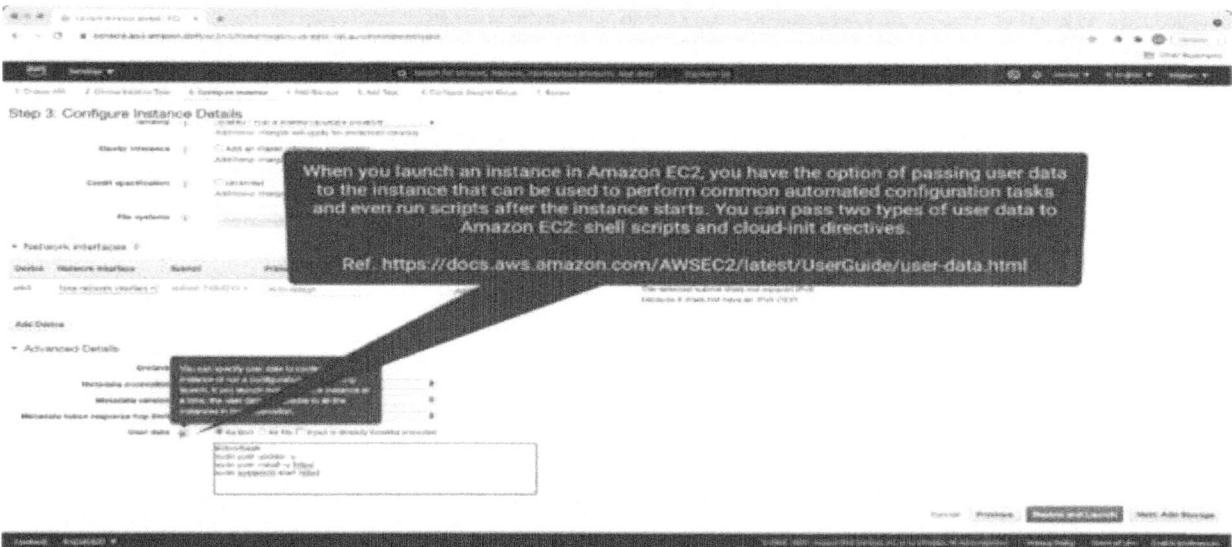

EC2 configure instance -- user data

In this, the first line is about using the bash shell. The second line is to update OS – it's always good practice to update the OS. In case if there is any security patch that has been released but is not yet available in AMI, which could lead to potential security risks. The third line is about installing an HTTP web server. And the last line starts the server. Additionally, whenever this EC2 instance stops and starts again, the httpd daemon will be started, which means the webserver will be started automatically at the server startup.

![KEY POINTS]

- You can bootstrap EC2 instances using an EC2 User data script. Bootstrapping means launching commands when a machine starts. The script is only run once at the launch of the instance.
- EC2 user data is used to automate boot tasks such as applying OS updates, installing software, downloading common files from the internet, or any other tasks you would like to perform at instance launch.
- The EC2 User Data Script runs as the root user.

Step 4: Add Storage

EC2 instance -- add storage

The next step is to add storage. The default 8 Gb is OK for our learning of setting up a web server

Step 5: Add Tags
The next step is to add tags. This is optional. However, if you would want, you can add, for example, you can add "name" as a key and "Apache Web Server Test" as a value.

Step 6: Configure Security Group
The next step is about configuring the security group.

What is a Security Group?
The security group is a mechanism to control inbound and outbound connections to the launched EC2 machine. For example, what type of traffic and sources are allowed to make the connection on the launched ec2 instance? For example, is inbound FTP connection allowed? If allowed, is it allowed from all IP addresses or selected IP addresses?

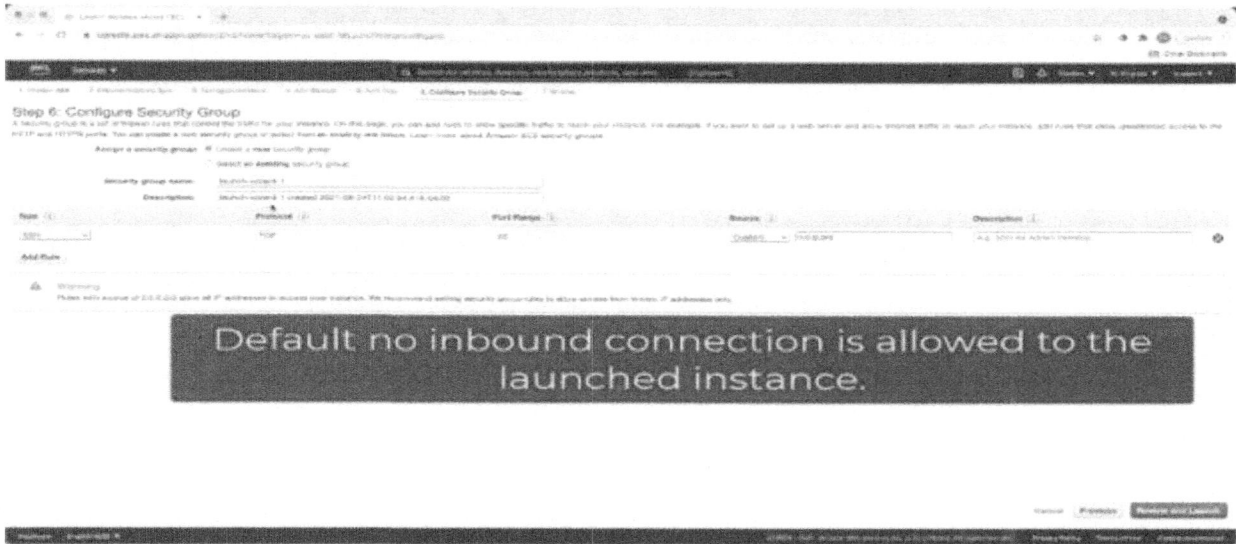

Default no inbound connection is allowed to the launched instance.

With regards to default settings, no inbound connection is allowed to a launched EC2 instance.

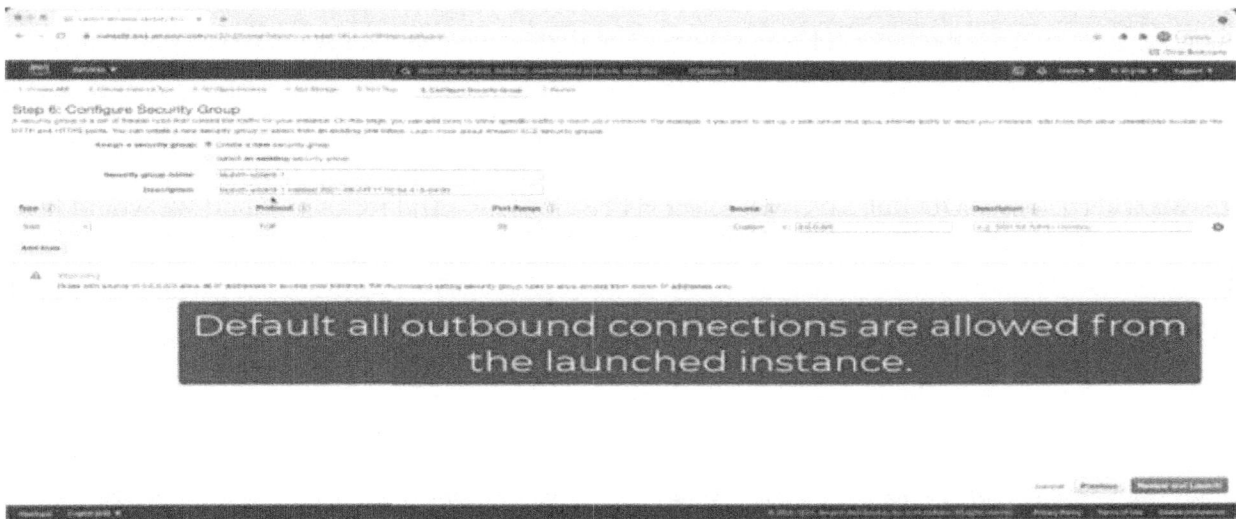

Default all outbound connections are allowed from the launched instance.

configure security group

Default, all outbound connections are allowed from a launched EC2 instance. That being the case, we need to set up inbound connections for this instance. We will create a new security group and name it: apache-web-server-test-sg. For the description, we will add "Apache web server security group to learn how to launch a web server on EC2."

Rules for Inbound Connections

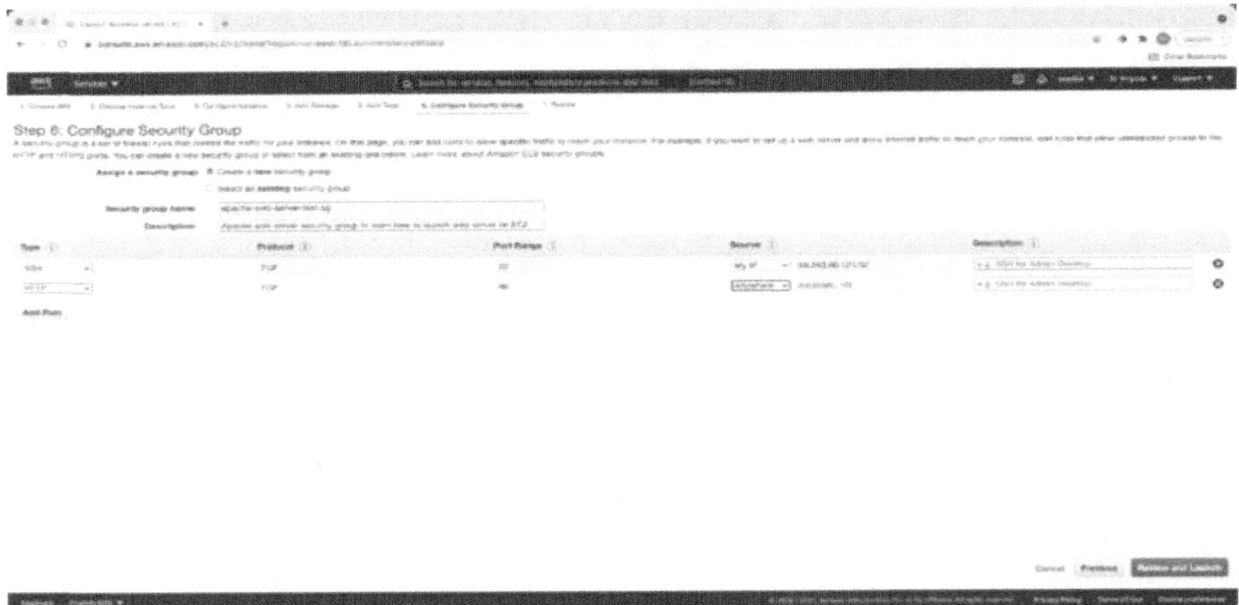

rules for inbound connection

Now let's add a rule for the inbound connections. The first is, we need to open a port to make an ssh connection to the launched ec2 instance from the local Mac machine.

Change the source IP so that ssh connection can only be done from your machine only. So, change the Source to your IP. And secondly, you need to open an HTTP connection port for the webserver. Here, we will click on ADD Rule. We will select HTTP on Type. And for Source and we would like the webserver to be accessed from anywhere, so, we will change Source to Anywhere.

Step 7: Review and Launch

Now click on Review, and then Launch.

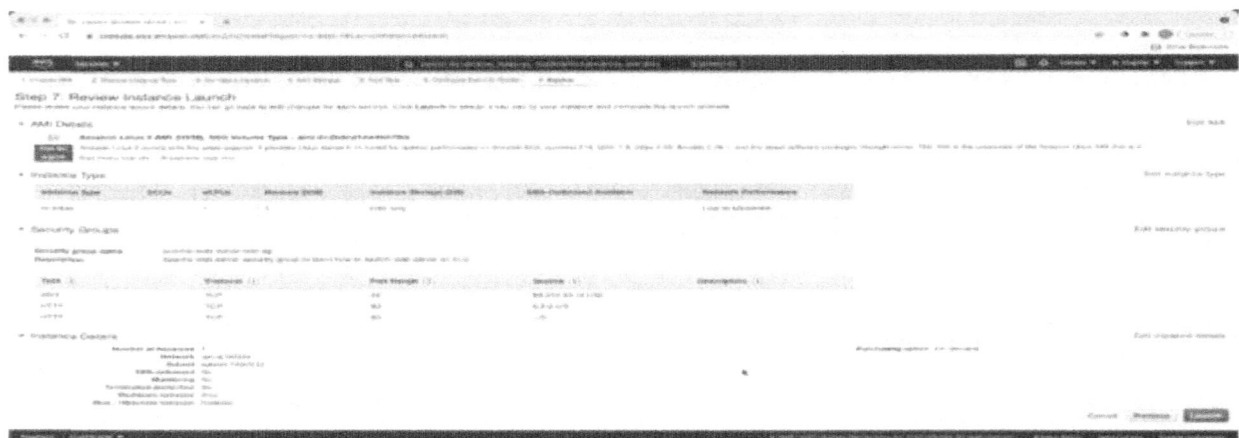

review and launch

We will create new key pair. You need key pair to make a ssh connection to the launched machine. Enter the name of the key pair for example. We will name it: ec2-web-server-test-key and download the new key pair. You will need to download the key pair. Otherwise, you will not be able to make the connection to the launched instance using your terminal.

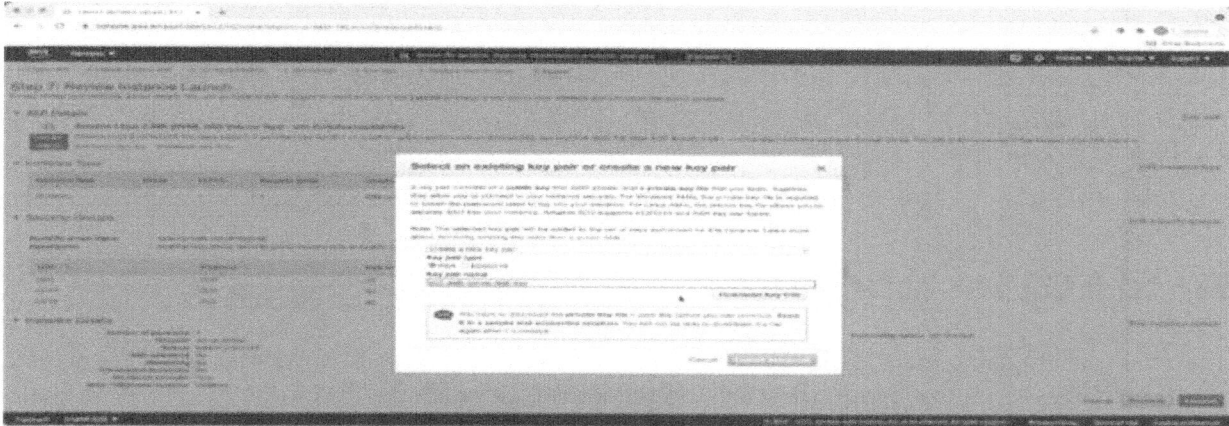

EC2 instance - key pair

Click on the Launch Instance button. It says that your instances are now launching.

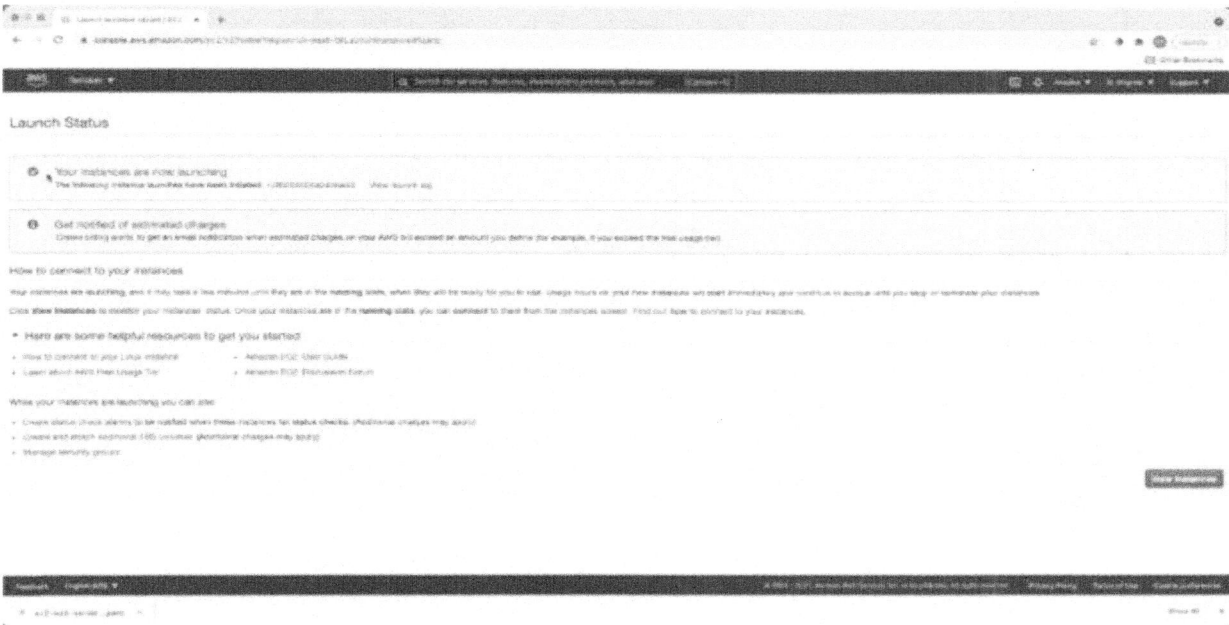

EC2 instance -- launch status

Test the Launched EC2 Instance

Let's get the public IP of the launched EC2 instance machine and open the browser to make sure if your instance is set up with an Apache web server.

A quick way to test is if your web server is installed and running is to click on the Open address. As you can notice, we got the Apache Web Server test page.

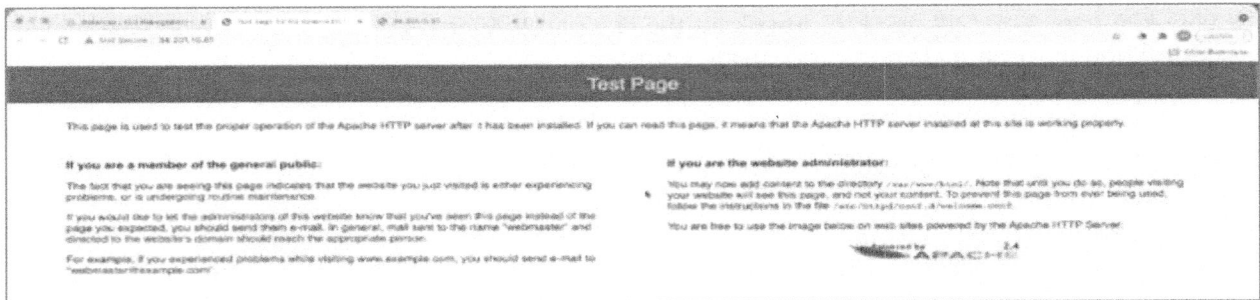

test launch instance

SSH to EC2 Instance

(In this example I'm using macOS) Now, let's learn how to use ssh connection to the EC2 instance from my local machine. Create a "temp" directory on the local Mac machine. From this directory, we will connect to launched EC2 instance using ssh. The steps are as follows:

- Let's open a Mac terminal window
- Create a temp directory on your machine and go to the temp folder.
- Copy the downloaded security key pair to this temp folder.
- Change the permission of the key file to ensure the key is not publicly viewable.

chmod 400 ec2-web-server-test-key.pem

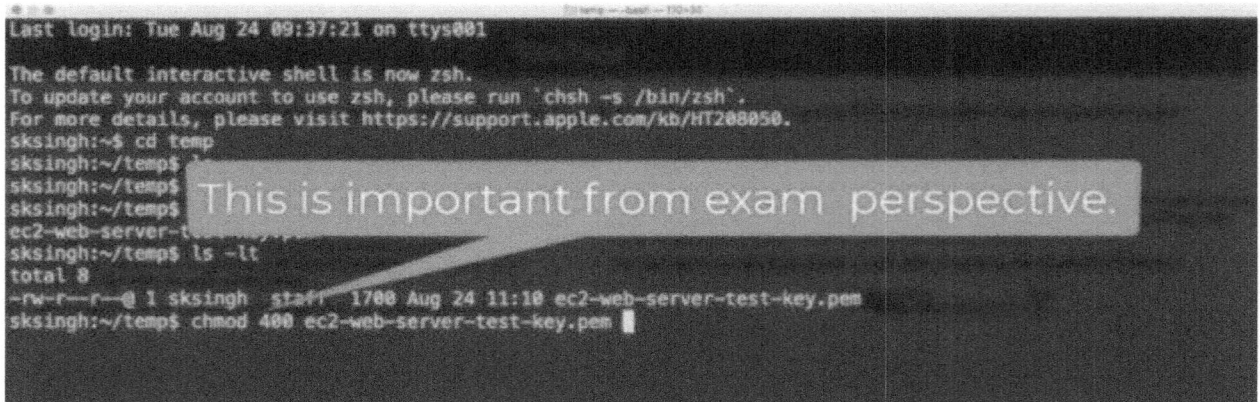

setting permission on the key file

Connect to the launched instance using its Public IP or DNS

For example:
ssh -i ec2-web-server-demo-key.pem ec2-user@ec2-18-205-160-41.compute-1.amazonaws.com

The syntax is "ssh -i key name ec2-user@ec2 instance Public IP Address or DNS name."
The default username for the Amazon Linux EC2 instance is *ec2-user*.

ssh to the launched EC2 instance

Let's go to the directory where the web server is installed: /var/www/html.
And create a test.html file. Just add a line "this a web server test page."

sample test.html file

Test the webserver, by adding http://<Public IP Address>/test.html in the URL

As you can notice, test.html is displayed in the browser.

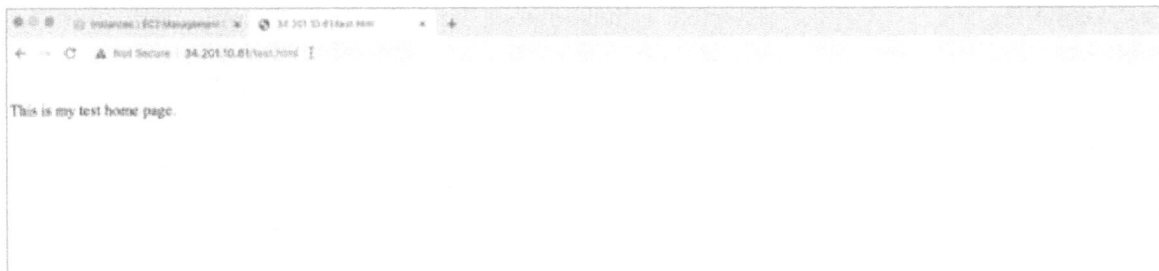

Connect to EC2 From AWS Management Console

You can also connect to an EC2 instance from the AWS Management console.

list of running EC2 instance

Amazon EC2 Instance Connect

Amazon EC2 Instance Connect provides a straightforward way to connect to your Linux instances using Secure Shell (SSH). With EC2 Instance Connect, you use AWS IAM policies to control SSH access to your instances. Thus, it removes the need to share and manage SSH keys.

KEY POINTS

- Connect to your EC2 instance from within your browser
- No need to use the key file -- a temporary key is uploaded onto EC2 by AWS
- Works only out-of-the-box with Amazon Linux 2
- Make sure the port 22 is open

Stop, Reboot, or Terminate

You can stop, reboot, or terminate a launched EC2 instance. It's a good practice to stop/terminate an On-Demand instance if you don't need it -- as on AWS, we typically pay based on the usage: pay-as-you-go pricing model.

EC2 Hibernate

An EC2 instance can be stopped, restarted, or terminated. When an EC2 is stopped, the data on disk (EBS) is kept intact at the next start. When an EC2 instance is terminated, any EBS volume, if "Delete on Termination" has been checked (on AWS Management Console), is deleted at the termination.

When an EC2 starts, first the OS boots, then the EC2 User Data script runs, then your application starts and caches get warmed up –as you can see, starting an EC2 instance can take time depending on your EC2 User Data and application.

If you would like to make an EC2 instance restart faster, you can enable "hibernate" as an additional stop behavior. When an EC2 instance is hibernated, the instance in-memory (RAM) state is preserved, which helps in faster booting of the instance as the OS is not stopped and restarted. Essentially, the RAM state is written to a file on the root EBS volume. The root EBS volume must be encrypted.

You can use EC2 Hibernate in use cases that deal with long-running processes, saving the RAM state, or services that take time to initialize.

Other important points about EC2 Hibernate:

- EC2 Instance RAM must be less than 150 GB.
- It is not for bare metal instances.
- Root volume must be EBS and encrypted.
- It is available for On-Demand, Reserved, and Spot Instances.
- An EC2 instance cannot be hibernated for more than 60 days.

Features of Amazon EC2

Features of Amazon EC2

Amazon EC2 provides the following features:

- Virtual computing environments, known as *instances*
- Preconfigured templates for your instances, known as *Amazon Machine Images (AMIs)*, that package the bits you need for your server (including the operating system and additional software)
- Various configurations of CPU, memory, storage, and networking capacity for your instances, known as *instance types*
- Secure login information for your instances using *key pairs* (AWS stores the public key, and you store the private key in a secure place)
- Storage volumes for temporary data that's deleted when you stop, hibernate, or terminate your instance, known as *instance store volumes*
- Persistent storage volumes for your data using Amazon Elastic Block Store (Amazon EBS), known as *Amazon EBS volumes*
- Multiple physical locations for your resources, such as instances and Amazon EBS volumes, known as *Regions* and *Availability Zones*
- A firewall that enables you to specify the protocols, ports, and source IP ranges that can reach your instances using *security groups*
- Static IPv4 addresses for dynamic cloud computing, known as *Elastic IP addresses*
- Metadata, known as *tags*, that you can create and assign to your Amazon EC2 resources
- Virtual networks you can create that are logically isolated from the rest of the AWS Cloud, and that you can optionally connect to your own network, known as *virtual private clouds* (VPCs)

Screenshot from: https://docs.aws.amazon.com/AWSEC2/latest/UserGuide/concepts.html

EC2 Use Cases

Use cases

Run cloud-native and enterprise applications

Amazon EC2 delivers secure, reliable, high-performance, and cost-effective compute infrastructure to meet demanding business needs.

Scale for HPC applications

Access the on-demand infrastructure and capacity you need to run HPC applications faster and cost-effectively.

Develop for Apple platforms

Build, test, and sign on-demand macOS workloads. Access environments in minutes, dynamically scale capacity as needed, and benefit from AWS's pay-as-you-go pricing.

Train and deploy ML applications

Amazon EC2 delivers the broadest choice of compute, networking (up to 400 Gbps), and storage services purpose-built to optimize price performance for ML projects.

Screenshot reference: https://aws.amazon.com/ec2/

EC2 User Data

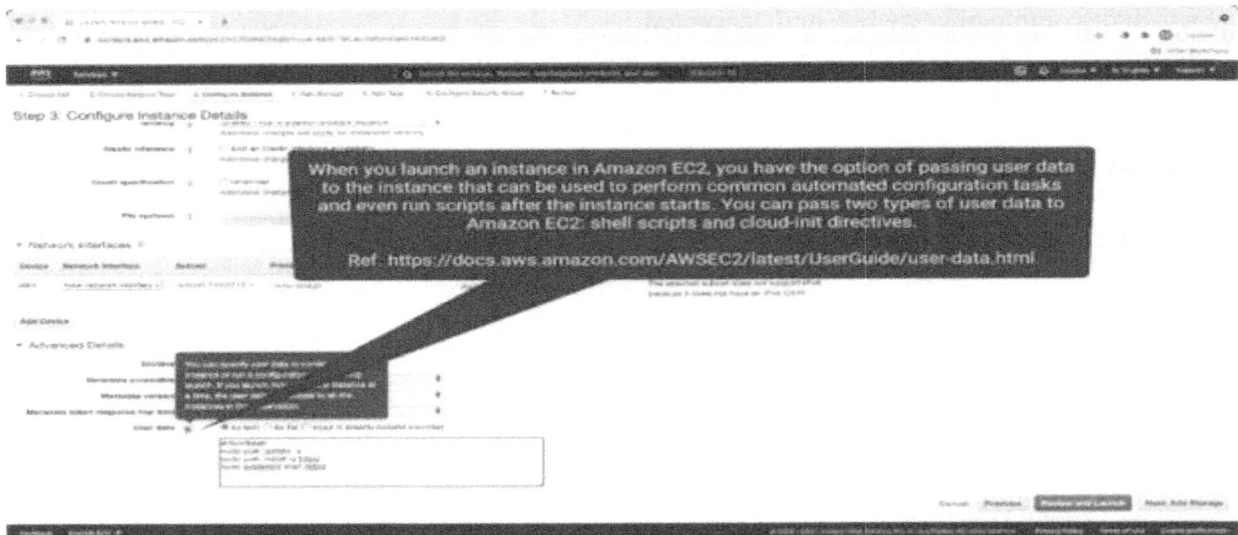

EC2 configure instance -- user data

When you launch an instance, you can pass user data to the instance that can be used to perform common automated configuration tasks such as applying OS updates, installing software, and even running scripts after the instance starts.

Launch Template

A launch template is an Amazon Elastic Compute Cloud (EC2) feature that reduces the number of steps required to create an AWS instance by capturing all launch parameters within one resource.

EC2 Instance Metadata

AWS EC2 Instance Metadata allows EC2 instances to "learn information about themselves" without using an IAM Role. The metadata available from your EC2 instance provides important information about the running EC2 instance, such as instance ID, public IP address, AMI ID, user data, and much more. The data about your instance can be used to configure or manage the running instance.

The URL is: *http://169.254.169.254/latest/meta-data*

You can retrieve the IAM Role name from metadata, but you cannot retrieve the IAM Policy.

Please note: *Metadata is the information about the EC2 instance; however, Userdata is the launch script of the EC2 instance.*

AMI Overview

An AMI (Amazon Machine Image) is a customization of an EC2 instance. You add your own software, configuration, operating system, monitoring tools in an AMI. It helps in faster boot and configuration time because all your software is pre-installed. AMIs are scoped for a specific AWS Region. You can copy an AMI from one AWS Region to another AWS Region.

Besides having your own AMI, which you make and maintain yourself, there are also AMIs provided by AWS and AMIs available in **AWS Marketplace** (made by someone else, potentially for selling purposes).

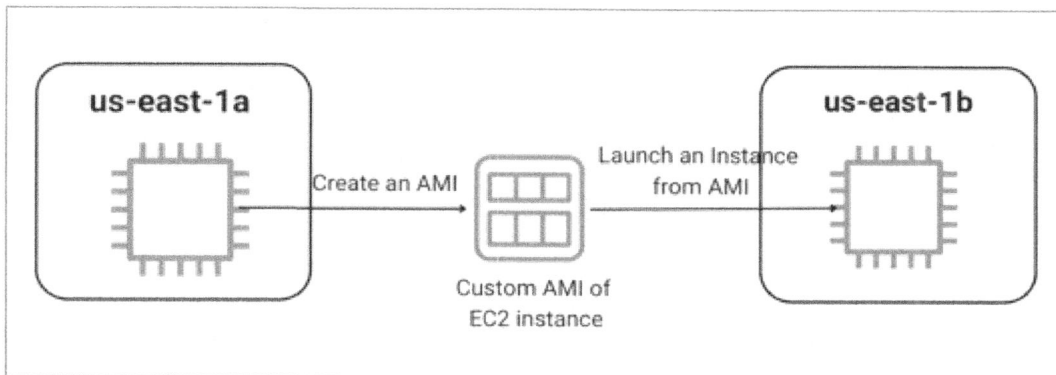

You can launch an EC2 instance using your own AMI. Or, you can launch an EC2 instance from a public AMI provided by AWS, which is very common when you launch an EC2 instance. In addition, you can also use AMIs having specific software pre-installed from AWS Marketplace to launch an EC2 instance.

Though you can create AMI using a running EC2 instance, it is better to stop the instance and then create an AMI for data integrity purposes. When you create an AMI, it will also create an EBS snapshot will also be created.

Introduction to EC2 Security

Before understanding EC2 Security Group, let's first look into two related topics: public vs private IP, and elastic IP.

Public vs. Private IP

In computing networking, two hosts to communicate with each other require a unique IP address. Each machine on the network is recognized by its unique IP address. There are two versions of IP address IPv4 (for example, 74.34.45.98) or IPv6 (for example, 4ff2:1800:4545:4:200:f7ff:fe22:64cf). In this book, we will be using IPv4; the reason is that IPv4 is still the most common format used online. IPv6 is newer and more used in IoT. With IPv4 address, 3.7 billion different addresses ((([0-255]. [0-255].[0-255].[0-255]) are possible.

Regarding public IP address, a host to be identified on the Internet(www) must have a public IP address. Each public IP address must be unique across the web (www). In other words, two machines cannot have the same public IP address. With public address, they can be geo-located easily.

Regarding private IP addresses, with a private IP address, a host can be identified on a private network only. The private IP address must be unique across the private network. However, two different private networks can have the same private IP. For example, the private internal network of two different companies can have the same IPs. Machines on the private network (which have only private IPs) can connect to the Internet using NAT Gateway (used to translate the machine's private IP to a public IP) + Internet Gateway (a proxy). Some routers can perform both NAT and Internet Gateway functions in one device. Only a specified range of IP addresses can be used as private IPs.

Elastic IP

When you launch an EC2 instance in a public subnet, the instance gets assigned a public IP, which is fine because AWS doesn't charge for assigning a public IP address to an EC2 instance. However, when you stop and restart an EC2 instance, the public IP address assigned to the instance can be changed. As you can notice, this is a problem if you are running for example, a web server hosted on an EC2 instance, and you stop it for some maintenance and restart it, and if the IP address is changed, then your users will not be able to access your web servers until you make the appropriate changes to the DNS entry or let the users know your new IP address. This – change of public IP address -- is a problem for a commercial website.

To avoid this change of public IP address assigned to an EC2 instance, when you stop and restart the EC2 instance, you can use an elastic IP. An Elastic IP is a fixed public IPv4 IP, you can get it from AWS and assign it to your instance. It's free if it is assigned to an EC2 instance. You will be charged if the EC2 instance is not running which has an Elastic IP assigned. An Elastic IP can be assigned to one EC2 instance at one time.

Within the AWS cloud environment, AWS states that the Elastic IP is used for dynamic cloud computing. The understanding this distinction is important. If an EC2 instance goes down, and you want to maintain your IP address. An Elastic IP is a combination of a public IP address and a static IP address. It allows you to continue to advertise AWS instances within your AWS network infrastructure or outside with a DNS entry.

With an Elastic IP address, you can mask the failure of an EC2 instance or software by remapping the elastic IP address to another instance in your account. You can only have 5 Elastic IPs in an AWS account (you can ask AWS to increase). In general, using Elastic IP is not common and reflects poor architectural decisions unless your business use case (public and static IP) requires it.

KEY POINTS

- An Elastic IP is a combination of a public IP address and a static IP address.

- You will be charged if the EC2 instance is not running which has an Elastic IP assigned. An Elastic IP can be assigned to one EC2 instance at one time.

- You can only have 5 Elastic IPs in an AWS account (you can ask AWS to increase)

Elastic Network Interfaces (ENI)

ENIs are essentially virtual network cards you can attach to your EC2 instances. ENIs are used to enable network connectivity of your EC2 instances.

When you launch an EC2 instance, your instance will be attached to an ENI – eth0, the default interface. However, more than one ENI can be attached to an EC2 instance. Having more than one connected to an EC2 instance allows the instance to communicate on two different subnets.

A common use case for ENIs is the setting up of management networks. This way, you would have public-facing applications like web servers in a public subnet. Still, you would lock SSH access down to a private subnet on a secondary network interface using an ENI assigned to the secondary network.

This way, you would connect using a VPN to the private management subnet, then can administrate your servers as usual.

EC2 Security Group

Security groups are fundamental to the network security of EC2 instances. EC2 Security groups control how traffic is allowed into or out of EC2 instances. Security groups only contain "allow" rules. Security group rules can reference by IP (which IP address is allowed) or by the security group (which security group is allowed).

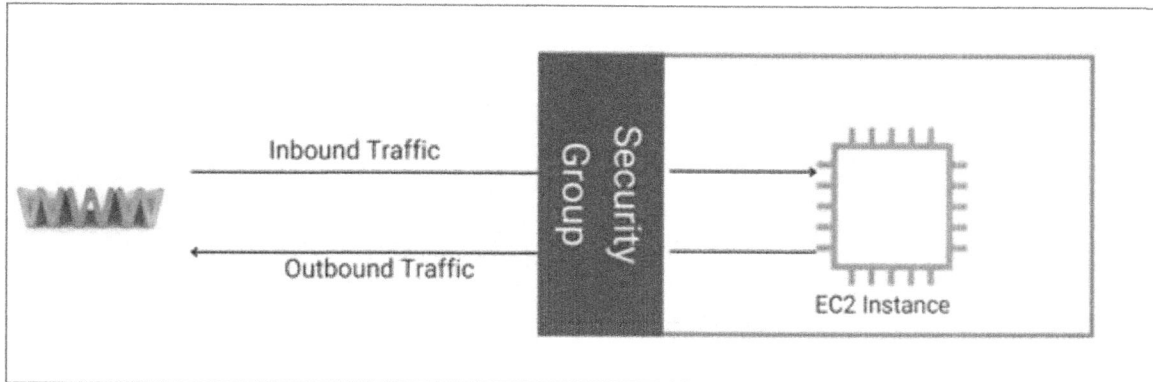

As you can notice in the above diagram, the security group is acting as a firewall for inbound and outbound traffic to the EC2 instance.

Security grou... ▽	IP version ▽	Type ▽	Protocol ▽	Port range ▽	Source ▽	Description
sgr-0b5b6cb5fb...	IPv4	HTTPS	TCP	443	0.0.0.0/0	–
sgr-0f384a1b8b...	IPv4	HTTP	TCP	80	0.0.0.0/0	–
sgr-05a39a2a54...	IPv4	SSH	TCP	22	69.253.60.121/32	–

As you can notice in the above screenshot of a security group, the security group allows inbound traffic at port 80 (HTTP) and port 443 (HTTPS) from any IP address. Additionally, the security group allows traffic at port 22 (SSH) only from a specific IP address. If this security group is attached to an EC2 instance, only ports 80, 443, and 22 are allowed to accept inbound traffic. Rest all other ports are blocked for any incoming traffic.

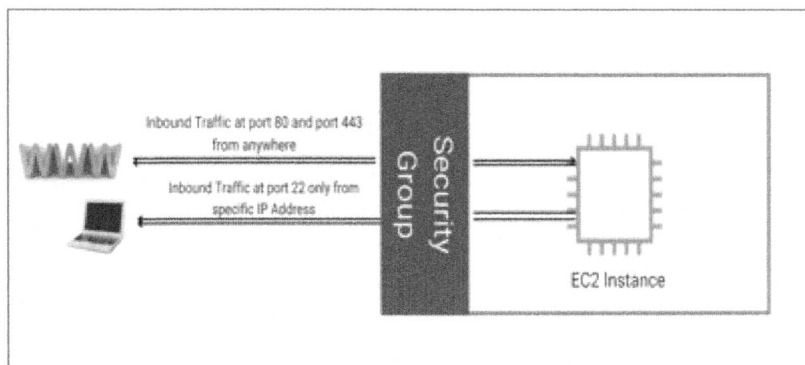

The diagram above is another way to understand the screenshot of the security group.

The diagram above is another way to understand the screenshot of the security group. All inbound is blocked by default. All outbound traffic is allowed. In other words, if you launch an EC2 instance and assign a default security group, all inbound traffic will be blocked and all outbound traffic will be allowed.

KEY POINTS

- A security group can also reference security groups when configuring rules.

- Security groups are stateful — if you send a request from your instance, the response for that request is allowed to flow in irrespective of inbound security group rules on that EC2 instance.

- Its scope is with a VPC in a Region. In other words, a security group can be assigned to any EC2 instances of the VPC to which the security group is associated.

- A security group is attached to multiple instances within a VPC.

- If your application is not accessible and it times out, it could be an issue related to security group rules.

- If your application gives a "connection refused" error, it's an application error, or the instance is not launched.

- Data transfer into EC2 instances from the Internet is free. However, data transfer OUT to the Internet from EC2 instances is not free.

- Data transfer OUT from an EC2 instance to Amazon CloudFront is Free

Amazon S3
Object storage built to retrieve any amount of data from anywhere

5 GB of S3 standard storage
for 12 months with the AWS Free Tier

Get Started with Amazon S3

Connect with an Amazon S3 specialist

Scale storage resources to meet fluctuating needs with 99.999999999% (11 9s) of data durability.

Store data across Amazon S3 storage classes to reduce costs without upfront investment or hardware refresh cycles.

Protect your data with unmatched security, compliance, and audit capabilities.

Easily manage data at any scale with robust access controls, flexible replication tools, and organization-wide visibility.

Chapter 14. Simple Storage Service (S3)

You will learn the following in this chapter:
- Introduction of S3
- Types of storage systems
- Features of S3
- S3 Bucket
- Creating S3 Bucket and S3 Bucket Name
- Uploading object to S3 Bucket
- S3 Bucket versioning
- S3 Bucket encryption
- Public access of S3 bucket
- Encryption for Objects in Transit
- Encryption for Objects at Rest
- SSE-S3
- SSE-KMS
- SSE-C
- Client-Side Encryption
- S3 Security
- Preventing Accidental Deletion of Objects
- S3 Pre-Signed URLs
- S3 Access Logs
- Networking, Logging & Audit, and User Security
- S3 CORS
- S3 Replication
- S3 Use Cases

As we know that IaaS is one of the main cloud computing types. In IaaS, cloud providers, provide infrastructure such as virtual servers, virtual storage services over the Internet. You already learned EC2 which is AWS IaaS cloud computing type of service to launch virtual servers on the cloud. Like EC2, S3 (Simple Storage Service) is also an AWS IaaS cloud computing type of service. S3 provides a virtual storage service on the AWS cloud platform. In the chapter, we learn about the introduction to S3 and do hands-on to upload an image on S3.

Amazon S3 Basic Fundamentals

Amazon S3 is one of the main building blocks of AWS. It is advertised as "infinitely scaling" storage. It's a widely popular AWS service. Many websites use Amazon S3 as a storage backbone. Many AWS services use Amazon S3 as an integration as well.

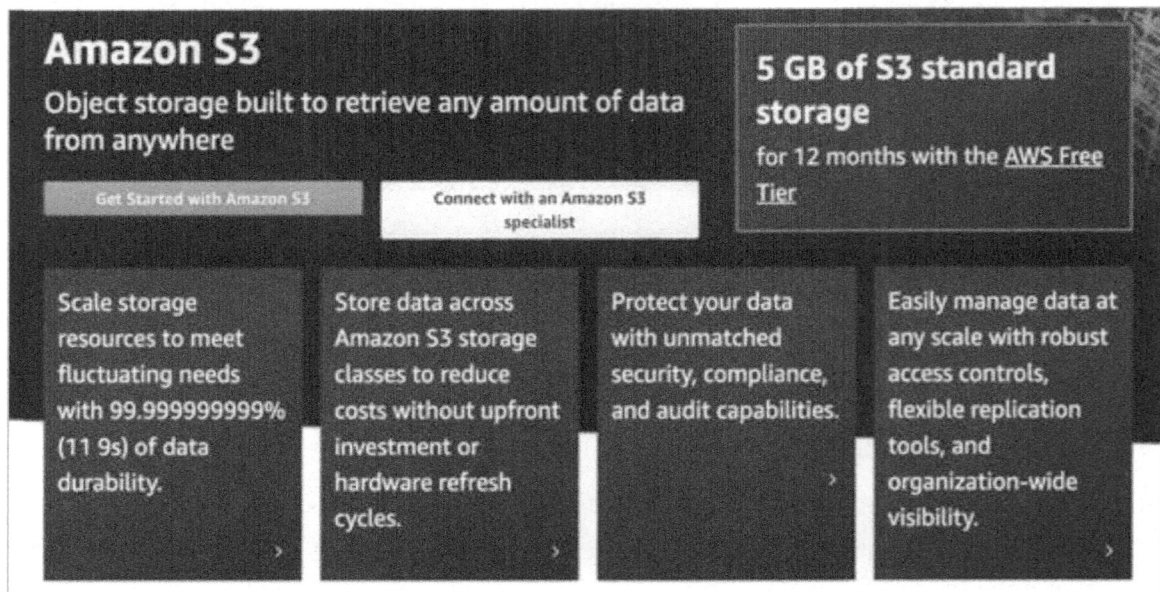

Screenshot from: https://aws.amazon.com/s3/

Essentially, S3 is a cloud storage service of AWS. The first noticeable point about S3 is that it is object storage built to store and retrieve any amount of data from anywhere. S3 provides a set of APIs to store and retrieve data on the cloud. A few terms such as object storage, scalability, data availability, security, performance, compliance, and durability are essential to understand S3 to have an excellent conceptual understanding of what S3 is. Let's first understand about object storage system as S3 is an object storage service.

S3 is an Object Storage Service

Let's understand the phrase object storage because this is the key to understanding S3. Regarding storage, I guess we are more familiar with file storage, which is a type of storage system used by operating systems. However, S3 is not a file storage service – it is an object storage service – this is a crucial concept to keep in mind.

Objects are the Distinct Units

The question, then, is: what is object storage or object-based storage? In object storage, objects are the distinct units to manage and manipulate data storage. Or, in more simple words, data storage is managed as objects.

No Folder or Hierarchy Concept

In object storage, there is no folder or hierarchy concept like we have in file storage systems. Instead, in an object storage system, everything is stored in a flat address space, which is also known as storage pool. In AWS, this storage pool has a particular name – called "bucket."

Metadata

Another essential point about object storage is metadata. Metadata about objects are attached with stored objects, which is one of the reasons that we can do high performant analytics on AWS.

That's the reason even though we don't have any idea about objects' content, still, because metadata is attached to objects, we can query objects.

Object Storage Systems can be Scaled Out

Another feature of an object storage system is that object storage systems can be scaled out. This is the key reason the S3 storage system has virtually unlimited scalability.

Types of Storage Systems

There are two types of storage systems: classic scale-up storage that most of us are familiar with as it is used in file-based storage systems. The other one is scale-out which is closely related to object storage systems.

Classic Scale-up Storage

In a scale-up system, the storage scalability is limited by how many maximum disks can be attached to storage controllers – you cannot add more storage if the machine has reached the limit of how many maximum disks can be attached.

Scale-out System

On the other hand, with a scale-out system, you have a cluster of machines forming a storage address space called Storage Pool or Bucket in AWS terms. To increase storage capacity, just add more machines, which makes scale-out systems virtually unlimited scalable.

> *Object storage characteristics, such as storing objects in flat address space, metadata, and scale-out are the critical factors in driving S3 features.*

Amazon S3 Overview

Buckets

Amazon S3 allows users to store objects (files) in "buckets" (directories). Buckets must have a **globally unique name**. Buckets are defined at the Region level.

Regarding the naming convention for buckets, a bucket name must start with a lowercase character or a number and must be between 3-63 characters long. No uppercase and underscore characters are allowed. A bucket name cannot be an IP address.

Objects

Each S3 object (file) has a key. The key is the FULL path, for example, s3://my-bucket/**file_1.txt**, s3://my-bucket/**my_folder/another_folder/file_2.txt**.

The key comprises *prefix* + **object name**, for example, s3://my-bucket/*my_folder/another_folder/***file_3.txt**.

One important point to remember about S3 objects is that there is no concept of **"directories"** within buckets though the S3 UI may give you an impression of thinking otherwise. It's just an S3 object key with very long names that contain slashes ("/").

The S3 object's value is the content of the body. The maximum object size is 5TB, and if you upload an object of more than 5GB, you must use "multi-part upload."

The S3 object also contains metadata, a list of text key/value pairs. The metadata can be system or user metadata. The S3 object also contains tags that are Unicode key/value pairs – up to 10. The S3 object tag is useful for security or lifecycle. The S3 object also contains Version ID if versioning is enabled.

S3 Object Versioning

You can version your files on S3 – it is enabled at the bucket level. It is a best practice to version your buckets. Versioning protects against unintended deletes – it provides the ability to restore a version. It provides the ability to roll back to a previous version easily.

An important point to remember is that any file not versioned before enabling "versioning" will have "null" as a version. Suspending versioning does not delete the previous versions.

S3 Features

Object Storage System
Since S3 is an object storage system, and object storage systems have virtually unlimited scalability, as we talked earlier, that being the case, S3 has theoretically virtual unlimited scalability, which is a sort of logical conclusion.

Max Size of an Object on S3
Each object is stored in a bucket, and there is a limitation for the maximum size of the object which can be stored in a S3 bucket. The limit is 5TB what it means you cannot upload an object larger than 5TB on S3.

Fully Qualified Domain Name
Each S3 bucket gets a fully qualified domain name, and you use the fully qualified domain of a bucket to access objects in a S3 bucket.

Data Availability
S3 replicates data or content of the S3 Bucket in a minimum of three availability zones within a selected region.

Since availability zones are physically separate, the replication of data on the additional availability zones helps increase the degree of availability if there is any device failure or facility issue at the data center of an availability zone. For instance, since data are replicated on two additional AZs, data can be sustained even though data are lost concurrently in two facilities.

Security

S3 provides many securities-related features. For instance, you can store data in an encrypted form using different types of encryption mechanisms.

Performance

In S3, you can store data in a region nearest to your location. That way, you will get low latency, which leads to better performance.

Compliance

S3 has the feature of cross-region replication, which can manage regulatory compliance or keep a copy of data in case of a region failure.

Durability

Another final keyword here that I would like to bring your attention to is durability. S3 has 11 9's (99.999999999) durability, which means if you store 100 billion objects in S3, you will lose one object at most.

Creating S3 Bucket

Let's do a hands-on exercise of creating an S3 bucket uploading a file on S3.

Let's log in to the AWS Management Console. Now, go to the S3 service home page.

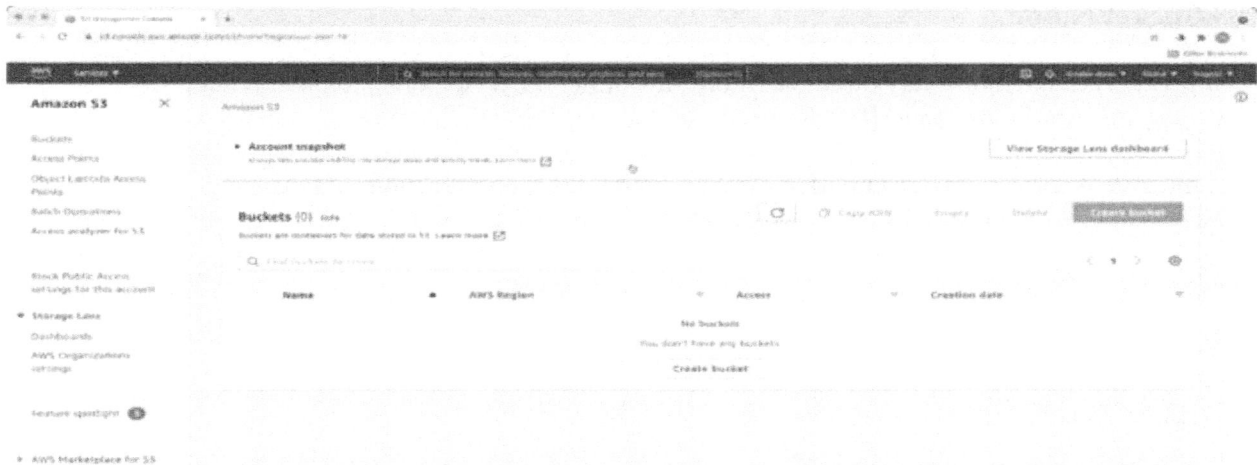

I would like to bring your attention to the top right corner. The first is the account name. You will see your account name here.

Then, the next placeholder is for AWS Region. Since S3 is a global service, it doesn't show any specific region – it says global. I'm on this page to upload an image. But I don't see any option to upload the image.

Here comes an interesting point that is related to the object storage concept. Since S3 is object-based storage, we need to create a storage pool to store objects. This storage pool is called Bucket.

We first need to create a bucket to upload the image, because currently there is no bucket listed in my account.

Click on Create bucket button.

Now I'm on the Create Bucket page. First, I need to enter the bucket name. Let's talk about bucket names– bucket names must be unique within a partition.

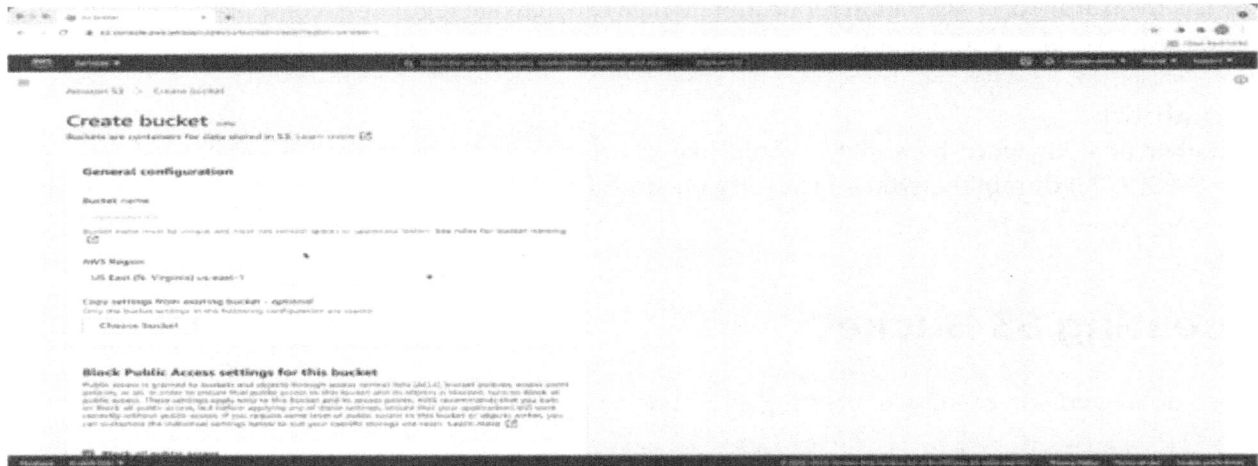

S3 Bucket Name

Bucket names must be unique within a partition. A partition is a grouping of AWS Regions. For example, AWS currently has three partitions: aws (Standard Regions), aws-cn (China Regions), and aws-us-gov (AWS GovCloud [US] Regions).

Let me give Bucket name knodax-demo-test Usually, it's a good technique to use a domain name in a bucket name, which usually avoids the possibility of name collision.

Next is AWS Region. This is where your actual data is stored.

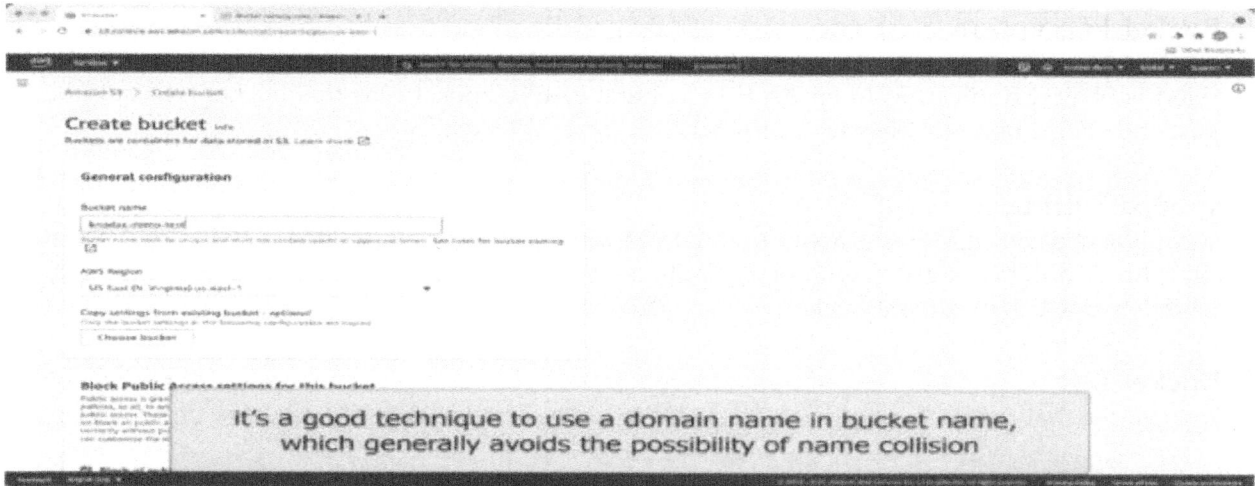

It's a good technique to use a domain name in bucket name, which generally avoids the possibility of name collision

Select the region which is nearest to your location to have low latency and good performance.

Your default region will be displayed; you can change it. However, I'll keep it as it is, as this is my nearest region.

Public Access for Bucket

Next is public access for this bucket. I'll block all public access, as this is my private bucket. I don't want the content of this bucket to be shared.

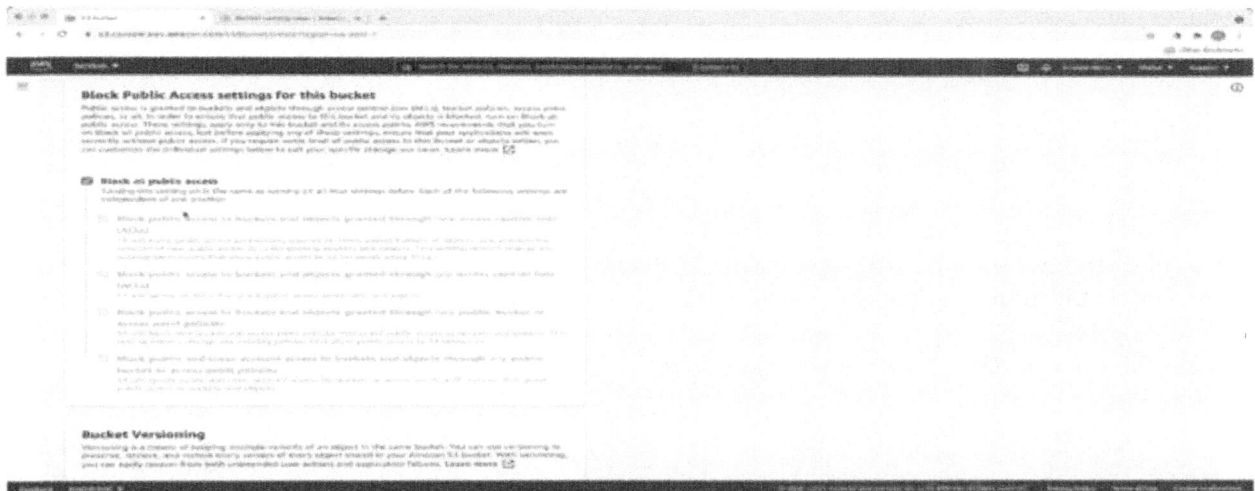

If I were using this bucket to store my website contents, I would have unchecked this box, which would have allowed public access.

S3 Bucket Versioning

Next is the bucket versioning; the *Disable* option is fine. But if you have a use case where you would want previous versions to be retained to recover from unintended user actions, you will check the enable radio button.

S3 Bucket Encryption

The next option is about whether you would want the content of this bucket to be encrypted. For me, Disabled is okay. I don't need to encrypt the content of this bucket – as this bucket will only have images, and encryption will be extra overhead to impact performance.

Advanced Settings

Next is advanced settings. This is about if you don't want objects to get deleted in the bucket. Disable option is fine. I don't have any regulatory compliance sort of data in this bucket which I would like to be not deleted. Click on Create Bucket.

S3 Bucket List

As you can see that the bucket has been created. I'm on the knodax-demo-test bucket page.

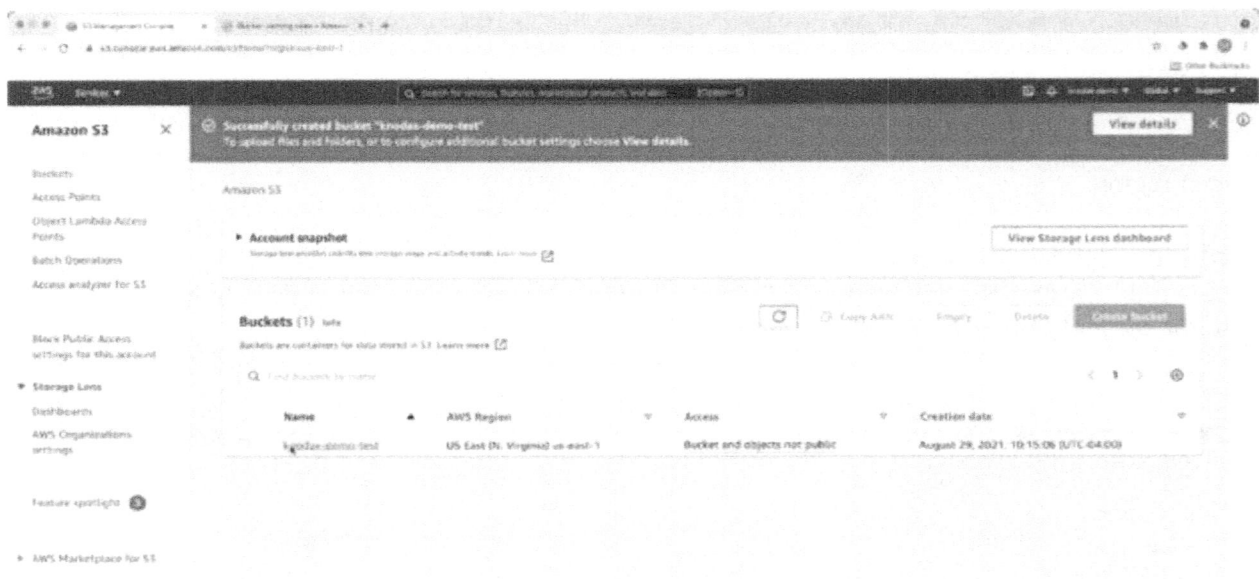

If you select the bucket, you can see options to delete the bucket and empty the bucket. You cannot delete a bucket if there is any object in the bucket.

Click on the Bucket. Now I'm on the bucket page.

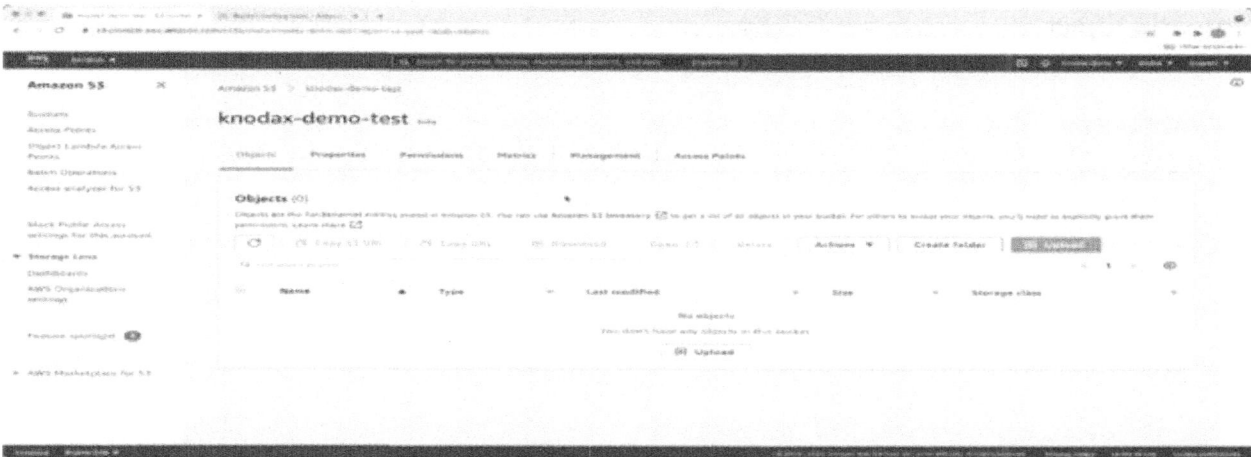

Let me click on the upload button to upload an image that I have.

Now I'm on the Upload page.

Upload Object to S3 bucket

Click on the Add files button to upload files. You also have the option to add a folder if you would like to add your content in a folder.

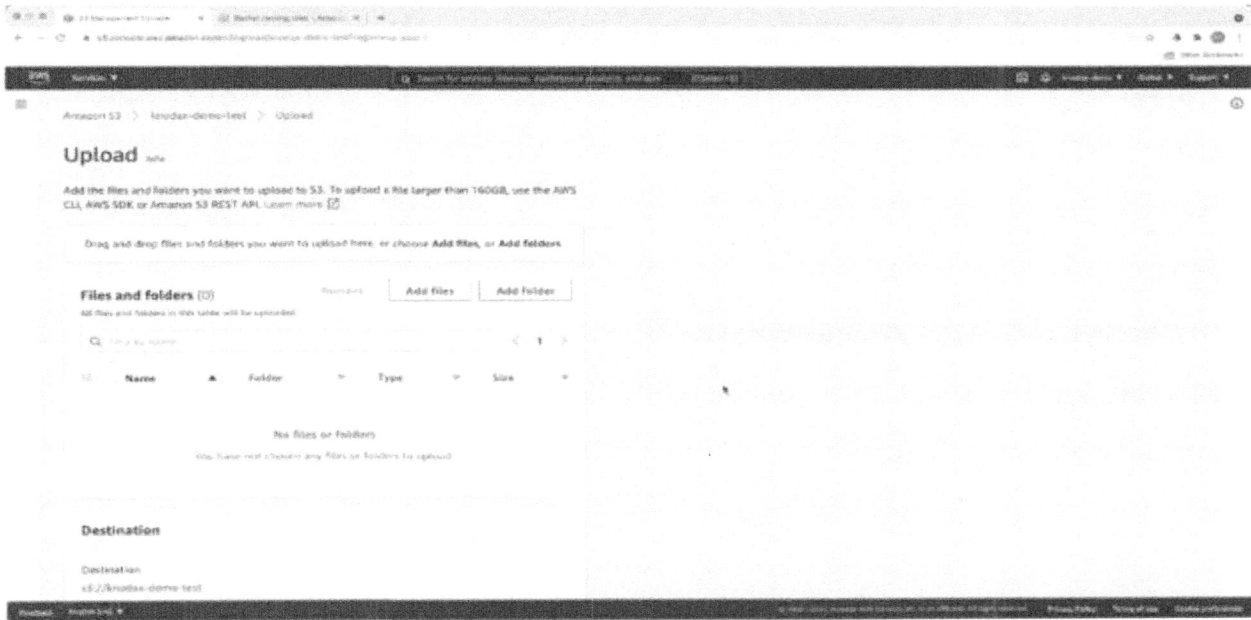

Please note that creating a folder will not make it a file storage system. It will just mimic the structure of a file system – s3 is an object storage system. The folder structure becomes key for the object, which is used to find the object.

Let me click on Add files; I'll add an AWS image.

Upload Object

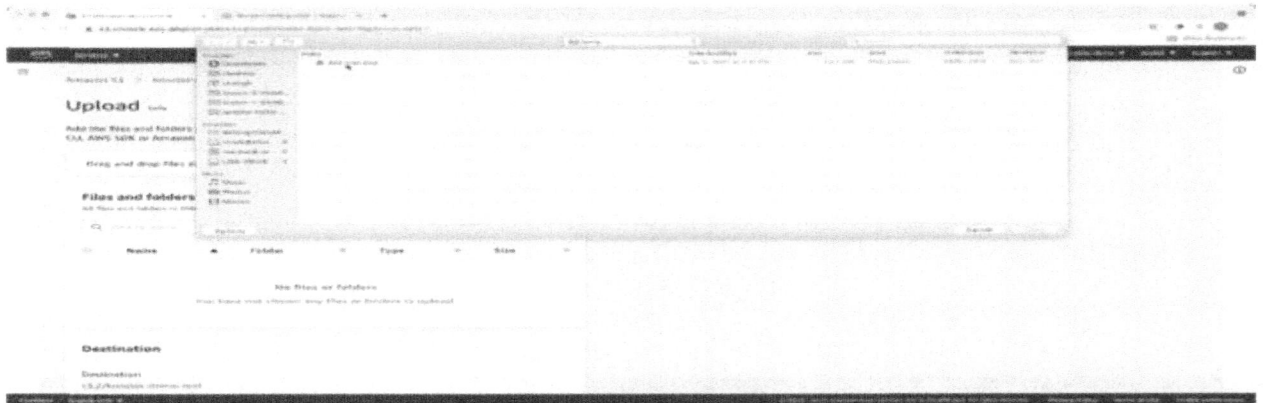

Click on upload.

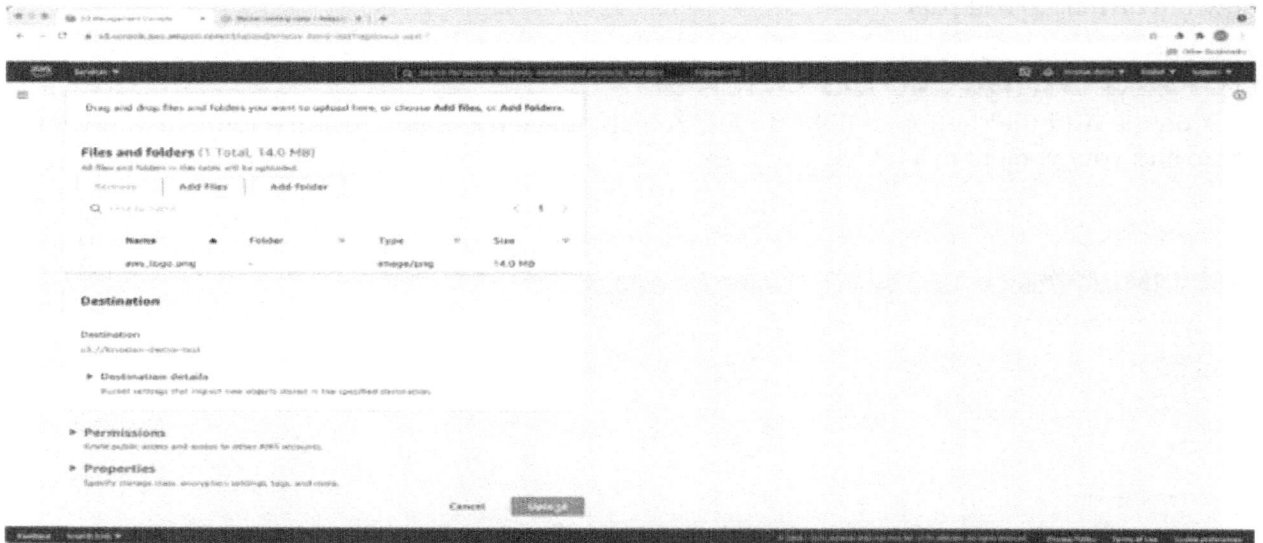

Now the image is getting uploaded – upload is successful.

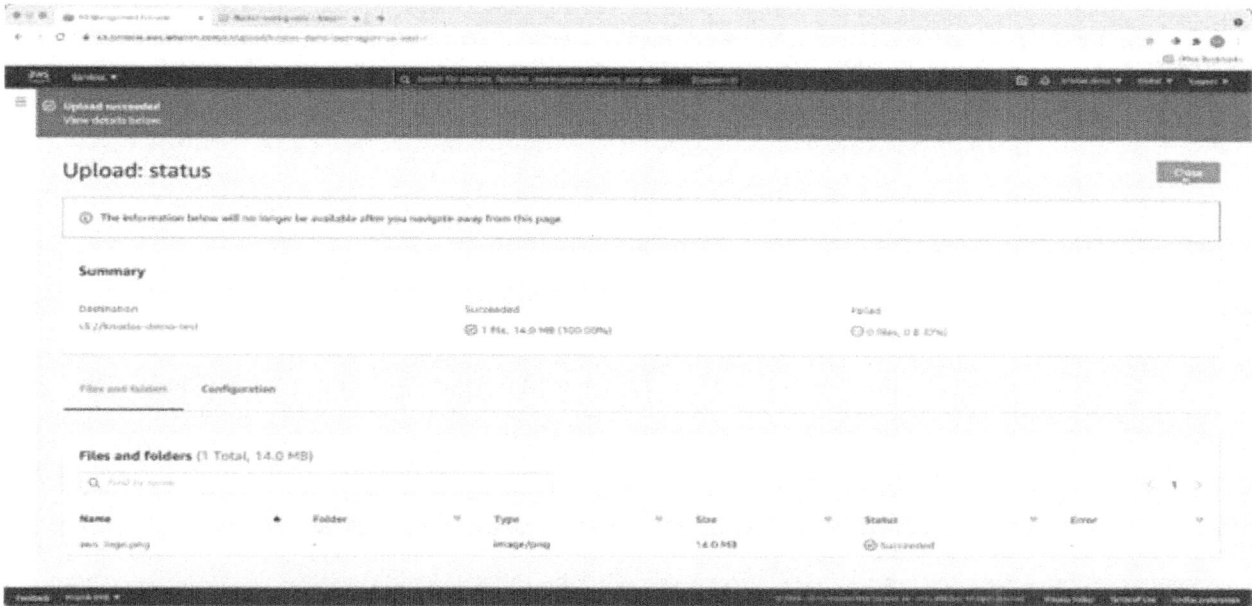

Click on close and view the uploaded image. Next, select the image and click on the image link.

Uploaded Object Details

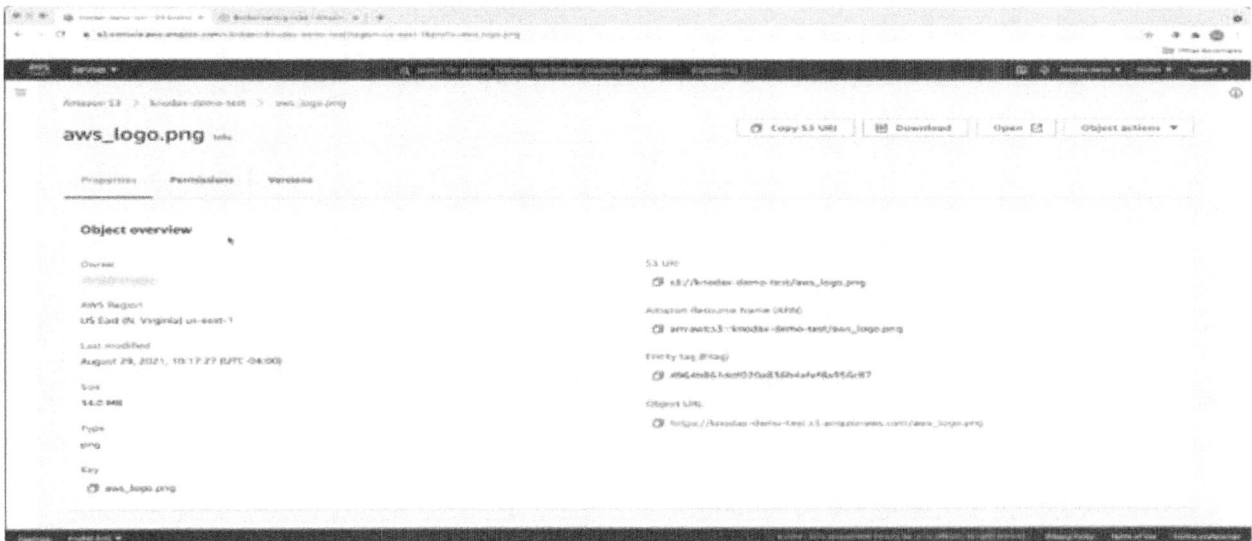

On the page, details about the image are displayed, for instance, Owner, AWS Region, last modified, size, type, key, S3 URI, a unique fully qualified domain name to access the image.

You will use this URI if you write code to access the image from your Java or Python code.

ARN

Next is ARN, which is used to manage permissions on the object – for instance, ARN can be used in IAM to set access permissions about this object.

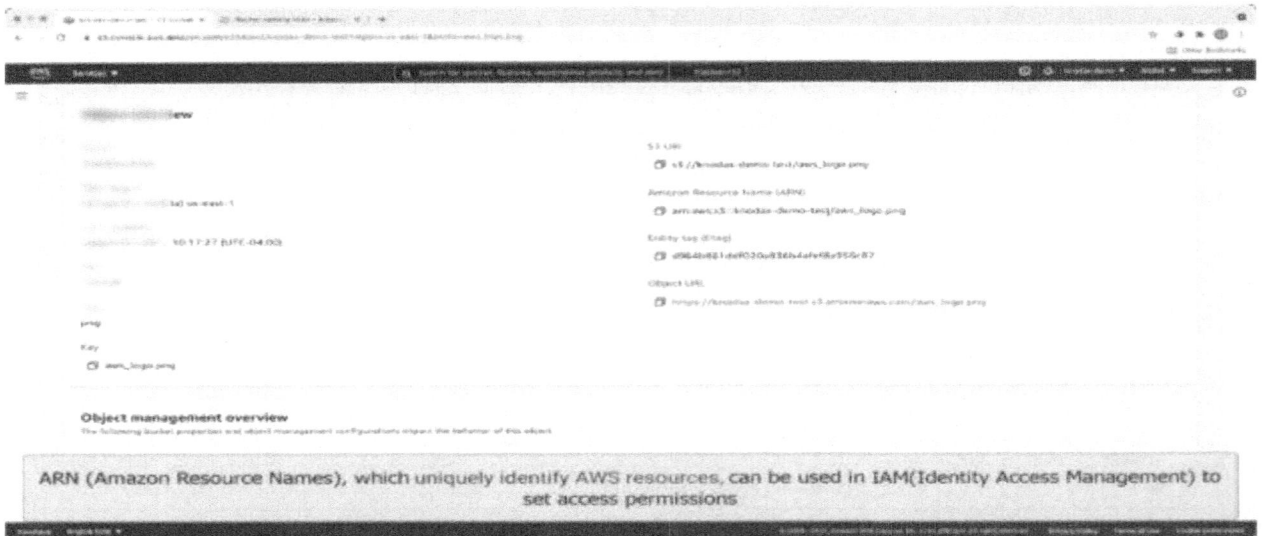

ARN (Amazon Resource Names), which uniquely identify AWS resources, can be used in IAM(Identity Access Management) to set access permissions

Etag

Then Etag, which is the md5 checksum of that file. It is used to find out if the object has been modified, which is used in caching.

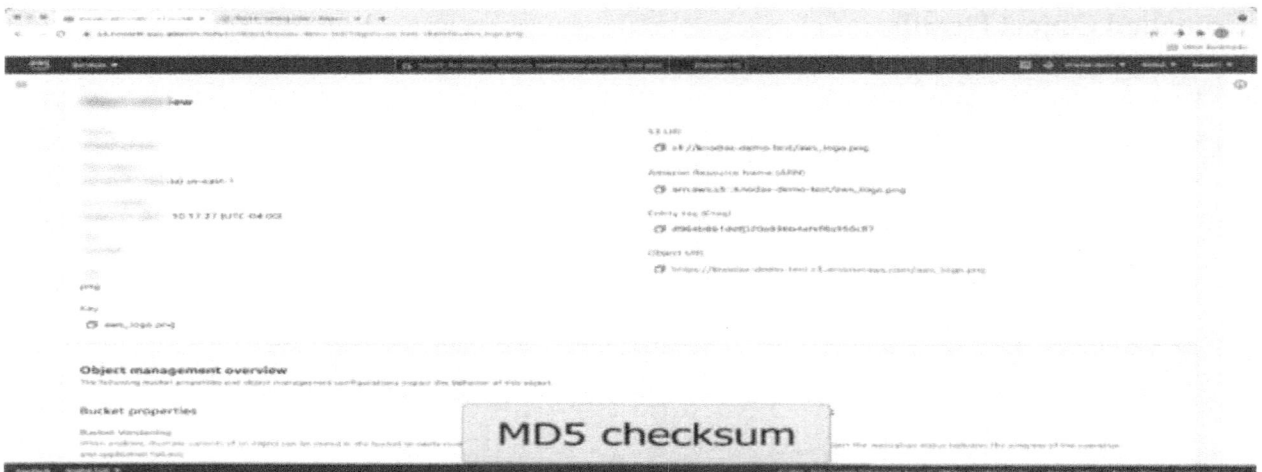

MD5 checksum

View the Uploaded Object

Let's click on the open URL to view the image.

This is the AWS image that I uploaded.

Protecting Data in Transit and at Rest on S3

You can protect data in transit using SSL/TLS or client-side encryption. To protect data at rest in Amazon S3, you can use Server-Side Encryption and Client-Side Encryption.

Encryption for Objects in Transit

Amazon S3 exposes HTTP endpoint, which is not-encrypted, and HTTPS, which provides encryption in transit. Encryption in flight is also called SSL/TLS.

You are free to use either HTTP or HTTPS endpoint; however, HTTPS endpoint is recommended.

HTTPS is mandatory for SSE-C.

Encryption for Objects at Rest

There are four methods of encrypting objects on S3:
- SSE-S3: encrypts S3 objects using keys handled & managed by AWS.
- SS3-KMS: leverages AWS Key Management Service (KMS) to manage encryption keys.
- SSE-C: you use it when you want to manage your own encryption keys.
- Client Side Encryption

For the certification exam, it is important to understand which ones are used for which situation.

SSE-S3

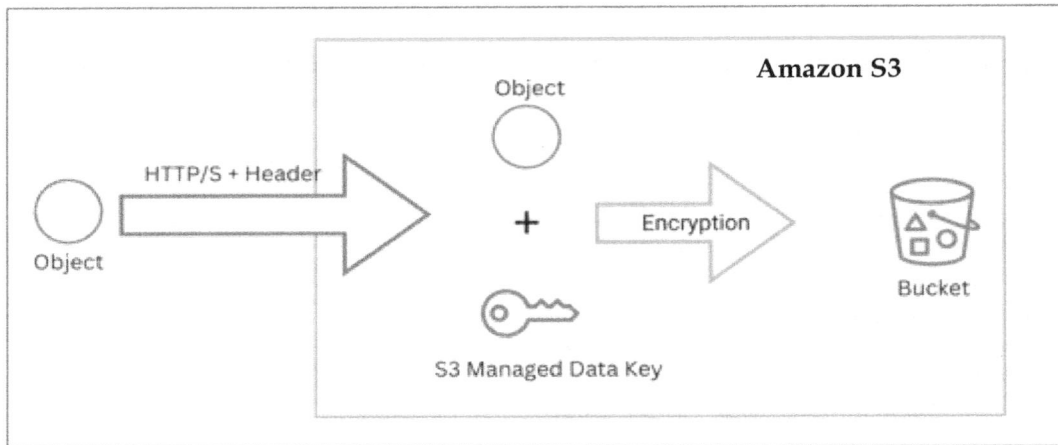

This encryption method of encrypting S3 objects uses keys handled and managed by Amazon S3. The object is encrypted on the server side using AES-256 symmetric encryption. The HTTP request must have custom HTTP Header field: "x-amz-server-side-encryption": "AES256"

SSE-KMS

This encryption method of encrypting S3 objects uses keys handled and managed by KMS. AWS KMS offers you centralized control over the cryptographic keys to protect your data. The service is also integrated with AWS CloudTrail, which allows you to audit who used which keys, on which resources, and when.

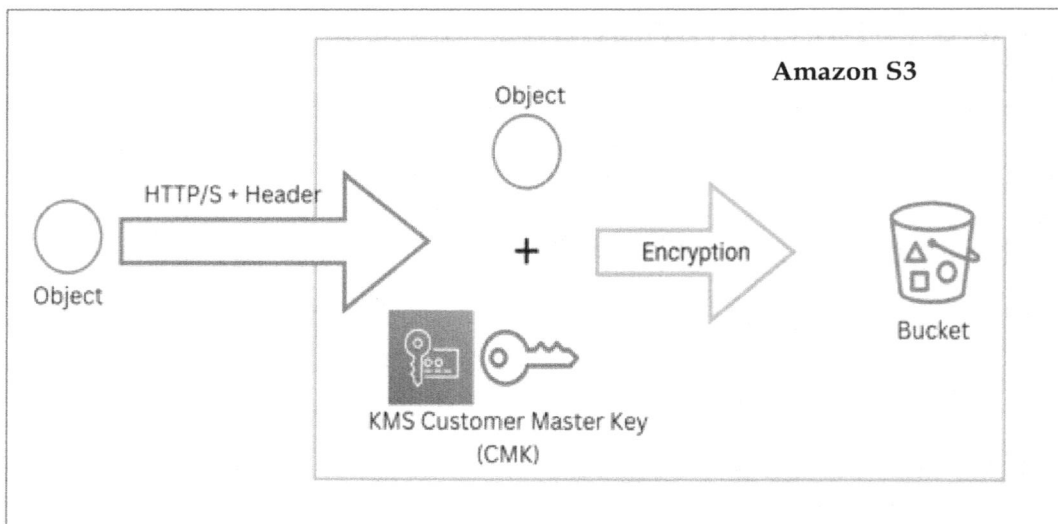

The object is encrypted on the server side using AES-256 symmetric encryption. The HTTP request must have custom HTTP Header field: "x-amz-server-side-encryption": "aws:kms"

SSE-C

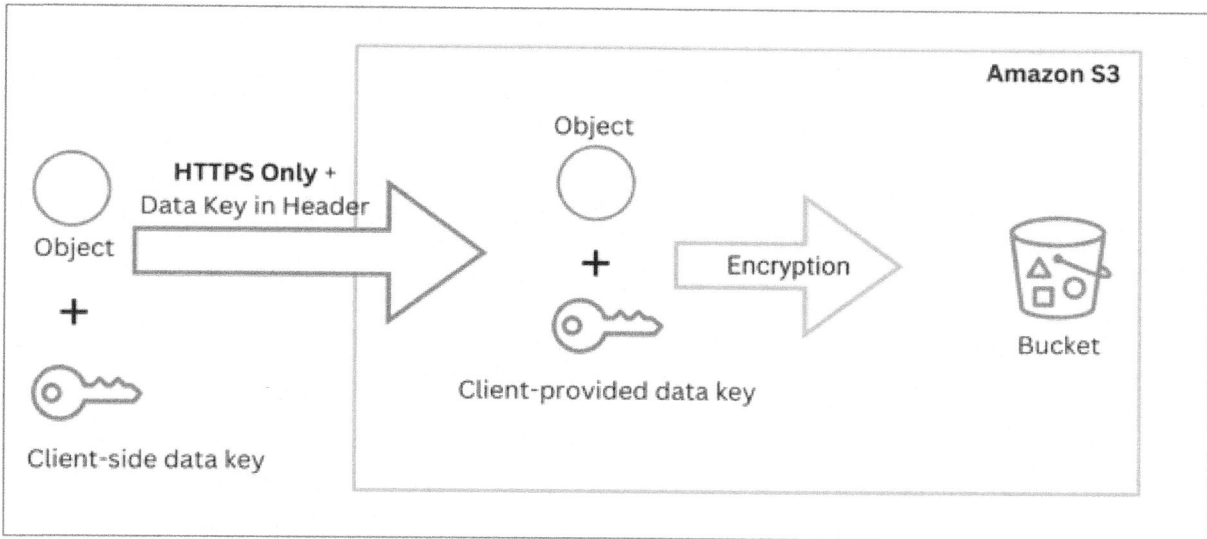

This method uses server-side encryption using data keys fully managed by the customer outside of AWS. Amazon S3 does not store the encryption key that you provide.

In this method, HTTPS must be used, and an encryption key must be provided in HTTP headers for every HTTP request.

Client-Side Encryption

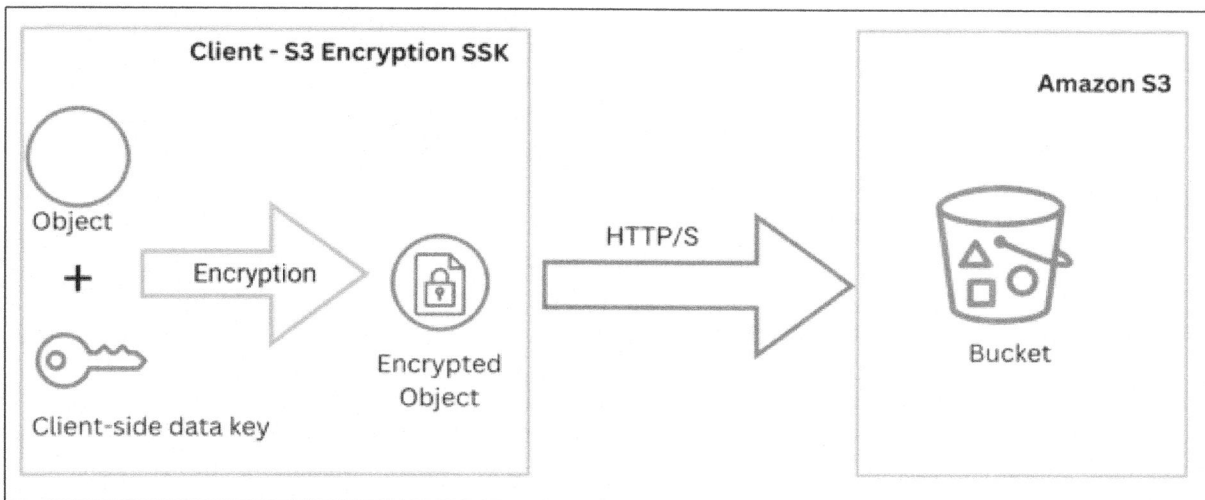

In this encryption method, clients must encrypt data themselves before sending it to S3, and clients must decrypt data themselves when retrieving from S3. The customer fully manages the keys and encryption cycle. Client library such as the Amazon S3 Encryption Client is used.

S3 Security

There are two ways to secure S3 access. One is the User Based, and the other is Resource Based. In User Based S3 security, IAM Policies are assigned to the user, which defines which API calls are allowed for a specific user.

The other type of S3 Security is Resource Based; we can provide a more fine-grain ACL (Access Control List) at the object level. Or, we can provide ACL at the bucket level – more coarse-grained control.

Please keep in mind that an IAM principal can access an S3 object if:
- The user IAM permissions allow it, OR if the resource policy ALLOWS it
- And there is no explicit DENY

S3 Bucket Policies

S3 Bucket Policies are JSON based. You define the bucket policy in a JSON document. The following are the main elements of an S3 policy document:

Resources: provide buckets and objects ARNs that are controlled by the policy document
Actions: What set of API calls are Allowed or Denied, for example, "GetObject"
Effect: Policy allows "Allow" or "Deny" the Action
Principal: Which account or user this policy is applied to

```
{
  "Version": "2012-10-17",
  "Statement": [
    {
      "Sid": "PublicRead",
      "Effect": "Allow",
      "Principal": "*",
      "Action" : [
        "s3:GetObject"
      ],
      "Resoruce": [
        "arm:aws:S3:::myExampleBucket/*"
      ]
    }
  ]
}
```

The question is when to use S3 Bucket for a policy instead of IAM permissions to control the S3 access.
- Use the S3 bucket policy when you need to grant public access to the bucket.
- You need to force objects to be encrypted at upload time.
- You need to grant cross-account access.

S3 Default Encryption vs. Bucket Policies

One way to force encryption is to use a bucket policy and refuse any API call to PUT an S3 object without encryption headers Another way is to use the "default encryption" option in S3.

Please note that the Bucket Policy is evaluated first before "default encryption."

Preventing Accidental Deletion of Objects

Enable MFA Delete on the S3 bucket

You can configure MFA delete on a bucket to help ensure that the data in your bucket cannot be accidentally deleted. Enabling MFA Delete can be used to provide an additional layer of security. By default, all requests to your Amazon S3 bucket require your AWS account credentials. However, suppose you enable Versioning with MFA Delete on your Amazon S3 bucket. In that case, two forms of authentication are required to permanently delete a version of an object: your AWS account credentials and a valid code from an authentication device in your physical possession.

Only the bucket owner (root account) can enable/disable MFA Delete.

You will need MFA to:
- permanently delete an object version
- suspend versioning on the bucket

You will not need MFA for:
- enable versioning
- listing deleted versions

Enable Versioning on the S3 bucket

You can version your files on S3 – it is enabled at the bucket level. It is a best practice to version your buckets. Versioning protects against unintended deletes – it provides the ability to restore a version. It provides the ability to roll back to a previous version easily.

When a user deletes an object in an S3 bucket, all subsequent requests will no longer be able to retrieve the object. However, all versions of that object will continue to be stored in your S3 bucket, and those versions of the object can be retrieved.

S3 Pre-Signed URLs

You can generate pre-signed URLs using AWS SDK or CLI. For downloads, you can use CLI, for example, *aws s3 presign s3://my-bucket/file.txt.*

You can generate a pre-signed URL programmatically using the AWS SDKs for .NET, Java, Ruby, JavaScript, PHP, and Python.

For uploads, you must use AWS SDK to generate a pre-signed URL programmatically using the AWS SDKs for .NET, Java, Ruby, JavaScript, PHP, and Python. The generated pre-signed URL that you or anyone that you give can use to upload objects on S3.

Pre-signed URLs are valid for a default of 3600 seconds. You can, however, change timeout with the – expires-in [TIME_BY_SECONDS] argument.

Users who are provided a pre-signed URL inherit the permissions of the AWS user who generated the URL.

Some use cases of pre-signed URLs:
- Allow only logged-in users to download your premium videos from your S3 bucket.
- Allow a user to temporarily upload a file to a specific location in a bucket.
- Allows an ever-changing list of new users to download files by generating URLs dynamically.

S3 Networking, Logging & Audit, and User Security

VPC endpoint
When your applications running on EC2 instances need access to objects on S3 buckets, you can use VPC endpoints to simplify access to S3 from within a VPC without going through the internet. When you create an S3 VPC endpoint, you can attach an endpoint policy to it that controls access to the bucket.

S3 Access Logs & Audit
For audit purposes, you may need to log all access to S3 buckets. Any request made to S3 from any account authorized or denied can be logged. The log data can be analyzed using data analysis tools (for example, Aetna) for analyzing access patterns.
The Amazon S3 server access log format at:
https://docs.aws.amazon.com/AmazonS3/latest/dev/LogFormat.html

Please note: *Do not set your logging bucket to the monitored bucket. It will cause to create a logging loop, and your bucket size will grow exponentially.*

S3 access API calls can be logged in AWS CloudTrail. Amazon S3 is integrated with AWS CloudTrail. CloudTrail captures a subset of API calls for Amazon S3 as events. If you don't configure a trail, you can still view the most recent events in the CloudTrail console in Event history.

User Security
In a versioned bucket, MFA Delete can be required to prevent the accidental deletion of objects. You can use Pre-Signed URLs to keep URLs valid for a limited time, for example, premium video service for logged-in users.

S3 Websites
You can use an S3 bucket to host a static website and have them accessible via the Internet.
The website URL pattern using S3 bucket:
<bucket-name>.s3-website-<AWS-Region>.amazonaws.com
Or
<bucket-name>.s3-website.<AWS-Region>.amazonaws.com

Make sure the bucket is public; otherwise, your users will get a 403(forbidden) error.

CORS
Browsers have implemented many security features to have us safe browsing. CORS stands for Cross-Origin Resource Sharing. This web browser-based mechanism allows requests to other origins while visiting the main origin. The requests from the other origin are not allowed unless the other origin allows requests using CORS Headers (for example, Access-Control-Allow-Origin).

An origin is a scheme (protocol), host (domain), and port (implied port is 443 for HTTPS and 80 for HTTP), for example, https://www.example.com.

The same origin examples:

http://example.com/warehouse/inventories, http://example.com/crm/customerLists

The different origin examples: http://warehouse.example.com/inventories, http://crm.example.com/customerLists

By default, browsers allow us to embed most content from other websites, such as images, CSS, and JavaScript (exceptions iframes). They also look into any side effects and stop any requests with side effects. This is where CORS and SOP come into play.

Browsers allow SOP, which is the **S**ame **O**rigin **P**olicy. On the other hand, if the request is made from the other origin, the browser looks into the CORS Headers to see if access is allowed.

Let's take an example to understand a hypothetical security risk if browsers didn't have a CORS policy. Some online user visits their online bank site, and the bank may store a cookie on the user's browser so that the user doesn't have to enter his user and password. Suppose that the user visits another website; that website may use the cookie to log in to the bank and perform a transfer outside of the user's account by making an AJAX call. As you can understand, this is where the browser's CORS policy comes into play, which, by default, disallows any request from the origin that creates a side effect.

Reference: https://medium.com/@electra_chong/what-is-cors-what-is-it-used-for-308cafa4df1a

To instruct the browser to expose server responses to HTTP requests from a certain origin, the web server must respond to the request to the additional HTTP response header, 'Access-Control-Allow-Origin:<origin>'. Alternatively, the web server may expose its responses to all origins by specifying a value of "*", for example, "Access-Control-Allow-Origin: *" – which is not considered a safe option.

The browser first sends a preflight request, which is an OPTIONS request Web servers that wish to support CORS requests must respond to preflight requests.

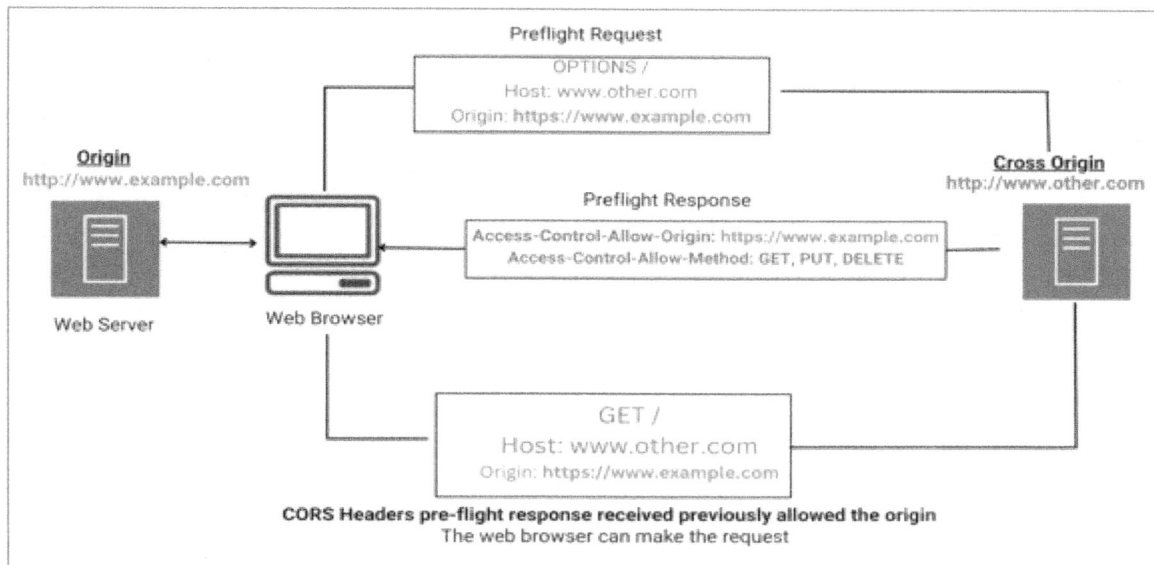

Preflight Request
OPTIONS /
Host: www.other.com
Origin: https://www.example.com

Origin
http://www.example.com

Cross Origin
http://www.other.com

Preflight Response
Access-Control-Allow-Origin: https://www.example.com
Access-Control-Allow-Method: GET, PUT, DELETE

Web Server   Web Browser

GET /
Host: www.other.com
Origin: https://www.example.com

CORS Headers pre-flight response received previously allowed the origin
The web browser can make the request

In this diagram, the origin, http://www.example.com, would like to make a cross-origin (http://www/other.com) request. The browser first sends a preflight request to the server of cross-origin (http://www/other.com), asking if the cross-origin request is fulfilled. As you can see in the pre-flight response, it allows the origin (www.example.com) for GET, PUT, and DELETE methods. Therefore, the browser address http://www.example.com (origin) can access http://www.other.com (cross-origin).

S3 CORS

If a client makes a cross-origin request on an S3 bucket, we need to enable the correct CORS header. As we discussed earlier, you can allow for a specific origin or for "*" (all origins).

For example:

In this example, the CORS configuration for an S3 bucket, which has been configured to host a static website, allows cross-origin PUT, POST, and DELETE requests from the http://www.example.com origin.

S3 Replication

Both cross Region (CRR) and same Region replication (SRR) can be performed. The versioning must be enabled in the source and destination for replication. Buckets can be in different accounts. Replication is done asynchronously. We need to give proper IAM permissions to S3.

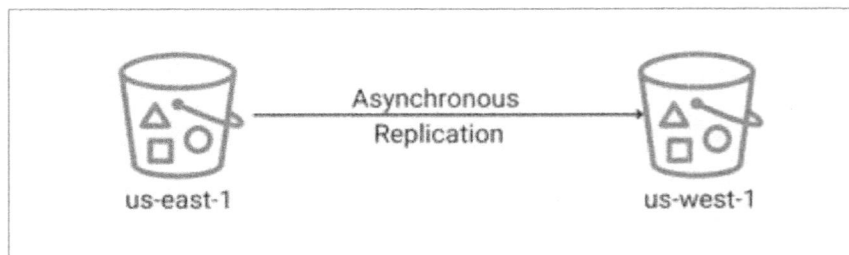

When you activate replication, only new objects after activation will be replicated. You can, optionally, replicate existing objects using S3 Batch Operation. S3 Batch Operation replicates existing objects and objects that have failed replication.

There is no chaining of replication. If Bucket 'X' has replication into Bucket 'Y' and bucket 'Y' has replication into Bucket 'Z.' Then, the bucket objects from X will not be replicated on bucket Z.

For delete operations, delete markers can be replicated from the source to the target. This is an optional setting.

S3 Cross Region Replication (CRR) User Cases:
compliance, reduced latency access, and replication across accounts

S3 Same Region Replication (SRR) User Cases:
log aggregation, live replication between production and test environments

S3 Use Cases

Use cases

Build a data lake	Back up and restore critical data	Archive data at the lowest cost	Run cloud-native applications
Run big data analytics, artificial intelligence (AI), machine learning (ML), and high performance computing (HPC) applications to unlock data insights.	Meet Recovery Time Objectives (RTO), Recovery Point Objectives (RPO), and compliance requirements with S3's robust replication features.	Move data archives to the Amazon S3 Glacier storage classes to lower costs, eliminate operational complexities, and gain new insights.	Build fast, powerful mobile and web-based cloud-native apps that scale automatically in a highly available configuration.

Reference:
https://aws.amazon.com/s3/

Section 3. AWS Advanced

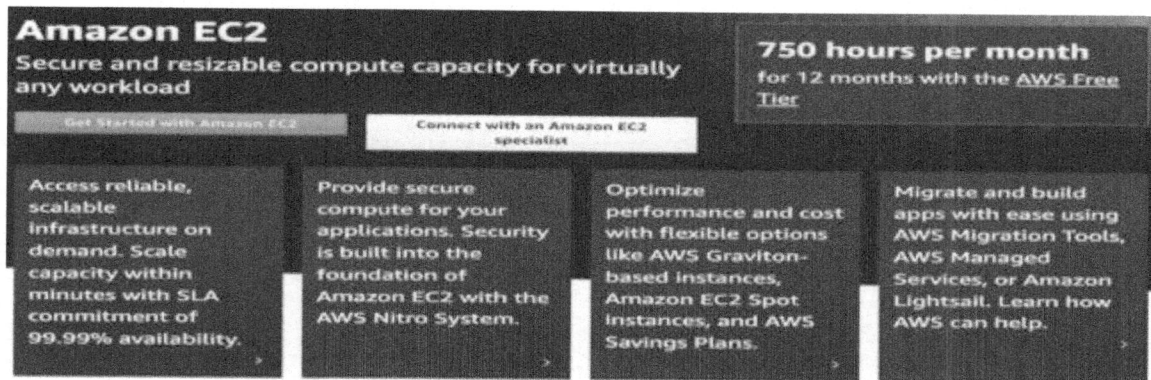

Amazon EC2
Secure and resizable compute capacity for virtually any workload

750 hours per month
for 12 months with the AWS Free Tier

Get Started with Amazon EC2

Connect with an Amazon EC2 specialist

Access reliable, scalable infrastructure on demand. Scale capacity within minutes with SLA commitment of 99.99% availability.

Provide secure compute for your applications. Security is built into the foundation of Amazon EC2 with the AWS Nitro System.

Optimize performance and cost with flexible options like AWS Graviton-based instances, Amazon EC2 Spot instances, and AWS Savings Plans.

Migrate and build apps with ease using AWS Migration Tools, AWS Managed Services, or Amazon Lightsail. Learn how AWS can help.

Chapter 15. EC2 Advanced

You will learn the following in this chapter:
- EC2 Instance Types
- General Purpose Instance
- Compute Optimized Instance
- Memory Optimized Instance
- Storage Optimized Instance
- Accelerated Computing Instance
- EC2 Instance Additional Features
- EC2 Instance Purchasing Options
- On-Demand Instance
- Reserved Instance
- Convertible Reserved Instances
- Scheduled Reserved Instances
- Spot Instances
- Spot Fleets
- Dedicated Host
- Dedicated Instance
- EC2 Savings Plans
- Placement Groups
- Cluster Placement Group
- Spread Placement Group
- Partition Placement Group

EC2 Instance Types

You can use different types of EC2 instances such as General Purpose, Compute Optimized, Memory Optimized, Storage Optimized, and Storage Optimized Instance for different use cases.

AWS has the following naming convention for an EC2 instance: **m2.4xlarge** (**m**: instance class, **2**: generation, **4xlarge**: size within the instance class)

General Purpose Instance

The General Purpose instances are great for a diversity of workloads such as *web servers or code repositories*. It balances between compute, memory, and networking. For example, t2.micro is a general-purpose EC2 instance.

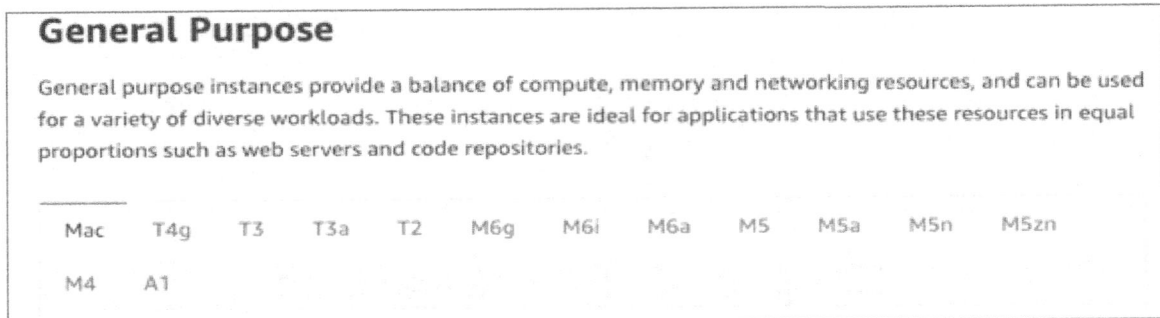

General Purpose

General purpose instances provide a balance of compute, memory and networking resources, and can be used for a variety of diverse workloads. These instances are ideal for applications that use these resources in equal proportions such as web servers and code repositories.

Mac	T4g	T3	T3a	T2	M6g	M6i	M6a	M5	M5a	M5n	M5zn
M4	A1										

Screenshot from: https://aws.amazon.com/ec2/instance-types/

Compute Optimized Instance

The Compute Optimized instances are designed for compute-bound applications that benefit from high-performance processors. The use cases include compute-intensive applications such *as batch processing workloads, media transcoding, high performance web servers, high performance computing (HPC), scientific modeling & machine learning, and dedicated gaming servers.*

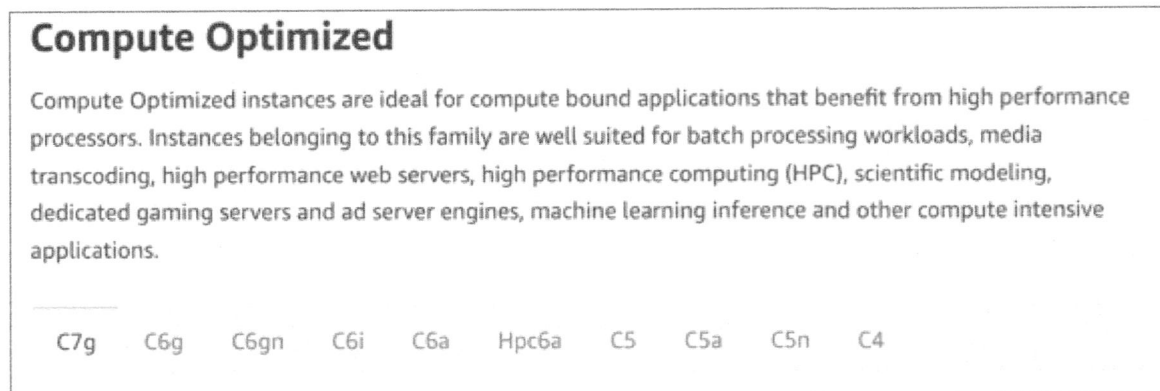

Compute Optimized

Compute Optimized instances are ideal for compute bound applications that benefit from high performance processors. Instances belonging to this family are well suited for batch processing workloads, media transcoding, high performance web servers, high performance computing (HPC), scientific modeling, dedicated gaming servers and ad server engines, machine learning inference and other compute intensive applications.

C7g	C6g	C6gn	C6i	C6a	Hpc6a	C5	C5a	C5n	C4

Screenshot from: https://aws.amazon.com/ec2/instance-types/

Memory Optimized Instance

The Memory Optimized instances are designed to deliver fast performance for workloads that process large data sets in memory. Memory-optimized instances offer a large memory size for memory-intensive applications such as in-memory applications, in-memory databases, or in-memory analytics solutions.

The use cases include *high-performance relational/non-relational databases, distributed web scale cache stores, in-memory databases optimized for BI (business intelligence), and applications performing real-time processing of big unstructured data.*

Memory Optimized

Memory optimized instances are designed to deliver fast performance for workloads that process large data sets in memory.

R6a	R6g	R6i	R5	R5a	R5b	R5n	R4	X2gd	X2idn	X2iedn	X2iezn

X1e	X1	High Memory	z1d

Screenshot from: https://aws.amazon.com/ec2/instance-types/

Storage Optimized Instance

The Storage Optimized instances are designed for workloads that require high sequential read and write access to very large data sets. Examples of large data sets could be Hadoop distributed computing, massively parallel processing, data warehousing, and log processing applications. The Storage Optimized instances are optimized to deliver tens of thousands of low-latency, random I/O operations per second (IOPS) to applications. The Storage Optimized instances offer the best/GB-storage and price/disk-throughput across other EC2 instances.

The use cases include *high-frequency online transaction processing (OLTP) systems, relational & NoSQL databases, the cache for in-memory databases (for example, Redis), data warehousing applications, and distributed file systems.*

These instances are well suited for the following:

- Massive parallel processing (MPP) data warehouse

- MapReduce and Hadoop distributed computing

- Log or data processing applications

Screenshot from:
https://docs.aws.amazon.com/AWSEC2/latest/UserGuide/storage-optimized-instances.html

Screenshot from: https://aws.amazon.com/ec2/instance-types/

Accelerated Computing Instance

The Accelerated Computing instance family uses hardware accelerators, or co-processors, to perform some functions, such as floating-point number calculation and graphics processing, more efficiently than in software running on CPUs. Amazon EC2 provides three types of Accelerated Computing instances: GPU compute instances for general-purpose computing, GPU graphics instances for graphics-intensive applications, and FPGA programmable hardware computes instances for advanced scientific workloads.

EC2 Instance Types Examples

Instance Type	Memory	vCPU	Storage	Network Performance
t2.micro	1.0 GiB	1 vCPUs for a 2h 24m burst	EBS only	Low to Moderate
r6g.medium	8.0 GiB	1 vCPUs	EBS only	Up to 10 Gigabit
c6gd.medium	2.0 GiB	1 vCPUs	59 GB NVMe SSD	Up to 10 Gigabit
m3.medium	3.75 GiB	1 vCPUs	4 GB SSD	Moderate
t2.small	2.0 GiB	1 vCPUs for a 4h 48m burst	EBS only	Low to Moderate
m6g.medium	4.0 GiB	1 vCPUs	EBS only	Up to 10 Gigabit
m1.medium	3.75 GiB	1 vCPUs	410 GB HDD	Moderate
m1.small	1.7 GiB	1 vCPUs	160 GB HDD + 900MB swap	Low
x2gd.medium	16.0 GiB	1 vCPUs	59 GB NVMe SSD	Up to 10 Gigabit
m6gd.medium	4.0 GiB	1 vCPUs	59 GB NVMe SSD	Up to 10 Gigabit
is4gen.medium	6.0 GiB	1 vCPUs	937 GB NVMe SSD	Up to 25 Gigabit

Source: https://instances.vantage.sh

EC2 Instance Additional Features

Amazon EC2 instances provide several additional features such as burstable performance instances, multiple storage options, and placement groups to help you deploy, manage, and scale your applications.

Burstable Performance Instances

Besides choosing EC2 instances from Fixed Performance instance families (for example, M6, C6, and R6), you can also choose from Burstable Performance Instance families (for example, T3). Burstable

Performance EC2 Instances provide a baseline level of CPU performance with the ability to burst above the baseline. Many applications related to web servers, developer environments, and small databases benefits from Burstable Performance Instance families as they don't need consistently high CPU levels but benefit significantly from full access to high-speed CPUs when needed.

Multiple Storage Options

When it comes to selecting storage options for Amazon EC2, it allows you to choose between multiple storage options based on your requirements.

Amazon EBS

Amazon EBS (Elastic Block Storage) is a durable, block-level storage volume that you can attach to an Amazon EC2 instance. You can use Amazon EBS as a primary storage device if your use case requires frequent and granular updates. For example, Amazon EBS is the recommended storage option for running a database on Amazon EC2.

Amazon EBS provides three volume types to best meet your workloads' needs: General Purpose (SSD), Provisioned IOPS (SSD), and Magnetic.

General Purpose (SSD)

General Purpose (SSD) is the new, SSD-backed, general purpose EBS volume type that is recommended default choice for customer. They are suitable for many workloads, including small to medium-sized databases, development, and test environments, and boot volumes.

Provisioned IOPS (SSD)

Provisioned IOPS (SSD) volumes offer storage with consistent and low-latency performance. They are designed for I/O-intensive applications such as large relational or NoSQL databases.

Magnetic

Magnetic volumes provide the lowest cost per gigabyte of all EBS volume types. They are ideal for workloads where data is accessed infrequently and applications where the lowest storage cost is important.

Instance Storage

Many Amazon EC2 instances can also include storage located inside the host computer, referred to as instance storage. Instance storage provides temporary block-level storage for Amazon EC2 instances. Therefore, the data on instance storage persists only during the life of the associated Amazon EC2 instance.

Amazon S3

In addition to block-level storage via Amazon EBS or instance storage, you can also use Amazon S3 for highly durable object storage.

EBS-optimized instances with Provisioned IOPS

Customers can launch selected Amazon EC2 instance types as EBS-optimized instances for an additional, low, hourly fee. EBS-optimized instances enable EC2 instances to use the IOPS provisioned on an EBS volume fully. The dedicated throughput minimizes contention between Amazon EBS I/O and other traffic from your EC2 instance, providing the best performance for your EBS volumes. In addition, EBS-optimized instances are designed for use with all EBS volumes.

When attached to EBS-optimized instances, Provisioned IOPS volumes can achieve single-digit millisecond latencies. It is recommended to use Provisioned IOPS volumes with EBS-optimized instances or instances that support cluster networking for applications with high storage I/O requirements.

EC2 Instance Purchasing Options

On-Demand Instance

As the name says, An On-Demand Instance is an instance that you use on-demand. You have complete control over its lifecycle — you decide when to launch, stop, hibernate, start, reboot, or terminate it. There is no long-term commitment required when you purchase On-Demand Instances. There is no upfront payment when using On-Demand instances. You can pay by the hour or the second (minimum 60 seconds) depending on which instances you run, with no long-term commitment.

On-demand instances are not interrupted.

On-Demand instances are recommended for the following types of use cases:
- When you prefer the low cost and flexibility of EC2 On-Demand, you can start, stop, hibernate, or terminate an EC2 instance at any time. There is no upfront cost, and there is no long-term commitment.
- When your use case requires a short-term, spiky, unpredictable load pattern, you don't want the instances to be interrupted.
- When developing or testing an application on an EC2 instance, On-Demand instances can be an optimal choice.

KEY POINTS

- Pay for what you use:
    - Linux or Windows - billing per second, after the first minute
    - All other OS - billing per hour
- Most costly option but there is no upfront payment
- No long-term commitment
- Recommended for short-term and un-interrupted workloads

Reserved Instance

Reserved Instances offer you significant savings on your Amazon EC2 costs compared to On-Demand Instance pricing. For example, Reserved Instances save you up to 75% compared to On-Demand Instances.

Reserved Instances is a billing discount applied to the use of On-Demand Instances in your account -- they are not physical instances. Reserved Instanced can be purchased for a one-year or three-year commitment. You get a more significant discount when you choose a three-year commitment offering. When using Reserved Instances, you will be charged for the entire duration, irrespective of your usage.

You cannot use Reserved Instances for using server-bound software licenses. Reserved instances are not interrupted.

- You can get up to 72% discount compared to On-Demand instances
- You reserve specific instance attributes (Instance Type, Region, Tenancy, OS)
- Reservation Period: 1 year (discount) or three years (more discount)
- Payment Options: No Upfront (discount), Partial Upfront (more discount), All Upfront (most discount)
- Reserved Instance's Scope: Regional or AZ
- Recommended for always up a steady-state type of applications, such as databases, web servers
- buy and sell in the Reserved Instance Marketplace

Convertible Reserved Instances

Convertible Reserved Instances provide you additional flexibility, such as using different instance families, operating systems, or tenancies over the Reserved Instance term. In addition, Convertible Reserved Instances offer you a significant discount compared to On-Demand Instances. You can purchase Convertible Reserved Instances for a 1-year or 3-year term.

Convertible Reserved Instances can be helpful when workloads are likely to change. The Convertible Reserved Instances option enables you to choose an instance (as per the allowed instance family, type of Convertible Reserved Instances) for your workload without paying extra.

Please review difference between Standard and Convertible Reserved Instances

Standard vs. Convertible offering classes

PDF   RSS

When you purchase a Reserved Instance, you can choose between a Standard or Convertible offering class.

Table 1 - Comparison of standard and Convertible Reserved Instances

Standard Reserved Instance	Convertible Reserved Instance
One-year to three-year term.	One-year to three-year term.
Enables you to modify Availability Zone, scope, networking type, and instance size (within the same instance type) of your Reserved Instance. For more information, see Modifying Reserved Instances.	Enables you to exchange one or more Convertible Reserved Instances for another Convertible Reserved Instance with a different configuration, including instance family, operating system, and tenancy. There are no limits to how many times you perform an exchange, as long as the target Convertible Reserved Instance is of an equal or higher value than the Convertible Reserved Instances that you are exchanging. For more information, see Exchanging Convertible Reserved Instances.
Can be sold in the Reserved Instance Marketplace.	Cannot be sold in the Reserved Instance Marketplace.

Screenshot from: https://docs.aws.amazon.com/whitepapers/latest/cost-optimization-reservation-models/standard-vs.-convertible-offering-classes.html

- You can change the EC2 instance type, instance family, OS, scope, and tenancy
- You can get up to 66% discount

Scheduled Reserved Instances

Scheduled Reserved Instances helps you reserve the capacity in advance. It enables you to purchase capacity reservations that recur daily, weekly, or monthly, with a specified start time and duration, for a one-year term. They are a good choice for workloads that do not run continuously but run on a regular schedule.

Standard Reserved instances are a good choice for workloads that run continuously. This is a good option for the production environment to save some money than on-demand instances. Scheduled Reserved instances, however, are designed for workloads that recur daily, weekly, or monthly and are purchased for a one-year term. AWS says that Scheduled Reserved Instances provide a 5-10% savings over On-Demand instances used for this exact purpose.

Spot Instances

Spot Instance lets you use spare EC2 capacity at a meager price – up to 90% off the price of On-Demand instances. Because Spot Instances enable you to request unused EC2 instances at steep discounts, it helps lower your Amazon EC2 costs. You can get Spot Instances at up to a 90% discount compared to On-Demand prices.

You could use Spot Instances for the various stateless, fault-tolerant applications that don't get impacted if they terminate suddenly. For example, if you have an ETL batch job that can be interrupted and resumed to start from the point where it stopped, you can be a good candidate for using Spot Instances if you are looking to save costs for running these types of jobs. On the hand, since these instances can be terminated at short notice, Spot Instances are not suitable for workloads that need to run at a specific point in time or if the workload result is impacted because of sudden termination of its execution.

To get an EC2 Spot Instance, you define the max spot price, and you get the instance during the current spot price < max. The hourly spot price varies based on offer and capacity. If the current spot price > your max price, you can choose to stop or terminate your instance with a 2-minute grace period.

The other strategy is "block" spot. You can "block" spot instances for a specified time frame (1 to 6 hours) without interruptions. In rare situations, the instance may be reclaimed.

Spot Instances can be used in the following scenario:
- Suppose your application has flexibility for its start and stop time. In other words, it's ok if your application is stopped, interrupted, or terminated at any time. The reason is spot instances are acquired using the bidding process. Therefore, there is a probability that you may not get the spot instance at the price you bid. Additionally, spot instances can be terminated because of the bidding nature of acquiring instances.
- If you are looking for a large number of computing resources immediately, you can use Spot Instances.

Terminating Spot Instances

When Amazon EC2 interrupts a Spot Instance, it terminates the instance by default unless you specify a different interruption behavior, such as stop or hibernate.

You can only cancel Spot Instance requests that are open, active, or disabled. Canceling a Spot Request does not terminate spot instances. You must first cancel a Spot Request and then terminate the associated Spot Instances.

EC2 Spot Instance Pricing

The screenshot given below about EC2 Spot Instance Pricing History in us-east-1 Regionshows the average savings.

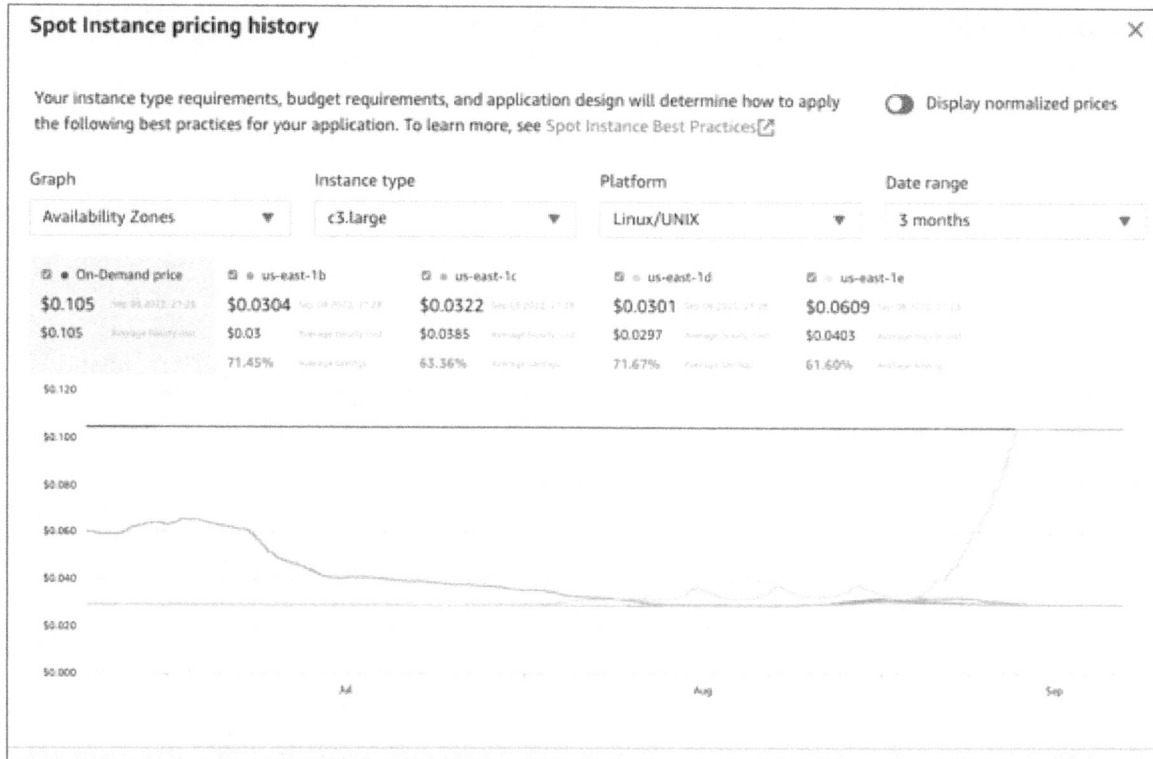

https://us-east-1.console.aws.amazon.com/ec2/v2/home?region=us-east-1#SpotInstances:

Spot Fleets

Spot Fleet is a collection of sets of Spot Instances and On-Demand Instances (optional). The Spot Fleet will try to match the target capacity with price constraints. You can define possible launch pools: instance type (t3.xlarge), OS, and Availability Zone. You can have multiple launch pools. Spot Fleet stops launching instances when reaching capacity or max cost.

Strategies to allocate Spot Instances:
- Lowest price: the lowest price from the allocated pool (cost optimization, short workload)
- Diversified: instance distribution across all pools (great for availability, long workloads)
- Optimized Capacity: pool with the optimal capacity for the number of instances
- Spot Fleets automatically request Spot Instances with the lowest price.

KEY POINTS

- You can get a discount of up to 90% compared to On-Demand instances
- You can "lose" your spot instance at any point of time if your max price is less than the current spot price
- Good use case for workloads that are resilient to failure: batch jobs, image processing, data analysis, or workloads having a flexible start and end time
- It is the MOST cost-efficient instance in AWS
- It is not suitable for critical jobs or databases

Dedicated Host

EC2 Dedicated Hosts is a physical server with EC2 instance capacity fully dedicated for your use. In addition, Amazon EC2 Dedicated Hosts allow you to use your eligible software licenses from vendors such as Microsoft and Oracle on Amazon EC2. This concept, also known as BYOL (bring your licenses), helps you get the flexibility and cost-effectiveness of using your licenses, along with the simplicity, resiliency, and elasticity of AWS.

An Amazon EC2 Dedicated Host is a physical server fully dedicated for your use. It can help in addressing corporate compliance requirements as well.

With respect to pricing, Dedicated Hosts can be purchased On-Demand at an hourly rate and can be purchased as Reservations with 70% off from the On-Demand price.

KEY POINTS

- A fully dedicated physical server to your workloads with EC2 instance capacity
- Use cases: companies that have strong regulatory or compliance needs, use your existing server-bound software licenses (per-socket, per-core software licenses)
- Purchasing Options:
  - On-demand -- pay per second for active Dedicated Host
  - Reserved -- 1 or 3 years (payment options of no upfront, partial upfront, all upfront)
- It is the most expensive option

Dedicated Instance

Dedicated Instances run in Amazon VPC on EC2 hardware that is dedicated to a single customer. Dedicated Instances are physically isolated at the hardware level for each AWS account. In other words, Dedicated Instances that belong to different AWS accounts are physically isolated at the hardware level from one another. However, Dedicated Instances may share hardware with other instances from the same AWS account that are not Dedicated Instances. With respect to pricing, Dedicated Instances On-Demand can save you up to 70% by purchasing Reserved Instances or save up to 90% by purchasing Spot Instances.

Please review the difference between Dedicated Hosts and Dedicated Instances

Differences between Dedicated Hosts and Dedicated Instances

Dedicated Hosts and Dedicated Instances can both be used to launch Amazon EC2 instances onto physical servers that are dedicated for your use.

There are no performance, security, or physical differences between Dedicated Instances and instances on Dedicated Hosts. However, there are some differences between the two. The following table highlights some of the key differences between Dedicated Hosts and Dedicated Instances:

	Dedicated Host	Dedicated Instance
Billing	Per-host billing	Per-instance billing
Visibility of sockets, cores, and host ID	Provides visibility of the number of sockets and physical cores	No visibility
Host and instance affinity	Allows you to consistently deploy your instances to the same physical server over time	Not supported
Targeted instance placement	Provides additional visibility and control over how instances are placed on a physical server	Not supported
Automatic instance recovery	Supported. For more information, see Host recovery.	Supported
Bring Your Own License (BYOL)	Supported	Not supported

Screenshot from: https://docs.aws.amazon.com/AWSEC2/latest/UserGuide/dedicated-hosts-overview.html

KEY POINTS

- Instances are run on the hardware dedicated to you
- Instances may share the hardware with other instances in the same account
- You have no control over instance placement -- instances can move to another hardware after stop/start
- You cannot use Dedicated Instances for using server-bound software licenses.

EC2 Savings Plans

Using EC2 Saving Plans, you can get a discount (up to 72% - same as RIs) based on long-term usage. You need to commit to a certain type of usage, for example, $15/hour for 1 or 3 years. Any usage beyond EC2 Savings Plans is billed at the On-Demand price. The plan is locked to a specific instance family & AWS region (e.g., M5 in us-east-1). The plan is flexible across Instance Size (e.g., m5.xlarge, m5.2xlarge), OS (e.g., Linux, Windows), and Tenancy (Host, Dedicated, Default).

EC2 Capacity Reservations

You can reserve On-Demand instances capacity in a specific AZ for any duration. You always have access to EC2 capacity when you need it. There is no time commitment -- create/cancel anytime. You don't get any billing discounts. You're charged at an On-Demand rate whether you run instances or not. It is suitable for short-term, uninterrupted workloads that need to be in a specific AZ.

Free Tier

In this option, you get 750 hours each month for one year. Use only EC2 Micro instances in Free Tier.

Which purchasing option is right for you?

Ok, you have gone through different purchasing options; you may be wondering which purchasing option is suitable for your use case. Here are some main points from the analogy of staying in a hotel.

- **On-Demand**: You pay the full price when coming in and staying in the hotel whenever you like
- **Reserved**: It is like planning before -- you may get a good discount if you plan to stay for a long time.

- **Savings Plans**: Pay a specific amount per hour for a specific period and stay in any room type.
- **Spot Instances**: Imagine a scenario where the hotel allows people to bid for available rooms, and the highest bidder gets the room. However, you can be sent out whenever another highest bidder gets the room.
- **Dedicated Hosts**: You book an entire physical building of the hotel.
- **Capacity Reservations**: You book a room for a period at full price even if you don't stay in the hotel.

Price Comparison Example

Instance Type: t3.large
AWS Region: us-east-1

On-Demand	$0.0832
Spot Instance (Spot Price)	$0.0262 - $0.0288 (up to 69% off)
Reserved Instance (1 year)	$$0.052 (No Upfront) - $0.049 (All Upfront)
Reserved Instance (3 years)	$0.036 (No Upfront) - $0.031 (All Upfront)
EC2 Savings Plan (1 year)	$0.06 (No Upfront) - $0.056 (All Upfront)
Reserved Convertible Instance (1 year)	$0.060 (No Upfront) - $0.056 (All Upfront)
Dedicated Host	On-Demand Price
Dedicated Host Reservation	Up to 70% off
Capacity Reservations	On-Demand Price

KEY POINTS

- **Dedicated Host** – need to reserve an entire physical server; you can control instance placement.
- **Dedicated Instance** – no other customers will share underlying hardware
- **Reserved (1 & 3 years)**
  - **Reserved Instance** – use case for long workloads
  - **Convertible Reserved Instances**– use case for long workloads with flexible instances
- **Savings Plans (1 & 3 years)** – use case for long workload, commitment to an amount of usage
- **On-Demand Instances** – use case for short workload, predictable pricing, pay by second
- **Spot Instances** – use case for short workloads, cheap, less reliable as can lose instances
- **Capacity Reservations** – reserve capacity in a specific AZ for any duration

Placement Groups

Depending on your use case, you sometimes want control over the EC2 Instance placement strategy. That strategy – controlling where EC2 instances are placed – can be defined using placement groups. When you launch a new EC2 instance, the launched EC2 instance is placed in such a way as to minimize correlated failures. In order to minimize co-related failures, EC2 service spreads out your EC2 instances across underlying hardware. You can also use placement groups to influence the placement of a group of interdependent instances to meet your workload's needs. For example, depending on the type of workload, you can use a cluster placement group, partition placement group, or spread placement group.

Cluster Placement Group

Cluster placement groups bring instances close together inside an Availability Zone. Cluster placement groups are recommended for applications that benefit from low network latency, high network throughput, or both.

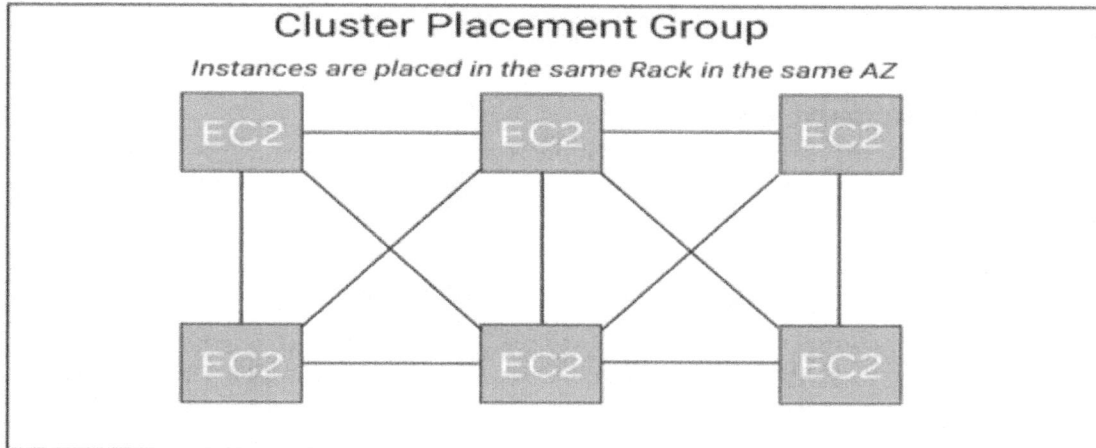

For example, HPC applications are typically deployed in cluster placement groups to achieve the low-latency network performance necessary for tightly coupled node-to-node communication.

KEY POINTS

- pros: you would get excellent network connectivity
- cons: If the rack fails, all the instances fail at the same time
- use cases: big data job that needs to be completed fast; an application that requires extremely low latency with high network throughput

Spread Placement Group

A spread placement group is a group of instances that are each placed on distinct racks -- each rack having its own network and power source.

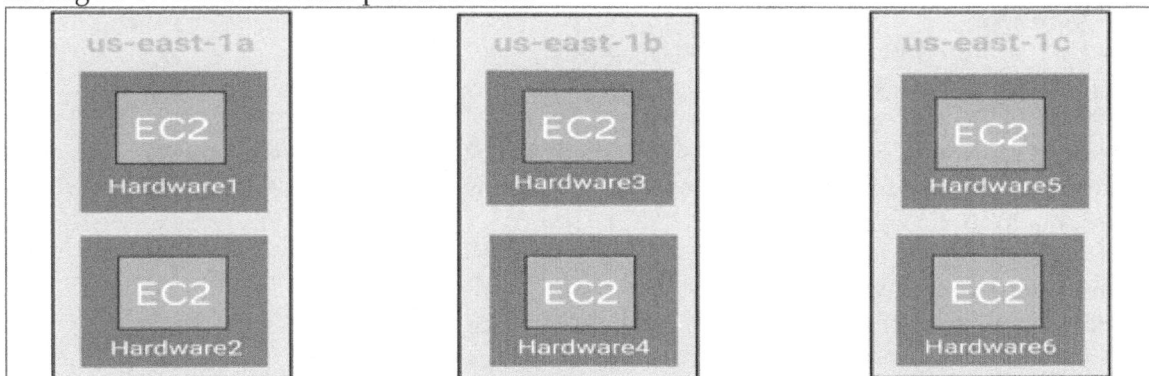

The instances are placed across distinct underlying hardware to reduce correlated failures. In a spread placement group, you can have a maximum of seven running instances per Availability Zone per group.

- pros: instances can span across AZ; reduces the risk of a simultaneous failure; EC2 instances run on different physical hardware
- cons: limited to 7 instances per AZ per placement group
- use cases: applications that need to maximize high availability; critical applications where each instance must be isolated from failure from each other

Partition Placement Group

A partition placement group spreads your instances across logical partitions such that groups of instances in one partition do not share the underlying hardware with groups of instances in different partitions.

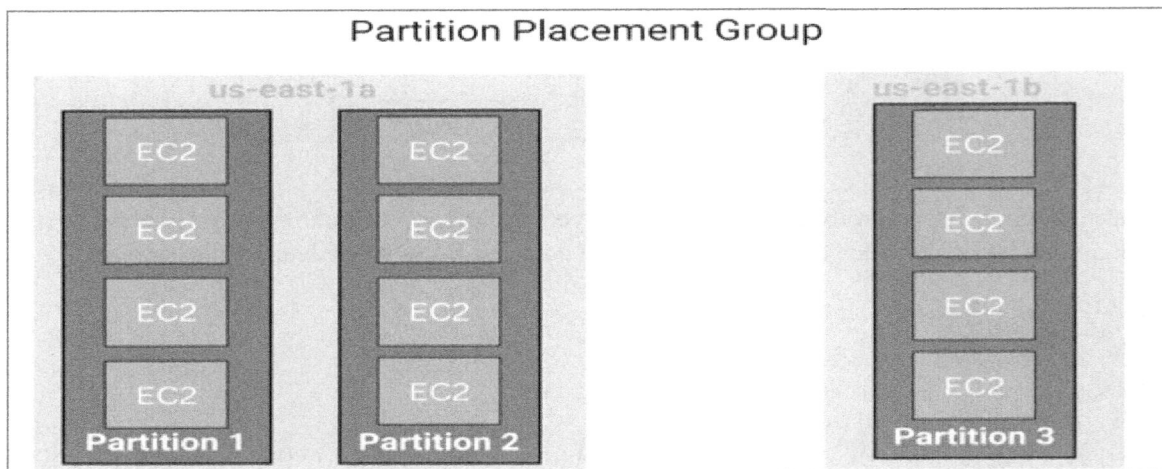

A partition placement group is typically used by large distributed and replicated workloads. For example, Hadoop, Cassandra, and Kafka clusters use a partition placement group. A partition placement group can have a maximum of seven partitions per Availability Zone.

KEY POINTS

- Can span across multiple AZs in the same AWS Region
- Up to 7 partitions per AZ
- Up to 100s of EC2 instances
- Instances in a partition do not share racks with the instances in the other partitions.
- A partition failure can affect many instances in the same partition but won't affect other partitions
- Use cases: Hadoop, Cassandra, Kafka

Some common ports to know:
Port 22 => SSH (Secure Shell); used to log into a Linux instance
Port 21 => FTP (File Transfer Protocol; used for uploading files to server
Port 22 => SFTP (Secure File Transfer Protocol); used for uploading files to server securely
Port 80 => HTTP; used to access websites without SSL
Port 443 => HTTPS; used to access websites with SSL

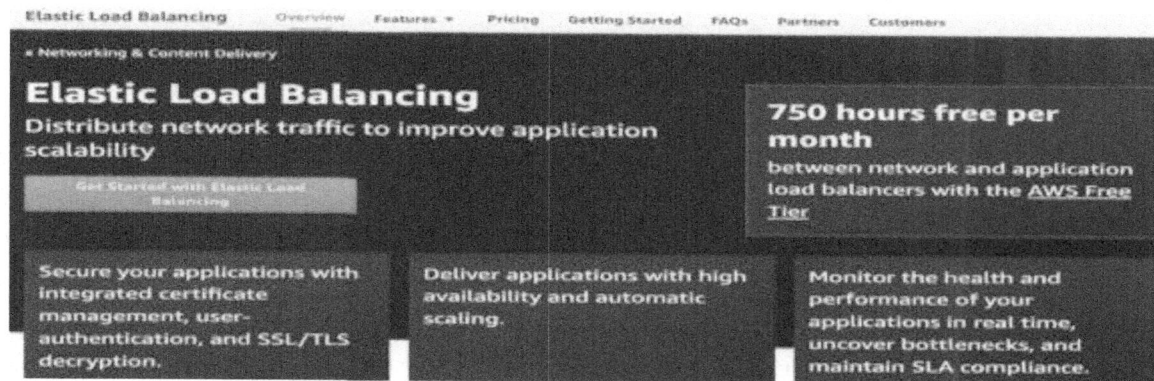

Chapter 16. Elastic Load Balancing

You will learn the following in this chapter:
- Scalability & High Availability
- What is load balancing?
- Types of Load Balancer on AWS
- Classic Load Balancer
- Application Load Balancer
- Network Load Balancer
- Gateway Load Balancer
- Cross-Zone Load Balancing
- Elastic Load Balancer Security
- Sticky Sessions
- Connection Draining
- AWS Auto Scaling
- Launch Template
- Auto Scaling with CloudWatch Alarms
- Dynamic Scaling for Amazon EC2 Auto Scaling

Scalability & High Availability

Scalability means an application or system can handle more loads by adapting itself without impacting performance. There are two types of scalabilities: horizontal and vertical. The term "horizontal scalability" is similar to the term "elasticity" in a cloud environment. Though the term "scalability" is linked to the term "availability," availability is different.

Vertical Scalability

With respect to EC2, vertical scalability means increasing the size of the EC2 instance. For example, if your application runs on t2.micro, then vertically scaling means running the application to, say, t2.large instance. Vertical scalability is a typical use case for systems that are monolithic type or non-distributed. Usually, vertical scalability is used to scale the performance of databases. For example, AWS RDS and ElastiCache services can be scaled vertically. Vertical scalability has a limitation on how much the system can be scaled. That being the case, vertical scalability depends on the hardware limit.

A "vertical scalable" system is considered constrained on resources such as CPU, RAM, and storage, which negatively impacts the overall system's performance. Therefore, to improve this system's implementation by the "vertical scalable" mechanism means adding more resources such as CPU, RAM, and storage. However, since there is still no addition of a machine or node, making the system vertical scalable doesn't improve the fault tolerance of the overall design.

Let's try to understand Vertical Scalability from an example. Suppose that you have hired a junior typist to type an easy, which took some time which is ok to you. Now suppose you have a research paper to get typed, and you would like your research paper to be typed sooner; you would hire a senior typist and let the senior typist do the typing to complete the job sooner. This is an example of vertical scaling– replacing one with another, which is more resourceful and efficient -- if the workload increases and you would like to maintain the same performance level when you have less workload.

Horizontal Scalability

Horizontal scalability means increasing the number of instances or systems (servers) for your application. Horizontal scaling implies distributed system. In other words, it is common for distributed systems to utilize horizontal scaling to scale them – very common for web applications / micro-services / event-driven systems.
When cloud computing was not mainstream, horizontally scaling systems was a more involved and time-consuming process. But with Amazon EC2, horizontal scaling systems and managing them become easier and faster.

A "horizontally scalable" system increases its resource capacity by adding more nodes or machines to the system. Comparing a horizontally scalable system with a scalable vertical design, the former is preferred to scale the systems. The reason is that a horizontally scalable system helps increase the degree of fault tolerance of the overall strategy and helps improve performance by enabling parallel execution of the workload and distributing that workload across multiple machines.

Horizontal scalability helps increase in making the system horizontally scalable. In a horizontally scalable system, since more machines are added to increase the pool of resources, thus if one machine goes down, the other machine is allocated to process the workload of the failed machine. Thus, helping to increase the degree of fault tolerance of fault the overall system.

Let's try to understand Horizontal Scalability from the previous example. Suppose you have hired a junior typist to type an easy, which took some time and is ok to you. On the other hand, suppose you have a research paper to get typed, and you would like your research paper to be typed sooner; you would hire two additional junior typists to do the typing to complete the job sooner. This is an example of horizontal scaling– adding more resources of a similar type -- if the workload increases and you would like to maintain the same performance level when you have less workload.

High Availability

High availability usually goes together with horizontal scaling. Regarding AWS, high availability means running applications or systems in at least two data centers (in other words, two Availability Zones). The main objective of high availability is to let the applications or systems survive even in case of data center loss. High availability can be passive, for example, in the case of Multi-AZ set up of an RDS. On the other hand, high availability can be active when you use horizontal scaling.

High Availability & Scalability for EC2 Instances

Let's understand vertical scaling for EC2 instances. If you need vertical scaling, increase the instance size -- you can scale up or down. For example, you can vertically scale up an EC2 instance from "t2.nano, 0.5G RAM, 1 vCPU" to an EC2 instance: "t3.large, 8 GB RAM, 2 vCPU".

If you need horizontal scaling, increase the number of EC2 instances (another term "scale out") or decrease the number of instances (another term "scale in"). Run or deploy the same application or system across multi-AZ for high availability.

What is load balancing?

Load balancers are servers that forward traffic to multiple servers (e.g., EC2 instances).

Why use a load balancer

To manage the scalability and high availability of your applications, Load Balancer is an excellent architectural choice. Load balancers spread the load across multiple downstream instances. They help expose a single point of access to your application. Load balancers also provide SSL termination (HTTPS) termination for your websites. Load balancers can enforce stickiness with cookies which helps session management when applications are deployed on multiple servers. Load Balancers can handle failures of downstream instances seamlessly. A load balancer also does regular health checks of downstream instances. Load balancers help provide high availability across multiple availability zones. Load balancers separate public traffic from private traffic.

Elastic Load Balancing

Elastic Load Balancer automatically distributes traffic (incoming) across multiple targets in one or more Availability Zones (AZs) on EC2 instances, containers, and IP addresses.

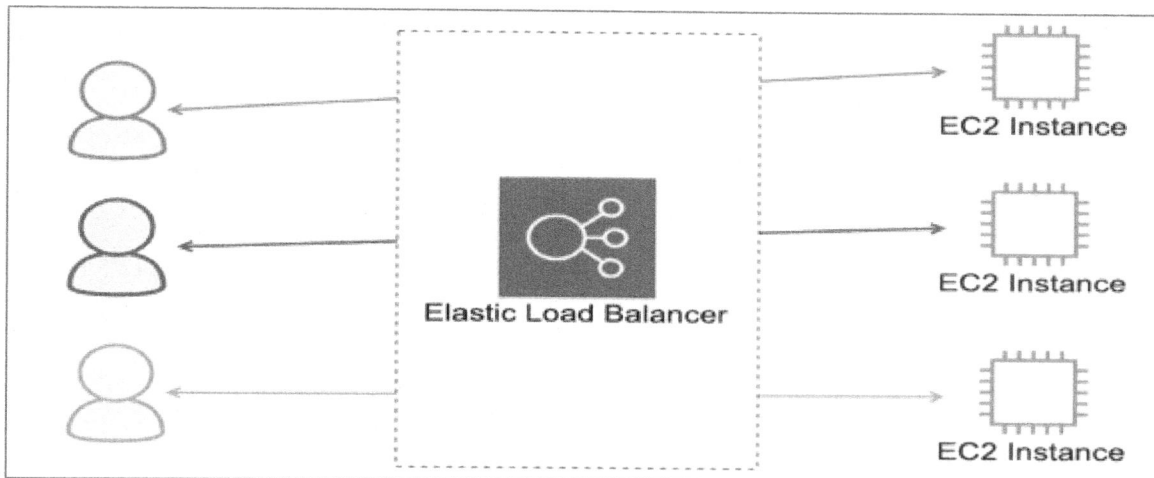

An Elastic Load Balancer is a managed load balancer. Since it is a managed load balancer, AWS takes responsibility for upgrades, maintenance, and high availability. AWS provides only a few configuration knobs to make a change in the default configuration. Though you can set up your own load balancer, which can cost less, it is much effort.

The elastic load balancer is integrated with many AWS services. For example, it is integrated with EC2, EC2 Auto Scaling Groups, Cloud Watch, AWS Global Accelerator, Amazon ECS, AWS Certificate Manager, Route53, and AWS WAF.

Health Checks are extremely critical for Load Balancers. The health check enables the load balancer to find out if instances it forwards traffic are healthy, i.e., available to reply to requests.

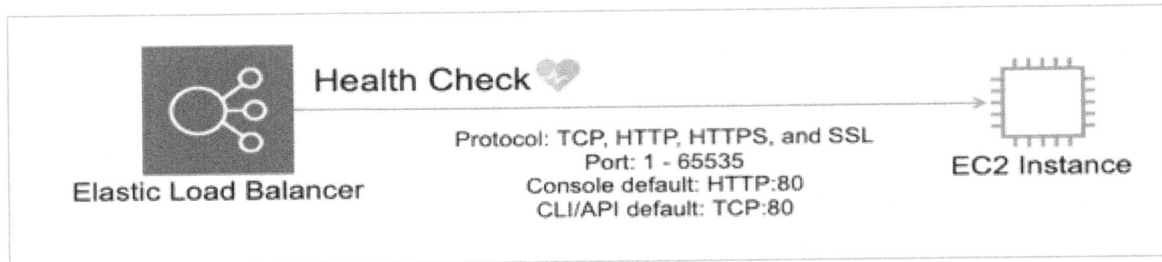

The health check is done using TCP, HTTP, HTTPS, and SSL protocol, and you can use any port in the range of 1 to 65535. The default for a web application would be HTTP on port 80 (CLI/API default: TCP:80) and a path of /index.html. If the response received is not 200 (OK), then the instance is considered to be unhealthy. By monitoring the health of its registered targets, it routes traffic only to the healthy target.

Elastic Load Balancer can scale out and scale in as incoming traffic changes – increases or decreases-- over time.

There are different types of load balancers that Elastic Load Balancing supports. These load balancers are: Application Load Balancer, Network Load Balancer, Gateway Load Balancer, and Classic Load Balancer. The type of balancer you select depends on your need -- select the one that best fits your requirement.

Types of Load Balancer on AWS

AWS has four kinds of elastic (managed) load balancers.
- Classic Load Balancer: It is v1 (old generation) and was launched in **2009.** It supports TCP (i.e., layer 4), HTTP, and HTTPS (i.e., layer 7) traffic.
- Application Load Balancer (ALB): It was launched in 2016. It supports HTTP, HTTPS, and Web Socket traffic, i.e., layer 7 – application layer.
- Network Load Balancer (NLB): it was launched in 2017. It supports TCP, TLS (i.e., secure TCP), and UDP traffic, i.e., layer 4 – transport layer.
- Gateway Load Balancer (GWLB): It was launched in 2020. It operates at layer 3 (Network layer) – IP Protocol.

Overall, it is recommended to use the newer generation (Application, Network, and Gateway) load balancers as they provide more features. Some load balancers can be set up as **internal** (private) or **external** (public) ELBs.

Classic Load Balancer

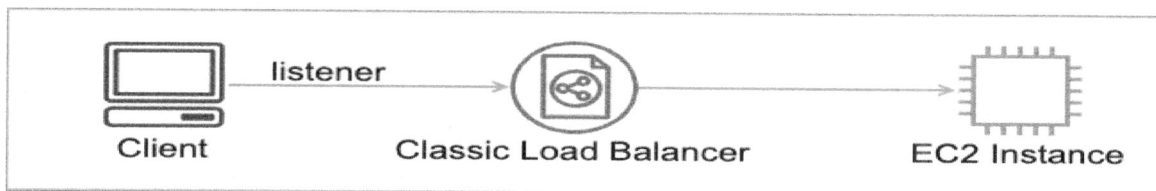

Classic Load Balancer offers basic load balancing across multiple EC2 instances and operates at both the request level and connection level. It is intended for applications that are built for the classic EC2 instances.

KEY POINTS

- Supports TCP (Layer4), and HTTP & HTTPS (Layer 7)
- Health checks are TCP and HTTP based

Application Load Balancer

Application Load Balancer operates at layer 7, which is the request level. It can route traffic to targets such as EC2 instances, containers, IP addresses, and Lambda functions. It can provide load balancing to multiple applications across machines (target groups). It can also provide load balancing to various applications on the same machine. ALB provides support for HTTP/2 and Web Socket as well.

You can add multiple target groups and have rules for the ALB to forward the request to the different target groups. For example, you can set routing based on the path in the URL (example.com/orders & example.com/cart), or routing based on the hostname in the URL (one.example.com & two.example.com), or routing based on the query string, headers (example.com/order?id=101). This routing to multiple targets based on rules makes ALB more efficient. However, if you compare it with using (Classic Load Balancer) CLB, you will have to set up multiple CLBs for multiple applications.

The application servers, where ALB forwards the HTTP request, can't know the IP address of the client directly. The client IP can be obtained from the value of the X-Forwarded-For header. The application servers can also get the port (from the X-Forwarded-Port header) and proto (from the X-Forwarded-Proto header).

Application Load Balancers are very good for the use cases for load balancing micro-services & container-based applications.

HTTP traffic – Path-based Routing

As you can see in the diagram, which is for the external ALB handling HTTP traffic. there are two target groups added to the ALB, and the rule is that when the URL path is /order, the ALB forwards to the target group where the order microservice application is deployed.

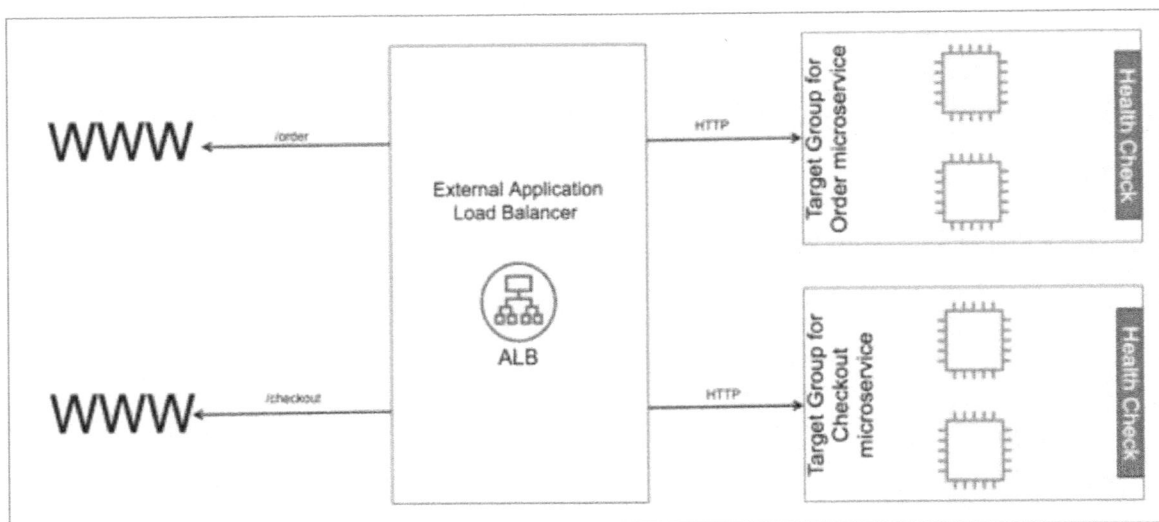

And when the path is /checkout, the ALB forwards the request to the target group where the checkout microservice application is deployed.

Target Groups

Application Load Balancer can forward traffic to multiple target groups. It can forward HTTP traffic to the target group of EC2 instances running HTTP-based applications and ECS tasks running on containers. The target group of EC2 instances can also be managed by Auto Scaling Group. The IP address of registered EC2 instances must be private IPs. Application Load Balancer can also forward HTTP traffic to the target group of the AWS Lambda function. The HTTP request is translated to a JSON event for AWS Lambda. Health checks are at the target group level.

Query Strings / Parameters Routing

The diagram given is an example of external ALB routing HTTP traffic to different target groups based on the query string in the HTTP request.

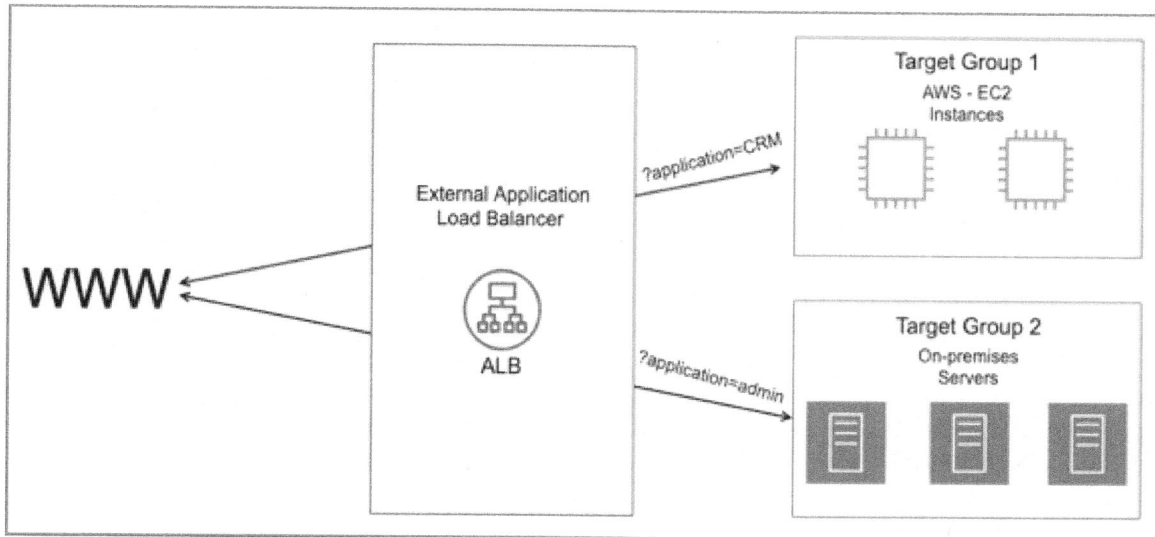

The ALB forwards HTTP requests to the target group of EC2 instances if the *application* request parameter is *CRM; if* the *application* request parameter is *admin,* the ALB forwards the HTTP request to on-premises servers.

KEY POINTS

- The application load balancer is ideal for advanced load balancing of HTTP and HTTPS traffic. It is particularly useful to load balance requests for modern application architectures, including microservices and container-based applications.
- The application load balancer operates at layer 7 -- request level. It routes traffic to targets – EC2 instances, containers, IP addresses, and Lambda functions -- based on the content of the request.
- The application load balancer simplifies and improves the application's security by ensuring that the latest SSL/TLS ciphers and protocols are used at all times.
- ALB can do host based, path based, and query string/parameter based routing .

Network Load Balancer

Network Load Balancers (NLB) work at layer 4, forwarding incoming TCP & UDP traffic to EC2 instances. Network Load Balancers can handle millions of requests per second. They are low latency ELBs (~100 ms) compared with ALB (~400 ms). The Network Load Balancer has one static IP per Availability Zone and allows support of Elastic IP. NLBs are used in use cases that require extremely high performance for TCP and UDP traffic. NLS is not included in AWS Free Tier.

NLB Layer 4 Traffic

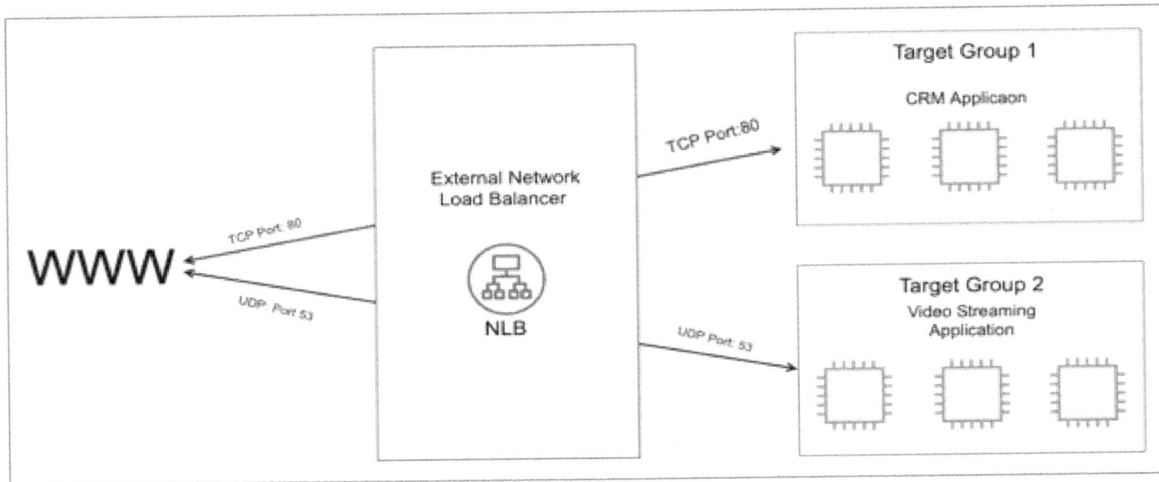

To illustrate further, in this diagram, NLB is forwarding layer 4 traffic to two target groups: one target group is running a CRM application deployed on EC2 instances, and the other target group is running a video streaming application deployed on EC2 instances. Now the rule on NLB is to forward TCP traffic on port 80 to the target group 1 (CRM application), and the other is to forward UDP traffic on port 53 to the target group 2 (video streaming application).

NLB Target Groups

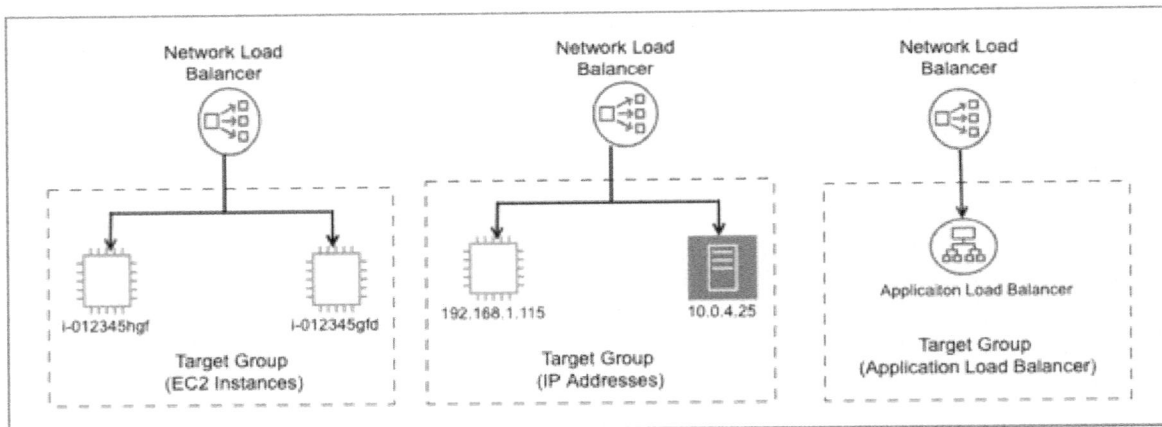

NLB target groups: EC2 instances, IP addresses (must be private IPs), and Application Load Balancer, as shown in the diagram. The target group's health checks support TCP, HTTP, and HTTPS protocols.

KEY POINTS

- The Network Load Balancer operates at the Layer 4 -- connection level. Based on IP protocol data, it routes connections to targets – EC2 instances, microservices, and containers – within VPC.
- The Network Load Balancer is ideal for load balancing of both TCP and UDP traffic.

- The Network Load Balancer is capable of not only handling millions of requests per second but can also maintaining ultra-low latency.
- The Network Load Balancer is optimized to handle sudden and volatile traffic patterns using a single static IP address per AZ.

ALB or NLB?

Suppose you have web servers behind Load Balancer. ALB is the best choice – because you have the flexibility of forwarding traffic in many ways: path, the query string parameter. You don't get this flexibility on NLB because NLB operates at the network layer – just forwards based on the protocol. For example, if NLB gets TCP traffic at port 80, it can forward it to a CRM web application, and if it gets UDP traffic, it can forward it to a video streaming or gaming application. NLB is expensive compared to ALB.

NLB operates at the network layer, which can deal with raw traffic and network spikes. Because of this reason, if your goal is to reduce network latency and increase the routing throughput of traffic – NLB is an excellent choice. Another reason if you want to get end-to-end encryption is that NLB is your choice, as ALB doesn't have end-to-end encryption -- SSL is terminated at the ALB.

ALB is often the best option in most use cases, e.g., balancing traffic based on functionality and traffic load is not heavy. If you have traffic in millions per second, NLB is the way to go. If you need to balance traffic based on functionality.

Gateway Load Balancer

Gateway Load Balancers help you deploy, scale, and manage systems such as firewalls, intrusion detection and prevention systems, and deep packet inspection systems. A Gateway Load Balancer operates at the network layer (layer 3) of the OSI model. It listens for all IP packets across all ports and forwards traffic to the target group specified in the listener rule.

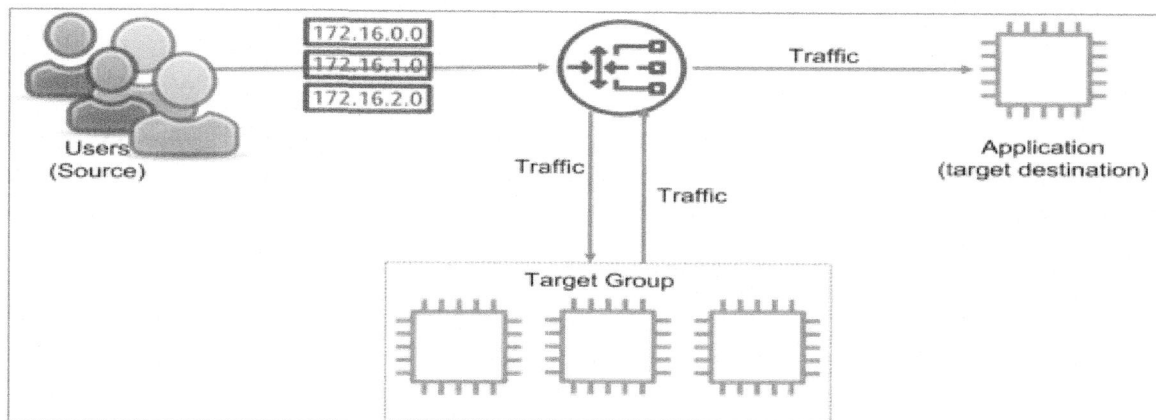

Gateway load balancer combines a Transparent Network Gateway, which is a single entry and exit for all traffic, and a load balancer that distributes traffic to virtual appliances. The gateway load balancer uses the GENEVE protocol on port 6081.

Gateway Load Balancers use Gateway Load Balancer endpoints to exchange traffic across VPC boundaries securely. A Gateway Load Balancer endpoint is a VPC endpoint that provides private connectivity between virtual appliances in the service provider VPC and application servers in the service consumer VPC.

Gateway Load Balancer target groups: EC2 instances, IP addresses (must be private IPs).

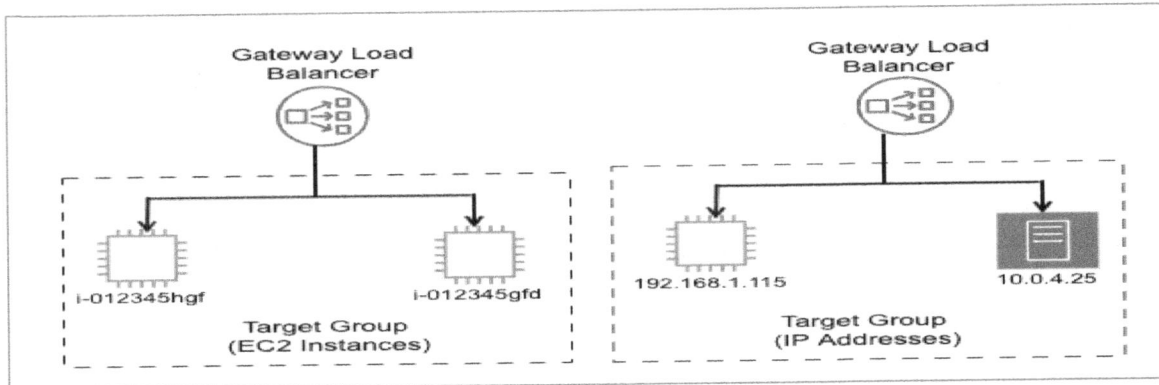

Load Balancer Security Groups

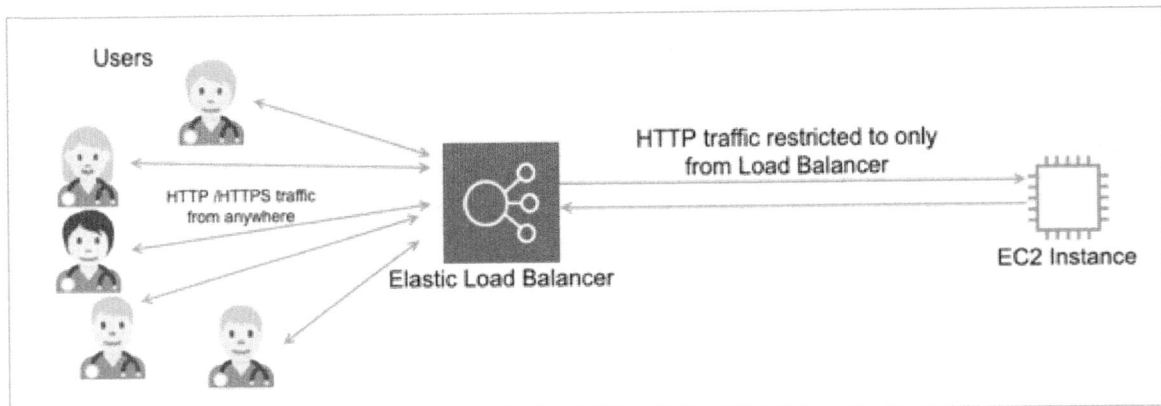

A typical internet-facing Application Load balancer (ALB) will have a security group with rules to allow traffic on port 80 (HTTP) and port 443 (HTTPS) from anywhere. And registered EC2 instances behind the ELB get traffic only from the security group of ALB.

Cross-Zone Load Balancing

In order to maintain high availability, it is common to deploy ELB in multiple AZs with EC2 instances spread across multiple AZs. Now the question is, how ELBs distribute requests when multiple ELBs are involved? There are two scenarios: one is when cross-zone balancing is enabled, and the other is when there is no cross-zone balancing.

When cross-zone balancing is enabled, each load balancer instance distributes requests evenly across all registered instances in all AZs.

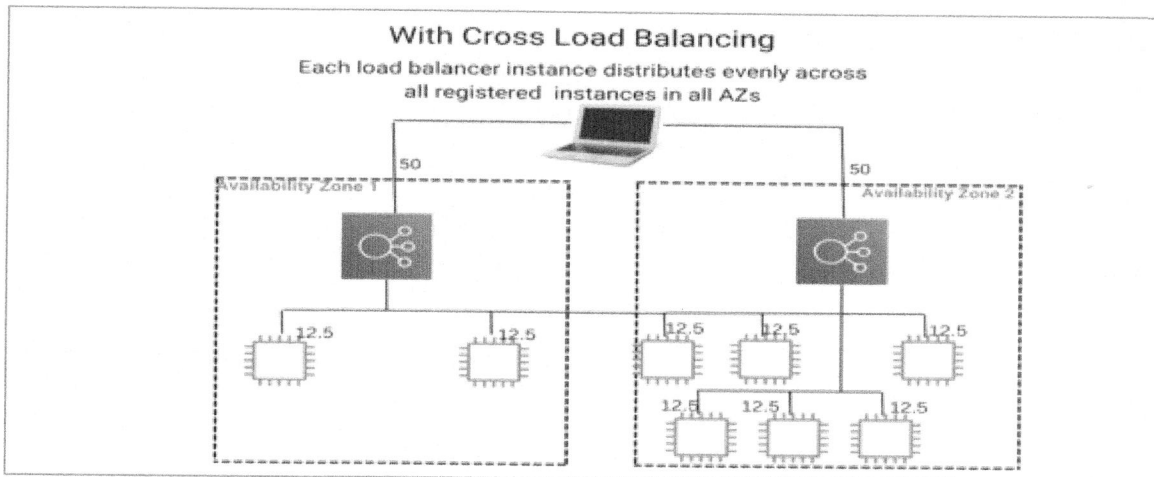

With Cross Load Balancing
Each load balancer instance distributes evenly across
all registered instances in all AZs

However, when there is no cross-zone load balancing, requests are distributed evenly only within registered instances of each ELB instance.

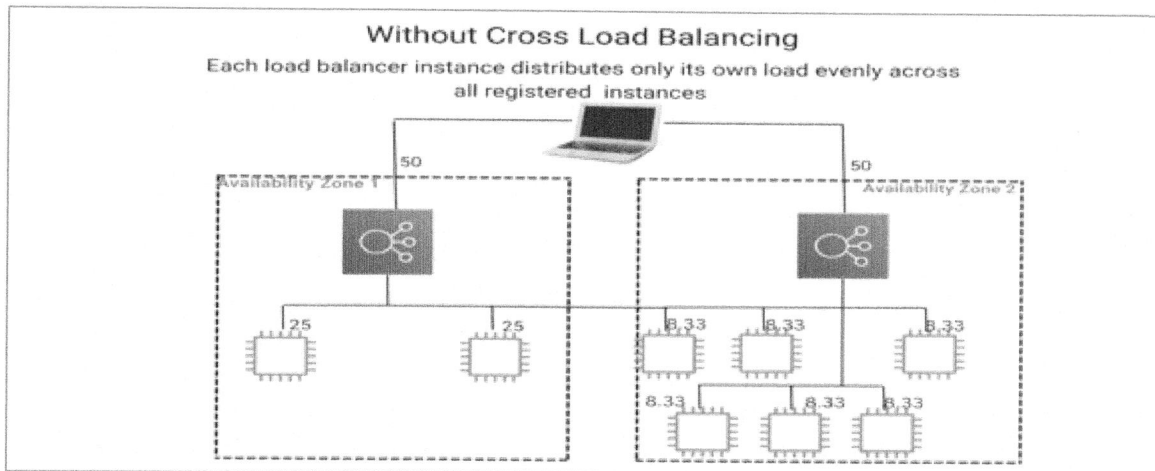

Without Cross Load Balancing
Each load balancer instance distributes only its own load evenly across
all registered instances

Cross-Zone Load Balancing Feature Support

Now let's see which ELB types allow cross-zone load balancing. In ALB, it's always on and can't be disabled, and there is no charge for inter-AZ data transfer. In NLB, it is disabled by default, and there are charges for inter-AZ data transfer if cross-zone balancing is enabled. In a classic load balancer, it is disabled by default. However, like ALB, there is no charge for inter-AZ data transfer if cross-zone balancing is enabled.

Elastic Load Balancer Security

Security of ELB is extremely important, particularly if the ELB is external and takes client requests directly before forwarding them to a target group. Let's first look into SSL / TLS basics.

SSL/TLS basics

An SSL (Secure Socket Layer) certificate encrypts in-flight (data in transit) traffic between the client and the ELB. TLS (Transport Layer Security) is a new version of SSL, and nowadays, TLS is used. However, SSL is such a famous term that people still use SSL instead of TLS.

SSL/TLS certificates are used to secure network communications and establish the identity of websites. Public SSL certificates are issued by Certificate Authority (CA), e.g., GoDaddy, Letsencrypt (open source), Symantec, and Digicert. An SSL certificate has an expiry date, and it must be renewed otherwise, the certificate will not be valid.

SSL Certificate – Load Balancer

The Elastic Load Balancer uses an X.509 certificate (SSL/TLS certificate), a public/private key-based encryption. You can manage SSL certificates using ACM (AWS Certificate Manager). Using ACM (AWS Certificate Manager), you easily provision, manage, and deploy public and private SSL/TLS certificates for use with AWS services and your internally connected resources.

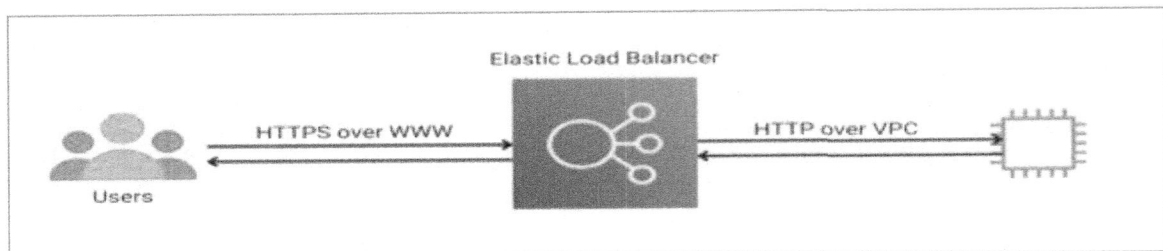

You can also add your SSL/TLS certificates provided by Certifying Authority. In order to use HTTPS listener, you must specify an SSL/TLS certificate. You can also add multiple SSL/TLS certificates if your ELB handles multiple domains (host-based routing). Clients can use SNI (Server Name Indication) to specify which host they would like to send the HTTPS request.

SNI (Server Name Indication)

When you have more than one web application (example1.com, example2.com) hosted on a single web server host, the client accessing any application using an IP address may get the wrong certificate. This is because in TLS/SSL, handshaking is done before sending the request.

SNI is handy in this use case where more than one web application (example1.com, example2.com) is hosted on a single web server host. SNI allows user devices to see the correct SSL certificate they are trying to reach if the web server hosts more than one web application on the same IP address.

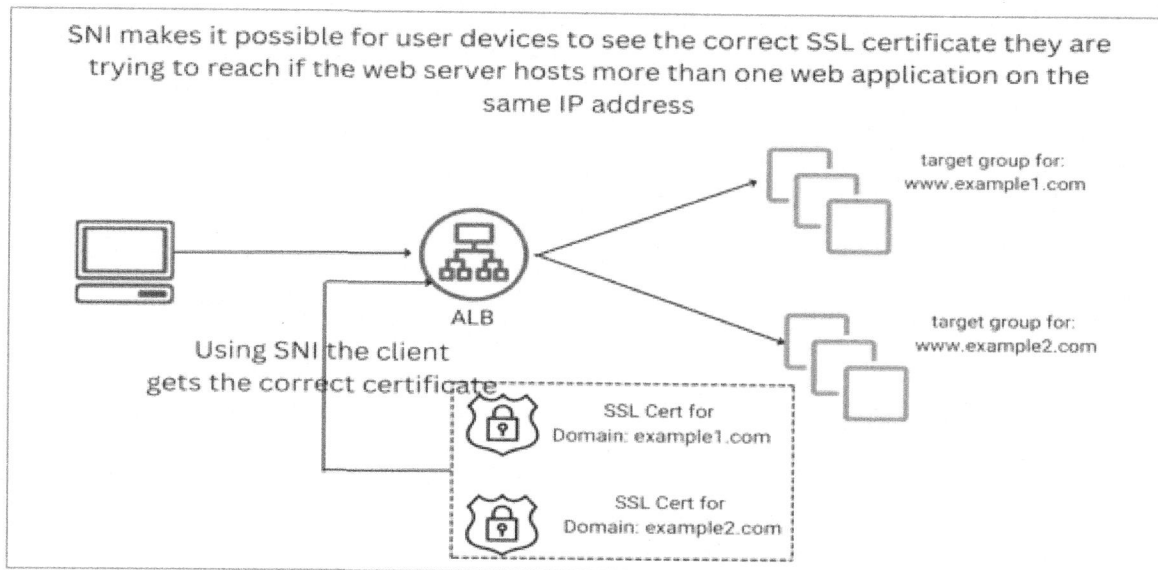

SNI makes it possible for user devices to see the correct SSL certificate they are trying to reach if the web server hosts more than one web application on the same IP address

SNI is an extension for the TLS protocol. SNI is included in the TLS/SSL handshake process to ensure that client devices can see the correct SSL certificate for the website they are trying to reach. In addition, the extension makes it possible to specify the website's hostname, or domain name, during the TLS handshake, instead of when the HTTP connection opens after the handshake.

More simply put, SNI makes it possible for a user device to open a secure connection with https://www.example.com even if that website is hosted in the same place (same IP address) as https://www.example1.com, https://www.example2.com, and https://www.example3.com.

Elastic Load Balancers – SSL Certificates

Classic Load Balancer (CLB) supports only one SSL certificate. In other words, you cannot use SNI with CLB. You need to use multiple CLBs if you are using multiple host names.

Application Load Balancer (ALB) and Network Load Balancer support multiple listeners and multiple SSL certificates using SNI.

Sticky Sessions (Session Affinity)

Session management is one of the challenges of deploying your web application on multiple instances behind load balancers. For example, if you don't manage sessions properly when your application is deployed on multiple machines (e.g., EC2 instances), one user's shopping cart may be seen by the other user. Or the server may create a brand-new session for every request, thus losing everything stored in the previous encounter of the user with the application if the user would like to, for example, maintain a shopping cart before final checkout.

There is a term called stickiness in session management; the term implies that the same client is always redirected to the same instance during a session behind a load balancer. In other words, sticky sessions are a mechanism to route requests from the same client to the same target.

Elastic Load Balancers support sticky sessions. Stickiness is defined at a target group level; the session stickiness works for Classic Load Balancers and Application Load Balancers.

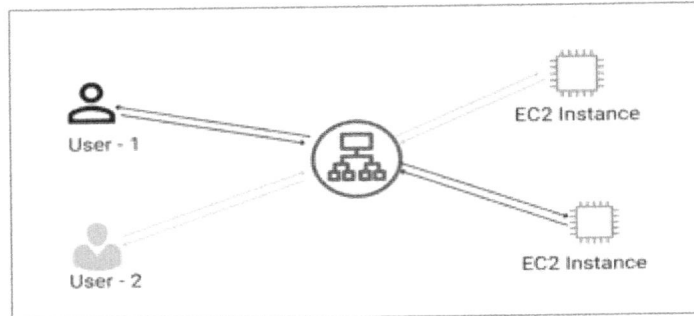

The session "cookie" is used for stickiness and has an expiration date that you can programmatically control. Enabling sickness may imbalance the load over the backend EC2 instances – in modern architecture, stateless web services are preferred over stateful web services.

Application vs. Duration-Based Cookies

There are two types of Application-based Cookies: Custom cookies and Application Cookies. The target generates custom cookies. It can include any custom attributes required by the application. The Cookie name must be specified individually for each target group. You cannot use AWSALB, AWSALBAPP, and AWSALBTG – these are reserved by the ELB. The load balancer generates the Application Cookies, and the Cookie name is AWSALBAPP.

The load balancer generates the Duration-based Cookies, and the Cookie name is AWSALB for ALB and AWSELB for CLB.

Connection Draining

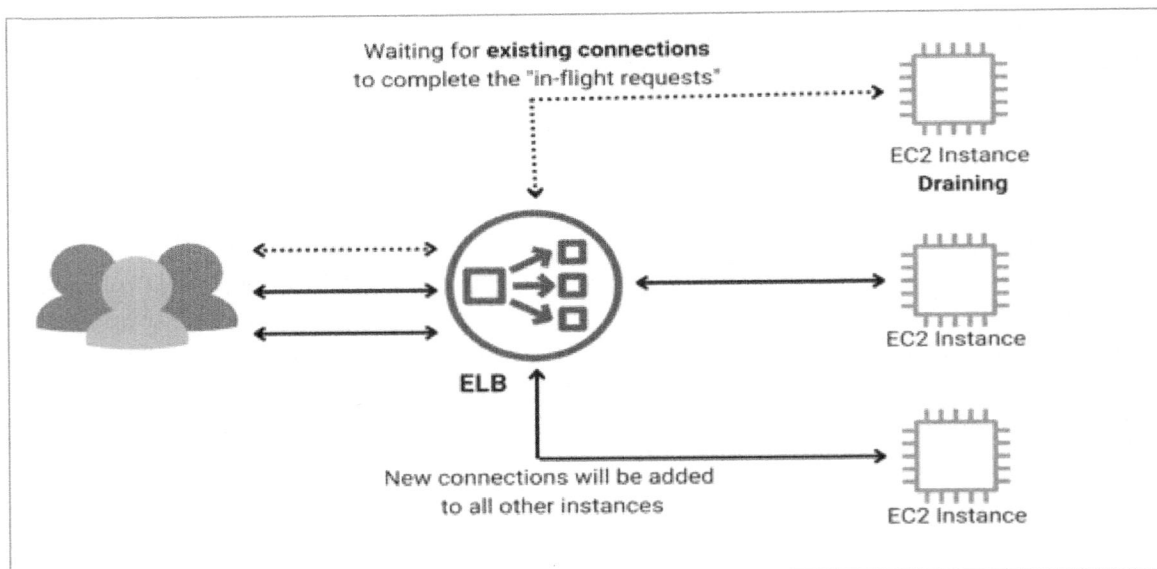

Connection Draining, an ELB feature, is a process that ensures that existing and in-progress requests are given sufficient time to complete when a VM is removed from a target group or when an endpoint is removed. When the timeout duration is reached, all remaining connections to the VM are closed.

With Connection Draining enabled, if an EC2 instance fails health checks, the ELB will not send any new request to the unhealthy EC2 instance. However, the ELB will still allow existing "in-flight" requests to be complete for the duration of the configured timeout.

"Connection Draining" is used for CLB; for ALB and NLB, it is called "Deregistration Delay."

Duration can be between 1 to 3600 seconds (default: 300 seconds). It can also be disabled. You can also set the duration timeout to smaller if the application's request/response cycle is short.

AWS Auto Scaling

If you have deployed applications on production, you know how the load on your websites and application can change – in general, it varies – except for some particular types of applications with a fixed number of users. In the cloud environment, you can quickly create and get rid of servers.

Auto Scaling helps handle the varied load most efficiently with minimal impact on performance. Auto Scaling does it by scaling out (i.e., add EC2 instances) to match an increased load and scaling in (i.e., remove EC2 instances) to match a decreased load. Auto Scaling ensures a minimum and a maximum number of EC2 instances running in the Auto Scaling Group (ASG) and allows automatic registration of new instances to a load balancer. It also re-launches an EC2 instance if an instance in the ASG is terminated (e.g., if unhealthy).

AWS Auto Scaling provides monitoring to your applications and automatically adjusts capacity to maintain steady, predictable performance at the lowest possible cost. In addition, you can quickly set up auto-scaling using AWS Auto Scaling across multiple services.

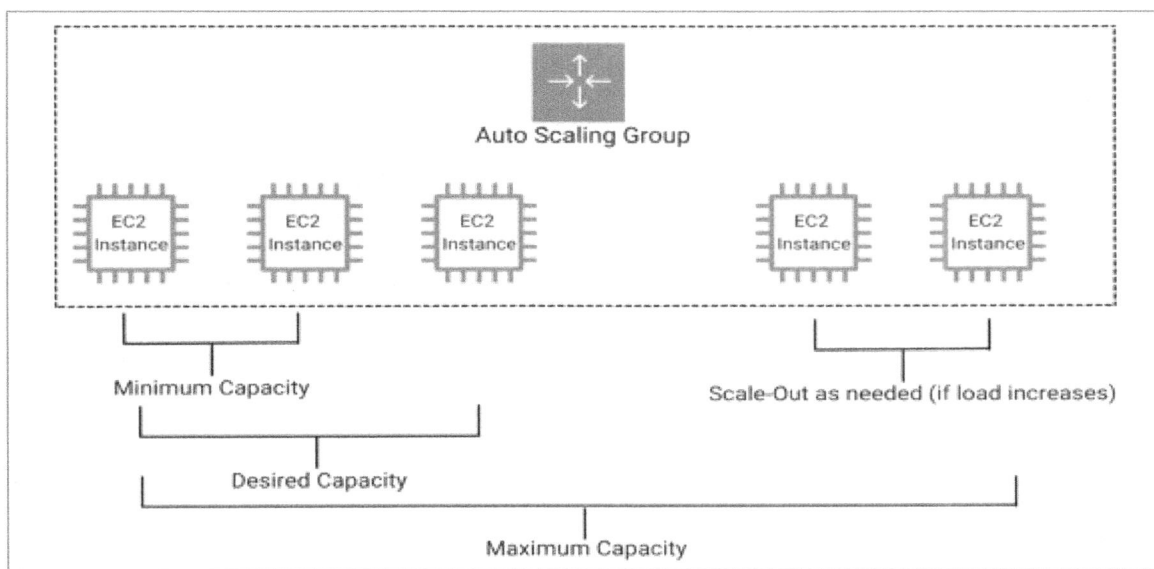

As shown in the above diagram, in ASG, you can configure minimum, desired, and maximum capacity.

Desired capacity: ASG's desired capacity represents the initial capacity of the Auto Scaling group at the time of creation. An ASG attempts to maintain the desired capacity. To do so, it starts by launching the number of instances specified for the desired capacity and maintains this number of instances as long as there are no scaling policies or scheduled actions attached to the ASG.

Minimum capacity: ASG's minimum capacity represents the minimum group size. When scaling policies are set, an ASG cannot decrease its desired capacity lower than the minimum size limit.

Maximum capacity: ASG's maximum capacity represents the maximum group size. When scaling policies are set, an Auto Scaling group cannot increase its desired capacity higher than the maximum size limit.

An Auto Scaling group always tries to maintain its desired capacity. However, in cases where an EC2 instance terminates unexpectedly -- for example, because of a Spot Instance interruption, a health check failure, or human action -- the ASG automatically launches a new instance to maintain its desired capacity.

The service provides a simple and powerful UI to configure and set up auto-scaling. You can use auto-scaling with Amazon EC2 instances, Spot Fleets, Amazon ECS tasks, Amazon DynamoDB, and Amazon Aurora Replicas. With AWS Auto Scaling, your applications get the right resources at the right time.

For AWS Auto Scaling -- There is no additional cost. You only pay Amazon CloudWatch monitoring fees and the AWS resources needed to run your applications.

You should use Auto Scaling to manage to scale for multiple AWS resources across multiple AWS services. Using AWS Auto Scaling to configure scaling policies for all scalable resources is faster than managing scaling policies for individual resources. It's also easier to configure scaling policies, as AWS Auto Scaling includes predefined scaling strategies that simplify the setup of scaling policies. In addition, Amazon EC2 Auto Scaling works with Application Load Balancers and Network Load Balancers, including their health check feature.

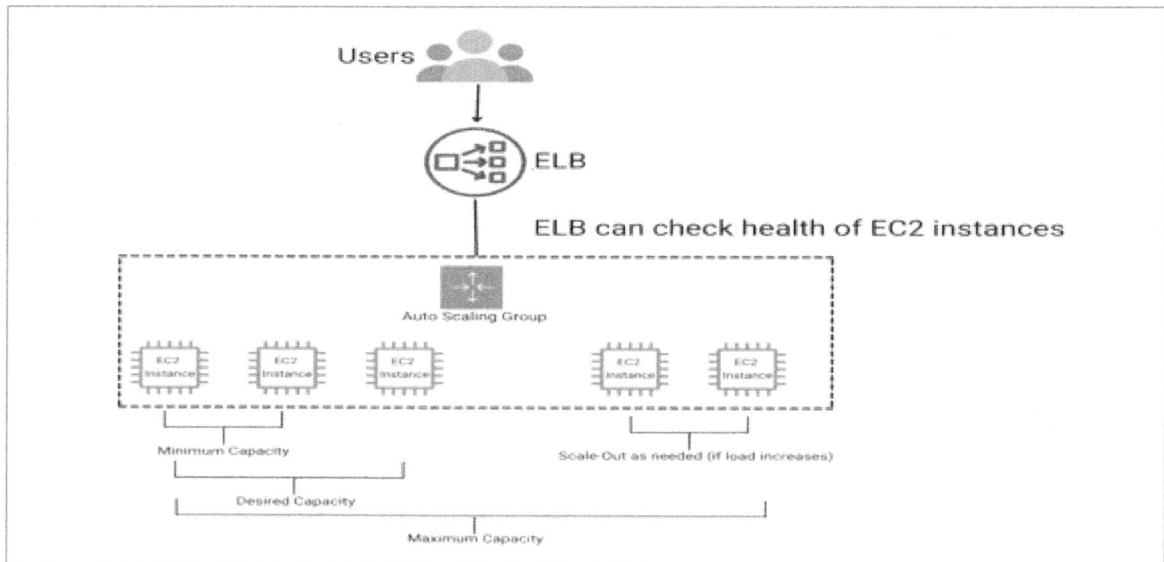

Though you don't have to use ELB to use Auto Scaling, you can use the EC2 health check to identify and replace unhealthy instances. It is common; however, the use case where ASG is fronted with ELB. The reason is that ELB provides a single point of entry for web applications for all the EC2 instances and forward the load based on how the target group is configured and can ensure the traffic is forwarded only to healthy instances.

Launch Template

We talked about a minimum, desired, and maximum size for an Auto Scaling Group. Another important attribute of ASG is the Launch Template (older "Launch Configuration" is deprecated).

Before creating an ASG using a launch template, you must create a launch template with the parameters required to launch an EC2 instance. Therefore, in order to create an Auto Scaling group, you need a launch template.

A launch template includes:
- AMI + instance type compatible with AMI
- EC2 User Data
- Key pair to use when connecting to instances (e.g., SSH)
- Security group to allow relevant access to instances to connect to from an external network
- EBS Volumes
- IAM Roles for EC2 instances
- network and subnet information
- custom tags (key-value pair) to the instances and volumes.

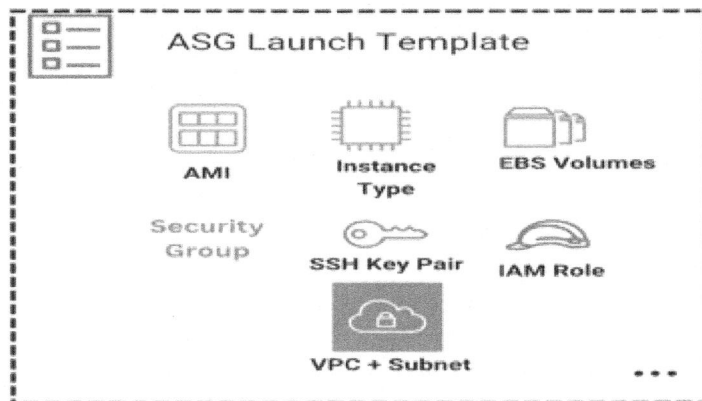

Auto Scaling with CloudWatch Alarms

In addition to knowing about a minimum, desired, and maximum size and about the Launch Template, the other important attribute is scaling policies. In other words, what and how scaling is triggered in an Auto Scaling Group.

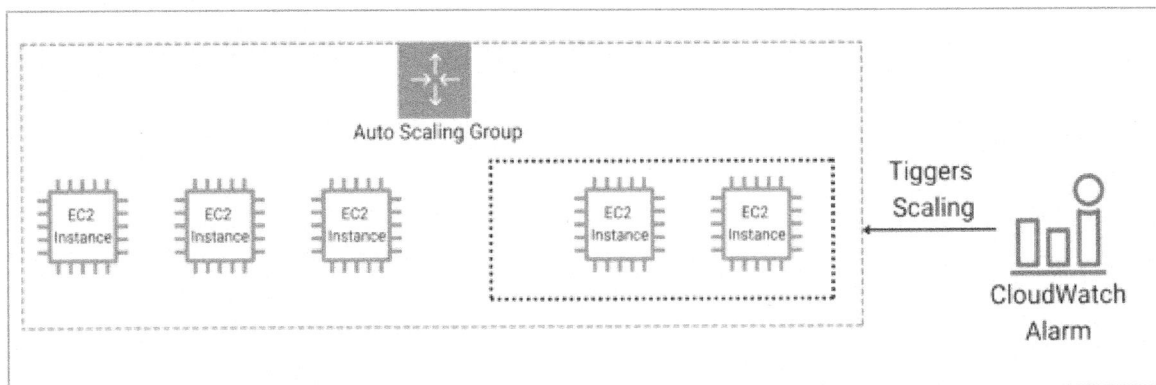

It is possible to scale an Auto Scaling Group using CloudWatch alarms. Scaling works using CloudWatch alarms because CloudWatch alarm monitors metrics such as average CPU utilization,

I/O metric, or any custom metric. Then the alarm triggers auto-scaling if the scaling rule fires. For example, if CPU utilization exceeds 70%, launch one additional instance in the ASG. Metrics such as Average CPU are computed by considering CPU performance for all ASG instances.

We can set scale-out policies (launch additional instances in ASG) and scale-in policies (terminate instances in ASG) by configuring CloudWatch alarms based on the CloudWatch monitoring metrics.

Dynamic Scaling for Amazon EC2 Auto Scaling

Dynamic scaling helps scale the capacity of your Auto Scaling group as traffic changes occur. Amazon EC2 Auto Scaling supports Target tracking scaling, Step scaling, and Simple scaling.

Target tracking scaling: This is the simplest to set up. For example, increase and decrease the current capacity of the group based on an Amazon CloudWatch metric and a target value -- keep the average ASG CPU at around 40%. It works similarly to how your thermostat maintains your home's temperature—you select a temperature, and the thermostat does the rest.

Step scaling: Increase and decrease the group's current capacity based on a set of scaling adjustments, known as step adjustments. For example, add two more instances when a CloudWatch alarm is triggered (e.g., CPU > 70%).

Simple scaling: Increase and decrease the group's current capacity based on a single scaling adjustment, with a cooldown period between each scaling activity. For example, remove one instance when a CloudWatch alarm is triggered (e.g., CPU < 30%).

Suppose you are scaling based on a metric that increases or decreases proportionally to the number of instances in an Auto Scaling group. In that case, it is recommended to use target tracking scaling policies. Otherwise, you use step scaling policies.

By default, a new ASG starts without any scaling policies. When you use an ASG without any form of dynamic scaling (e.g., target scaling, simple/step scaling), the ASG doesn't scale independently unless you set up scheduled scaling or predictive scaling.

Scheduled Actions: You can also use Scheduled Actions in scenarios where you anticipate a scaling based on known usage patterns, for example, increasing minimum capacity to 12 at 7 pm on Fridays.

Predictive Scaling: Predictive Scaling continuously forecasts load and schedule scaling ahead based on the generated prediction.

KEY POINTS

Good metrics to scale on:
- CPU utilization: Average CPU utilization across your instances
- RequestCountPerTarget: To make sure the number of requests per EC2 instance is stable
- Average Network In / Out: If you're application is network bound (for example, CloudWatch 120,000,000 in Network In means => 120MB / 60s => 2 MB/s => 16 Mbps)

Scaling Cooldowns

After a scaling activity (launching or terminating instances) happens, there is a cooldown period (default 300 seconds). During the cooldown period, the ASG will not launch or terminate additional instances to allow for metrics to stabilize. The cooldown period intends to prevent an ASG from launching or terminating additional instances before the effects of previous activities are visible

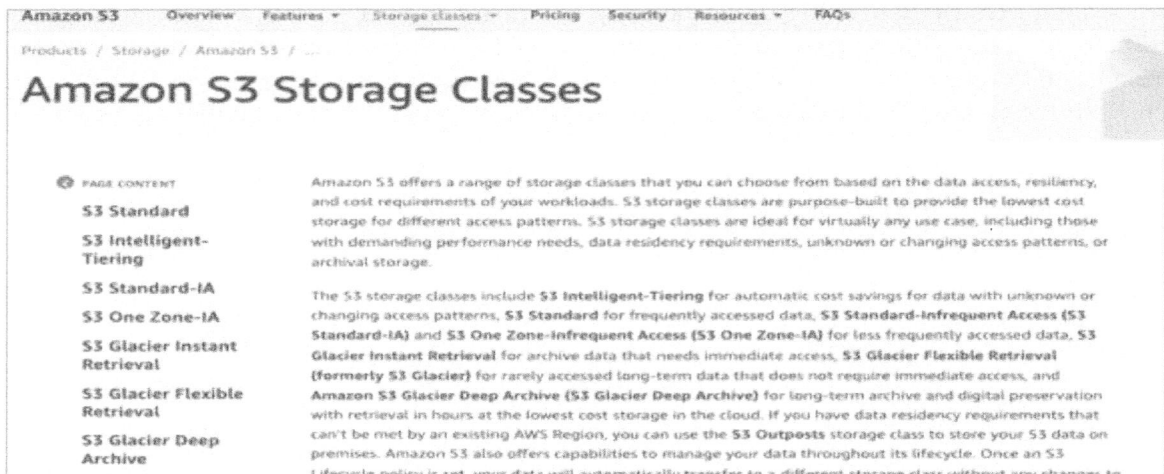

Chapter 17. Advanced S3

You will learn the following in this chapter:
- Amazon S3 Standard – General Purpose
- Amazon S3 Standard - Infrequent Access (IA)
- Amazon S3 Standard - One Zone-IA
- Amazon S3 Glacier Storage Classes
- Amazon S3 Glacier Deep Archive
- Amazon S3 Intelligent-Tiering
- Moving Between Storage Classes
- S3 Lifecycle Rules
- S3 Performance
- S3 Select and Glacier Select
- S3 Event Notifications
- S3 Event Notifications using Amazon EventBridge
- S3 Requester Pays
- S3 Glacier Vault Lock
- S3 Object Lock
- S3 Access Points
- S3 Object Lambda
- S3 Batch Operations
- S3 Storage Classes Key Matrix
- S3 Storage Classes Availability Matrix
- S3 Storage Classes Data Retrieval Times Matrix

In the previous chapter, we discussed the introduction to S3 in quite detail. In this chapter, we will look into various S3 Storage Classes: Amazon S3 Standard -- General Purpose, Amazon S3 Standard – Infrequent Access (IA), Amazon S3 One Zone-Infrequent Access, Amazon 3 Glacier Instant

Retrieval, Amazon S3 Glacier Flexible Retrieval, Amazon S3 Glacier Deep Archive, Amazon S3 Intelligent Tiering.

The S3 objects can be moved between classes **manually** or using **S3 Lifecycle** configurations.

Before looking at each S3 Storage Class in detail, let's first understand about durability and availability of objects stored on S3.

S3 Durability
S3 provides high durability (99.999999999% or 9's) for objects stored across Multiple AZs. In simple words, for example, if you store 10,000,000 objects on S3, you can, on average, expect to incur a loss of a single object once in every 10,000 years. This 9's durability applies to all storage classes.

S3 Availability
It is a measure of how readily available a service is. S3 availability percentage varies depending on storage class. For example, S3 Standard has 99.99% availability – which means S3 may not be available for 53 minutes a year.

Amazon S3 Standard – General Purpose
S3 Standard offers highly durable, available, and performance object storage for frequently accessed data. S3 Standard has a retrieval time (first-byte latency) of milliseconds. It provides 99.99% availability. It is used for frequently accessed data with low latency and high throughput.

Because S3 Standard delivers low latency and high throughput, S3 Standard is appropriate for a wide variety of use cases, including cloud applications, dynamic websites, content distribution, mobile and gaming applications, and big data analytics. However, the S3 Standard storage class is not used to store secondary backup copies of on-premises data. Data stored in S3 Standard - is used for General Purposes and for frequently accessed data.

Amazon S3 Standard - Infrequent Access (IA)
Amazon S3 Standard-IA (Standard-Infrequent Access) is for data that is accessed less frequently but requires rapid access when needed. S3 Standard-IA offers highly durable, high throughput, and low latency of S3 Standard, with a low per GB storage price and per GB retrieval fee. It provides 99.99% availability.

This combination of low cost and high performance makes S3 Standard-IA ideal for long-term storage, backups, and as a data store for disaster recovery files. It can be used for backups, but it is more expensive than S3 One Zone - Infrequent Access. Hence, S3 One Zone - Infrequent Access is a better option for secondary backup copies.

Amazon S3 Standard - One Zone-IA
S3 One Zone-IA Storage Class is used for data that is accessed less frequently. However, when needed, it requires rapid access. Unlike other S3 Storage Classes, which store data in a minimum of three AZs, S3 One Zone-IA stores data in a single AZ, and it costs 20% less than S3 Standard-IA.

It provides high durability (99.999999999%) and 99.5% Availability in a single AZ, and data is lost when AZ is destroyed.

S3 One Zone-IA is very good for the use cases of customers who want a lower-cost option for infrequently accessed data but do not need the availability and resilience of S3 Standard or S3 Standard-IA. Additionally, S3 One Zone-IA is a good choice for storing secondary backup copies of on-premises data or easily re-creatable data. You can also use it as cost-effective storage for data that is replicated from another AWS Region using S3 Cross-Region Replication.

An example is thumbnail storage. However, S3 One Zone-IA offers less availability than S3 Standard, but that's not an issue for storing thumbnails since the thumbnails can be regenerated easily.
In a use case where the thumbnails are rarely used but need to be rapidly accessed when required, S3 One Zone-IA could be the best choice.

Amazon S3 Glacier Storage Classes

Amazon S3 Glacier is a secure, durable, and extremely low-cost S3 Storage Class for data archiving and long-term backup. It is designed to deliver 99.999999999% durability. Amazon S3 Glacier provides comprehensive security and compliance capabilities that can help meet even the most stringent regulatory requirements. S3 Glacier has a retrieval time (first-byte latency) of minutes or a few hours.

Amazon S3 Glacier is optimized for infrequently used data, or "cold data." Data stored in S3 Glacier is automatically server-side encrypted using 256-bit Advanced Encryption Standard (AES-256) with keys maintained by AWS.

Amazon S3 Glacier Storage Classes pricing has two components: price for storage and object retrieval cost.

Amazon S3 Glacier Instance Retrieval
Retrieval: Millisecond retrieval; great for data accessed once a quarter
Storage: Minimum storage duration of 90 days

Amazon S3 Glacier Flexible Retrieval (formerly Amazon S3 Glacier):
Retrieval: Expedited (1 to 5 minutes), Standard (3 to 5 hours), Bulk (5 to 12 hours) – free
Storage: Minimum storage duration of 90 days

Amazon S3 Glacier Deep Archive – for long-term storage:
Retrieval: Standard (12 hours), Bulk (48 hours)
Storage: Minimum storage duration of 180 days

Amazon S3 Glacier Deep Archive

Amazon S3 Glacier Deep Archive is the lowest-cost Storage Class offering. Its typical use case supports long-term retention of data that may be accessed once or twice a year. It is designed for customers that retain data sets for 7-10 years or longer to meet regulatory compliance requirements — particularly those in highly-regulated industries, such as Financial Services, Healthcare, and Public Sectors.

S3 Glacier Deep Archive can also be used for backup and disaster recovery cases. It is also a cost-effective and easy-to-manage alternative to magnetic tape systems, whether they are on-premises libraries or off-premises services. It has a retrieval time (first-byte latency) of 12 to 48 hours.

S3 Glacier Deep Archive complements Amazon S3 Glacier, which is ideal for archives where data is regularly retrieved, and some of the data may be needed in minutes. All objects stored in S3 Glacier Deep Archive are replicated and stored across at least three geographically-dispersed AZs, protected by 99.999999999% of durability, and can be restored within 12 hours.

S3 Glacier Deep Archive Overview

Amazon S3 Glacier Deep Archive (S3 Glacier Deep Archive)

S3 Glacier Deep Archive is Amazon S3's lowest-cost storage class and supports long-term retention and digital preservation for data that may be accessed once or twice in a year. It is designed for customers — particularly those in highly-regulated industries, such as the Financial Services, Healthcare, and Public Sectors — that retain data sets for 7-10 years or longer to meet regulatory compliance requirements. S3 Glacier Deep Archive can also be used for backup and disaster recovery use cases, and is a cost-effective and easy-to-manage alternative to magnetic tape systems, whether they are on-premises libraries or off-premises services. S3 Glacier Deep Archive complements Amazon S3 Glacier, which is ideal for archives where data is regularly retrieved and some of the data may be needed in minutes. All objects stored in S3 Glacier Deep Archive are replicated and stored across at least three geographically-dispersed Availability Zones, protected by 99.999999999% of durability, and can be restored within 12 hours.

Key Features:

- Designed for durability of 99.999999999% of objects across multiple Availability Zones
- Lowest cost storage class designed for long-term retention of data that will be retained for 7-10 years
- Ideal alternative to magnetic tape libraries
- Retrieval time within 12 hours
- S3 PUT API for direct uploads to S3 Glacier Deep Archive, and S3 Lifecycle management for automatic migration of objects

Amazon S3 Intelligent-Tiering

The S3 Intelligent-Tiering storage class is designed to optimize costs by automatically moving data to the most cost-effective access tier-based access patterns change without performance impact or operational overhead. It works by storing objects in two access tiers: one tier that is optimized for frequent access and another lower-cost tier that is optimized for infrequent access. S3 Intelligent-Tiering has a retrieval time (first-byte latency) of milliseconds.

It works by storing objects in four access tiers: two low latency access tiers optimized for frequent and infrequent access and two optional archive access tiers designed for asynchronous access that are optimized for rare access. Objects uploaded or transitioned to S3 Intelligent-Tiering are automatically stored in the Frequent Access tier.

S3 Intelligent-Tiering works by monitoring access patterns and then moving the objects that have not been accessed in 30 consecutive days to the Infrequent Access tier. Once you have activated one or both of the archive access tiers, S3 Intelligent-Tiering will automatically move objects that haven't been accessed for 90 consecutive days to the Archive Access tier and then after 180 consecutive days of no access to the Deep Archive Access tier. If the objects are accessed later, S3 Intelligent-Tiering moves the objects back to the Frequent Access tier.

There are no retrieval fees when using the S3 Intelligent-Tiering storage class and no additional tiering fees when objects are moved between access tiers within S3 Intelligent-Tiering. It is the ideal storage class for data sets with unknown storage access patterns, like new applications, or unpredictable access patterns, like data lakes.

Moving Between Storage Classes

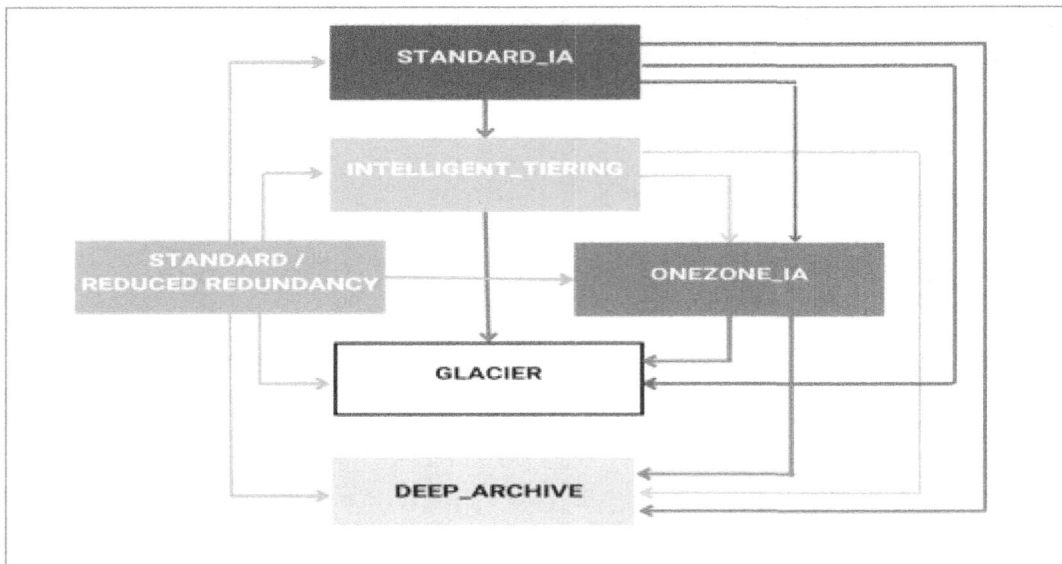

You can transition S3 objects between storage classes. The diagram shows how objects can be transitioned from one storage class to another. For objects that are accessed **infrequently**, you can move them to STANDARD_IA. For objects you don't need in the immediate or near future, you can move them to GLACIER or DEEP_ARCHIVE.

Moving objects can also be automated using a **lifecycle configuration**.

How objects automatically move between Access Tiers based on usage
- Frequent Access tier (automatic): default tier
- Infrequent Access tier (automatic): objects not accessed for 30 days
- Archive Instant Access tier (automatic): objects not accessed for 90 days
- Archive Access tier (optional): configurable from 90 days to 700+ days
- Deep Archive Access tier (optional): configurable from 180 days to 700+ days

S3 Lifecycle Rules

To store objects cost-effectively throughout their lifecycle, you can transition them manually. You can also configure their *S3 Lifecycle* to automate transition.   An *S3 Lifecycle configuration* is a set of rules that define actions that Amazon S3 applies to a group of objects.

Rules can be created for a certain prefix (for example, as s3://mybucket/mp4/*) or for a certain object tag (for example, Department: Marketing).

There are two types of S3 Lifecycle actions:

Transition actions

It defines when objects are transitioned to another storage class. For example, you might decide to move objects to Standard IA class 60 days after creation or move to Glacier for archival six months after creating them.

Expiration Actions
It defines actions when to expire objects -- Amazon S3 deletes expired objects. For example, expiration actions can be used to delete old version files (if versioning is enabled). Expiration Actions can be used to delete incomplete multi-part uploads. You can set Access Log files to delete after 365 days using expiration actions.

S3 Lifecycle Rules Use Case Examples

Use Case 1:
You have a social media web application deployed on an EC2 instance. The application generates a thumbnail image when a profile picture is uploaded to the S3. These thumbnails can be easily created and only need to be kept for 30 days. The user should be able to retrieve their uploaded profile image immediately for up 30 days. After 30 days, the user can wait up to 6 hours. How would you design the S3 Lifecycle Rules for this use case?

The profile images (source images) can be stored on the S3 Standard Storage class, with a lifecycle configuration rule to transition to Glacier after 30 days. S3 thumbnails can be stored on S3 One Zone-IA with a lifecycle configuration to expire them after 30 days -- S3 deletes expired objects.

Use Case 2:
You have a rule in your company about objects stored on S3 that, for up to 20 days, users should be able to recover deleted objects immediately – although this may happen rarely. After 20 days and for up to 365 days, deleted objects should be recoverable within 48 hours.

To recover deleted objects, you need to enable S3 versioning so that deleted objects are hidden by a "delete marker" and can be recovered. You can transition these "noncurrent versions" to S3_IA. From S3_IA, you can transition these "noncurrent versions" to DEEP_ARCHIVE.

S3 Storage Class Analytics
To help set Lifecycle Rules, you can set up S3 Analytics to help determine when to transition objects. It takes about 24 to 48 hours for the first star -- The report is updated daily. S3 Analytics does not work for One Zone-IA and Glacier.

S3 Performance

Baseline Performance
Amazon S3 automatically scales to a high request rate with a latency of 100 to 200 milliseconds. Your application accessing S3 objects can achieve at least **3500 PUT/COPY/POST/DELETE and 5,500 GET/HEAD requests per second per prefix in a bucket**. There are no limits to the number of prefixes in a bucket.

To get an idea about prefixes in a bucket, let's see some examples:

Object path	prefix
bucket/folder1/subfolder1/file1	/folder1/subfolder1
bucket/folder1/subfolder2/file1	/folder1/subfolder2

bucket/1/file	/1/
bucket/2/file	/2/
Bucket/3/file	/3/

In the example of the prefix above, if you can spread your reads across all five prefixes evenly, you can achieve 27,500 requests per second for GET and HEAD requests.

Impact of KMS on the baseline performance

S3 baseline performance may be impacted if you use KMS by the KMS limits. When you upload object, it calls the GenerateDataKey KMS API, and when you download, it calls the Decrypt KMS API. The KMS quota depends on the AWS Regions. You can request a quota increase using the Service Quota Console.

Multi-Part Upload

Multi-Part upload is recommended for files that are greater than 100 MB. However, you must use multi-part upload for files greater than 5GB. Multi-part uploads parallelize uploads which help speed up uploads.

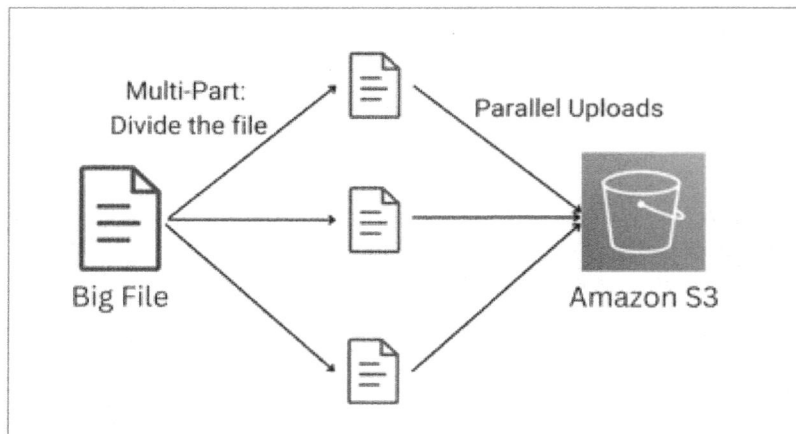

S3 Transfer Acceleration

S3 Transfer Acceleration increases transfer speed by transferring files to an AWS Edge Location, which will then forward the data to the S3 bucket in the target AWS Region. S

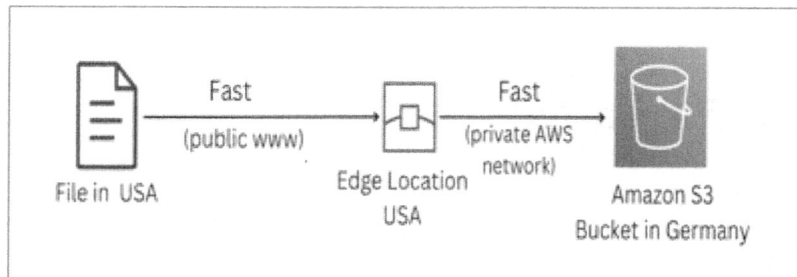

3 Transfer Acceleration is compatible with Multi-part uploads.

S3 Byte-Range Fetches

Amazon S3 allows you to fetch different byte ranges from within the same object and thus helps achieve higher aggregate throughput vs. an entire object request.

It parallelizes GET requests by requesting specific byte ranges.

In addition, fetching smaller byte ranges of a large object also allows an application to improve resilience when these requests are interrupted by providing the retry times.

It can be used to speed up downloads by breaking into parts – downloading each part parallelly.

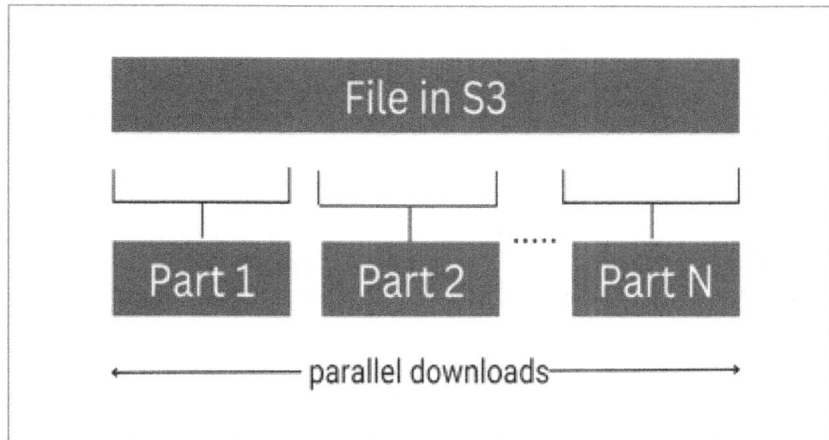

Byte-range fetch can also be used to retrieve only partial data, for example, if you would like to retrieve the head (first XX bytes) of the file.

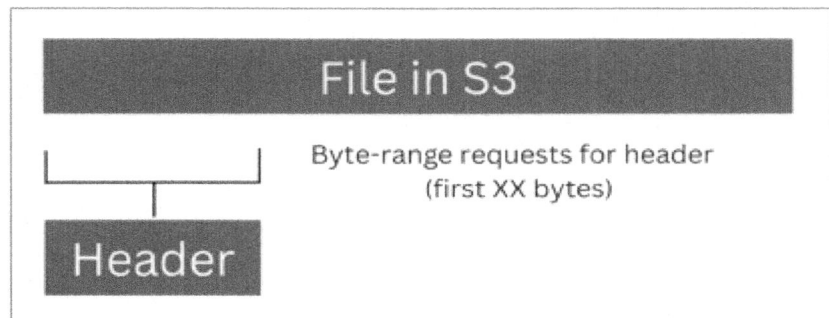

S3 Select and Glacier Select

S3 Select is a powerful feature where it enables applications to retrieve only a subset of data from an object (for example, a subset of records from a CSV file) by using simple SQL expressions.

By using S3 Select to fetch only data needed for your application, you can achieve major performance improvement – as much as 400%.

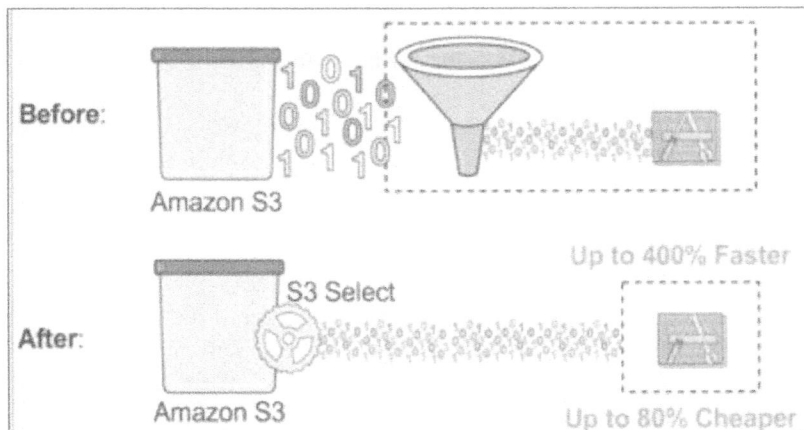

For example: "select * from s3object s where s.\"Country (Name)\" like '%United States%'"

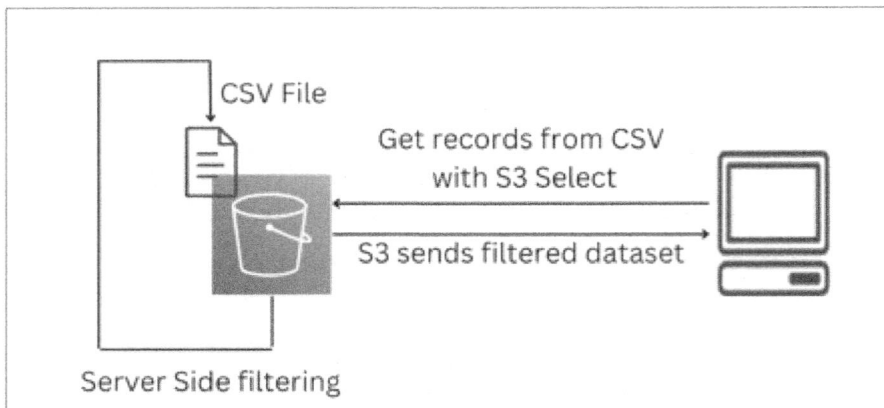

It retrieves a subset of data using SQL expression by performing server-side filtering.

It can filter by rows and columns – which results in less data transfer over the network and less CPU cost on the client side.

You can also retrieve cold data stored in Glacier within minutes. Glacier Select allows you to perform filtering directly against a Glacier object using standard SQL statements.

S3 Event Notifications

You can use Amazon S3 Event Notifications (e.g., S3:ObjectCreated, S3:ObjectRemoved, S3:ObjectRestore, S3:Replicatio) to get notifications when certain events occur in your S3 bucket.

To enable S3 event notifications, add an event notification configuration (including destinations where you want S3 to send the notifications) about the events you want Amazon S3 to publish.

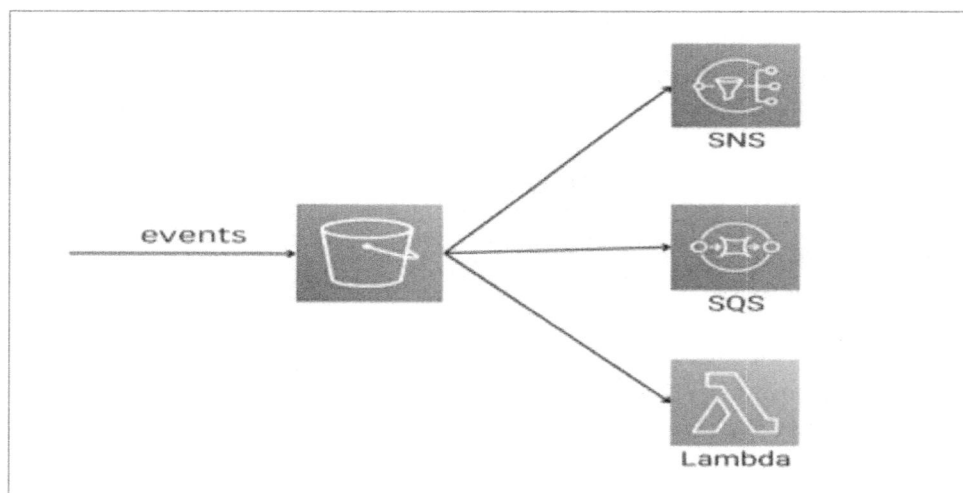

For example, when a file is uploaded by your external data vendor, you can use S3 event notification to publish the event to SNS, SQS, and AWS Lambda. You can also use S3 event notifications to generate thumbnails of images uploaded to S3. This is a useful S3 feature to set up event-driven workflow integration.

You can also perform object name filtering (*.jpg). You can create as many "S3 events" as desired.

S3 event notifications typically publish events in seconds but sometimes can take a minute or longer.

S3 Event Notifications using Amazon EventBridge

Using Amazon EventBridge, you can integrate S3 to build applications that react quickly to changes in your S3 objects. In other words, you can now configure S3 Event Notifications to deliver to EventBridge directly.

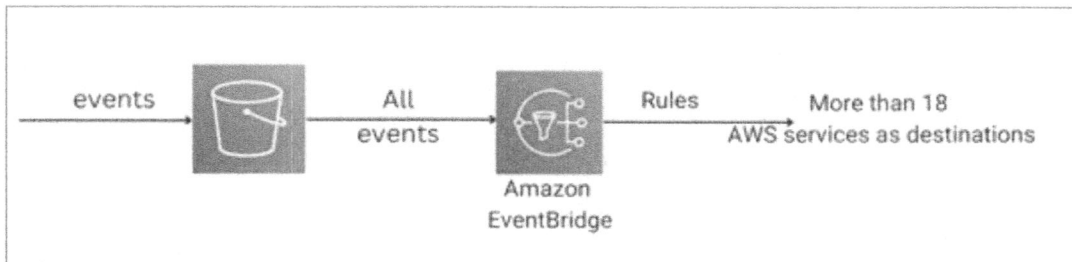

You can set up advanced filtering options with JSON rules. You can add multiple destinations, e.g., Step Functions, Kinesis Streams, and Firehose. EventBridge makes it much easier than creating your own fan-out mechanism. In addition, it will also help you to deal with enterprise-scale situations where independent teams want to do their own event processing.

You get reliable delivery, and can archive and replay events.

S3 Requester Pays

In general, the S3 bucket owner is responsible for paying for all S3 storage and data transfer costs associated with their bucket. However, you can configure a bucket to be a Requester Pays bucket.

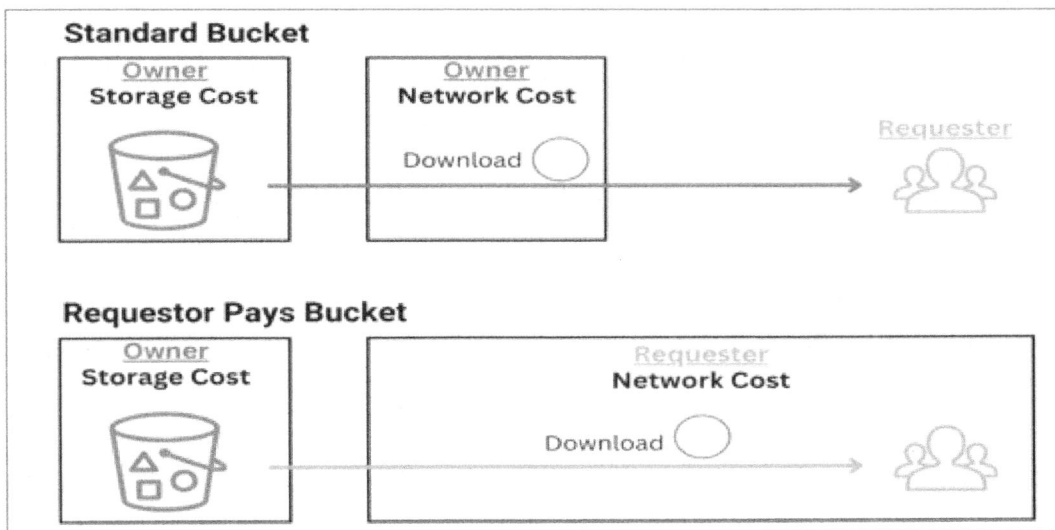

With Requestor Pays Bucket, the requestor – instead of the bucket owner – pays the cost of the request and data to download from the bucket. The bucket owner is always responsible for paying the cost of storing data.

The feature is helpful if you would like to share large datasets with other accounts. The requestor must be authenticated in AWS -- the requestor cannot be anonymous.

S3 Glacier Vault Lock

S3 Glacier Vault Lock helps you adopt controls such as "write once read many" (WORM).

You can easily deploy and enforce compliance controls for individual S3 Glacier vaults with a Vault Lock policy.

You can lock the policy from future edits. **After a Vault Lock policy is locked, the policy can no longer be changed or deleted.**

It is helpful for compliance and data retention.

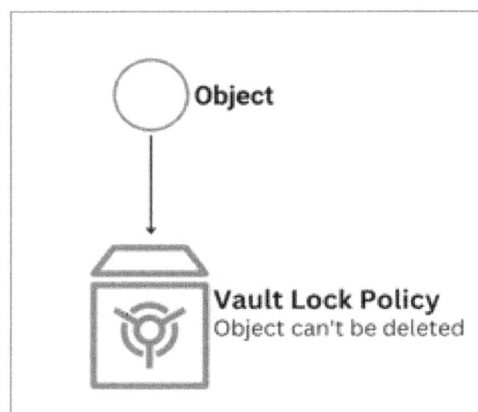

S3 Object Lock

With S3 Object Lock, you can adopt the WORM (write-once-read-many) model for storing objects. You can use Object Lock to help prevent objects from being deleted or overwritten for a fixed amount of time or indefinitely.

For Object Lock to work, versioning must be enabled for the bucket to work-- it only works in the versioned bucket.

Object Lock provides two ways to manage object retention: retention periods and legal holds.

Retention period — Specifies a fixed period during which an object remains locked and WORM-protected and can't be overwritten or deleted. The retention period can be extended.

Legal hold — Protects object indefinitely -- it has no expiration date. It is independent of the retention period. For example, a lock can be freely placed and removed using the s3:PutObjectLegalHold IAM permission.

S3 Access Points

As the number of your users and data grows, managing access to your S3 buckets becomes a complicated task. Provisioning access policies (who and where to access these objects) to these users could get become complicated as well.

AWS added a feature called Access Points on S3 to resolve this current problem. With this feature, each user can have a dedicated access point on a bucket. And each Access Point gets its own DNS, and policy to limit who can access it.

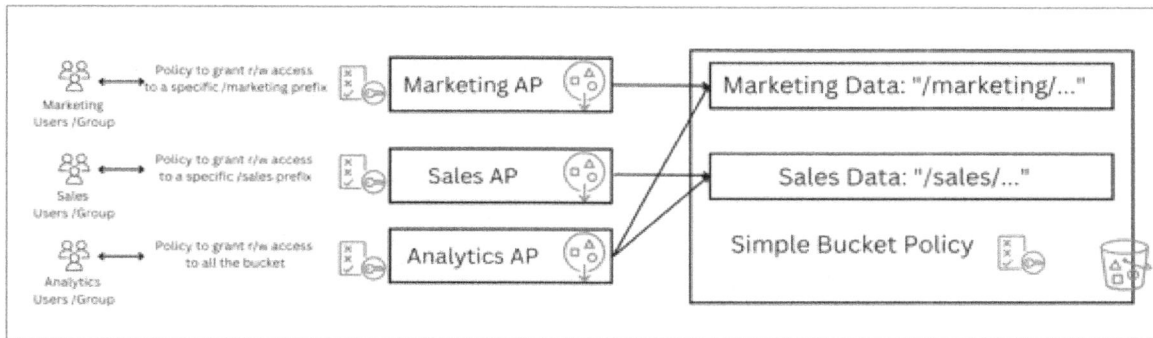

Access Points can simplify things in terms of provisioning access to different users.

This is quite helpful when you have large data sets on a bucket that are accessed by different users and/or applications. An Access Point can also be restricted to a particular VPC which is very useful if you have tight data security requirements.

S3 Object Lambda

S3 Object Lambda enables you to add your own custom code to process data (such as transform, and enrich data) retrieved from S3 before returning it to the caller application. S3 Object Lambda uses AWS Lambda functions to process your data retrieved from S3. S3 Object Lambda allows you to easily present multiple views from the same dataset. On the top of the S3 bucket, we create S3 Access Point and S3 Object Lambda Access Points.

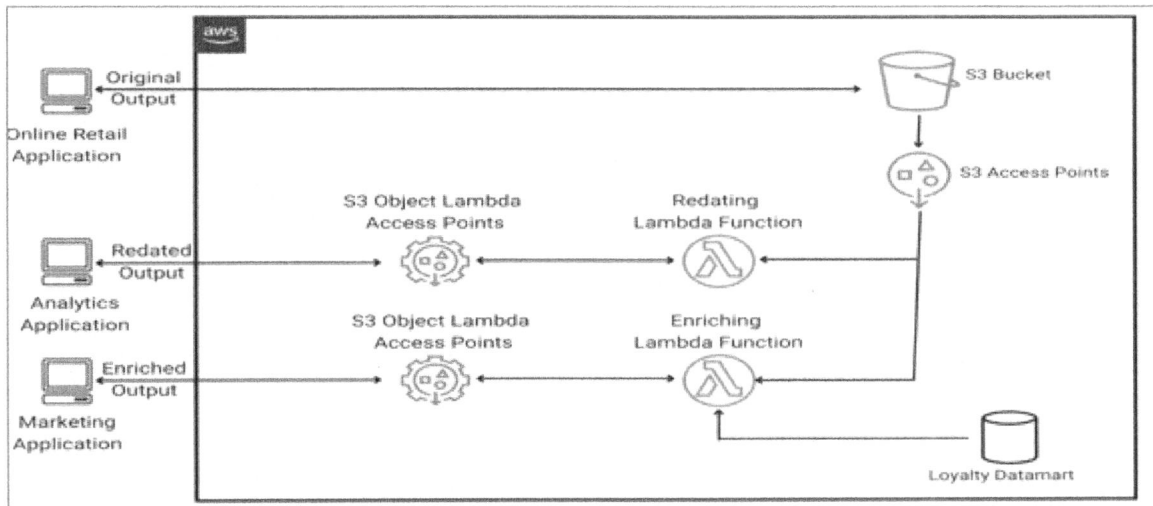

Regarding use cases of S3 Object Lambda, S3 Object Lambda makes it easier to redate personally identifiable information for analytics before returning fetched original S3 data to the client application. It can also help you easily convert S3 data across data formats, such as converting XML into JSON, resizing, and watermarking images on the fly using caller-specific details, such as the user-requested object, before returning to the client application.

S3 Batch Operations

S3 Batch Operations is a managed solution that can perform bulk actions on existing S3 objects (across billions of objects and petabytes of data) with a single request. S3 Batch Operations can perform operations such as:

- modify object metadata & properties
- copy objects between S3 buckets
- encrypt objects
- modify ACLs and tags
- restore objects from S3 Glacier
- invoke AWs Lambda function to perform custom actions on objects

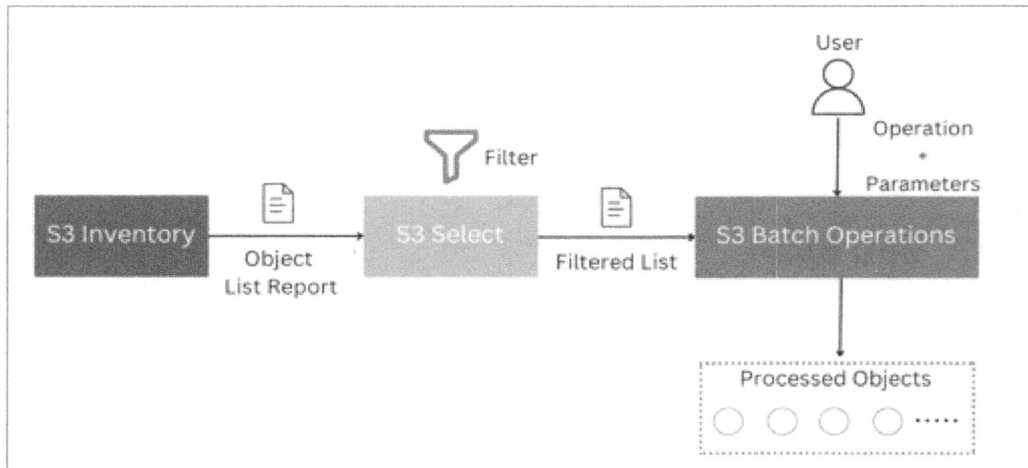

A job consists of the list of objects, the action to perform, and the optional parameters. S3 Batch Operations manages retries, tracks progress, sends completion notifications, and generates reports. It delivers events to AWS CloudTrail for changes made and tasks executed.

You can use S3 Inventory to get an object list and use S3 Select to filter your objects.

S3 Storage Classes Key Matrix

	S3 Standard	S3 Intelligent-Tiering*	S3 Standard-IA	S3 One Zone-IA†	S3 Glacier	S3 Glacier Deep Archive
Designed for durability	99.999999999% (11 9's)	99.999999999% (11 9's)	99.999999999% (11 9's)	99.999999999% (11 9's)	99.999999999% (11 9's)	99.999999999% (11 9's)
Designed for availability	99.99%	99.9%	99.9%	99.5%	99.99%	99.99%
Availability SLA	99.9%	99%	99%	99%	99.9%	99.9%
Availability Zones	≥3	≥3	≥3	1	≥3	≥3
Minimum capacity charge per object	N/A	N/A	128KB	128KB	40KB	40KB
Minimum storage duration charge	N/A	30 days	30 days	30 days	90 days	180 days
Retrieval fee	N/A	N/A	per GB retrieved	per GB retrieved	per GB retrieved	per GB retrieved
First byte latency	milliseconds	milliseconds	milliseconds	milliseconds	select minutes or hours	select hours
Storage type	Object	Object	Object	Object	Object	Object
Lifecycle transitions	Yes	Yes	Yes	Yes	Yes	Yes

S3 Storage Classes Availability Matrix

Please review this illustration for S3 Storage Classes availability. You don't need to memorize the actual numbers, just remember that S3 One Zone-IA offers the lowest availability:

	S3 Standard	S3 Intelligent-Tiering*	S3 Standard-IA	S3 One Zone-IA†	S3 Glacier	S3 Glacier Deep Archive
Designed for durability	99.999999999% (11 9's)	99.999999999% (11 9's)	99.999999999% (11 9's)	99.999999999% (11 9's)	99.999999999% (11 9's)	99.999999999% (11 9's)
Designed for availability	99.99%	99.9%	99.9%	99.5%	99.99%	99.99%
Availability SLA	99.9%	99%	99%	99%	99.9%	99.9%
Availability Zones	≥3	≥3	≥3	1	≥3	≥3
Minimum capacity charge per object	N/A	N/A	128KB	128KB	40KB	40KB
Minimum storage duration charge	N/A	30 days	30 days	30 days	90 days	180 days
Retrieval fee	N/A	N/A	per GB retrieved	per GB retrieved	per GB retrieved	per GB retrieved
First byte latency	milliseconds	milliseconds	milliseconds	milliseconds	select minutes or hours	select hours
Storage type	Object	Object	Object	Object	Object	Object
Lifecycle transitions	Yes	Yes	Yes	Yes	Yes	Yes

S3 Storage Classes Data Retrieval Times Matrix

Please review this illustration for S3 Storage Classes data retrieval times. You don't need to memorize the actual numbers, just remember that S3 Glacier Deep Archive takes the most time to retrieve data:

	S3 Standard	S3 Intelligent-Tiering*	S3 Standard-IA	S3 One Zone-IA†	S3 Glacier	S3 Glacier Deep Archive
Designed for durability	99.999999999% (11 9's)	99.999999999% (11 9's)	99.999999999% (11 9's)	99.999999999% (11 9's)	99.999999999% (11 9's)	99.999999999% (11 9's)
Designed for availability	99.99%	99.9%	99.9%	99.5%	99.99%	99.99%
Availability SLA	99.9%	99%	99%	99%	99.9%	99.9%
Availability Zones	≥3	≥3	≥3	1	≥3	≥3
Minimum capacity charge per object	N/A	N/A	128KB	128KB	40KB	40KB
Minimum storage duration charge	N/A	30 days	30 days	30 days	90 days	180 days
Retrieval fee	N/A	N/A	per GB retrieved	per GB retrieved	per GB retrieved	per GB retrieved
First byte latency	milliseconds	milliseconds	milliseconds	milliseconds	select minutes or hours	select hours
Storage type	Object	Object	Object	Object	Object	Object
Lifecycle transitions	Yes	Yes	Yes	Yes	Yes	Yes

Reference:

https://aws.amazon.com/s3/storage-classes/

Amazon Route 53

A reliable and cost-effective way to route end users to Internet applications

Chapter 18. Amazon Route 53

You will learn the following in this chapter:
- DNS
- Routing Policy
- Latency Routing Policy
- AWS Weighted Routing Policy
- AWS Simple Routing Policy
- Failover Routing Policy
- Geolocation Routing Policy
- Geoproximity Routing Policy
- Multi-Value Answer Routing Policy
- Route 53 Health Checks

Amazon Route 53 is a highly available and scalable cloud-based Domain Name System (DNS). It provides an extremely reliable and cost-effective way to route traffic to Internet applications by translating names like www.example.com into an IP address like 192.0.2.1 that computers use to connect. Let's understand some basic concepts related to Route 53 before diving into this interesting chapter.

DNS (Domain Name System)

DNS (or Domain Name System) is the protocol that maps human-friendly URLs into machine IP addresses. In other words, if, for example, you enter www.example.com into the browser, the DNS system is responsible for providing the machine IP address of the domain name. DNS is the backbone of the Internet.

DNS related terms

Domain Registrar: a business, e.g., Amazon Route 53, GoDaddy, that handles the reservation of domain names and the mapping of IP addresses for those domain names.

DNS Records: It is the mapping of domain names and IP addresses. For example, if you visit google.com, your device sends a DNS request to the ISP, and then ISP uses DNS records to find out the IP address of the google.com domain. There are many types of DNS records, e.g., A, CNAME, SOA, and NS.

Zone File: It contains DNS records.

Name Server: Names servers essentially make up the DNS. They contain multiple types of DNS records and translate a URL into an IP address. There are four types of name servers: Recursive (also known as Resolver) server, Root name server, TLD name server, and Authoritative server.

Top Level Domain (TLD): A domain name is hierarchical – the TLD (Top Level Domain) is the last part of the domain name, for example, .com, .edu, .in, .gov, .org.

Second Level Domain (SLD): A domain name is hierarchical – the SLD (Second Level Domain) is the second part of the domain name, for example, amazon.com, microsoft.com, etc.

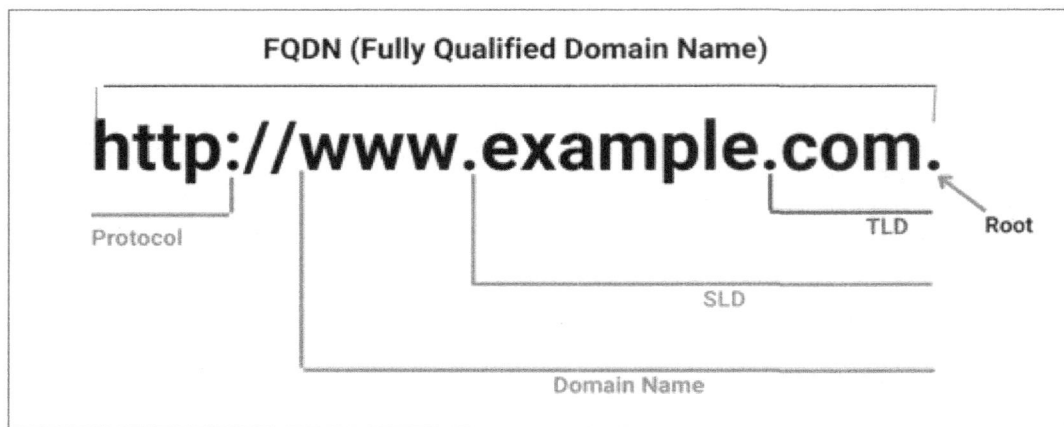

FQDN: A fully qualified domain name is written as a list of domain labels separated using the "." character. A domain name is hierarchical. The top hierarchy in an FQDN begins with TLD, e.g., .com, .edu. For instance, in the FQDN www.example.com, com, which is TLD, is directly under the root zone, example is nested under com, and finally, www is nested under example.com.

The root zone, the topmost layer of every domain name, is the DNS root zone, is expressed as an empty label and can be represented in an FQDN with a trailing "." (dot), such as www.example.com..

If you enter trailing "." in the browser, the browser will ignore it. A trailing dot is generally implied in FQDN and often omitted by most applications.

How DNS works?
You enter a human-friendly domain (for example, example.com) of a website into the browser address bar. If the IP address for this domain (for example, 93.184.216.34) is not cached in the local machine, the machine sends a DNS request to the local DNS Server. This local DNS server could be your company's or ISP's DNS server. If the IP address is found in the cache of the local DNS server, it is sent to your machine, and your browser can directly communicate to the example.com website.

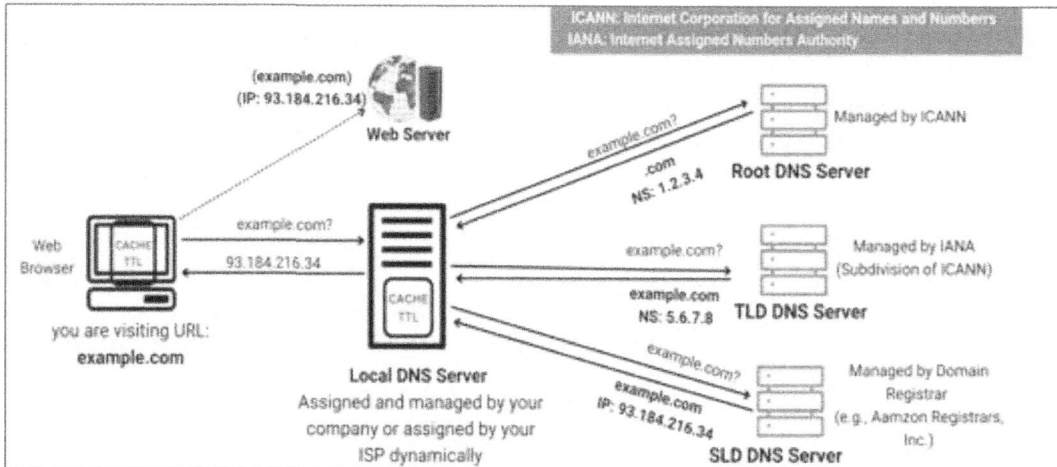

If the IP address of example.com is not found in the cache of the local DNS server, the local DNS server first sends a request to the Root DNS server to locate the TLD DNS server (".com"). Then sends a DNS request to this TLD DNS server to find the SLD DNS server of example.com. Then sends a DNS request to the SLD DNS server to find the IP address of example.com. Finally, this IP address is sent to your machine, and your browser can directly communicate with the example.com website.

Domain Registrar vs. DNS Service

You buy or register your domain name (for example, example.com) from a domain registrar, typicallypaying an annual charge. When purchasing the domain name, you will also be typically provided with various renewable options. Some well-known examples of domain registrars are GoDaddy and Amazon Registrar Inc.

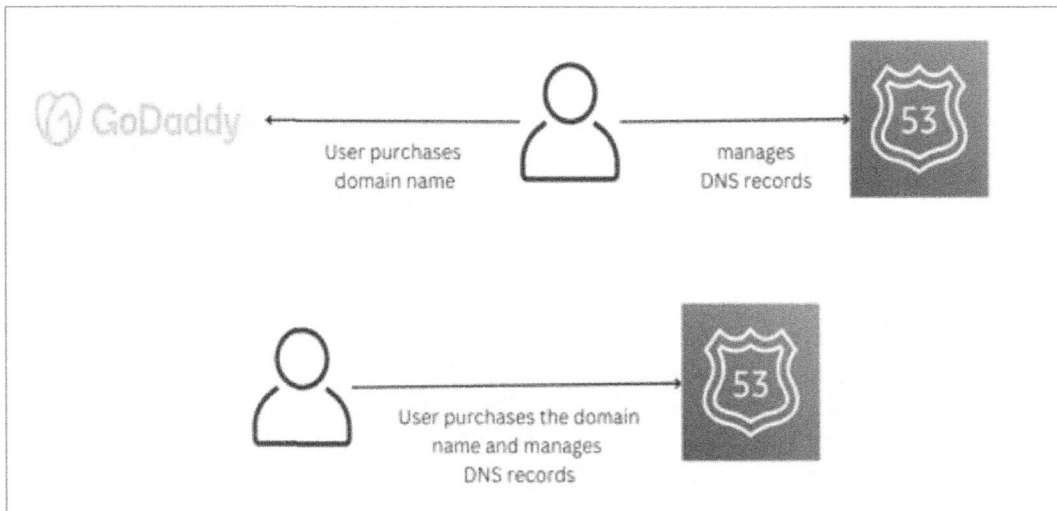

The domain registrar usually provides you DNS service to manage your DNS records. However, you are free to use another service to manage your DNS records. For example, you can use a domain name from GoDaddy and use Route 53 to manage your DNS records.

3rd Party Registrar and Amazon Route 53 DNS Provider

As discussed above, you can buy a domain name from a 3rd party and use Route 53 as the DNS service provider. To use your purchased domain from the 3rd party in Route 53, you create a Hosted Zone in Route 53 and update NS records on the 3rd party website with Route 53 Name Servers.

Nonetheless, generally, it is convenient to purchase the domain name and manage the DNS records from the same provider; for example, purchase a domain from Amazon Registrar and manage DNS records on Route 53.

The key point is that domain registrar and DNS Service are two different concepts. Every domain registrar usually provides some DNS features.

Route53 Introduction

You may be curious why it is named: Route 53 – "53" is the traditional DNS port number.

Amazon Route53 is a highly available, scalable, fully managed, and Authoritative DNS. The Authoritative DNS implies that the customer (you) can update the DNS records. Route 53 is also a Domain Registrar and allows you to check your resources' health.

Route 53 is the only AWS service that provides 100% SLA.

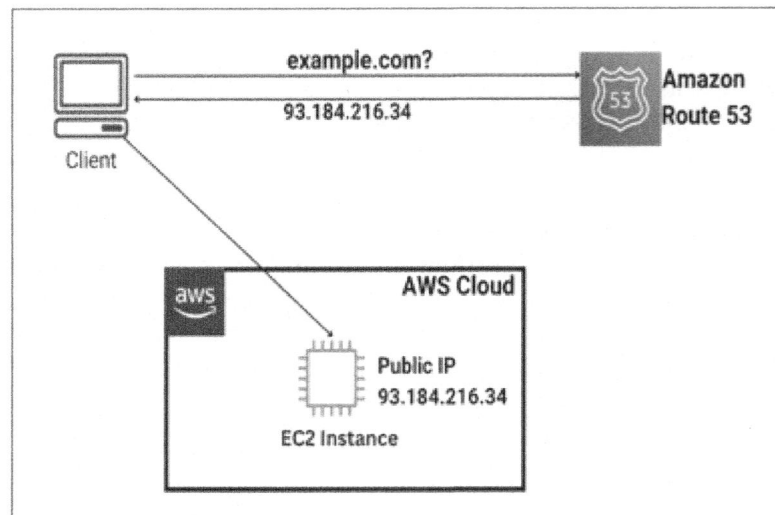

Route 53 Record

Each Route 53 record contains the followings:
- Domain/Subdomain name, for example, example.com
- RecordType, for example, A or AAAA
- Value, for example, 93.184.216.34
- Routing Policy: it decides how Route 53 responds to queries
- TTL: the amount of time the DNS record is cached at the DNS resolvers

Route 53 supports the following DNS records types:
- A, CNAME, NS, MX, SOA, TXT (common ones)
- SPF, SRV, CAA, DS, NAPTR, PTR, AAAA

Route 53 Record Types

Let's go through some common record types:

A – maps a hostname to an IPv4 address

AAAA – maps a hostname to an IPv6 address

CNAME – It is a canonical name (CNAME) record. It is merely an alias or nickname of a primary host that a host is known by -- it is not its real name. For instance, if you have a domain name like example.com but want your users to access the site using its 'www' part (www.example.com), you can create a CNAME record pointing to example.com.

You can't create a CNAME record for the top node of a DNS namespace. So, you can't create for example.com, but you can create www.example.com.

What are the use cases of CNAME records? First, you can use a CNAME record to redirect multiple domains to a single IP address. For example, if you are migrating from example.com to example.net, you can use CNAME to record to redirect your users to the new domain name(example.net). You can also use CNAME records to map several sub-domains (e.g., crm.example.com, store.example.com) to the main domain name (example.com) if you have many websites running on the same machine.

NS -- Name Servers for Hosted Zone. A Name Server is a part of DNS that contains records that point a domain name to a certain server. For example, ns-216.awsdns-27.com is one of Route 53 name servers (NS).

MX -- Mail Exchange (MX) record directs email to a mail server. An MX record indicates how email messages should be routed for SMTP. Like CNAME records, an MX record must always point to another domain.

Route 53 Hosted Zones

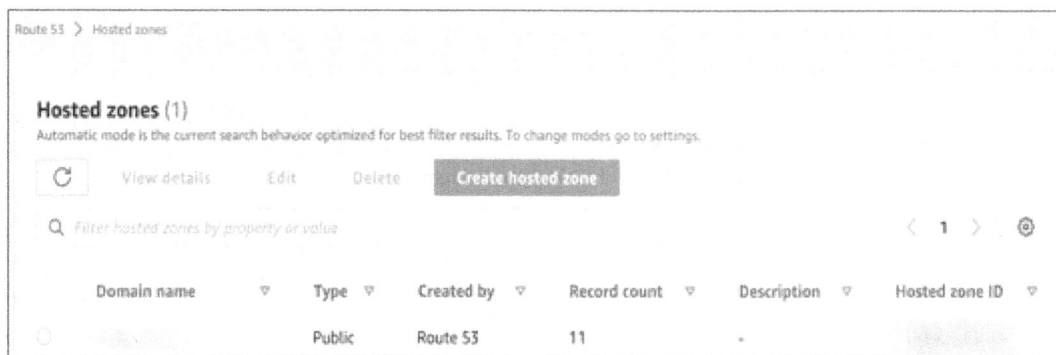

A Host Zone is a container for records, e.g., A, CNAME, MX records, that define how to route traffic to a domain and its subdomains. There are public-hosted zones and private-hosted zones.

Public Hosted Zone

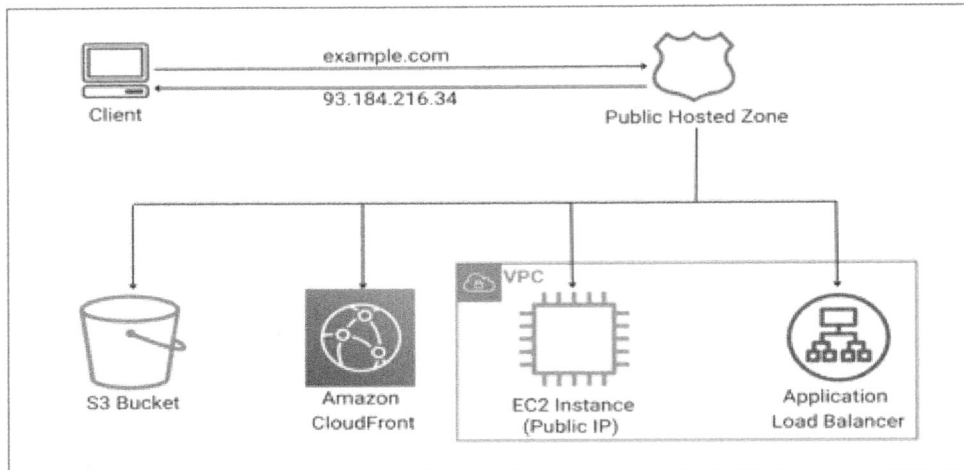

A Public Hosted Zone contains records specifying how to route traffic on the Internet. As the name says, Public Hosted Zones are used for public domain names.

Private Hosted Zone

A Private Hosted Zone contains records specifying how to route traffic within one or move VPC. As the name says, Private Hosted Zones are used for private domain names. You create a hosted zone for a domain, for example, example.com, and then create records to let Amazon Route 53 know how you want traffic to be routed for that domain within and among your VPCs. For each VPC you want to associate with a Route 53 Private Hosted Zone, change the "enableDnsHostnames" and "enableDnsSupport" VPC settings to true.

On the pricing front, you pay $0.50 per hosted zone/month for the first 25 hosted zones.

Route 53 – TTL (Time to Live) for Records

Time to Live is the idea from the caching concept – to avoid going to the source each time -- instead read from the cache, thus improving response time by reducing latency and fetch. However, to avoid reading stale data, it is also important to invalidate the cache and get the latest from the original true source. TTL is the duration after which the record is invalidated, and the latest value is fetched.

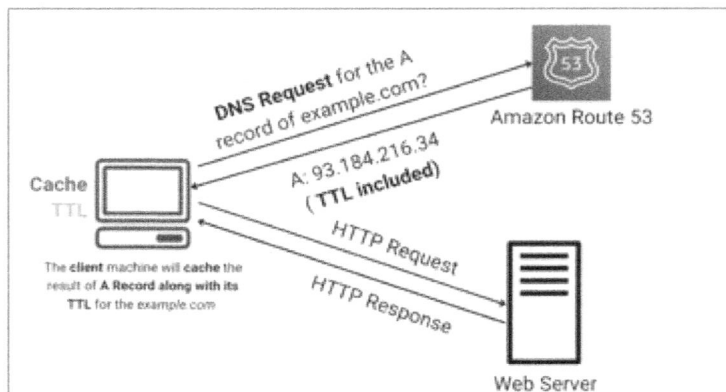

Though Route 53 provides a default value for records, you can provide your own depending on your use case. Keeping high TTL, for example, 24 hours, would help receive traffic on Route 53, but there would be the possibility of outdated records. Keeping low TTL, for example, 60 seconds, would lead to more traffic to Route 53 but less possibility of reading the outdated record.

Except for an alias record, TTL is mandatory for each DNS record.

CNAME vs. Alias

Another important concept to understand about Route 53 is the difference between CNAME and an alias. Many AWS resources, e.g., Load Balancer, CloudFront, etc., expose their hostname on the AWS platform. For example, let's say you have an ELB with hostname lbI-5432.us-east-1.elb.amazonaws.com, and you would like to access this ELB using, say, with the domain name app. example.com. So you can set up a CNAME record for the domain name app. example.com in your hosted zone that will point to the elastic load balancer's hostname.

An important point to remember about a CNAME record is that it points a hostname (api.example.com) to another hostname (api-v1.example.com). And CNAME is used only for non-root domains. In other words, you cannot create a CNAME record, for example, which would map example.com to api.example.com.

An "alias" record points a hostname to an **AWS Resource; for** example, api.example.com points to api-v1.example.com. Another example would be pointing a domain to an S3 bucket (static S3 website). It can be used both for root and non-root domains. It is free of charge, and it provides native health checks.

The diagram shows how a DNS record points to a static website hosted on an S3 bucket. Notice that this is an A record with an alias enabled. With "alias" enabled, A record type points to an AWS resource.

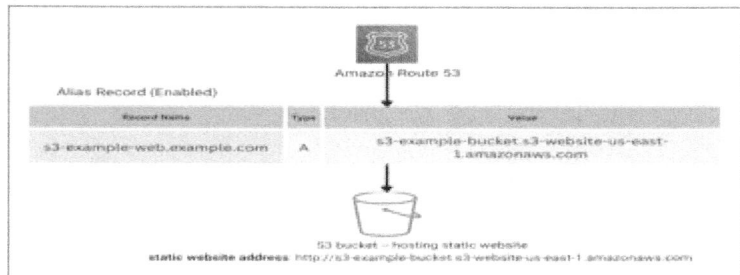

Unlike CNAME, it can be used for the top node (hostname). For example, example.com can point to an AWS resource by creating an A record with an alias. Alias record is always of type A(IPv4) or AAAA(IPv6) for AWS resources.

You can't set TTL with a record having an alias enabled.

The following are the AWS resource types that can be used as an Alias target: S3 static websites, Elastic Load Balancers, CloudFront Distributions, API Gateway, Elastic Beanstalk, Route 53 record (in the same hosted zone), VPC Interface Endpoints, and Global Accelerator accelerator.

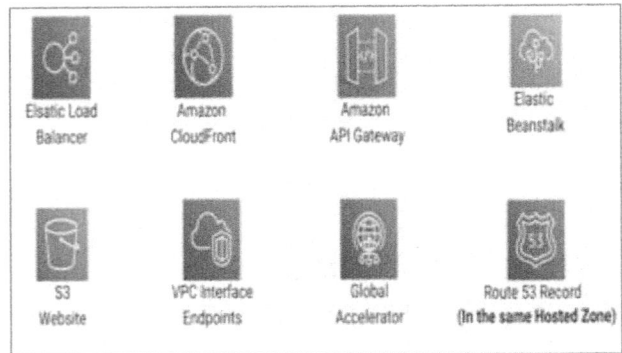

Routing Policy

Route 53 Routing Policy defines how Route 53 responds to DNS queries. The one thing to note is that the term "routing" in "routing policy" is not the same as in Load Balancer routing, which routes the traffic. This routing is about responding to DNS queries – not about routing traffic.

Route 53 supports the following Routing Policies: Simple, Weighted, Failover, Latency, Geolocation, Multi-Value Answer, and Geoproximity.

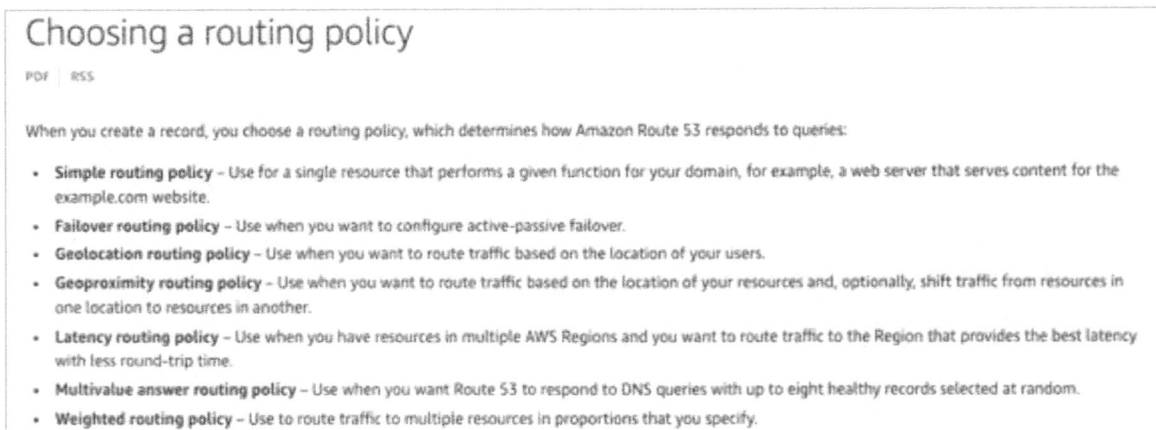

Screenshot from:
https://docs.aws.amazon.com/Route53/latest/DeveloperGuide/routing-policy.html

Simple Routing Policy

Route 53 Simple Routing Policy is the most basic routing policy. With Route 53 Simple Routing, you typically route traffic to a single resource, for example, to a web server for your website. It is defined as using an A record to resolve a single resource without specific rules. In other words, Route 53 Simple Routing lets you configure standard DNS records with no particular Route 53 routing, such as weighted or latency.

A Simple Routing Policy is typically used to route to a single resource.

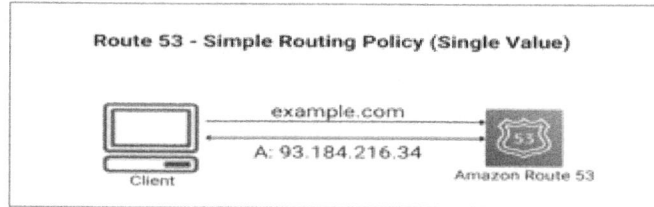
Route 53 - Simple Routing Policy (Single Value)

example.com
A: 93.184.216.34
Client
Amazon Route 53

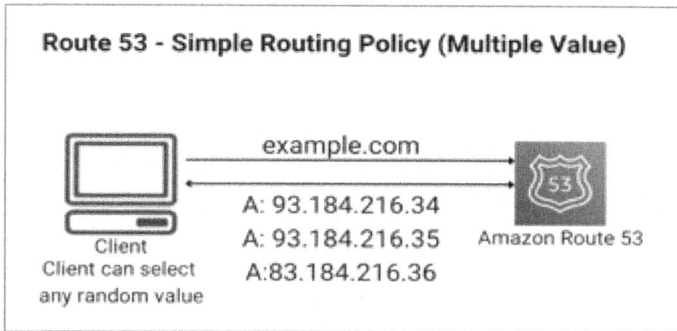
Route 53 - Simple Routing Policy (Multiple Value)

example.com
A: 93.184.216.34
A: 93.184.216.35
A:83.184.216.36
Client
Client can select
any random value
Amazon Route 53

You can specify multiple values in the same record. If multiple values are returned, a random one is selected by the client.

When Alias is enabled, you need to specify only a single AWS Resource. Health checks are not performed when using the Simple Routing Policy.

Weighted Routing Policy

The Route 53 Weight Routing Policy is used to route traffic to multiple resources in the proportions that you specify. The policy controls what percentage of requests go to each specific resource. You assign each record a relative weight – the sum of weight doesn't need to be 100.

The Weighted Routing Policy lets you associate multiple resources with a single domain name (example.com) or subdomain name (acme.example.com) and choose how much traffic is routed to each resource.

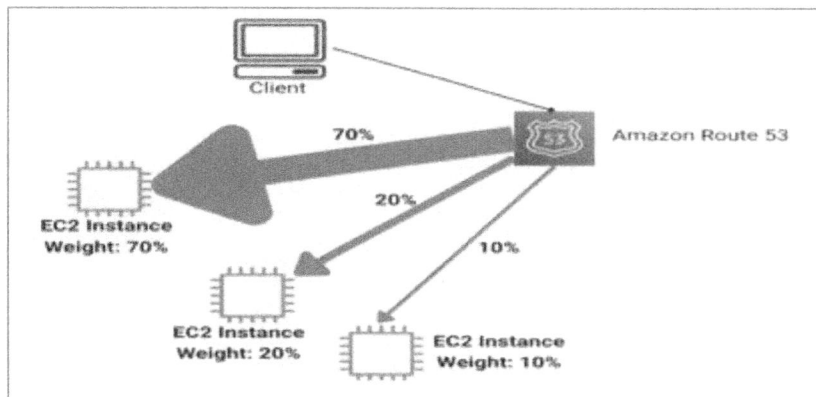
Client
70%
20%
10%
Amazon Route 53
EC2 Instance Weight: 70%
EC2 Instance Weight: 20%
EC2 Instance Weight: 10%

Weight for a specific record

Percentage of total Traffic = --

Sum of all weights for all records

If you would like to stop sending traffic to a resource – assign a weight of 0. One interesting point to remember is that if each record is assigned a weight of 0, each associated resource will get equal distribution of the total traffic.

Each DNS record entry in the Hosted Zone must have the same name and type, and each record can be associated with a health check.

The typical use cases of a Weighted Routing Policy are load balancing between AWS Regions and testing new application versions (A/B testing).

Latency-Based Routing Policy

Use the Latency Routing policy when you would like to get the best latency with less round-trip time with resources in multiple AWS Regions. This routing policy is very helpful when you need to minimize the effect of latency to improve the overall performance of users.

Suppose your application is hosted in multiple AWS Regions. In that case, you can use a latency routing policy to improve your users' performance. The latency routing policy serves the AWS Region requests with the lowest latency. To use latency-based routing, you create latency records for your resources in multiple AWS Regions.

When Route 53 receives a DNS query for your domain or subdomain (example.com or acme.example.com), it determines which AWS Regions you've created latency records. Next, the routing policy determines which AWS Region gives the user the lowest latency. And then, it selects a latency record for that Region. Finally, Route 53 responds with the value from the selected record, such as the IP address for a web server.

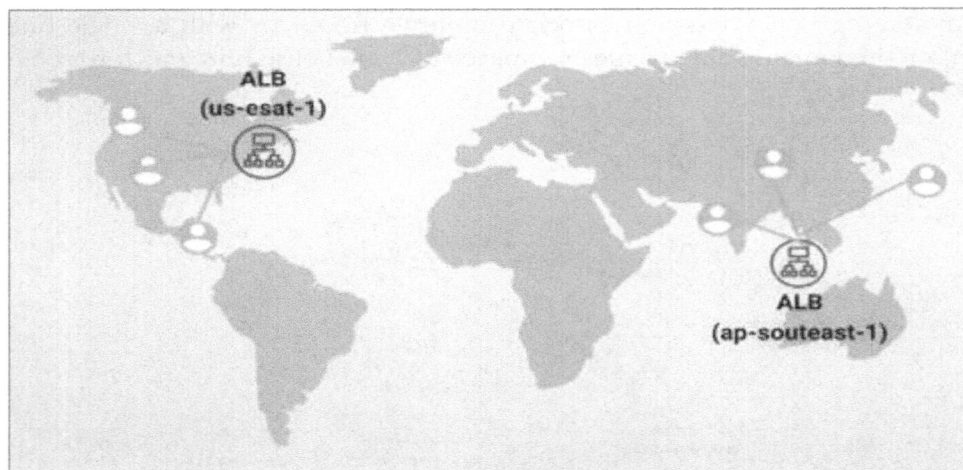

As you can notice from the diagram, the Latency-based Routing Policy redirects to the resource with the least latency from the user. Latency is based on the traffic between users and AWS Regions. Users are directed to the resource in the AWS Region that provides the least latency with respect to the resource they are trying to connect. Records can be associated with Health Checks, and the policy provides failover capability.

Failover (Active-Passive) Routing Policy

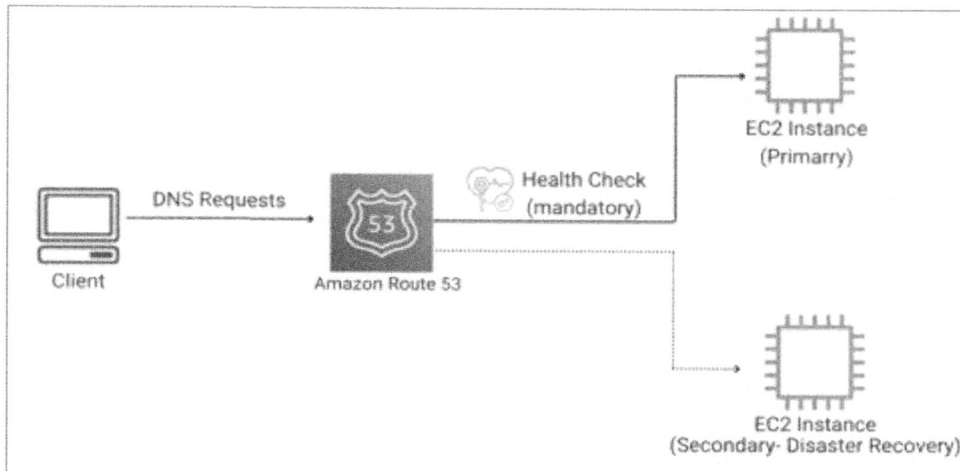

Failover Routing lets you route traffic based on if the resource is healthy or not. It lets you route traffic to a resource when the resource is healthy or to a different resource when the resource is unhealthy. This routing policy is used when you want to configure active-passive failover.

Geolocation Routing Policy

The first important point is that Geolocation Routing Policy differs from the Latency-based Routing Policy – this routing policy is based on user location. In other words, since Route 53 is a DNS service, the Geolocation Routing Policy enables Route 53 to respond to DNS queries based on the user's geographic location.

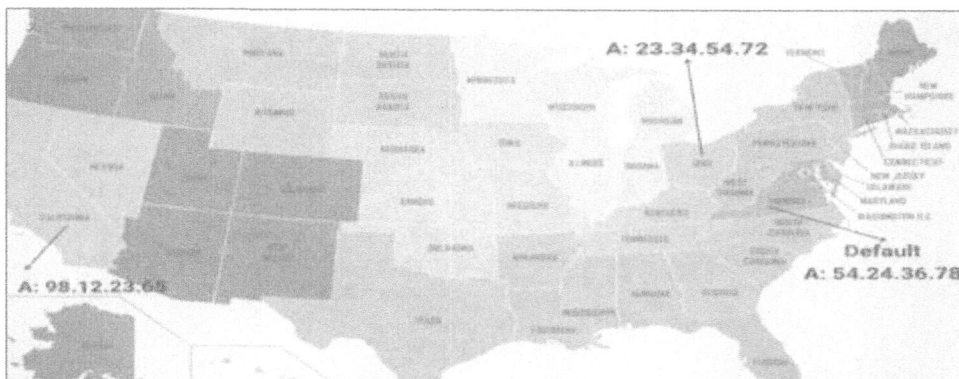

When configuring, we specify user geographic location by Continent, Country, or US State. If there is any overlap, the most precise location is considered. You also should create a "Default" record to handle a use case when there is no match on location.

As you can notice in the above diagram, users from California state and Ohio have been assigned an A record. There is a default A record that is in the Virginia location – which means users who are not assigned based on the geolocation policy in either California or Ohio will be assigned the default record.

Geolocation Routing Policy can be associated with Health Checks.

You can use Route 53 Geolocation Routing Policy to localize content and present some or all of the website in the user's language. You can also use Route 53 Geolocation Routing Policy to restrict content distribution to the locations based on the distribution rights.

Geoproximity Routing Policy

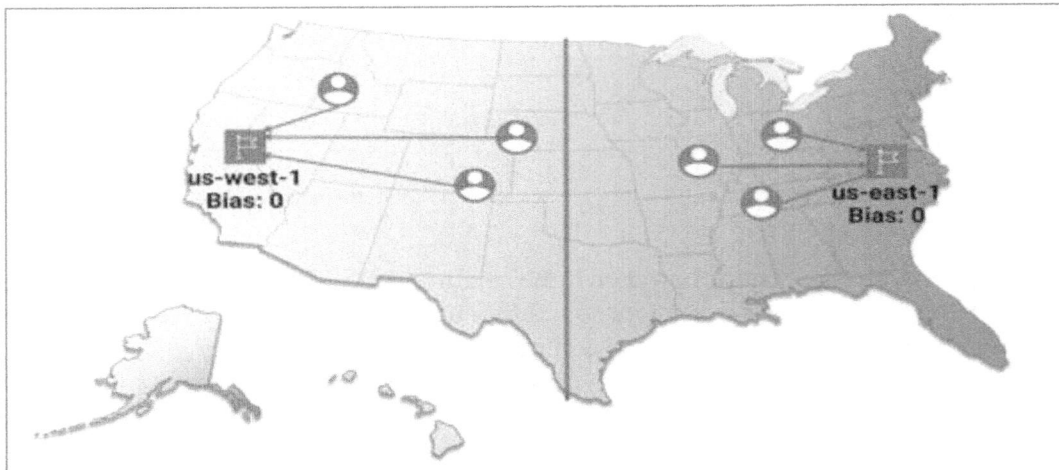

Geoproximity Routing Policy routes traffic to your resources based on the geographic location of users and resources. This policy has the ability to shift more traffic to resources based on the defined bias.

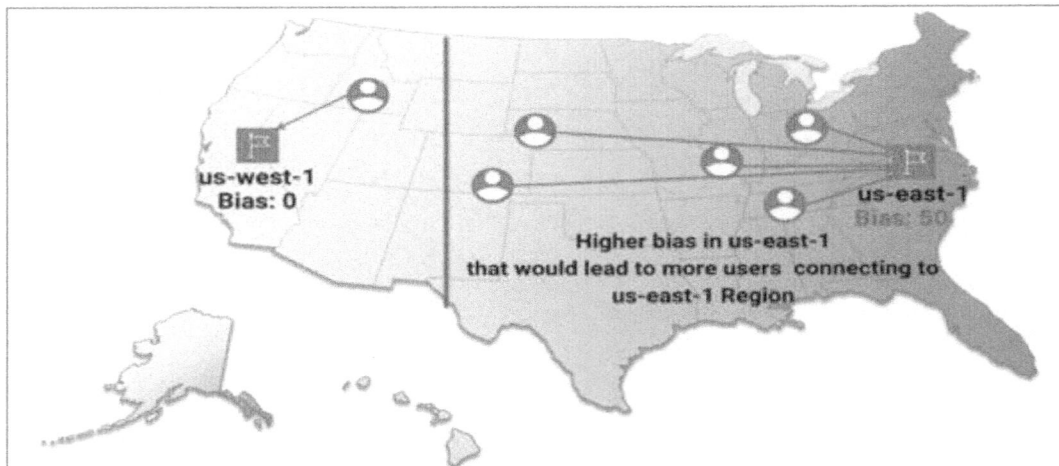

To change the size of a geographic region, specify bias values. To expand – more traffic to the resource – specify a value between 1 to 11. To shrink – means less traffic to the resource – specify a value between -1 to -99.

Resources can be AWS resources -- you need to specify AWS Region. And resources can be non-AWS as well -- you need to specify Latitude and Longitude.

You need to use Route 53 Traffic Flow to use this feature.

Multi-Value Answer Routing Policy

Multi-value Answer Routing Policy is used when routing traffic to multiple resources. Records can be associated with Health Checks – which return values only for healthy resources. For each Multi-Value query, up to 8 healthy records are returned. Please note that Multi-Value is not a substitute for having an ELB. (Ref: https://docs.aws.amazon.com/Route53/latest/DeveloperGuide/routing-policy-multivalue.html)

Name	Type	Value	TTL	Set ID
www.example.com	A record	192.168.23.34	60	Web Set 1
www.example.com	A record	198.78.101.4	60	Web Set 2
www.example.com	A record	204.10.112.5	60	Web Set 3

Route 53 Health Checks

Amazon Route 53 health checks monitor the health of your resources as web applications or other AWS resources. Additionally, you can configure (optionally) CloudWatch alarms so that you receive notifications when a resource becomes unavailable based on how you configured the metrics for the health checks.

In simple words, Route 53 Health checks enable requests not to be directed to a resource having issues processing user requests, for example, if the resource is down. HTTP Health Checks are only for public resources. Health checks are integrated with CloudWatch metrics.

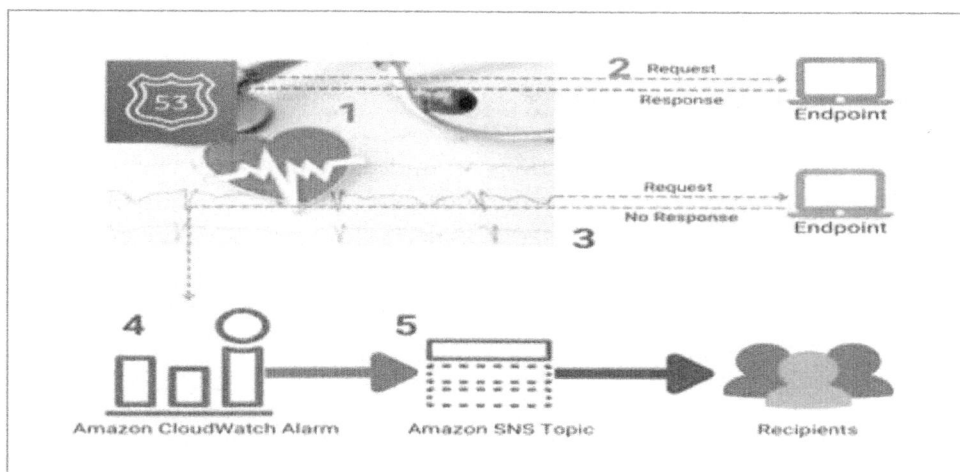

The above diagram is an overview of how health checking works if you want to be notified when a resource becomes unavailable.

You specify a health check to define how you want it to work, such as the IP address or domain name of the endpoint, protocol (HTTP, HTTPS, or TCP), the request interval you want Route 53 to send a health check request to an endpoint, how many times in a row requests fail to consider the resource unhealthy (failure threshold). Optionally, specify how you want to be notified if the endpoint is unhealthy. When you configure a notification, Route 53 sets up CloudWatch alarms. CloudWatch uses SNS topics to send notifications.

Types of Route 53 Health Checks
Health checks enable automated DNS Failover. There are four types of Route 53 Health checks: Health checks that monitor an endpoint, Health checks that monitor other health checks (calculated health checks), Health checks that monitor CloudWatch alarms, and Amazon Route 53 Application Recovery Controller.

With regards to Health checks that monitor an endpoint, you can monitor the endpoint for applications, servers, and other AWS resources by specifying either an IP address or the domain name. Then, based on the health check interval you specify, Route 53 sends requests to your application, server, or other AWS resources to ensure that the endpoint is reachable, available, and functional.

For calculated health checks, you can create a health check of health checks whether Route 53 considers other checks healthy or not. One of the use cases of this type of health check is when you have multiple resources performing similar functions, for example, the same web application deployed on many EC2 instances. And your primary concern is ensuring that the minimum number of instances is healthy. You create a health check for each resource and then create health checks that monitor the status of the other health checks and notify only when the number of resources drops below a specified threshold.

The other type of Health check is monitoring CloudWatch alarms. You can create CloudWatch alarms that monitor the CW (CloudWatch) metrics, for example, the number of throttled read events for DynamoDB or RDS alarms.

With regards to Amazon Route 53 Application Recovery Controller, it provides insights into if your applications and resources are ready for recovery and then helps you manage and coordinate failover.

How Route 53 determines the status of health checks that monitor an Endpoint

Route 53 has health checkers in various locations around the world. You choose the location of the health checkers you want Route 53 to use to monitor the health of the endpoint. You also need to specify the internal health check-- every 10 seconds (leads to higher cost) or every 30 seconds. The point is that health checkers don't coordinate with one another as they are in different data centers. There could be the possibility that you see several requests per second regardless of the interval you choose.

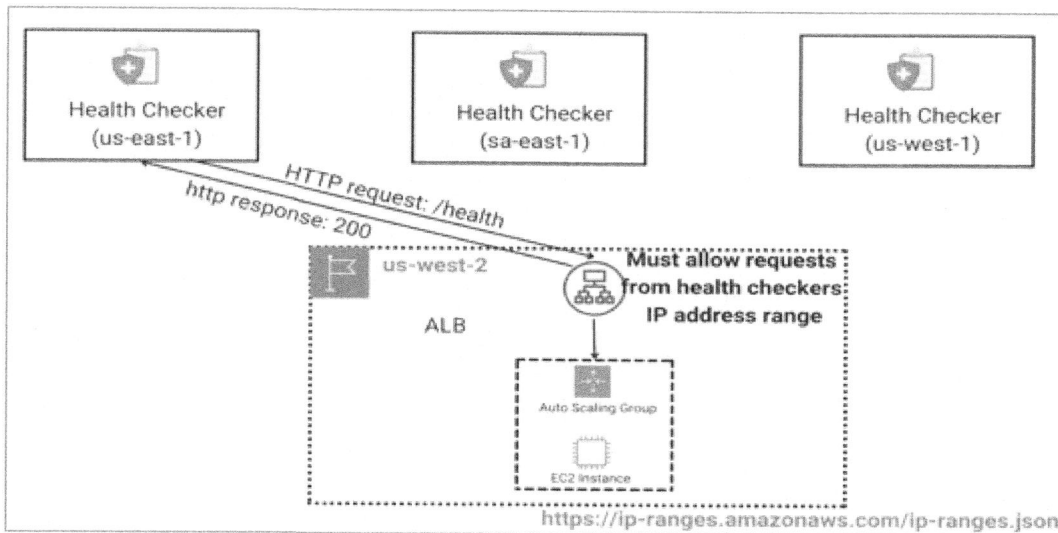

Each health checker evaluates the health of each endpoint based on two values: response time(can be slow or fail to respond) and whether the endpoint responds to the number of consecutive health checks that you specify. The response time used by an individual health checker to find out if an endpoint is healthy depends on the type of health check.

If more than 18% of health checkers report the endpoint is healthy, Route 53 considers the endpoint healthy; otherwise, the endpoint is considered unhealthy.

Health checks pass only when the endpoint responds with the 2xx and 3xx status codes. Health checks can be set up to pass or fail based on the text in the first 5120 bytes of the response.

You also need to configure your router/firewall to allow incoming health check requests from the Route 53 Health Checkers.

How Route 53 determines the status of health checks that monitor other health checks (calculated health checks)

A health checker can perform monitoring the status of other health checks; this type of check is called a calculated health check. In this type of health check, two terms are used: *parent health check* and *child health check*. The health check that does monitoring is called a parent health check, and the health check that is monitored is called a child health check. One parent health check can monitor up to 255 child health checks. You need to specify how many child health checks must pass to make the parent pass.

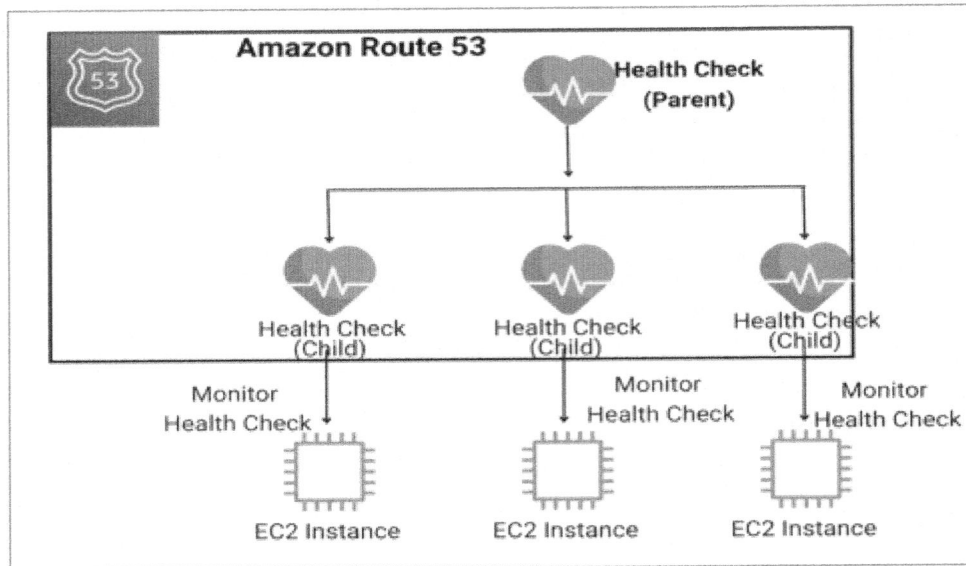

Now let's see how a calculated health check works. Route 53 sums all the child health checks that are healthy and compares with the number of specified health checks that must be healthy for the parent health check to be considered healthy.

Route 53 Health Checks of Resources in Private Hosted Zones

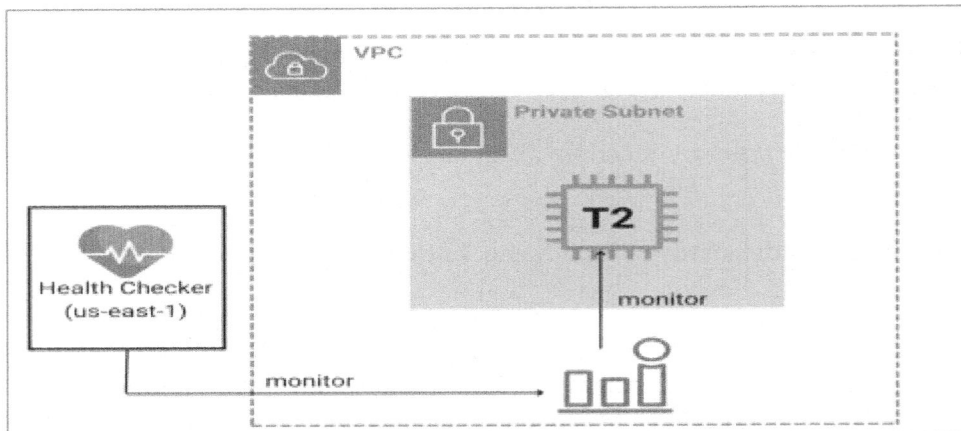

Route 53 health checkers are outside the VPC and cannot access a private endpoint, a private VPC, or an on-prem resource. To perform health checks in this scenario, you can create a CloudWatch metric and associate a health check that checks the alarm itself.

References:
https://aws.amazon.com/route53/pricing/

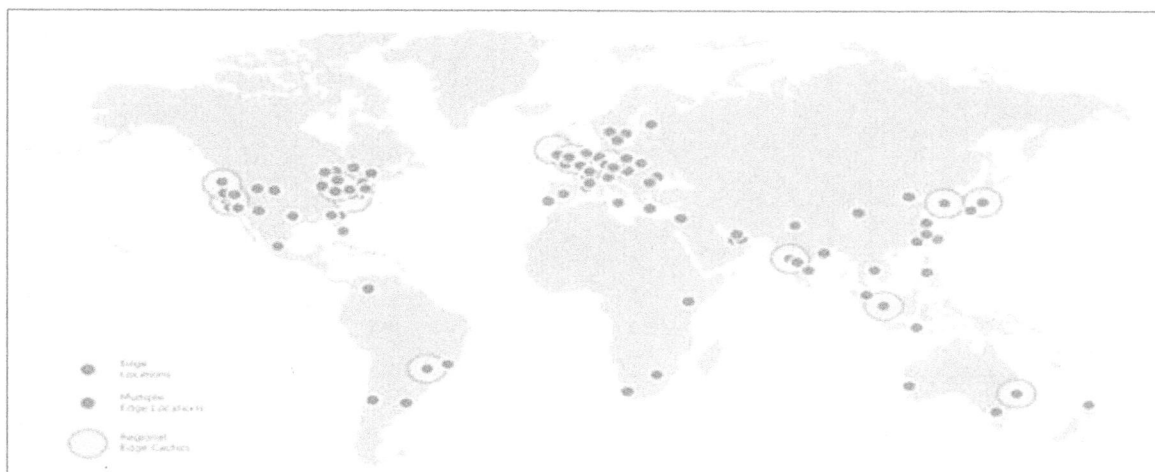

Chapter 19. AWS Global Cloud Infrastructure (Part II)

You will learn the following in this chapter:
- Amazon CloudFront
- CloudFront Origins
- CloudFront Geo Restriction
- CloudFront – Cache Invalidations
- Amazon CloudFront with Route 53
- Global Accelerator
- Amazon S3 Transfer Acceleration (S3TA)

Amazon CloudFront

Most of the services that AWS offers are Region specific. But few services, by definition, need to be in a global scope because of the underlying service they offer. AWS IAM, Amazon CloudFront, Route 53 and WAF are some of the global services.

Amazon CloudFront is a fast content delivery network (CDN) service that securely delivers data, videos, applications, and APIs to customers globally with low latency, high transfer speeds, all within a developer-friendly environment.

You can use Amazon CloudFront to improve the performance of your website. CloudFront makes your website files (such as HTML, images, and video) available from Point-of-Presence locations around the world. There are 216 Point-of-Presence locations (data centers) globally – called Edge Locations.

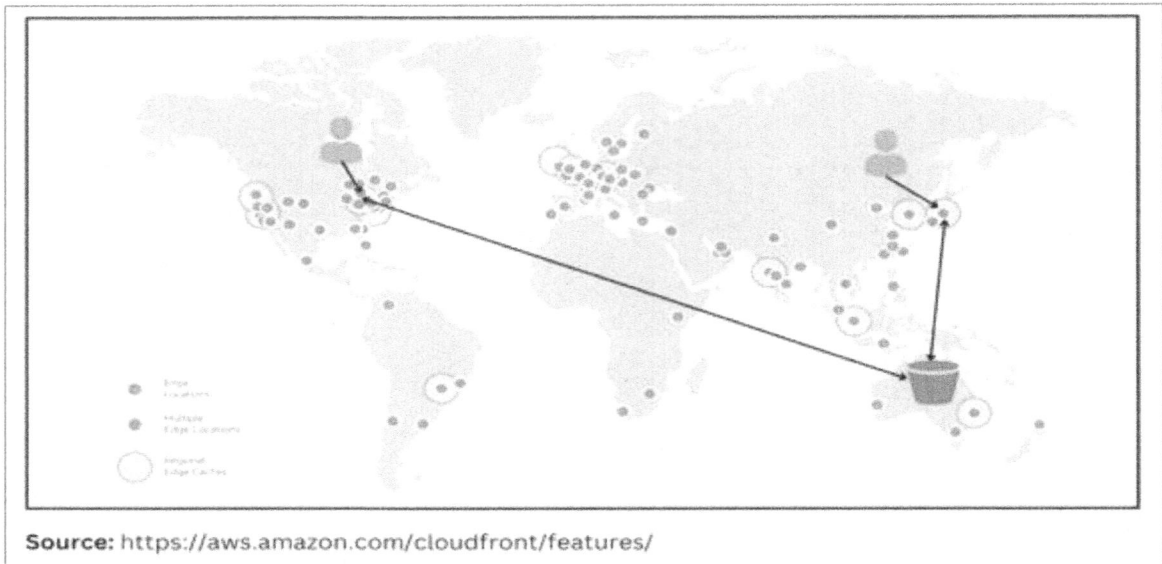

Source: https://aws.amazon.com/cloudfront/features/

When a visitor requests a file from your website, CloudFront automatically redirects the request to a copy of the file at the nearest edge location. This results in faster download times than if the visitor had requested the content from a data center that is located farther away.

It provides DDoS protection, integration with Shield, AWS Application Firewall. It can expose external HTTPS and can talk to internal HTTPS backend.

CloudFront at High Level

When a visitor requests a file from S3 or a custom origin (for example, a web application), CloudFront automatically redirects the request to a file copy at the nearest edge location. If the result is already cached, it is served from the cache.

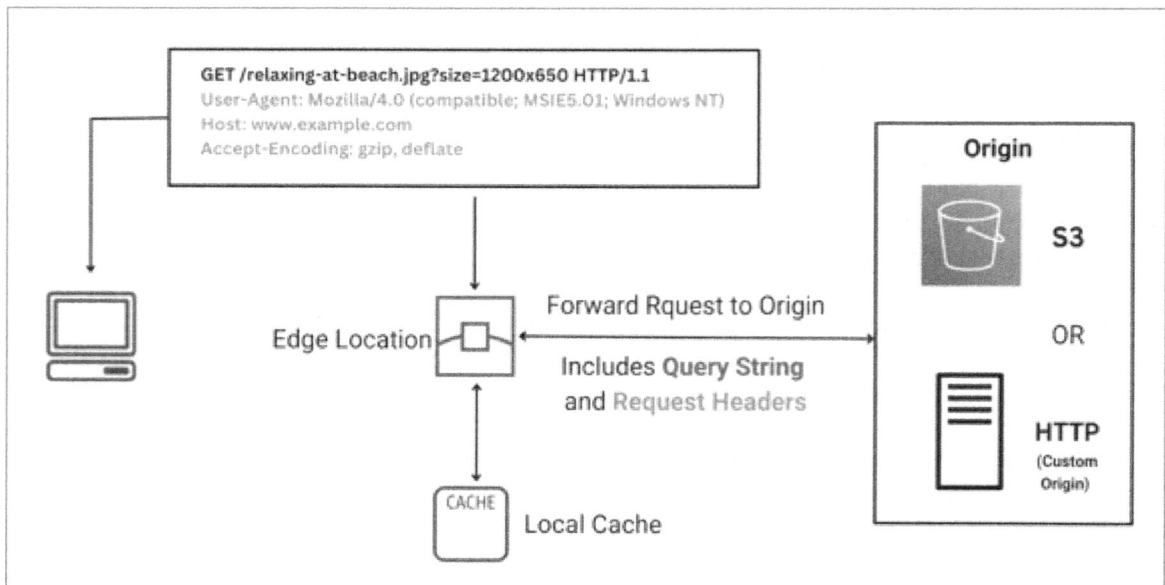

Otherwise, CloudFront forwards the request to Origin, which includes query strings and request headers. The result is also cached, so the next time the result is returned from the cache. The CloudFront caching at the edge location improves the retrieval performance compared to if the visitor had requested the content from a data center farther away.

CloudFront Origins

CloudFront origin is the location where content is stored and from which CloudFront gets content to provide to its viewers when requested.

S3 Bucket as CloudFront Origin

We can use S3 Bucket as CloudFront origin for distributing files and caching them at the edge locations.

We can provide enhanced security with CloudFront Origin Access Identity (OAI). The OAI is the primary way to make CloudFront access private content stored in S3. Without it, CloudFront is like an anonymous user, it only has access to content everybody else has access to.

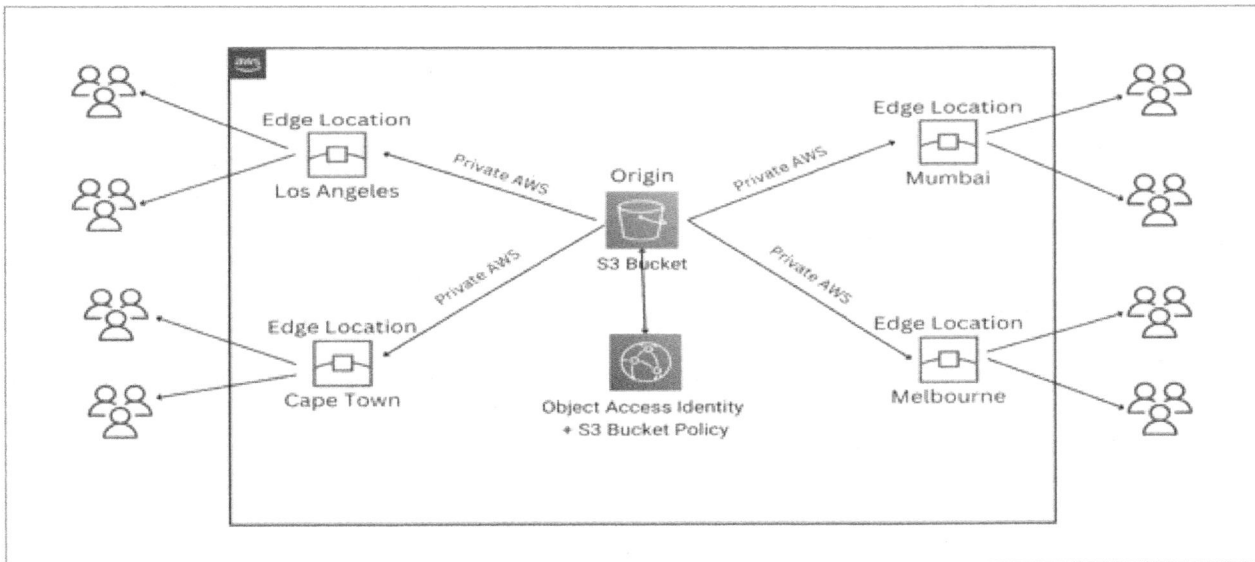

CloudFront can be used as an ingress to upload files to S3.

To specify an origin, use S3OriginConfig to specify an Amazon S3 bucket that is not configured with static website hosting.

Custom Origin (HTTP) as CloudFront Origin

A web server running on an EC2 instance can be a Custom Origin for CloudFront, also an Application Load Balancer. An Amazon S3 origin configured as a website endpoint is also considered a custom origin.

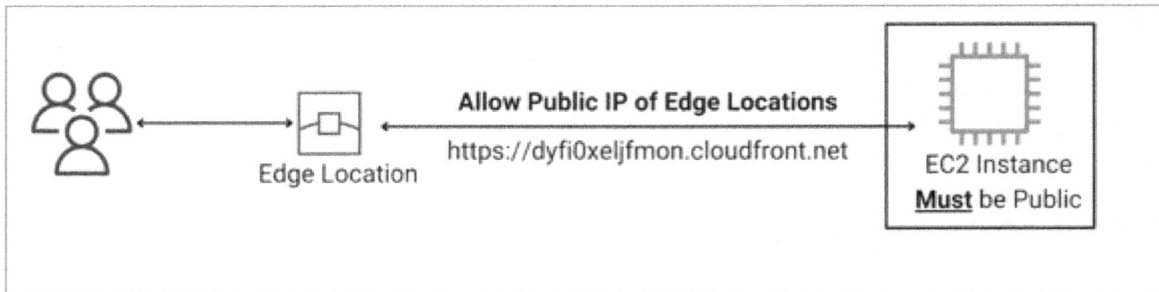

In the diagram above, the web application running on an EC2 instance is a custom origin for the CloudFront distribution. The instance must be public – accessible from WWW over HTTP.

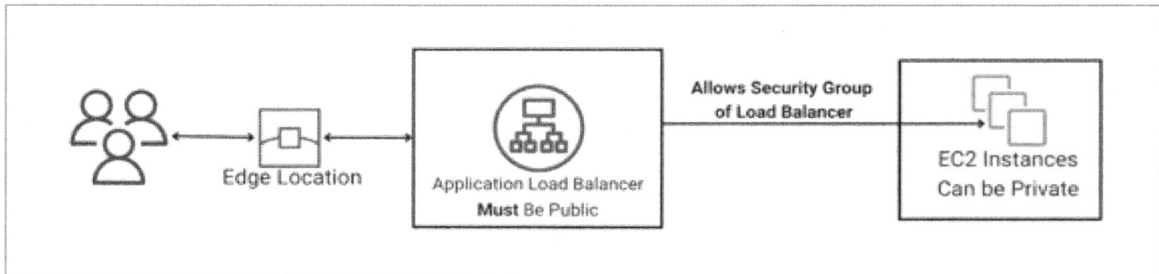

In the diagram above, Application Load Balancer is the origin of the CloudFront distribution.

The important point to note is that the custom origin must support the HTTP protocol.

CloudFront Geo Restriction

You can provide restrictions using CloudFront based on Geo location. In other words, you can restrict who can access your distribution.

You can allow your users to access your content only if they are in one of the countries on a list of approved countries (Whitelist). On the same token, you can also prevent your users from accessing your content if they are in one of the countries on a blocklist of banned countries (Blacklist). The "country" is determined using a 3rd party Geo-IP database.

Regarding the use case of Geo-based content restriction, you can use it for copyright laws to control access to content based on geolocation.

Global Users for Applications

When we deploy an application for global users, users access it over the public Internet. Depending on where users are located, this can add lots of latency due to many hops.

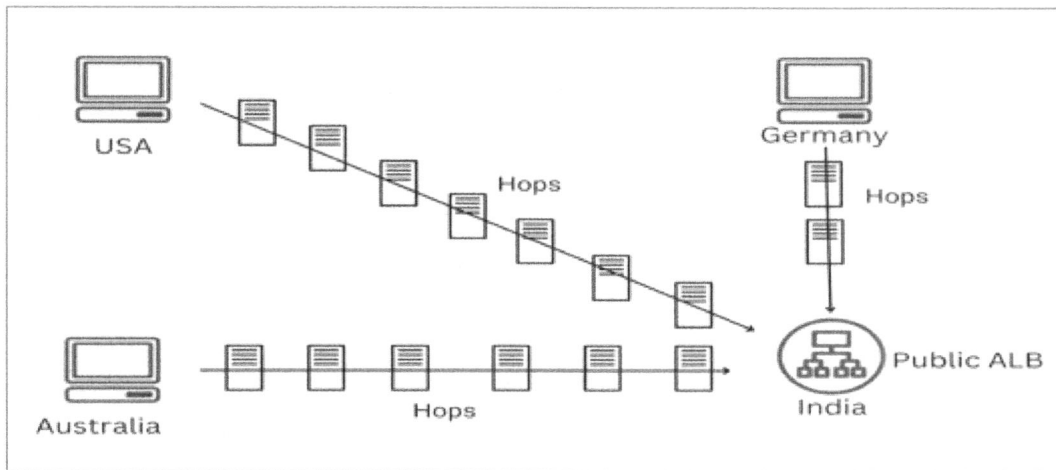

Unicast IP vs. Anycast IP

You may find these two terms in the context of networking.

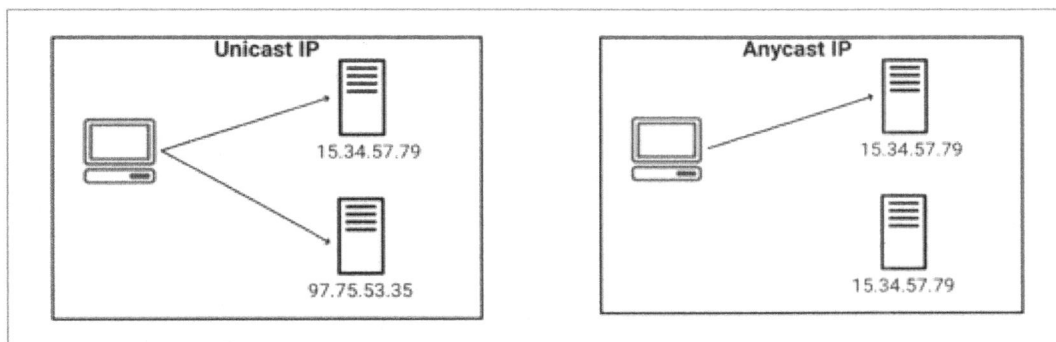

In Unicast IP, each server is assigned a unique IP address. However, in Anycast IP, all servers are assigned the same IP address, and the client is routed to the nearest one.

CloudFront vs. S3 Cross Region Replication

CloudFront is a Global Edge (Edge Locations) network. Files are cached based on TTL (Time-to-Live) – maybe a day. CloudFront is good for the use case of static content that must be available everywhere.

S3 Cross Region Replication, on the other hand, must be set up for each Region you want files to be replicated, and files are updated in near real-time. It is Read Only. It is good for dynamic content that needs to be available at low latency in a few Regions.

CloudFront Pricing

CloudFront Edge locations are worldwide, and the cost of data out per edge location varies. You can reduce the number of edge locations for cost reductions.

There are three price classes:
1. Price Class ALL: all regions – best performance
2. Price Class 200: most regions, but excludes the most expensive regions

3. Price Class 100: only the least expensive regions

	North America (United States, Mexico, Canada)	Europe and Israel	South Africa, Kenya, and the Middle East	South America	Japan	Australia and New Zealand	Hong Kong, Indonesia, the Philippines, Singapore, South Korea, Taiwan, and Thailand	India
Price Class All	Yes	Yes	Yes	Yes	Yes	Yes	Yes	Yes
Price Class 200	Yes	Yes	Yes	No	Yes	No	Yes	Yes
Price Class 100	Yes	Yes	No	No	No	No	No	No

Source: https://docs.aws.amazon.com/AmazonCloudFront/latest/DeveloperGuide/PriceClass.html

CloudFront – Cache Invalidations

CloudFront caches the content at the Edge locations. If you update the back-end origin, CloudFront doesn't know about the update and will only get the refreshing content after the TTL has expired.

However, you can force a full or partial cache refresh, thus bypassing the CloudFront Cache TTL, by performing a CloudFront Invalidation. For example, you can invalidate all files (*) or a unique path (/images/*).

Amazon CloudFront with Route 53

AWS hosts CloudFront and Route 53 services on a distributed network of proxy servers in data centers throughout the world called edge locations. Using the global Amazon network of edge locations for application delivery and DNS service plays an important part in building a comprehensive defense against DDoS attacks for your dynamic web applications.

How AWS Shield, WAF, and CloudFront with Route 53 help mitigate DDoS attacks

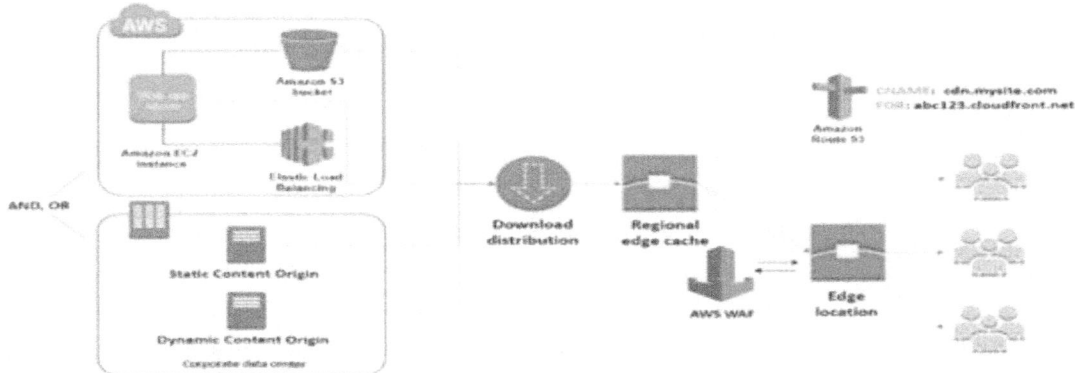

How AWS Shield, CloudFront, and Route 53 work to help protect against DDoS attacks

To help keep your dynamic web applications available when they are under DDoS attack, the steps in this post enable AWS Shield Standard by configuring your applications behind CloudFront and Route 53. AWS Shield Standard protects your resources from common, frequently occurring network and transport layer DDoS attacks. Attack traffic can be geographically isolated and absorbed using the capacity in edge locations close to the source. Additionally, you can configure geographical restrictions to help block attacks originating from specific countries.

The request-routing technology in CloudFront connects each client to the nearest edge location, as determined by continuously updated latency measurements. HTTP and HTTPS requests sent to CloudFront can be monitored, and access to your application resources can be controlled at edge locations using AWS WAF. Based on conditions that you specify in AWS WAF, such as the IP addresses that requests originate from or the values of query strings, traffic can be allowed, blocked, or allowed and counted for further investigation or remediation. The following diagram shows how static and dynamic web application content can originate from endpoint resources within AWS or your corporate data center. For more details, see How CloudFront Delivers Content and How CloudFront Works with Regional Edge Caches.

Reference:
https://aws.amazon.com/blogs/security/how-to-protect-dynamic-web-applications-against-ddos-attacks-by-using-amazon-cloudfront-and-amazon-route-53/

Global Accelerator

Suppose we have a public-facing application on AWS, for example, in a Region in Europe. We have users outside that environment who would like to connect to that application. We would like to make that experience as good as possible for those users.

AWS Global Accelerator is a network layer service that you can deploy in front of your Internet-facing applications to improve availability and performance for your globally distributed users. You deploy Global Accelerator between users on the Internet and the public-facing applications deployed and hosted on AWS. Then, the Global Accelerator allows an optimized experience for those users. In addition, it can optimize user experience both for TCP and UDP types of applications.

It leverages the AWS internal network to route the traffic to your application. 2 Anycast IPs are created for your application. The Anycast IP sends traffic directly to Edge locations. The Edge locations then send the traffic to your application.

218

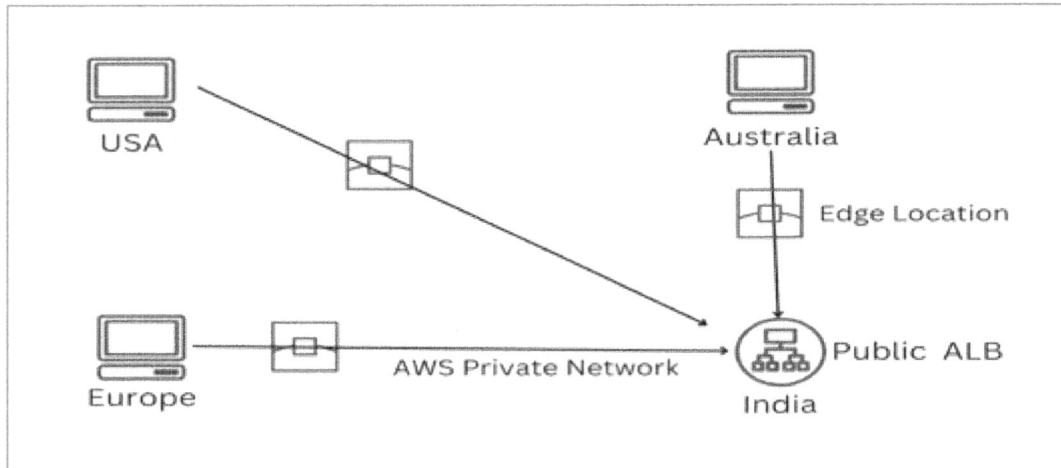

AWS Global Accelerator is a service that improves the availability and performance of your applications with local or global users. It provides static IP addresses that act as a fixed entry point to your application endpoints in a single or multiple AWS Regions, such as your Application Load Balancers, Network Load Balancers, or Amazon EC2 instances. AWS Global Accelerator uses the AWS global network to optimize the path from your users to your applications, improving the performance of your traffic by as much as 60%.

AWS Global Accelerator is a networking service that helps you improve the availability and performance of the applications that you offer to your global users. Global Accelerator improves performance for a wide range of applications over TCP or UDP by proxying packets at the edge to applications running in one or more AWS Regions. Global Accelerator is a good fit for non-HTTP use cases, such as gaming (UDP), IoT (MQTT), or Voice over IP, as well as for HTTP use cases that specifically require static IP addresses or deterministic, fast regional failover.

Like CloudFront, it uses AWS Global network and edge locations for enhanced performance. However, it's an overall performance enhancer than an upload speed accelerator. You cannot use Global Accelerator to speed up media file uploads into S3.

The question is: why does it matter?

Suppose we have web applications deployed on the AWS, and we have users worldwide who want to access the application. Since the traffic needed to travel to many networks or many hops, such as their ISPs and some other carriers, this is possibly impacted by Internet weather conditions. In other words, you don't control the end-to-end experience of that user.

When you deploy AWS Global Accelerator, you bring your remote user as close as possible to the AWS backbone. And from there, the traffic will use the uncongested managed AWS backbone to the actual service running in an AWS Region.

- Global Accelerator is a good fit for non-HTTP use cases, such as gaming (UDP), IoT (MQTT), or Voice over IP, as well as for HTTP use cases that specifically require static IP addresses or deterministic, fast regional failover.
- It provides static IP addresses that provide a fixed entry point to your applications and eliminate the complexity of managing specific IP addresses for different AWS Regions and Availability Zones.
- AWS Global Accelerator and Amazon CloudFront use the same edge locations.
- A regional ELB load balancer is an ideal target for AWS Global Accelerator. AWS Global Accelerator complements ELB by extending these capabilities beyond a single AWS Region, allowing you to provide a global interface for your applications in any number of Regions.
- AWS Global Accelerator works with Elastic IP, EC2 Instances, ALB, NLB, and public and private network
- It provides consistent performance by intelligently routing to provide the lowest latency and fast regional failover.
- There is no issue with the client cache because the IP doesn't change.
- It uses AWS internal network.
- It performs health checks of your applications.
- It helps make your application global – failover takes less than 1 minute for unhealthy instances
- Only 2 external IPs need to be whitelisted.
- It provides DDoS protection using AWS Shield.

Exam Tip:
Please review the differences between CloudFront and Global Accelerator:

Amazon S3 Transfer Acceleration (S3TA)

Amazon S3 Transfer Acceleration (S3TA) is a file transfer service over long distances between the source location and your Amazon S3 bucket. It is fast, easy, and secure. S3 Transfer Acceleration leverages Amazon CloudFront's globally distributed AWS Edge Locations. As data arrives at an AWS Edge Location, data is routed to your Amazon S3 bucket over an optimized network path.

Amazon S3 Transfer Acceleration is designed to optimize transfer speeds from across the world into S3 buckets. So if you are uploading to a centralized bucket from geographically dispersed locations, or if you regularly transfer GBs or TBs of data across continents, you may save hours or days of data transfer time with S3 Transfer Acceleration.

Benefits

Move data faster over long distances

S3TA can accelerate long-distance transfers to and from your Amazon S3 buckets. The longer the distance between your client application (mobile, web application, or upload tool) and the target S3 bucket, the more S3TA can help. And if S3TA would not accelerate a transfer, you are not charged.

Reduce network variability

For applications interacting with your S3 buckets through the S3 API from outside of your bucket's region, S3TA helps avoid the variability in Internet routing and congestion. It does this by routing your uploads and downloads over the AWS global network infrastructure, so you get the benefit of our network optimizations.

Shorten the distance to S3

S3TA shortens the distance between client applications and AWS servers that acknowledge PUTS and GETS to Amazon S3 using our global network of hundreds of CloudFront Edge Locations. We automatically route your uploads and downloads through the closest Edge Locations to your application.

Maximize bandwidth utilization

S3TA on average fully utilizes your bandwidth for transfers, and minimizes the effect of distance on throughput. This helps to ensure consistently fast performance to Amazon S3 regardless of your client's location.

Screenshot from: https://aws.amazon.com/s3/transfer-acceleration/

CloudFront vs S3 Transfer Acceleration

AWS CloudFront is for content delivery; on the other hand, S3 Transfer Acceleration is for faster transfers and higher throughput to S3 buckets -- mainly for uploads. Amazon S3 Transfer Acceleration is an S3 feature that accelerates uploads to S3 buckets using AWS Edge locations - the same Edge locations as in the AWS CloudFront service.

CloudFront vs. Global Accelerator

Both of them use the AWS Global Network and AWS Edge locations around the world, and both of them are integrated with AWS Shield for DDoS protection.

CloudFront:

CloudFront improves performance for cacheable content (such as images and videos) and dynamic content (such as API acceleration and dynamic site). The content is served from Edge locations.

Global Accelerator:

It improves performance for a wide range of applications over TCP or UDP. It is a good fit for non-HTTP use cases such as gaming (UDP), IoT (MQTT), or Voice over IP (VoIP). It is good for HTTP use cases that require static IP addresses and use cases that require deterministic, fast regional failover.

Q: How is AWS Global Accelerator different from Amazon CloudFront?

A: AWS Global Accelerator and Amazon CloudFront are separate services that use the AWS global network and its edge locations around the world. CloudFront improves performance for both cacheable content (such as images and videos) and dynamic content (such as API acceleration and dynamic site delivery). Global Accelerator improves performance for a wide range of applications over TCP or UDP by proxying packets at the edge to applications running in one or more AWS Regions. Global Accelerator is a good fit for non-HTTP use cases, such as gaming (UDP), IoT (MQTT), or Voice over IP, as well as for HTTP use cases that specifically require static IP addresses or deterministic, fast regional failover. Both services integrate with AWS Shield for DDoS protection.

Reference: https://aws.amazon.com/global-accelerator/faqs/

AWS storage services

Object, file, and block storage

Amazon Simple Storage Service (S3)

Object storage with industry-leading scalability, availability, and security for you to store and retrieve any amount of data from anywhere.

Amazon Elastic File System (EFS)

A simple, serverless, elastic, set-and-forget file system for you to share file data without managing storage.

FSx — Amazon FSx

Fully managed, cost-effective file storage offering the capabilities and performance of popular commercial and open-source file systems.

Amazon Elastic Block Store (EBS)

Easy to use, high-performance block storage service for both throughput and transaction-intensive workloads at any scale.

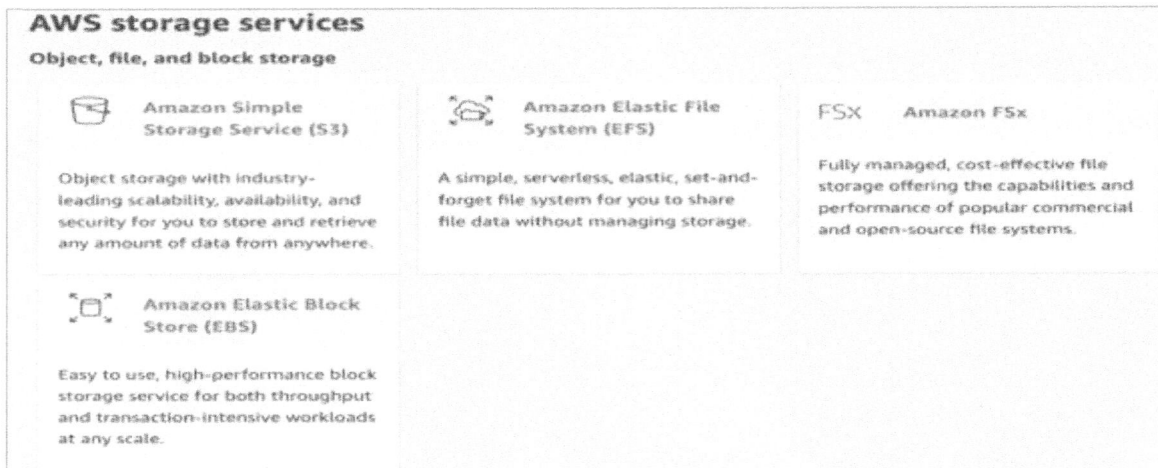

Chapter 20. Advanced Storage On AWS

You will learn the following in this chapter:
- Amazon EFS
- Amazon EBS
- Instance Store
- AWS Snow Family
- AWS OpsHub
- Amazon FSx
- AWS Storage Gateway
- AWS Transfer Family
- AWS DataSync

Amazon EFS (Elastic File System)

Amazon EFS provides a simple, scalable, fully managed elastic NFS file system for use with AWS services and on-premises resources. It is a file storage service for use with Amazon EC2. It provides a file system interface, file system access semantics, and concurrently accessible storage for up to thousands of Amazon EC2 instances. It is built to scale on-demand to petabytes of storage without disrupting applications. It can automatically grow and shrink as you add and remove files, eliminating the need to provision and manage capacity to accommodate growth.

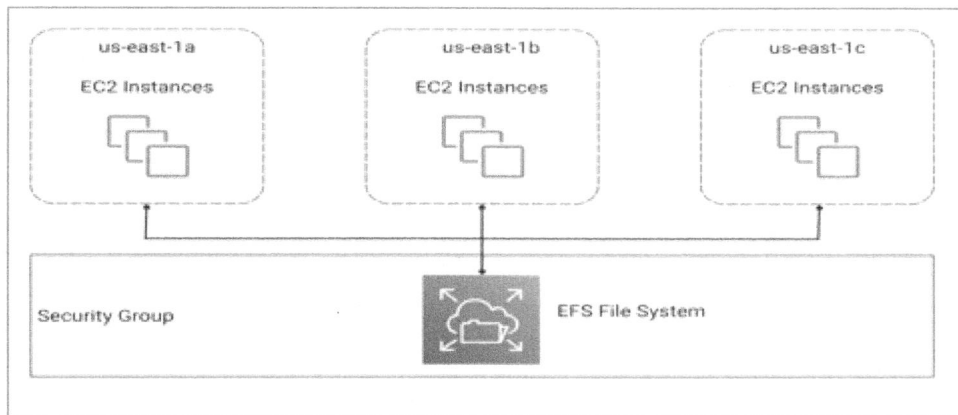

Amazon EFS is a regional service storing data within and across multiple Availability Zones (AZs) for high availability and durability. Amazon EC2 instances can access your file system across AZs, regions, and VPCs, while on-premises servers can access using AWS Direct Connect or AWS VPN. Amazon EFS is designed to provide massively parallel shared access to thousands of Amazon EC2 instances, enabling your applications to achieve high levels of aggregate throughput and IOPS with consistent low latencies.

To access EFS file systems from on-premises, you must have an AWS Direct Connect or AWS VPN connection between your on-premises datacenter and your Amazon VPC. You mount an EFS file system on your on-premises Linux server using the standard Linux mount command for mounting a file system.

The service is designed to be highly scalable, highly available, and highly durable. Amazon EFS file systems store data and metadata across multiple Availability Zones in an AWS Region. EFS file system can be mounted on instances across multiple Availability Zones.

EFS Use Cases

Amazon EFS is well suited to support a broad spectrum of use cases from home directories to business-critical applications, for example, big data analytics, web serving and content management, application development and testing, media and entertainment workflows, database backups, and container storage. Customers can use EFS to lift-and-shift existing enterprise applications to the AWS Cloud.

EFS Storage Classes

Amazon EFS Standard and Standard-IA storage classes

Amazon EFS offers two storage classes: the Standard storage class and the Infrequent Access storage class (EFS IA). The Standard storage class is used for frequently accessed files.

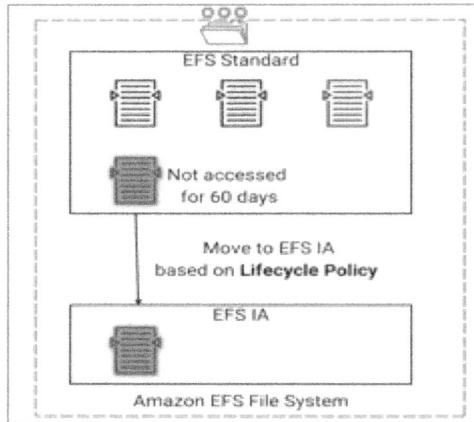

On the other hand, the Infrequent Access storage class (EFS-IA) is used for files that are accessed infrequently. EFS-IA provides price/performance that's cost-optimized for files that are not accessed every day. By simply enabling EFS Lifecycle Management on your file system, files not accessed according to the lifecycle policy you choose will be automatically and transparently moved into EFS IA.

Amazon EFS One Zone and EFS One Zone-IA storage classes

If you are looking for continuous data availability within a single Availability Zone, then EFS One Zone and One Zone–IA storage classes are designed for that purpose. The Standard is good for multi-AZ and the production environment. However, EFS One Zone is a great fit for dev – backup is enabled by default for added data protection. EFS One Zone–Standard is used for frequently accessed files. The customer data is initially written to One Zone–Standard for One Zone storage classes. The EFS One Zone–IA storage class helps reduce storage costs for files not accessed daily.

Comparing Amazon EFS storage classes

The following table compares the storage classes, including their availability, durability, minimum storage duration, and other considerations.

Storage class	Designed for	Durability (designed for)	Availability	Availability zones	Other considerations
EFS Standard	Frequently accessed data requiring the highest durability and availability.	99.999999999% (11 9's)	99.99%	>=3	None
EFS Standard–Infrequent Access (IA)	Long lived, infrequently accessed data requiring the highest durability and availability.	99.999999999% (11 9's)	99.99%	>=3	Per GB retrieval fees apply.
EFS One Zone	Frequently accessed data that doesn't require highest levels of durability and availability.	99.999999999% (11 9's)*	99.90%	1	Not resilient to the loss of the Availability Zone.
EFS One Zone-IA	Long lived, infrequently accessed data that doesn't require highest levels of durability and availability.	99.999999999% (11 9's)*	99.90%	1	Not resilient to the loss of the Availability Zone. Per GB retrieval fees apply.

*Because EFS One Zone storage classes store data in a single AWS Availability Zone, data stored in these storage classes may be lost in the event of a disaster or other fault that affects all copies of the data within the Availability Zone, or in the event of Availability Zone destruction.

Amazon EFS Overview:

Amazon Elastic File System (Amazon EFS) provides a simple, scalable, fully managed elastic NFS file system for use with AWS Cloud services and on-premises resources. It is built to scale on demand to petabytes without disrupting applications, growing and shrinking automatically as you add and remove files, eliminating the need to provision and manage capacity to accommodate growth.

Amazon EFS offers two storage classes: the Standard storage class, and the Infrequent Access storage class (EFS IA). EFS IA provides price/performance that's cost-optimized for files not accessed every day. By simply enabling EFS Lifecycle Management on your file system, files not accessed according to the lifecycle policy you choose will be automatically and transparently moved into EFS IA. The EFS IA storage class costs only $0.025/GB-month*.

While workload patterns vary, customers typically find that 80% of files are infrequently accessed (and suitable for EFS IA), and 20% are actively used (suitable for EFS Standard), resulting in an effective storage cost as low as $0.08/GB-month*. Amazon EFS transparently serves files from both storage classes in a common file system namespace.

Amazon EFS is designed to provide massively parallel shared access to thousands of Amazon EC2 instances, enabling your applications to achieve high levels of aggregate throughput and IOPS with consistent low latencies.

Amazon EFS is well suited to support a broad spectrum of use cases from home directories to business-critical applications. Customers can use EFS to lift-and-shift existing enterprise applications to the AWS Cloud. Other use cases include: big data analytics, web serving and content management, application development and testing, media and entertainment workflows, database backups, and container storage.

Amazon EFS is a regional service storing data within and across multiple Availability Zones (AZs) for high availability and durability. Amazon EC2 instances can access your file system across AZs, regions, and VPCs, while on-premises servers can access using AWS Direct Connect or AWS VPN.

- EFS One Zone storage class is used to store data in a single AWS Availability Zone. Data stored in this storage class may be lost in the event of an Availability Zone destruction.
- EFS is a file system service and not an object storage service.
- It uses POSIX file system.
- EFS file system scales automatically, pay-per-use – no capacity planning.
- EFS uses NFSv4.1 protocol
- EFS uses security group to control access to EFS
- EFS is compatible with Linux based AMI (not Windows)
- It allows encryption at rest using KMS
- Amazon EFS cannot be used as a boot volume for Amazon EC2 instances. For boot volumes, Amazon Elastic Block Storage (Amazon EBS) volumes are used.
- You will pay a fee each time you read from or write data stored on the EFS (Infrequent Access storage class). The Infrequent Access storage class is cost-optimized for files accessed less frequently. Data stored on the Infrequent Access storage class costs less than Standard, and you will pay a fee each time you read from or write to a file.
- EC2 instances can access files on an EFS file system across many Availability Zones, Regions and VPCs

Reference:
https://aws.amazon.com/efs/faq/
https://aws.amazon.com/efs/pricing/

Amazon EBS

An EBS (Elastic Block Store) Volume is a network drive that can be attached to an EC2 instance. An EC2 instance can persist its data on an EBS Volume. An EBS Volume can only be mounted to one EC2 instance at a time. An EBS Volume is bound to a specific AZ. If we need to understand EBS Volume with an analogy, consider them like a "network USB drive."

Amazon Elastic Block Store (EBS) is an easy-to-use, high-performance block storage service designed for use with Amazon EC2 for both throughput and transaction-intensive workloads at any scale. EBS can be used with a broad range of workloads such as enterprise applications, containerized applications, big data analytics, and many others. EBS volumes are designed for mission-critical systems; they can be replicated within an Availability Zone (AZ) and can easily scale to petabytes of data. You can attach an available EBS volume to one instance that is in the same Availability Zone as the volume.

EBS volumes cannot be accessed simultaneously by multiple EC2 instances. An EBS can only be mounted to one EC2 instance at a time, so this option is not correct for the given use case.

Amazon EBS volumes are not encrypted, by default. You can configure your AWS account to enforce the encryption of the new EBS volumes and snapshot copies that you create. Encryption (at rest and during transit) is an optional feature for EBS and has to be enabled by the user.

Volume Type

Amazon Elastic Block Store (Amazon EBS) provides persistent block storage volumes for use with Amazon EC2 instances. Each Amazon EBS volume is automatically replicated within its Availability Zone to protect you from component failure -- thus, offering high availability and durability. With Amazon EBS, you can scale your usage up or down within minutes — all while paying a low price for only what you provision. The fundamentals charges for EBS volumes are the volume type (based on performance), the storage volume in GB per month provisioned, the number of IOPS provisioned per month, the storage consumed by snapshots, and outbound data transfer.

EBS Volumes are characterized based on size and throughput (IOPS). The following are the main categorization of EBS Volume Types:

- **gp2 / gp3 (general-purpose SSD):** These are general-purpose SSD volumes that balance price and performance for various workloads.

- **io1 / io2 (highest-performance Provisioned IOPS SSD):** These are the highest-performance SSD volumes for low-latency and high-throughput workloads.

- **st1 (throughput optimized HDD):** These are low-cost HDD volumes designed for frequently accessed, throughput-intensive workloads.

- **sc1(cold HDD):** These are low-cost HDD volumes designed for less frequently accessed workloads.

Only gp2/gp2 and io1/io2 can be used as boot volumes.

EBS snapshots

An EBS snapshot is a point-in-time copy of your Amazon EBS volume. In other words, an EBS Snapshot is used to make a backup of your EBS Volume.

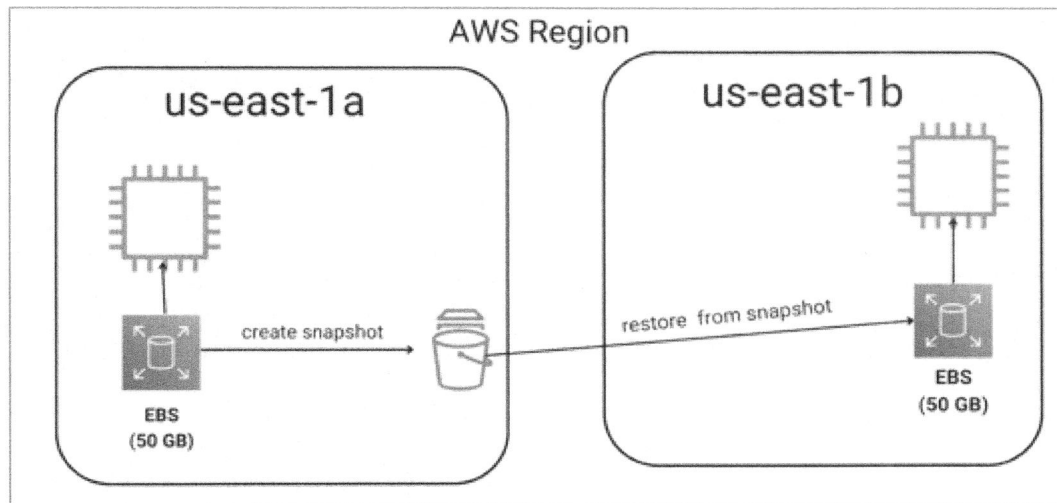

You can create an EBS Snapshot of an EBS Volume attached to an EC2 instance. However, it is recommended to create an EBS Snapshot when the volume is detached. EBS Snapshots can be copied over from across AZ or Region.

EBS snapshots are one of the components of an AMI, but EBS snapshots alone cannot be used to deploy the same EC2 instances across different Availability Zones (AZs).

EBS Snapshots Features

EBS Snapshot Archive – You can move an EBS Snapshot to an "archive tier" that is 75% less expensive. It takes about 24-72 hours to restore from the archive.

Recycle Bis for EBS Snapshots – You can set up rules to retain deleted snapshots, which helps recover deleted snapshots in case of accidental deletion. The duration of retention is from 1 day to a year.

Fast Snapshot Restore (FSR) – This feature forces full snapshot initialization to have no latency on the first use.

The important point to keep in mind about an EBS Volume:

It is a network drive – not a physical drive. Since it is not a physical drive -- it is a network drive-- attached to an EC2 instance, it uses a network to communicate with the EC2 instance, and the communication with EC2 over the network may cause a bit of latency. However, since an EBS Volume is a network drive, it has the advantage of the easy swap if we compare it with a drive that is physically attached to a machine. In other words, an EBS Volume can be quickly detached and attached to another EC2 instance.

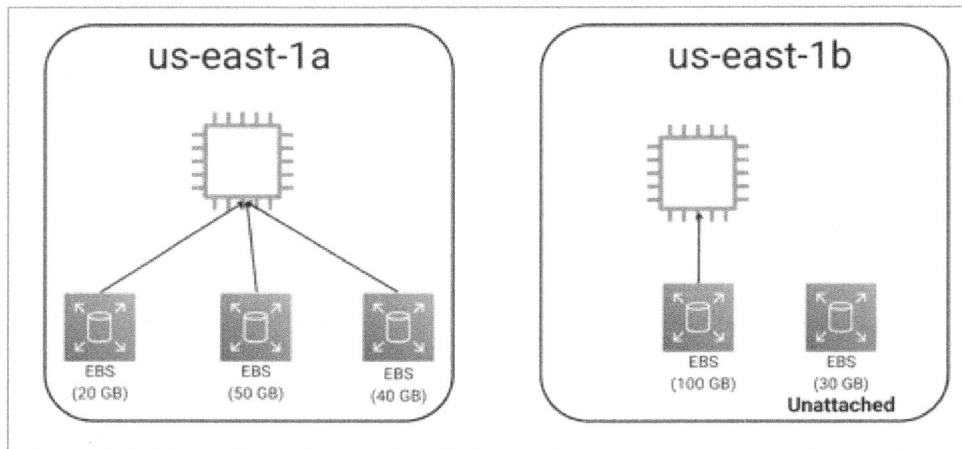

It is associated or locked to an AZ. An EBS Volume is locked to an AZ and cannot be attached to an EC2 instance in some other AZ. For example, an EBS Volume present in us-east-1a cannot be used in the us-east-1b. To move an EBS Volume, you will need to create a snapshot of the EBS Volume first.

It has a provisioned capacity (in GB and IOPS). An EBS Volume has a provisioned capacity –the size in GB and IOPS. You get billed based on the provisioned capacity of an EBS Volume. You can increase provisioned capacity of an EBS Volume.

EBS Volume Types Features

(ref: https://aws.amazon.com/ebs/features/)

The following table shows use cases and performance characteristics of current generation EBS volumes:

Solid State Drives (SSD)					
Volume Type	EBS Provisioned IOPS SSD (io2 Block Express)	EBS Provisioned IOPS SSD (io2)	EBS Provisioned IOPS SSD (io1)	EBS General Purpose SSD (gp3)	EBS General Purpose SSD (gp2)*
Short Description	Highest performance SSD volume designed for business-	Highest performance and highest durability	Highest performance SSD volume designed for latency-sensitive	Lowest cost SSD volume that balances price performance for a wide variety of	General Purpose SSD volume that balances price

	critical latency-sensitive transactional workloads	SSD volume designed for latency-sensitive transactional workloads	transactional workloads	transactional workloads	performance for a wide variety of transactional workloads
Durability	99.999%	99.999%	99.8% - 99.9% durability	99.8% - 99.9% durability	99.8% - 99.9% durability
Use Cases	Largest, most I/O intensive, mission critical deployments of NoSQL and relational databases such as Oracle, SAP HANA, Microsoft SQL Server, and SAS Analytics	I/O-intensive NoSQL and relational databases	I/O-intensive NoSQL and relational databases	Virtual desktops, medium sized single instance databases such as Microsoft SQL Server and Oracle, latency sensitive interactive applications, boot volumes, and dev/test environments	Virtual desktops, medium sized single instance databases such as Microsoft SQL Server and Oracle, latency sensitive interactive applications, boot volumes, and dev/test environments
API Name	io2	io2	io1	gp3	gp2
Volume Size	4 GB – 64 TB	4 GB – 16 TB	4 GB - 16 TB	1 GB - 16 TB	1 GB - 16 TB
Max IOPS/Volume**	256,000	64,000	64,000	16,000	16,000
Max Throughput*/Volume**	4,000 MB/s	1,000 MB/s	1,000 MB/s	1,000 MB/s	250 MB/s
Max IOPS/Instance	260,000	160,000**	260,000	260,000	260,000
Max Throughput/Instance	7,500 MB/s	4,750 MB/s**	7,500 MB/s	7,500 MB/s	7,500 MB/s
Latency	sub-millisecond	single digit millisecond	single digit millisecond	single digit millisecond	single digit millisecond
Price	$0.125/GB-month $0.065/provisioned IOPS-month up to 32,000 IOPS $0.046/provisioned IOPS-month from 32,001 to 64,000 $0.032/provisioned IOPS-month for greater than 64,000 IOPS		$0.125/GB-month $0.065/provisioned IOPS-month	$0.08/GB-month 3,000 IOPS free and $0.005/provisioned IOPS-month over 3,000; 125 MB/s free and $0.04/provisioned MB/s-month over 125	$0.10/GB-month
Dominant Performance Attribute	IOPS, throughput, latency, capacity,	IOPS and volume durability	IOPS	IOPS	IOPS

	and volume durability			

*Default volume type
**Not currently supported by EC2 R5b instances
***Volume throughput is calculated as MB = 1024^2 bytes

Hard Disk Drives (HDD)		
	Throughput Optimized HDD (st1)	Cold HDD (sc1)
Short Description	Low cost HDD volume designed for frequently accessed, throughput intensive workloads	Lowest cost HDD volume designed for less frequently accessed workloads
Durability	99.8% - 99.9% durability	99.8% - 99.9% durability
Use Cases	Big data, data warehouses, log processing	Colder data requiring fewer scans per day
API Name	st1	sc1
Volume Size	125 GB - 16 TB	125 GB - 16 TB
Max IOPS/Volume**	500	250
Max Throughput*/Volume**	500 MB/s	250 MB/s
Max IOPS/Instance	260,000	260,000
Max Throughput/Instance	7,500 MB/s	7,500 MB/s
Price	$0.045/GB-month	$0.015/GB-month
Dominant Performance Attribute	MB/s	MB/s

* st1/sc1 based on 1 MB I/O size
** volume throughput is calculated as MB = 1024^2 bytes

EBS Multi-Attach (io1/io2 EBS Volume Types)

Using io1/io2 EBS Volume types, you can attach the same EBS volume to multiple EC2 instances in the same AZ --- up to 16 EC2 instances at a time. Each instance has full read & writes access permissions to the attached EBS Volume.

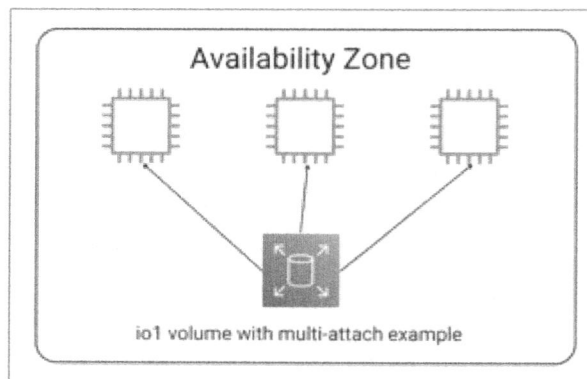

io1 volume with multi-attach example

EBS Multi-Attach can be a good use case in a clustered Linux environment to achieve higher application availability. Applications need to manage concurrency when writing to the EBS Volume. It would help if you used a cluster-aware filesystem when using EBS Multi-Attach.

EBS Encryption

When you attach an encrypted EBS Volume, you get the following features.
- Snapshots of an encrypted volume are encrypted.

- If you copy an unencrypted snapshot to an encrypted EBS Volume, it allows encryption.
- Data at rest is encrypted.
- Data movement between the EBS Volume and the EC2 instance is encrypted.
- Encryption and decryption are handled behind the scenes transparently – you don't need to do anything extra except configure your volume to use encrypted EBS Volume.
- Encryption has minimal impacts on the latency of the application running on an EC2 instance.
- EBS encryption uses keys from KMS – uses an AES-256 encryption algorithm.

How to encrypt an unencrypted EBS Volume

Create an EBS Snapshot of the EBS Volume. Then, encrypt the EBS Snapshot using copy.
Create a new EBS Volume from this encrypted Snapshot. The new EBS Volume will also be encrypted.
Now, you can attach the newly created encrypted volume to the original EC2 instance.

- EBS volumes can only be mounted with Amazon EC2.
- EBS volume can be attached to a single instance in the same Availability Zone whereas EFS file system can be mounted on instances across multiple Availability Zones.
- Amazon EBS Snapshots are a point in time copy of your block data. For the first snapshot of a volume, Amazon EBS saves a full copy of your data to Amazon S3. EBS Snapshots are stored incrementally, which means you are billed only for the changed blocks stored.
- When using EBS direct APIs for Snapshots, additional EC2 data transfer charges will apply only when you use external or cross-region data transfers.
- Snapshot storage is based on the amount of space your data consumes in Amazon S3. Because Amazon EBS does not save empty blocks, it is likely that the snapshot size will be considerably less than your volume size. Copying EBS snapshots is charged for the data transferred across regions. After the snapshot is copied, standard EBS snapshot charges apply for storage in the destination region.
- Data transfer-in is always free, including for EBS volumes.

Instance Store

As discussed above, EBS Volumes are network drives with good but "limited" performance because of implicit latency due to dependency on the network. If you need a high-performance hardware disk, your choice is EC2 Instance Store. An instance store provides temporary block-level storage for your EC2 instance. Instance storage is located on disks that are physically attached to the host computer.

EC2 Instance Stores provide better I/O performance. You need to be aware that EC2 Instance Stores are ephemeral. What it means is that if the EC2 instance is stopped, you lose the data stored on EC2 Instance Store. Also, you risk losing data if there is any hardware failure.

An instance store is a good option when you need storage with very low latency, but you don't need the data to persist when the instance terminates. An Instance Store is ideal for the temporary storage of information that frequently changes, such as buffers, caches, scratch data, and other temporary content, or for data that is replicated across a fleet of instances, such as a load-balanced pool of web servers. As Instance Store volumes are tied to an EC2 instance, they are also single AZ entities.

EC2 Instances Store Overview:

Reference:

https://docs.aws.amazon.com/AWSEC2/latest/UserGuide/InstanceStorage.html

EBS vs. EFS

Let's discuss the differences between EBS and EFS to clarify these AWS storage types.

EBS Volumes
- It can be attached to only one instance at a time.
- It is locked at the AZ level.
- If you are using gp2, I/O performance increases as the disk size increases
- If you are using io1, I/O performance can increase independently
- To migrate an EBS Volume across AZ, first take a snapshot, then use the snapshot to restore from the EBS Volume.
- It's a good idea to make an EBS snapshot when the load on the system is low, as EBS snapshot use IO.

EFS
EFS can be mounted 100s of instances across AZs. It is a good storage option when you have clustered instances. It is used only for Linux instances as it uses the POSIX file system. EFS is a bit expensive than EBS. However, you can leverage EFS-IA for cost savings.

AWS Snow Family

AWS Snow Family are highly secure, portable devices to collect and process data at the edge and migrate data into and out of AWS. We can classify them into two categories: Data Migration and Edge Computing.

Data Migration:

Snowcone   Snowball Edge   Snowmobile

Edge Computing:

Snowcone   Snowball Edge

Data Migrations with AWS Snow Family

When transferring data to S3, there are a few challenges, such as limited connectivity, limited bandwidth, high network cost, shared bandwidth (can't maximize the line), and connection stability.

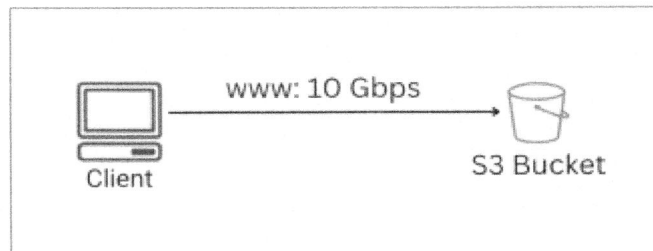

The table below shows will give you an idea of how much time it takes to transfer different sizes of data over connections with different speeds.

	Time to Transfer		
	100 Mbps	**1 Gbps**	**10 Gbps**
10 TB	12 days	20 hours	3 hours
100 TB	124 days	12 days	30 hours
1 PB	3 years	124 days	12 days

AWS Snow Family are offline devices that can perform data migrations.

If it takes more than a week to transfer data over the network, use Snowball device

AWS Snowball Edge

AWS Snowball Edge provides physical data transport solutions to help move TBs or PBs of data in or out of AWS. As you can see, this is an alternative to data transfer over the network – Snowball Edge makes it faster to move TBS or PBs of data and saves on paying network fees.

It is a type of Snowball device which contains onboard storage and compute power for some selective AWS capabilities. The Snowball Edge can also do local processing and edge-computing workloads besides transferring data between your local environment and the AWS Cloud.

You pay per data transfer job. It provides block storage and Amazon S3-compatible object storage.

There are two types of Snowball Edge devices: Snowball Edge Storage Optimized and Snowball Edge Compute Optimized.

Snowball Edge Storage Optimized provides 80 TB HDD capacity for block storage and S3-compatible object storage, and 1 TB of SATA SSD for block volumes.

Snowball Edge Compute Optimized provides 42 TB of HDD capacity for block storage and S3-compatible object storage.

What are the use cases of Snowball Edge? You can use Snowball Edge for disaster recovery, cloud migration of large data, and data center decommissioning, machine learning, video analysis, analytics, and local computing stacks.

AWS Snowcone

AWS Snowcone is the smallest member of the AWS Snow Family --weighing in at 4.5 pounds (2.1 kg). It is rugged & secure and can withstand harsh environments. AWS Snowcone is equipped with 8 TB of usable storage, while AWS Snowcone Solid State Drive (SSD) supports 14 terabytes of usable storage.

Snowcone is designed for data migration needs up to 8 TB per device in environments where the space is constrained or where AWS Snowball devices will not fit. Its small form factor makes it a perfect fit for small spaces where you need portability or where network connectivity is unreliable. Use Snowcone where Snowball does not fit due to a space-constrained environment.

You can use Snowcone in backpacks or for IoT, vehicular, or drone use cases. Like AWS Snowball, Snowcone has multiple layers of security and encryption. You can use either of these services to run edge computing workloads, or to collect, process, and transfer data to AWS.

It can be sent back to AWS offline. Or it can be connected to the Internet and use AWS DataSync to transfer data.

AWS Snowmobile

AWS Snowmobile is an Exabyte-scale data transfer service. It is a 45-foot-long ruggedized shipping container pulled by a semi-trailer truck. It can move extremely large amounts of data such as video libraries, image repositories, or even a complete data center migration to AWS.

Each Snowmobile has 100 PB of capacity -- you can transfer up to 100PB per Snowmobile. It provides high security: temperature controlled, GPS enabled, and 24/7 video surveillance. It is a better alternative than Snowball if you transfer more than 10 PB.

Data Migrations Feature Comparison

	Snowball Edge (Storage Optmized)	Snowcone	Snowmobile
Storage Capacity	80 TB usable	8 TB Usable	< 100 PB
Migration Size	UP to petabytes, offline	Up to 24 TB, online and offline	Up to exabytes, offline

AWS Snow Family Using Process

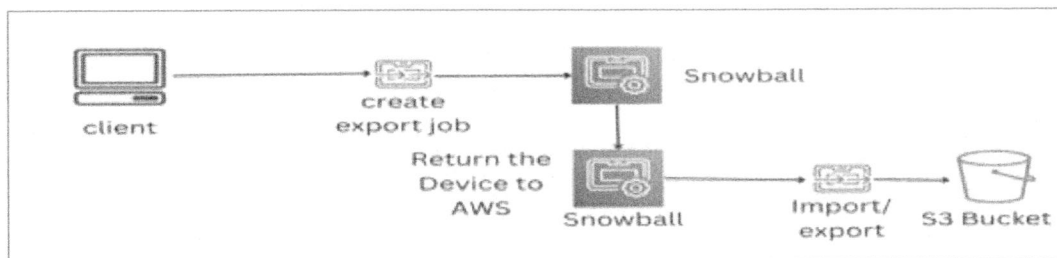

Following are the steps for using AWS Snow Family.

1. Request Snowball device from the AWS Console
2. Install the Snowball client / AWS OpsHub on your servers
3. Connect the Snowball to your servers and copy the files
4. Ship the device back to the AWS
5. Data will be loaded into an S3 bucket
6. Data will be completely wiped out

Edge Computing

Edge computing is about processing data closer to where it is being generated – it could be on a truck on the road, a ship on the sea, or an underground mining station. These locations may have limited or no internet access and limited or no easy access to computing power.

AWS can set up a Snowball Edge / Snowcone device for edge computing. And we can also ship the device back to AWS for transferring data.

Use cases of edge computing: preprocessing of data, machine learning at an edge location, transcoding media streams.

Snow Family Edge Computing

Snowcone
It provides 2 CPUs and 4GB of memory. It can be used as wired or wireless.

Snowball Edge – Compute Optimized
It provides 52 vCPUs and 208 GiB of RAM, and an optional GPU. The GPU can be useful for video processing or machine learning.

Snowball Edge – Storage Optimized
It provides up to 40 vCPUs and 80 GiB of RAM.

On all of them, you can run EC2 instances and AWS Lambda functions (using AWS IoT Greengrass).

AWS OpsHub

In the past, in order to use AWS Snow Family devices, we needed a CLI (Command Line Interface). Customers operated Snowball devices by either entering commands into a command-line interface or by using REST APIs. Now with AWS OpsHub, you have an easier way to deploy and manage even large fleets of Snowball devices, all while operating without an internet connection.

Now, we can use AWS OpsHub, which is a software you install on your computer, to manage your Snow Family devices such as:
- Transferring files
- Launching and managing instances running on Snow Family devices
- Monitor device metrics
- Launch compatible AWS services on your devices, for example, EC2 instances, and AWS DataSync.

AWS OpsHub is a graphical user interface you can use to manage your AWS Snowball devices. Thus it enables you to rapidly deploy edge computing workloads and simplify data migration to the cloud. With just a few clicks in AWS OpsHub, you have the full functionality of the Snowball devices at your fingertips; you can unlock and configure devices, drag-and-drop data to devices, launch applications, and monitor device metrics.

AWS OpsHub takes all the existing operations available in the Snowball API and presents them as a simple graphical user interface. This interface helps you quickly and easily migrate data to the AWS Cloud and deploy edge computing applications on Snow Family Devices.

Solution Architecture: Use case of Snowball to Glacier

You cannot import files to Amazon Glacier directly. You must first use Amazon S3, then apply the Lifecycle policy at the Bucket.

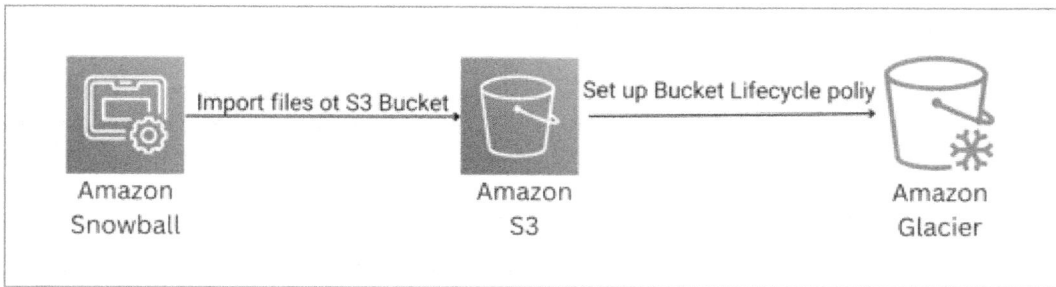

Amazon FSx

Amazon FSx makes it easy to launch 3rd party high-performance file systems on AWS. It is **a fully managed shared storage** service.

You can choose from four types of widely used file systems:

- FSx for Lustre
- FSx for Windows File Server
- FSx for NetApp ONTAP
- FSx for OpenZFS

FSX for Lustre (Built on the world's most popular high-performance file system.)	FSX for Windows File Server (Built on Windows Server.)
FSx for NetApp ONTAP (Built on NetApp's popular ONTAP file system)	FSx for OpenZFS (Built on the popular OpenZFS file system.)

Amazon FSx for Windows

Amazon FSx for Windows File Server is fully managed, highly reliable, and scalable file storage accessible over the industry-standard Service Message Block (SMB) protocol and Windows NTFS. In addition, it supports Microsoft Active Directory, ACLs, and user quotas. It supports Microsoft's Distributed File System (DFS) Namespaces, which groups files across multiple FS.

In addition, Amazon FSx provides high throughput levels and sub-millisecond latencies. It can scale up to 10s of GB/s and millions of IOPS. In storage, it supports SSD and HDD.

Amazon FSx is accessible from Windows, Linux, and macOS compute instances and devices. It can be accessed from your on-premises infrastructure – VPC or Direct Connect. It can be configured to be Multi-AZ for high availability. Data is backed up daily on S3.

Amazon FSx for Lustre

Amazon FSx for Lustre is fully managed shared storage with the scalability and performance of the popular Lustre file system. The name Lustre is derived from the words "Linux" and "Cluster." It is a type of parallel distributed file system for computing at large-scale. FSx for Lustre is only compatible with Linux.

It has seamless integration with S3. For example, it can "read S3" as a file system and write the output of the computations back to S3.

It can be accessed from your on-premises infrastructure – VPC or Direct Connect.

Amazon FSx for Lustre can be used for compute-intensive workloads such as high-performance computing (HPC), machine learning, and media processing.

Amazon FSx for NetApp ONTAP

Amazon FSx for NetApp ONTAP is a fully managed service that provides NetApp's popular ONTAP file system on AWS.

The file system is compatible with NFS, SMB, and iSCSI protocols. You can move workloads running on ONTAP or NAS to AWS.

It works with: Linux, Windows, macOS, VMWare Cloud on AWS, Amazon Workspaces & AppStream 2.0, Amazon EC2, ECS, and EKS.

The storage shrinks and grows automatically. You can do Point-in-time instantaneous cloning, which helps test new workloads.

Amazon FSx for OpenZFS

It is a managed OpenZFS file system on AWS. The file system is compatible with NFS (v3, v4, v4.1, v4.2). You can move workloads running on ZFS to AWS.

It works with: Linux, Windows, macOS, VMWare Cloud on AWS, Amazon Workspaces & AppStream 2.0, Amazon EC2, ECS, and EKS.

Provides up to 1,000,000 IOPS with less than 0.5 seconds of latency. You can do Point-in-time instantaneous cloning, which helps test new workloads.

Hybrid Cloud for Storage

As you can notice, based on the previous discussions, there are many storage options available. However, AWS pushing for a "hybrid cloud" in which some part of your infrastructure is on the cloud, and the other part of the infrastructure is on-premises.

The reason for this push is due to the long cloud migrations cycle, security & compliance requirements, and the organizations IT strategy.

The question is how you would go about the hybrid cloud. In other words, how would you expose S3 data, which is AWS proprietary technology, to on-preemies? AWS Storage Gateway.

Cloud Native AWS Storage Options

AWS has provided many cloud-native options for block, file, and object storage. For example, if you are looking for a typical OS-style block storage, you have EBS and EC2 Instance Store (non-persistent but varies fast).

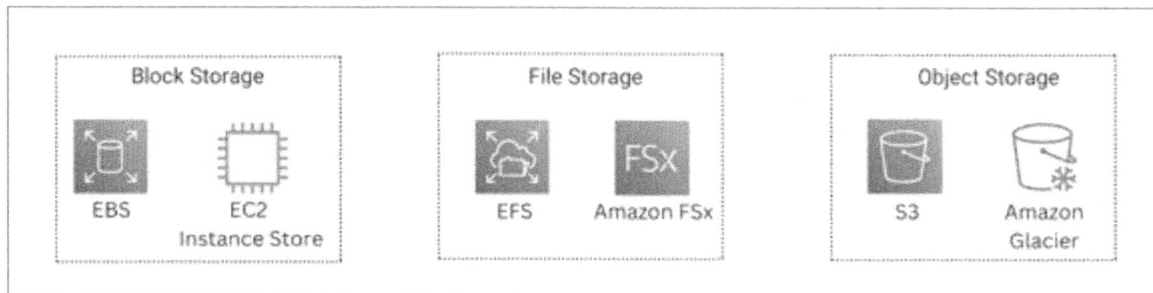

If your use case requires file-based storage, you have EFS and Amazon FSx. And for object storage, such as images and videos, you can use Amazon S3 and Amazon Glacier(long-term, inexpensive storage).

AWS Storage Gateway

AWS Storage Gateway is a hybrid cloud storage service that connects your existing on-premises environments with the AWS Cloud. It gives you on-premises access to virtually unlimited cloud storage. All data transferred between the gateway and AWS storage is encrypted using SSL.

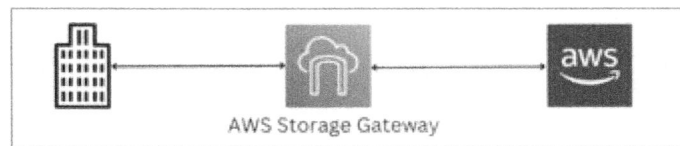

AWS Storage Gateway service provides different types of gateways – **Amazon S3 File Gateway, Amazon FSx File Gateway, Volume Gateway, and Tape Gateway.** These storage gateways seamlessly connect on-premises applications to cloud storage, caching data locally for low-latency access.

AWS Storage Gateway use cases are **disaster recovery, backup & restore tiered storage, on-premises cache & low-latency files access.**

Customers use Storage Gateway to simplify storage management and reduce costs for key hybrid cloud storage use cases. These include moving tape backups to the cloud, reducing on-premises storage with cloud-backed file shares, providing low latency access to data in AWS for on-premises applications, as well as various migration, archiving, processing, and disaster recovery use cases. However, data transfer through AWS Storage Gateway takes longer, even with great bandwidth. Moreover, to transfer 50 PBs of data, will be more expensive than using AWS Snowmobile.

Storage Gateway provides a standard set of storage protocols such as iSCSI, SMB, and NFS. This flexibility of storage protocols allow you to use AWS storage without rewriting your existing applications. You can take point-in-time snapshots of your Volume Gateway volumes in the form of EBS snapshots. Using this approach, you can easily supply data from your on-premises applications to your applications running on Amazon EC2 if you require additional on-demand computing capacity for data processing or replacement capacity for disaster recovery. However, Storage Gateways cannot be used for continuous replication-based disaster recovery.

Amazon S3 File Gateway

The Amazon S3 File Gateway is one of the Storage Gateway types. The S3 File Gateway is used to integrate on-premises IT infrastructure to Amazon S3. For example, you can use S3 File Gateway -- using NFS and SMB protocol -- to copy on-premises data such as files to Amazon S3. The S3 File Gateway caches the most recently used data.

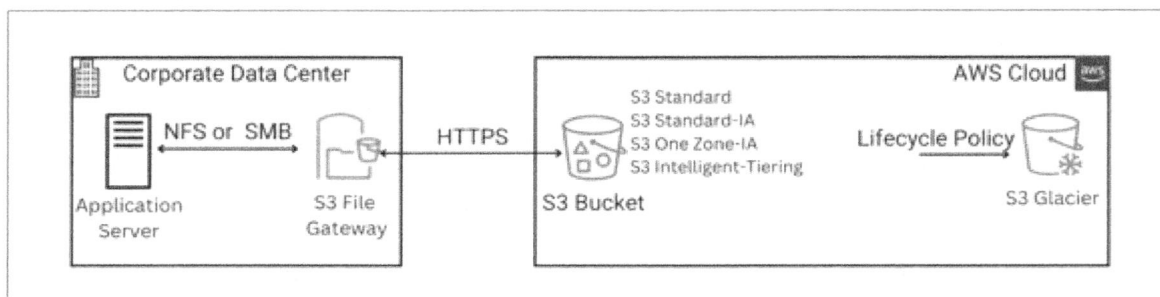

You can take advantage of different S3 storage classes to cost-effectively manage accessibility, durability, and retention. It supports S3 Standard, S3 Standard IA, S3 One Zone-IA, and S3 Intelligent Tiering. Then using the bucket Lifecycle policy, the files can be moved to Glacier for long-term archival.

The IAM policy is applied when S3 File Gateway accesses the S3 Bucket.

Regarding the use case of File Gateway, you can use File Gateway to manage a hybrid workload, which requires access to both on-premises and AWS Cloud environments. The File Gateway can be used for big data analytic use cases. For example, you can use File Gateway to copy on-premises data to S3. And there, you leverage AWS services such as EMR, Athena, or Glue to build and run ETL jobs or can perform ad hoc analytics.

You can also leverage AWS machine learning services such as SageMaker, Forecast, and Rekognition to build and run machine models.

You can also use data copied on S3 as backup copy by applying various retention policies.

Amazon FSx File Gateway

It provides native access to Amazon FSx for Windows File Server, in addition to providing a local cache for frequently accessed data. It has Windows native compatibility. For example, it is compatible with SMB, NTFS, and Active Directory.

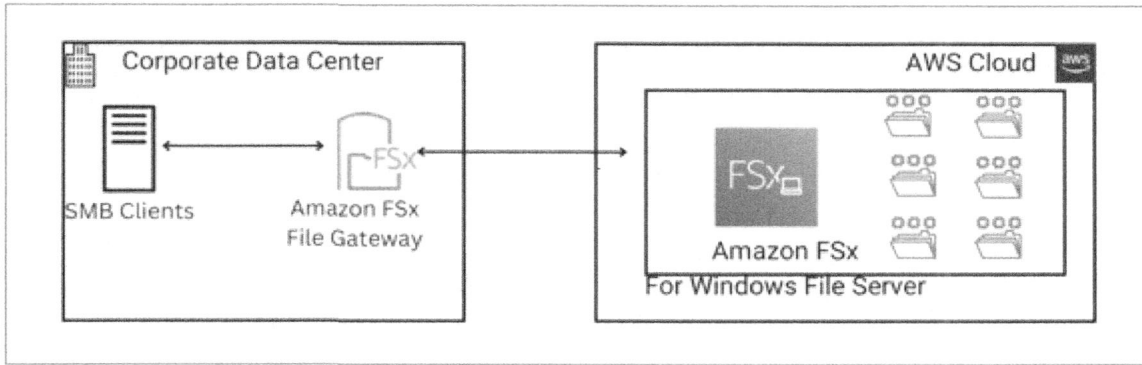

It is useful for group file shares and the home directory.

Volume Gateway

The Volume Gateway offers your on-premises application to access iSCSI block storage, such as EBS volume backed by S3.

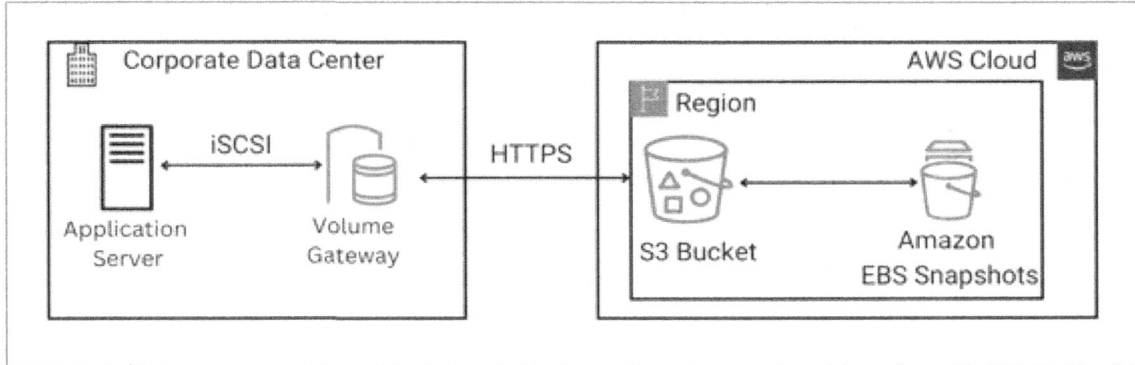

Regarding use cases of Volume Gateway, you can use Volume Gateway to create EBS snapshots of the on-premises application to be used as a backup copy. The backup copy can also be integrated with the AWS Backup service. In addition, this snapshot can be used in case of disaster recovery. You can also use the EBS snapshot to migrate and run your workload on the AWS Cloud. The Volume Gateway can also be used in cloud migration.

Tape Gateway

The Tape Gateway helps offload your tape back up to the AWS Cloud without disturbing your existing on-premises backup workflow. The Tape Gateway allows you to continue to rely on the current backup workflow, yet you can copy your data to Amazon S3 and then archive it to Glacier as a backup. In addition, this Tape Gateway is compatible with typical backup applications such as Dell EMC NetWorker and Microsoft System Center Data Protection Manager.

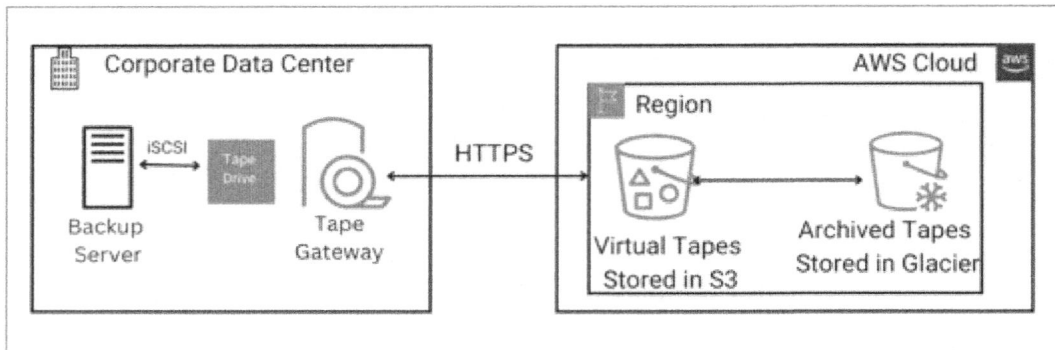

With regards to the use case of the Tape Gateway, you can use the existing working tape backup workflow to back up your on-premises on S3. the traditional tape backup process has many issues, such as shipping tapes sometimes being costly.

Imagine a use case where tape backs need to send to Singapore from the US east coast data center ASAP. How much cost would it be? Or the process has high costs, time, and money. Also, using the backup in case of disaster recovery was a time-consuming process. There was concern about the hardware and durability as well. The Tape Gateway makes the process of backup data on the AWS Cloud easy, efficient, and cost-effective.

AWS Storage Gateway– Hardware Appliance

In order to use Storage Gateway, you need on-premises virtualization. However, many times, branch offices, R&D departmental workgroups, or industrial sites lack the on-premises infrastructure to run virtualization such as hypervisors, server clusters, and networked storage systems.

The AWS Storage Gateway Hardware Appliance is a physical, standalone, validated server configuration for on-premises deployments. It comes pre-loaded with Storage Gateway software (File Gateway, Volume Gateway, Tape Gateway). It has all the required CPU, memory, network, and SSD cache resources for creating and configuring File Gateway, Volume Gateway, or Tape Gateway.

The Appliance is designed to provide you with a simple out-of-the-box experience that does not require any additional infrastructure and is managed from the AWS Console or API.

It can be dropped in and rapidly set up, providing local applications access to virtually unlimited cloud storage for a wide variety of use cases.

AWS Transfer Family

It is a fully managed service for file transfers into and out of Amazon S3 or Amazon EFS using FTP protocol.

It supports the following protocols:
- AWS Transfer for FTP (File Transfer Protocol)

- AWS Transfer for FTPS (File Transfer Protocol over SSL)
- AWS Transfer for SFTP (Secure File Transfer Protocol)

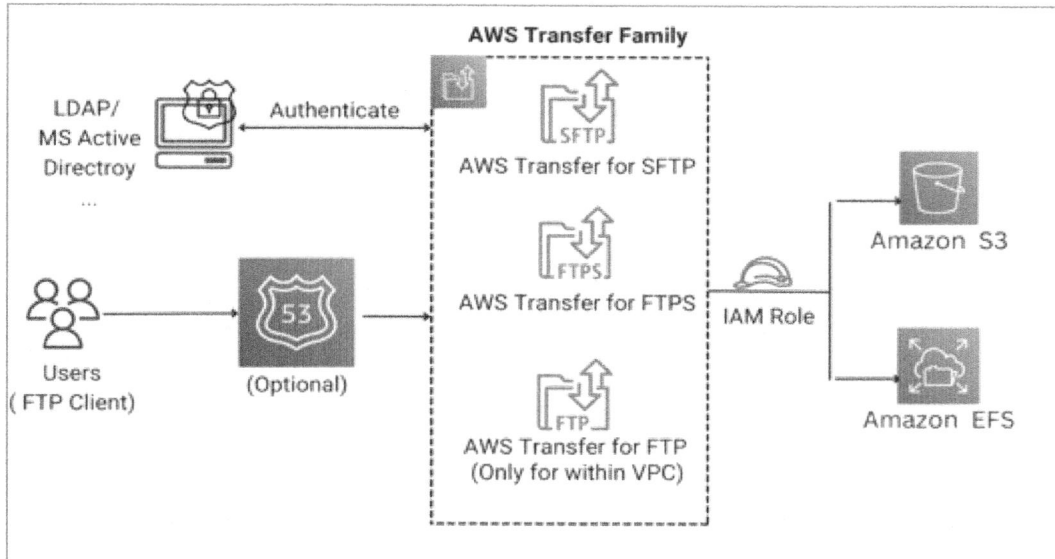

You pay per provisioned endpoint per hour and data transfer costs in GB. It stores and manages users' credentials within the service. It integrates with existing authentication systems, e.g., Microsoft Active Directory, LDAP, Okta, and Amazon Cognito.

AWS Transfer Family use cases: sharing files and data sets in large complex enterprise systems such as CRM, ERM

AWS DataSync

AWS DataSync, an online data transfer service, simplifies, automates, and accelerates moving data between on-premises storage systems and AWS storage services and between AWS storage services. AWS DataSync can copy data between NFS and SMB file servers, HDFS, on-premises object storage, AWS Snowcone devices, Amazon S3 buckets, Amazon EFS file systems, Amazon FSx for Windows File Server file system, Amazon FSx for Lustre file systems, Amazon FSx for OpenZFS file systems.

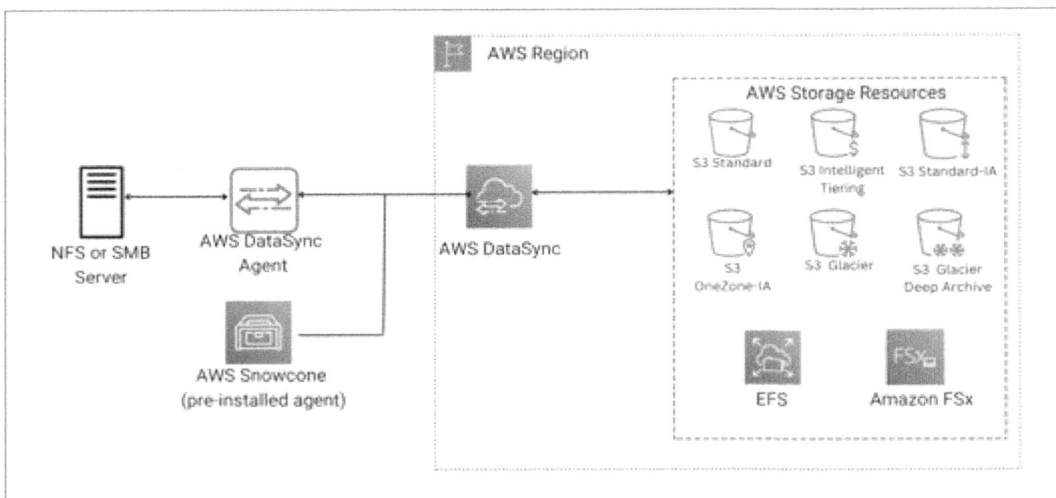

AWS DataSync using NFS/SMB to S3, EFS, FSx

You can use AWS DataSync for data transfers from on-premises systems into or out of AWS for processing. AWS DataSync can help speed up your critical hybrid cloud storage workflows in industries that need to move active files into AWS quickly. DataSync provides timely delivery to ensure dependent processes are not delayed. In addition, you can specify exclude filters, include filters, or both, to determine which files, folders, or objects get transferred each time your task runs.

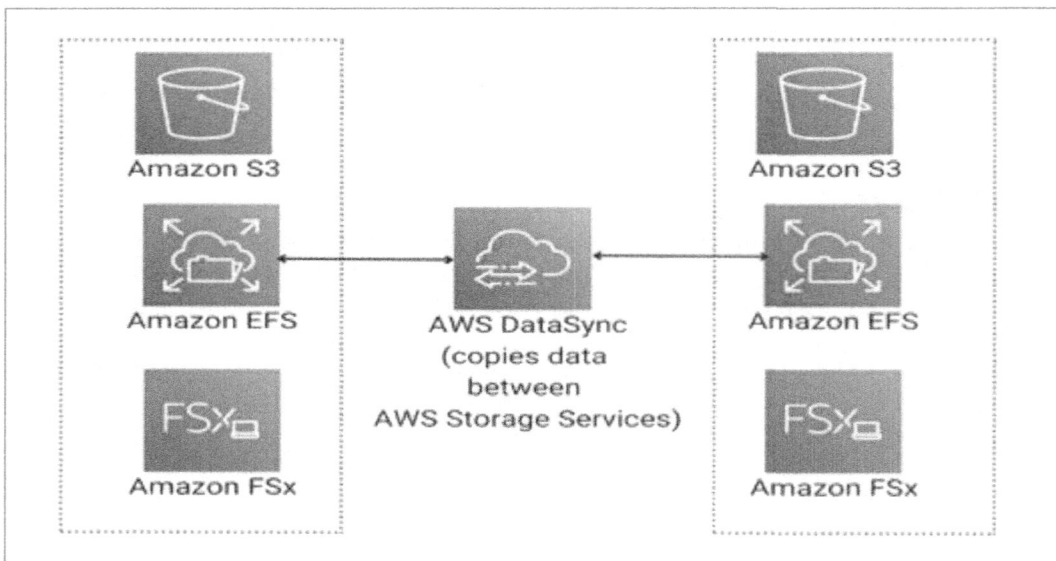

AWS DataSync – Copies Data Between AWS Storage Services

AWS DataSync employs an AWS-designed transfer protocol — decoupled from the storage protocol — to accelerate data movement. The protocol optimizes how, when, and what data is sent over the network. Network optimizations performed by DataSync include incremental transfers, in-line compression, sparse file detection, and in-line data validation and encryption.

Chapter 21. AWS Monitoring, Audit, and Performance

You will learn the following in this chapter:
- Amazon CloudWatch
- CloudWatch Logs
- CloudWatch Alarms
- Amazon EventBridge
- CloudWatch Insights
- AWS CloudTrail
- AWS Config
- AWS Personal Health Dashboard
- AWS Service Health Dashboard

Amazon CloudWatch

Amazon CloudWatch is an AWS monitoring and observability service. AWS CloudWatch service helps you monitor your applications and resource optimizations, respond to system-wide performance changes and provide a unified view of operation health by providing data and actionable insights.

There are many components or features of the CloudWatch service. Amazon CloudWatch is an excellent service for building Resilient systems. If you are looking for resource performance monitoring, events, and alerts – CloudWatch is a go-to service. For example, you can configure a CloudWatch alarm that sends an email message using Amazon SNS when CPU utilization crosses the threshold of 80%.

Looking for resource performance monitoring, events, and alerts; think CloudWatch.

It has Dashboard, Alarms, Logs, Metrics, X-Ray traces, Events, Application monitoring, and Insights sections – these are the main sections.

The CloudWatch service collects data in logs, metrics, and events. After collecting the data, the service provides a unified view of AWS resources, applications, and services that run on AWS and on-premises servers. You can use CloudWatch to detect anomalies or anomalous behavior in your environment. You can set alarms. You can view logs. You can view metrics, take automated action, troubleshoot issues, and discover insights to keep your applications running as best as possible with respect to performance, resource utilization, and cost.

How it works

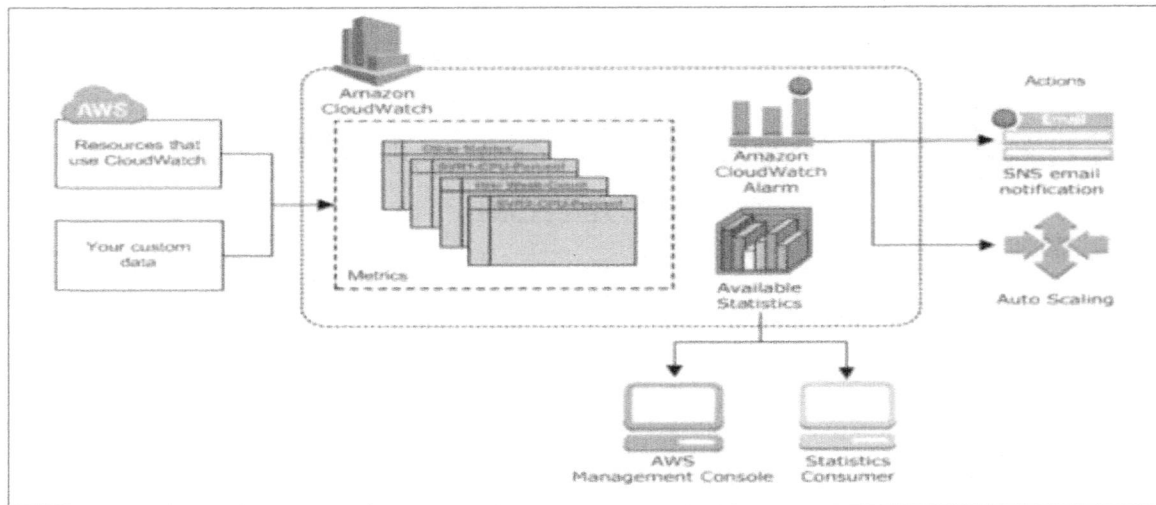

Reference: https://docs.aws.amazon.com/AmazonCloudWatch/latest/monitoring/cloudwatch_architecture.html

Amazon CloudWatch service is essentially a metrics repository. AWS services, such as Amazon EC2, put all kinds of data logs (CloudWatch term is metrics) into the repository, and you can get statistics based on those metrics. For example, EC2 puts data for 38 different types of metrics.

You can also send custom log data (custom metrics) from your applications to CloudWatch, for example, from AWS Lambda or EMR. In that case, you can retrieve statistics on these metrics.

You can configure the CloudWatch alarm to trigger based on different metrics or criteria met. For example, you can stop, start, or terminate an Amazon EC2 instance when specific criteria are met.

Metrics are stored separately in regions, but you can use CloudWatch cross-Region functionality to aggregate statistics from different Regions.

So, the main idea about the CloudWatch system is that services put log data, which can be monitored, acted upon, and analyzed, to tune the system to work the way you want the resource utilization to optimize the performance and reduce your overall cost.

CloudWatch Console

Now let's look into the CloudWatch console to get an idea about various features of the CloudWatch service. First, the CloudWatch console or home page shows the summary of what's going on with different resources if any recent alarms are fired. This page is more geared to if you have configured alarms in your account, for example, a Billing alarm to get a notification you bill is crossing 75% of your total budget for the current month.

CloudWatch Home page

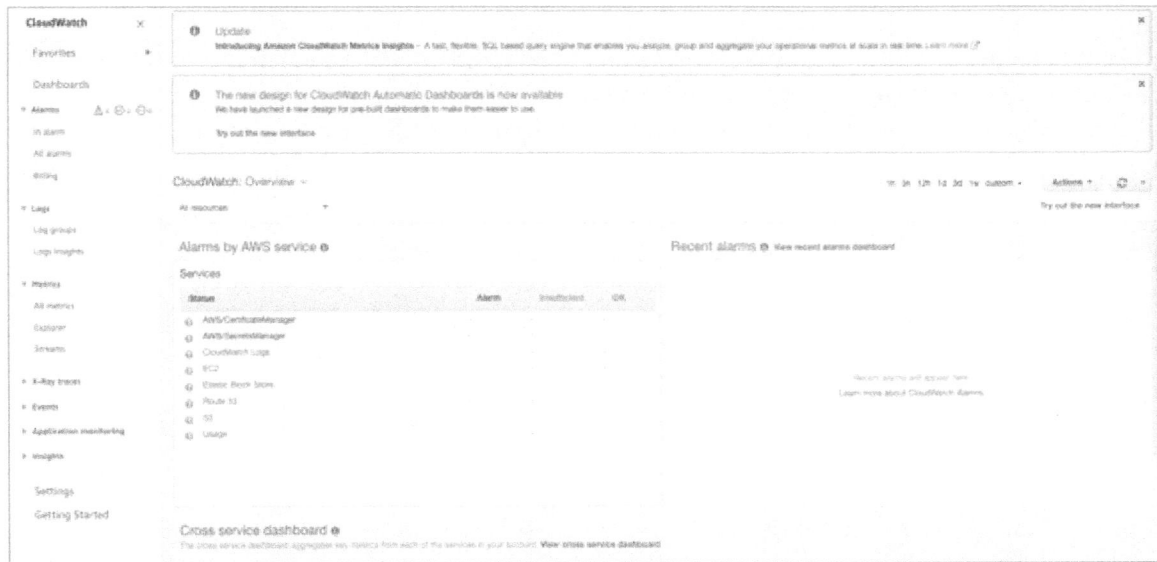

CloudWatch can be considered an umbrella service consisting of many small components or features. As you can see in the screenshot above on the left side, they are many. It has Dashboard, Alarms, Logs, Metrics, X-Ray traces, Events, Application monitoring, and Insights sections – these are the main sections.

AWS CloudWatch Dashboard

With this feature, you can create a custom dashboard based on your requirements for the kind of metrics you are interested in, particularly resources. For example, if you are interested in EC2 instances CPU utilization metrics or ConsumeWriteCapacityUnits metrics of DynamoDB. You can set up various graphs of resources you are interested in to look at a glance to idea about the assessment of the health of the resources. There is a lot to it – you can add live data to the dashboard. In summary, with the dashboard, you can quickly get the health of your system.

Alarm

We have the Alarm section, which is very useful for getting the notification as an event happens. This notification can help you take appropriate action. For example, you can set up a Billing alarm to get a notification if your bill crosses 75% of your total budget for the current month.

Logs

The logs section is handy for assessing what's going on in your application. The Logs section is separated into two groups: Log groups and Insights.

Log groups are just data dumps for your log files. Insights is a relatively new feature where you can run SQL-looking queries to search through log files. It is very powerful -- you can run regular expression types of query, group, etc.

This is very handy as searching through logs for particular information is a bit challenging as there may be log files in 100 or 1000.

Metrics

The Metrics is a very important and very useful section. You can get very extensive idea about your AWS resources and applications by looking at various metrics data of various AWS resources. You can cut data based on the period and conclude by looking at multiple graphs about what's happening with your AWS resources in your AWS account. Tons of metrics are by default, available to you.

Events

The Events are divided into two sections Rules and Event Buses. You can create a Rule and add an event pattern to hook that to a Lambda function, or you can add a scheduled event such as running a Lambda function every 30 min. You can configure it to pass input to the Lambda function as well. The Event Buses section is related to event delegation.

X-Ray traces

X-Ray traces is a distributed tracing tool. If you have a microservices-based application deployed and would like to help troubleshoot issues related to microservices, this tool could be very helpful. You can instrument the code to log the aspect using CloudWatch log, for example, logging requests and the response of a microservices call. The X-Ray service can then access these logs to troubleshoot performance-related issues on this microservice.

KEY POINTS

- Amazon CloudWatch service provides metrics for almost **every** service in AWS
- Metric is a variable (data about the performance of your systems) to monitor, such as CPU Util, I/O, etc.
- Dimension (instance id, environment, etc.) is an attribute of a metric
- By default, many services provide free metrics for resources (such as Amazon EC2 instances, Amazon EBS volumes, and Amazon RDS DB instances).
- Amazon CloudWatch can load all the metrics in your account (both AWS resource metrics and application metrics that you provide) for search, graphing, and alarms.
- Metric data is kept for 15 months, allowing you to view up-to-the-minute and historical data.

CloudWatch Metric Streams

You can use metric streams to continually stream CloudWatch metrics to a destination, such as Amazon S3, Amazon Redshift, Amazon OpenSearch, and third-party service providers with near-real-time delivery and low latency. Additionally, you can filter metrics to only stream a subset of them.

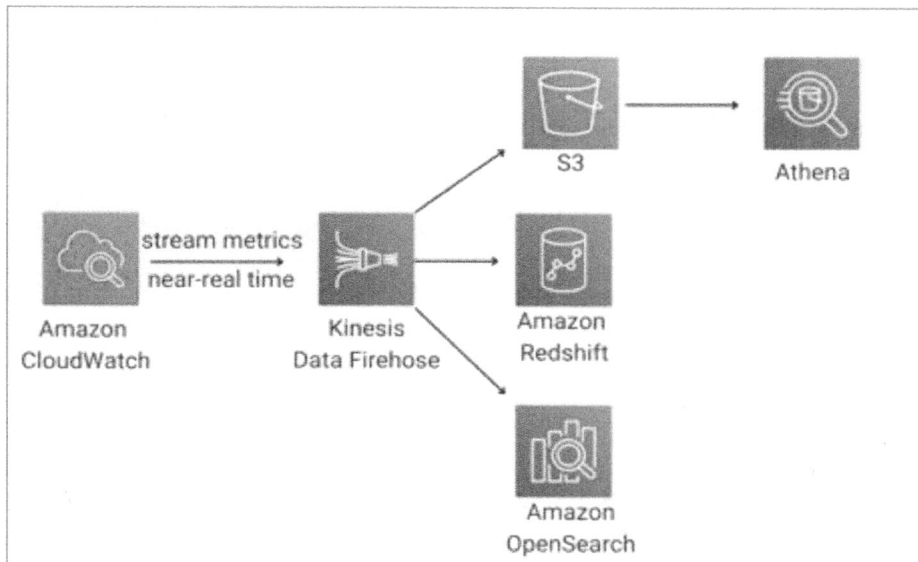

There are two main use cases of the CloudWatch metric streams: data lake and third-party providers.

You can ingest metric streams to your data lake, such as S3, and combine them with the other billing and performance data to create rich data for analytics.

You can also integrate with third-party providers (such as Datadog, Dynatrace, Splunk, etc.) to monitor, troubleshoot, and analyze your applications using the streamed CloudWatch data.

CloudWatch Logs

CloudWatch Log groups are data dumps for your log files representing an application. You can define log expiration policies (such as never expire, 30 days, etc.)

A log stream is a sequence of events sharing the same source. Each separate source of logs in CloudWatch Logs makes up a different log stream.

CloudWatch Logs can send logs to Amazon S3, Kinesis Data Streams, Kinesis Data Firehose, AWS Lambda, and OpenSearch.

Reference: https://docs.aws.amazon.com/AmazonCloudWatch/latest/logs/Working-with-log-groups-and-streams.html

CloudWatch Sources

You can use Amazon CloudWatch Logs to monitor, store, and access your log files from the following log sources:

Amazon EC2 instances, Elastic Beanstalk, ECS, AWS CloudTrail, API Gateway, Route 53 (log DNS queries), AWS Lambda (function logs), VPC Flow Logs.

CloudWatch Logs Metric Filter & Insights

You can use **metric filter** expressions on CloudWatch Logs. For example, find a specific IP, or find the count of the number of "ERROR" in logs.

You can also use **metric filters** to trigger CloudWatch alarms.

CloudWatch Log Insights is a relatively new feature where you can run SQL-looking queries to search through log files. It is very powerful -- you can run regular expression types of query, group, etc.

This is very handy as searching through logs for particular information is a bit challenging as there may be log files in 100 or 1000. And searching for information through many files is a bit process involved.

CloudWatch Logs – S3 Export

You can export CloudWatch Logs data to Amazon S3. You can export CloudWatch Logs to Amazon S3.

You can do the following:
- Export log data to S3 buckets that KMS encrypts.
- Export log data to S3 buckets with S3 Object Lock enabled with a retention period.

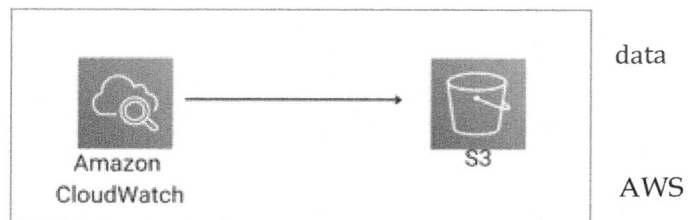

You can also export using API: The API call is CreateExportTask.

```
aws logs create-export-task --profile ExportIAMUser --task-name
"cloudwatchtos3400" --log-group-name "cloudwatchtos3" --from
1331290400000 --to 1331290800000 -destination "testsample-bucket-
100" --destination-prefix "log-output"
```

It takes around 5 to 10 minutes for logs to be available in CloudWatch after a function invocation.

So, if you want real-time / near real-time, you need to use a logs subscription to access a real-time feed of log events and have it delivered to streaming services (Kinesis) and AWS Lambda.

CloudWatch Logs Subscriptions

So, suppose you want real-time / near real-time. In that case, you need to use a logs subscription to access a real-time feed of log events and have it delivered to other services such as an Amazon Kinesis stream, an Amazon Kinesis Data Firehose stream, or AWS Lambda for custom processing, analysis, or loading to other systems.

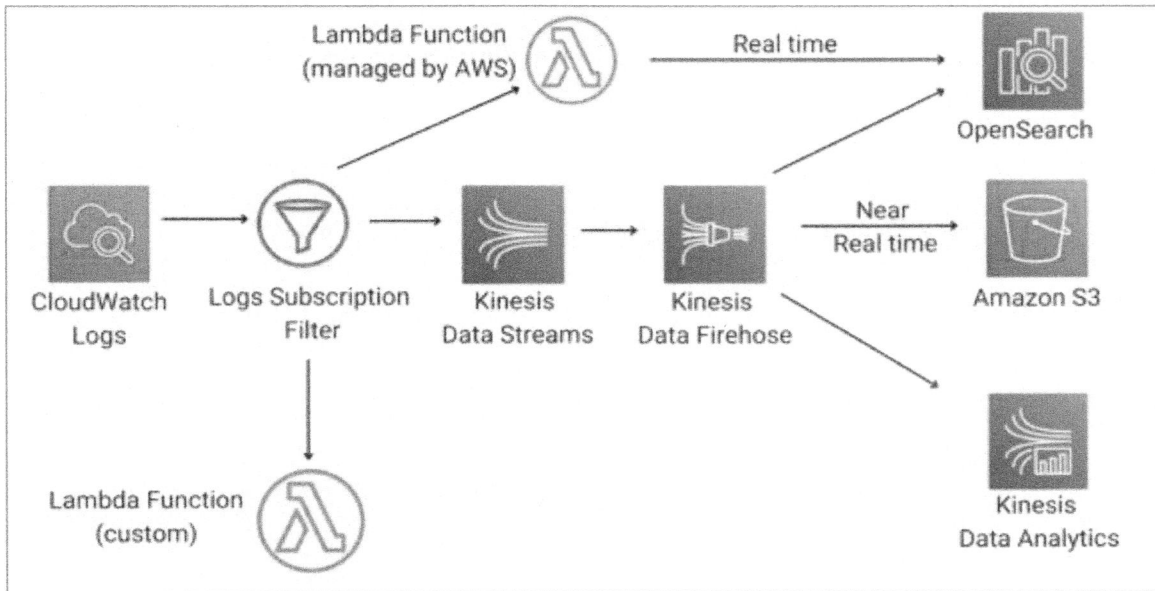

CloudWatch Logs Aggregation

Amazon CloudWatch can't aggregate data across Regions. Metrics are completely separate between Regions. However, you can aggregate statistics for your EC2 instances with detailed monitoring enabled. Instances that use basic monitoring are separate.

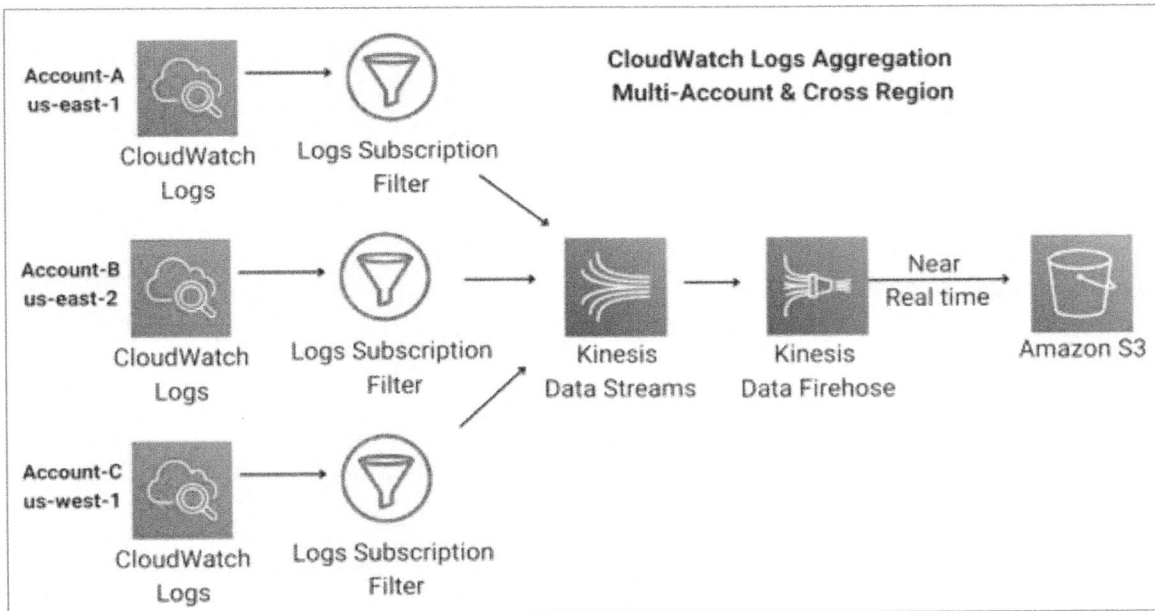

You can create cross-account cross-Region dashboards to summarize your CloudWatch data from multiple AWS accounts and multiple Regions into one dashboard.

You can create a cross-account programmatically as well.

To create a cross-account cross-Region dashboard, you need to enable at least one sharing account and monitoring account.

CloudWatch Logs for EC2

If you need to push logs from an EC2 instance to CloudWatch --- you will have to use the CloudWatch Logs agent. By default, EC2 instances don't push logs to CloudWatch.

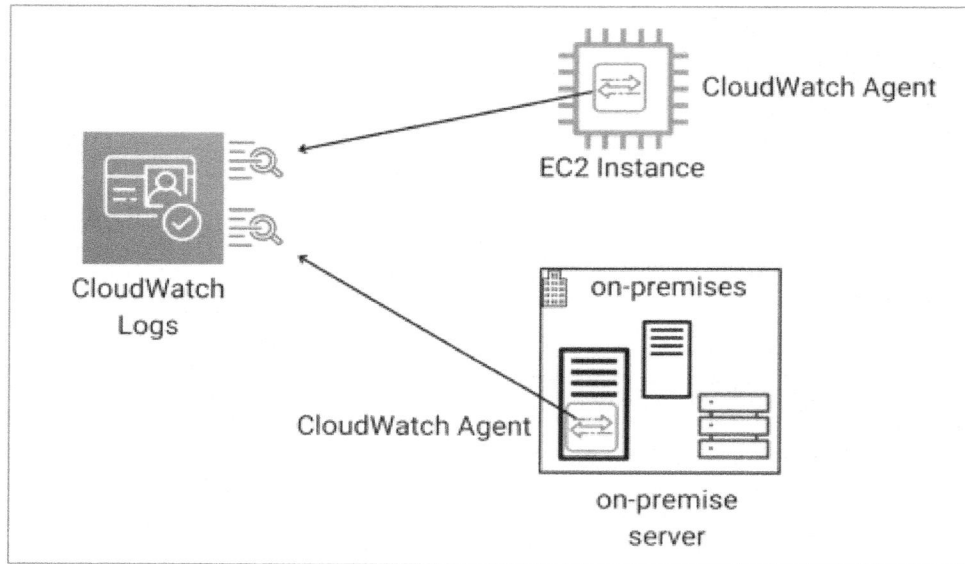

You need to run a CloudWatch agent on EC2 to push the log files you want. The CloudWatch Logs agent provides an automated way to push log data to CloudWatch from Amazon EC2 instances. The log agent includes a script that initiates the process of pushing log data and a plug-in to the AWS CLI that pushes log data.

Make sure IAM permissions are correct. The CloudWatch log agent can be set up on-premises too.

CloudWatch Logs Agent & Unified Agent

- They are used to send logs from virtual servers such as from EC2 instances and on-premises servers.

- CloudWatch logs agent is the old version of the agent. It can only send logs to CloudWatch Logs.

- The Unified CloudWatch agent enables you to collect both logs and advanced system-level metrics, such as disk metrics, RAM, CPU, disk I/O, processes, network, etc., from Amazon EC2 instances with one agent. It offers support across operating systems, including servers running Windows Server.

- You can use centralized configuration using SSM Parameter Store.

CloudWatch Alarms

CloudWatch alarms are used to trigger notifications for any metric. There are various options, such as sampling, %, max, min, threshold, etc.

You can create *metric* and *composite* alarms in Amazon CloudWatch.

- A *metric alarm* watches a single CloudWatch metric or the result of a math expression based on CloudWatch metrics.

- A *composite alarm* includes a rule expression that considers the alarm states of other alarms you have created. The composite alarm goes into an ALARM state only if all conditions of the rule are met.

Metric alarm states

A CloudWatch Metric Alarm is always in one of three states:

OK: The metric or expression is within the defined threshold.
ALARM: The metric or expression is outside of the defined threshold.
INSUFFICIENT_DATA: The alarm has just started, the metric is not available, or not enough data is available for the metric to determine the alarm state.

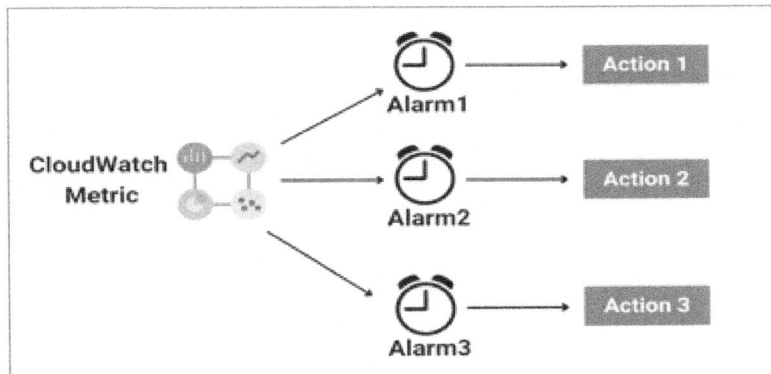

Evaluating an alarm

When you create an alarm, you specify the following settings based on which CloudWatch evaluates when to change the alarm state:

- **Period** (in seconds or minutes) is the time to evaluate the metric or expression to create each data point.
- **Evaluation Periods** are the number of the most recent periods or data points to evaluate to determine the alarm state.
- **Datapoints to Alarm** is the number of data points within the Evaluation Periods that must be breached to cause the alarm to trigger any associated action.

The minimum resolution supported by CloudWatch is **one-second** data points, a high-resolution metric. You can also store metrics for one minute.

Sometimes metrics are received at varying intervals, such as three or 5-minute intervals.

If you set the alarm on a high-resolution metric, you can specify an alarm for **10 seconds or 30 seconds, or** any multiple of 60 seconds.

Alarm Actions
The common targets for CloudWatch alarm actions are **Amazon SNS, Amazon EC2, or EC2 Auto Scaling.**

You can specify an alarm's actions when it changes state between the states (OK, ALARM, and INSUFFICIENT_DATA.

- **Send notification to SNS:** The most common type of alarm action is to send a notification by sending a message to an SNS topic. You can do almost anything once you get a notification on SNS.
- **Stop, Terminate, Reboot, or Recover an EC2 instance**: Alarms based on EC2 metrics can be used to stop, terminate, reboot, or recover an EC2 instance.
- **Trigger Auto Scaling Action:** Alarms can also be used to scale an Auto Scaling group.

Reference:

https://docs.aws.amazon.com/AmazonCloudWatch/latest/monitoring/AlarmThatSendsEmail.html

Amazon EventBridge
It was formerly called **CloudWatch Events**. Amazon EventBridge is the preferred way to manage your events. Both CloudWatch Events and EventBridge use the same underlying service and API; however, EventBridge provides more features. Changes you make in either CloudWatch or EventBridge will appear in each console.

Amazon EventBridge, a serverless event bus, makes it easier to build event-driven applications. It helps scale the event-driven applications using events generated from your applications, SaaS applications, and AWS services.

CloudWatch Alarms watch a single metric and respond to changes in that metric. Events can respond to actions or some other change in your AWS environment.

Amazon CloudWatch Events delivers a near real-time stream of system events that describe changes in AWS resources. You can quickly set up Amazon CloudWatch Events using simple rules.

Amazon EventBridge delivers real-time data streams from event sources such as AWS services, SaaS apps, microservices, or custom apps to targets like AWS Lambda and other SaaS applications.

When building application architectures for event-driven applications, you can set up routing rules to determine where to send your data to react in real-time to the event sources, with event publishers and consumers completely decoupled.

Use cases of Amazon EventBridge are re-architecting for speed, monitoring, and auditing, extending functionality via SaaS integrations, and customizing SaaS with AI/ML.

CloudWatch Event

Events in Amazon CloudWatch Events are represented as JSON objects. An example CloudWatch event JSON is shown below.

All CloudWatch events have the same top-level fields. The ones appearing in the example above are never absent.

The contents of the top-level detail field are different depending on which service generated the event and what the event is. The combination of the source and detail-type fields serves to identify the fields and values found in the detail field.

CloudWatch Event Examples

Schedule: Cron jobs (scheduled scripts)

You can create rules that self-trigger on an automated schedule in CloudWatch Events using cron or rate expressions. All scheduled events use a UTC zone, and the minimum precision for schedules is 1 minute.

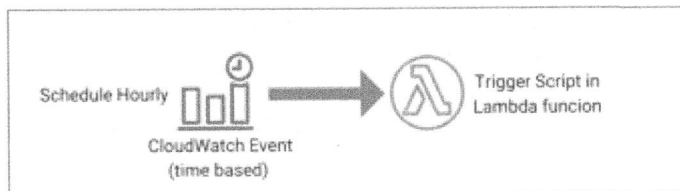

Event Pattern: Event rules to react to a service doing something

You can create a CloudWatch Events rule that triggers an event emitted by an AWS service.

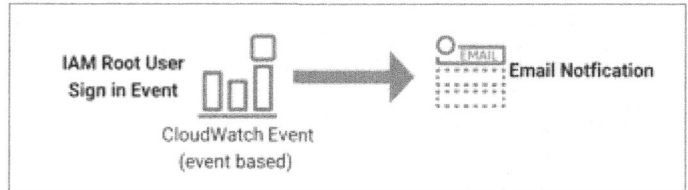

For example, on CloudWatch Console, you can configure it. For example, on the CloudWatch Console, choose Event Pattern, and build an event pattern to match events by service. For Service Name, choose the service that emits the event to trigger the rule. For Event Type, choose the specific event that is to trigger the rule. For Targets, choose Add Target and choose the AWS service that is to act when an event of the selected type is detected. For example, trigger Lambda functions, or send SQS/SNS messages.

Amazon EventBridge Rules

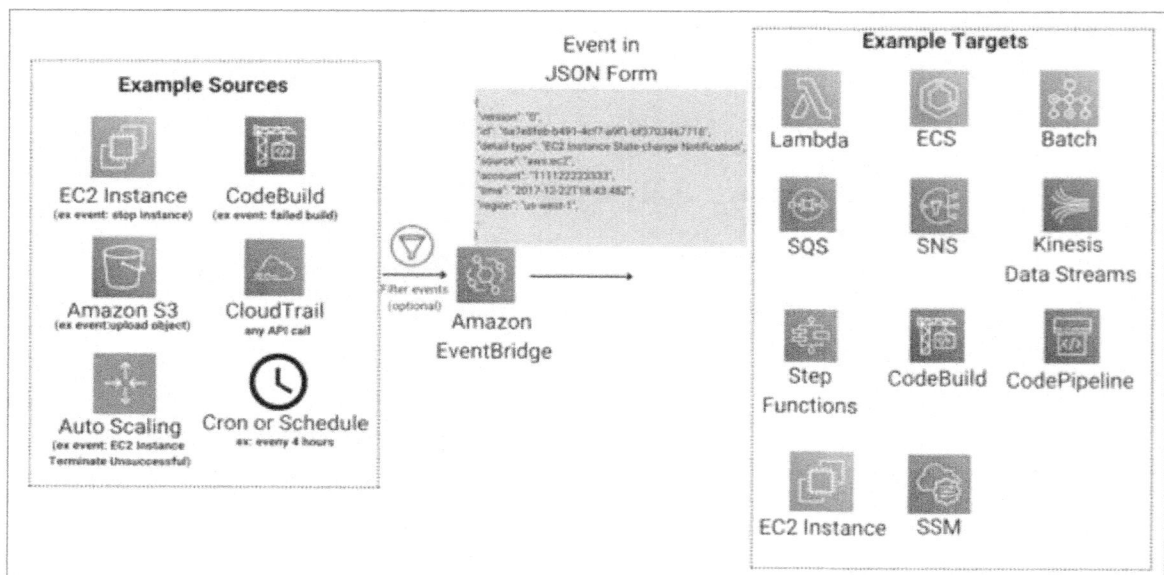

You can set up an Event Rule. For example, for Service Name, choose the service that emits the event to trigger the rule. For Event Type, choose the specific event that is to trigger the rule. For Targets, choose Add Target and choose the AWS service that is to act when an event of the selected type is detected. For example, trigger Lambda functions, or send SQS/SNS messages.

- You can filter events, which is optional.
- Events are passed in JSON form.

Amazon EventBridge Event Bus

- An event bus receives events, uses rules to evaluate them, applies configured input transformation, and sends them to the appropriate target(s). default event bus in each account receives events from AWS services.

any

then

The

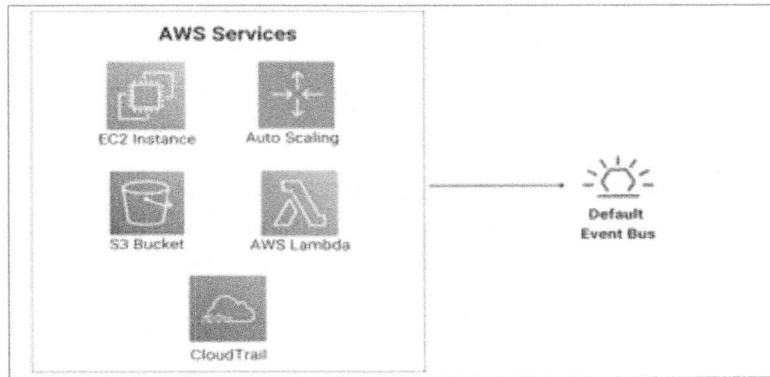

- EventBridge provides an option to create SaaS event buses and custom event buses on top of the default bus.

- The SaaS event bus is used to channel through events triggered by SaaS platforms.

- A custom event bus can receive events from your custom applications and services.

- You can configure EventBridge to send and receive events between accounts. You can specify which AWS accounts can send events or receive events from the event bus in your account.

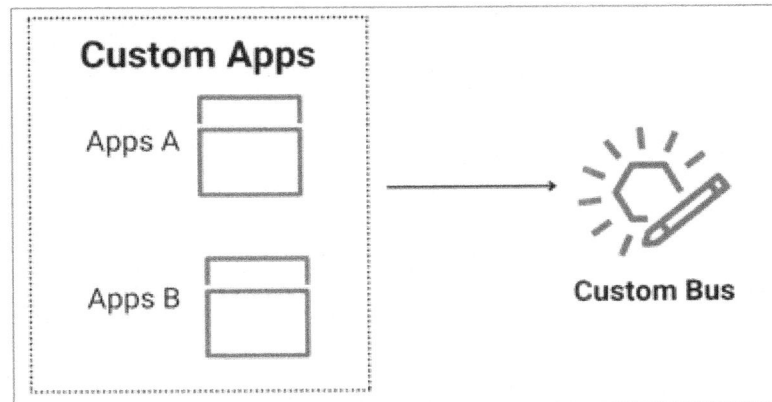

- Event buses can be accessed by other AWS accounts using Resource-based Policies.

- A custom event bus sends events to or receives events from a different Region to aggregate events in a single location.

- You can archive all or filter events sent to an event bus indefinitely or set a period. You can replay archived events.

Reference:
https://docs.aws.amazon.com/eventbridge/latest/userguide/eb-cross-account.html
https://docs.aws.amazon.com/eventbridge/latest/userguide/eb-saas.html

Amazon EventBridge Schema Registry

- A schema defines the structure -- An EventBridge schema defines the structure of events that are sent to EventBridge. It helps in advance how data of an event is structured in the event bus.

- EventBridge provides schemas for all events that are generated by AWS services. In addition, EventBridge can analyze the events in your bus and infer the schema. Schema can be versioned.

- You can also create or upload custom schemas.

- The Amazon EventBridge Schema Registry allows you to discover, create, and manage schemas for events on EventBridge. EventBridge schemas can be versioned.

- Once you have a schema for an event, you can download code bindings for popular programming languages, which can help speed up development.

Amazon EventBridge Resource-based Policy

You can configure EventBridge to send and receive events between accounts. You can specify which AWS accounts can send events or receive events from the event bus in your account.

Event buses can be accessed by other AWS accounts using Resource-based Policies. Resource-based policies manage permissions for a specific event bus. For example, you can allow/deny events from another AWS account or AWS Region.

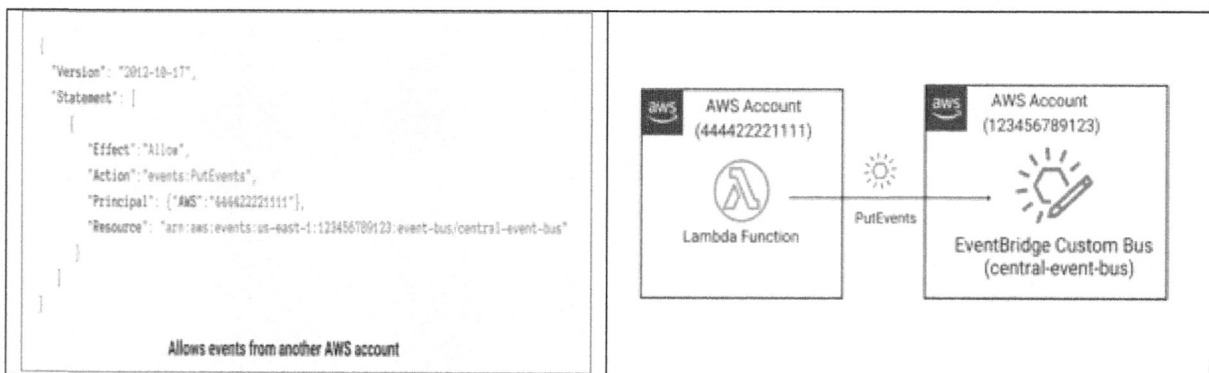

Use case: You can apply Resource-based policies to aggregate all events from your AWS Organization in a single AWS account or AWS region.

CloudWatch Insights

CloudWatch Container Insights

- Container Insights collects, aggregates, and summarizes metrics and logs from your containerized applications and microservices.

- Container Insights is available for **ECS, EKS, and Kubernetes platforms on Amazon EC2**. It also supports collecting metrics from clusters deployed on **Fargate** for both Amazon ECS and Amazon EKS.

- Container Insights also provides diagnostic information, such as container restart failures, to help you isolate and resolve issues quickly.

- You can also set CloudWatch alarms on metrics that Container Insights collects.

- Metrics collected by Container Insights are charged as custom metrics.

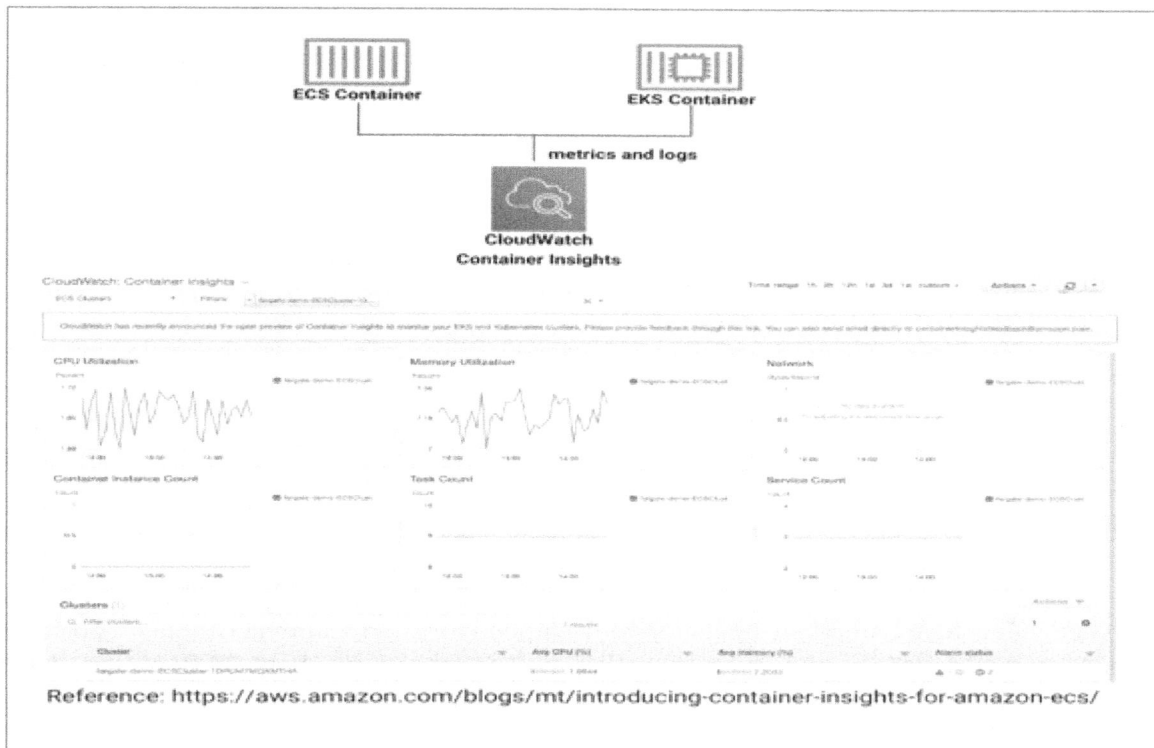

Reference: https://aws.amazon.com/blogs/mt/introducing-container-insights-for-amazon-ecs/

- In Amazon EKS and Kubernetes, Container Insights uses a containerized version of the CloudWatch agent to discover all the running containers in a cluster.

- Amazon provides CloudWatch agent container image on Amazon ECR.

CloudWatch Lambda Insights

- It is a monitoring and troubleshooting solution for serverless applications on AWS Lambda.

- It collects, aggregates, and summarizes system-level metrics, including CPU time, memory, disk, and network usage.

- It also collects, aggregates, and summarizes diagnostic information such as cold starts and Lambda worker shutdowns to help isolate issues and resolve them quickly for your Lambda functions.

- Lambda Insights uses a new CloudWatch Lambda Insights extension, which is provided as a Lambda layer.

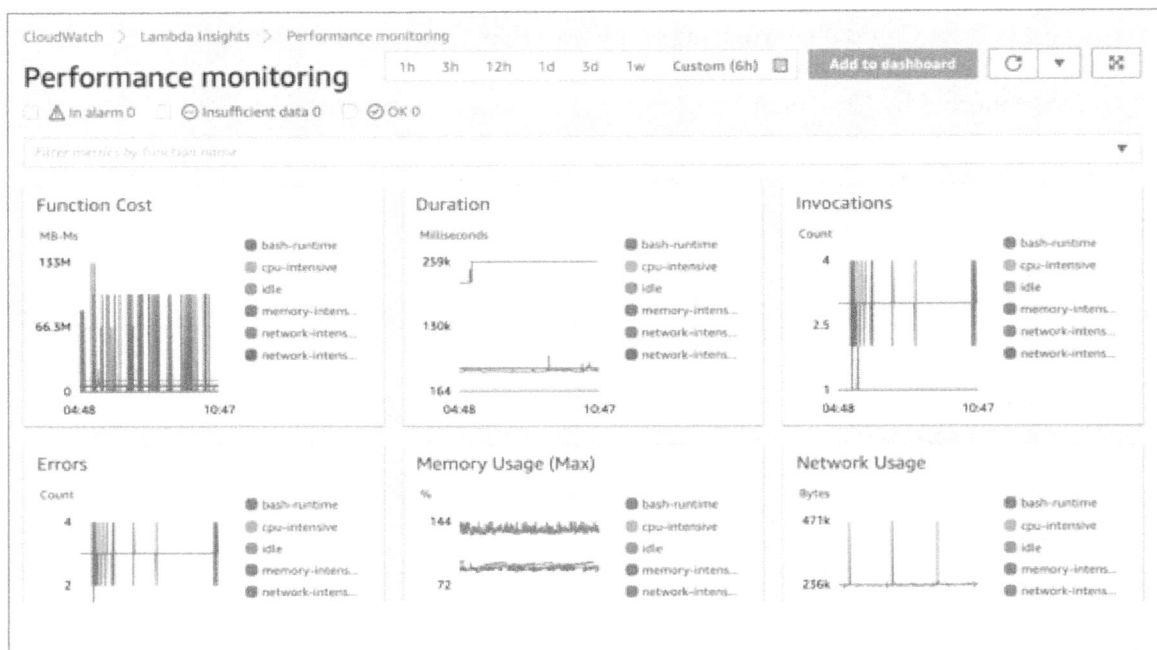

Reference: https://docs.aws.amazon.com/lambda/latest/dg/monitoring-insights.html

- When you enable Lambda Insights for your Lambda function, Lambda Insights reports eight metrics per function, and every function invocation sends about 1KB of log data to CloudWatch.

- You only pay for the metrics and logs reported for your function by Lambda Insights.

- You can use Lambda Insights with any runtimes supporting Lambda extensions.

CloudWatch Contributor Insights

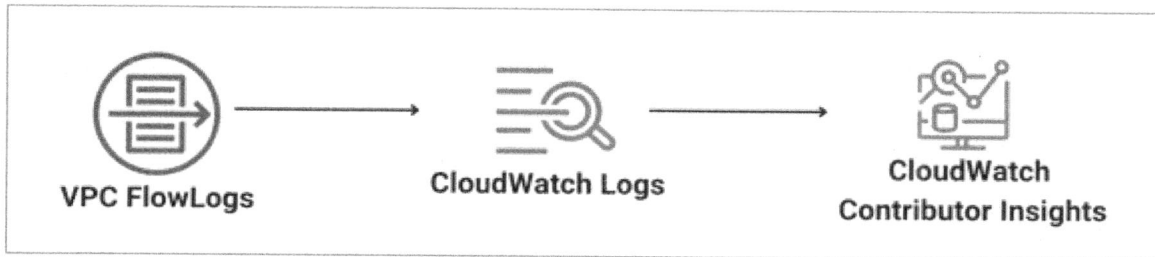

VPC FlowLogs → **CloudWatch Logs** → **CloudWatch Contributor Insights**

It analyzes time-series data to find the top contributors influencing system performance.

For example, you can use Contributor Insights to analyze log data and create time series that provides information about contributors. For example, you can find the top N, the total number of unique contributors, and their usage.

The findings help you find top talkers and understand contributors impacting system performance. For example, you can find rogue hosts, the heaviest network users, or the URLs that generate the most errors.

Rules:
You can use sample rules that AWS has created when you use the AWS Management Console. In addition, you can build your rules from scratch.

Rules define the log fields you want to use to define contributors, such as IP Address. You can also filter the log data to find and analyze the behavior of individual contributors.

All rules analyze incoming data in real-time.

CloudWatch also provides built-in rules you can use with their AWS services to analyze metrics.

CloudWatch Application Insights

It facilitates observability for your applications and underlying AWS resources. For example, it provides automated dashboards that show potential problems with monitored applications to help isolate ongoing issues.

CloudWatch Application Insights is powered by Amazon SageMaker and other AWS technologies.

The Application Insights' enhanced visibility into the health of your applications helps reduce the mean time to repair (MTTR) to troubleshoot your application issues.

It provides additional insights that point to a possible root cause and steps for resolution for common problems in .NET and SQL application stacks, such as application latency, SQL Server failed backups, memory leaks, large HTTP requests, and canceled I/O operations.

It has built-in integration with AWS SSM OpsCenter allows you to send findings and alerts to SSM OpsCenter to resolve issues by running the relevant Systems Manager Automation document.

CloudWatch Insights Key Summary

CloudWatch Container Insights
Summarizes metrics and logs. Works with ECS, EKS, Kubernetes on EC2, Fargate

CloudWatch Lambda Insights
Summarizes system-level detailed metrics to troubleshoot serverless applications.

CloudWatch Contributors Insights
Find "Top-N" contributors, rogue hosts, the heaviest network users, or the URLs that generate the most errors.

CloudWatch Application Insights
Provides automated dashboards that show potential problems with monitored applications.

AWS CloudTrail

- Visibility into your AWS account activities are crucial to the security and operational best practices. AWS CloudTrail helps you enable governance, compliance, and operational risk auditing of your AWS account.

- You can use CloudTrail for all things related to account activity across your AWS infrastructure, such as view, search, download, archive, and analyze.

- You can get a history of events / API calls made within your AWS Account by AWS Management Console, AWS SDK, AWS CLI, and AWS Services.

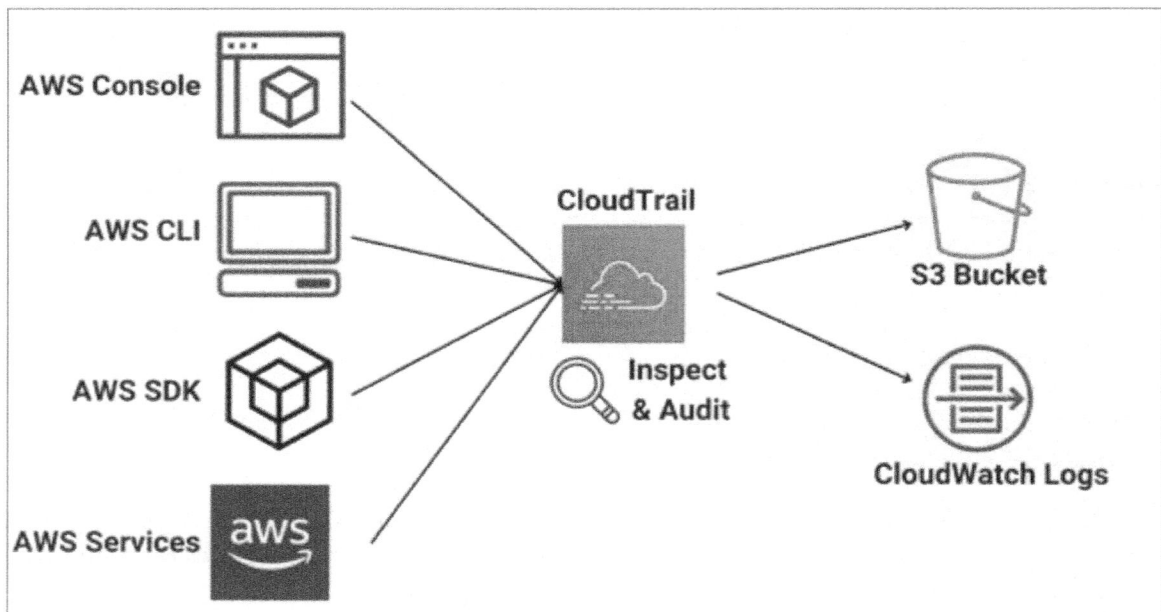

- You can put logs from CloudTrail into CloudWatch Logs or S3.

- You can integrate CloudTrail into applications using the API, automate trail creation for your organization, check the status of trails you create, and control how users view CloudTrail events.

- A trial can be applied to All Regions (default) or a single Region.

- If a resource is deleted in AWS, to investigate, look into CloudTrail first!

CloudTrail Events

Management Events

- Management Events are Operations that are performed on resources in your AWS account. For example, configuring security, configuring rules for routing data, or setting up logging.

- By default, trails are configured to log management events.

- You can separate Read Events -- which don't modify resources -- from Write Events -- which may modify resources.

Data Events

- CloudTrail data events (also known as "data plane operations") show the resource operations performed on or within a resource in your AWS account.

- For example, Amazon S3 object-level activity, such as GetObject, DeleteObject, and PutObject; or AWS Lambda function execution activity, which is invoking an API.

- You can separate Read and Write Events.

CloudTrail Insights Events

You can enable CloudTrail Insights to detect unusual activity in your account, such as inaccurate resource provisioning, hitting service limits, bursts of AWS IAM actions, or gaps in periodic maintenance activity.

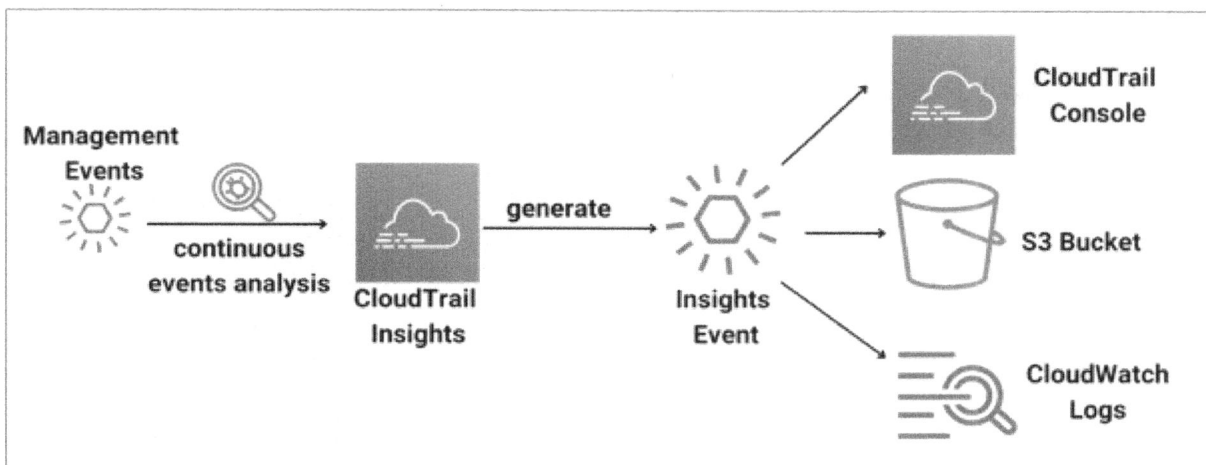

CloudTrail Insights analyzes normal management events to create a baseline. And then continuously analyzes write events to detect unusual patterns and anomalies that appear in the CloudTrail console. Events are sent to Amazon S3 and Amazon CloudWatch logs.

CloudTrail Events Retention

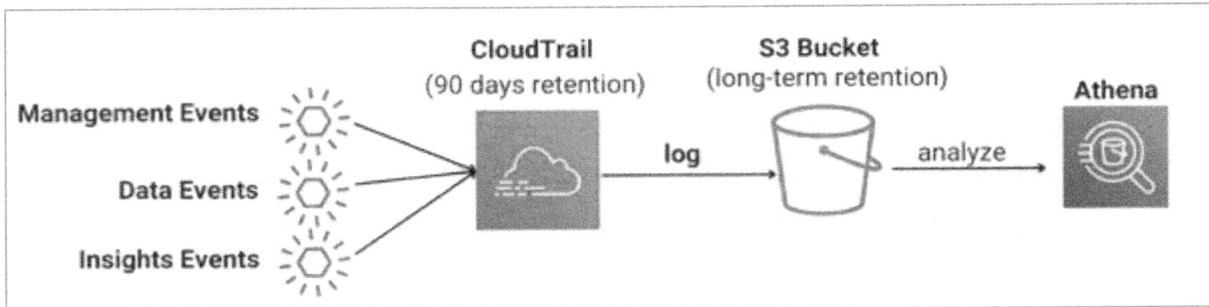

By default, CloudTrail retains logs for the last 90 days. If you want to store events beyond 90 days, log them to S3. You can use Athena to query and analyze them.

Intercept API Calls

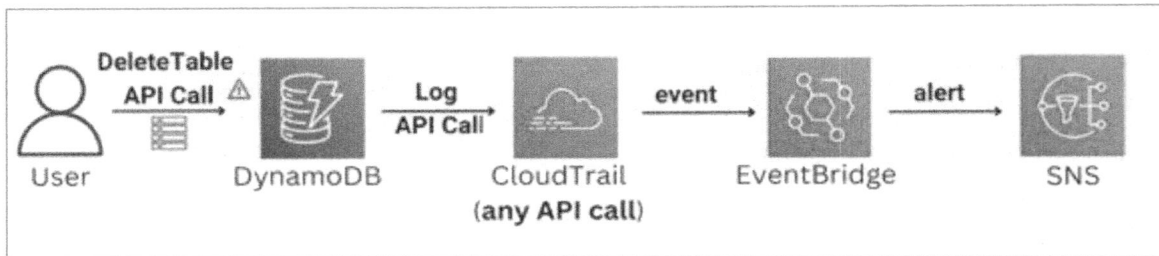

You can use CloudTrail, EventBridge, and SNS to intercept API calls and get notified in which you are interested, such as if a DeleteTable API call is executed.

AWS Config

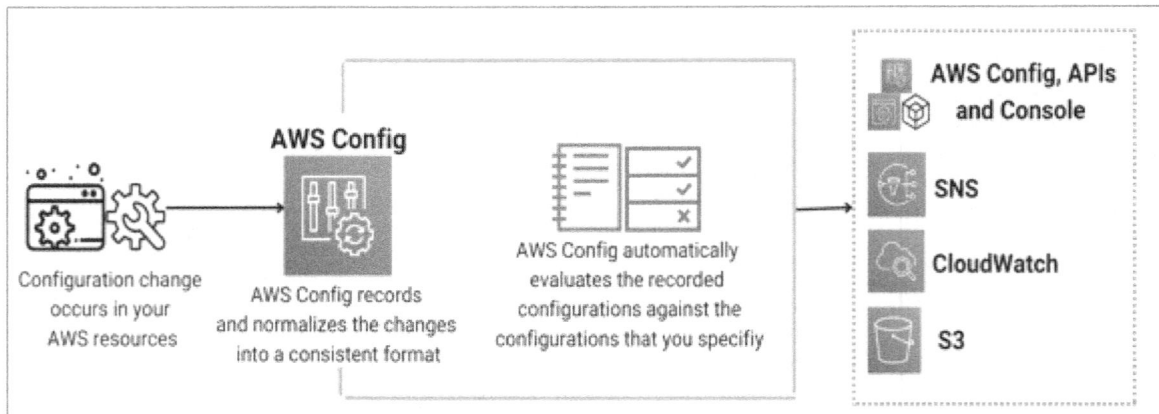

AWS Config continually assesses, audits, and evaluates the configurations and relationships of your resources.

That way, it helps with auditing and recording compliance of your AWS resources and recording configurations and changes over time.

It simplifies operational troubleshooting by correlating configuration changes to particular events in your accounts.

For example, questions that AWS Config can answer:
- Is there unrestricted SSH access to my security groups?
- Do my buckets have any public access?
- How has my ALB configuration changed over time?

When changes occur, you can access change history and compliance results using console or APIs, CloudWatch Events, or SNS alerts. You can deliver change history and snapshot files to your S3 bucket, which you can analyze by Athena.

AWS Config is a per-region service. It can be aggregated across regions and accounts.

KEY POINTS

- You can view compliance of a resource over time
- You can view the configuration of a resource over time
- You can view CloudTrail API calls of a resource over time
- It evaluates your AWS resource configurations for desired / compliance settings
- It sends notifications whenever an AWS resource is created, modified, or deleted

Config Rules

AWS Config Rules evaluates the configuration settings of your AWS resources.

Rules can be evaluated or triggered when AWS Config detects a configuration change or at a regular interval that you choose, for example, every 12 hours.

There are two types of Config Rules: AWS Config Managed Rules and AWS Config Custom Rules.

AWS Config Managed Rules: Managed rules are predefined, customizable rules created by AWS Config. The AWS Config console provides a list of all available managed rules -- there are over 84 of them currently.

AWS Config Custom Rules: You can create custom rules using Guard (Guard GitHub Repository) or Lambda functions. For example: evaluate if each EBS disk is of type gp2 or evaluate if each EC2 instance is t2.micro.

AWS Lambda uses custom code invoked by events published by an event source, which AWS Config invokes when the custom rule is initiated.

AWS Config Rules does not prevent actions from happening -- no deny.

Pricing:

- There is no free tier
- $0.003 per configuration item recorded/region
- $0.001 per config rule evaluation/region

Config Rules Notifications

Let's look into two typical notification use cases:

- You can EventBridge to trigger notifications when AWS resources have become non-compliant due to configuration changes.

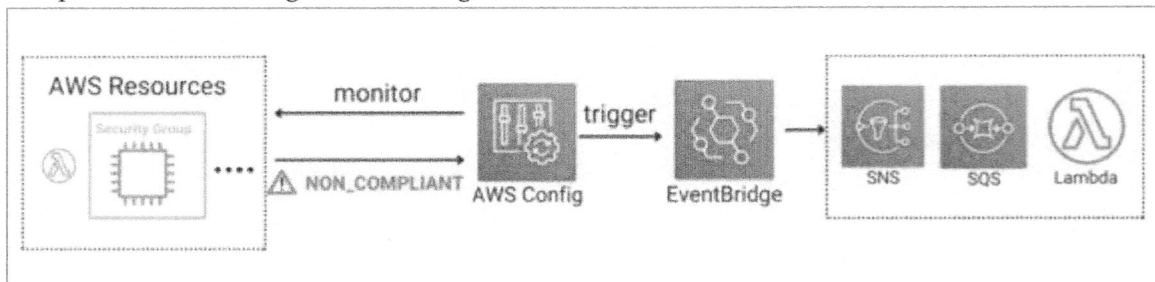

- You can send configuration changes and compliance state notifications to SNS for all events. You can also use SNS Filtering or filter on the client side.

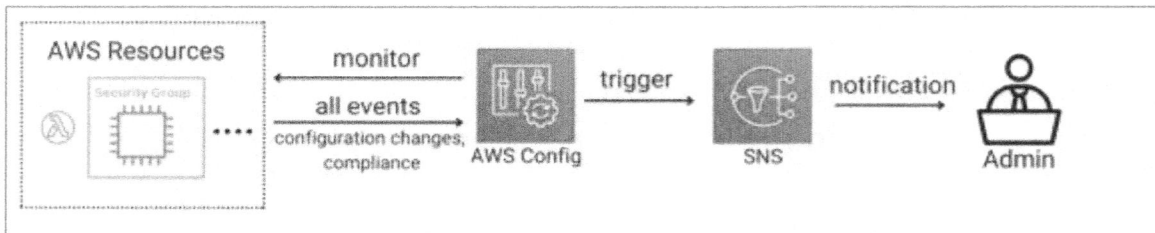

Config Rules Remediations

- You can automate the remediation of non-compliant resources using SSM Automation Documents.
- You can use AWS-Managed Automation Documents or create custom Automation Documents.
- You can create custom Automation Documents that invoke a Lambda function.
- You can set Remediation Retries if the resource is still non-compliant after auto-remediation

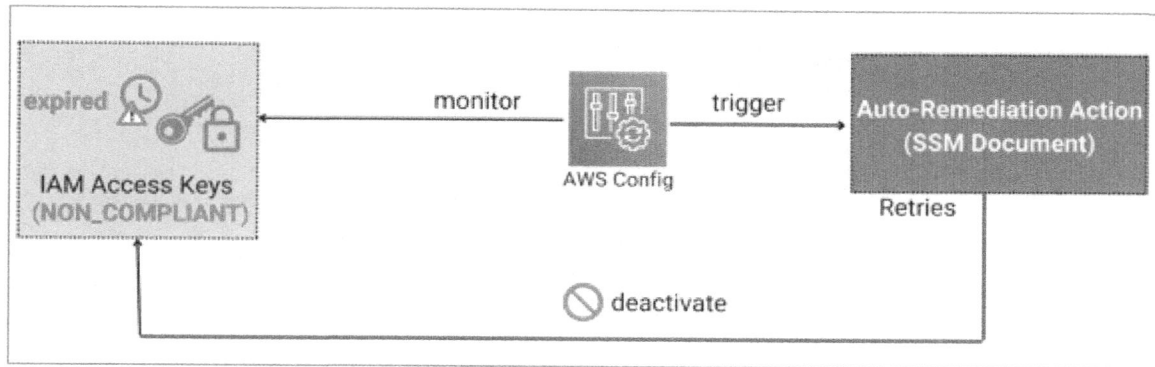

CloudWatch vs CloudTrail vs Config

CloudWatch: Used for **performance monitoring**, events & alerts, log aggregation & analysis.

CloudTrail: Used to **record API calls**. You can define trails for specific resources. It's a global service.

Config: Used to record **configuration changes**, evaluate configuration changes against compliance rules, and get a timeline of changes and compliance.

AWS Service Health Dashboard

The AWS Service Health Dashboard is an AWS general service event dashboard where you can view the overall health of AWS services. In other words, the AWS Service Health Dashboard is the single place to find out about the availability and health of AWS services.

In addition, you can view the overall status of AWS services. Amazon Web Services publishes up-to-the-minute information on service availability using its Health Dashboard page. You can check the page to get current status information about AWS services or subscribe to an RSS feed to be notified about any interruption of AWS services.

The page can be accessed via the URL - https://status.aws.amazon.com/.

AWS Personal Health Dashboard

AWS Personal Health Dashboard offers alerts and remediation guidance when AWS is having issues that might impact your workloads or any other access issues. While the Service Health Dashboard provides the general availability status of AWS services, Personal Health Dashboard gives you a personalized view of the performance and availability of the AWS services underlying your AWS resources.

With Personal Health Dashboard, alerts are triggered by changes in the health of AWS resources. The alerts provide you with event visibility and guidance to help quickly diagnose and resolve issues. For example, in the event of an AWS hardware failure, which impacts one of your EBS volumes, you will get an alert that includes a list of your affected resources and a recommendation to restore your volume.

Section 4. AWS RDS and Databases

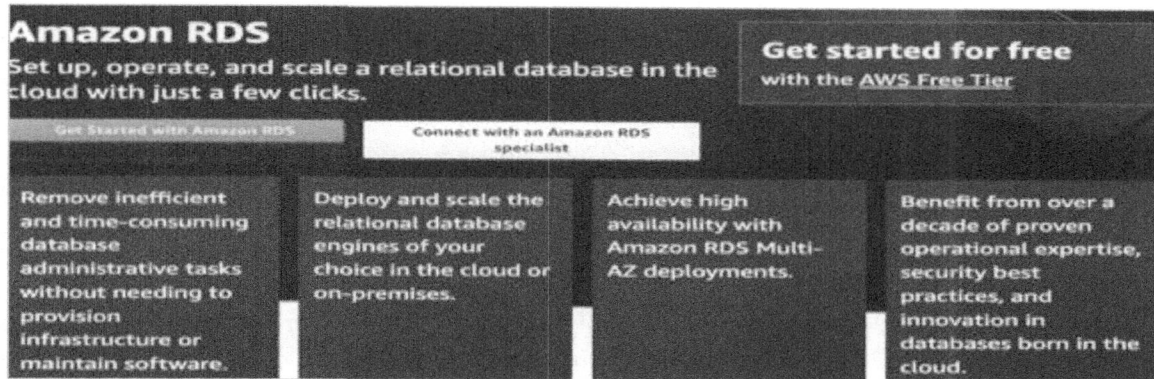

Chapter 22. AWS RDS and Cache

You will learn the following in this chapter:
- Amazon RDS
- RDS Multi-AZ
- RDS Read Replica
- Amazon Aurora
- Amazon ElastiCache
- Amazon Athena
- Amazon RedShift

Amazon RDS

Amazon RDS (Relational Database Service), which is AWS **managed** relational database cloud service, offers an easier way to set up, operate, and scale a relational database on the AWS platform. In other words, Amazon RDS allows you to create databases in the cloud that are managed by AWS. You can choose from six familiar database engines: Amazon Aurora (AWS proprietary database), PostgreSQL, MySQL, MariaDB, Oracle Database, and SQL Server.

Amazon RDS provides cost-efficient, resizable capacity and is optimized for memory, performance, and I/O. It automates time-consuming tasks such as hardware provisioning, database setup, patching, and backups. It frees you to focus on your applications so you can give them the fast performance, high availability, security, and compatibility they need. It minimizes relational database management by automation. It creates multiple instances for high availability and failovers.

Amazon RDS provides a selection of instance types optimized to fit different relational database use cases. You can create RDS instance types comprising varying CPU, memory, storage, and networking capacity combinations. RDS allows you to choose the appropriate mix of resources to optimize the database for your use case by selecting the correct instance type and size.

RDS vs. Deploying Database on EC2

Since RDS is a managed service, AWS performs many routine database maintenance tasks for you, such as automatic provisioning, os patching, continuous backups, restore to specific timestamp (point-in-time restore), read replicas to improve read performance, multi-AZ setup for disaster recovery (DR).

But you can't make an SSH connection to your DB instances.

Amazon RDS Features

- As the RDS instances are optimized for memory, performance, or I/O, therefore the performance of the AWS-managed RDS instance is better than a customer-managed database instance.

- Customers use Amazon RDS databases primarily for online-transaction processing (OLTP) workload, while Redshift is used primarily for reporting and analytics.

- It is not a NoSQL Database service.

- It cannot be used to take the load off databases. However, ElastiCache is often used with RDS to take the load off from RDS.

- Amazon RDS is a regional service.

- Amazon RDS protects database performance by avoiding suspending I/O activity on your primary during backup by backing up from your standby instance.

- Amazon RDS enhances durability by using synchronous replication technologies in Multi-AZ to keep the standby database instance up to date with the primary.

- Amazon RDS increases availability by deploying a standby instance in a second AZ and achieves fault tolerance in case of an AZ or database instance failure.

Availability and durability

Automated backups

The automated backup feature of Amazon RDS enables point-in-time recovery for your database instance. Amazon RDS will backup your database and transaction logs and store both for a user-specified retention period. This allows you to restore your database instance to any second during your retention period, up to the last five minutes. Your automatic backup retention period can be configured to up to thirty-five days.

Learn more »

Database snapshots

Database snapshots are user-initiated backups of your instance stored in Amazon S3 that are kept until you explicitly delete them. You can create a new instance from a database snapshots whenever you desire. Although database snapshots serve operationally as full backups, you are billed only for incremental storage use.

Multi-AZ deployments

Amazon RDS Multi-AZ deployments provide enhanced availability and durability for database instances, making them a natural fit for production database workloads. When you provision a Multi-AZ database instance, Amazon RDS synchronously replicates your data to a standby instance in a different Availability Zone (AZ).

Learn more »

Automatic host replacement

Amazon RDS will automatically replace the compute instance powering your deployment in the event of a hardware failure.

Lower administrative burden

Easy to use

You can use the AWS Management Console, the Amazon RDS Command Line Interface, or simple API calls to access the capabilities of a production-ready relational database in minutes.

Amazon RDS database instances are pre-configured with parameters and settings appropriate for the engine and class you have selected. You can launch a database instance and connect your application within minutes. DB Parameter Groups provide granular control and fine-tuning of your database.

Automatic software patching

Amazon RDS will make sure that the relational database software powering your deployment stays up-to-date with the latest patches. You can exert optional control over when and if your database instance is patched.

Learn more »

Best practice recommendations

Amazon RDS provide best practice guidance by analyzing configuration and usage metrics from your database instances. Recommendations cover areas such as database engine versions, storage, instance types, and networking. You can browse the available recommendations and perform a recommended action immediately, schedule it for their next maintenance window, or dismiss it entirely.

Learn more »

Screenshot reference: https://aws.amazon.com/rds/

Please go through all the features of Amazon RDS.

Database Storage Auto Scaling

Amazon RDS helps increase database storage dynamically. When RDS detects that database storage runs out of free storage, it scales automatically. That way, it avoids going through the effort of manually scaling your database storage.

Auto-scaling of database storage is useful for applications with unpredictable workloads. Therefore, all RDS engines support auto-scaling of database storage.

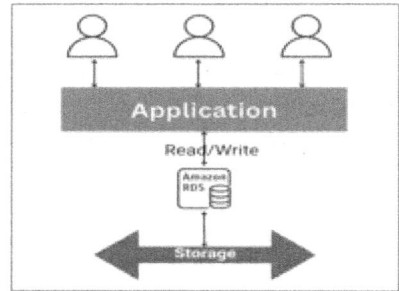

You have to set up a maximum storage threshold, the maximum limit for database storage. Then it automatically scales storage if free storage < 10% of allocates storage, low storage lasts at least 5 minutes, or 6 hours have elapsed since the last modification.

RDS Multi-AZ Deployments

Amazon RDS Multi-AZ deployments provide increased performance, availability, durability, and automatic failover for RDS database instances. This helps in managing database workloads.

When you provision a Multi-AZ RDS Instance, Amazon RDS automatically creates a primary DB Instance. The Amazon RDS then synchronously replicates the data to the standby instance in a different Availability Zone (AZ). In case of an infrastructure failure, Amazon RDS performs an automatic failover to the standby so that database operations can be resumed as soon as the failover is complete. Automatic database failover can complete as quickly as 60 seconds with zero data loss and no manual intervention. Since the endpoint for your DB Instance doesn't change after a failover, the application can resume its database operation without needing manual administrative intervention.

.

How it works

In an Amazon RDS Multi-AZ deployment, Amazon RDS automatically creates a primary database (DB) instance and synchronously replicates the data to an instance in a different AZ. When it detects a failure, Amazon RDS automatically fails over to a standby instance without manual intervention.

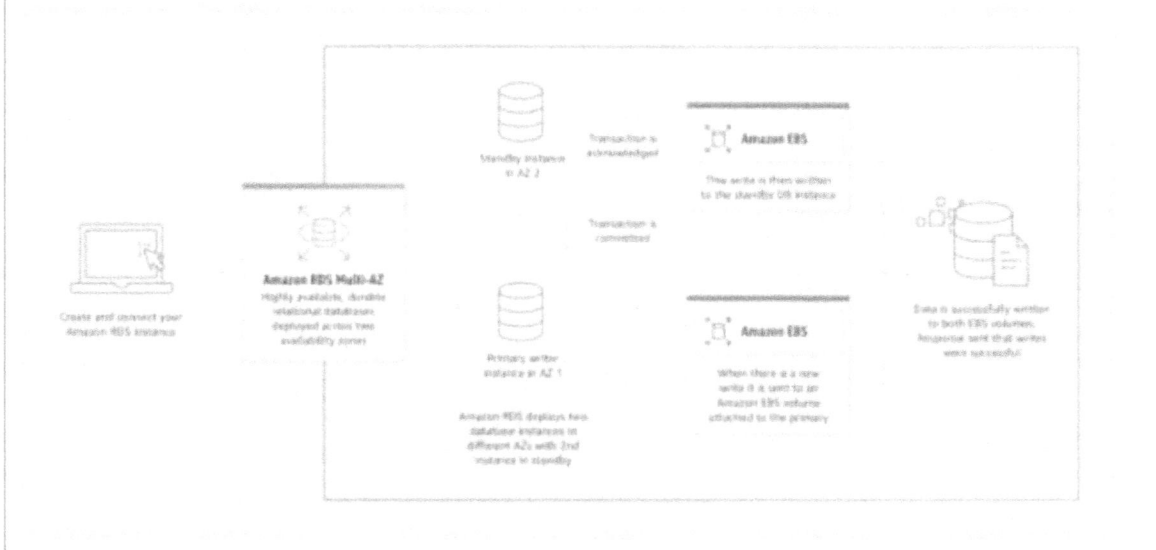

Screenshot from: https://aws.amazon.com/rds/features/multi-az/

RDS Multi-AZ with One Stand-By Database

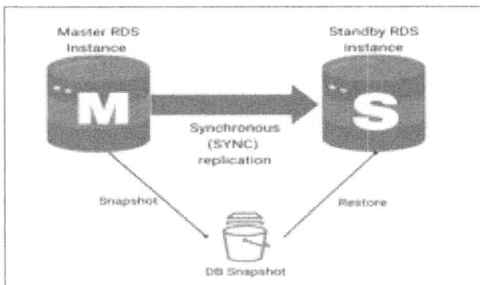

Setting up multi-AZ with a stand-by database from a single AZ is a zero-downtime operation – you don't need to stop the database. Just click on "modify" for the database. Then internally, a snap is taken, a new DB is restored from the snapshot in a new AZ, and synchronization is established between the two databases.

Amazon RDS Multi-AZ with one standby

Automatic fail over	Protect database performance	Enhance durability	Increase availability
Support high availability for your application with automatic database failover that completes as quickly as 60 seconds with zero data loss and no manual intervention.	Avoid suspending I/O activity on your primary during backup by backing up from your standby instance.	Use Amazon RDS Multi-AZ synchronous replication technologies to keep data on your standby database instance up to date with the primary.	Enhance availability by deploying a standby instance in a second AZ, and achieve fault tolerance in the event of an AZ or database instance failure.

Screenshot from: https://aws.amazon.com/rds/features/multi-az/

Read Replicas for Read Scalability

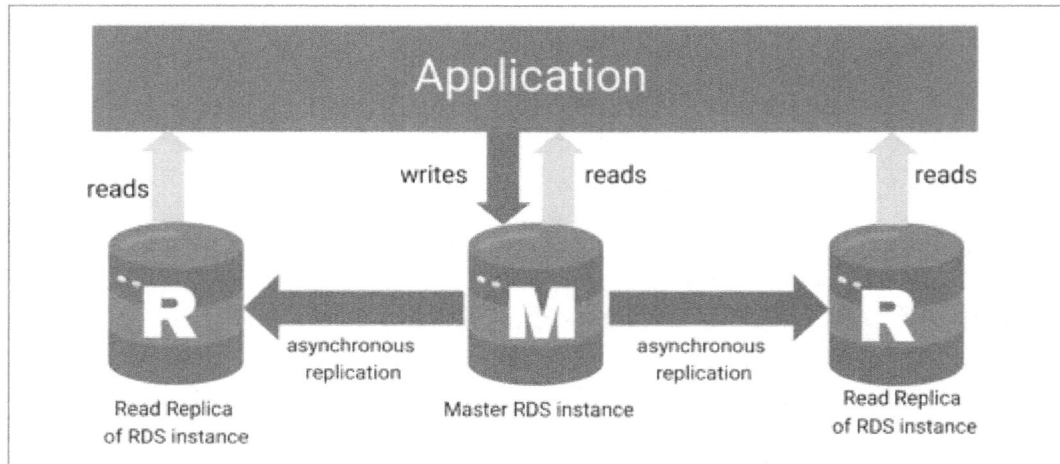

You can also configure the database in RDS read replica mode with automatic failover to the standby. Read replicas allow you to create read-only copies that are synchronized with your master database. There is no standby available while using read replicas. In case of infrastructure failure, you have to manually promote the read replica to be its own standalone DB Instance, which means that the database endpoint would change.

You can configure up to 5 Read Replicas. Read Replicas can be within AZ, cross AZ (multi-AZ), or cross Region. Replication is performed asynchronously, which makes reading operations from Read Replicas eventually consistent. Read Replicas can be promoted to the primary database. Applications must need to update the connection string to leverage Read Replicas.

Read Replicas Use Cases

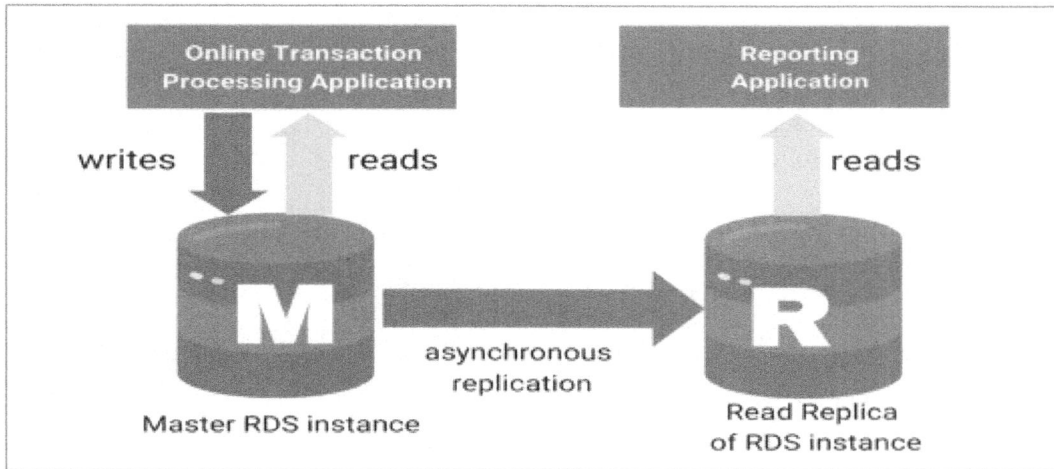

RDS Replicas has an excellent use case for applications suffering from performance issues – particularly those using the database for both OLTP and reporting purposes (for example, running analytical queries having complex join operations on a large dataset during the peak transaction period). For example, you can create Read Replica to run your reporting application workload from the Read Replicas, and your OLTP application will be unaffected. Thus, you will have improved performance in both: OLTP and Reporting applications. *Read Replicas are used only for SELECT(=read) – not for INSERT, UPDATE, DELETE.*

Read Replicas – Data Transfer Cost

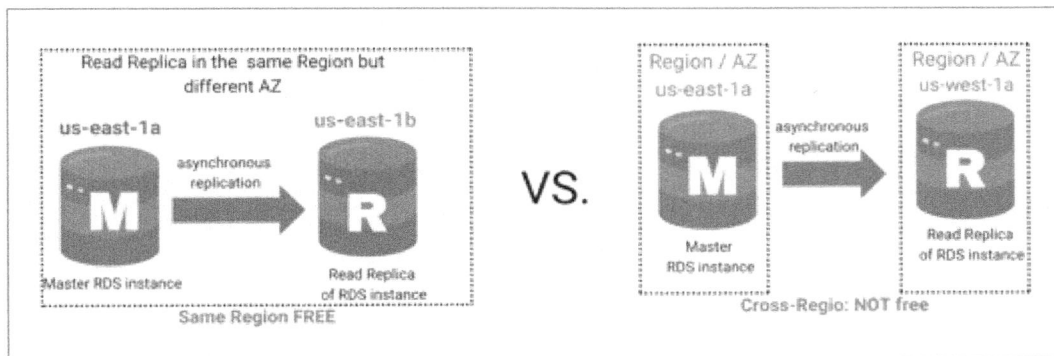

In AWS, there is a data transfer cost over the network when data travels from one AZ to another. For RDS Read Replicas, the data transfer within Region across AZ is free. However, when Read Replicas are in a different Region, there is a data transfer cost.

RDS Multi-AZ Disaster Recovery

RDS multi-AZ setup can be used to manage disaster recovery to manage failover in case of loss of AZ, loss of network, instance, or storage failure. When failover is detected, the application automatically failovers to the standby database – by DNS pointing to the new standby RDS instance. You need to use synchronous replication to set up a standby database of the RDS master instance. Disaster recovery helps increase the availability of applications. Since Multi-AZ replication is free, managing disaster recovery in the same Region is free with respect to data transfer.

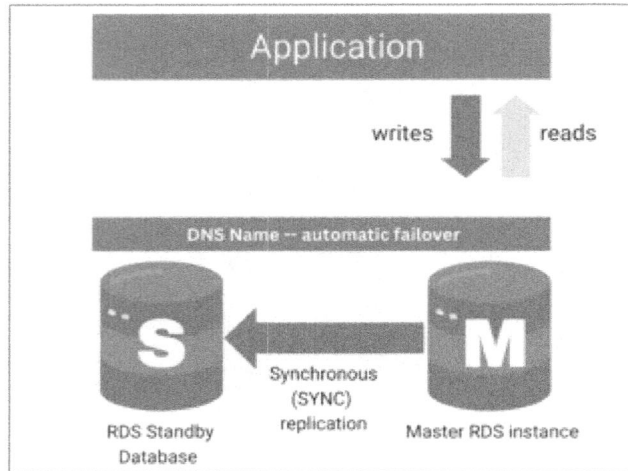

Read Replica improves database scalability, improve read performance as well as Disaster Recovery

Amazon RDS makes it easy to set up, operate, and scale an RDMS database on the AWS cloud platform. With the Read Replica concept, you can Read Replies of an RDS instance, which allows you to create read-only copies that are synchronized with the master database. Read Replicas are used to improve the read performance of an RDS instance. You can also place your Read Replica database in a different AWS Region closer to your users for better performance. Read Replicas are an example of horizontal scaling of resources. You can also cross-Region Read Replicas. Using a cross-Region Read Replica can also help ensure that you get up and running if you experience a regional availability issue in case of a disaster.

To understand the RDS disaster recovery capabilities in more detail, you can refer to this excellent AWS blog:
https://aws.amazon.com/blogs/database/implementing-a-disaster-recovery-strategy-with-amazon-rds/

RDS Custom

Amazon RDS Custom is a managed database service for applications that need more control of the underlying operating system and database environment. For example, users can SSH into the EC2 instance to customize the operating system and database environment for managed Oracle and Microsoft SQL Server databases.

To understand RDS Custom, in other words, the "RDS" includes automation of setup, operation, and scaling of the database. And the "Custom" includes access to the underlying database and

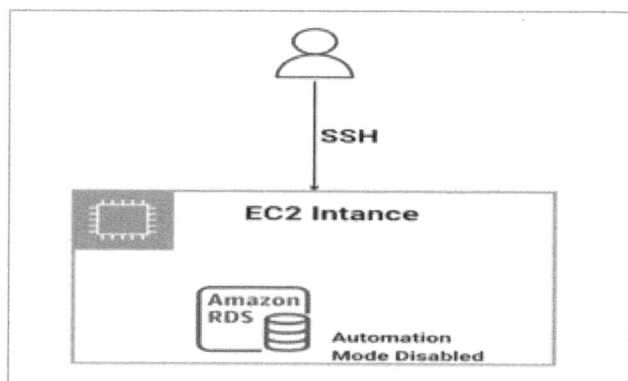

OS to configure settings, install patches, enable the native feature, and access the underlying EC2 instance using SSH.

The key highlighted differences to keep in mind between RDS and RDS Custom are:
- In RDS, the entire database and the OS is managed by OS—fully managed.
- In RDS Custom, you can get full admin access to the underlying OS and the database.

In order to use RDS Custom, deactivate Automation Mode to perform customization. It's better to take a snapshot of the database before making the change.

RDS Backups

RDS provides manual snapshots and automated backups. The important points to keep in mind about RDS backups:
- Daily full automated backup of the database is performed during the maintenance window.
- Transaction logs are backed up every 5 min interval.
- You can restore from the backup taken 5 min ago.
- The retention period for automated backup is between 1 to 35 days.
- You can set the retention period to 0 to disable automated backups.

- Manual DB snapshots are triggered by the user.
- Retention of manual backup is as long as you want to keep the backups.

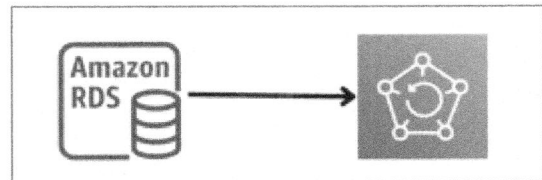

Note: If your RDS database is stopped, you will still pay for storage. If you plan to stop your DB for a long time, it's better to make a snapshot and restore it from the snapshot.

RDS Restore

Restoring from a backup creates a new database.

To restore the MySQL RDS database from the backup stored on Amazon S3, follow the following steps:
- Create a backup of your database
- Copy the backup to S3
- Restore from the backup file on S3 onto a new RDS instance running MySQL

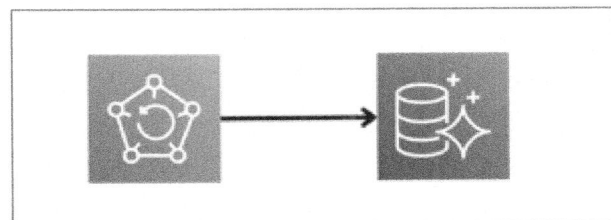

Amazon RDS Proxy
Essentially RDS proxy manages connection issues for your applications in situations where many open connections to the database server, and many possibly open and close database connections at a high rate, can create exhaustion for database memory and compute resources.

Amazon RDS Proxy serverless, autoscaling, highly available (multi-AZ) database proxy for RDS makes applications more scalable, more resilient to database failures, and more secure.

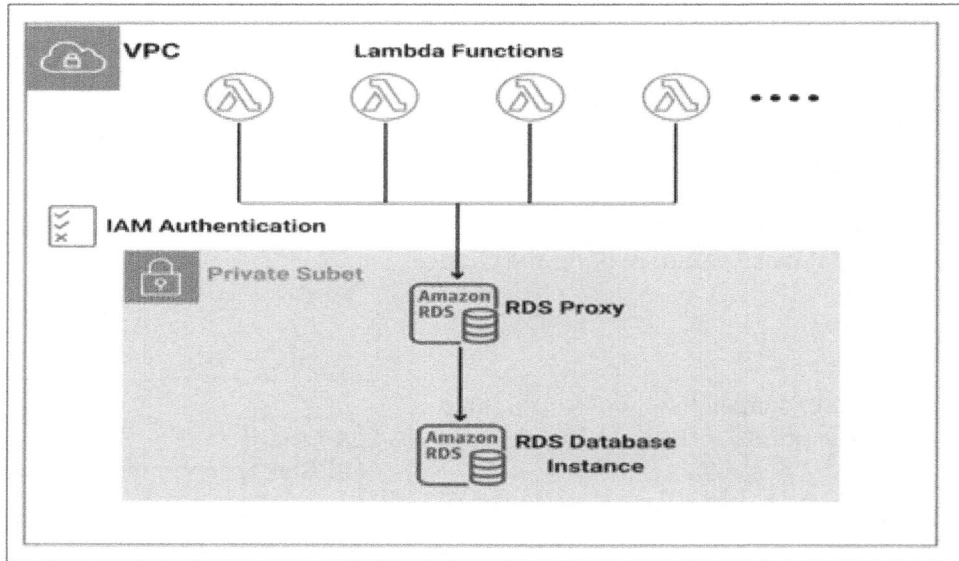

Amazon RDS Proxy allows applications to pool and share database connections, thus improving database efficiency by reducing the stress on database resources (e.g., CPU, RAM) and minimizing open connections (and timeouts). RDS Proxy helps failover times for Aurora and RDS databases to be reduced by up to 66%. It supports RDS (MySQL, PostgreSQL, MariaDB) and Aurora (MySQL, PostgreSQL).

It enforces IAM Authentication for databases and securely stores credentials in AWS Secrets Manager.

RDS Proxy is never publicly accessible – it is in a private subnet and must be accessed from the VPC.

Amazon Aurora

Amazon Aurora is a proprietary database from AWS -- not an open-source database. Both Postgres and MySQL databases are supported as Aurora databases, which means if you have an existing database in Postgres or MySQL, you can also leverage Amazon Aurora. Amazon Aurora is highly optimized for the cloud.

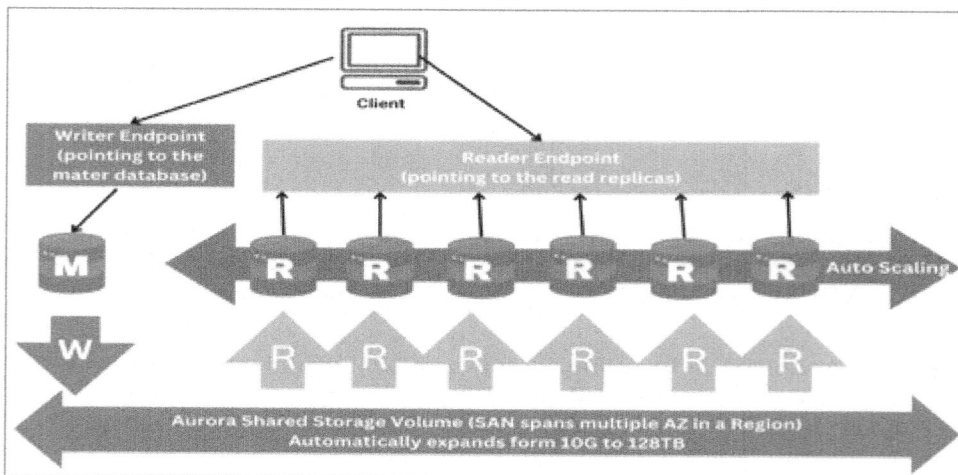

Amazon Aurora is an RDMS that combines the speed and reliability of high-end commercial databases with the simplicity and cost-effectiveness of open-source databases. Amazon Aurora MySQL performance is up to five times the throughput of open-source MySQL, and Amazon Aurora PostgreSQL delivers up to three times the throughput of open-source PostgreSQL.

Amazon Aurora self-manages database size needs – by automatically growing in increments of 10GB to up to 128TB. Amazon Aurora can have 15 replicas, while MySQL has five replicas.

Amazon Aurora database high-level architecture is based on the separation of concern. What it means is that storage and computing are separated. This helps make data highly available and safe even if some or all of the DB instances in the cluster become unavailable.

Amazon RDS manages your Amazon Aurora DB instances, handling time-consuming tasks such as provisioning, patching, backup, recovery, failure detection, and repair. You only pay a monthly charge for each Amazon Aurora database instance you use. There are no upfront costs or long-term commitments required.

Amazon Aurora costs about 20% more than the RDS – but provides a high-performance database.

High Availability for Amazon Aurora

High Availability of Aurora DB Instances
When setting up Aurora DB using single-master replication, you can create up to 15 read replicas, also known as reader instances. These reader instances can offload some of the work from the primary instance by taking read-intensive operations to process SELECT queries. This mechanism is known as failover, which helps maintain high availability.

Aurora, when detecting database problems, automatically activates the failover mechanism when necessary. One important point to note is that even though the primary instance changes due to failover, the connect string stays as the connection string points to the cluster endpoint --- not the actual instance. This indirection (connecting to the cluster endpoint) makes the failover process almost transparent from the client's perspective.

High Availability of Aurora DB Instances
When setting up Aurora DB using single-master replication, you can create up to 15 read replicas, also known as reader instances. These reader instances can offload some of the work from the primary instance by taking read-intensive operations to process SELECT queries. This mechanism is known as failover, which helps maintain high availability.

Aurora, when detecting database problems, automatically activates the failover mechanism when necessary. One important point to note is that even though the primary instance changes due to failover, the connect string stays as the connection string points to the cluster endpoint --- not the actual instance. This indirection (connecting to the cluster endpoint) makes the failover process almost transparent from the client's perspective.

Amazon Aurora Auto Scaling with Aurora Replicas

Amazon Aurora Auto Scaling feature automatically adjusts the number of Aurora Replicas provisioned for an Aurora DB cluster using single master replication. This helps your Aurora DB cluster to handle a sudden increase in the number of connections or workload. Aurora scale-in provisioned Aurora Replicas – when there is a decrease in the number of connections or workload, Aurora removes redundant Aurora Replicas to avoid paying you for unused provisioned instances.

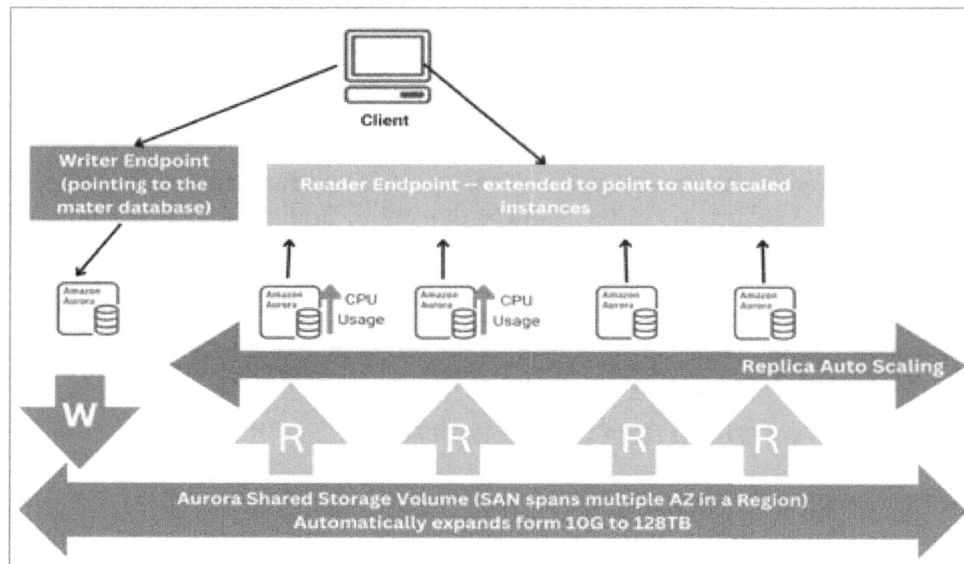

You define and apply an auto-scaling policy. The policy defines the minimum and the maximum number of Aurora Replicas in the cluster. Then based on the CloudWatch metrics and target values, Aurora Auto Scaling adjusts the replicas up or down. For example, when you define a scaling policy that uses the predefined average CPU utilization metric. Then such a policy can keep CPU utilization at, or close to, a specified percentage of utilization, such as 60 percent. To achieve the CPU utilization at, or close to, a specified percentage of utilization, more replicas can be added or removed (if redundant).

Amazon Aurora Endpoints

In practical use cases, Amazon Aurora typically involves a cluster of DB instances instead of a single instance. When connecting to the cluster of DB instances, you will not directly connect to these instances. Instead, you will use an intermediary handler called *endpoint*. You will use the hostname and port of the endpoint to connect to your Aurora DB cluster.

Aurora uses this mechanism to provide an abstraction to connection management. That way, you don't have to hardcode all connection URLs (Aurora-specific URL, hostname and port) or write your logic for load-balancing and rerouting connections when one or more DB instances are unavailable.

Depending on the tasks, as different instances or groups of instances perform different roles, the Aurora DB cluster points these different groups of instances into different types of endpoints, For example, writer endpoint, reader point, and custom endpoint.

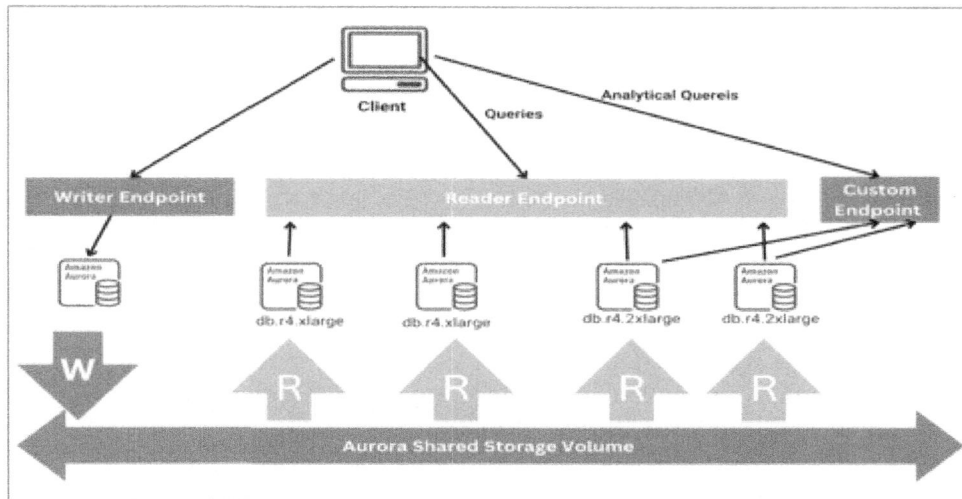

As you can see, there are three types of endpoints available in the Amazon Aurora DB cluster: **writer endpoint (or cluster endpoint), reader point, and custom endpoint.** Using endpoints, you can map each connection to the appropriate instance or group of instances based on their use case.

A writer endpoint connects to the current primary DB instance for the DB cluster. This endpoint is the only one that can perform write operations such as DDL statements. As you can notice, since this is the only endpoint that can execute DDL statements, the cluster endpoint is the one you connect to when you first set up a cluster or when your cluster contains a single DB instance.

A reader endpoint provides load-balancing support for read-only connections to the DB cluster. It is recommended to use a reader endpoint for reading operations, such as SQL queries, as it reduces the overhead on the primary DB instance.

A custom endpoint for an Aurora cluster represents a set of DB instances that you choose. You define which instances this endpoint refers to and decide what purpose the endpoint serves; for example, you could have a custom endpoint for running analytical queries. The Reader Endpoint is generally not used after defining a Custom Endpoint.

KEY POINTS

- Aurora stores six copies of the data across 3 AZs
- 4 out of 6 copies are used for writing, and 3 out of 6 used for reading
- Aurora database storage is stripped across 100s of volumes
- It does self-healing with a peer-to-peer connection
- Automatic failover for master in less than 30s
- Up to 15 Aurora Read Replicas
- Support for Cross Region Replication

Amazon Aurora Serverless

Amazon Aurora Serverless is an on-demand, automated autoscaling based on actual usage (your application's needs). In other words, you can run your database on AWS without managing database capacity – no capacity planning is needed. It is good for use cases having infrequent, intermittent, or unpredictable workloads.

You pay on a per-second basis when the database is active. You can migrate between standard and serverless configurations with a few steps in the Amazon RDS console.

The client connects to a *proxy fleet* that routes the connection to a fleet of DB instances that are automatically scaled, and Aurora manages the connections automatically. The proxy fleet enables continuous connections as Aurora Serverless scales the resources automatically based on the minimum and maximum specified capacity.

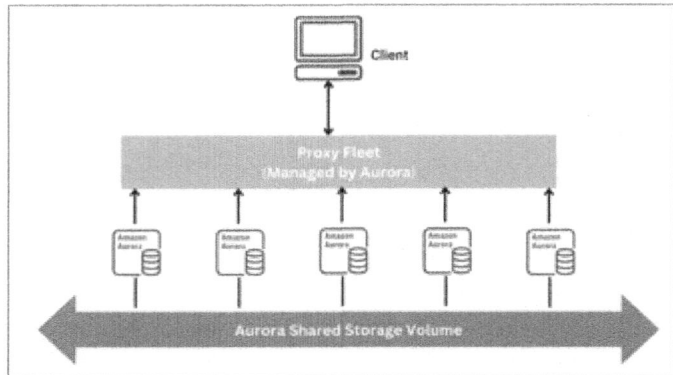

In Aurora Serverless, scaling is rapid because it uses a pool of "warm" resources that are always ready to process workloads. It also supports automatic pause where the DB cluster can be paused after no activity for a specified period – the default is minutes. The pausing of the DB cluster can be disabled.

Aurora Multi-Master

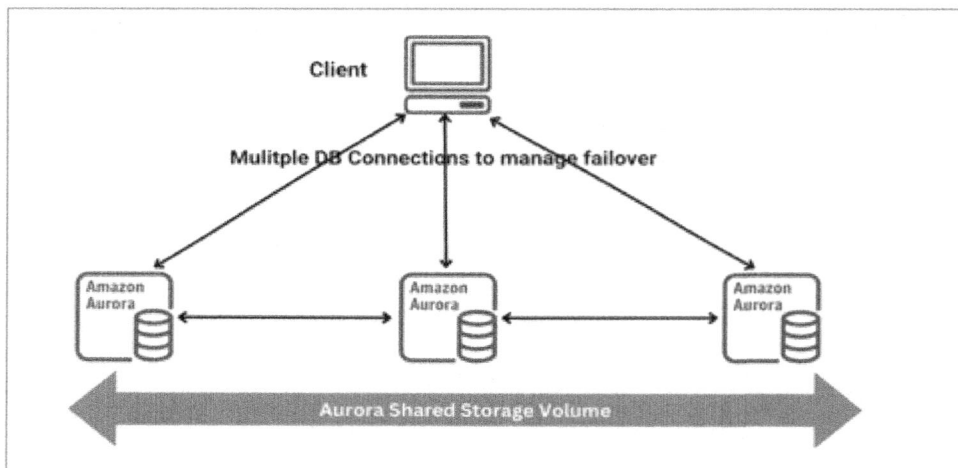

A typical Aurora DB cluster is a single-master cluster. In a single-master cluster, one primary or master instance performs all write operations (for example, DDL), and any other DB instances are read-only. If the master instance becomes unavailable, the failover mechanism promotes one of the read-only (read replicas) instances as the new master (writer).

Every node performs R/W – vs. promoting a read replica as the new master in a single-master cluster in a multi-master cluster. In a multi-master cluster, when a writer DB instance becomes unavailable, another writer DB instance immediately takes over the work of the failed instance. This type of availability is referred to as *continuous availability* to distinguish it from high availability (with brief downtime during failover).

Amazon Aurora - Global

Critical workloads in some domains, such as financial and travel, have strict availability requirements and may need to tolerate Region-wide outages. Amazon Aurora Global Database is a good fit for use cases related to global applications. Amazon Aurora Global Database allows a single database to span multiple AWS Regions by replication – without impacting DB performance. In addition, it enables fast local reads with latency in each Region and provides disaster recovery from Region-wide outages.

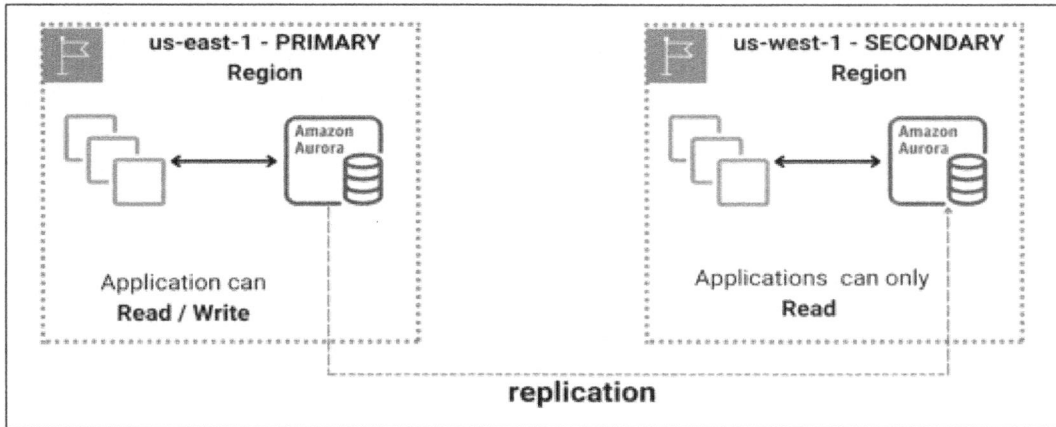

Amazon Aurora Global Database is a good fit for use cases of globally distributed applications, allowing a single Amazon Aurora database to span to multiple AWS Regions.

Using storage-based replication with a typical latency of less than 1 second, Aurora replicates DB data without impacting database performance, enables fast local reads with low latency in each Region, and provides disaster recovery from Region-wide outages. In Aurora Global, there is one Primary Region handling read and write and up to 5 secondary read-only Regions with 16 Read Replicas per secondary Region.

One of the secondary Regions can be promoted to handle read and write operations in less than 1 minute in case of an unlikely event of a Regional degradation or outage.

Amazon Aurora Machine Learning

Amazon Aurora machine learning enables you to add ML-based predictions to your applications via SQL queries – you don't need prior ML experience. it provides integration between Aurora and AWS ML services that are simple, optimized, and secure. Thus you don't need to build custom integrations or move data around.

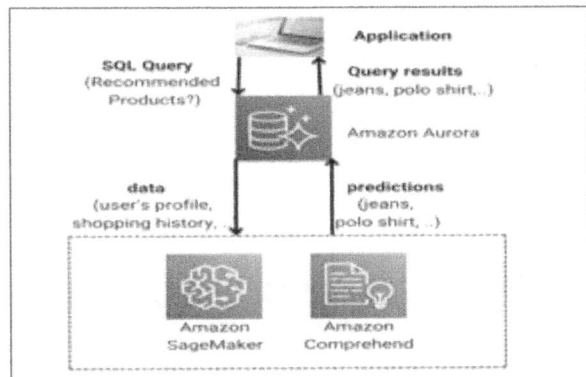

When you run an SQL based ML query, Aurora calls Amazon SageMaker for ML algorithms or Amazon Comprehend for sentiment analysis. That way, your application doesn't need to call these services directly – Aurora takes care of running the ML query for you.

Aurora machine learning use cases are fraud detection, ads targeting, sentiment analysis, and product recommendations.

Amazon Aurora Backups

Amazon Aurora provides manual snapshots and automated backups. The important points to keep in mind about Aurora backups:

- Daily full automated backup of the database
- The retention period for automated backup is between 1 to 35 days.
- You cannot disable automated backups.

- Manual DB snapshots are triggered by the user.
- Retention of manual backup is as long as you want to keep the backups.

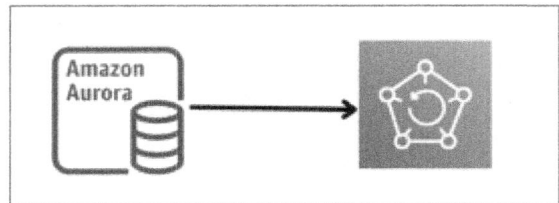

Amazon Aurora MySQL DB Cluster Restore

Restoring from a backup creates a new database.

To restore the Aurora DB cluster from the backup stored on Amazon S3, follow the following steps:

- Create a backup of your database using Percona XtraBackup
- Copy the backup to S3
- Restore from the backup file on S3 onto a new Aurora DB cluster running MySQL

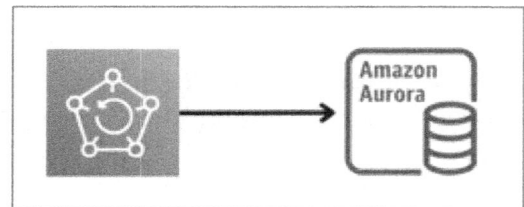

Amazon Aurora Database Clone

You can create a new Aurora database cluster from an existing one by cloning it with the option provided in the AWS Management Console. It is faster than taking a snapshot and restoring from the snapshot. The cloned database is distributed and replicated across 3 AZs, like all Aurora databases.

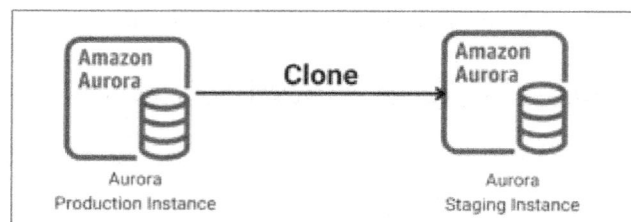

There is no charge for cloning operation -- you will only be charged for additional storage space if you make data changes.

Amazon RDS & Aurora DB Security

Both at-rest and in-flight encryption are provided. For at-rest encryption, both master and replica can be encrypted using AWS KMS. It must be defined at the time of launching the instance. If the master database is not encrypted, the replica is cannot be encrypted. To encrypt an unencrypted database, take the DB snapshot and restore it as encrypted. For in-flight encryption, TLS-ready is the default. Use AWS-TLS root certificates for the client side.

IAM roles are used to connect databases – no username/password.

Security Groups control network access to your RDS and Aurora cluster. You cannot connect to SSH – except when using RDS Custom. For logging, audit logs can be enabled and sent to CloudWatch Logs for longer retention.

Amazon ElastiCache

The concept is related to some extent to RDS. In a way, RDS is to get managed relational database -- ElastiCache is to get managed Redis or Memcached.

Caches are in-memory data stores with really high performance and extremely low latency. Caches are very helpful in boosting the performance of databases having read-intensive workloads. It also helps to make your application stateless.

Amazon ElastiCache is a web service that makes it easy to deploy, operate, and scale an in-memory cache in the cloud. The service improves the performance of web applications by allowing you to retrieve information from fast, managed, in-memory caches, instead of relying entirely on slower disk-based databases.

If EC2 instances are intensively reading data from a database, ElastiCache can cache some values to take the load off the database.

Amazon ElastiCache allows you to set up seamlessly, run, and scale popular open-Source compatible in-memory data stores in the cloud. Build data-intensive apps or boost the performance of your existing databases by retrieving data from high throughput and low latency in-memory data stores. Amazon ElastiCache is a popular choice for real-time use cases like Caching, Session Stores, Gaming, Geospatial Services, Real-Time Analytics, and Queuing. ElastiCache cannot be used for online analytical processing.

AWS takes care of the maintenance of OS, patching, optimizations, setup, configurations, monitoring, failure recovery, and backups.

If you are planning to refactor your application to use ElastiCache, it involves heavy application code changes.

ElastiCache DB Cache Solution Architecture

When applications utilize Amazon ElastiCache to build an in-memory cache, the data is first looked into the cache. If it is found, it is fetched from there – this is a very fast operation as this is retrieved from the in-memory cache. Building an in-memory cache on top of RDS off-loads many read operations if the data is found in the cache.

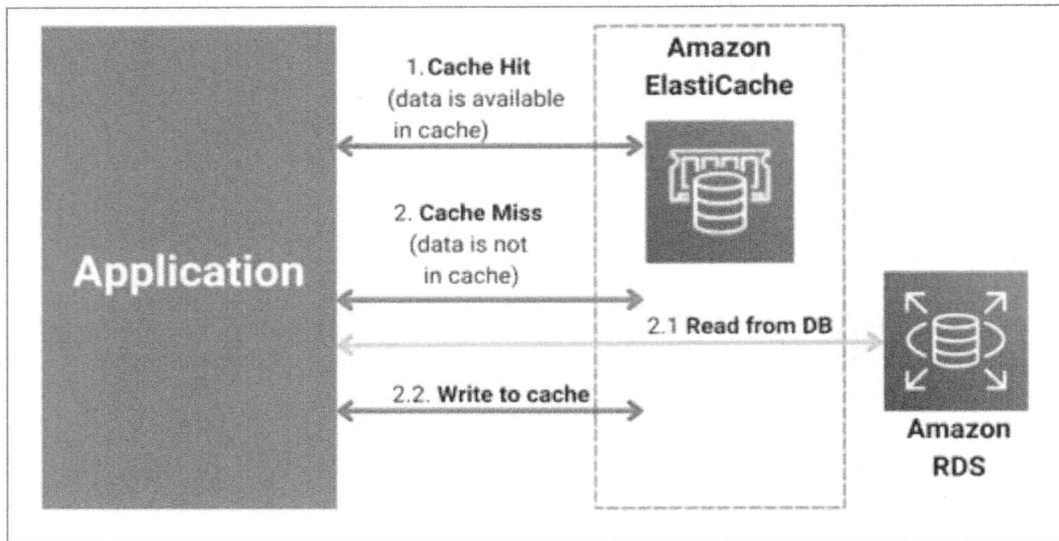

On the other hand, if the data is not found in the cache, it is fetched from Amazon RDS and then written to the cache. So that next time, if the same data needs to be looked at, it can be fetched from the cache, thus improving the overall response time (fetch time and latency).

The only challenge in building a cache is invalidation – when to invalidate data so that client gets the latest. Having an invalidation strategy is a must to make sure that the most current data is read. Usually, master types of records or data such as product catalogs that remain constant for a while or change less frequently if implemented using a cache improve the application's overall performance.

ElastiCache User Session Store Solution Architecture

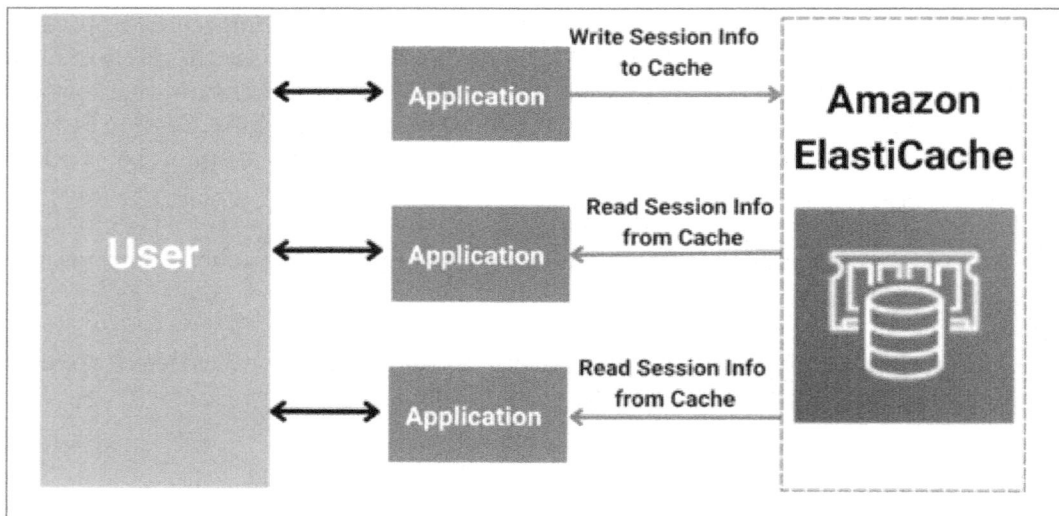

Implementing a user session cache is another use case of ElastiCache, where user session information such as user details, shopping cart (for example, in eCommerce), etc., is stored in the cache. The next time, the session information for the user, is retrieved from the cache, which improves the overall performance of the application.

ElastiCache – Security

ElastiCache (Redis and Memcached) does not support IAM authentication, and IAM policies on ElastiCache are only used for AWS API-level security.

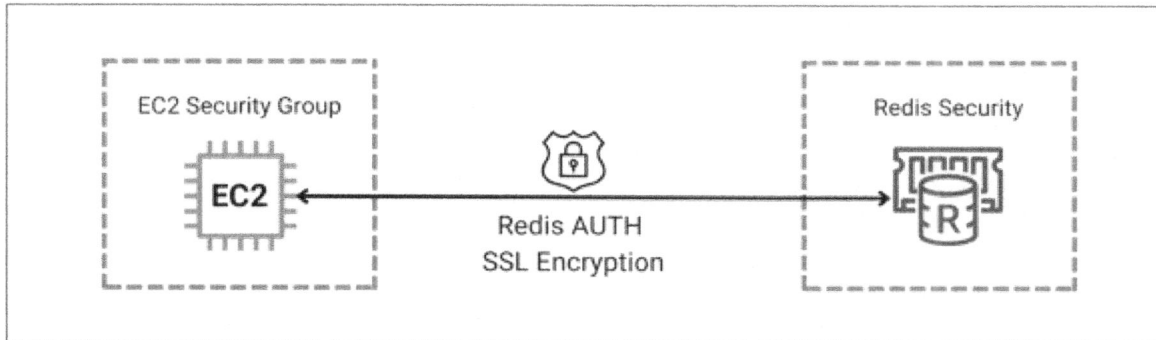

For Redis authentication, you use the **Redis AUTH** command. To provide an extra level of security, you can require that users enter a token (password) on a token-protected Redis server when you set up a Redis cluster. In addition, Redis supports SSL for in-flight encryption.

Memcached supports SASL-based authentication, which is for Simple Authentication and Security Layer. It provides a means of adding authentication support to connection-based protocols, such as the Memcached client binary protocol. It works via an API call that is added to the client, which is used for authenticating a given user. Once a user is authenticated, the system provides a security layer between the client protocol and connection.

ElastiCache – Redis Vs. Memcached

Redis

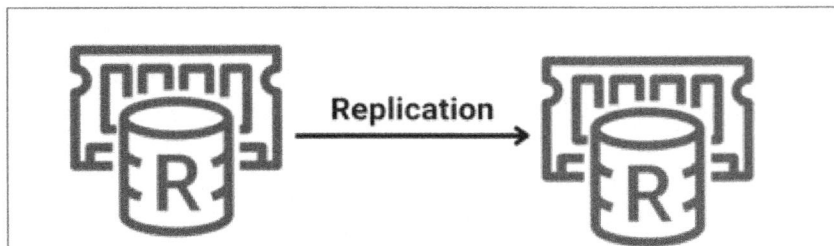

- Provides Read Replicas to scale reads provides high availability using replication
- Provides data durability using AOF (Append Only File) persistence
- Provides backup and restore features
- Provides multi-AZ with auto-failover

Memcached

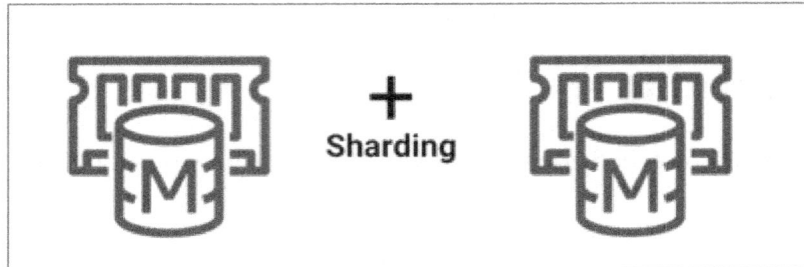

- It doesn't provide persistence
- It doesn't provide high availability (no replication)
- It doesn't provide backup and restore
- It is a multi-node architecture -- uses sharding to partition data

The screenshot (https://aws.amazon.com/elasticache/redis-vs-memcached/) provides more comparison between Redis vs Memcached:

	Memcached	Redis
Sub-millisecond latency	Yes	Yes
Developer ease of use	Yes	Yes
Data partitioning	Yes	Yes
Support for a broad set of programming languages	Yes	Yes
Advanced data structures	-	Yes
Multithreaded architecture	Yes	-
Snapshots	-	Yes
Replication	-	Yes
Transactions	-	Yes
Pub/Sub	-	Yes
Lua scripting	-	Yes
Geospatial support	-	Yes

ElastiCache – Redis Use Case

One of the use cases of Redis is in implementing leaderboards in gaming applications. Implementing leaderboards in gaming applications is computationally complex.

When using Redis, each time when a new participant is added, it is ranked in real-time and then added in the correct order with the help of Redis Sorted Sets that guarantee both uniqueness and element order.

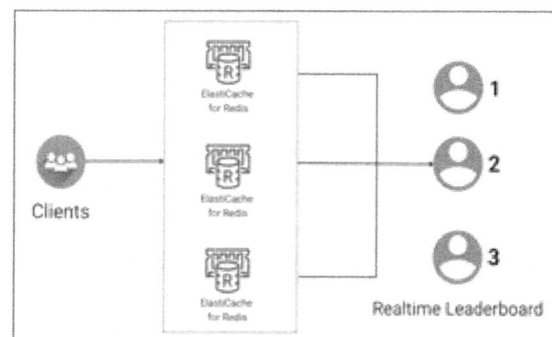

Chapter 23. AWS Databases

You will learn the following in this chapter:
- Database types
- High Level Summary of RDS, Aurora, ElastiCache, DynamoDB, S3
- Amazon DocumentDB
- Amazon Neptune
- Amazon Keyspaces
- Amazon Quantum Ledger Database (QLDB)
- Amazon Timestream
- Amazon Managed Blockchain

Introduction

AWS has many managed databases; sometimes, deciding which one to choose becomes a little challenging. The question is, which one is the right database for your solution's architecture? The answer to this depends on the answers to many questions, such as:
- Is your database read-intensive, write-intensive, or is it balanced? What is the throughput requirement? Does the load on the database vary -- does it need to scale?
- What is the database size, and for how long does the data need to be stored? Will the database grow? What is the average object size? How is the database accessed?
- What is the durability of data? What is the source of truth of data?
- What are latency requirements? Does it have concurrent users?
- What is the availability requirement – how long can the database be down without impacting business?
- What are backup and recovery requirements?
- Does the database have global users?
- What is the data model? How will you query the data? Do the query operations involve joining tables? Is the data model structured or semi-structured?
- Does it have a strong schema? Is the schema flexible? Is it used for reporting, transactions, or search operations? Is it RDBMS or NoSQL?
- What is licensing cost? Would you like to switch to a Cloud Native database such as Amazon Aurora?

Database Types

AWS has the following database types.

RDBMS (Relational Database Management System)

RDBM is a very common database type and has been a solid battle-tested database for many decades, particularly for OLTP (On-Line Transaction Processing) use cases. RDBM databases are accessed using SQL and are very good for OLTP systems.

Examples: Amazon RDS and Aurora.

NoSQL Database

NoSQL databases mean you don't need SQL queries to access NoSQL databases. Though over the years, at times, it's difficult to find feature-wise differences between NoSQL and RDBMS. For example, some NoSQL databases allow transactions.

Nonetheless, these databases are a good choice if you need a globally distributed, highly available, highly scalable, and high throughput database. NoSQL databases are also a good option where the schema is evolving and not fixed – for example, semi-structured schema such as JSON. NoSQL databases are a great choice to model distributed joins (not for join operation).

Examples: **DynamoDB (~JSON), ElastiCache** (in-memory cache, key/value **pairs), Neptune (graphs** database**), DocumentDB** (supports **MongoDB** workload**), Keyspaces** (supports A**pache Cassandra** workload**)**

Object Storage

An object storage stores data as objects. The object data storage architecture is designed to handle large amounts of unstructured data. It designates data as distinct units, along with any metadata that describes the file and a unique identifier that can be used to locate and access each data unit.

Examples: Amazon S3 for regular object storage and Amazon Glacier for backups and archives

Data Warehouse

A data warehouse is a database that extracts (filters), transforms (sometimes without any transformation), loads copies of transaction data from disparate transactional systems, and provisions them for analytical use. The critical distinction is that data warehouses are designed to handle analytics and reporting (BI) requirements.

Examples: RedShfit (OLAP), Athena, EMR

Search Database

A search database is a type of database dedicated to searching content as free text or unstructured searches. It is built for indexing and querying information. Search databases use indexes to categorize similar characteristics among data and facilitate search capability.

Example: OpenSearch (JSON) (forked from Elasticsearch)

Graph Database

Graph databases are designed and built to store and navigate relationships. Relationships are first-class citizens in graph databases -- they display relationships between data. Most of the value of graph databases is derived from how relationships are presented and navigated.

Example: Amazon Neptune

Ledger Database

Ledger databases are architected to provide and maintain the integrity of all data to be protected for the entire lifetime. As with a traditional ledger, ledger databases preserve historical data. If a record is updated in the database, its previous original value is protected (an immutable record) as it is in a history table. In addition, the ledger database provides a history of all changes made to the database over time.

Example: Amazon Quantum Ledger Database

Time Series Database

Time-series database is a sequence of data points (measurements or events) collected over time intervals that are tracked, monitored, down-sampled, and aggregated over time.

Example: Amazon Timestream

Amazon RDS – High-Level Summary

- It is a managed database. You can launch PostgreSQL, MySQL, Oracle, SQL Server, and MariaDB databases.
- You can provision RDS instance size, EBS volume type & size.
- As the RDS instances are optimized for memory, performance, or I/O, the performance of the AWS-managed RDS instance is better than that of a customer-managed database instance.
- Customers use Amazon RDS databases primarily for online-transaction processing (OLTP) workload.

- It is not a NoSQL Database service.
- Amazon RDS is a regional service.

- It provides auto-scaling for storage.
- It has support for Read Replicas and Multi-AZ.
- Amazon RDS increases availability by deploying a standby instance in a second AZ and achieves fault tolerance in case of a failure in an AZ or database instance.
- Amazon RDS enhances durability by using synchronous replication technologies in Multi-AZ to keep the standby database instance up to date with the primary.

- It provides automated backup with a point-in-time restore feature (up to 365 days)
- You can also take a manual DB snapshot for longer-term recovery.
- It provides managed and scheduled maintenance (with downtime).
- Amazon RDS protects database performance by avoiding suspending I/O activity on your primary during backup by backing up from your standby instance.

- It provides support for IAM authentication.
- It has integration with Secrets Manager.
- It provides security through IAM, Security Groups, KMS, and SSL. (In transit).

Use Case: RDBMS database, OLTP system

Amazon Aurora – High-Level Summary

- It has compatible APIs for PostgreSQL and MySQL. In other words, you can easily port your PostgreSQL and MySQL databases to Amazon Aurora.

- Its architecture separates storage and compute – in other words, compute, and storage are decoupled.

- It delivers high performance and availability with up to 15 low-latency read replicas, point-in-time recovery, continuous backup to Amazon Simple Storage Service (Amazon S3), and replication across three Availability Zones (AZs).

- Data is stored in 15 low-latency read replicas across 3 AZs -- highly available, auto-scaling

- It provides self-healing -- failover typically completes within 30 seconds. If a DB instance or AZ becomes unavailable, Aurora will automatically recreate the DB instance in a different AZ.

- Provides custom endpoints for reader and writer DB instances

- The security, monitoring, and maintenance features are the same as you get in RDS.

Aurora Serverless
Amazon Aurora and Aurora Serverless are two different. The main difference is that the Aurora Serverless configuration enables automated capacity scaling. It is good for use cases related to unpredictable/intermittent workloads with no capacity planning.

Aurora Multi-Master
An Amazon Aurora multi-master setup allows you to configure a pair of masters in an active-active read-write configuration. This setup can later be scaled up on demand. In Aurora multi-master clusters, each instance can perform both read and write operations. If you contrast this with single-master, multi-master clusters are best suited for segmented workloads, such as for multitenant applications. It is good for use cases where you need continuous writes failover -- high write availability.

Aurora Global
Aurora Global Database lets you quickly scale database reads to global users worldwide by placing it close to your users. It provides up to 16 DB Read Instances in each region, with typical cross-region replication latency of less than 1 second.

Aurora Machine Learning
Amazon Aurora machine learning enables you to perform ML using SageMaker & Comprehend on Aurora via the familiar SQL programming language, so you don't need to learn ML. You can integrate

your Aurora DB cluster with Amazon Comprehend or Amazon SageMaker, or both, depending on your needs.

Aurora Database Cloning

Aurora clone is a quick and cost-effective way to create a duplicate aurora cluster -- new cluster from an existing one. It is faster than restoring a snapshot.

Use case

The same as RDS. However, Aurora provides flexibility and many features, better performance, and less maintenance.

Amazon ElastiCache – High-Level Summary

- It is an in-memory data store service with sub-millisecond latency.

- It is managed Redis or Memcached. Both are key-value in-memory cache services. Redis offers more features and can also be used as a primary database.

- You must provision an EC2 instance. Amazon ElastiCache instances can only be accessed through an Amazon EC2 instance.

- It provides Read Replicas (maximum five). The read endpoint offers a single endpoint for distributing queries across replica nodes. Read replicas are maintained using Redis asynchronous replication.

- It provides support for clustering (Redis) and Multi-AZ. Multi-AZ differs from RDS as there is no standby, but a Read Replica is promoted as primary if the primary goes down.

- It provides security through IAM, Security Groups, KMS, Redis Auth.

- It supports backup, snapshot, and point-in-time restore features.

- it provides managed and scheduled maintenance.

Use Case

Key/Value store, cache results for DB queries, store session data for websites users, read-intensive applications

Amazon DynamoDB– High-Level Summary

- It is a managed serverless NoSQL database that provides milliseconds of latency.
- It provides two options for capacity: provisioned capacity (default) with optional auto-scaling, and the other one is on-demand.
- It is highly available, multi-AZ (default).
- Read and Writes are decoupled – RCU (Read Capacity Unit) and WCU (Write Capacity Unit) usages are calculated separately.
- It also supports transactions.

- For cache, it provides DAX, which improves read latency to microsecond (from millisecond)
- IAM is used to manage access control (authentication, authorization).
- You can also use DynamoDB for event processing by enabling streams and integrating DynamoDB streams (when an item changes) to AWS Lambda or Kinesis Data Streams for processing.
- It provides a Global Table feature with active-active replication to improve read latency for global users.
- Automated backups for up to 35 days with point-in-time recovery (PITR). It also provides on-demand backups.
- You can export data to S3 without using RCU within the PITR window (35 days) and import from S3 without using WCU.
- The maximum item size is 400KB.
- Excellent fit if your schema is changing rapidly.

Use Case
serverless applications, near real-time streaming applications, and distributed serverless cache.

Amazon S3– High-Level Summary

- It is an object storage of key-value type. It is good for bigger objects but not so good for smaller objects (latency 100 - 200 milliseconds).
- It is serverless and scales infinitely.
- Maximum object size is 5TB.
- You can version objects by enabling versioning.
- You can use the MFA Delete option to help manage accidental deletes.
- It provides encryption, replication, and access logs.
- The access control can be managed by using an IAM policy.
- Provides many options for encryption at rest, such as SSE-S3, SSE-KMS, SSE-C, and client-side encryption. For encryption in transit: TLS is used.
- **S3 Storage Classes**: S3 Standard, S3 Intelligent-Tiering, S3 Standard-IA, and S3 One Zone-IA, S3 Glacier
- **S3 Batch operations:** S3 Batch operations can copy and tag objects at scale (billions of objects and petabytes of data) with a single request.
- **Amazon S3 Inventory**: You can use Amazon S3 Inventory to audit and report on your objects' replication and encryption status to manage compliance and regulatory needs.
- You can use Multi-part Upload and S3 Transfer Acceleration to optimize upload performance.
- **Multi-part Upload**: Multipart upload enables you to upload a single object as a set of multiple parts. The minimum allowable part size is 1 MB, and the maximum is 4 GB. In general, for objects over 100 MB, you should consider using multipart uploads.
- **S3 Transfer Acceleration**: S3 Transfer Acceleration is designed to optimize upload performance worldwide. It is a bucket-level feature that allows fast and easy transfers of files over long distances into an S3 bucket.
- **S3 Event Notifications**: You can automate certain event handling in S3 by enabling the Amazon S3 bucket to send a notification message to destinations such as SNS, SQS, Lambda, and EventBridge, whenever those events occur.

Use Cases:
Static large files, key-value store for large files, static website hosting

Amazon DocumentDB

In application code, data is often represented in JSON because it is an efficient and intuitive data model for developers in many use cases. Document databases help developers easily store, query, and index JSON data in their application code.

As Amazon Aurora is an AWS implementation of PostgreSQL and MySQL, DocumentDB is an AWS implementation for MongoDB. DocumentDB supports MongoDB workload. It is fully managed and highly available with replication across 3 AZ.

The storage and compute are decoupled in Amazon DocumentDB, which allows each to scale independently. For example, it automatically scales to workloads with millions of requests per second. In addition, Aurora storage automatically grows in increments of 10GB up to 64 TB.

Amazon Neptune

Amazon Neptune is a fully managed graph database service and is considered a NoSQL database type. Not only does a graph database make it easy to build graph models, but it also makes it easy to build and run applications that work efficiently well with highly connected datasets.

For example, you can model a social network as a graph dataset:
*   Users have friends
*   Posts have comments
*   Comments have likes from users
*   Users share and like posts

Amazon Neptune is optimized for complex queries. It can store up to billions of relationships and query the graph with milliseconds latency.

Amazon Neptune is highly available across 3 AZs, with Read Replicas up to 15. it allows replication, continuous backup to Amazon S3, and point-in-time recovery.

It supports HTTPS and encryption at rest. It is fully managed, which helps you offload typical database management tasks such as hardware provisioning, patching, configuration, or backups.

Amazon Neptune supports popular graph models such as Property Graph and W3C's RDF and their respective query languages, Apache TinkerPop Gremlin and SPARQL. Thus, it allows you to build queries that easily navigate highly connected datasets.

Amazon Neptune is tailor-built for use cases like Knowledge Graphs, Identity Graphs, Fraud Detection, Recommendation Engines, Social Networking, Life Sciences, etc. Amazon Neptune is not for relational databases.

Amazon Keyspaces

Amazon Keyspaces is the right solution if you want to run your Cassandra application code on AWS. Amazon Keyspaces is a scalable, highly available Apache Cassandra-compatible service that allows you to run your Cassandra workloads on AWS. You can use CQL (Cassandra Query Language) to access data.

Amazon Keyspaces is a managed service -- you don't have to install, maintain, or operate the software. You don't have to manage scalability, either. It automatically scales tables up and down in response to application traffic.

Data is encrypted by default in Amazon Keyspaces, enabling you to back up your table data continuously along with point-in-time recovery. It also provides backup, Point-in-Time Recovery (PTR) for up to 35 days.

Tables are replicated three times across multiple AZs. It provides single-digit millisecond latency, 1000s of requests per second at any scale.

It provides two choices for capacity: On-demand mode or provisioned mode with auto-scaling.

Use Cases

- high-speed data processing -- for applications that require single-digit millisecond latency, such as industrial equipment maintenance, trade monitoring, fleet management, and route optimization.

- Move your Cassandra workloads to the cloud.

- Data store for applications -- store information about devices for the Internet of Things (IoT) applications

Amazon Quantum Ledger Database

Amazon Quantum Ledger Database (QLDB) is a serverless, scalable, and fully managed ledger database. It provides immutable (no entry can be removed or modified) and verifiable transaction logs -- each entry is cryptographically verifiable. It provides 2-3x better performance than familiar ledge blockchain frameworks.

Ledgers are generally used to record a history of financial transactions in an organization. Many organizations build financial applications with ledger-like functionality to maintain an accurate history of their financial transactions data, for example, tracking the history of credits and debits in banking transactions. Ledger applications are often implemented by creating custom tables for storing audit trails of financial transactions created in relational databases.

Amazon QLDB is a new class of databases that eliminates the need to develop complex ledger-like applications. With QLDB, you can store data about financial activity and easily verify any unintended modifications to the data using cryptography.

QLDB provides SQL-like API, a flexible document data model, and full transaction support. In addition, QLDB's streaming capability offers a near real-time flow of your data stored within QLDB, which helps develop event-driven workflows and real-time analytics. The data can also be replicated for other AWS services to support advanced analytical processing.

Use Cases
- Financial transactions: Store financial transactions, such as credit and debit transactions

- Maintain claims history: Track a claim over its lifetime and cryptographically verify data integrity to make it resilient against data entry errors and manipulation.

- Reconcile supply chain systems: Record the history of each transaction, such as details of every batch manufactured, shipped, stored, and sold from facility to store

Amazon Timestream

Amazon Timestream is a fully managed, fast, scalable, serverless time series database that makes it easy to store and analyze trillions of events daily, particularly for IoT and operational applications.

Amazon Timestream saves you time and costs in managing the lifecycle of time series data. It keeps recent data in memory and moves historical data to a cost-optimized storage tier based on user-defined policies. The recent data is kept in memory, and historical data is kept in cost-optimized storage.

It provides scheduled queries and multi-measure records. It is compatible with SQL. It provides built-in time series analytics functions, which help you identify patterns in your data in near real-time.

It can automatically scale up/down to adjust capacity. It is up to 1,000 times faster with as little as 1/10th the cost of relational databases.

It provides encryption in transit and at rest.

Use cases
IoT apps, operational applications, real-time analytics

Amazon Managed Blockchain

Amazon Managed Blockchain is a fully managed service that allows you to join public networks or set up and manage scalable private networks using popular open-source frameworks. Amazon Managed Blockchain eliminates the overhead required to create the network or join a public network and automatically scales to meet the demands of thousands of applications running millions of transactions.

While QLDB is a ledger database purpose-built for customers who need to maintain a complete and verifiable history of data changes in an application that they own and manage in a centralized way, QLDB is not a blockchain technology. Instead, blockchain technologies focus on enabling multiple parties to transact and share data securely in a decentralized way; without a trusted, central authority.

Every member in a network has an independently verifiable copy of an immutable ledger, and members can create and endorse transactions in the network.

Section 5. Serverless

Chapter 24. Serverless Computing

You will learn the following in this chapter:

- What is Serverless Computing?
- Serverless Computing Features
- Serverless Computing Backend Service Types
- Serverless Computing Stack
- AWS Serverless Services
- Serverless Computing: Pros & Cons
- Serverless Computing: Use Cases
- AWS Lambda
- Lambda@Edge
- Amazon DynamoDB
- DynamoDB Accelerator (DAX)
- DynamoDB Stream
- AWS API Gateway
- AWS Step Functions

In software engineering, abstraction is a powerful tool to hide what varies. Serverless computing is a modern computing paradigm primarily germinated from the power of abstraction. Serverless computing -- a modern cloud computing paradigm – is getting popular quickly. In this chapter, we will learn what serverless computing is, its features, use cases, pros & cons, and serverless in AWS. Let's start with what serverless computing is.

What is Serverless Computing?

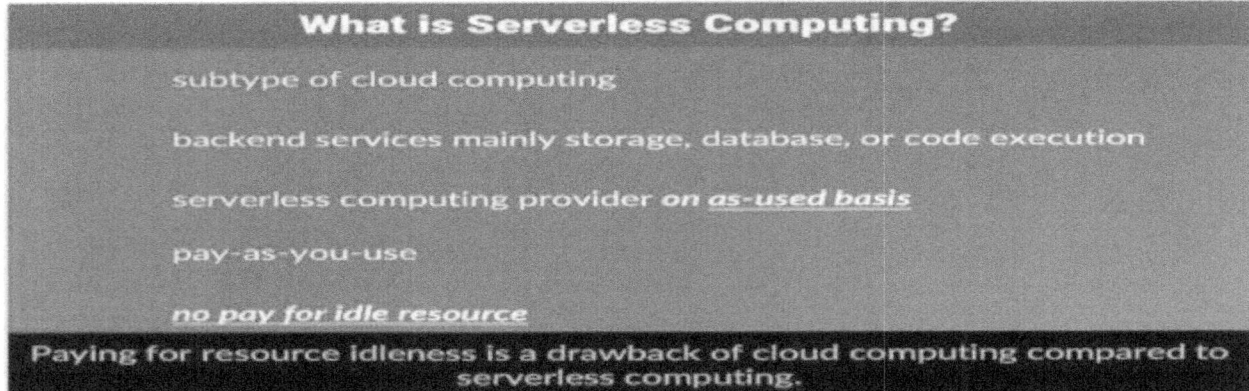

What is Serverless Computing?

subtype of cloud computing

backend services mainly storage, database, or code execution

serverless computing provider *on as-used basis*

pay-as-you-use

no pay for idle resource

Paying for resource idleness is a drawback of cloud computing compared to serverless computing.

Serverless computing is a subtype of cloud computing. It is a new paradigm in which developers don't have to manage servers anymore -- instead, they deploy code, for example, functions. Initially, serverless was considered a Function-as-a-Service, and AWS Lambda pioneered serverless. However, now serverless includes anything managed, such as databases, messaging, and storage.

The interesting point to note is that word serverless in the term serverless computing is a misnomer; servers are an essential component of the computing process in serverless computing. In other words, Serverless doesn't mean there are no servers. Servers are there -- you just don't manage, provision, or see them.

The question is then how it differs from regular computing. In serverless computing, we deal with an abstraction layer. In other words, we don't deal with or manage the server or operating system directly, which we would do in traditional computing or cloud computing. This abstraction layer sets up an illusion of serverless.

Let's understand that further. Suppose we have a use case to create a thumbnail image when an image is uploaded to a particular folder on the server. We develop a web service and deploy the code on the server, and the program is working fine – which means the web service is creating thumbnail images of the uploaded images.

This thumbnail processing application is working fine. But we have an issue that we get billed from the cloud provider for the instance even though the server is idle most of the time. The reason is that the average number of images processed each hour is around five (5 images/hour), and the processing time is 1 second. So, this is where we (as a software engineer) would need to think about a solution where we would pay only for the actual processing time, not for the idle time of the server.

And that's where serverless computing fits in. In serverless computing, servers are made available on-demand to process the request, and you would only be billed for the processing time. Serverless computing vendors have different cloud services, classifying them as serverless computing types.

Serverless Computing Features

Automatic Provisioning of Computing Resources

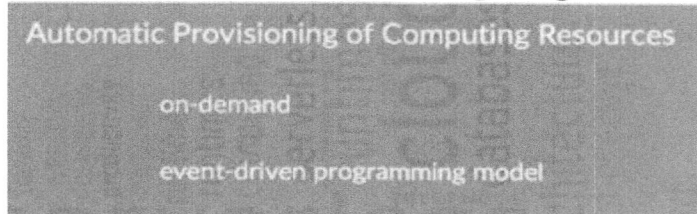

Serverless vendors automatically provision computing resources needed to run code both on-demand or in response to the trigger of an event in an event-driven programming model.

Elastic Scalability

Not only does it automatically provision computing resources, but serverless computing also has the feature of elastic scalability. It means computing resources are scaled up to meet the demand of increased requests to maintain service level agreements (SLA) without degradation in performance to maintain quality output. Conversely, it scales down as the number of requests goes down and shuts down completely when there is no request. The idea of elastic scalability saves costs, and it helps vendors efficiently utilize resources.

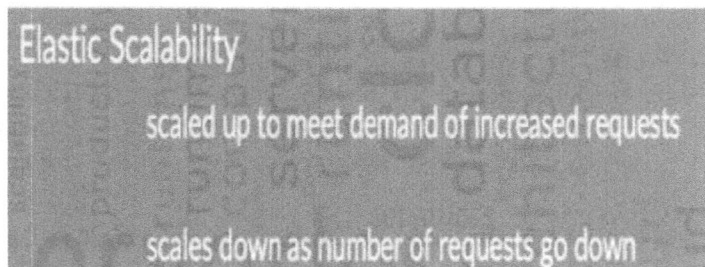

Faster Delivery Code

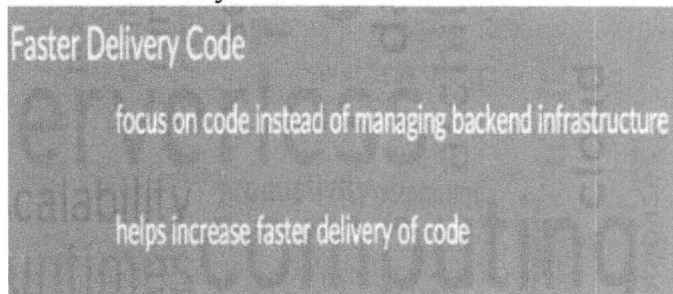

Another feature is productivity. To be more specific, it is about the faster delivery of code. In serverless architecture, engineers would have to focus on code instead of managing backend cloud infrastructure and tasks such as provisioning, scaling, patching, and other related things. As a result, serverless computing helps increase faster delivery of code. The serverless computing provider manages backend cloud infrastructure and operational tasks such as provisioning servers, scaling, patching.

Serverless Computing Backend Service Types

Mainly database, storage, function-as-a-service (FaaS) are the type of backend services in serverless computing. Serverless computing (serverless architecture) is well suited in event-driven and stream processing-related applications because these applications have some critical quality attributes to consider. These quality attributes are scalability and latency; the other is, at times, idleness (for example, an online store may not get any online order in some time duration) attributes.

The other type of backend service in serverless computing is the API gateway. The API gateway manages (delegates) HTTP call to web services such as routing, rate limits, CORS, and authentication. Or in other words, API Gateway delegates HTTP requests to the code block implemented as function-as-a-service (FaaS). Essentially, these web services are wrappers over the FaaS code.

Serverless Computing Stack

We understood serverless computing and types of backend services that qualified as serverless computing. Now, let's know how we can combine and use these backend services -- which form a serverless computing stack -- to implement serverless computing use cases. An understanding serverless stack will help us rationalize how to combine different back-end services to design and build serverless architectural solutions. Serverless computing stack mainly includes function-as-a-service (FaaS), database and storage, event-driven & stream processing, and API gateway. We will look at each of them in this section.

Function-as-a-Service (FaaS)

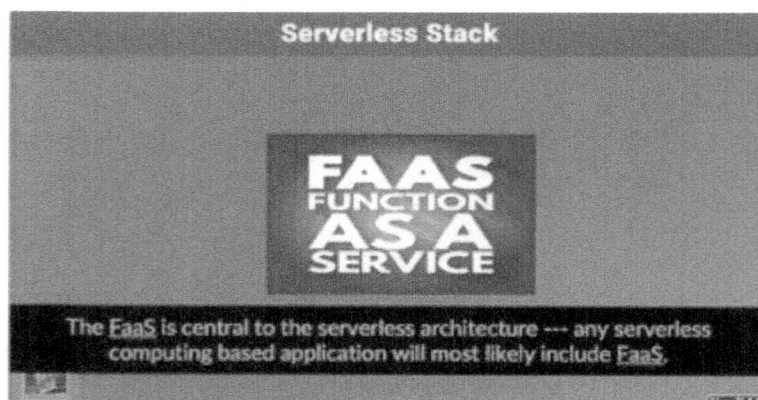

The function-as-a-service (FaaS) is central to the serverless architecture. FaaS, which is central to the serverless architecture, deals with the application code in the serverless stack. Therefore, any serverless computing-based application will most likely include FaaS.

To understand function-as-a-service from the serverless stack, let's look into the diagram shown below. Let's assume in this diagram that the web application shown in the diagram is implemented using serverless architecture.

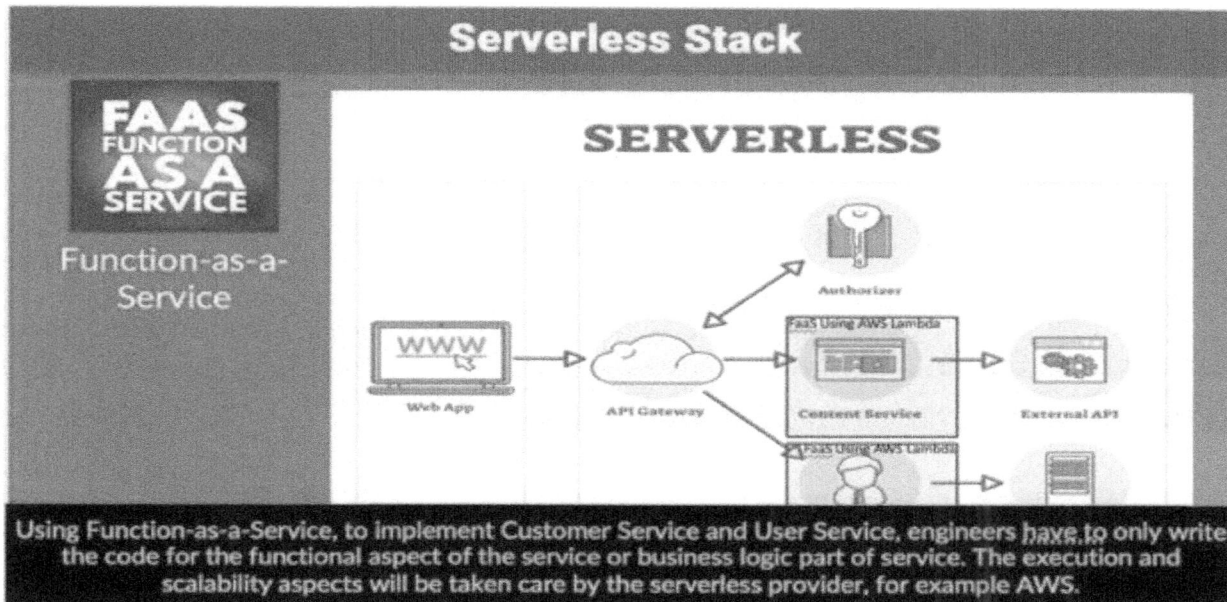

Serverless Stack

Function-as-a-Service

SERVERLESS

Using Function-as-a-Service, to implement Customer Service and User Service, engineers have to only write the code for the functional aspect of the service or business logic part of service. The execution and scalability aspects will be taken care by the serverless provider, for example AWS.

Let's focus on Customer Service and User Service. Customer Service is interacting with an external API. User Service is interacting with an external database for the user information, for example, user verification and new user registration. In this use case, since Customer and User services are not called very less (let's assume five requests/hour), we can leverage function-as-a-service, for example, AWS Lambda, from the serverless stack if you use the AWS cloud platform. That way, we would only pay for the processing time of serverless services instead of running a server that would be sitting idle most of the time.

Function-as-a-service (FaaS) of serverless computing is a massive plus if you look at it from the timesaving and productivity perspective. Using function-as-a-service, we would have to write only code for the functional aspect of the service or business logic part of the service, for example, to implement Customer Service and User Service. The execution and scalability aspects of the application will be taken care of by the serverless provider, for example, AWS.

Database and Storage

Let's look into other components of a serverless stack. In most enterprise-grade applications, database and storage are the foundation. We usually run a database instance (or storage such as AWS S3 commonly used in cloud-based data engineering applications) or instances on a separate server and build an abstraction layer to connect to the database. This abstraction layer is called Data Layer or Database Layer.

When applying serverless architecture, for the database and storage, instead of previsioning database instances with defined capacity or fixed storage space, we can use serverless database and storage services and pay for what we use. Additionally, serverless database and storage services will scale automatically. For example, using serverless architecture, User Service can store user registration in the serverless database such as DynamoDB or Amazon Arora to optimize the cost and scalability of User Service.

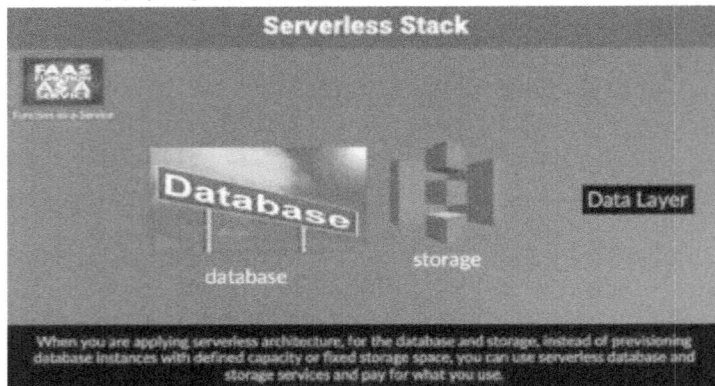

Event-Driven & Stream Processing

Another type of component in the serverless stack is event-driven and stream processing. If your application is event-driven or a stream processing application, you could use serverless architecture.

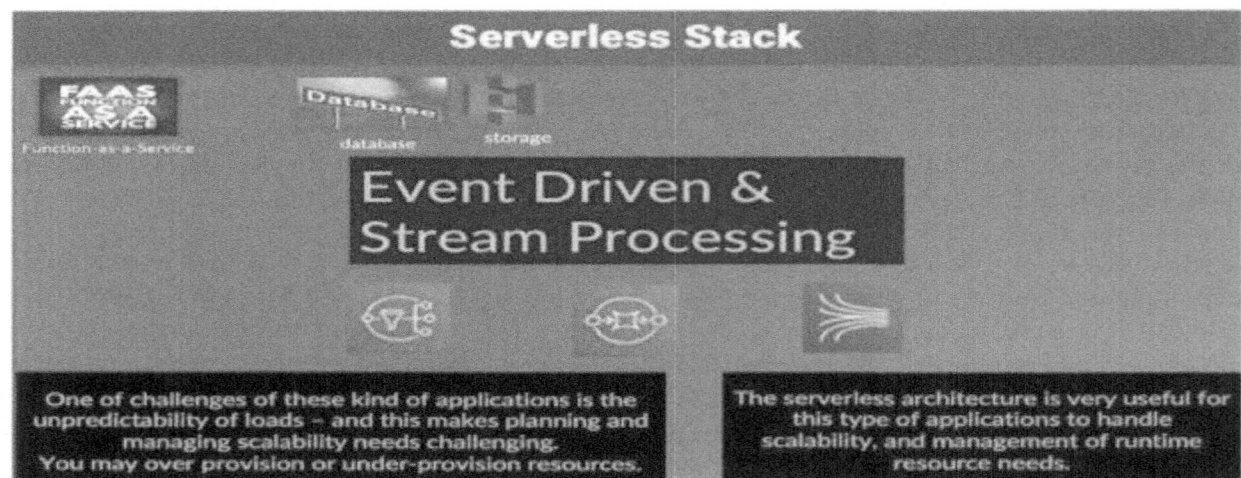

One of the challenges of these applications is the unpredictability of loads, which makes planning and managing scalability needs challenging. As a result, you may over-provision or under-provision resources. The serverless architecture is beneficial for these applications to handle scalability and manage runtime resource needs. AWS has many serverless services for event-driven and stream processing applications. For example, AWS SNS (Simple Notification Service), AWS SQS (Simple Queue Service), AWS Kinesis are some examples of serverless services.

API Gateway

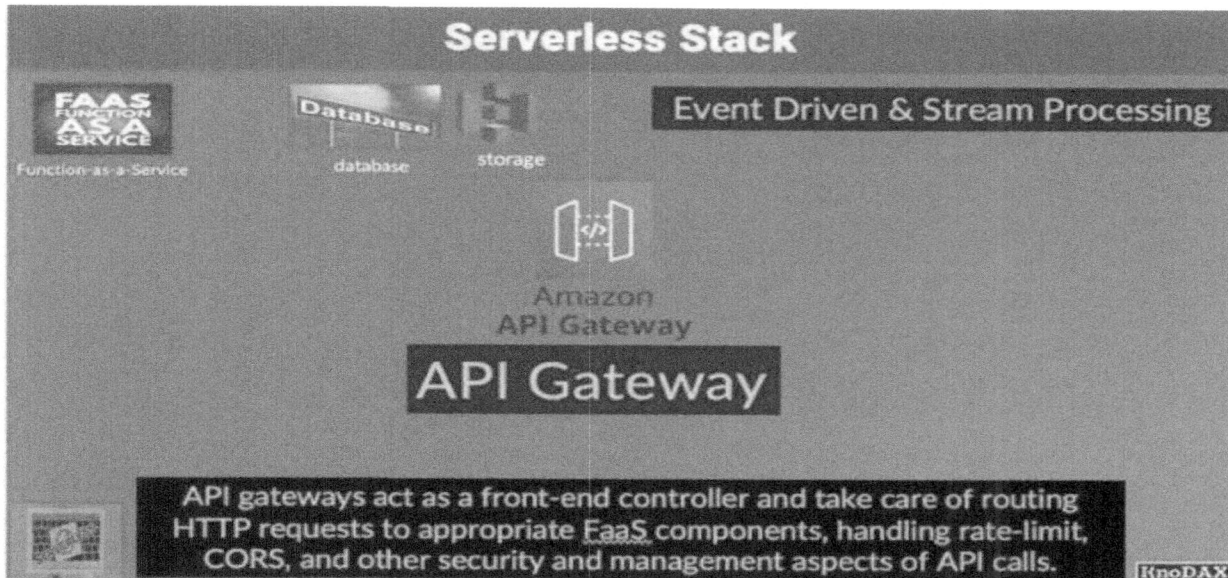

API gateways are another serverless architectural component. API gateways act as a front-end controller and take care of routing HTTP requests to appropriate FaaS components. Additionally, API gateways can handle rate limits, CORS, and other security and management aspects of API calls.

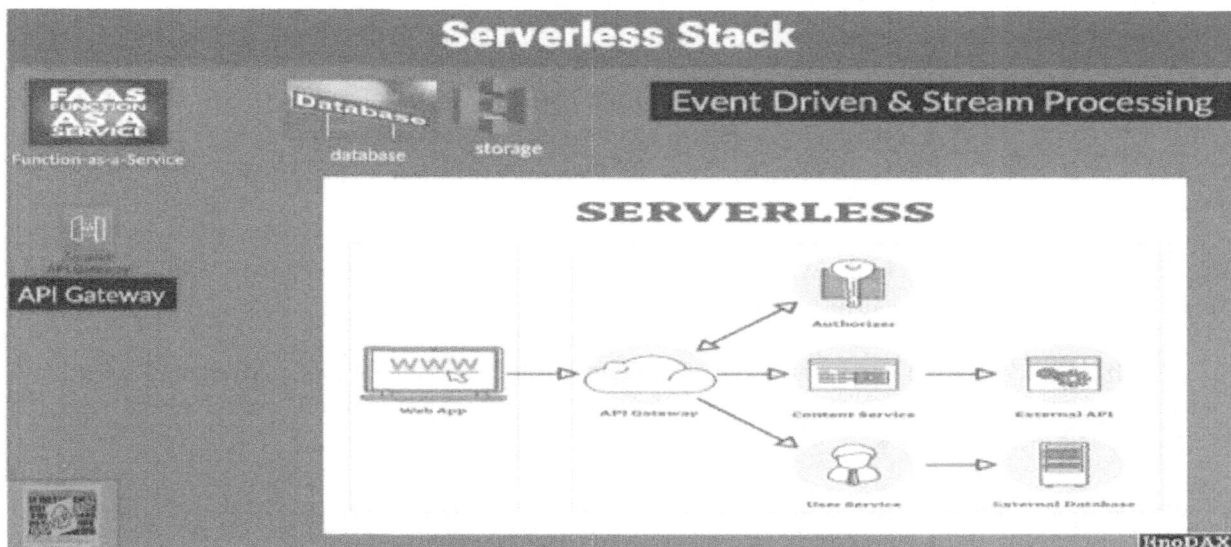

Coming back to this architecture diagram of User Management which we are looking into. The API gateway component in the diagram, as shown above, is a serverless component that handles the authentication of a user and other API management-related aspects. Imagine building the API gateway in a non-serverless way – as you can imagine, handling scalability will become a challenging engineering exercise.

AWS Serverless Services

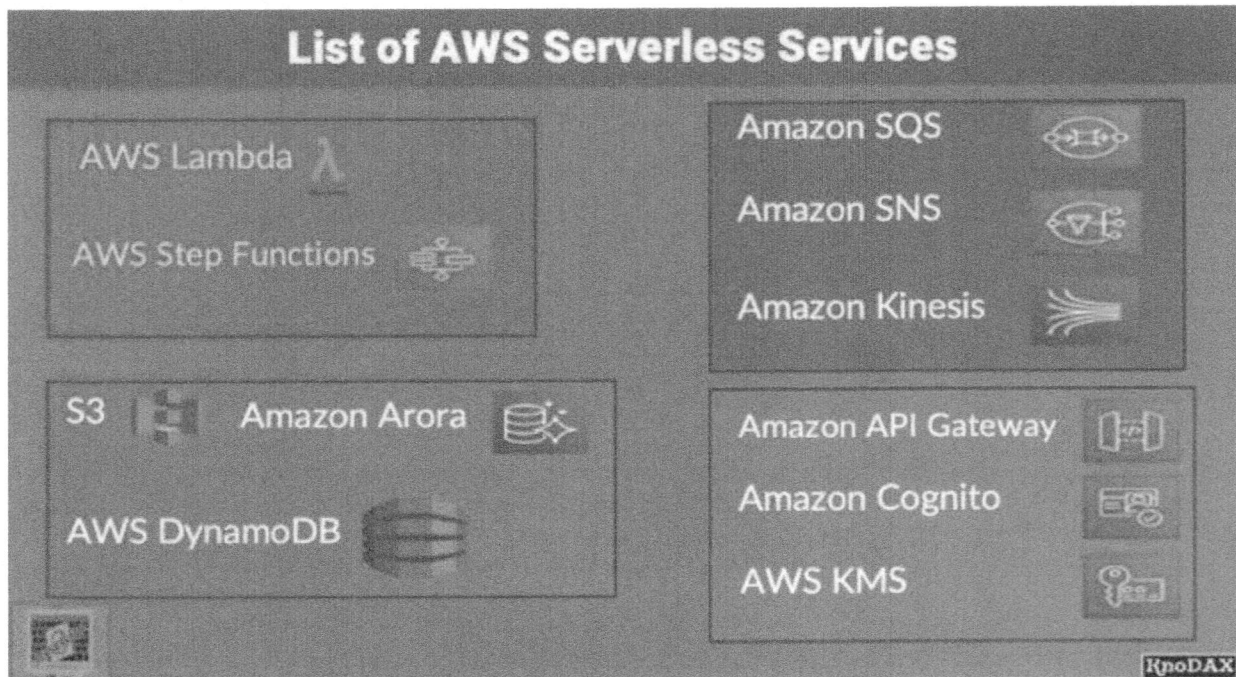

List of AWS Serverless Services

AWS Lambda λ

AWS Step Functions

S3   Amazon Arora

AWS DynamoDB

Amazon SQS

Amazon SNS

Amazon Kinesis

Amazon API Gateway

Amazon Cognito

AWS KMS

KnoDAX

Since AWS is a cloud provider and provides backend services for serverless computing. Let's discuss AWS backend services of serverless type.

In the code execution category, AWS provides AWS Lambda and AWS Step Functions. AWS Lambda is a fully FaaS type of serverless service, which is used to write code. For example, we can write AWS Lambda code in Java, Python, or Node.js and in many other languages to implement business functions.

AWS Step Functions is a visual workflow service that helps build serverless applications by orchestrating AWS services to automate business processes.

In the database and storage category, AWS has S3 (Simple Storage Service), Amazon Arora, and DynamoDB. Amazon Arora is a relational database service, and DynamoDB is a NoSQL service. These are all serverless services.

In event-driven and stream processing backend services, AWS has SQS (Simple Queue Service), SNS (Simple Notification Service), and Kinesis. SQS is AWS queuing service, SNS is a notification service, and Kinesis is a streaming service. Functionally, Kinesis is like Kafka.

The other services are Amazon API Gateway, Amazon Cognito. Amazon Cognito provides authentication, authorization, and user management-related functionalities to web and mobile applications. In addition, AWS KMS is an essential management service for encryption/decryption.

These are a few examples of AWS serverless services to give you an overview of serverless services from a serverless provider perspective.

Serverless Computing: Pros & Cons

Pros

The first is about cost. In general, serverless computing is a cost-effective solution for many application types—particularly web applications with an unpredictable number of requests. In a traditional cloud, we end up paying for the entire server resource, in which we may be paying for the unused or idle resources. But in serverless computing, we don't pay for idle resources.

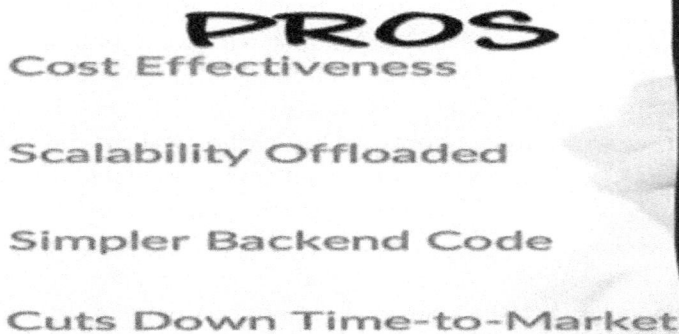

PROS

Cost Effectiveness

Scalability Offloaded

Simpler Backend Code

Cuts Down Time-to-Market

Next is scalability. Scalability is one of the main advantages of serverless computing. In serverless computing, engineers would not have to give much thought to scalability. We must design code to be scalable and stateless, though. And the serverless vendor would take care of making sure the system doesn't degrade as load increases.

Next on the list here is simpler backend code. As we know that function-as-a-service is one of the significant components of serverless architecture. Using FaaS, we can write highly cohesive code – implementing one and only one functional aspect. Since non-functional concerns are offloaded, this offloading simplifies the FaaS code.

And the last one we have is reduced time-to-market. Serverless architecture cuts down the significant time to market. Instead of planning and setting up servers for dev, test, and production, we can leverage serverless offerings from serverless providers -- thus saving huge in time.

You may wonder whether serverless computing doesn't have any drawbacks – yes, there are a few.

Cons

Let's talk about the cons of serverless before completing this topic – which is mainly latency in start-up and monitoring, debugging.

CONS

Cold Start Issue

Not a Good Solution Choice for Predictable Load

Monitoring and Debugging Challenges

Since to run FaaS optimally, the server must be running. However, if the server or container is not processing, the provider shuts down the server or container to save energy and computing resources. That being the case, when the subsequent request comes, the container needs to be started fresh – this start-up adds latency. The latency might be an issue if the load has lots of lags. However, if the requests are continuous, the restart will not be an issue. Serverless doesn't provide much cost savings for consistent or predictable workloads. However, it offers excellent protection for a sudden spike or unpredictable load patterns.

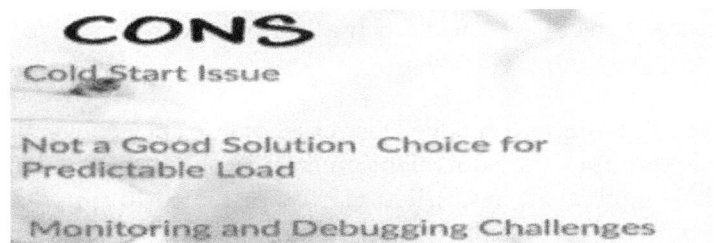

Another issue with serverless computing is related to monitoring and debugging. Monitoring and debugging is generally challenging in a distributed environment. For example, low-level debugging is tedious, mainly because of the abstraction of distributed cloud computing.

Serverless Computing Use Cases

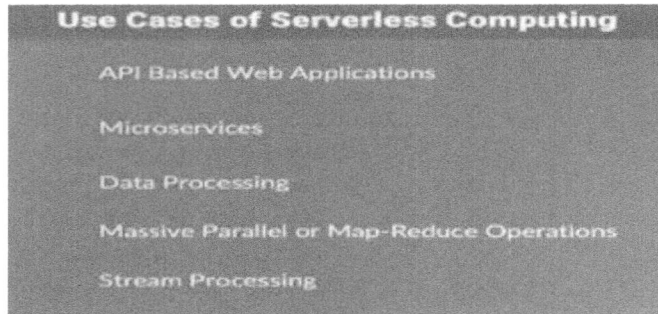

Use Cases of Serverless Computing

API Based Web Applications

Microservices

Data Processing

Massive Parallel or Map-Reduce Operations

Stream Processing

The first typical use case is API-based applications. For example, suppose we have a web application that has APIs driven backend. Here, we can use FaaS to write functional code for APIs that interact with the database, and we can front the FaaS code with an API gateway. Typically, in API-based web applications on the cloud, we can leverage serverless if the load is unpredictable or there is a chance of a sudden spike in load.

The following use case is about microservices. As we notice, nowadays, many microservices applications are built using containers. However, using serverless can be an advantage with a fast turnaround as we can write highly cohesive code using FaaS to implement microservices.

Another potential use case is related to ETL type of applications. Serverless computing is a good solution for ETL projects such as data cleaning, transformation, enrichment, and validation because of unpredictable data requirements. Building a real-time ETL application on the same token and a related concept is also a good use case for serverless. We can leverage FaaS to write code for enrichment, validation, cleaning, and orchestration. Applications inherently parallel in computation, such as map-reduce type of applications, are also a good use case for serverless computing.

AWS Lambda

In order to understand AWS Lambda in a very basic sense, let's start with Amazon EC2. Amazon EC2 provides us with virtual servers in the cloud. For example, if you need Linux servers to set up a web server, you don't need to start shopping for a physical server. We can launch a Linux server and set up a web server on AWS within a few minutes.

Now let's assume you have a use case for currency conversion -- where based on the user's input, you need to output the equivalent amount in the target currency, for example, 10 US Dollars to 10 US Dollars equivalent in UK Pound. You just need to run a Java code that gets input from an API and calls another API to find the equivalent amount in the target currency. Essentially, your real goal is to run a few lines of code – it could be written in Java, Python, or Node.js and in other programming languages supported by AWS Lambda. What if you have had some construct that allows you to do that instead of looking for a physical machine, set up the environment to run the code, deploy the code, and run the code – that's the type of use case where AWS Lambda fits in.

AWS Lambda enables you to run the code without you requiring a physical server. EC2 is about virtual servers, and AWS Lambda is about virtual functions – no servers to manage. Function executions are short executions -- limited by time, and they run on demand. Scaling is automated.

AWS Lambda enables you to execute code without provisioning or managing servers. Instead, you are charged based on the number of requests for your functions and the duration it takes for your code to execute. AWS Lambda executes code in response to events such as object uploads to S3, updates to DynamoDB tables, or other events such as website clicks.

Once you upload code to Lambda, Lambda handles all the capacity related to resource provisioning, scaling, patching, and administration of infrastructure to run your code. It also provides visibility into performance by publishing real-time metrics and logs to Amazon CloudWatch. Your job is only to write code.

You would like to generate an excellent user experience for your user. For example, maybe you would like to send a verification code to the user's phone when the user logs in to your site. Or perhaps you would like to validate the street address during credit card checkout. Or maybe you would like to generate a thumbnail available immediately as the user uploads pictures. Your backend code needs to run in response to an event for these to happen.

The real challenge here is to host servers, and to run the backend code is a bit involved and could be expensive. It requires you to estimate many servers' size, provision, and scale. You will also have to manage OS updates and apply patching for any security updates. On top of that, you will have to monitor the systems for any performance and availability issues.

What if you could write the code and hand it over to some execution infrastructure to run it for you without managing servers.

AWS Lambda fits the bill for this use case. *AWS Lambda is serverless event-driven compute service* -- compute service provides virtual servers, storage, and APIs that allow users to migrate workloads to virtual machines. AWS Lambda *lets you run code of virtually any application or backend service without provisioning or managing servers.*

The AWS Lambda doesn't require any upfront cost – it is a low-cost solution to run your code. In the AWS Lambda service, *y*ou *are charged based on the number of requests and time taken to execute the function (*measured in increments of 100ms). *Maximum execution time should not be more than 15 min per execution.*

To write code in AWS Lambda, you don't need to learn any new language. You can use most mainstream languages such as Java, Python, and Node.js to write your code and uploads your code and dependencies in the form of a zip file. In addition, there are many pre-functions, such as image conversion and file conversion. You can call other AWS services also from your code using AWS SDK.

Once you upload the code, you can select the event source to monitor, such as the S3 bucket and DynamoDB table. Then when an event occurs, the Lambda code will fire in response to an event.

Each Lambda function runs in its container. The container is allocated the necessary RAM and CPU capacity to run the function. When a function needs to run, Lambda deploys the code into a new container and then executes that container on a multi-tenant cluster of machines managed by AWS.

Lambda Features

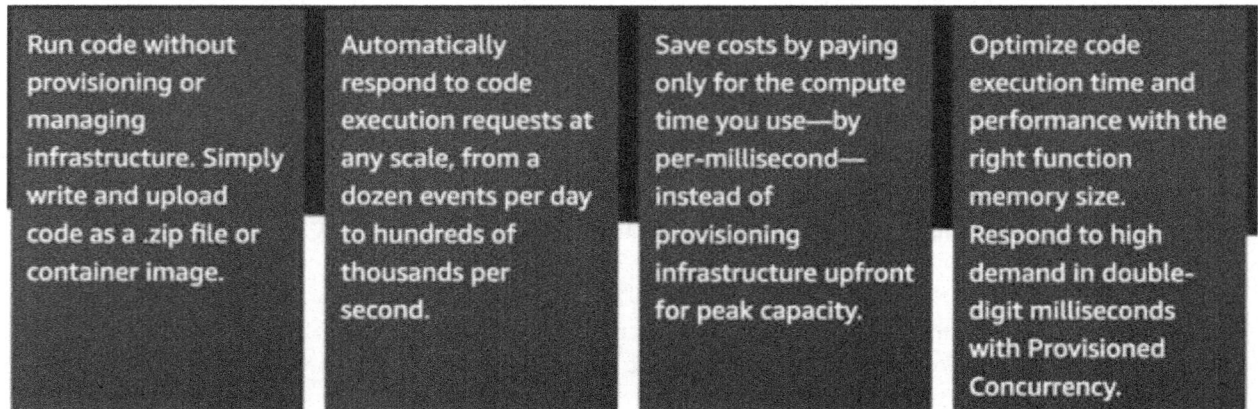

| Run code without provisioning or managing infrastructure. Simply write and upload code as a .zip file or container image. | Automatically respond to code execution requests at any scale, from a dozen events per day to hundreds of thousands per second. | Save costs by paying only for the compute time you use—by per-millisecond—instead of provisioning infrastructure upfront for peak capacity. | Optimize code execution time and performance with the right function memory size. Respond to high demand in double-digit milliseconds with Provisioned Concurrency. |

Screenshot from:
https://aws.amazon.com/lambda/

- AWS Lambda has flexible pricing. You pay per request and compute time. In AWS Free Tier, AWS Lambda provides 1,000,0000 AWS Lambda requests and 400,000 GBs of free compute time.
- It is integrated with many AWS services.
- It has support for many mainstream programming languages, such as
- Node.js, Python, Java, C#, Go, Ruby, Scala, Custom Runtime API (for example, Rust)
- It has monitoring support through AWS CloudWatch.
- If your function requires more resources, you can quickly get them. For example, you can easily assign up to 10 GB RAM to your Lambda function.

AWS Lambda Language Support

You can write AWS Lambda functions in the following languages:
Node.js, Python, Java, C# (.NET Core, Powershell), Golang, Ruby, Scala, Custom Runtime API (for example, Rust). Lambda container image must implement the Lambda Runtime API.

AWS Lambda Integrations

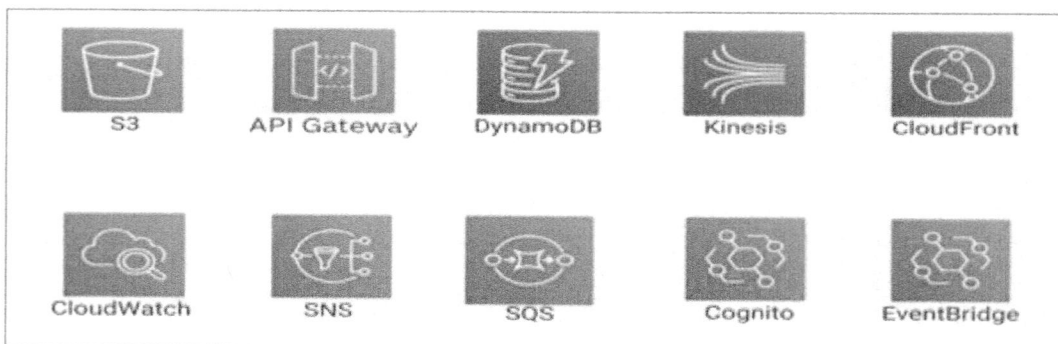

AWS Lambda has integration support with many AWS services, such as S3, API Gateway, DynamoDB, Kinesis, CloudFront, CloudWatch, SNS, SQS, Cognito, and EventBridge.

AWS Lambda Pricing

- AWS Lambda has flexible pricing. You pay per request and compute time.
- Your first 1,000,000 Lambda requests are free. You pay $0.20 per 1 million requests after that -- in other words, you pay $0.0000002 per request.

- About compute time, which is an increment of 1 millisecond, you get 400,000 GB seconds of compute time per month is free. After that, the compute cost is $0.00001667 for every GB-second used – in other words, if your function uses 1 GB of memory, you pay $0.00001667 for every second of compute time.

- As you can notice, it is usually very inexpensive to run AWS Lambda, which is why AWS Lambda is very popular.

- Lambda functions are short lived; the Lambda max timeout is **15 minutes.**

- You can change the amount of memory assigned to an AWS Lambda function. It is configurable -- the range is between 128 MB and **10,240 MB.**

- You can find AWS Lambda pricing information at: https://aws.amazon.com/lambda/pricing.

AWS Lambda Limits

Runtime Limits:
- You can assign memory between 128 MB to 10 GB – in 1 MB increments.
- The maximum execution time for AWS Lambda is 15 minutes.
- The environment variable maximum size is 4 KB.
- The function container's temporary space (/tmp) is between 512 MB to 10 GB.
- The maximum number of concurrent executions for the Lambda instance is 1000 (it can be increased). After the function code stops running, it can start handling another request – what it means is that the running Lambda function instance can again process 1000 concurrent requests.

Deployment Limits:
- The maximum compressed deployment size (compressed .zip) is 50 MB.
- The maximum uncompressed deployment size (code + dependencies) is 250 MB.
- You can use the "/tmp" directory to load other files at startup.

Note: These limits are for AWS Lambda per AWS Region.

Lambda@Edge

What if you want to run code closer to the users of your application to improve performance and reduce latency? Or, you want to implement request filtering before processing your request by the deployed application. Or, you have deployed CDN using AWS CloudFront, and you want to run a global AWS Lambda alongside. That's where Lambda@Edge fits.

You can use Lambda@Edge to deploy functions alongside your CloudFront CDN to build more responsive applications. With Lambda@Edge, you don't have to provision or manage infrastructure in multiple locations worldwide. In simple words, you don't need to manage servers as Lambda is deployed globally. It also helps to customize CDN content. You pay only for what you use.

Lambda@Edge Requests/Responses Filtering

You can use Lambda@Edge to change CloudFront requests and responses:

- after CloudFront receives requests from the user
- before CloudFront forwards the request to the origin
- After CloudFront receives the response from the origin
- Before CloudFront forwards the response to the user

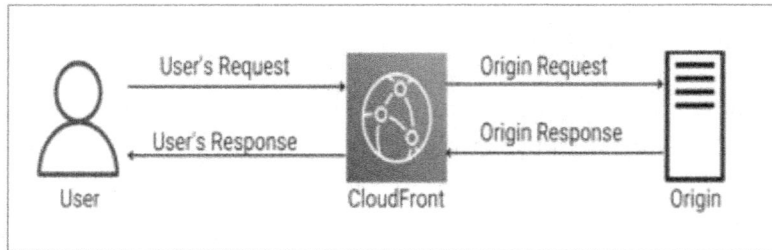

You can also generate the response for your users without ever sending the request to the Origin server.

Lambda@Edge as a Global Application
As you can notice in the diagram, when a user visits a website, the static contents are served from the S3 bucket, while requests for the dynamic content are sent to CloudFront as an API call.

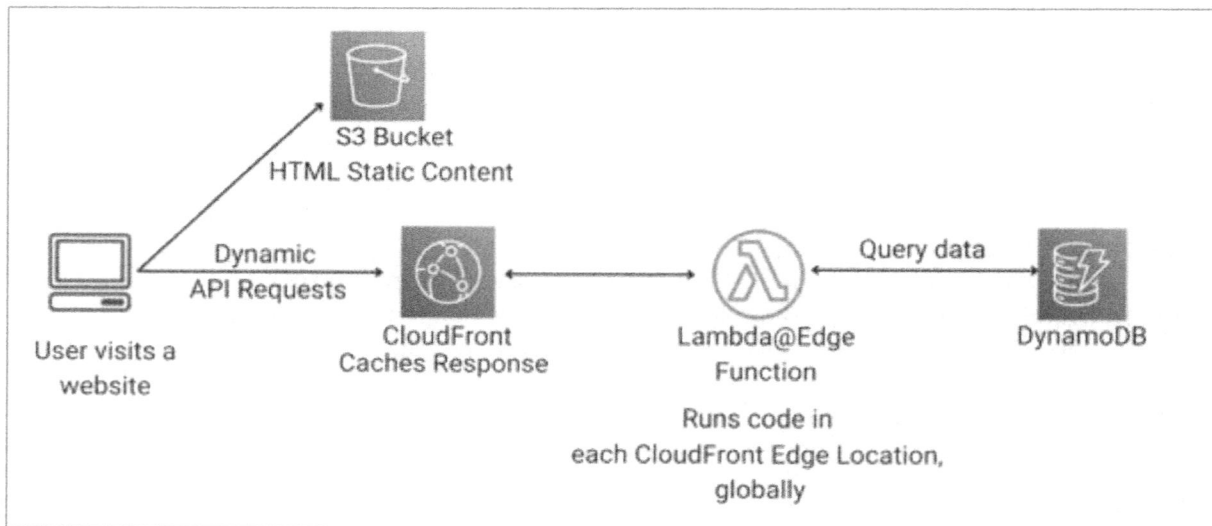

The CloudFront can send a cache response or forward the request to the Lambda@Edge function at the edge location, which returns the response after executing the function -- the CloudFront can cache the response. Thus Lambda@Edge improves the latency and overall performance of your applications for your global users.

Lambda@Edge Use Cases

We can use Lambda@Edge in the following use cases: dynamic web applications with edge processing for global applications, website security & privacy, search engine optimization (SEO), A/B testing, user authentication and authorization, user prioritization, user tracking & analytics, bot mitigation at the edge, real-time transformation, and intelligently route across origins and data centers.

Access Resources in a VPC

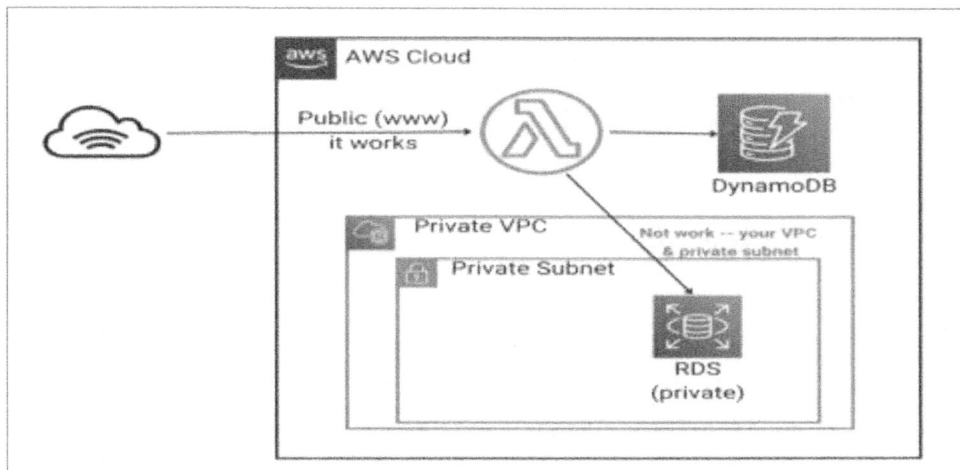

By default, AWS Lambda runs outside your own VPC – it runs in an AWS-owned VPC. Because of that, it cannot access resources in your VPC, such as RDS, ElastiCache, internal ELB, etc. In other words, A Lambda function outside of a VPC cannot access a resource inside a VPC.

To connect your Lambda function to the resources, such as RDS, in your private subnet, you must define the VPC ID, the subnets, and the security groups.

When you connect a Lambda function to a VPC, Lambda assigns your function to a Hyperplane ENI (Elastic Network Interface) for each subnet in your function's VPC configuration. Lambda creates a Hyperplane ENI for the first time when a unique subnet and security group combination is defined for a VPC-enabled function in an account.

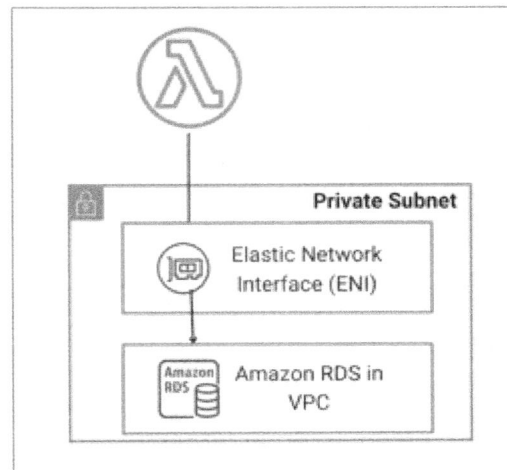

Reference: https://docs.aws.amazon.com/lambda/latest/dg/configuration-vpc.html

Lambda Multiple DB Connections – RDS Proxy

When Lambda functions directly access your database, they may open too many connections. Too many opened DB connections will impact DB performance -- potentially slowing down or not allowing new DB connections.

In this situation, use RDS Proxy. RDS Proxy improves scalability by pooling and sharing DB connections. It also improves availability and failover time by preserving connections. In addition, it also improves security by enforcing IAM authentication and storing credentials in Secrets Manager.

In order to use an RDS proxy, the Lambda function must be deployed in your VPC because RDS Proxy is never publicly accessible.

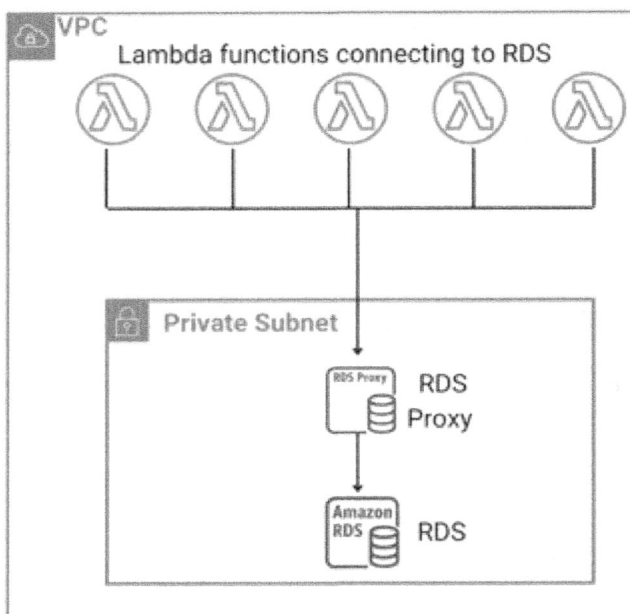

How Lambda Works – File Processing

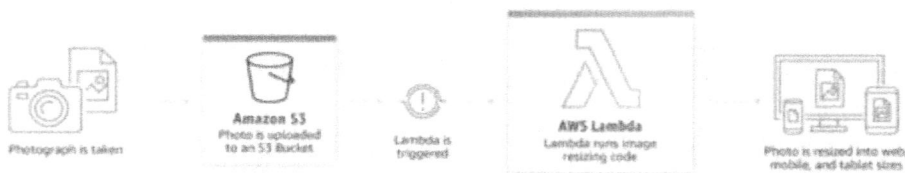

Use Amazon Simple Storage Service (Amazon S3) to trigger AWS Lambda data processing in real time after an upload, or connect to an existing Amazon EFS file system to enable massively parallel shared access for large-scale file processing.

How Lambda Works – Stream Processing

File processing   Stream processing   Web applications   IoT backends   Mobile backends

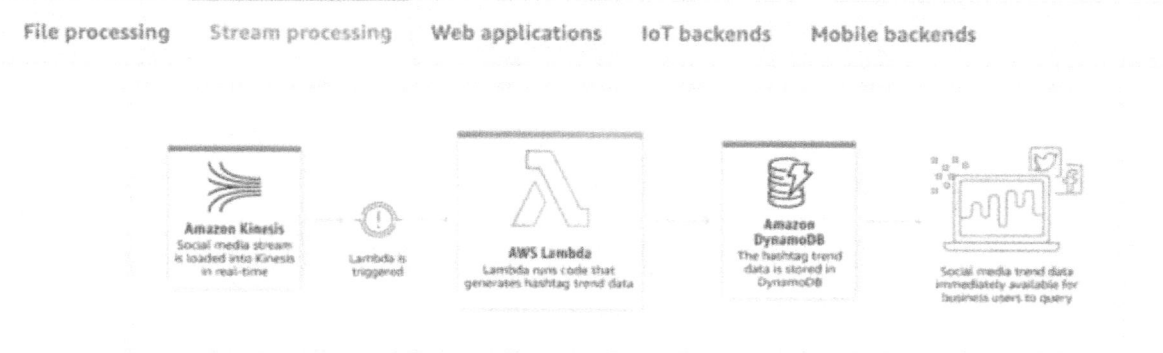

Use AWS Lambda and Amazon Kinesis to process real-time streaming data for application activity tracking, transaction order processing, clickstream analysis, data cleansing, log filtering, indexing, social media analysis, IoT device data telemetry, and metering.

How Lambda Works – Web applications

File processing   Stream processing   Web applications   IoT backends   Mobile backends

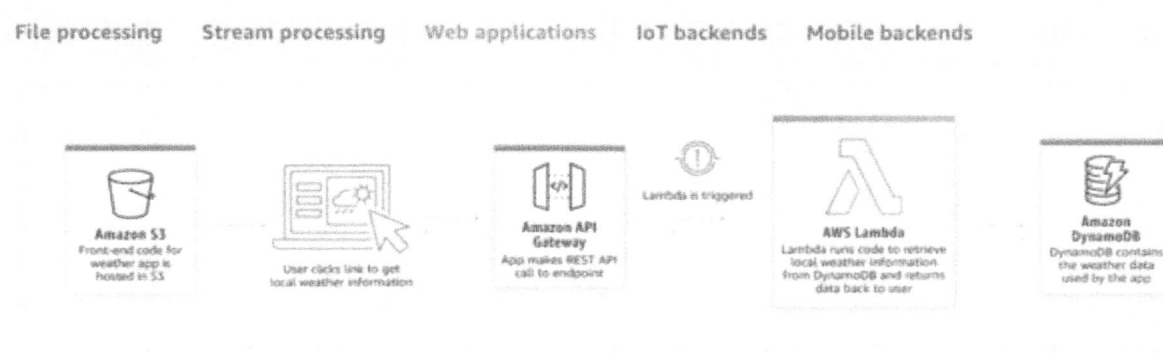

Combine AWS Lambda with other AWS services to build powerful web applications that automatically scale up and down and run in a highly available configuration across multiple data centers.

How Lambda Works – IoT backends

File processing   Stream processing   Web applications   IoT backends   Mobile backends

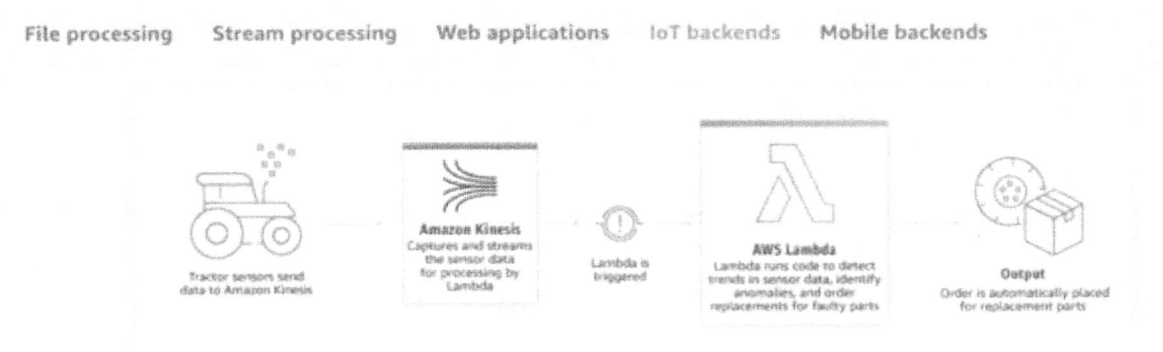

Build serverless backends using AWS Lambda to handle web, mobile, Internet of Things (IoT), and third-party API requests.

How Lambda Works – Mobile backends

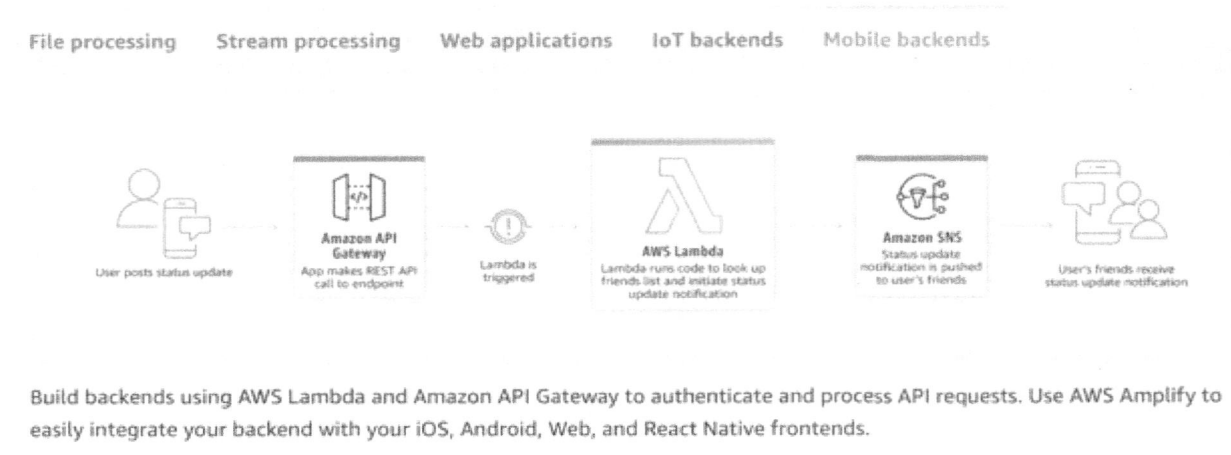

File processing   Stream processing   Web applications   IoT backends   **Mobile backends**

User posts status update | Amazon API Gateway — App makes REST API call to endpoint | Lambda is triggered | AWS Lambda — Lambda runs code to look up friends list and initiate status update notification | Amazon SNS — Status update notification is pushed to user's friends | User's friends receive status update notification

Build backends using AWS Lambda and Amazon API Gateway to authenticate and process API requests. Use AWS Amplify to easily integrate your backend with your iOS, Android, Web, and React Native frontends.

Amazon DynamoDB

Amazon DynamoDB is a fully managed (no maintenance or patching, always available), highly available NoSQL database with transactional support.

It is a multi-region, multi-active, durable database with built-in security, backup and restore, and in-memory caching for internet-scale applications. It also provides replication across multiple AZs.

It is fast and consistent in performance (single-digit millisecond latency). It delivers single-digit millisecond performance at any scale. It can scale to a massive workload. It can process millions of requests per second – trillions of rows and 100s of TB of storage. It can handle more than 10 trillion daily requests and support peaks of more than 20 million requests per second.

It is optimized for performance over consistency. Using this model, DynamoDB will look for the nearest and most available location to fulfill the read request during a read. DynamoDB keeps three replicas of the table in a geographically distributed fashion. That being the case, there is a possibility that during the read, the data in the nearest and available replica may still need to be updated with the latest.

The DynamoDB database has an eventual consistency model. When you request a strongly consistent read, DynamoDB returns a response with the most up-to-date data, reflecting the successful updates from all prior write operations. However, this consistency has some disadvantages: A strongly consistent read might not be available if there is a network delay or outage. DynamoDB may return a server error (HTTP 500) in this case. Strongly consistent reads may have higher latency than eventually consistent reads. Strongly consistent reads are not supported on global secondary indexes. Strongly consistent reads use more throughput capacity than eventually consistent reads.

Amazon DynamoDB Basics

DynamoDB is a collection of tables. Each table has a Primary Key – it must be defined at the table creation time. Once a primary key is defined on the table, it cannot be changed.

Each table can contain an infinite number of rows. Each table contains attributes, and additional attributes can be added over time. In addition, an item can be null. In many ways, attributes in DynamoDB tables are similar to fields or columns in other database systems. The maximum size of an item is 400 KB.

The supported data types are:
- Scalar Types – String, Number, Binary, Boolean, Null
- Set Types – String, Set, Number Set, Binary Set
- Document Types – List, Map

A Partition Key is a key that DynamoDB uses to partition your data into separate logical data shards. For example, when there is no Sort Key, then Primary Key also works as Partition Key.

Primary Key		Attributes	
Partition Key	Sort Key	Attribute	Attribute
user_id	**event**	**web_page**	**duration_in_sec**
x1234	click	cart	25
y1234	purchase	checkout	45
a1234	impression	product	15
b1234	view	home	35

You can also add a Sort Key and make the primary key a composite primary key: Partition Key + Sort Key. Adding a Sort Key allows storing multiple records with the same partition key value since the partition key + sort key forms a unique pair and stores the data with the same partition key in the same data shard. DynamoDB dynamically partitions (shards) data across all of the nodes in a cluster.

Read/Write Capacity Modes

There are two modes to define how much read/write capacity your table needs: on-demand and provisioned (default). The read/write capacity mode controls costs for read/write throughput and how you manage capacity. You can set the capacity mode for a table when creating the table -- you can change it later.

Provisioned Mode (default)

In provisioned Mode, you need to specify the number of reads/writes per second required for your application. You need to plan the capacity. You pay for provisioned Read Capacity Units (RCU) &

Write Capacity Units (WCU). You can also auto-scaling to adjust your table provisioned reads/writes capacity in response to your workload traffic change.

Provisioned Mode is a good option in the following use cases:
- You have predictable workloads
- You run applications whose workload is consistent or ramps up gradually.
- You can forecast the reads/writes capacity for your workloads.

On-Demand Mode
In On-Demand mode, read/writes are automatically scaled up/down with your workloads to maintain the throughput of single-digit millisecond latency. You don't need any capacity planning. You pay for what you use – it is more expensive.

On-Demand mode is a good option for use cases having unpredictable workloads or sudden steep spikes.

DynamoDB Accelerator (DAX)

Amazon DynamoDB Accelerator (DAX) is an in-memory cache for Amazon DynamoDB that provides up to 10 times performance improvement—from milliseconds to microseconds. It delivers this performance even when processing millions of requests per second.

DAX is fully managed and highly available. It does all the heavy lifting required to add an in-memory cache to accelerate the read performance of your DynamoDB tables. For example, developers don't have to manage cache invalidation (which is sometimes challenging), data population, or cluster management.

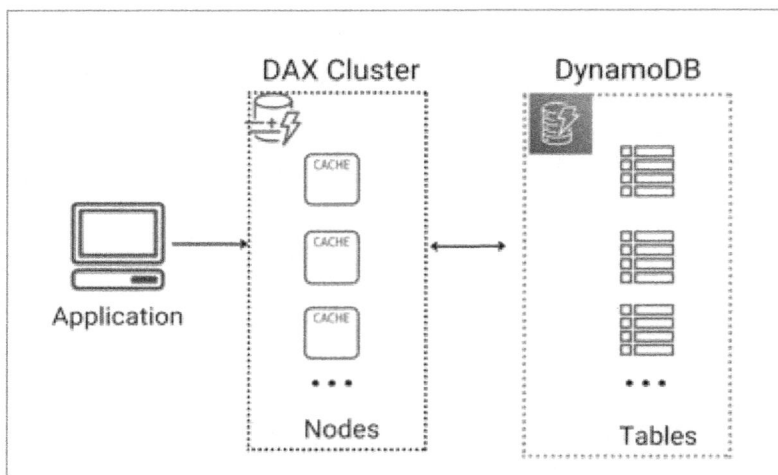

It helps solve read congestion or helps improve read performance by caching – provides **microseconds** latency for cached data.

You don't need to change any existing logic to use DAX – it is compatible with existing DynamoDB APIs.

The default TTL (Time-to-Live) for the DAX cache is **5 minutes**.

DynamoDB Accelerator (DAX) vs ElastiCache

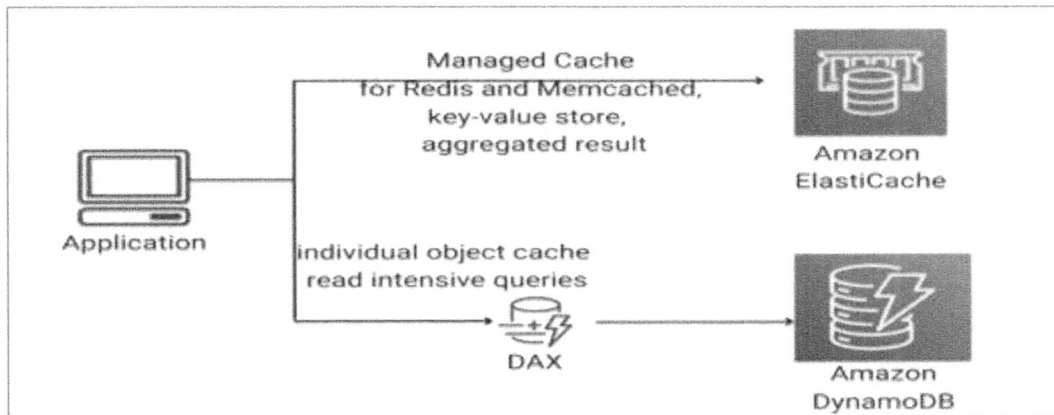

DynamoDB Stream

DynamoDB streams are an ordered flow of information about changes (create / update/ delete) to items in a DynamoDB table. You can use them to track change data capture (CDC) as it happens. Once you enable a stream (StreamEnabled: true) on a DynamoDB table, it captures any change to data items in the table.

```
"StreamSpecification": {
        "StreamEnabled": true,
        "StreamViewType": "NEW_AND_OLD_IMAGES"
}
```

DynamoDB Stream can be used in the following use cases: real-time usage analytics, inserting records into derivative tables, implementing cross-region replication, calling AWS Lambda on changes in table data, and reacting to changes in real-time (for example, sending welcome emails to users).

DynamoDB Streams vs Kinesis Data Streams

DynamoDB Streams	Kinesis Data Streams (New)
Retention: 24 hours	Retention: 1 year
Limited consumers	Consumers are scalable
Process streams using AWS Lambda or DynamoDB Steams Kinesis Adapter (Kinesis Adapter implements the Kinesis Data Streams interface of KCL)	Process streams using AWS Lambda, Kinesis Data Analytics, Kinesis Data Firehose

DynamoDB Stream Processing Solutions Architecture

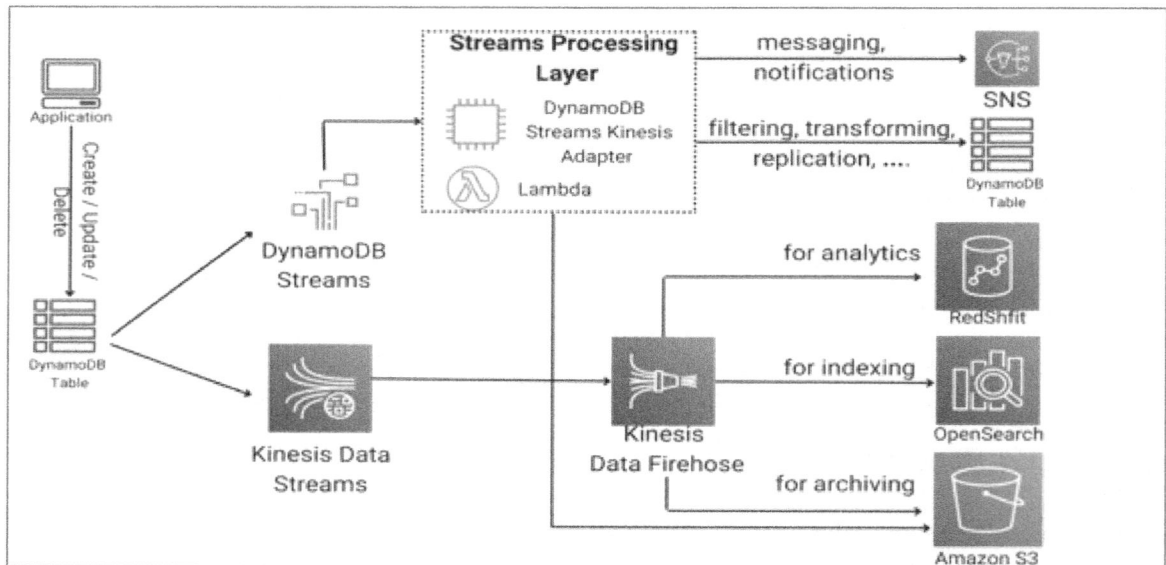

DynamoDB Global Tables

You can make a DynamoDB table accessible with low latency in multiple AWS regions by making it a Global Table, which enables applications to read and write to the tables in any region. DynamoDB Global tables are based on active-active replication. Global tables replicate your DynamoDB tables automatically across your choice of AWS Regions.

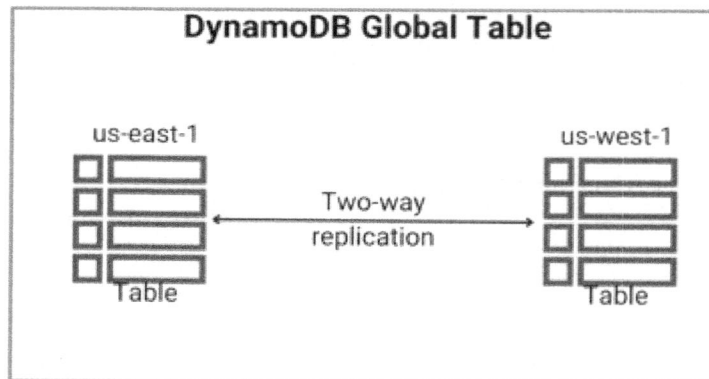

Global tables remove the complex work of replicating data between regions and resolving update conflicts, which enables you to focus on your application's business logic. In addition, global tables help make your applications highly available even in the unlikely event of the degradation of an entire Region.

You must enable DynamoDB Streams, a prerequisite for DynamoDB Global tables. You can set up DynamoDB Global tables in the AWS Management Console or use AWS CLI.

DynamoDB Time-to-Live (TTL)

Amazon DynamoDB Time to Live (TTL) feature allows you to define timestamp to determine when a table record is no longer needed. It automatically deletes records after an expiry timestamp without consuming any write throughput. The timestamp is in **seconds**, not in milliseconds.

The TTL must be enabled, and the TTL attribute name must be defined on the table. You can use the DynamoDB console or AWS CLI to enable Time to Live.

```
aws dynamodb update-time-to-live --table-name TTLExample --time-to-live-specification "Enabled=true,
AttributeName=ttl"
```

When TTL is enabled on a table, a scanner background (per-partition) process continuously checks the expiry status of items in the table by comparing it with the current time (in Unix epoch time format) in *seconds* to the value stored in the user-defined attribute of an item -- in order to delete expired items.

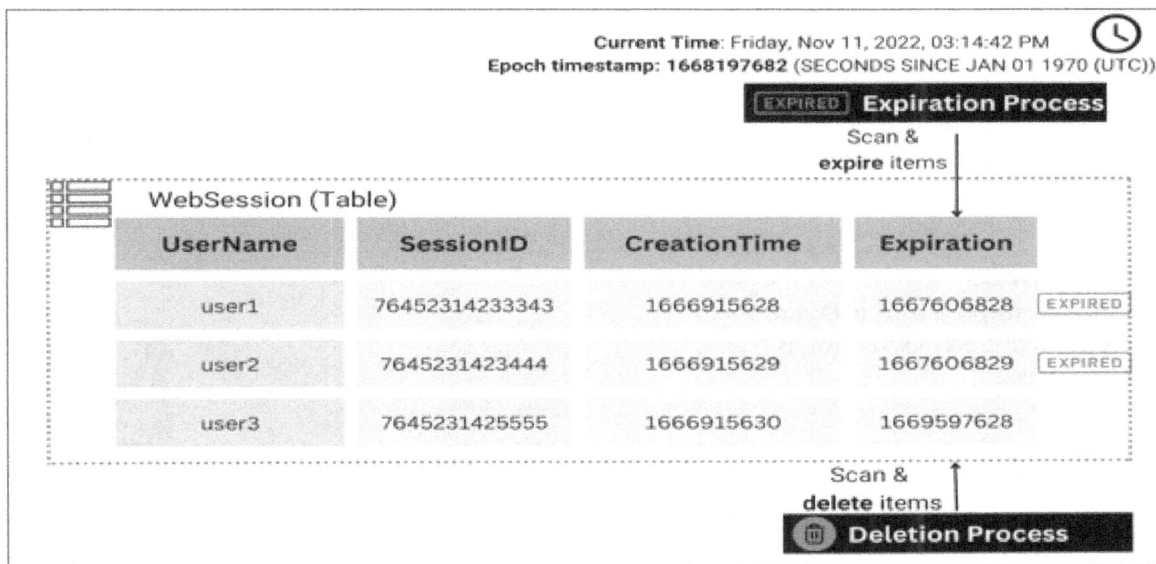

The use case for enabling TTL on DynamoDB tables is: to reduce data storage by keeping only current items, maintain regulatory obligations, and click stream data handling, for example, deleting use cookies records over 30 days old.

Backups for Disaster Recovery

Continuous Backups
You can enable continuous backups in the AWS Management Console, with an API call, or with the AWS CLI. Once enabled, DynamoDB can back up your table data with a granularity level per per-second, and you can restore to any single second from when PITR was enabled up to **35 days** prior. The recovery process creates a new table. The feature helps protect against accidental writes or deletes.

On-demand Backups

DynamoDB also provides on-demand backups, using which you can do full backups for long-term retention until deleted. It doesn't affect performance or latency. It can be configured and managed in AWS Backup (it enables cross-region copy). The recovery process creates a new table.

Integration With Amazon S3

DynamoDB data can be easily exported to S3, and data from S3 can be imported to the DynamoDB table.

Export to S3 (PITR must be enabled)

DynamoDB table data can be exported to S3 for any point time in the last 35 days to perform data analysis.

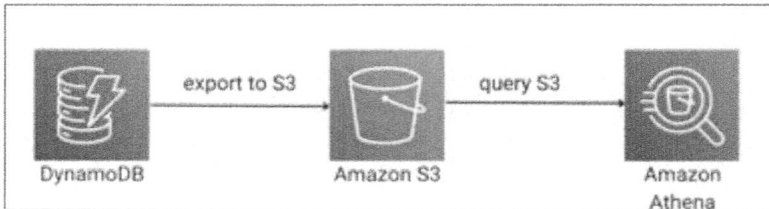

The export also can be used to retain for auditing. The export format can be DynamoDB JSON or ION format.

After exporting to S3, you can perform ETL on top of S3 data and publish the output by importing it back into the DynamoDB table.

The export process doesn't affect the read capacity of the table.

Import from S3

You can also import into a DynamoDB table from S3 in CSV, DynamoDB JSON, or ION format.

The import process creates a new DynamoDB table.

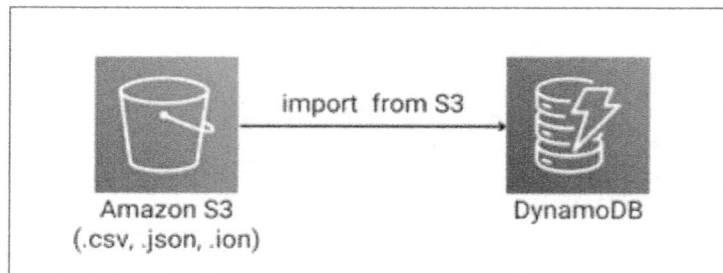

The import process doesn't affect any writing capacity.

Amazon API Gateway

Amazon API Gateway, a fully managed service, makes it easy for developers to develop, publish, maintain, monitor, and secure APIs at any scale. APIs are considered to be the "front door" for applications to access data, business logic, or functionality from backend services.

API Gateway offers a variety of benefits and capabilities such as a unified front door, security and governance built-in, standards built-in, regulatory compliance support, observability built-in, API lifecycle management, streamlined developer experience, performance at any scale, and pay-for-value pricing.

The following are the main features of API Gateway:

- You can create RESTful APIs and WebSocket APIs that enable real-time communication between applications using API Gateway.
- API Gateway supports containerized and serverless workloads and web applications as well.
- Using API Gateway with AWS Lambda means there is no infrastructure to manage.
- You can create API versioning for your APIs.
- You can set up different environments for APIs, such as Dev, Test, and Prod.
- You can use AWS APIs to authenticate and authorize your users.
- You can create API keys and handle request throttling.
- You can configure REST API endpoints with Swagger.
- You can transform and validate requests and responses from REST API calls.
- You can generate SDK and API specifications.
- You can cache API responses.

API Gateway Integrations Overview

Lambda Function

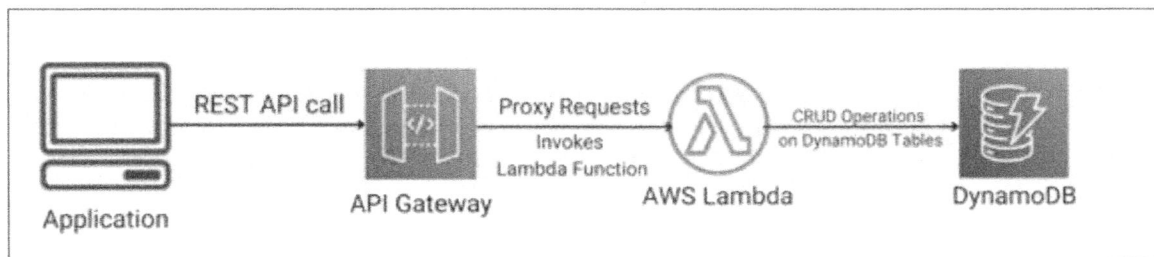

API Gateway can easily be integrated with AWS Lambda to invoke the Lambda function. Integration of API Gateway with AWS Lambda provides an easy way to expose REST API backed by AWS Lambda. In other words, you can easily expose backend functionality written in AWS Lambda as REST APIs using API Gateway with AWS Lambda.

AWS Service

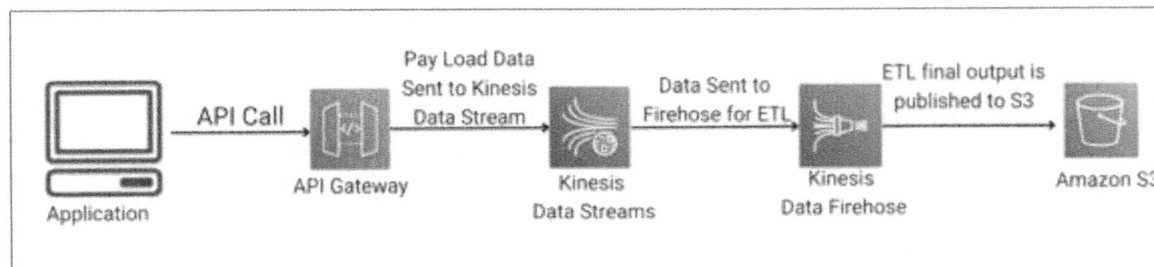

You can expose any AWS API through API Gateway. For example, you can start an AWS Step Function workflow and post a message to SQS using API Gateway.

API Gateway Endpoint Types

The API endpoint is a hostname for an API in API Gateway deployed in a specific Region. For example, the hostname is *{api-id}*.execute-api.*{region}*.amazonaws.com. The following types of API endpoints are supported in API Gateway.

Private API endpoint
The private API endpoints are exposed through interface VPC endpoints (ENI), allowing clients to access resources inside a VPC – in other words, they can be accessed only from VPC. Private APIs are isolated from the public internet.

Regional API endpoint
This is the default selection for HTTP and WebSocket API Gateway points. The Regional API endpoint type is deployed in the specified Region and intended to serve clients in the same AWS Region, such as EC2 instances. Or, when you want to route requests that are not in-region requests to an Amazon CloudFront distribution with a regional API Gateway endpoint as your origin for dynamic content. For in-Region requests, a regional endpoint avoids the unnecessary round trip to a CloudFront distribution. This is the default selection for HTTP and WebSocket API Gateway points.

Edge-optimized
This is a default type for RES API Endpoint -- used for global clients. API requests are routed through the nearest CloudFront Point of Presence (POP). This routing through POP typically improves latency for geographically diverse clients. The API Gateway, though, still is deployed in one AWS Region.

Security Best Practices Guidance

The following are the best practices guidance for securing your workloads when using API Gateway:

- Understand the AWS security and compliance Shared Responsibility Model
- Protect data in transit and at-rest
- Implement a strong identity and access foundation
- Minimize attack surface area
- Mitigate Distributed Denial of Service (DDoS) attack impacts
- Implement inspection and protection (inspect and filter your traffic)
- Enable auditing and traceability
- Automate security best practices:
- Apply security at all layers

Reference: https://d1.awsstatic.com/whitepapers/api-gateway-security.pdf

API Gateway User Authentication

One of the best security practices guidance is implementing a solid identity and access foundation. With that regard, you have the following options to authenticate users:
- Use IAM Roles – useful for internal applications.
- Use Amazon Cognito – useful for identifying external users, for example, mobile users.
- Custom authorizer – build your custom logic for user authentication.

Security integration with AWS Certificate Manager (ACM)

You can add HTTPS to your API endpoint by integrating with AWS Certificate Manager (ACM). The main points to consider with regard to API Gateway integration with ACM are as follows:

- The certificate must be in us-east-1 when using an Edge-Optimized endpoint type of API.
- The certificate must be in the API Gateway region when using a Regional endpoint type of API.
- You need to set up CNAME or A-alias record for your domain name in Amazon Route 53.

AWS Step Functions

AWS Step Functions is a visual workflow service to build serverless distributed applications, automate processes, orchestrate microservices (or Lambda functions), and build ETL and ML pipelines.

AWS Step Functions service can integrate with EC2, ECS, on-premises servers, API Gateway, SQS, and many other AWS services.

Its use cases are ETL, automating security and IT functions, orchestrating microservices, and training ML models.

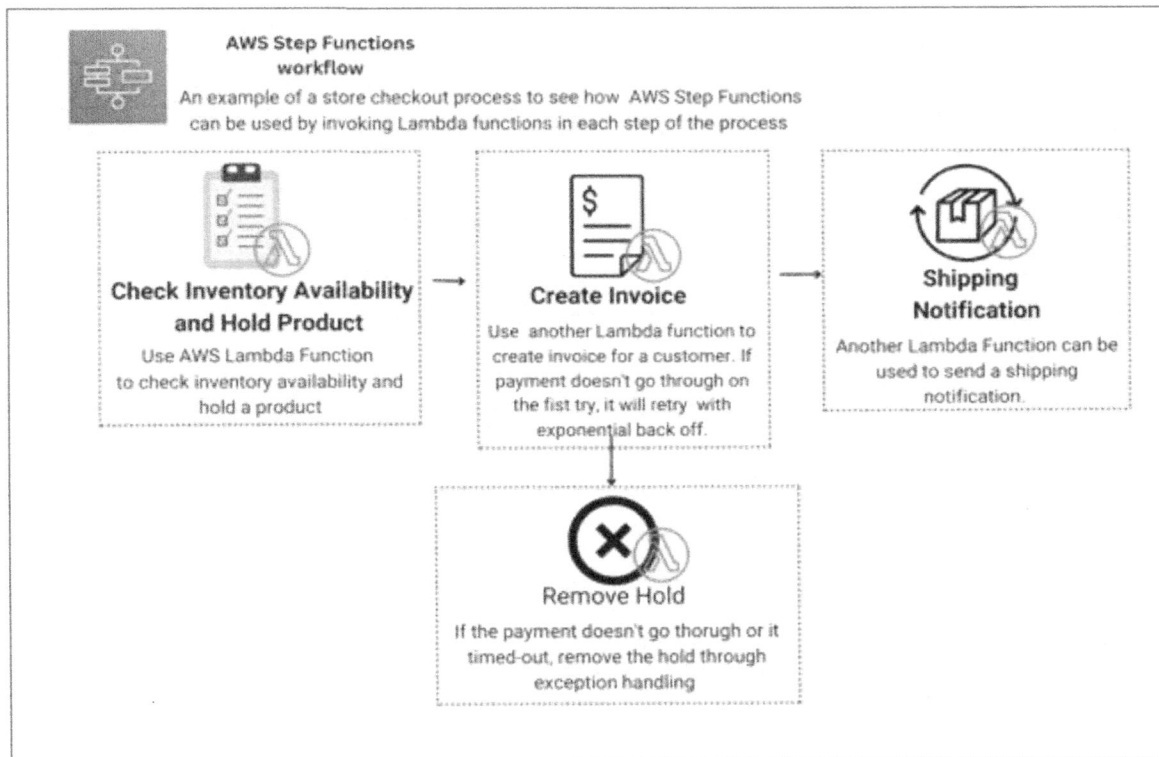

AWS Step Functions workflow

An example of a store checkout process to see how AWS Step Functions can be used by invoking Lambda functions in each step of the process

Check Inventory Availability and Hold Product

Use AWS Lambda Function to check inventory availability and hold a product

Create Invoice

Use another Lambda function to create invoice for a customer. If payment doesn't go through on the fist try, it will retry with exponential back off.

Shipping Notification

Another Lambda Function can be used to send a shipping notification.

Remove Hold

If the payment doesn't go thorugh or it timed-out, remove the hold through exception handling

The workflows (orchestration) can be sequential, parallel, or conditional. You can also add timeouts and error handling. You can also add a human approval feature in a workflow using Callback Task

Pattern (Reference: https://docs.aws.amazon.com/step-functions/latest/dg/callback-task-sample-sqs.html)

Summary

The serverless architecture stack provides a function-as-a-service component to write services without thinking about scalability issues. For example, it includes database and storage services without going through how many extra servers we need to handle additional loads. The serverless provider will take care of provisioning and scalability needs. And we only pay for the usage.

It provides services for event-driven and stream processing. However, in the non-serverless environment, we need to monitor and troubleshoot issues continuously and handle scalability issues. Therefore, there is always a possibility of over-provisioning or under-provisioning.

However, if you have worked on an event-driven or stream processing application in a non-serverless environment, you can easily understand how helpful serverless architecture is. We just focus on writing code for business logic or functional requirements and let serverless providers provide and manage runtime computing resources. Finally, we have an API gateway that fronts it with all kinds of things, such as request routing, rate limit, CORS, authentication, and many.

Chapter 25. AWS Integration & Messaging

You will learn the following in this chapter:
- Amazon SQS
- Amazon SNS
- Amazon Kinesis
- Kinesis Data Streams
- Kinesis Data Firehose
- Kinesis Data Analytics
- Amazon MQ

Introduction

In enterprises, it is common to have more than applications deployed. And often, these applications are integrated in some way to communicate with one another; for example, on an eCommerce platform, the Order Entry application can also be integrated with the Payment Processing service to process the customer's order. And the Order Entry application can be integrated with the Shipping application when the customer's payment is successfully processed.

At a high level, there are two patterns of communication when one application communicates with the other: synchronous and asynchronous.

Synchronous Communication Pattern

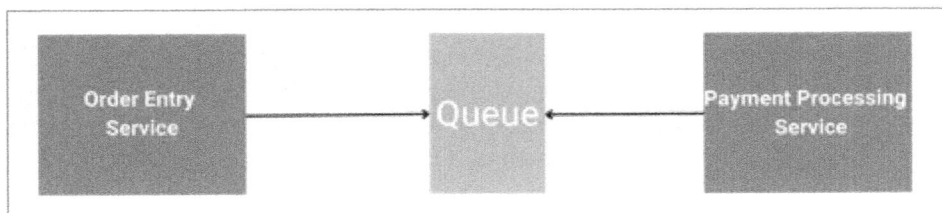

Asynchronous / Event-Based Communication Pattern
(Using Queue)

In synchronous communication, the caller waits for the result; however, in the asynchronous method of communication, the caller calls but doesn't wait for the response. In general, most method calls, typically by default, are synchronous – unless otherwise.

There is nothing special about when one application communicates with the other application – synchronously. The application calls the other application and waits for the result before processing to do anything – the caller application is considered blocked. However, the question is how the application communicates to the other application asynchronously. In asynchronous application-to-application communication, some form of middleware is typically used, such as Queue, which acts as a glue to integrate one application into another asynchronously.

For example, after receiving the order, the Order Entry service of the Order application publishes the order detail to the Order Queue. Then, instead of waiting for a response from the Payment Processing service, whether the payment was processed successfully or not, the Order Entry service gets ready to process the next order.

Challenges of Synchronous Connection Between Applications

Synchronous connections between applications get constrained when there is an unexpected or sudden increase in traffic. For example, suppose that if the Payment Processing service is slow, and the new orders keep coming, it can slow down the order entry if the two applications are synchronously connected. As a result, your customer support may start receiving calls from customers about being unable to place their orders.

To handle a situation like this or in a case like this, it's a good idea to integrate the applications asynchronously – decouple the two applications and use some middleware, such as a queue, to integrate them in a loosely coupled fashion. That way, both applications can scale independently – if one application is too busy, it will not cause the called application to be blocked.

To decouple the applications on the AWS, you can use the following services:
- SQS – Queue Model
- SNS – Pub / Sub Model
- Kinesis – Real-time Streaming Model

These services can scale independently from our application.

Amazon Simple Queue Service (SQS)

What is Queue?

A message queue is an asynchronous service-to-service (or application-to-application) communication method commonly used in modern architectures such as serverless and microservices. Producers send messages and store them in the queue until they are processed by polling consumers. These polling consumers continuously poll on queue to find out if any messages are available. Once messages are found in the queue, they are processed and deleted. Each message is processed only once by a consumer.

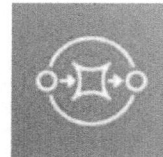

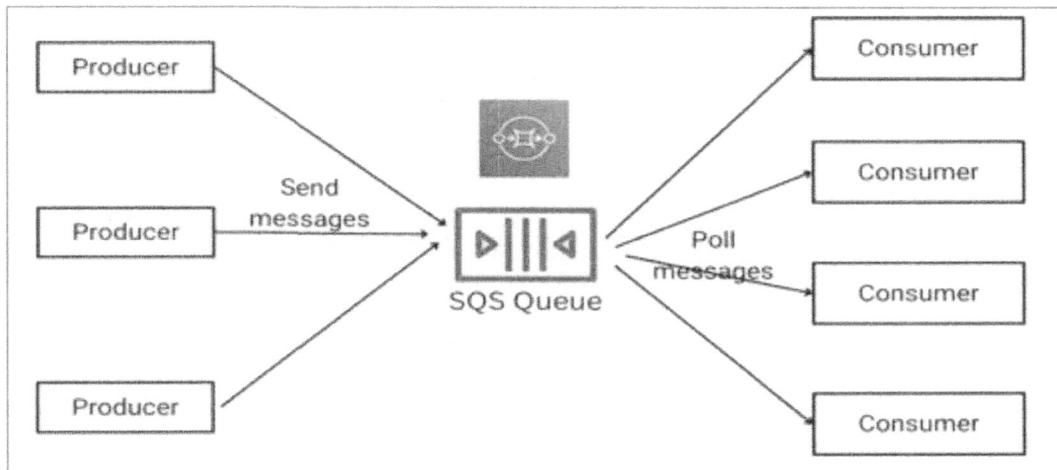

Amazon SQS Overview

Amazon Simple Queue Service (SQS) is a fully managed message queuing service of AWS. The Amazon Simple Queue Service enables you to build systems using decoupled components or modules. You can develop and scale microservices, distributed systems, and serverless applications. SQS offers two types of message queues - Standard queues vs. FIFO queues.

Using SQS, you can send, store, and receive messages between software components at any volume without losing or requiring other services to be available.

Amazon SQS uses a pull mechanism, i.e., the messages in the queue are available till a registered process pulls the messages to process them. This pull mechanism decouples the architecture since the second application does not need to be always available to process messages coming from application one.

Amazon SQS -- Standard Queue

It is the oldest offering – over ten years old. It is a fully managed service that integrates decoupled applications using asynchronous communication.

Let's look into AWS Standard Queue's important attributes:

- It provides unlimited throughput. We can publish an unlimited number of messages in an SQS queue.
- The default retention of messages is four days, and the maximum is 14 days.
- It provides low latency: < 10ms on publish and receive.
- The maximum message size is 256KB.

SQS Standard Queue can have duplicate messages. If you need to avoid duplicate messages, either handle them in code or use the FIFO queue.

The messages in SQS Standard Queue need not be in order. However, Standard queues provide **best-effort ordering** to ensure that messages are generally delivered in the same order as they're sent.

Producing Messages

You can produce messages to SQS using AWS SDK (SendMessage API). The sent message is persisted in SQS until deleted by a consumer. The default retention of messages is four days, and the maximum is 14 days.

For example, an SQS producer sends an order to be processed. An order might have an order ID, customer ID, line item, etc.

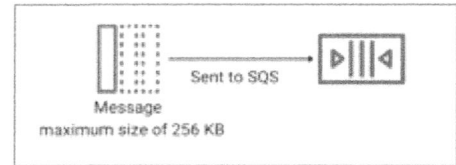

Message maximum size of 256 KB — Sent to SQS

SQS Standard provides unlimited throughput. For example, we can publish an unlimited number of messages in a Standard SQS queue.

Consuming Messages

SQS consumers, which can be running on EC2 instances. You could also have SQS consumers implemented as AWS Lambda. SQS consumers poll for SQS messages on an SQS Queue. One consumer can receive up to 10 messages at a time.

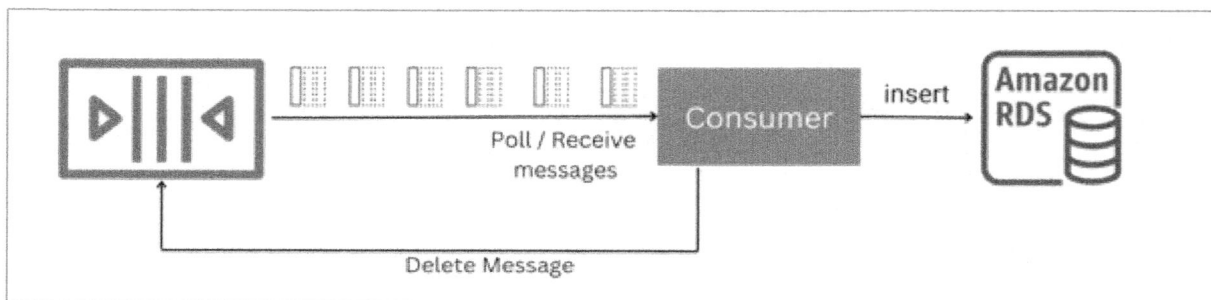

After receiving the message, the consumer does some form of processing. For example, the consumer can insert the message into an RDS database or invoke another program or application to check if the credit card company processes the customer's payment information.

After processing the message, the customer deleted the message using DeleteMessage API.

Suppose the consumer throws an exception (fails) before deleting the message, and your application doesn't call the DeleteMessage action to delete the message before the visibility timeout expires. In that case, the message becomes visible to other consumers and is received and processed again. To avoid duplicate processing, you should delete the message after processing it.

SQS Consumers on EC2 Instances

SQS consumers poll the SQS Queue in parallel for messages and process them in parallel.

Each message is delivered at least once.

There is a best effort on message ordering; however, the messages in SQS Standard Queue need not be in order.

Consumers delete messages after processing them.

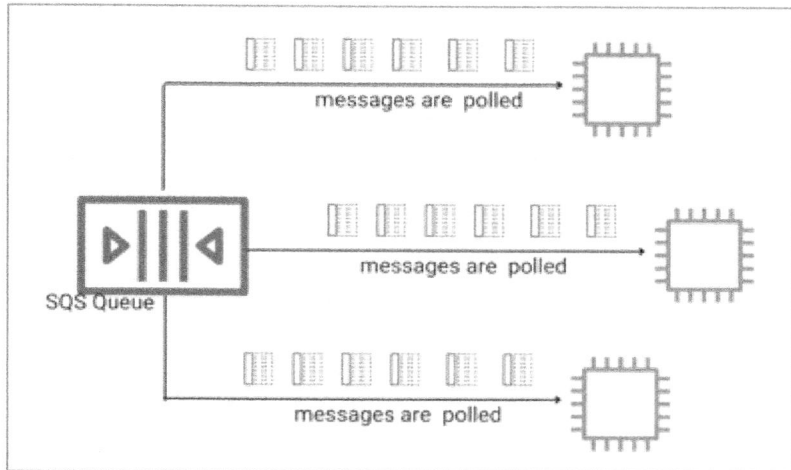

We can scale consumers by adding more consumers, for example, running more consumers on EC2 instances, to improve throughput.

SQS Security

SQS provides in-flight and at-rest security to SQS messages. It provides in-flight encryption using HTTPS API and at-rest encryption using KMS keys. It can provide client-side encryption if the client wants to perform encryption/decryption by itself.

IAM policies are used to regulate control to access SQS API.

With regards to SQS access policies, SQS access policies are similar to S3 bucket policies. With the help of SQS policies, we can allow cross-account access to SQS queues and other services to publish messages on SQS queues.

SQS Message Visibility

When a message is retrieved by the consumer, it becomes invisible to the other SQS consumers. By default, the SQS message visibility timeout is 30 seconds – which means that when a message is read, it should be processed within 30 seconds.

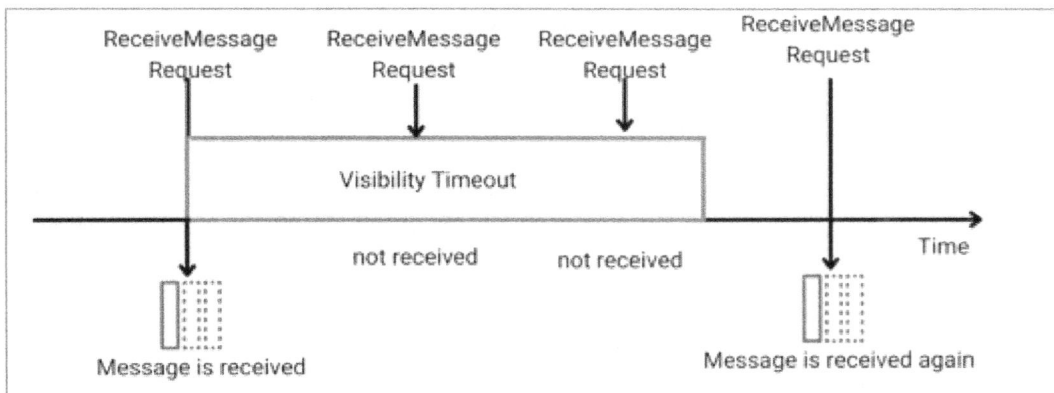

If the message cannot be processed and deleted within the visibility timeout period, it will be again visible on SQS for the consumers to poll, which add to the possibility that the message could be processed twice.

An SQS consumer could call the ChangeMessageVisibility API to increase visibility timeout. The important point to keep in mind when changing default message visibility is that if you increase the visibility timeout too high and the consumer crashes, then re-processing will take a longer time. If the visibility timeout is too low (for example, in seconds), we may process the message more than once – which can lead to duplicates.

Long Polling

Amazon SQS provides short and long polling to receive messages from an SQS queue. The default is short polling.

When using short polling, the Receive Message request queries only a subset of the servers and returns the response immediately. However, messages are available in the queue. In other words, it doesn't wait, even if messages are no message in the queue.

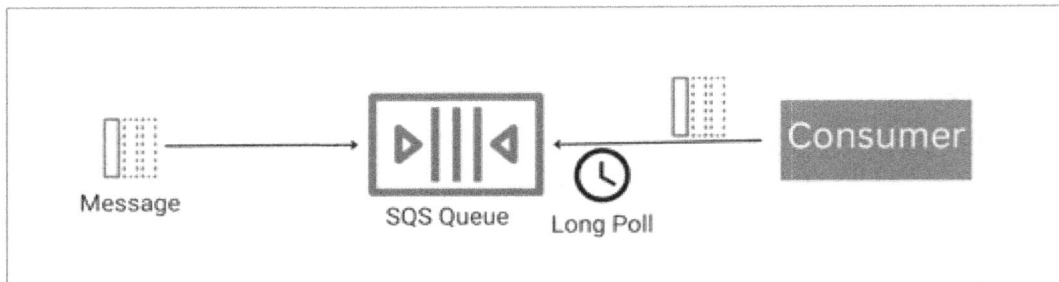

When using long polling, the Receive Message request queries all the servers. It returns the response if it collects at least one message available on the queue, up to the maximum number of messages specified in the request. The Long Polling sends an empty response only if the polling wait time expires.

The polling wait time can be between 1 sec to 20 sec (20 sec preferable). Long polling is preferable to short polling; long polling can be enabled at the queue level or the API level using WaitTimeSeconds.

Amazon SQS -- FIFO Queue

SQS FIFO (First-In-First-Out) queues have all the features of Standard SQS Queues. However, they are designed for use cases where the ordering of the messages is critical, and no messages should be processed more than once.

In other words, if your use case requires ordering in the processing of messages – messages should be processed in the order they are received. And, there should be no duplicate processing of messages – then Amazon FIFO SQS is the best fit for your use case.

It provides exactly-once semantics — by removing duplicates.

It provides through put of 300 messages/seconds without batches and 3000 messages/seconds with batches.

Scaling based on Amazon SQS

In some cases, depending on the SLA, you might need to scale your application to maintain the system's overall performance, to manage the processing if the load on the queue increases suddenly.

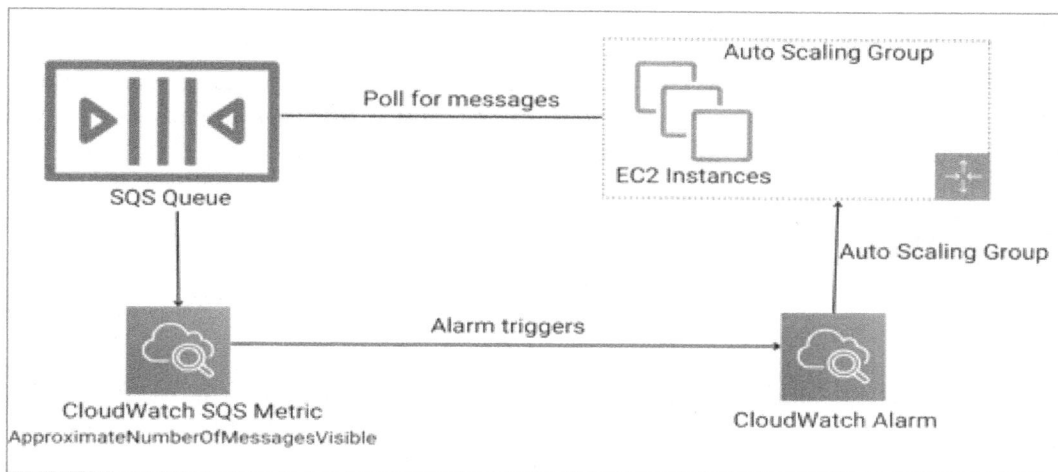

You can use CloudWatch and configure to scale out EC2 instances if for example, ApproximateNumberofMessaagesVisible exceeds to trigger the CloudWatch alarm, and scale in EC2 instances if the additional instances are not required.

SQS Use Case: Decoupling of Application Layers

One of the very common use cases of SQS is to decouple and integrate application layers using an SQS Queue. Integrating applications (or application layers) with SQS allows both applications to scale independently and easily measure and maintain their performance.

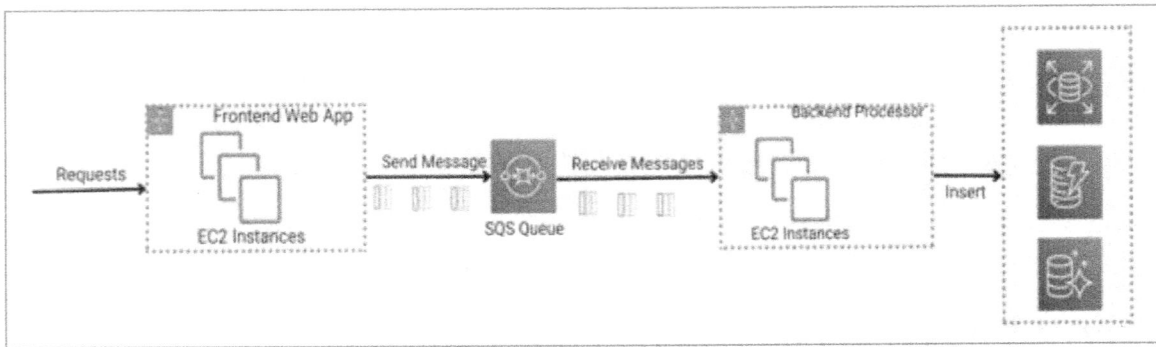

For example, in an eCommerce application, the front-end Order Entry service can take the order and send it to an SQS queue, then send the message to the user that your order has been received. Now, this order can be processed by the backend system (SQS consumers) later without impacting the front-end Order Entry service.

Imagine a scenario where both the backend and frontend order processing were tightly coupled synchronously. Then, if the database is down or the backend system has any issues, the system users would not be able to submit their orders – which you would try to avoid.

Amazon SNS

Amazon SNS is an essentially fully managed pub/sub messaging service of AWS. It is highly available, durable, and secure. Amazon SNS can help you decouple microservices, distributed systems, and serverless applications.

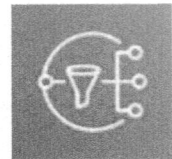

It is for both application-to-application (A2A) and application-to-person (A2P) communication. The A2A pub/sub functionality provides topics for high-throughput, push-based, many-to-many messaging between distributed systems, microservices, and event-driven serverless applications. Amazon SNS allows applications to send time-critical messages to multiple subscribers through a "push" mechanism, implying that the receiving applications have to be present and run to receive the notifications.

Amazon SNS provides message delivery from publishers to subscribers (also known as *producers* and *consumers*). Publishers communicate with subscribers by sending messages to a *topic*, a logical access point -- asynchronously. Clients -- such as Amazon Kinesis Data Firehose, Amazon SQS, AWS Lambda, HTTP, email, mobile push notifications, and mobile text messages (SMS) -- can subscribe to the SNS topic and receive published messages.

Suppose that an eCommerce platform, has an Order Service that is synchronously connected with Payment Service to process payment, Email Service to send an email to customer about their order, Shipping Service to prepare and ship the order and SQS Queue to send the message to integrate with the other part of the system such as CRM, SCP etc..

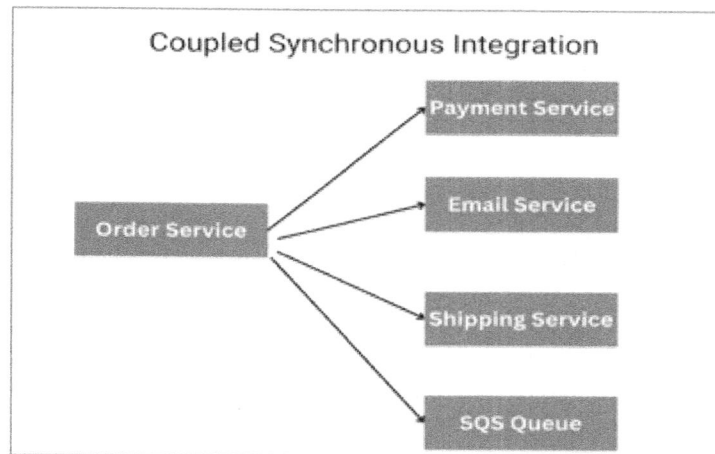

Coupled Synchronous Integration

The eCommerce application getting more orders and you getting complains that order entry process in slow. You talked to the engineering group and then it was decided to decouple the Order service from the other services and connect them asynchronously.

As you can that is a use case where you have one message needs to be processed by multiple consumers in a decoupled and asynchronous fashion. In Amazon SQS, one message on SQS Queue can only be processed by one consumer.

That's where Amazon SNS fits.

Amazon SNS is one of the key architectural components if you want to build scalable, decoupled application architecture or integrate applications in asynchronous communication patterns.

Using Amazon SNS, you can send one message to many subscribers. It is based on pub/sub (publishers/subscribers) model.

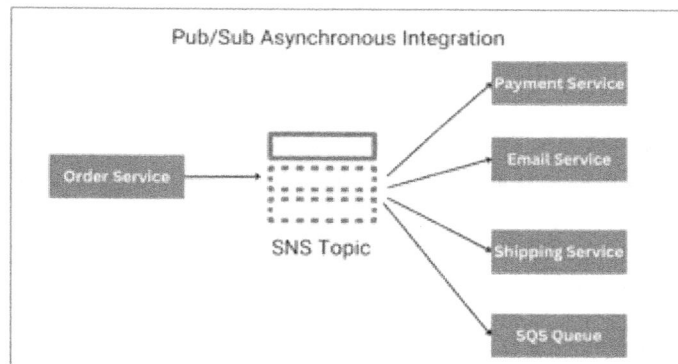

Pub/Sub Asynchronous Integration

Usually the term "event" is used in case of SNS and "event producers" send messaged to one SNS topic. In other words, you could many instances of Order service (for example, deployed on multiple EC2 instances) sending order events to an SNS topic. And as many "event receivers" (or subscriptions) as we want to can subscribe to the SNS topic. Each

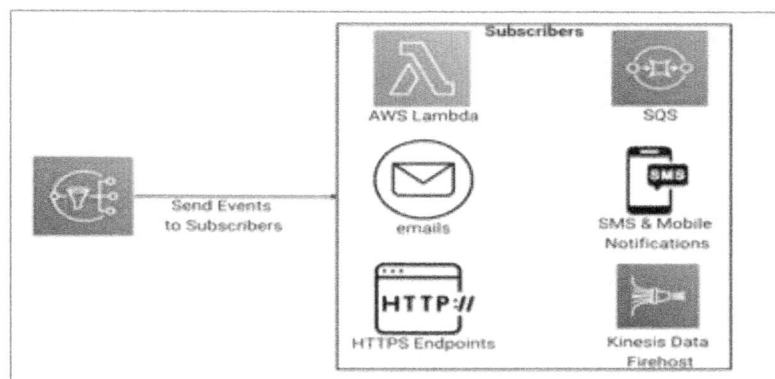

subscriber to the topic received all the events from the topic.

Each account can support up to 100,000 standard SNS topics and maximum 12,500,000 subscriptions per topic.

Amazon SNS can be integrated with many AWS services. For example, there are many AWS services that can publish events to SNS topics and from there subscribers of the SNS topics can receive those published events.

You can publish events on an SNS topic, using SDK.

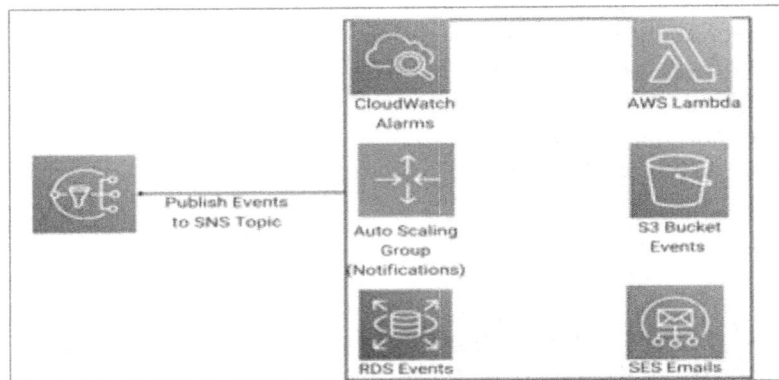

Amazon SNS Security

With regards to encryption, you can using HTTPS API to have in-flight encryption and for at-rest you use KMS keys to encrypt data at rest. You have option to use Client-side encryption if the client wants to perform encryption/decryption to itself.

You can use IAM access policies to regulated access to SNS API.

You can use SNS access policies for cross account access and allow other services (for example, S3) to write to an SNS topic

SNS and SQS Fan Out

You can use SNS and SQS in combination to Fan Out and make system highly scalable.

Once you push an event to an SNS topic, then SQS that are subscribers to the topic receives the event. From there each SQS queue, consumer can consume their events.

For example, Order Service publish a new order event to and SNS topic and from there Email Service SQS Service queue and Shipping Service SQS queue receive the same the order event. Then Email Service consumer reads from the event from the Email SQS Queue to sends email. Similarly, Shipping Service consumer reads from the Shipping SQS Queue to make the order ready for the shipping.

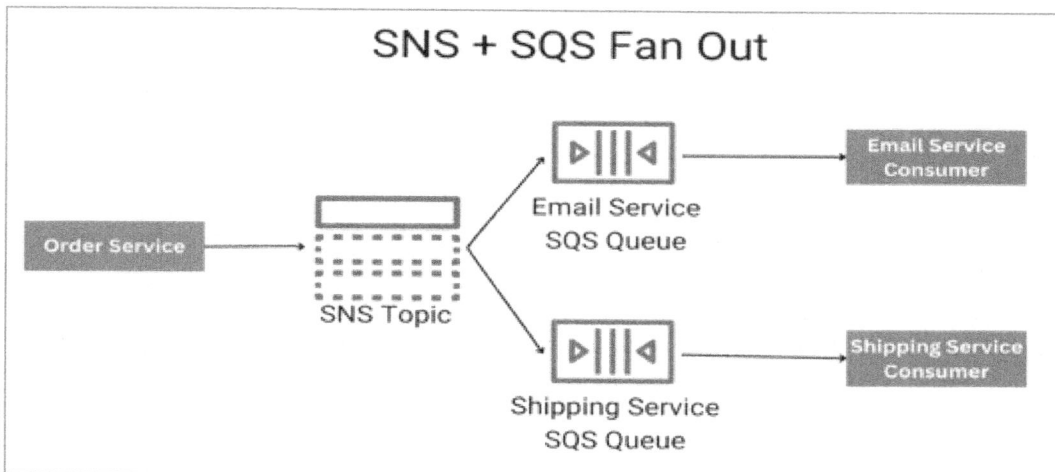

SNS + SQS Fan Out

The typical Fanout scenario with SNS and SQS is when a message published to an SNS topic is pushed to multiple endpoints by replicating it, such as Amazon SQS queues, HTTP(S) endpoints, Lambda functions, Kinesis Data Firehose delivery streams. This fanout architecture allows fully decoupled parallel asynchronous processing with no data loss.

Fan Out S3 Events

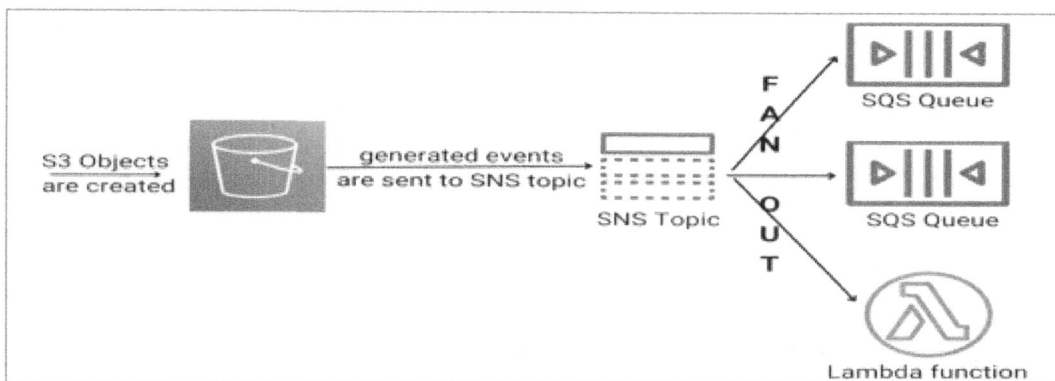

The typical way to fan out S3 events to multiple SQS queues is to use SNS. For example, if you want to send the same S3 event to many SQS queues, use fan-out. The S3 event notifications would go to an SNS topic instead of an SQS queue. And, the SNS would be responsible for fanning out those published messages out to as many queues as you want. As you can see in the diagram, the same S3 events are being sent to two separate SQS queues and Lambda function using SNS + SQS fan-out concept.

Fan Out Events to Multiple Destination Using SNS + KDF

You can also use SNS and Kinesis Data Firehose to build fan out events type of solutions architecture. For example, in an e-commerce application the Order Service can sent new order events to Kinesis Data Firehose (KDF) and KDP can replicate and fan out order events to S3 bucket and other KDF destination(s).

SNS + KDF Fan Out

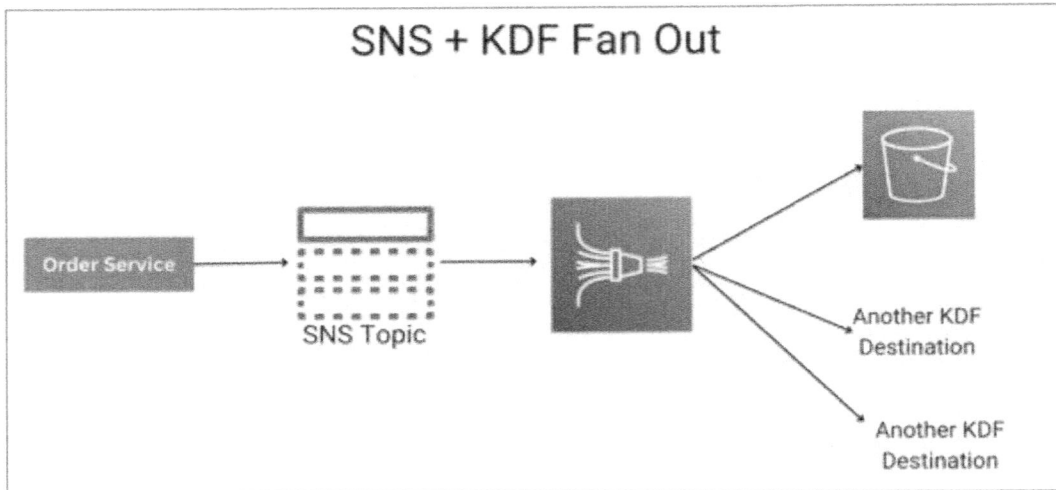

Amazon Simple Email Service (SES)

Amazon Simple Email Service (SES) is a cost-effective, flexible, and scalable email service which developers can use to send mail from within any application. You can configure Amazon SES quickly send email securely, globally, and at scale. It supports several email-related use cases such as transactional, marketing, or mass email communications.

Amazon Kinesis

Kinesis is a set of services to ingest, process, and analyze real-time streaming events such as application logs, metrics, website clickstreams, video stream, and IoT telemetry data and much more.

Amazon Kinesis enables you to process and analyze data as it arrives and responds instantly instead of the old classic style of data collection, where you have to wait until all your data is collected before the processing can begin. Kinesis allows you to process and analyze the data as it arrives and responds quickly.

These ingest, processes, and analysis of real-time streaming data help you get timely insights so that you can make better management decisions or react quickly.

Kinesis is a set of services: there are four main components of Amazon Kinesis that can be used to accomplish different tasks using their AWS services.
- Kinesis Data Streams – to ingest, process and store data streams
- Kinesis Firehose – to load data streams into AWS data stores
- Kinesis Data Analytics – to analyze data streams with SQL or Apache Flink
- Kinesis Video Streams – to collect, process, and store video streams

Kinesis Data Streams

One of the components of Amazon Kinesis, it is a serverless streaming data service that is used to ingest, process and store data streams at any scale. Amazon Kinesis Data Streams lets you build custom applications that process or analyze streaming data for specialized needs.

For example, you can continuously add various data types such as clickstreams, application logs, and social media to an Amazon Kinesis data stream from hundreds of thousands of sources. Within seconds, the data will be available for your Amazon Kinesis Applications to read and process from the stream.

Amazon Kinesis Data Streams help continue processing the incoming streaming data. For example, it is about transforming the data before publishing it to a data store, running real-time metrics and analytics, or deriving more complex data streams for further processing. The following are typical use cases: real-time metrics and reporting, real-time data analytics, complex stream processing, accelerated log, and data feed intake.

Producers such as AWS services, microservices, logs, or mobile apps and IoT sensors built using AWS SDK and KPL (Kinesis Producer Library) send data records to Kinesis Data Stream and consumers consume data record to build streaming applications using AWS services (such as Kinesis Data Firehose, Kinesis Data Analytics, AWS Lambda), open-source frameworks, and custom applications.

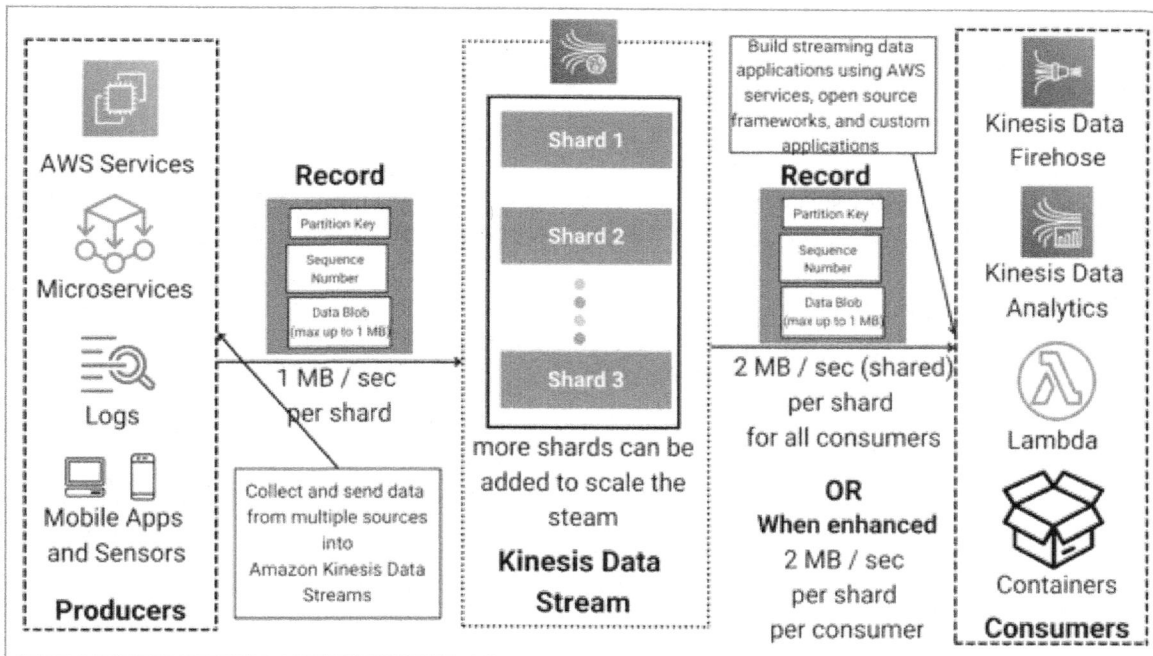

Some Key Concepts

Data Producer

It is an application that published data records in real-time as they are generated to a Kinesis data stream. The data records contain partition key the determine which shard ingests the data record.

Data Consumer
A data consumer is a distributed Kinesis application or an AWS service that retrieves data records from all shards.

Data Stream
A data stream is a logical grouping of shards – no bounds on the number of shards within a data stream. Data will be retained for 24 hours by default or optionally up to 365 days.

Shard
- A shard contains an ordered sequence of records that are ordered by their arrival time -- it is an append-only log.
- One shard can ingest 1000 data records/sec or 1MB/sec. You can add more shards to increase your ingestion capability.
- When using enhanced fan-out, one shard provides 1MB/sec input and 2MB/sec output. On the other hand, when there is no enhanced fan-out, a shard provides 1MB/sec of input and 2MB/sec of output. And this output is shared with any consumer not using enhanced fan-out.
- When creating a stream, you need to specify the number of shards. The number can be changed at any time. For example, when you can create a stream with three shards and if you add 5 consumers using enhanced fan-out. This stream can provide up to 30 MB/sec of total data output (3 shards x 2MB/sec x 5 data consumers). When consumers are not using enhanced fan-out, this stream provides a throughput of 2MB/sec input and 4MB/sec output.
- Shard-level metrics can be monitored in Amazon Kinesis Data Streams.

Data record
It is the unit of data stored in an Amazon Kinesis stream. A record contains: a sequence number, partition key, and data blob -- the maximum size of a data blob is 1 MB.

Partition key
A partition key is typically a meaningful identifier, such as a customer ID or timestamp. The partition key is also used to segregate and route data records to different shards of a stream.

For example, assuming you have a data stream with three shards (Shard 1, Shard 2, and Shard 3) for three different customers. You can configure your data producer to use three partition keys (customer-A, customer-B, and customer-C) so that all data records with partition key customer-A key are added to Shard 1 and all data records with partition key customer-B are added to Shard 2, and all data records with partition key customer-C are added to Shard 3.

Sequence number
It is a unique identifier for each record and is assigned by Amazon Kinesis Data Streams when a data producer calls PutRecord or PutRecords API to add data to an Amazon Kinesis data stream.

KEY POINTS

- Kinesis Data Stream has default retention of 24 hours and optionally up to 365 days.

- It has ability to replay or preprocess ingested data.
- Data records ingested in Kinesis are **immutable**.
- Data records with the **same partition key** go to the **same shard**.
- You can use AWS SDK, KPL (Kinesis Producer Library), Kinesis Agent for producers.
- For consumers, you can use consumers such as AWS Lambda, Kinesis Data Firehose, Kinesis Data Analytics. Or you can write your own using KCL (Kinesis Client Library) and AWS SDK.

Kinesis Data Streams Capacity Mode

Kinesis Data Stream capacity mode determines the management and charges of your data stream. You have two choices: **an on-demand** mode and a **provisioned** mode.

In **on-demand** mode, no need to provision or manage the capacity – the default provisioned capacity is 4 MB / second or 4000 records/second. It scales automatically based on the observed throughput of the last 30 days. You pay per stream/hour and data in/out per GB.

In provisioned mode, you decide the number of shards to provision and scale them manually or using API. Each shard gets a throughput of 1 MB / second or 1000 records per second. In addition, each shard gets 2 MB / second out – classic or enhanced fan-out. Charges are based on per shard provisioned / hour.

Security in Kinesis Data Streams

You can get both encryptions at rest and encryption in flight. Encryption in flight is provided using HTTPS, and encryption at rest can be provided using KMS.

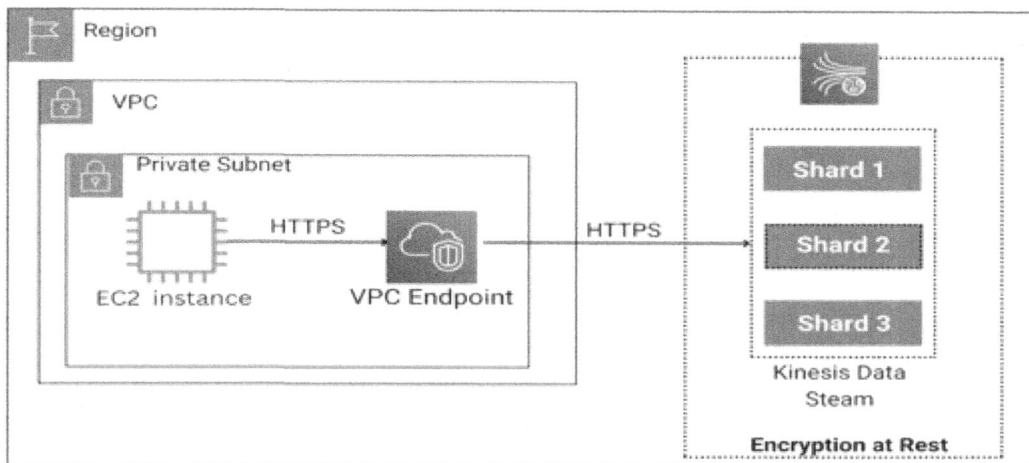

VPC Endpoints are available for Kinesis to access Kinesis Data Stream within VPC. You can monitor API calls using CloudTrail. IAM policies can be used to control access and authorization to Kinesis Data Streams.

Use Cases

Stream log and event data: Collect terabytes daily from applications and service logs, clickstream, sensor, and in-app user events data to generate metrics, power live analytic dashboards, and push data into data lakes.

Run real-time analytics: Build applications real-time analytics for high-frequency event data, such as clickstream data, to build insights in seconds -- not days, using AWS Lambda or Amazon Kinesis Data Analytics.

Power event-driven applications: By using AWS Lambda build event-driven applications to respond to or adjust the immediate occurrence of events in your environment at any scale.

Kinesis Data Firehose

Amazon Kinesis Data Firehose is an ETL (extract, transform, and load) service that collects, transforms, and delivers streaming data to data lakes, data stores, and analytics services. It is a fully managed service – which means no administration from the user side, automatic scaling, and serverless.

In terms of how it works, the input data records (**max record size 1MB**), such as logs, clickstream, IoT, sales, and orders records, are **extracted** to the Kinesis Data Firehose. The extraction is done using AWS SDK / KPL (Kinesis Producer Library), Kinesis Data Stream, Kinesis Agent, and 20+ AWS services.

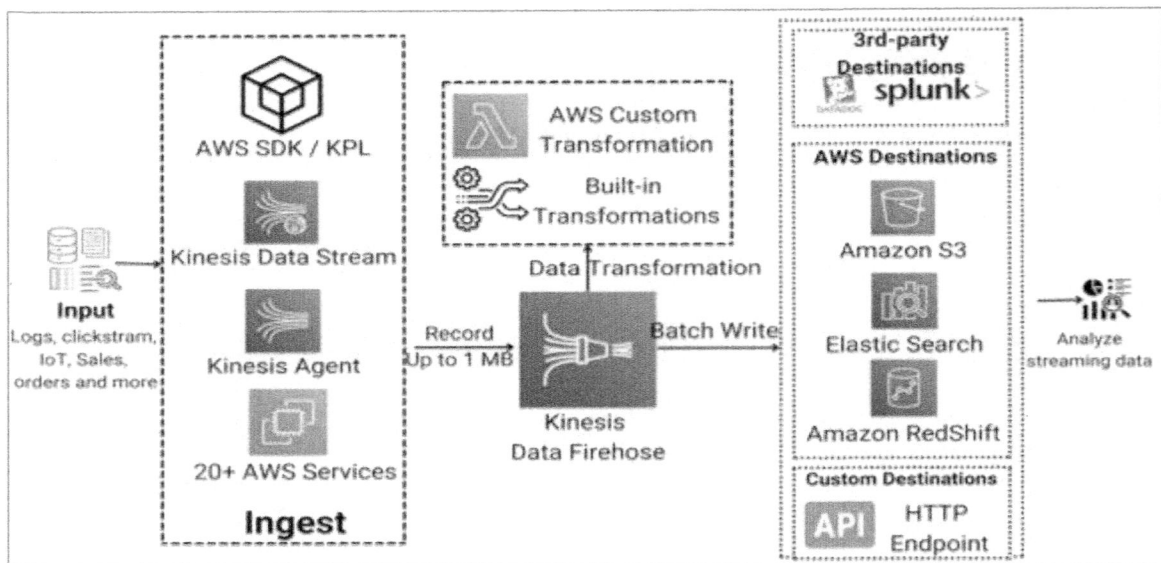

Then the data can be **transformed** using AWS custom transformation or Kinesis built-in transformation. The transformation is optional. The transformed data is then **loaded** to AWS destinations such as Amazon S3, Elastic Search, Amazon RedShift, custom destination using HTTP endpoint for the machine, or 3rd party destinations such Splunk and Datadog to run analytic queries, build machine learning models, and get insights.

KEY POINTS

- It is an ETL service. It provides near real time processing -- up to 1 MB of data at a time can be extracted into Kinesis Firehose.
- You pay for data going through Firehose.

- It supports many data formats, including conversions, compression and transformation – custom transformations are supported using AWS Lambda.
- Transformed data can be loaded into AWS destinations (RedShift, Amazon S3, Elasticsearch), 3rd party (Splunk, Datadog), or custom HTTP endpoints.
- When perform ETL, failed data or all data can be sent to a backup S3 bucket.

Kinesis Data Streams vs Kinesis Data Firehose

Kinesis Data Streams	Kinesis Data Firehose
Streaming service to ingest at scale	Load streaming data into S3 / RedShift/ Elasticsearch/ 3rd party/ custom HTTP
You write custom code for producers and consumers.	It is fully managed.
It is real time service.	It is near real time service -- latency time of minimum 60 seconds.
You can manage scaling by splitting/merging shards.	It provides automatic scaling.
Data retention is up to 365 days – default is 24 hours.	There is no data storage – it is a straight ETL service.
The stored (ingested) data can be replayed.	Since there is no data storage, there is no replay of data.

Kinesis Data Analytics

Kinesis Data Analytics is the easiest way to preform real-time analytics on Kinesis Streams using SQL. It is fully managed – so you don't need to provision any server.

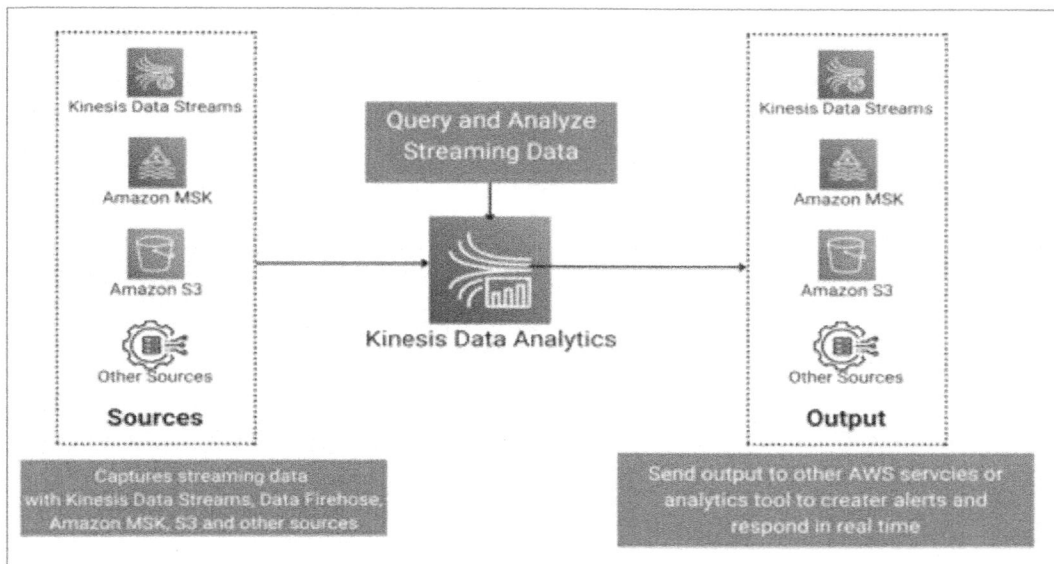

You can create streams by running real-time queries.

Kinesis Data Analytics use case are as follows:

Deliver streaming data in seconds: You can use Kinesis Data Analytics to develop applications that transform and ingest data to Amazon S3 and other AWS services.

Create real-time analytics: It is very useful for time-sensitive use cases where you need to continuously query and analyze data in real time and produce insights continuously.

Perform stateful processing: You can use it for anomaly detection based on historical data trends using long-running stateful computations.

Data Record Ordering

Amazon Kinesis

Consider a scenario where a trucking company has hired you to modernize the architecture of their tracking system so that trucks' locations can be tracked in real-time and displayed on a dashboard.

The trucking company has 75 trucks that travel in US and Canada.   They send their GPS coordinates continually to AWS.

To accurately track and display each truck's location, you need to maintain the order of location data of each truck in the Kinesis.

How would you ensure that each truck's location data in the Kinesis shards is ordered? You will have to use truck_id as partition_key for each data record. The data records having the same partition_key are ingested into the same shard.

Amazon SQS

If you are using Standard SQS, there is ordering of messages. For SQS FIFO, messages are consumed in the order they are sent with only one consumer, if there is no Group ID. If you would like to scale consumers but would like to grouped if the messages are related to each other use Group ID. Group ID concept in SQS FIFO is similar to Partition Key in Kinesis.

Comparison of SQS, SNS, Kinesis

SQS	SNS	Kinesis
Based on "pull" – consumers pull data from the queue	Based on "push" – data is pushed to subscribers. Up to 12,500,000 subscribers.	Standard: pull, 2 MB/shard Enhanced fan-out: push, 2 MB per shard / consumer
Data is deleted after it has been processed.	Data is not persisted – lost if it is not delivered.	Data can be replayed and deleted after X days.
Ordering is guaranteed only on FIFO queues.		Ordering is available at shard level. Data with the same Partition Key is delivered to the same shard.
No need to provision throughput	You can have up to 100,000 topics	shards to temporarily store data records -- the default is 24 hours (optionally 1 to 365 days).

Amazon MQ

If you have worked on Apache Active MQ, Amazon MQ is the managed Apache Active MQ.

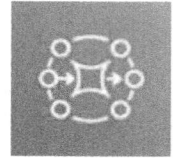

If you have on-premises applications that are using Apache Active MQ, or using open protocols such as MQTT, AMQP, STOMP, Openwire, and WSS, and you are planning to transition to AWS. The instead of re-engineering the applications to use SQS an SNS, you can use Amazon MQ.

- Amazon MQ doesn't scale as much as SQS or SNS.
- Amazon MQ runs on a dedicated machine – it can also run in High Availability (HA) mode with failover.

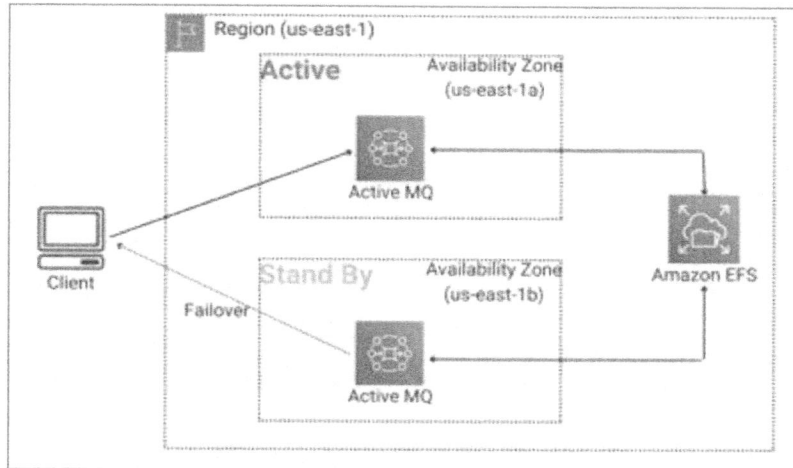

- Amazon MQ has both features: queue (~SQS) and topics(~SNS).

Section 6. Container & CI/CD

Chapter 26. Container

You will learn the following in this chapter:
- Docker Introduction
- Docker Terms
- Docker VS. Virtual Machine
- Docker Image Repository
- Containers Management on AWS
- Amazon ECS
- EC2 Launch Type
- Fargate Launch Type
- IAM Roles for Amazon ECS
- Load Balancer with Amazon ECS
- Amazon ECS Service Auto Scaling
- ECS on EC2 and Fargate
- When to use ECS on EC2 and when to use Fargate
- Amazon ECR
- Amazon EKS
- AWS App Runner

Docker Introduction

The basic concept behind Docker is to run an application -- and al its dependencies -- completely isolated as if -- only your application -- is running on a server.

Moreover, the process of deploying and running an application should be repeatable. Therefore, an image -- to achieve this concept -- is used. This image contains all the source code and dependencies. This image is run each time the application needs to be run.

Docker is a virtualization technology. The Docker-like virtual machines not only allow you to run applications in a different environment, but it does more. Therefore, it is one of the critical DevOps technologies.

Using Docker, we can package application source code into a Docker image, including operating system libraries and all dependencies required to run the application. The Docker image can run in any Docker environment. The runtime environment of the Docker image is called a Docker container.

Docker uses resource isolation – like how processes are isolated -- in the operating system kernel to run multiple containers on the same operating system.

Use Case

Docker is an excellent fit for microservices architecture, where you can run each microservice in an isolated container and scale them independently if needed by launching a separate container. Also, Docker is a good fit for the POC (proof of concept) type of work, for example, if you have a use case to set up a test environment of Apache Web Server on your local machine.

Docker on OS

In the diagram, on a server (could be EC2 instance), a Docker container for Java, a Docker container for Apache Webserver, a Docker container for MySQL, and Docker container for NodeJS are running in an isolated container environment as if each of them is running on a separate machine.

If we had installed Java, MySQL, Apache Webserver, and NodeJS in a classic way (without their Docker containers), each of them would run just as a separate process – not with a completely separate environment of OS, RAM, and CPU on the same server.

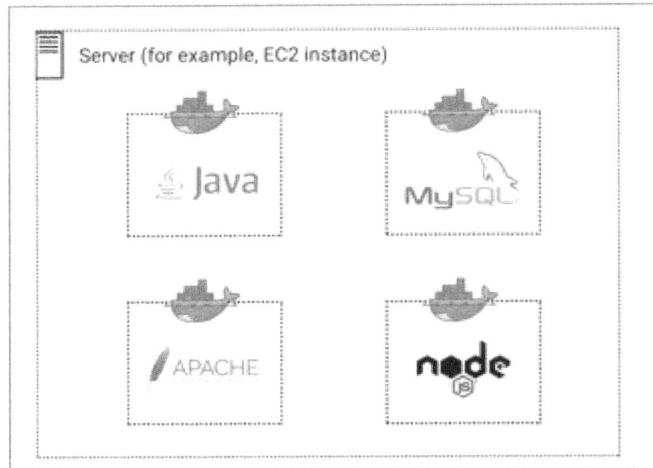

Docker Terms

Dockerfile

It is a text document containing all the commands to build a Docker image, including operating system libraries, application source code, and dependencies. These commands are like Linux command line commands, as you can notice in a Dockerfile given below in a screenshot. The Dockerfile in the screenshot gets the latest Ubuntu image, updates the image, installs OpenJDK version 8. Then copies the jar file into /usr/local/bin directory. And finally sets an entry point to run the jar file.

Docker Image

The Dockerfile contains the source code of a Docker image, as you can see in the image above. Once you have Dockerfile, you build the docker image from the Dockerfile by running the Docker command docker build. Thus, you could think of the docker image as a compiled version of Dockerfile. Docker images you can push to Docker Hub, which is a Docker registry, for redistribution.

Docker Container
Docker containers are runtime instances of Docker images. When you apply the command "docker run <Docker Image Name>," it creates a Docker container of that image which is the run time instance of the Docker image. You can stop the Docker container, restart it or remove it.

Docker Hub
Docker Hub is a registry provided by Docker to maintain and distribute Docker images. After building a Docker image, you can push it to the Docker Hub if you would like to share it with the public.

Docker VS. Virtual Machine

Since the host kernel is shared among Docker containers, applications only ship with the minimum needed to run. Docker containers share many of their resources with the host system. As a result, a container typically requires less RAM and CPU time than a virtual machine. This makes Docker applications more lightweight to deploy and relatively faster to start than those running on a virtual machine environment.

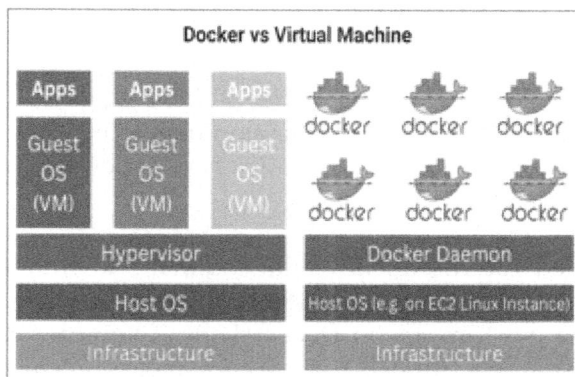

The other significant difference is that if an application is designed to run in a Docker environment on Windows, it can't run on Linux or vice versa. However, Virtual machine applications are not subject to this constraint.

Docker Image Repository

Docker images are stored in Docker repositories, such as DockerHub (https://hub.docker.com), a public Docker repository to store and distribute Docker images. You can also store docker images as private images on DockerHub. You can find base images for many technologies or OS for example, Ubuntu, Apache Kafka, MySQL, Hadoop etc.

On AWS, Amazon ECR (Amazon Elastic Container Registry) is the container registry to store docker images. It is a private repository. However, there is also a public ECR called Amazon ECR Public Gallery (https://gallery.ecr.aws).

Getting Started with Docker

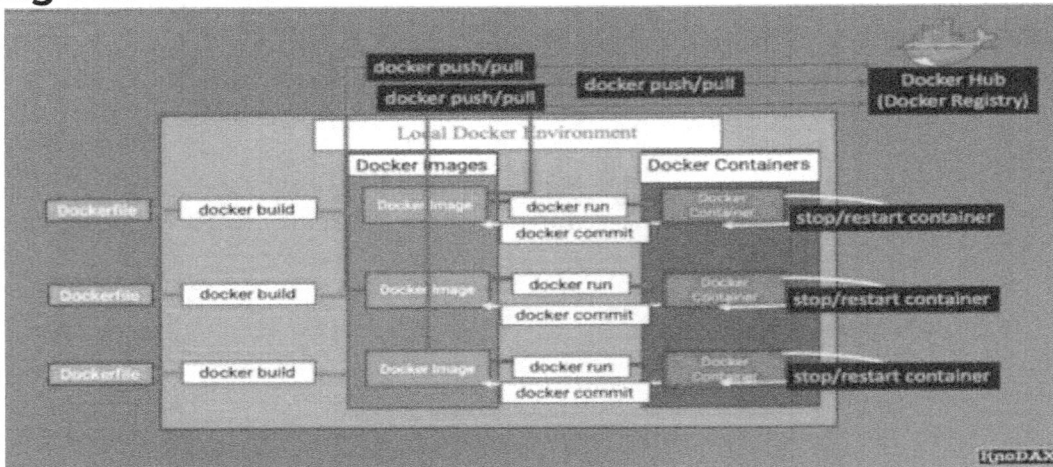

Let's get a high-level understanding of the Docker system based on this diagram. In this diagram, you notice there is a Dockerfile. Depending on your applications, you may have many Dockerfiles to build custom Docker images.

Then you run docker build command to build Docker images from the Dockerfile. Once the images are built you can run Docker containers from the Docker images. If you would like to push the images, can push images to Docker Hub. If you can also pull images from Docker Hub. You can stop and restart the stopped Docker container. You can also apply a docker commit to save the image if the Docker container is modified.

Simplistic View of Getting Started with Docker

This is a very simplistic view of getting started with Docker. In the diagram, we have a Dockerfile, the script which allows us to run a java jar file in a Docker container.

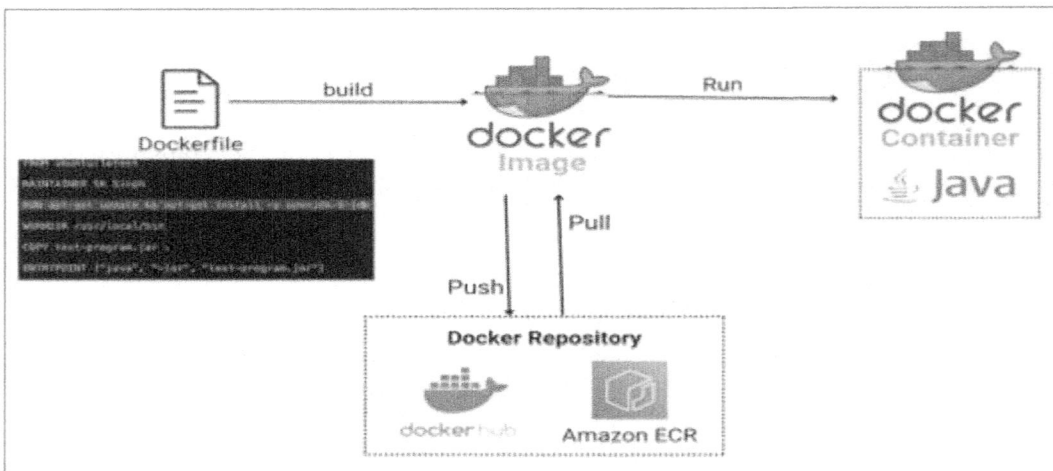

In the first step, we take the Dockerfile, which contains a script, and 'build' the docker image. Once the docker image is built, we 'push' the image into a Docker repository (DockerHub / Amazon ECR). Next, we 'pull' the Docker image from the repository and run the image, which starts the Docker container and runs the Docker image.

Containers Management on AWS

AWS offers services that enable you to store and manage your container images securely. In addition, it provides orchestration of container images that manage when and where to run your containers. Lastly, it provides a flexible compute engine to help provide power to run your containers.

That being said, AWS has broadly organized container management into three categories: registry, orchestration, and compute.

Registry

Amazon Elastic Container Registry

Amazon ECR is a fully-managed container registry that enables developers to store container images.

Orchestration

Amazon Elastic Container Service

Amazon ECS is a fully managed container orchestration service that enables you to run containerized applications.

Amazon Elastic Kubernetes Service

Amazon EKS is a fully managed Kubernetes service that enables to run containerized applications using Kubernetes.

Compute

AWS Fargate

AWS Fargate is a serverless compute engine for containers that make it easy for you to focus on building your applications as opposed to thinking about provisioning and managing your containers.

Amazon EC2

You can run containers on virtual machine infrastructure with full control over configuration and scaling.

AWS App Runner

AWS App Runner is a fully managed service that enables developers to quickly deploy containerized web applications and APIs. It is auto-scaled, and you don't need any prior infrastructure experience to deploy containerized web applications and APIs when using AWS App Runner.

Tools

AWS also provides tools to modernize and manage containers.

AWS App2Container

It is a command-line tool for modernizing .NET and Java applications into containerized applications.

AWS Copilot

Like AWS App2Container, it is also a command-line interface that enables developers to launch and manage containerized applications on AWS.

Amazon ECS

Amazon ECS is a fully managed container orchestration service that enables you to run containerized applications – essentially, it is used to launch Docker containers on AWS.

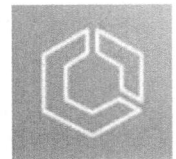

Launching Docker containers, in ECS terms, is considered to be launching ECS Tasks on an ECS cluster.

An **Amazon ECS Cluster** is a logical group of ECS tasks and services. Your ECS tasks and services are run on infrastructure registered to an ECS cluster. The ECS cluster infrastructure capacity can be provided by AWS Fargate, EC2 instances, or an on-premise server or VM.

When you first use Amazon ECS, a default cluster is created for you, but later on, you can create multiple ECS clusters to keep your resources separate.

An **ECS Task Definition** contains settings like exposed port, docker image, CPU shares, memory requirement, the command to run, and environmental variables.

After you create an ECS Task definition for your application, you can specify the number of tasks to run on the ECS cluster. An **ECS Service** runs and maintains your desired number of tasks in an ECS cluster.

An **ECS Task** is a running container with the settings defined in the Task Definition. It can be considered an "instance" of a Task Definition.

The Amazon **ECS Agent** allows container instances to connect to your clusters. The ECS container agent runs on each EC2 instance within an ECS cluster and sends telemetry data about the tasks and resource utilization of that EC2 instance to the Amazon ECS service. It also can start and stop tasks based on requests from ECS.

There are two types of ECS Launch: EC2 Launch type and Fargate Launch type.

EC2 Launch Type

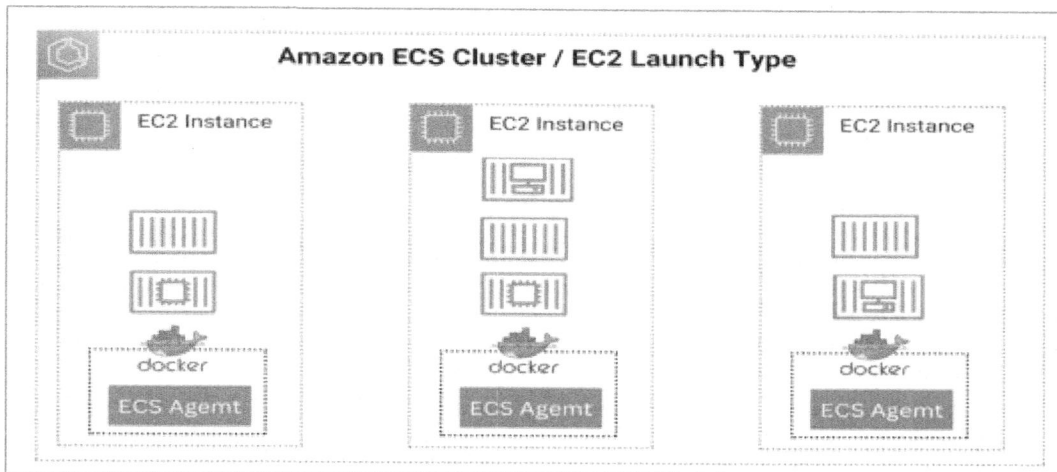

Amazon ECS Cluster / EC2 Launch Type

- In ECS Launch Type, you must provision and maintain the EC2 infrastructure – setting up EC2 instances for ECS.
- Each EC2 instance must also run ECS Agent to connect to ECS cluster. The ECS Agent sends telemetry data about the tasks and resource utilization of that EC2 instance to the Amazon ECS service.

Fargate Launch Type

Fargate is an operational mode within Amazon Elastic Container Service (ECS) that abstracts out host ECS clusters and servers running containers away from the user- offering serverless container management.

Amazon ECS Cluster / Fargate Launch Type

The Fargate Launch type is another way to launch the ECS cluster on AWS to launch your containers. You **do not need to provision the infrastructure (no need to manage EC2 instances)** – when using Fargate Launch. It is **serverless**.

You create ECS Task definitions, and AWS ECS Service runs ECS Tasks for you based on your Task definition of how much CPU/RAM containers need. In order to scale your containers, increase the number of tasks – no need to launch separate EC2 instances.

IAM Roles for Amazon ECS

The two important points here are that we need to assign **an EC2 Instance Profile** to the EC2 instance (applicable to EC2 Launch type only) and **EC2 Task Role** to the ECS Tasks.

EC2 Instance Profile (EC2 Launch type only)

An EC2 instance profile contains IAM Role that you can use to pass role information to an EC2 instance at the time the EC2 instance starts. It can contain only one IAM role -- this limit of one role per instance profile cannot be increased. However, you can remove the existing role, then add a different IAM role to an EC2 instance profile.

The ECS Agent uses the EC2 Instance Profile to pull Docker images from ECR, make API calls to ECS Service, send container logs to CloudWatch Logs, and refer to Secrets Manager or SSM Parameter Store for sensitive data.

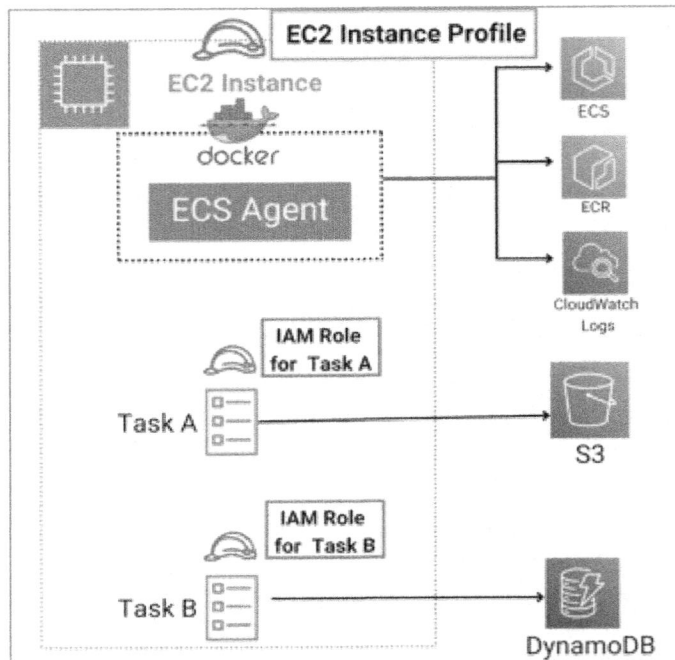

ECS Task Role

We can assign each ECS Task to have a specific IAM Role, for example, IAM Role to write to S3 for an ECS Task and a separate IAM Role to write to DynamoDB for another ECS Task. Task Role is defined in the **Task Definition**. Use different IAM Roles for different AWS Services for your ECS Task.

Load Balancer with Amazon ECS

Working with Amazon ECS, you may need to scale and load balance your containers – particularly for enterprise applications with a large user base.

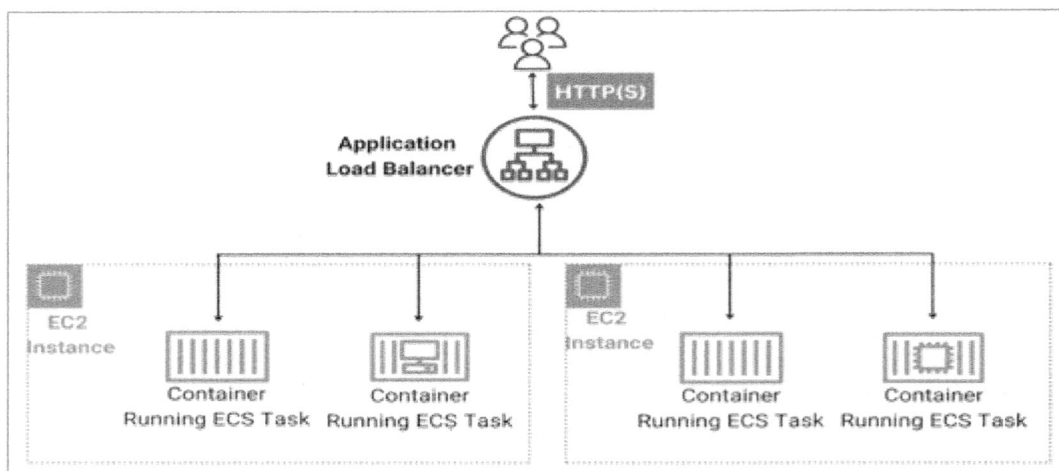

With Amazon ECS, **Application Load Balancers** are supported and work for most cases. However, if you need high throughput / high performance for your use cases, you use **Network Load Balancers,** or you can pair with **AWS Private Link.**

Elastic Load Balancers are supported but not recommended.

EFS with Amazon ECS

You can mount EFS file systems on ECS tasks – works for both EC2 and Fargate Launch types. Tasks in Availability Zone (AZ) can share the data in the same EFS file system.

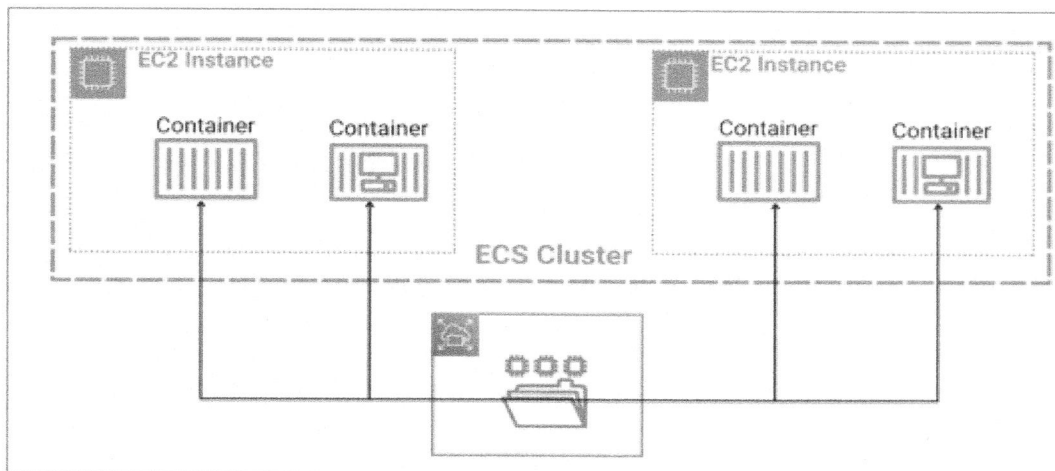

Mounting the EFS file system on containers running in Multi-AZ allows shared storage for your containers in the Multi-AZ scenario. Please note: you cannot mount S3 as a file system.

Amazon ECS Service Auto Scaling

ECS Service Auto Scaling is the ability to automatically increase or decrease the desired count of tasks in ECS service. Amazon ECS uses the AWS Application Auto Scaling to provide auto-scaling.

Amazon ECS publishes CloudWatch metrics of average CPU and memory usage about your ECS service. Using the average CPU and memory usage and other CloudWatch metrics, such as ALB request count per target, you can scale out your ECS service (add more tasks). The scaling helps to deal with high demand at peak times or scale in (reduce to run fewer tasks) to reduce costs during low utilization of ECS service.

Amazon ECS Service supports the following types of auto-scaling:

Target Tracking
Increase or decrease the number of tasks based on the target value of a specific CloudWatch metric.

Step Scaling
Increase or decrease the number of tasks based on the scaling adjustment that varies depending on the size of the CloudWatch alarm breach.

Scheduled Scaling
Increase or decrease the number of tasks based on specified dates and times – to manage predictable changes.

An important point to note is that **ECS Service Auto Scaling is not EC2 Auto Scaling.** EC2 Auto Scaling is at the instance level; however, ECS Service Auto Scaling is at the ECS Task level.

Fargate Auto Scaling is much easy to set up because of being Serverless.

ECS on EC2 and Fargate

AWS ECS is a container management service that facilitates the management of Docker containers. In order to launch compute infrastructure, you have two options: ECS on EC2 or Fargate.

When using EC2 to launch ECS, you will have to set up EC2 instances separately, such as installing the ECS agent and setting up Auto Scaling. However, when using AWS Fargate to run containers, you don't need to deal with Amazon EC2 instances to manage servers or clusters. For example, you no longer have to provision, configure, or scale clusters of VMs to run containers.

When you run your ECS tasks and services with the Fargate launch type, you package your application in containers, specify the OS, CPU, and memory requirements, configure networking, define IAM policies, and launch the application. Each Fargate task has its own isolation boundary and does not share the underlying kernel, CPU resources, memory resources, or elastic network interface with another task.

When to use ECS on EC2 and when to use Fargate

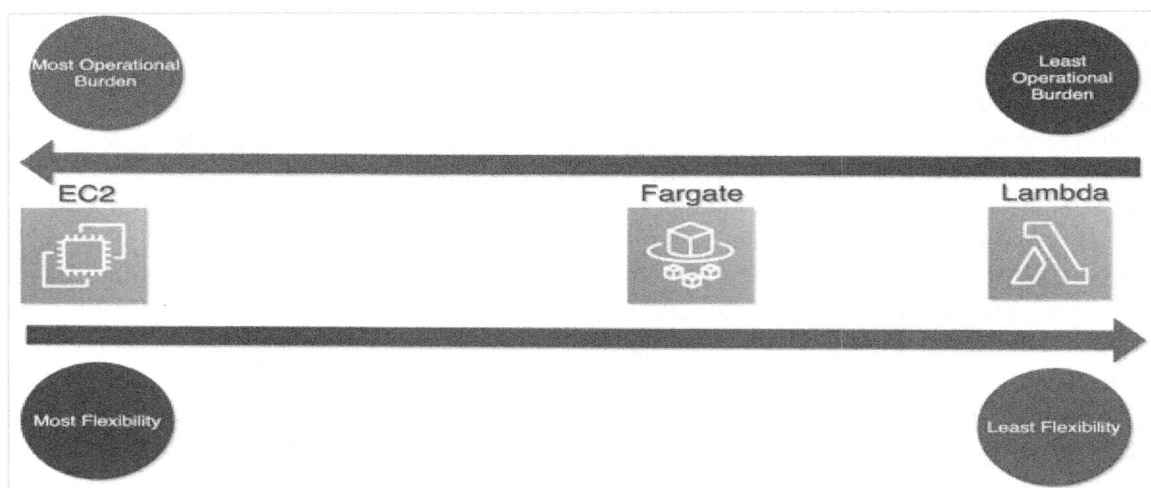

Screenshot from:
https://medium.com/thundra/getting-it-right-between-ec2-fargate-and-lambda-bb42220b8c79

If you would like to have explicit control of the running container, ECS on EC2 is a better option. If you would like to have flexibility, Fargate is the way to go. If you have spare EC2 instances, for example, Reserved EC2 instances, you can save on cost when using ECS on EC2. If you don't have time to set up an EC2 instance, for example, installing an ECS agent and setting up Auto Scaling, Fargate is the quickest option. In Fargate, you pay based on the provisioned compute resources.

When using EC2, you specify EC2 infrastructure. Typically, you launch one ECS task on an EC2 machine. However, depending on your task requirements and available capacity on the EC2 instance, you can run more than one task on the EC2 instance.

EC2 on ECS, you have the self-managed infrastructure; in the case of Fargate, you have AWS-managed infrastructure.

Amazon ECR

Amazon ECR (Elastic Container Registry) is a fully managed container registry service offering high-performance hosting that enables you reliably deploy Docker images and artifacts anywhere.
The repository

Amazon ECR has both private and public repository (public gallery: https://gallery.ecr.aws/).

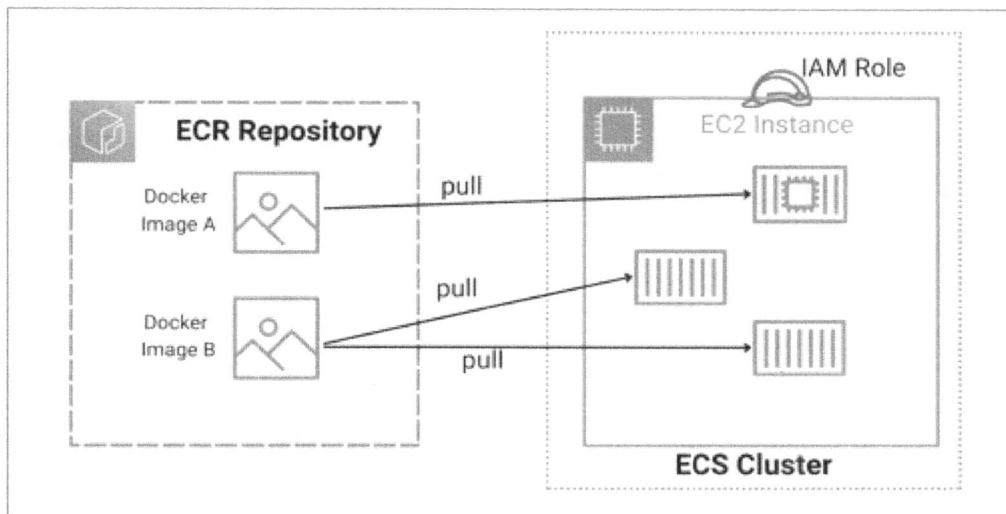

- It is fully integrated with ECS and backed by Amazon S3.
- Access to the Amazon ECR is controlled through IAM policy.
- Amazon ECR supports image vulnerability scanning, versioning, image tags, and image lifecycle.

Amazon EKS

Kubernetes, also known as KBs, is an open-source system for automating deployment, scaling, and managing containerized (usually Docker) applications.

It's an alternative to ECS -- if you need to automate deployment, scaling, and management of containerized (usually Docker) applications at scale.

Amazon EKS (Elastic Kubernetes Service) is a way to launch managed Kubernetes clusters on AWS and on-premises data centers. In the AWS cloud, Amazon EKS automatically manages the scalability and availability of the Kubernetes control plane nodes. On-premises, EKS provides integrated tooling and simple deployment.

- EKS supports EC2 if you want to deploy worker nodes or Fargate if want to deploy serverless containers.
- Kubernetes is cloud-agnostic – it can be used in any cloud such as Azure, GCP and others.
- If you would like to deploy EKS cluster in multiple AWS regions, deploy one EKS cluster per region.
- Collect logs and metrics using CloudWatch Container insights.
- Use Case: if your company is already using Kubernetes on premises on in another cloud and wants to migrate to AWS using Kubernetes.

Terms Related to EKS

Worker Nodes

Worker nodes in the Kubernetes cluster run containerized applications and handle networking to ensure that traffic between applications within and across the Kubernetes cluster and from outside the cluster is properly facilitated. Worker Nodes are the physical servers or VMs that comprise a Kubernetes Cluster.

Pods

Pods are the smallest and most basic deployable objects in Kubernetes. Pods contain one or more containers. A Pod represents a single running process instance in the Kubernetes cluster. When a Pod runs multiple containers, the containers share the Pod's resources.

Control Plane

Kubernetes control plane manages worker nodes and pods in the Kubernetes cluster.

Kubernetes Cluster

A Kubernetes cluster is a set of worker nodes that run containerized applications. Every Kubernetes cluster has at least one worker node—the worker node(s) host the Pods, which are the application workload components.

Difference Between Docker and Kubernetes

- While Docker is a container runtime, Kubernetes is a platform for running and managing different types of container runtimes such as Docker and any other implementation of the Kubernetes CRI (Container Runtime Interface).
- The Kubernetes server can run locally within your Docker instance –it is a single-node cluster and not configurable. Therefore, it is used only for local testing.
- While the containers promise to code once and run anywhere, Kubernetes orchestrate and manage all your container resources from a single control plane.

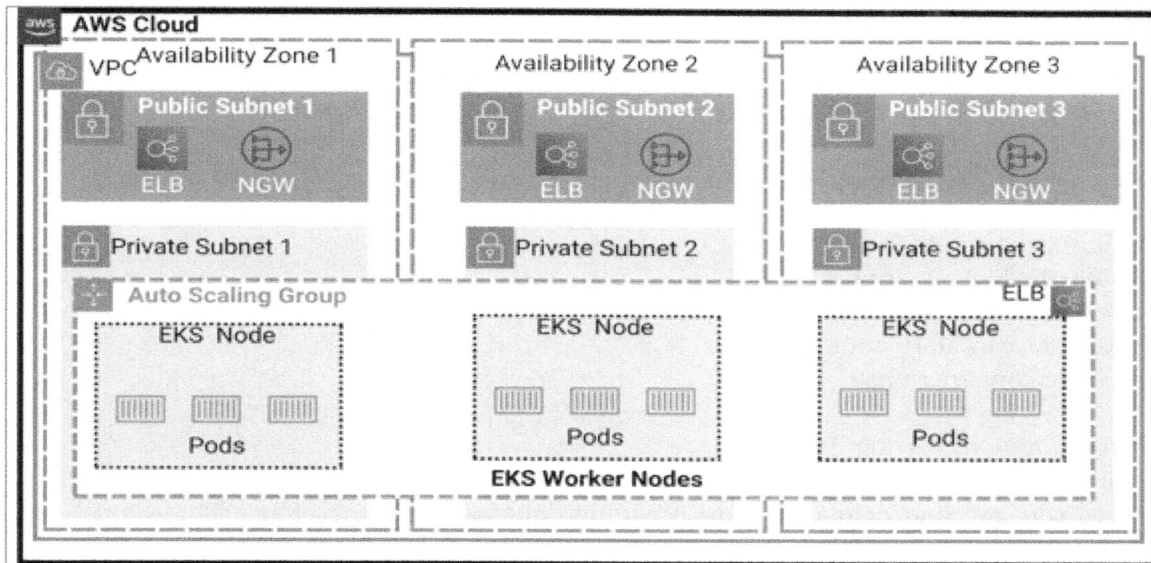

Amazon EKS Node Types

Managed Node Groups
It creates and manages nodes (EC2 instances for you. Nodes are part of Auto-Scaling Group (ASG) managed by EKS. It supports On-Demand or Spot EC2 instances.

Self-Managed Nodes
These nodes are created by and registered to the EKS cluster and managed by an ASG. You can use pre-built AMI, for example, Amazon EKS Optimized AMI. It supports On-Demand or Spot EC2 instances.

AWS Fargate
If you are using the AWS Fargate node type, no maintenance and node management are required.

Amazon EKS – Data Volumes

You need to specify the **StorageClass** manifest on your EKS cluster. It leverages a **Container Storage Interfaces (CSI)** compliant driver.

Amazon EKS supports Amazon EBS, Amazon EFS (works with Fargate), Amazon FSx for Lustre, and Amazon FSx for NetApp ONTAP.

AWS App Runner

AWS App Runner is a fully managed service that makes it easy to deploy web applications and APIs at scale. You don't need any infrastructure experience to deploy web applications and APIs at scale when using AWS App Runner. It automatically builds and deploys web apps. You can start with the source code or container image.

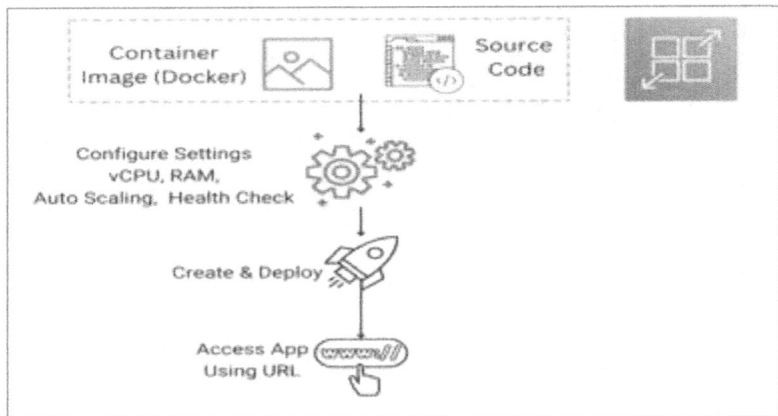

It provides automatic scaling, high availability, load balancer, and encryption. You can connect to a database, cache, and message queue services.

With regards to the AWS App Runner use case, you can use it to deploy web apps, APIs, microservices, or rapid production deployments.

Chapter 27. AWS CI/CD Services

You will learn the following in this chapter:
- AWS CodeCommit
- Amazon CodeStar
- AWS CodeBuild
- AWS CodeArtifact
- AWS Quick Starts
- AWS OpsWorks
- AWS CloudFormation
- AWS Elastic Beanstalk

AWS CodeCommit

AWS CodeCommit is a fully managed, secure source control service that hosts git-based repositories. You can create a git repository, add files, clone a repository, create a pull request, and merge pull requests to the branch. In other words, using AWS CodeCommit, you can do all sorts of git operations that you usually do as a developer.

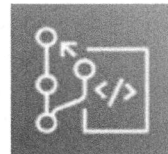

AWS CodeStar

AWS CodeStar provides a unified interface to bring all AWS CI/CD-related services under one service.

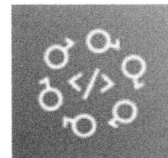

It brings together the following services:
- AWS CodeCommit is essentially a managed git source code repository in AWS.
- AWS CodeBuild, which is like Jenkins. It builds the code and runs tests, and creates deployable artifacts.
- AWS CodeDeploy is an automated software deployment service to deploy your code on an EC2 instance or Elastic Beanstalk.
- AWS Code Pipeline checks out the code, builds it, tests it, and then deploys the code. It is a managed CI/CD pipeline.

Amazon CodeGuru

Every day, millions of developers analyze codes and find issues to help solve performance issues, yet code issues still occur. This results in additional infrastructure costs and poor customer satisfaction.

Amazon CodeGuru is a developer tool powered by machine learning that provides intelligent recommendations for improving code quality by identifying applications' most expensive lines of code. You can add Amazon CodeGuru to your workflow to identify expensive lines of code to reduce cost. When you add a pull request, Amazon CodeGuru will analyze code from the repository for the critical issues and provides a recommendation report. The report shows why the issue is flagged, the cost of incurring, and suggestive resolution steps.

CodeGuru Reviewer uses machine learning to help identify critical issues such as security vulnerabilities and hard-to-find bugs during application development and provides recommendations to improve code quality.

CodeGuru Profiler pinpoints an application's most expensive lines of code by helping developers understand the runtime behavior of their applications, identify and remove code inefficiencies, and improve performance. In addition, it significantly decreases compute costs.

How it works

Integrate CodeGuru Reviewer and Profiler to your development pipeline to improve code quality and optimize performance for applications

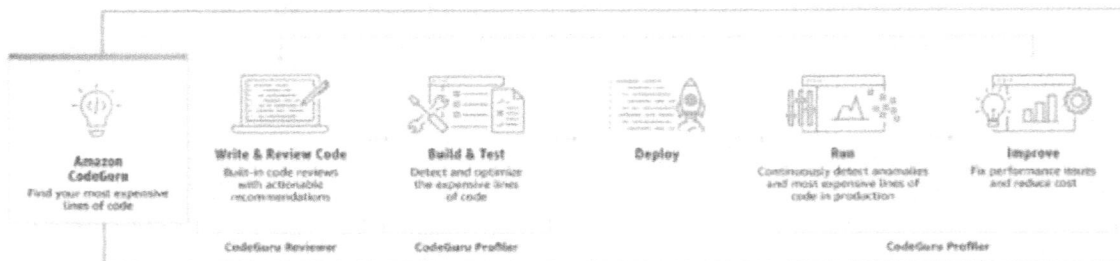

Screenshot from: https://aws.amazon.com/codeguru/

AWS CodeBuild

AWS CodeBuild, which is a fully-managed continuous integration (CI) service, compiles source code, runs tests, and produces software packages ready to deploy. With AWS CodeBuild, you don't need to provision, manage, and scale your build servers. Instead, AWS CodeBuild scales and performs multiple builds concurrently. This helps in builds not left waiting in a queue.

AWS CodeArtifact

AWS CodeArtifact, which is a fully managed artifact repository service, can be used by organizations of any size to publish, store, and share software deployment artifacts used in their software development lifecycle. AWS CodeArtifact can be configured to automatically fetch application code and its dependencies from public artifact repositories. CodeArtifact works with commonly used package managers and builds tools such as maven, gradle, npm, pip, thus making it easy to integrate into your existing software development workflows.

AWS Quick Starts

AWS Quick Starts: AWS Quick Starts is a collection of toolkits for various use cases built by AWS solution architects and partners to automate build and deployment by employing AWS best practices. Not only using AWS Quick Starts will make sure that the solution is employing AWS best practices, but it will also help save time in the build and deployment of the solution. It uses CloudFormation templates; recently, the support of Terraform templates has been added as well. As of this writing, there are around 200 AWS Quick Starts solutions for various use cases. AWS Quick Starts uses open-source software.

Reference:
https://aws.amazon.com/quickstart

AWS OpsWorks

AWS OpsWorks is an integrated DevOps application management solution for DevOps and IT admins. AWS OpsWorks can help you model, control, and automate the deployment and management of applications of all shapes and sizes. It is a tool to automate application management, such as automated instance scaling and health monitoring.

Managing operations of applications such as -- provisioning, deployment, configuration, monitoring, scaling, securing, and manually -- is error-prone and time taking. Automating your infrastructure gets your application to your users faster and helps you manage scaling, reliability, and complexity, and protects your application from failure and downtime. As your application grows, routine operational tasks can become even more time-consuming and error-prone. Changing applications -- such as adding features and other configuration changes due to business or environment change -- manually are error and takes time. Automating operational tasks takes away heavy lifting, and that helps you focus on development.

It provides lots of flexibility in application architecture and other things like packaging, and software configuration, including resources such as storage and databases that your application needs. OpsWorks makes it easier to add features and change the configuration of an application, server scaling, deployment, and database setup. It provides a way to quickly configure and deploy your application using Java, Apache, PHP, Ruby, and MySQL. It has a management console, SDKs, and API.

It is simple -- AWS OpsWorks is easy to use, and you can quickly get started and productive. You can become productive -- it reduces errors with conventions and scripted configurations. It is flexible -- it simplifies deployments of any scale and complexity with any software that has scripted installation. It is powerful -- it reduces cost and time with automation. With an event-driven configuration system, it supports customizable deployment, rollback, patch management, Auto Scaling, and more. Finally, it is secure -- it enables fine-grained permissions.

With OpsWorks, you model your application as stacks consisting of layers. A stack can be considered to consist of the cloud infrastructure and applications that you want to manage together. How to set up and configure a set of instances and related resources is defined by layers. Layers are blueprints defining how to set up and automate EC2 instances and resources. Then you have instances where you define how to scale: manually, with 24/7 instances, or automatically with load-based or time-based instances. Then, deploy your application to specific instances and customize the deployment with Chef resources. OpsWorks provides blueprints for common components such as Ruby, PHP, Java, Node.js, Amazon RDS, HAProxy, MySQL, and Memcached.

You can also define your own layer for any technology the way you want using Chef recipes. After you define all the layers, your application stack needs to choose an operating system and instance type. OpsWorks will pull the code from a repository -- once your stack is up and running -- and deploy it on your instances. And you will have the instance up and running based on the layer you define. You can scale your application based on time of day, average CPU utilization, memory utilization, or load.

You may be having a question about how it is different than Elastic Beanstalk or CloudFormation. OpsWorks is one of the few ways you can deploy applications on AWS. With various tools to deploy applications on AWS, the differentiation really comes to the level of convenience and control you need.

Elastic Beanstalk is a tool for building web apps and web services. If you want to upload and go and don't want to customize the environment, Beanstalk may be your tool. CloudFormation is a building block service that lets you provision and manages almost any AWS resource using domain-specific language and doesn't provide out-of-the-box application functionality such as deployments. On the other, OpsWorks is a powerful end-to-end solution, offering you an easy way to deploy and manage applications of any size, skill, and complexity without sacrificing control. It provides help in the complete application management lifecycle, including resource management, configuration management, application deployment, software updates, monitoring, and access control.

OpsWorks is free – no additional charge. You pay only for the resources you need to store and run.

AWS OpsWorks for Chef Automate

AWS OpsWorks for Chef Automate is a fully managed configuration management service that hosts Chef Automate, a suite of automation tools from Chef for configuration management, compliance and security, and continuous deployment. OpsWorks also maintains your Chef server by automatically patching, updating, and backing up your server. OpsWorks eliminates the need to operate your own configuration management systems or worry about maintaining its infrastructure. OpsWorks gives you access to all of the Chef Automate features, such as configuration and compliance management, which you manage through the Chef console or command line tools like Knife. It also works seamlessly with your existing Chef cookbooks.

Choose AWS OpsWorks for Chef Automate if you are an existing Chef user. Learn more »

AWS OpsWorks for Puppet Enterprise

AWS OpsWorks for Puppet Enterprise is a fully managed configuration management service that hosts Puppet Enterprise, a set of automation tools from Puppet for infrastructure and application management. OpsWorks also maintains your Puppet master server by automatically patching, updating, and backing up your server. OpsWorks eliminates the need to operate your own configuration management systems or worry about maintaining its infrastructure. OpsWorks gives you access to all of the Puppet Enterprise features, which you manage through the Puppet console. It also works seamlessly with your existing Puppet code.

Choose AWS OpsWorks for Puppet Enterprise if you are an existing Puppet user. Learn more »

AWS CloudFormation

AWS CloudFormation allows you to use programming languages or a simple text file to model and provision all the resources needed for your applications across all Regions and accounts in an automated and secure manner. CloudFormation is a building block service that lets you provision and manages almost any AWS resource using domain-specific language and doesn't provide out-of-the-box application functionality such as deployments.

Looking for infrastructure as code; think CloudFormation.

AWS Elastic Beanstalk

There are some common challenges that developers have to deal with, for example, managing infrastructure, deploying code, configuring databases, load balancers, and scaling issues.

Most web applications typically have the same architecture, including the Application Load Balancer and Auto Scaling Group. Developers want their code to run consistently, even across different environments.

Elastic Beanstalk is a developer-centric service to deploy an application on AWS. AWS Elastic Beanstalk is a PaaS (Platform-as-a-Service) type of AWS service that is used for deploying and scaling web applications. This AWS service takes your application code and deploys it while provisioning the compute resources required for the application to run.

It uses components such as EC2, Application Load Balancer (ASG), RDS, and many. It is a managed service – it automatically handles capacity provisioning, load balancing, scaling, application health monitoring, etc. The application developer is only for the code – the rest of the other aspects are taken care of by Elastic Beanstalk. The developer still has full control over the configuration.

AWS Elastic Beanstalk helps deploy and scale web applications that are developed with Java, NET, PHP, Node.js, Python, Ruby, Go, and Docker on familiar web servers such as Apache, Nginx, Passenger, and IIS. You simply upload the code, and Elastic Beanstalk automatically handles the deployment, from capacity provisioning, load balancing, and auto-scaling to application health monitoring. Elastic Beanstalk qualifies as a Platform-as-a-Service cloud computing type.

Elastic Beanstalk is free --you only pay for AWS resources you need to deploy and run the application.

Section 7. Data & Analytics

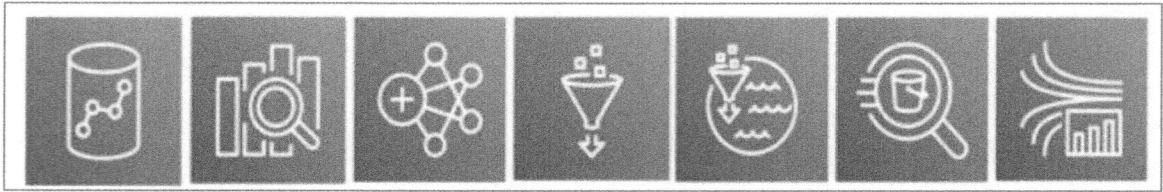

Chapter 28. Data & Analytics

You will learn the following in this chapter:
- Amazon Athena
- Amazon Redshift
- Amazon OpenSearch
- Amazon EMR
- Amazon QuickSight
- AWS Glue
- AWS Lake Formation
- Kinesis Data Analytics

Amazon Athena

- Amazon Athena is a serverless interactive query service to analyze data in Amazon S3 using standard SQL. It is serverless, so you don't have to manage any infrastructure and pay only for the queries you run.

- It is easy to use -- define the schema of your data on S3 and start querying using standard SQL -- most results are delivered within seconds.

- It uses standard SQL – built on Presto which is 5-10 times faster than Hive.

- It supports CSV, JSON, ORC, Avro, and Parquet file formats.

- Athena out-of-the-box is integrated with AWS Glue Data Catalog, which enables you to create a unified metadata repository across various services and crawl data sources to discover schemas.

- It is commonly used with Quicksight to visualize queried data via advanced interactive dashboards.

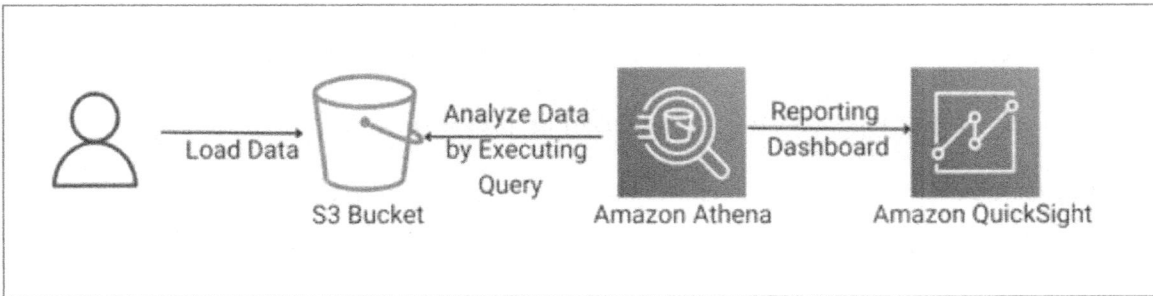

Use cases: business intelligence, analytics & reporting, analyze VPC Flow Logs, ELB Logs, and CloudTrail trails.

Guidelines for Better Query Performance

Columnar Data
- Use columnar data for cost savings, as columnar data drastically reduces the overall disk I/O requirements for analytical queries.
- ORC or Parquet file formats are recommended – both are columnar data file formats.

Use Larger Files and Compress Data
Use larger files (> 128 MB) to reduce the overhead of keeping metadata information for many smaller files in memory. Combine smaller files to minimize the number of files and compress them (for example, bzip2, gzip, snappy) to reduce the file size.

Partition Datasets
Partition datasets in S3 to improve query performance.

For example:
S3://yourBucket/pathToTable/<partition_column_name>=<value>
                          /<partition_column_name>=<value>
                          /<partition_column_name>=<value>
                          /…

For example: s3://yourBucket/sales/region=USA/year=2021/month=01/

Amazon Redshift
- Amazon Redshift is a fully managed, petabyte-scale, cloud-based, Mass Parallel Processing (MPP) data warehouse service. It is designed for large-scale data set storage and analysis.

- It is based on **PostgreSQL** – however, it is not used for OLTP. It is **OLAP** (online analytical processing).

- It provides **10x better performance** than other data warehouses. It allows you to run complex analytic queries against **terabytes to petabytes of structured data** -- using sophisticated query optimization.

- It uses **columnar data** storage & massively **parallel query** execution.

- It has a pay-as-you-go pricing model based on provisioned instances.

- BI tools such as Amazon Quicksight or Tableau can be integrated with it.

- **Compared with Amazon Athena**: Redshift is a relational database best suited for tabular data; Athena is better for semi-structured and unstructured data.

- For cost savings, you can provision the node size in advance by using Reserve Instances.

- **Encryption**: Encryption is an optional setting in Amazon Redshift. When you enable encryption for a cluster, the data blocks and system metadata are encrypted for the cluster and its snapshots.

Amazon Redshift only supports Single-AZ deployments:

> **Q: Does Amazon Redshift support Multi-AZ Deployments?**
>
> Currently, Amazon Redshift only supports Single-AZ deployments. You can run data warehouse clusters in multiple AZ's by loading data into two Amazon Redshift data warehouse clusters in separate AZs from the same set of Amazon S3 input files. With Redshift Spectrum, you can spin up multiple clusters across AZs and access data in Amazon S3 without having to load it into your cluster. In addition, you can also restore a data warehouse cluster to a different AZ from your data warehouse cluster snapshots.

Amazon Redshift High-Level Architecture

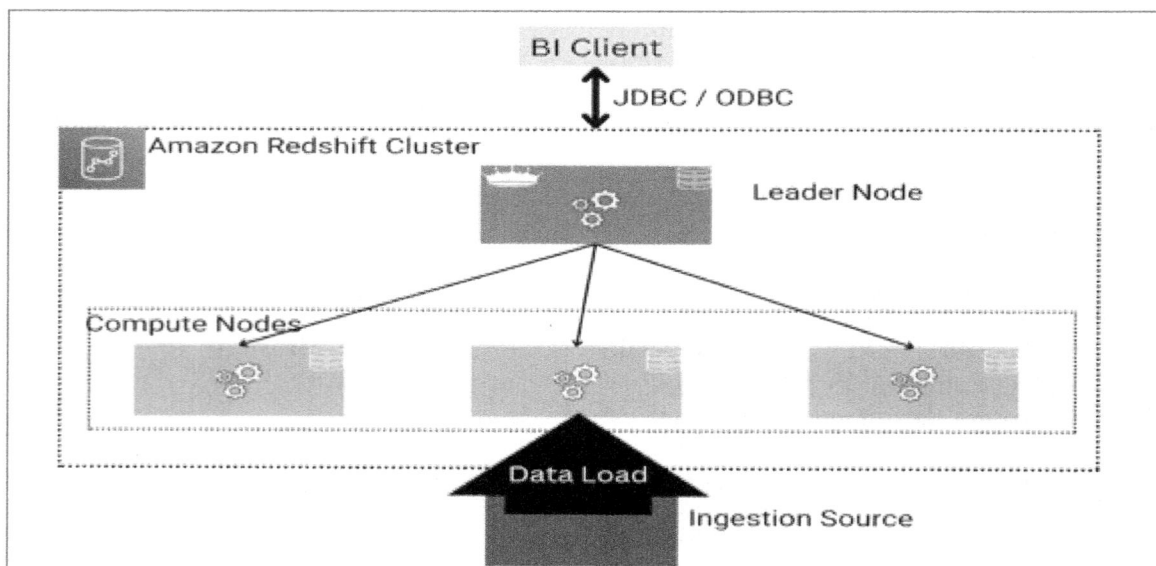

Client Applications

Amazon Redshift integrates with various data loading, BI (for example, Tableau or MicroStrategy), reporting, data mining, and analytics tools, or JDBC clients. It is based on open standard PostgreSQL so that most existing SQL client applications will work with minimal changes.

The client could exist on an instance inside of Amazon or it could also be remote on your own desktop or laptop.

Redshift Cluster

Redshift Data Warehouse is based on distributed computing and MPP – it is architected to work with a cluster of machines in practical use cases. A cluster is composed of one or more compute nodes. If a cluster has two or more nodes, an additional leader must communicate with compute nodes.

Leader Node

We have a Leader Node and many Compute Nodes in a Redshift cluster.

Leader Node's whole responsibility in life is to plan, coordinate and oversee the query execution. Based on the execution plan, the leader node compiles code, distributes the compiled code to the compute nodes, and assigns a portion of the data to each compute node. It manages communications with client programs as well.

Redshift architecture is very similar to Hadoop's architecture, where we have a master node or, in this case, Redshift, and we call it a leader node. The Leader Node figures out what needs to happen and then passes off that work to the compute nodes -- unless it is running in single-node mode. The Leader Node stores metadata and statistics -- that manage where the data is in the cluster -- these heavily affect the query performance.

There is one Leader Node per RedShfit cluster.

Compute Node

The leader node complies code, creates an execution plan, and assigns the code to individual compute nodes. **Compute Node** runs the complied code and sends results to the leader node for final aggregation.

Each compute node has its own dedicated CPU and memory. It maintains a subset of the data in columnar storage with redundant mirrors of each other. The compute nodes talk to each other and pass data back and forth. The leader node communicates with each and splits up part of the workload among compute nodes.

You can also have a Redshift cluster with just one node. In this case, we don't have any compute nodes. You always want to run a production workload with that.

Node Slices

A compute node is partitioned into slices, and each slice is allocated a portion of the node's memory and disk space, where it processes a part of the workload assigned to it. The leader node manages the data distribution to the slices, and slices work in parallel to complete the operation.

The node size of the cluster determines the number of slices per node.

When you create a table, you can optionally specify one column as the distribution key. The distribution key determines how the data is distributed on different slices. Defining a good distribution key **evenly distributes data across the slices**, enabling Amazon Redshift to use parallel processing to load data and run queries efficiently.

Internal Network
Amazon Redshift uses high-bandwidth connections, close proximity, and high-speed network communication between the leader and compute nodes. The compute nodes are put in a separated, isolated network, so that client applications never access them directly.

Databases
Amazon Redshift is based on PostgreSQL. Although it provides the same functionality as a typical RDBMS, Amazon Redshift is optimized for high-performance analysis and reporting of large datasets. In other words, Redshift should not be used for the production use cases of OLTP applications.

Redshift Managed Storage
AWS has added its new-generation redshift node type named RA3, which decouples the compute and storage enabling users to manage and scale independently based on needs. This architecture stores Redshift Data warehouse data in a separate tier -- Redshift Managed Storage (RMS).

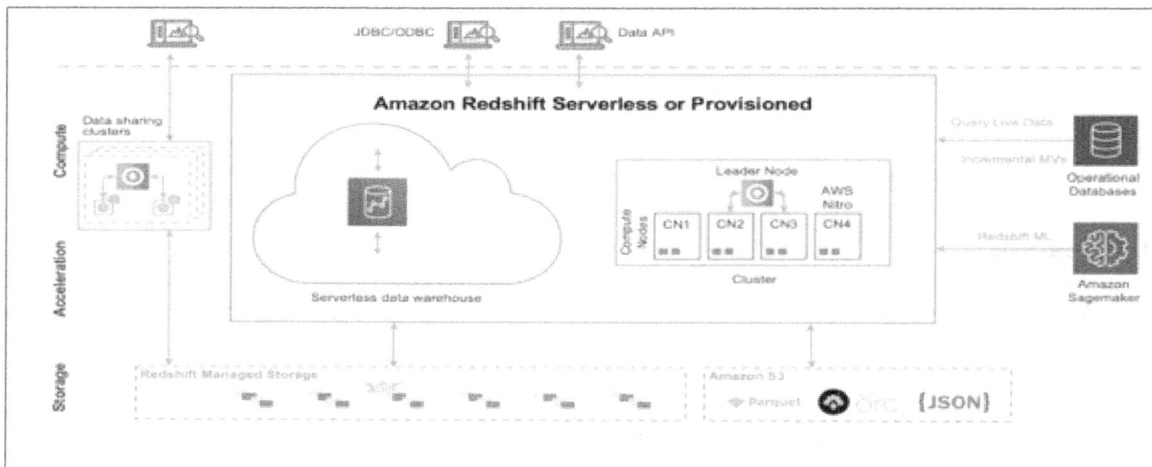

Image Source
https://docs.aws.amazon.com/redshift/latest/dg/c_high_level_system_architecture.html

RMS allows you to scale computing and storage independently, which enables you to size your cluster based only on your computing needs. RMS can scale your storage to petabytes using Amazon S3 storage. It uses high-performance SSD-based local storage as a tier-1 cache.

Redshift Snapshots & Disaster Recovery

- Snapshots are point-in-time backups of a cluster and are stored on S3. You can use a Snapshot to restore it in a new cluster.

- They are incremental – only what has changed is updated in each subsequent snapshot. You can configure Amazon Redshift to copy snapshots of a cluster to another AWS Region automatically.

- Amazon automates the snapshot process, by default, every 8 hours, every 5 GB per node of data changes, or whichever comes first. Alternatively, you can create a snapshot schedule about when automated snapshots are taken. The default retention period for automated snapshots is one day, but you can modify it using the Amazon Redshift console or programmatically using the Amazon Redshift API or CLI.

- You can disable automated snapshots by setting the retention period to zero. You can't disable automated snapshots for RA3 node types. You can set the retention of an RA3 node type snapshots between 1 to 35 days.

- Manual snapshots in Redshift are retained until you delete them.

- The important point is that Redshift doesn't have a "Multi-AZ" feature.

- You can configure the Amazon Redshift cluster to automatically (or manually) copy snapshots to another AWS region.

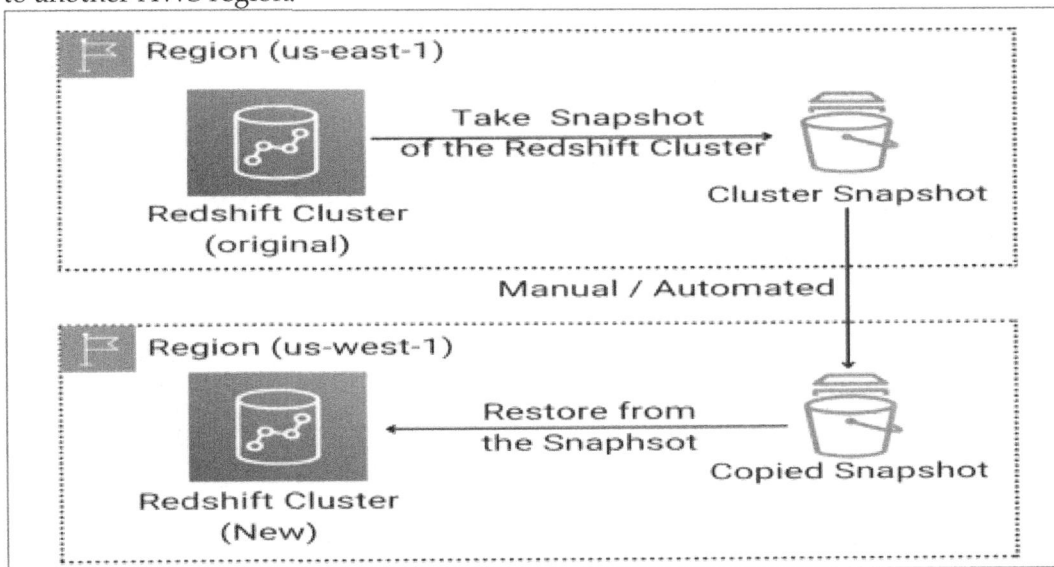

Data Loading into Redshift Cluster

You're also going to have an ingestion source -- this is where you will load the data. The ingestion source could be S3. It could be from your servers or other Amazon services like DynamoDB. You can load from anywhere, considering that one of the sources is an SSH type.

The data from the ingestion source goes directly to our compute nodes. It doesn't go through the Leader Node, so there's no bottleneck for the leader node. The data from the ingestion source is peppered throughout our cluster.

There are three ways you can load data into a Redshift Cluster.

From Amazon Kinesis Data Firehose	
From S3	 Sample S3 Copy Command: copy sales from 's3://mybucket/sales' iam_role 'arn:aws:iam::98754321013:role/testRedShiftRole';
Using JDBC from an EC2 instance, anywhere using SSH connection	

Redshift Spectrum

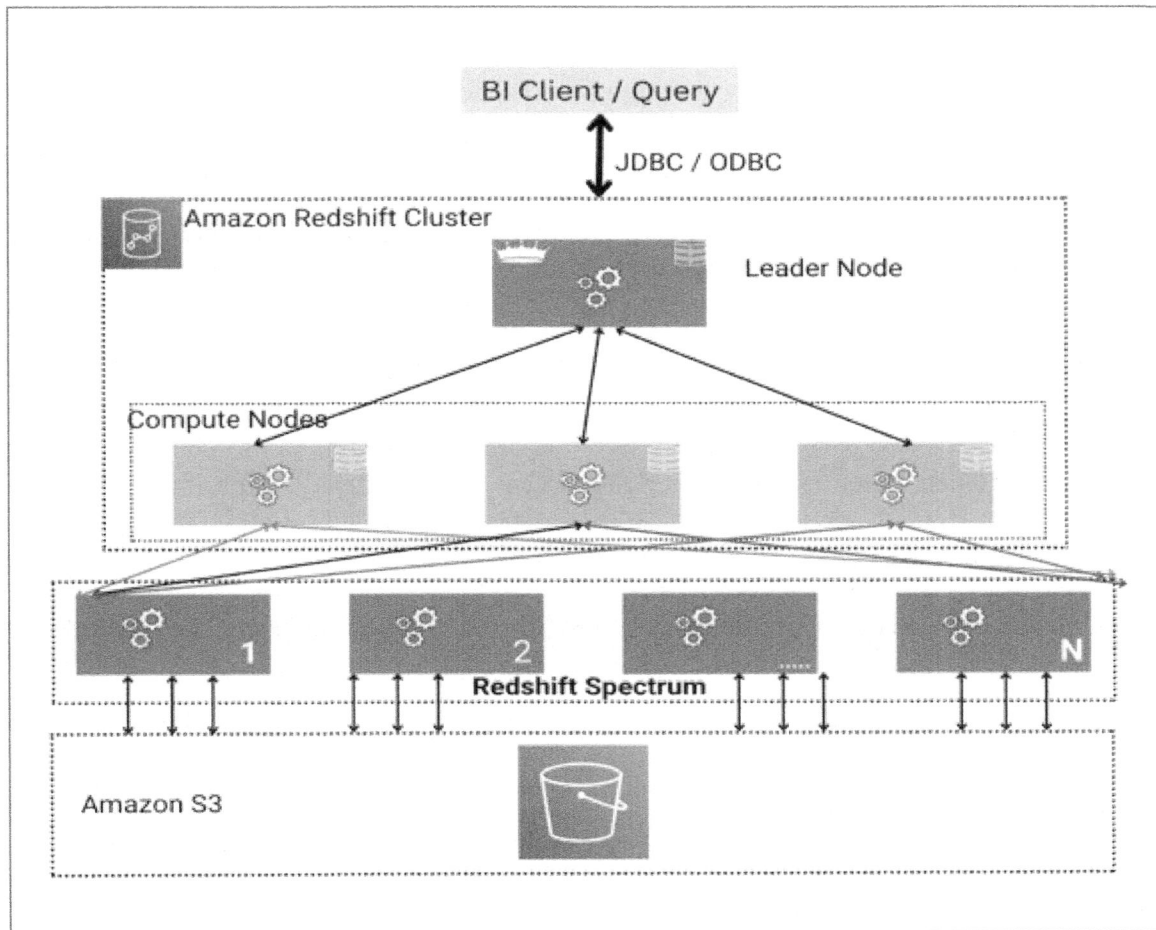

Amazon Redshift Spectrum enables you to efficiently query -- both structured and semi-structured data -- from Amazon S3 without having them load into the Amazon Redshift cluster. Redshift Spectrum queries employ MPP to run very fast against large datasets. Much of the processing in running queries occurs in the Redshift Spectrum layer, and most of the data remains in Amazon S3. Multiple clusters can concurrently query the same dataset in Amazon S3 without making copies of the data for each cluster.

Amazon OpenSearch

- On September 8, 2021, Amazon Elasticsearch Service was renamed to Amazon OpenSearch Service. In other words, if you are looking for an Amazon ElasticSearch service on AWS, look for Amazon OpenSearch.
- OpenSearch is a distributed, open-source search and analytics engine for all types of data, including textual, numerical, geospatial, structured, and unstructured. It is a fully managed service that makes it easy to deploy, secure, and run searches cost-effectively at scale.

- You can ingest data using Kinesis Data Firehose, AWS IoT, and CloudWatch logs. and other services. Once you have published data to OpenSearch and indexed the data, you can search any field, even partial matches.

- Amazon OpenSearch can be used for a broad set of use cases like real-time application monitoring, log analytics, and website search.

- It's common to use OpenSearch as a complement to another database particularly if your use case requires extensive and powerful searches on big data. You can publish data from Amazon DynamoDB into Amazon OpenSearch and have UI hooked up to the OpenSearch, where your users can search the results. For example, a prop-tech company can publish the results of its daily ETL job to the OpenSearch allowing its users to perform powerful searches on different fields about new properties on the market or any changes to the existing properties.

- Amazon OpenSearch is not a serverless service – it requires a cluster of instances.

- It has its query language – it doesn't support SQL.

- You can use Amazon Cognito and IAM for authentication and authorization, and for encryption, use KMS encryption and TLS.

- You can also use OpenSearch Dashboards with its database for visualization by running different searches.

- The Apache Lucene search library powers OpenSearch and supports several search and analytics capabilities, such as KNN, SQL, Anomaly Detection, Machine Learning Commons, Trace Analytics, full-text search, and more.

Loading streaming data into Amazon OpenSearch Service

From Amazon DynamoDB
You can use AWS Lambda to send data to your OpenSearch Service domain from Amazon DynamoDB.

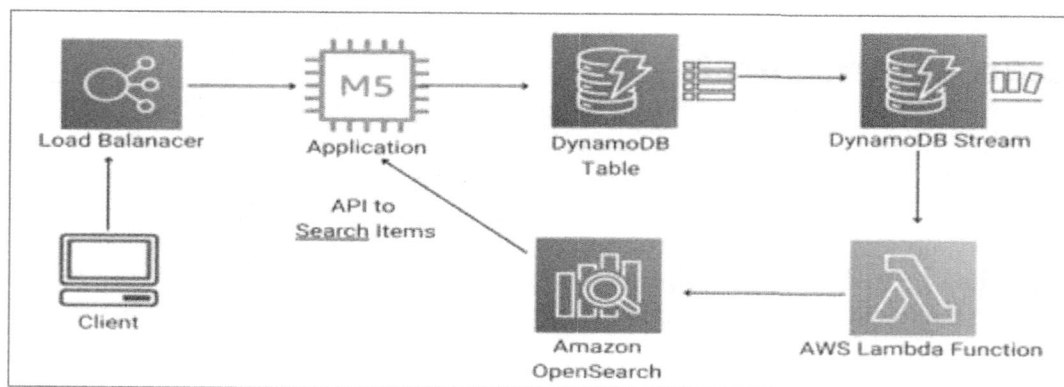

As a new data item arrives in a DynamoDB table (with stream enabled), it triggers an event notification to Lambda, executing your custom code to publish data on OpenSearch and perform the indexing.

From Amazon CloudWatch

You can load streaming data from CloudWatch Logs to your OpenSearch Service domain by using a CloudWatch Logs subscription. Using a CloudWatch Logs subscription, you can get access to a real-time feed of log events from CloudWatch Logs (you can also use a subscription filter) and have it delivered to other services such as an Amazon Kinesis stream, an Amazon Kinesis Data Firehose stream, or AWS Lambda for custom processing, analysis, or loading to other systems.

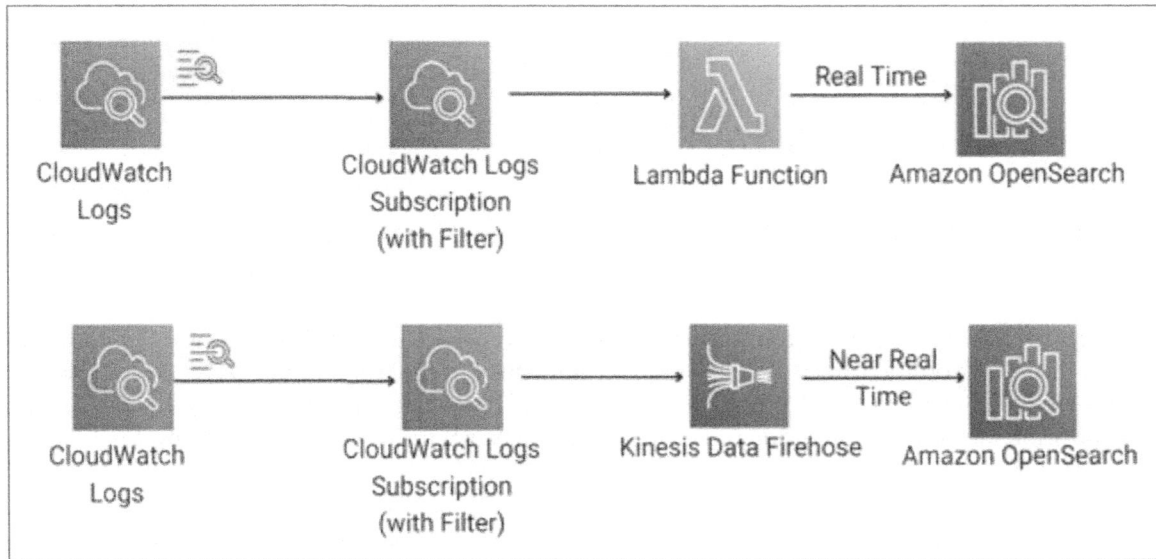

CloudWatch Logs sent to a receiving service through a subscription filter are base64 encoded and compressed with the gzip format.

From Amazon Kinesis Data Streams

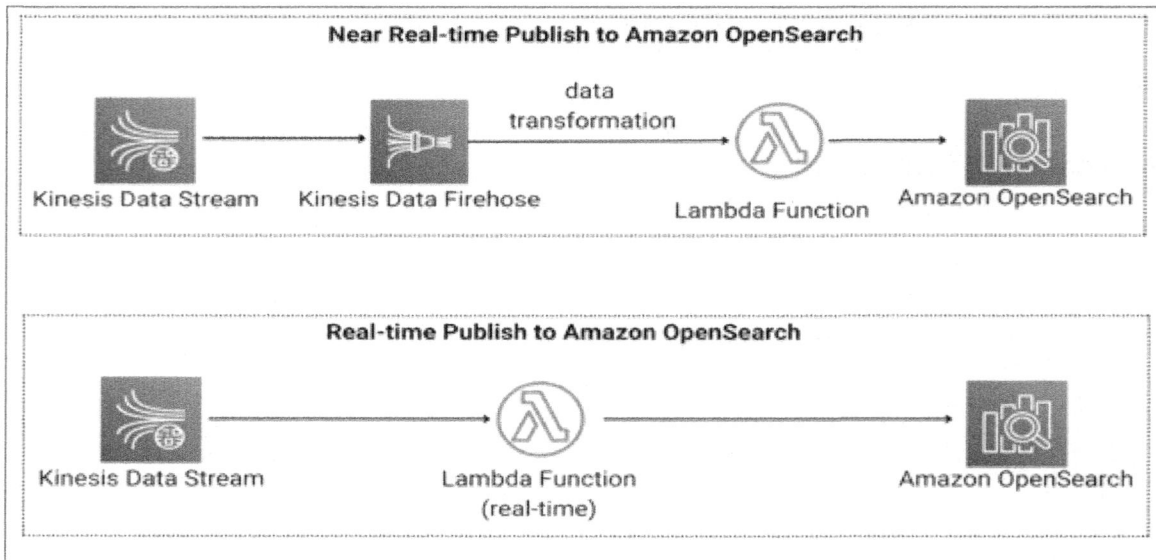

Near Real-time Publish to Amazon OpenSearch

Kinesis Data Stream → Kinesis Data Firehose → data transformation → Lambda Function → Amazon OpenSearch

Real-time Publish to Amazon OpenSearch

Kinesis Data Stream → Lambda Function (real-time) → Amazon OpenSearch

You can also publish and index data by ingesting from Kinesis Data Streams. There are two architectural choices here:

- (Near Real-time) The streaming data are sent to Kinesis Data Firehose. Kinesis Data Firehose can invoke your Lambda function to transform incoming source data and deliver the transformed data to the AWS Lambda function. The Lambda function does transformation and publishes data to Amazon OpenSearch, along with indexing the data to make it available for search.

- (Real-time) The streaming data are sent directly to a Lambda function, and the Lambda function publishes data to Amazon OpenSearch along with indexing the data to make it available for search.

(Reference:
https://docs.aws.amazon.com/opensearch-service/latest/developerguide/integrations.html)

Amazon EMR

- If you have worked on Hadoop, in simple words, you can think of it as a Hadoop service on AWS.
- EMR is a big data platform for petabyte-scale data processing, interactive analytics, and machine learning using open-source frameworks such as Apache Spark, Apache Hive, and Presto.
- It helps create Hadoop clusters for big data processing on AWS.
- When launching an EMR cluster, you will have various options to launch Apache Spark, HBase, Presto, Flink, and Hadoop. EMR takes care of all the provisioning and configuration.
- EMR clusters are highly scalable – you can add hundreds of EC2 instances. It provides also provides options for auto-scaling.
- You can run your EMR clusters by easily mixing Spot Instances with On-Demand and Reserved Instances using the EMR Instance Fleets feature.

- You can use a long-running cluster or a transient (temporary) cluster. If you configure your cluster to be terminated automatically, it is terminated after all the steps are complete. This is referred to as a **transient cluster**. If you configure the cluster to continue running even after processing completes, this type of cluster is referred to as a **long-running cluster**.

Use Cases
Perform big data analytics
Perform large-scale data processing and what-if analysis using statistical algorithms and predictive models to uncover hidden patterns, correlations, and trends in data.

Build scalable ETL data pipelines
Extract or collect data from various sources, filter/ process / transform it at scale, and publish it for consumption for applications and users.

Process real-time data streams
Process and analyze real-time events from streaming data sources by creating long-running, highly available, and fault-tolerant streaming data pipelines.

Accelerate data science and ML adoption
Analyze data using open-source ML frameworks. Connect to Amazon SageMaker Studio for large-scale model training, analysis, and reporting.

Amazon EMR Node Types
Master Node
The master node in EMR manages the cluster and monitors the instance groups' health. For example, the YARN ResourceManager service, which manages resource allocation to applications, runs on the master node. Likewise, the HDFS NameNode service, which tracks the status of jobs submitted to the cluster, runs on the master node.

Core Node
Core nodes run the Data Node daemon and also run the Task Tracker daemon. They perform other parallel computation tasks on data as well. For example, a core node runs YARN NodeManager daemons, Hadoop MapReduce tasks, and Spark executors. The master node manages core nodes.

Task Node **(Optional)**
Task nodes are optional. You can use task nodes to add more power to perform parallel computation tasks on data, such as Hadoop MapReduce tasks and Spark executors.

Commonly, Spot Instances are used to task nodes. As Spot Instances are commonly used to run task nodes, Amazon EMR has default functionality for scheduling YARN jobs to avoid running jobs failing when task nodes running on Spot Instances are terminated.

(Reference: https://docs.aws.amazon.com/emr/latest/ManagementGuide/emr-master-core-task-nodes.html)

Amazon EMR Purchasing Options
On-demand
Highly reliable, predictable, and won't be terminated.

Reserved
You can reserve nodes minimum of one year. It's a good option for cost savings if you have predictable usage for at least one year to have cost savings.

Spot Instances
It's an inexpensive option. However, it is less reliable, and instances can be terminated at any time.

Amazon QuickSight

- It is a serverless machine learning-powered business intelligence service to create interactive dashboards. Powered by machine learning, Amazon QuickSight enables users (particularly BI users) in your organization to understand your data by exploring through interactive dashboards, asking questions in natural language, or looking into patterns and outliers in your data.

- It is fast, automatically scalable, and embeddable. Its pricing is based on per session. It integrates with RDS, Aurora, Athena, Redshift, and S3.

- It does in-memory computation using the SPICE (Super-fast, Parallel, In-memory Calculation Engine) engine if data is imported into QuickSight. SPICE is the robust in-memory engine that Amazon QuickSight uses. It's engineered to perform advanced calculations and serve data rapidly -- in the Enterprise edition, data stored in SPICE is encrypted at rest.

- In the Enterprise edition, you can restrict access to data by setting up Column-Level security (CLS).
  (Reference: https://docs.aws.amazon.com/quicksight/latest/user/restrict-access-to-a-data-set-using-column-level-security.html)

- **Features**:
  Enable BI for everyone with QuickSight, perform advanced analytics with ML insights, and embed analytics to differentiate your applications

- **Benefits**
  Connect and scale all of your data, build customizable dashboards, leverage ML integrations for insights, enable true self-service BI for everyone, native AWS services integrations, no servers to manage, and pay by usage.

QuickSight Dashboard and Analysis
QuickSight Dashboard provides a read-only snapshot of analysis that you can share. It preserves the analysis's configuration, such as filtering, parameters, controls, and sorting.

You can share the analysis or the dashboard with users or groups. To share the dashboard, you must first publish it. Then, users who see the dashboard can also see the underlying data.

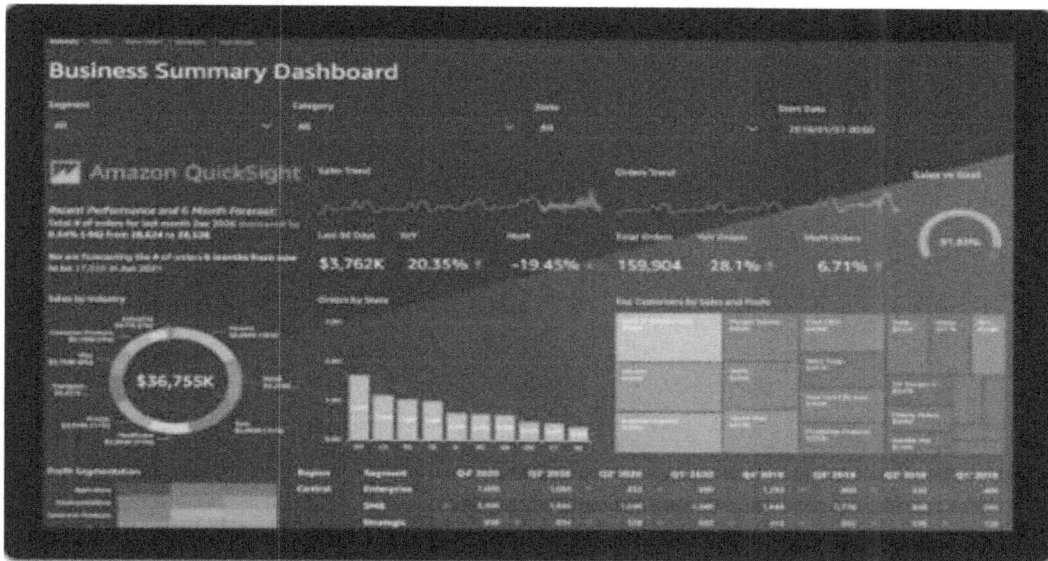

Image Source Reference: https://aws.amazon.com/quicksight/

You can define users in the Standard Version and groups in Enterprise Version. These users and groups only exist with QuickSight, not in IAM.

QuickSight Integrations

You can integrate a variety of data sources with Amazon QuickSight and import them for analyses.

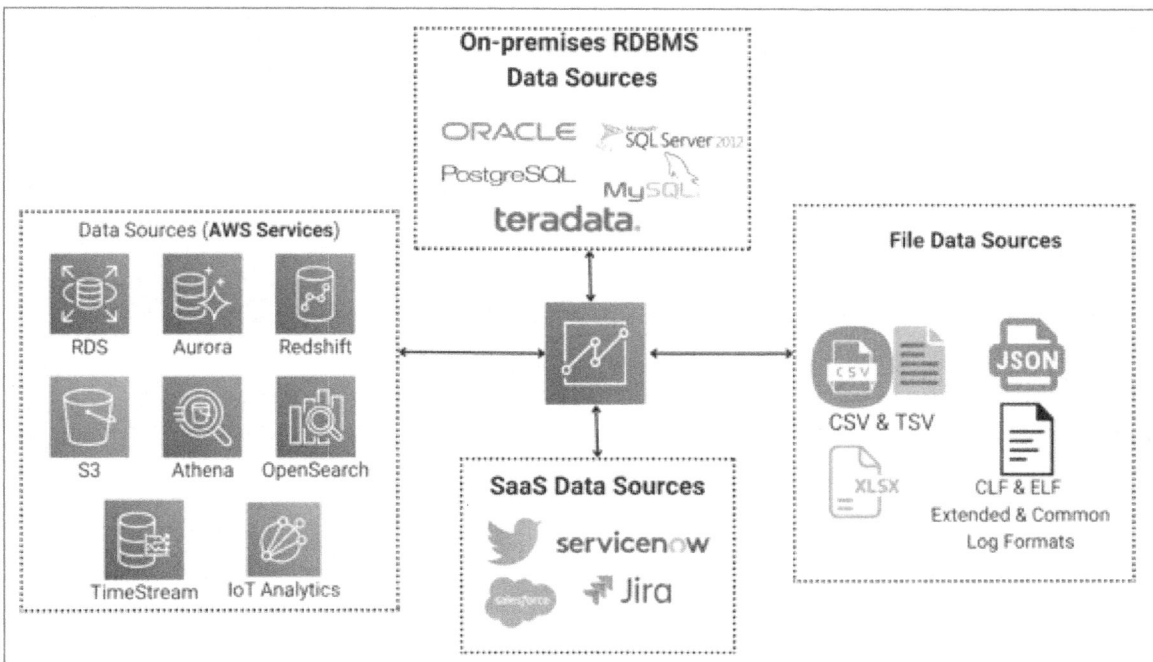

Reference: https://docs.aws.amazon.com/quicksight/latest/user/supported-data-sources.html

AWS Glue

AWS Glue is a managed ETL (Extract, Transform, and Load) service -- it is a serverless service for analytics, machine learning, and data engineering.

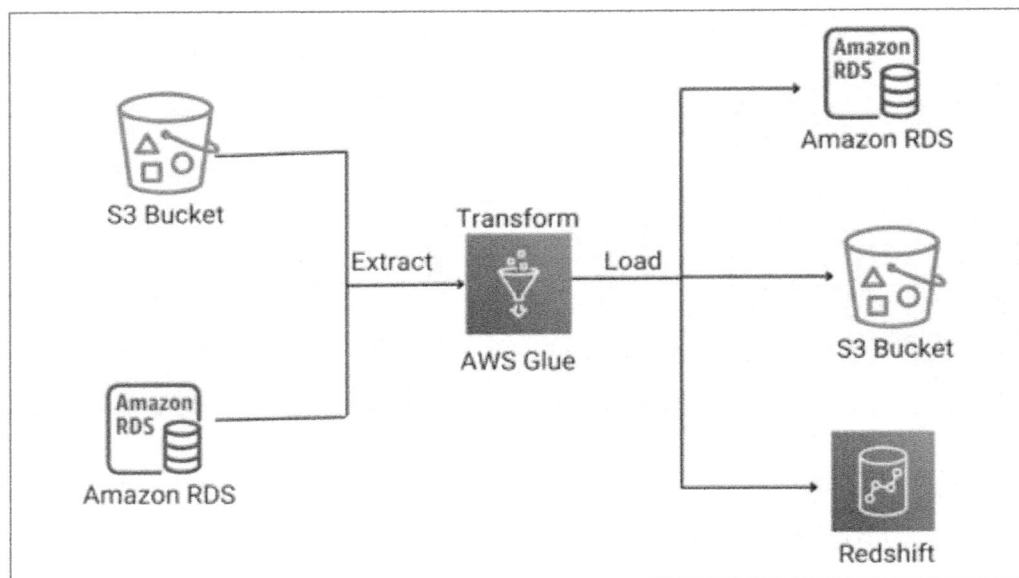

It makes it easy to discover, prepare, and combine data for data engineering or related tasks. AWS Glue can crawl your data sources to identify data formats and suggests schemas to store data.

The automatic generation of schema structure from the provided data sources saves time, which helps in the faster development of ETL jobs such as data extraction, pre-processing, transformations, and loading on the AWS Glue platform. Using AWS Glue, you can write Spark ETL jobs with data stored in S3, RDS, or on file using Python or Scala and set up the data pipeline in Glue to schedule ETL jobs.

In summary, AWS Glue automates much of the effort required for data integration. AWS Glue provides many of the modern capabilities needed for data integration, data analytics, machine learning, and data engineering so you can start analyzing your data and putting it to use in minutes instead of months.

You pay only for the resources consumed by your running jobs.

AWS Glue Features

Discover
- Discover and search across all your AWS data sets
- Automatic schema discovery
- Manage and enforce schemas for data streams
- Automatically scale based on workload

Prepare
- Deduplicate and cleanse data with built-in machine learning

- Edit, debug, and test ETL code with developer endpoints
- Normalize data without code using a visual interface
- Define, detect, and remediate sensitive data

Integrate
- Simplify Data Integration job development
- Built-in Job Notebooks
- Build complex ETL pipelines with simple job scheduling
- Apply and deploy DevOps best practices with Git integration
- Reduce costs for non-urgent workloads with flexible job execution

Transform
- Visually transform data with a drag-and-drop interface
- Clean and transform streaming data in-flight

AWS Glue related a few terms (good to know):
Glue Studio: It is UI for Glue to create, run and monitor ETL jobs in Glue.

Glue DataBrew: It cleans and normalizes data using pre-built transformation.

Glue Streaming ETL: It is built on Apache Spark Structured Streaming. It is compatible with Kinesis Data Streaming, Kafka, and MSK (Managed Kafka)

Glue Job Bookmarks: It prevents the re-processing of old data.

Glue Elastic View:
You can combine and replicate data across multiple data stores using SQL. It leverages a "virtual table" (materialized view). You don't need to write any custom code. AWS Glue monitors changes in the source data.

ETL Solutions Architecture Using Glue

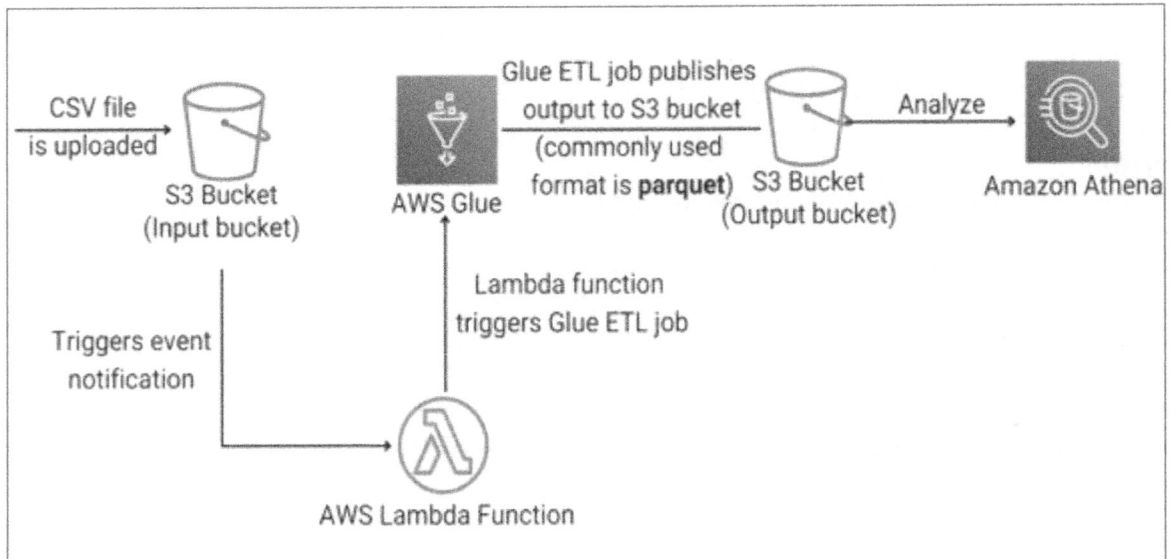

This is a Glue ETL use case diagram where a Glue ETL job (for example, a clean ETL job) is run when a file (for example, a CSV file) is uploaded to an S3 bucket.

When the file is uploaded, S3 sends a notification to AWS Lambda, and the Lambda function triggers the Glue ETL job, which finally publishes a parquet file to an S3 bucket. The file in the S3 bucket can be analyzed by Amazon Athena service.

AWS Glue Data Catalog

The AWS Glue Data Catalog provides a **metadata repository** where disparate systems can store and find metadata. You can then use the metadata from AWS Glue Data Catalog in your ETL job to query and consistently transform the data across various applications.

AWS Lake Formation

- Traditional data storage, such as data warehouses, including BI and analytics tools that organizations use to leverage, needs help getting the agility and flexibility required to deliver relevant business insights. That's the reason many organizations are moving to build a **data lake**.

- A data lake is an architectural approach related to data warehousing and data integration that allows you to store massive amounts of data in one central location so that it's readily available to be categorized, processed, analyzed, and consumed by diverse groups within your organization.

- Built on top of AWS Glue, AWS Lake Formation is a fully managed service enabling you to set up a data lake in days easily. A data lake is a central place to have all your data for analytics purposes.

- Using AWS Lake Formation, collect, clean, transform and ingest data into your Data Lake. It automates much complex manual strep such as collecting, cleaning, moving, and cataloging data.

- You can combine both structured and unstructured data in a data lake.

- It provides out-of-box source blueprints for S3, RDS, and NoSQL databases.

- You can also set up fine-grained access control (row level and column level) for your applications.

AWS Lake Formation in Action

The following diagram illustrates how data is loaded in AWS Lake Formation from data sources like Amazon S3, relational and NoSQL databases, and the data lake is built on Amazon S3.

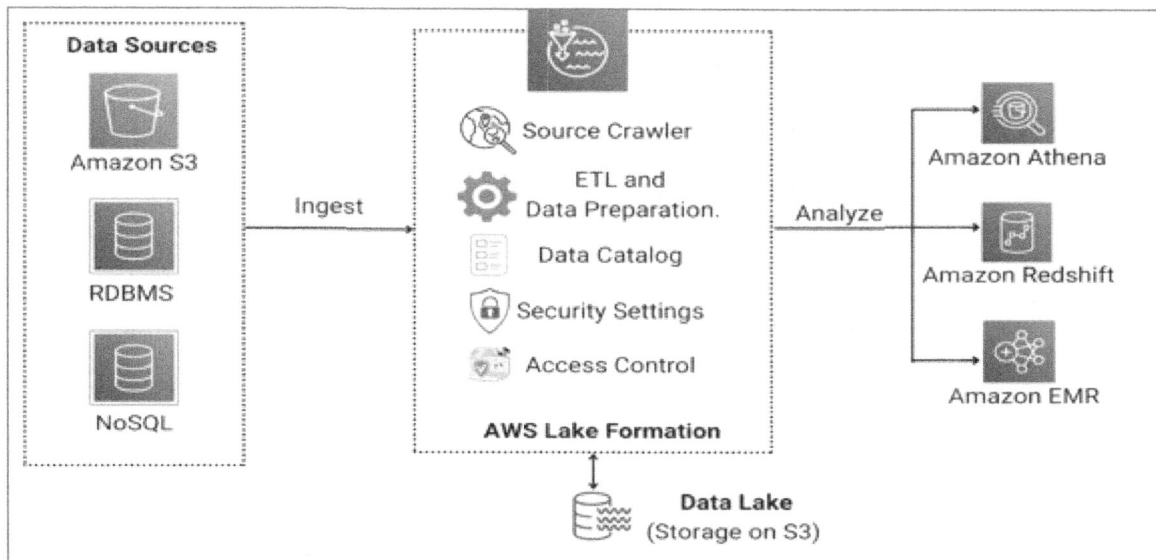

As the diagram shows, Lake Formation manages AWS Glue crawlers, AWS Glue ETL jobs, the Data Catalog, security settings, and access control. After the data is stored in the data lake, users can access it through their choice of analytics services, including Amazon Athena, Amazon Redshift, and Amazon EMR.

Kinesis Data Analytics

(Querying Streams of Data)

Kinesis Data Analytics is another system for querying streams of data continuously -- very similar conceptually to spark streaming. But it is specific to AWS Kinesis.

It is a service to perform real-time analytics on Kinesis Data Streams & Kinesis Firehose using SQL. It is a fully managed service and has automatic scaling. You pay for the actual consumption rate.

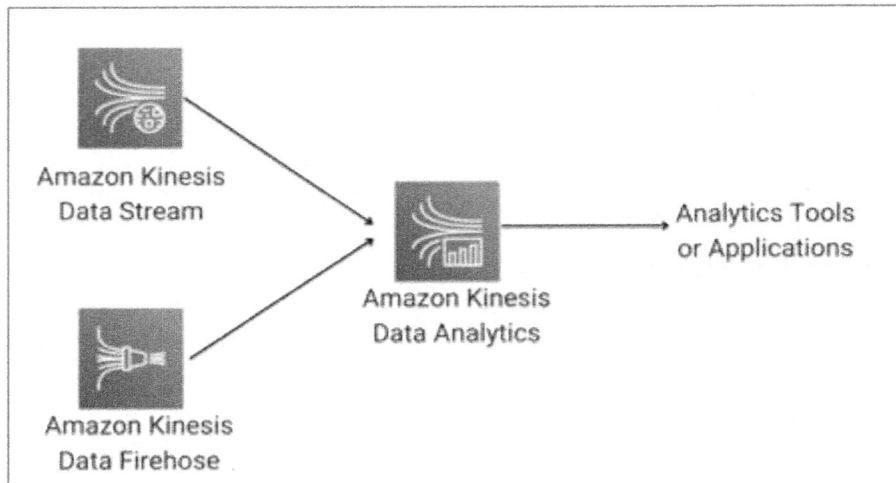

Conceptually it's very simple. Kinesis Data Analytics can receive data from either Kinesis Data Streams or a Kinesis Data Firehose stream. Like Spark streaming, you can set up windows of time to look back on and aggregate and analyze data across.

It's always receiving this never-ending stream of data, and you can write straight-up SQL to analyze that data, turn around, and spit out the results to some other stream, which might ultimately go to some analytics tools of your choice.

In more depth...

There are three main parts to Kinesis analytics. **source or input data**, and this is where the data to be streamed comes from. The input or source can be Kinesis streams or Firehose streams.

You can also optionally configure a reference data source to enrich your input data stream within the application. This will result in an application reference table. Maybe it's some lookup data you want to refer to within your SQL for your analytics job.

If you want to do that, you have to store your reference data as an object in an S3 bucket. And then, when your Kinesis analytics application starts, the Amazon Kinesis data analytics will read the Amazon S3 object and create an application table. You can refer to that data from there however you want.

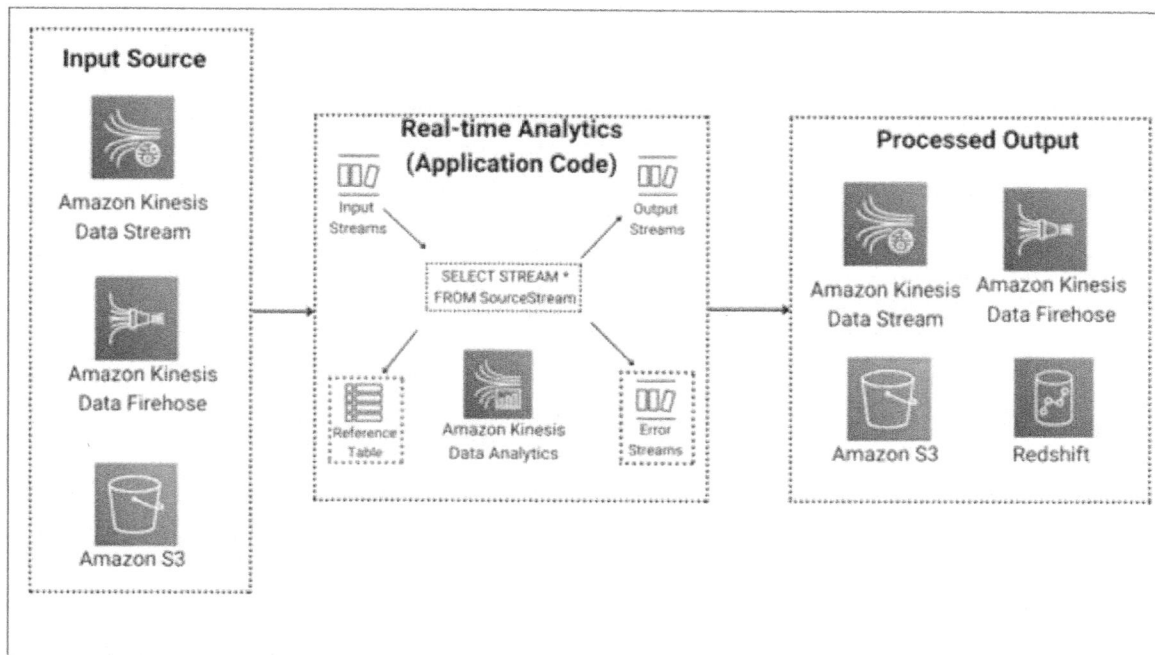

Then we have the real-time analytics or the application code itself sitting in the middle. That's where the actual analysis happens, which will perform real-time analytics just using straight-up SQL queries on your stream of information. The part that forms the analytics job is called the application code. These are just SQL statements that would be processed on the streaming data in reference tables. And again, it can operate over windows of time so he can look back through some fixed period.

As new data are being received, we have the destination going onto the output streams. And that's where the process data will go. So once the data is processed, the output can be sent to either Kinesis Data Streams again or Data Firehose. And from there, it can go off to wherever you want, like an S3 bucket or Amazon Redshift If you'd want to store that in a data warehouse.

AWS Lambda might be involved, too. If you want to use that as the glue between these services, do whatever you want. Also, if any errors are encountered, those are sent out to the errors stream.

Kinesis Data Analytics will automatically provide an in-application error stream for every application if your application has any issues while processing certain records like a type mismatch or later rival. That record will be written out to the error stream for you.

Reference Tables
You can add reference data from Amazon S3 to enrich streaming data. Suppose you're looking for an inexpensive way to join data for quick lookups within your Kinesis analytics job. Reference tables are a great way to do it again All you need to do is store a mapping file in S3, which is inexpensive, right? You could make that available as a reference table for Kinesis data analytics. You can use a join command to join that data from there.

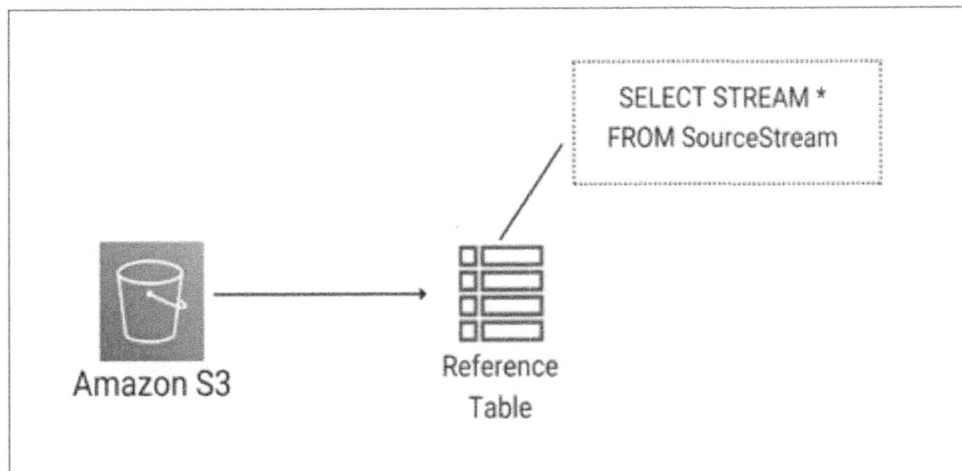

For example, Let's say you have one table with zip codes, but you want to actually look up the city associated with a given zip code You might have a reference table that associates zip codes with cities. And then, you can use a join command in SQL to join that data in to add that data to your output.

Remember. If you need an inexpensive way of doing joins in Kinesis Data Analytics' reference table is a great way to do it.

Kinesis Data Analytics and AWS Lambda
Kinesis data analytics now integrates with Lambda. What it means AWS Lambda can also be a destination for Kinesis data analytics. This gives you much flexibility.

For example. you can aggregate rows together, translate your data to a different format, enrich it with additional data, or even encrypt that data through an AWS Lambda function that operates on the output from Kinesis data analytics.

Also, by using Lambda, it opens up access to a lot of other services and destinations. For example, AWS Lambda can talk to many other services such as DynamoDB, Aurora, Redshift, SNS, SQS, or CloudWatch.

Kinesis Data Analytics with Apache Flink

You can use Apache Flink to process and analyze streaming data.

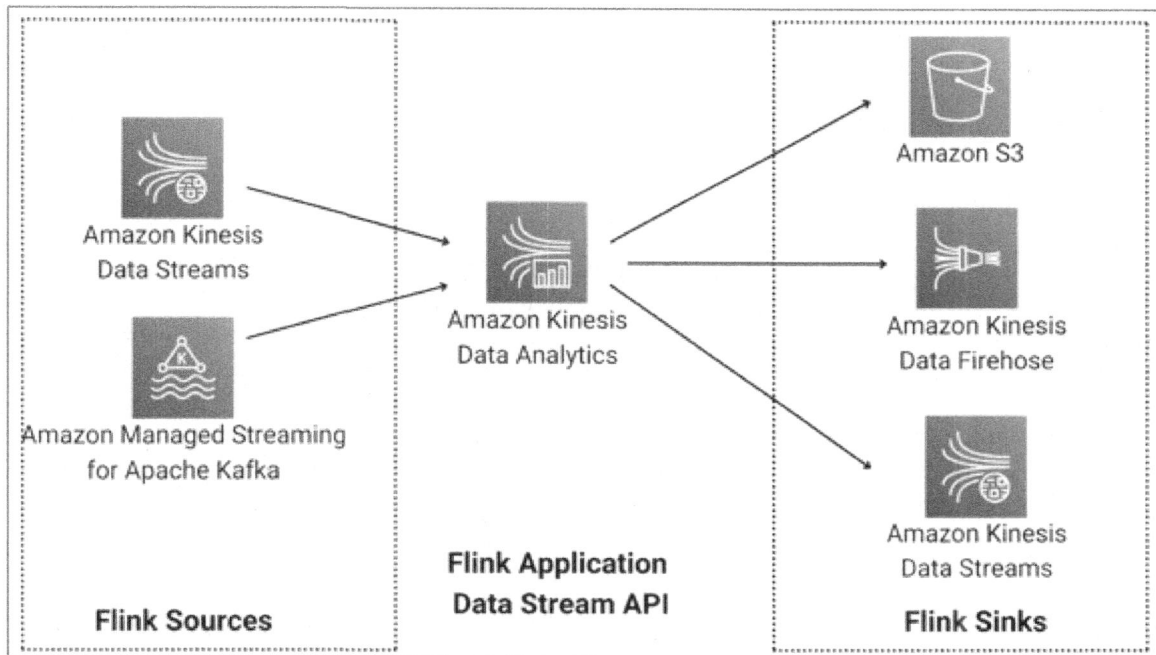

Conceptually Flink starts with what we call sources, which sound like where your data are coming from. In Kinesis Data Analytics for Flink, you can have a Kinesis Data Stream, or you can also have Amazon MSK, which is streaming for Apache Kafka as a valid Flink source.

These then get processed by your Flink application itself. It uses an API called Data Stream. And the Data Stream API allows you to talk to sources, apply processing on those sources, and then output them to what we call sinks. Supported sinks for Apache Flink include Amazon S3, Amazon Kinesis Data Streams, and Amazon Kinesis Data Firehose.

That's Kinesis data analytics for Apache Flink in a nutshell. Remember that it allows you to import your homegrown Flink applications into Kinesis data analytics using the data stream API. You can connect to Flink sources, including Kinesis Data Streams or MSK (Amazon Managed Streaming for Apache Kafka). That puts it to sinks that include Amazon S3, Amazon Kinesis Data Streams, and Amazon Kinesis Data Firehose.

Amazon Managed Streaming for Apache Kafka (Amazon MSK)

It is an alternative to Amazon Kinesis. It is a fully managed Apache Kafka service on AWS. It allows to create, update, and delete of Kafka clusters.

Kinesis Data Analytics Use Cases
- Time-series analytics
- Real-time dashboards
- Real-time metrics

Kinesis Data Analytics Cost Model

Pay for resources consumed (but it's not inexpensive)

- Charged by Kinesis Processing Unit (KPU) consumed per hour
- 1 KPU = 1 vCPU + 4 GB
- Serverless
- Scales automatically

It is serverless -- you pay for the resources as you consume. It scales up automatically, and you don't have to worry about the underlying resources needed to run your Kinesis analytics applications. However, it's not expensive, unlike AWS's other serverless services. So, make sure to shut down any analytics jobs to be safe once you're done using them.

Use IAM permissions to access streaming sources and designations

As far as security goes, you can use IAM permissions to access the streaming source and destination services that you're working with. You can configure IAM to allow your cases analytics application to talk to whatever upstream and downstream services it needs to communicate to.

Schema Discovery

There's also a cool feature in Kinesis analytics called schema discovery. And that's how the column names and your SQL are found. It can analyze the incoming data from your stream as you're setting it up.

RANDOM_CUT_FOREST

It's worth talking about RANDOM_CUT_FOREST. This is a SQL function offered by Kinesis data analytics that you can use within your data analytics application for anomaly detection on any numeric columns in a stream. It is a novel way of identifying outliers in a data set so you can handle them however you need to.

Reference:
https://d1.awsstatic.com/whitepapers/kinesis-anomaly-detection-on-streaming-data.pdf

Section 8. Machine Learning

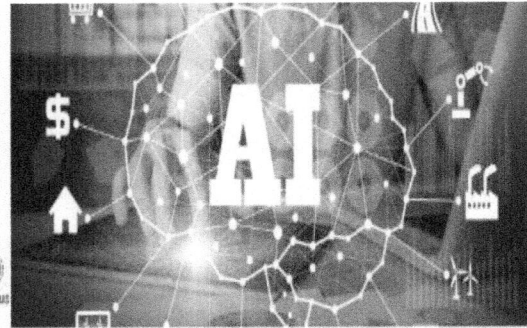

Chapter 29. AWS ML/AI Services

You will learn the following in this chapter:
- Introduction to ML/AI
- Amazon Rekognition
- Amazon Transcribe
- Amazon Polly
- Amazon Translate
- Amazon Lex
- Amazon Connect
- Amazon Comprehend
- Amazon SageMaker
- Amazon Forecast
- Amazon Kendra
- Amazon Personalize
- Amazon Textract
- Amazon Fraud Detector
- Amazon Sumerian

Introduction to ML/AI

Artificial Intelligence (AI), Machine Learning (ML), and Deep Learning (DL), though all three are related -- but there are differences.

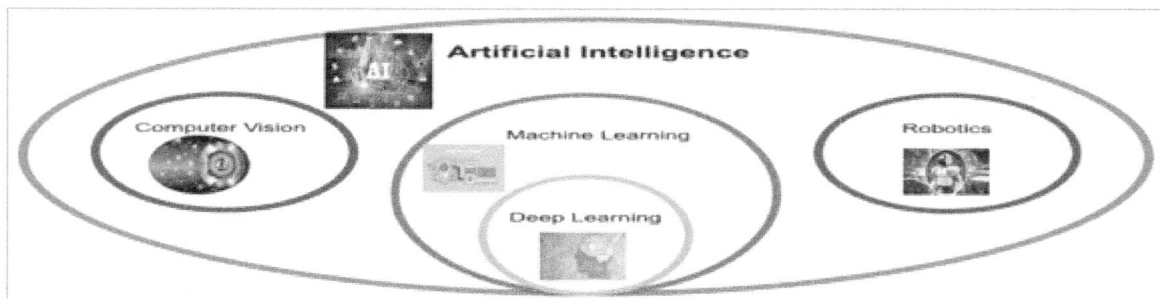

Artificial Intelligence

Artificial Intelligence (AI) is science that empowers computers to mimic intelligence of human such as decision making, text processing, and visual perception. AI is a broader or umbrella area of where machines are empowered to mimic human intelligence. AI encompasses several subfields such as machine learning, computer vision, and robotics.

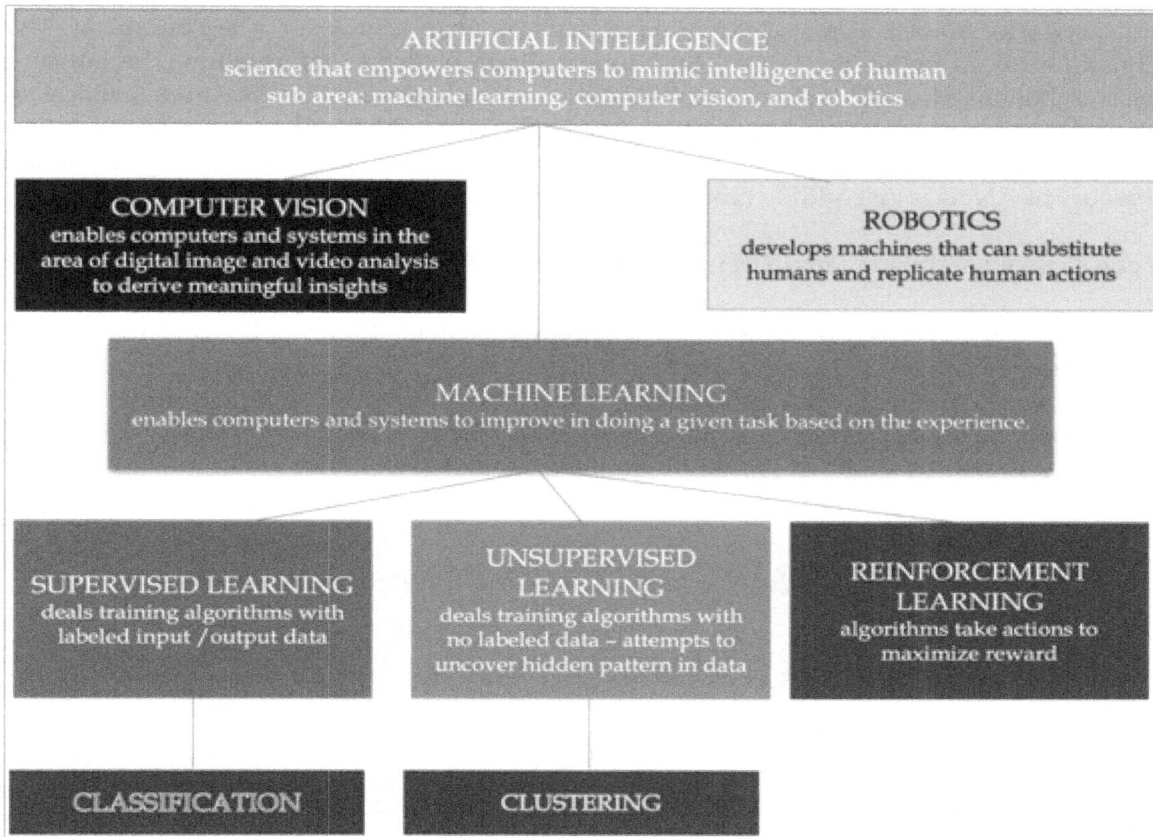

Machine learning

Machine learning is a subarea of AI that enables computers and systems to improve in doing a given task based on the experience. It is important to understand here is that all machine learning can be classified as AI ones. However, not all AI can be classified as machine learning -- there are some rule-based engines could be classified as AI but not as ML. The reason is since they do not learn from experience, therefore they are not considered to be on ML.

Computer vision

Computer vision is subarea of AI that enables computers and systems in the area of digital image and video analysis to derive meaningful insights and take actions or make recommendations based on that information.

If AI enables computers and systems to think, computer vision enables them to observe and understand.

Robotics is a subarea of AI or an interdisciplinary branch of computer science and engineering. Robotics develops machines that can substitute humans and replicate human actions.
Robots can be used in many situations for many purposes particularly where it's very difficult or risky for humans such as manufacturing processes, or where humans cannot survive for example, in space,

underwater, in high heat. Robots can take on any form, but some are made to resemble humans in appearance. (Reference: https://en.wikipedia.org/wiki/Robotics)

Deep Learning

Deep learning is specialized subarea of machine learning that is based on training of deep artificial neural network (ANNs) using a large dataset such as images or texts. The concept of ANNs is essentially inspired by human brain – how human brain processes information. The human brain consists of billions of neurons that communicate to each other using electrical and chemical signals that enables humans to see, observe, feel, and make decisions. ANNs are mathematically mimicked to work how human brain works – connecting multiple "artificial" neurons in a multilayered fashion. The beauty of ANNs is that adding more hidden layers to the network, makes the network deeper.

The questions what differentiates Deep Learning with Machine Learning.

- In Machine Learning the process is: (1) select the model to train and (2) features are extracting manually.
- In Deep Learning the process is: (1) select the architecture to network (2) features are extracted automatically by feeding in training data, such as image, along with the target class (label).

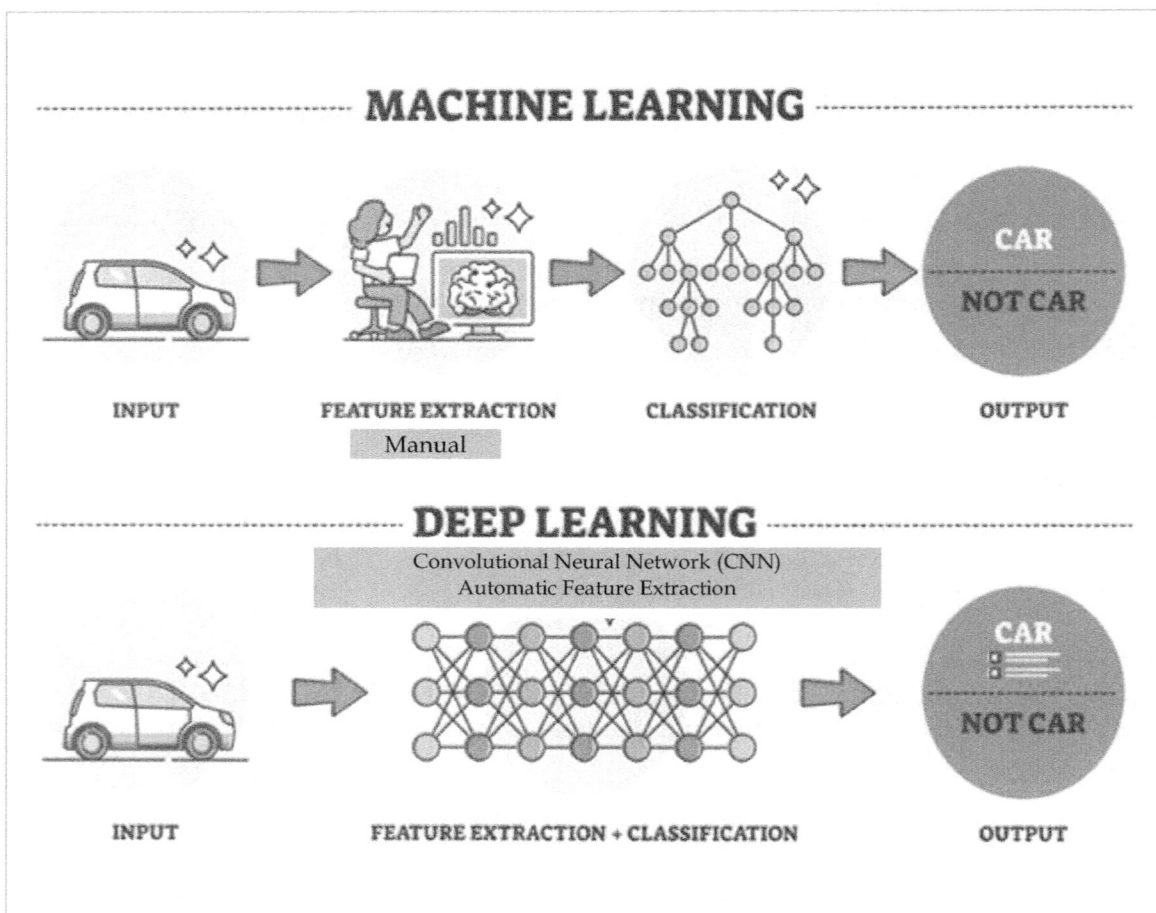

Amazon AI and ML Services

The Amazon AI and ML Services easily add intelligence to applications. Amazon has many Amazon AI and ML Services; we have listed some main ones below.

- Amazon Rekognition
- Amazon Transcribe
- Amazon Polly
- Amazon Translate
- Amazon Lex
- Amazon Comprehend
- Amazon Comprehend Medical
- Amazon SageMaker
- Amazon Forecast
- Amazon Kendra
- Amazon Personalize
- Amazon Fraud Detecto
- Amazon Textract
- Amazon Fraud Detector
- Amazon Sumerian

Amazon Rekognition

Extracting specific insights in images and videos is costly, time-intensive, prone to error, and hard to scale. Amazon Rekognition is a simple and easy service to quickly analyze pictures and videos stored on S3.

It is a fully managed computer vision service that helps automate your image and video analysis, thus avoiding manual inspection. In addition, the service employs proven and highly scalable deep learning technology. Using Amazon Rekognition, you can easily add image and video analysis capability to your applications through simple API endpoints.

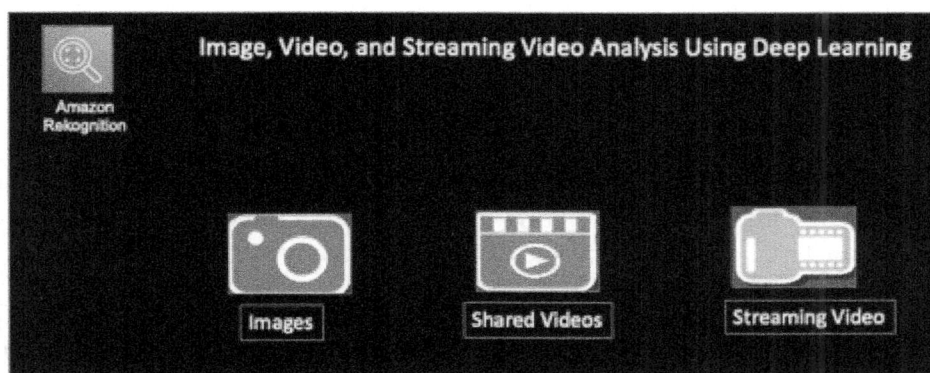

With Amazon Rekognition, you get highly accurate facial analysis. You can also perform analysis by matching objects, scenes, segments, and text detection in large numbers of images and videos.

You can automatically tag or label media content to make it searchable. Amazon Rekognition custom labels extend object detection capabilities further, allowing you to quickly train custom models by simply supplying labeled images unique to your business. For example, Amazon Rekognition can help you use custom labels to find images of related to your company, identify products and inventory on store shelves, or classify parts of your assembly line.

You can also flag any inappropriate content to enforce policies, comply with regulations, and protect your brand. You can identify and verify users such as customers and students by matching their faces with their identity document pictures, -- for example, picture ID -- using facial analysis.

Image Analysis

As discussed earlier, Amazon Rekognition has many features. For example, you can perform object and scene detection, facial analysis, face recognition, unsafe image detection, celebrity recognition, and extract text in an image.

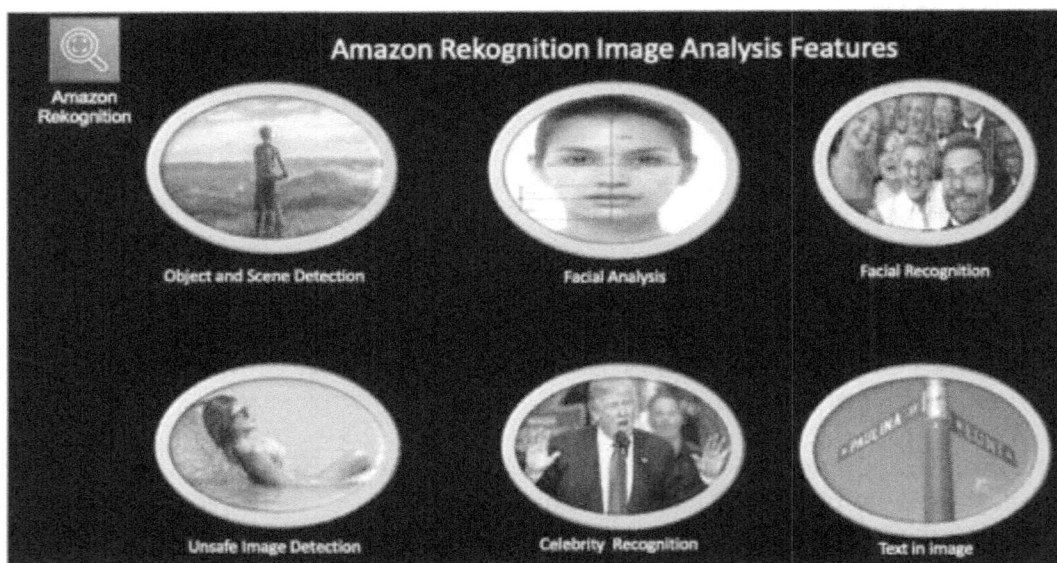

Let's look into a little about each feature of Amazon Recognition. With Amazon Rekognition object and scene detection, you can identify keywords that describe the content in an image from object detection like vehicle, sidewalk, or boat to scene descriptions like sunrise, sunset, or beach.

Another feature of Amazon Rekognition is that it lets you perform facial analysis. You just feed Amazon Rekognition an image. It will return many attributes about the photo, such as facial landmarks, emotion analysis, and demographic data like gender and age.

Another feature of Amazon Rekognition is face similarity detection and searching. Rekognition lets you match faces in an image against the index of images you've created. You can also find pictures of one face against faces in another photo, looking for the matches between the two. Rekognition also returns a similarity score which your application can use to determine the possibility of the correctness of the match.

Amazon Rekognition can recognize thousands of famous, noteworthy, and prominent individuals in their field. With each match, the service also provides relevant URLs for more information available.

If your application deals with user-contributed or user-generated content, you might want to ensure that images that your users share are flagged for explicit or suggestive content. Amazon Rekognition can help your image content moderation automatically. Each image moderation response includes a hierarchical list of moderation labels and confident scores, providing insight into the explicit or suggestive nature of the content in the image.

Amazon Rekognition makes it easy to locate and extract text found in a picture even when you're the picture contains real-world scenes like street signs, posts, or license plates. When analyzing the text in an image, Rekognition returns all the detected pieces of text, both individually and in a group, along with a confidence score for every detection.

The typical application architecture when building an application using Amazon Rekognition is for image search using custom labels is as follows:

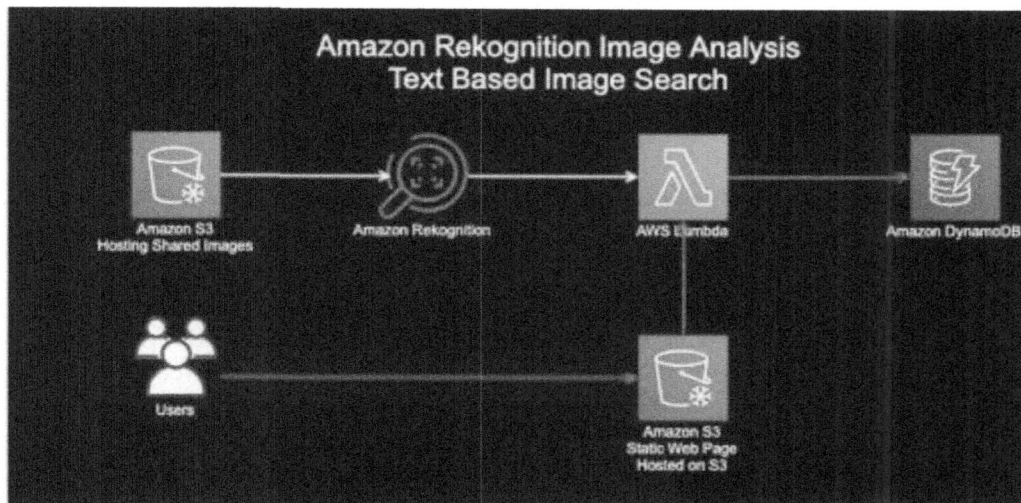

- The most interesting part is how we use Rekognition to extract relevant information from images so that we can store it in DynamoDB. To get this, we set up a simple pipeline that takes pictures uploaded into an S3 bucket and fires an event that causes an AWS Lambda function to execute.
- This Lambda function calls Rekognition to hit each image's APIs, *DetectLabels* API to detect objects and scenes detection, and *DetectFaces* API to perform face analysis. You could also use other APIs like the DetectText API to find text inside images or *DetectModerationLabels* API to perform unsafe content moderation to extend the application capability further.
- The Lambda function processes the results from API calls, stores the results into DynamoDB, and the results are ready to be queried by our web front end.
- Build a static HTML page for searching and filtering the images hosted on S3
- The search queries call a Lambda function via API Gateway to lookup images tagged with results we obtained via Amazon Rekognition. That is stored inside the DynamoDB.

This is a serverless and event-driven image analysis pipeline. With this setup, it's easy to scale. Furthermore, it is extremely cost-effective because we are not paying for any idle server time because of the serverless nature of the application.

Non-storage and Storage operation API Operations

Looking at the Amazon Rekognition API, there are two types of API operations: non-storage operation and storage operation. The non-storage operation APIs take the input and return the results without persisting in any state. The *DetectLabels* and *DetectFaces* endpoints are both examples of non-storage operations.

On the other hand, storage API operations persist some information to AWS servers to let you make additional API calls that rely on this information. For example, let's say you have a use case in which you need to build an application that will authenticate users by matching pictures of their faces against a set of profile pictures.

In this case, you will start by creating a collection on Rekognition to store all of the face data for your users. You do this using the API named *CreateCollection* endpoint. Then you want to analyze and remember the faces of all of your users.

Using the IndexFaces endpoint, you can pass in images and the collection's name you wish to Rekogniton to store the face vector metadata. Once you've done this, you can use the *SearchFacesByImage* API to search for faces in the picture to find any match in your collection. The *CreateCollection* and *IndexFaces* APIs are both storage API operations.

Many AWS customers are already leveraging Amazon Rekognition in their products. For example. Pinterest Rekognition to detect and extract the text found in images at scale.

Video Analysis

We have seen how Amazon Rekognition analyzes images – what about video analysis? There are countless opportunities to innovate and find actionable insights from the video content, from personal entertainment to physical security to in-store customer behavioral analysis.

The old classic video analysis technique was to sample still frames from a video feed, performing analysis on these images one at a time. In some cases, this approach can work, but there is a lot of opportunity for improvement here – and Amazon Rekognition does an excellent job of performing video analysis. Amazon Rekognition can perform analysis on videos stored on S3 and can perform analysis of streaming video content as well.

Video is all about motion over time -- this builds up context. For example, the adjacent frames are related, and a good analysis should consider this. It's hard to leverage this temporal context if we just perform a simple frame-by-frame analysis looking at an image in isolation. It doesn't surprise you that Amazon Rekognition does this type of analysis, but it does it in a way that preserves this context. As a result, you can perform object and activity detection, person tracking, facial analysis, unsafe video detection, celebrity recognition, and face recognition for video files.

Let's see how it works. Unlike Rekognition APIs operations for images, which return results immediately -- analyzing videos works asynchronously. We start by storing files on Amazon S3. Then, we call one of Recognition's asynchronous APIs like StartFaceDetection or StartCelebrityRecognition, by inputting the information for the location of video files on S3 and a resource identifier or ARN for the Amazon SNS topic.

After the analysis finished, Recognition published a notification on the topic we provided. We connect to this topic to invoke a Lambda function which then fetches the results from Rekognition using the next appropriate call like GetFaceDetection or GetCelebrityRecognition. When the Lambda function gets the results, it stores them in DynamoDB -- ready to be queried from a web app. The web app makes API Gateway calls to call the Lambda function to fetch the result from the DynamoDB.

Amazon Rekognition also can perform person tracking. The person tracking feature lets you follow a person throughout a video, learning their position in each frame and time stamp when they are seen in the video. It can also track people through frames when their faces are obscured or not facing the camera. The GetPersonTracking API returns this location information for each detected person and any detected facial landmarks for each person.

Rekognition also allows you to perform searches of detected faces against a collection of faces you've previously defined. For example, suppose you have defined a collection of faces with the CreateCollection API and populated it with results from the IndexFaces API. In that case, Rekognition can search your videos for matches against the collection using the FaceSearch APIs. The Amazon Recognition also lets you detect explicit or suggestive content in your videos, allowing you to flag or filter content based on the needs of your application.

Streaming Analysis

Amazon Rekognition can do video streaming analysis using Amazon Kinesis Video Streaming. Amazon Kinesis Video Stream is a secure and scalable service for streaming video from connected devices to AWS for analytics, machine learning, and other processing.

It automatically scales the infrastructure needed to ingest streaming video data from millions of devices. It also stores, encrypts, and indexes your video data in your streams and allows you to access it through easy-to-use APIs.

To send streaming video data into a Kinesis video stream, you need Producer SDKs. The Producer SDKs -- currently, there are Producer SDKs available for Java and C++ -- make it easy to stream video data to AWS securely. Then, once your streaming data is into the Kinesis Video Stream, you can point to Rekognition for analysis.

Let's see how this works.

There are three parts of a stream when you want to do video analysis. First is an Amazon Kinesis Video Stream to send your video stream content. You would like to use Producer SDK to make it easy to capture the stream from your devices and stream it directly to Kinesis Video Stream. The Producer SDK will also handle stream creation, token rotation, and other actions for reliable streaming. You will also take note of the ARN of Kinesis Video Stream to start receiving the content.

Next, you will need to create Kinesis Data Stream to store the result as Kinesis analyzes streaming video content. You will want to note down this ARN also. That takes care of setting up Source and Destination Kinesis Stream. Now you just need to connect them.

Amazon Rekognition has a built-in stream processer that can receive a video stream, analyze it, and send the results out as it processes the frame. So, start with creating a Rekognition video stream processor providing the ARNs for the incoming video streams and the outgoing data streams you created.

Then, Rekognition glues this process together and is ready to run, which triggers one of the Recognition video start APIs like StartPersonTracking or StartLabelDetection, for example. After completing all the parts needed, your application can now consume the data from Kinesis Data Streams.

Content Moderation

Using Amazon Recognition, you can detect content that is inappropriate, unwanted or offensive in images and videos. This feature can be used in social media, broadcast media, advertising, and e-commerce to help create a safer user experience.

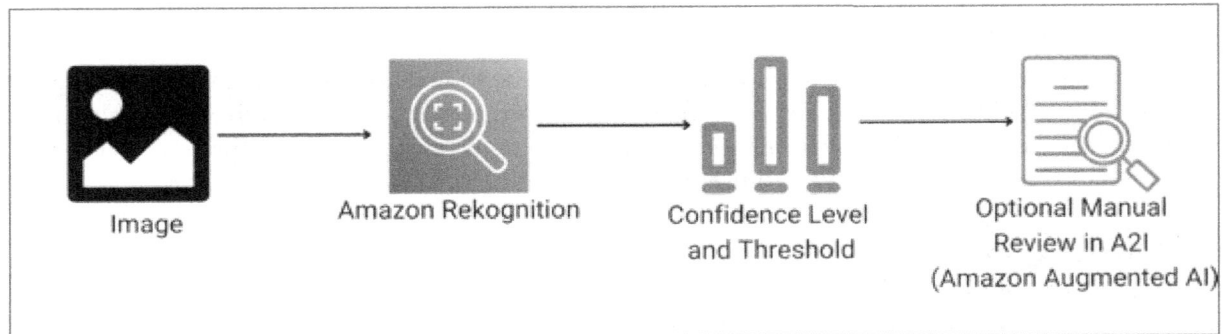

You can set a minimum confidence threshold for items that should be flagged. Flagged content can be manually reviewed in A2I (Amazon Augmented AI).

The content moderation feature also helps comply with regulations.

Use Cases

If your application or app contains user-generated or submitted content, you probably want to know if that content is free, explicit, or suggested. You can set up an automatic moderated pipeline like this.

If you upload your content on Amazon S3, you can trigger the Lambda function whenever new content is added to your storage bucket. In addition, the Lambda function can start Rekognition Detect Moderation Label's API. If it gets any label back, you can set the image to be reviewed by a human for selling to your users.

Another use case. Automatic sentiment analysis for a retail store. You can take a stream video feed from a retail store and have Rekognition perform real-time demographic and sentiment analysis on the faces of the people it sees in the store. You can keep this metadata on S3, periodically load it into RedShift, and plug it into Amazon QuickSight to quickly analyze the content and visualize trends, demographics, and customer sentiment over time.

As you can see, Amazon Rekognition lets you add the power of AI to image and video analysis capability to your application in minutes with only a few lines of code. For example, automatically extract and scene description, recognize and compare faces, detect suggestive and explicit video content, collect demographic details, track people in image and video streams, perform sentiment analysis, etc.

It's easy to get started and cost-effective too.

- Find objects, people, and text in images and videos
- Perform facial analysis and facial search for user verification
- Create a database of "familiar faces" or compare against celebrities
- Use cases: Labeling, Content Moderation, Text Detection, Face Detection and Analysis, Face Search and Verification, Celebrity Recognition

Amazon Transcribe

Amazon Transcribe service helps you quickly add high-quality speech-to-text capabilities to your applications. For example, you can quickly extract actionable insights from customer conversations.

In another use case, content producers can use this service to convert audio and video assets into fully searchable content automatically. For example, you can create subtitles for your broadcast content to increase accessibility and improve customer experience.

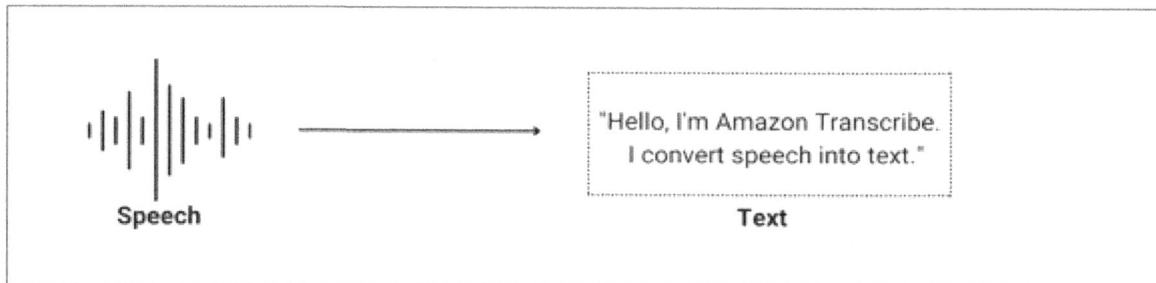

Speech → "Hello, I'm Amazon Transcribe. I convert speech into text." **Text**

Amazon Transcribe service can be used in the medical field as well. For example, doctors and practitioners can use Amazon Transcribe Medical to quickly document clinical conversations into electronic health record (EHR) systems for analysis.

KEY POINTS

- It uses a deep learning process called Automatic Speech Recognition (ASR) for automating speech-to-text conversion.
- Automatically removes Personally Identifiable Information (PII) using Redaction.
- Use cases: transcribe customer service calls, automate closed caption and subtitle, and generate metadata for media assets to create a fully searchable archive.

Amazon Polly

Amazon Polly is a Text-to-Speech (TTS) service that turns text into lifelike speech. It uses advanced deep-learning techniques to synthesize natural-sounding human speech, which helps developers build speech-enabled products -- applications that can talk.

"Hello, I'm Amazon Polly.
I convert text into lifelike speech."

Text   **Speech**

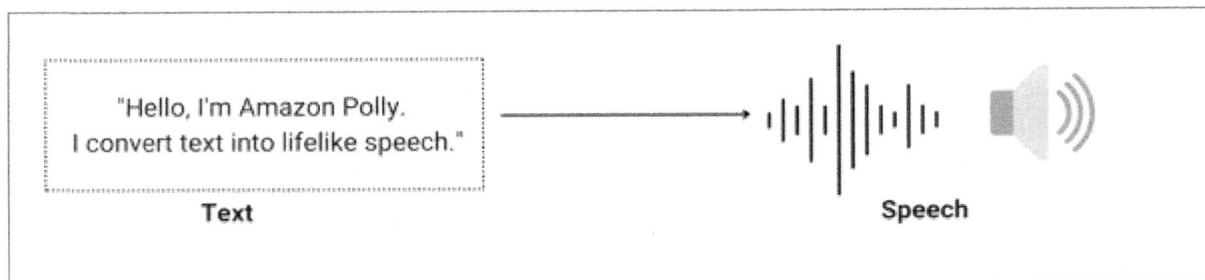

Using machine learning, Amazon Polly offers Neural Text-to-Speech (NTTS) voices, delivering advanced improvements in speech quality. Amazon Polly Brand Voice can also create a custom NTTS voice for your organization's exclusive use.

Lexicon & SSML

It can customize the pronunciation of words with pronunciation lexicons. For example, the acronym. AWS can be converted into speech as "Amazon Web Services." You need to upload lexicons

Additionally, you use generate speech from plain text or documents marked with Speech Synthesis Markup Language (SSML) – which enables more customization. For example, it can emphasize specific words or phrases and include breathing sounds and whispering.

KEY POINTS

- Turns text into lifelike speech
- Enables developers to build speech-enabled products

Amazon Translate

Amazon Translate is a natural machine translation that delivers fast, high-quality, affordable, and customizable **language translation**.

Amazon Translate differs from traditional statistical and rule-based translation algorithms. Instead, it uses natural machine translation, which uses deep learning models to provide more accurate and natural-sounding translations.

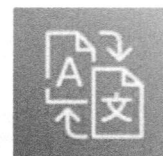

Translation

Source language

| Auto (auto) ▼ |

⇄

Target language

| Hindi (hi) ▼ |

Watching World Cup Soccer after every four years is really really entertaining and exciting.

हर चार साल बाद विश्व कप सॉकर देखना वास्तव में मनोरंजक और रोमांचक है।

| German (de) ▼ |

Alle vier Jahre eine Fußballweltmeisterschaft zu sehen, ist wirklich unterhaltsam und aufregend.

| Italian (it) ▼ |

Guardare la Coppa del Mondo di calcio ogni quattro anni è davvero divertente ed emozionante.

| French (fr) ▼ |

Regarder la Coupe du monde de football tous les quatre ans est vraiment amusant et passionnant.

| Portuguese (pt) ▼ |

Assistir a Copa do Mundo de Futebol a cada quatro anos é realmente divertido e emocionante.

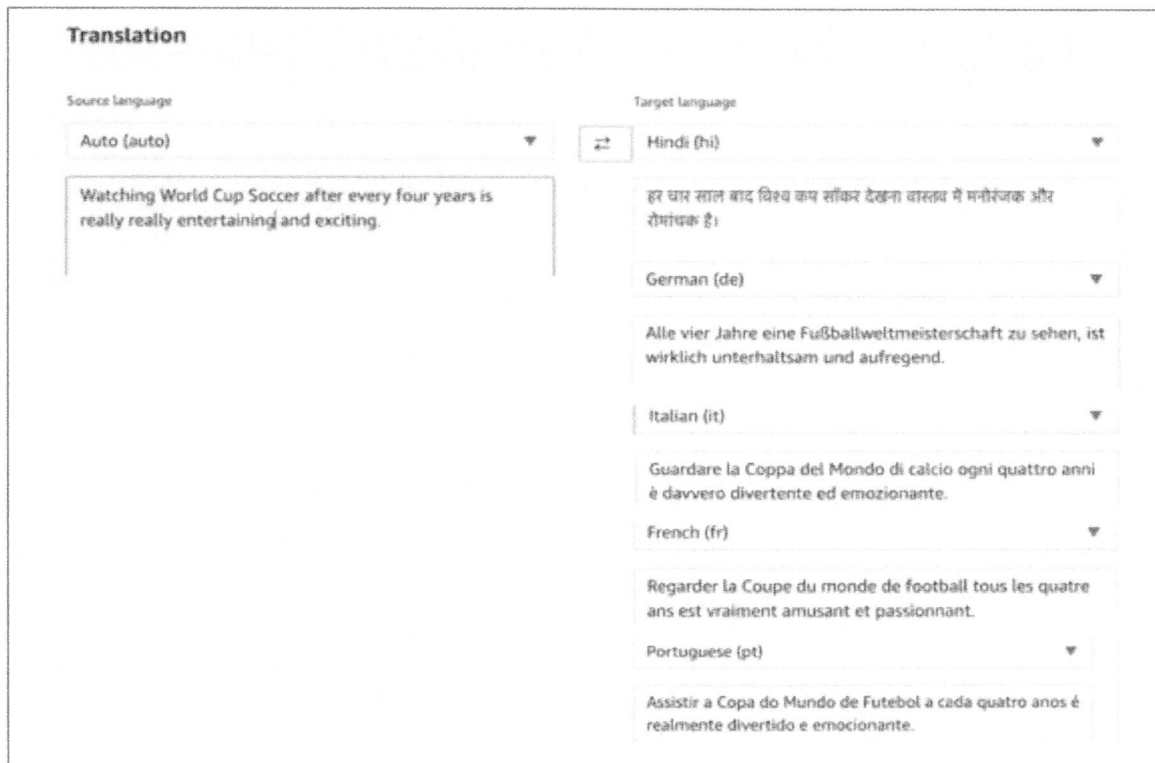

As a result, the Amazon Translate service can help you **localize content** such as websites and applications for your different types of diverse users. In addition, it can quickly translate large volumes of text for analysis and efficiently enable **cross-lingual** communication between users.

Amazon Lex

Amazon Lex is a service for building conversational interfaces into any application using voice and text.

It provides the advanced deep learning functionalities of automatic speech recognition (ASR) for converting speech to text, and natural language understanding (NLU) to recognize the text's intent, enabling you to build applications with highly engaging user experiences and lifelike conversational interactions.

Amazon Lex is a service for building conversational interfaces using voice and text. Powered by the same conversational engine as Alexa, Amazon Lex provides high-quality speech recognition and language understanding capabilities, enabling the addition of sophisticated, natural language 'chatbots' to new and existing applications.

Amazon Connect

It's a cloud-based virtual contact center -- it can create contact flows. Amazon Connect can be integrated with other CRM systems or AWS.

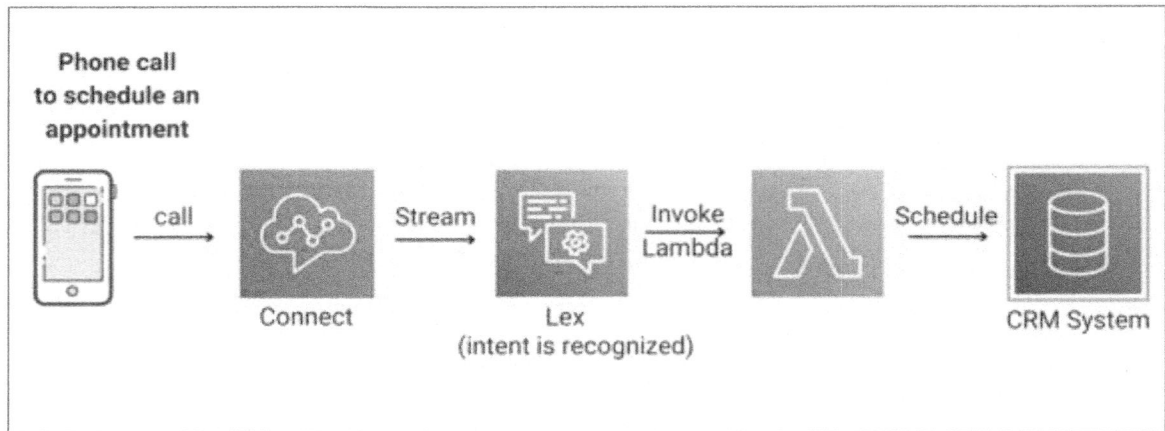

It's for free, 12 months, as part of the AWS Free Tier program. Users can get access to 90 minutes per month with the Free Tier.

Amazon Comprehend

- Amazon Comprehend is used for Natural-Language Processing (NLP).

- It can be used to apply natural-language processing (NLP) to uncover valuable insights and relationships in unstructured text. For example, it can mine business and call center analytics to detect customer sentiment and analyze customer interactions to categorize inbound support requests automatically.

- The service can also index and search product reviews by focusing on context and sentiment, not just keywords.

- You can also use the Amazon Comprehend service to secure documents by identifying and redacting Personally Identifiable Information (PII).

Amazon Comprehend Medical

Amazon Comprehend Medical detects and returns useful information in unstructured clinical text, e.g., physician's notes, discharge summaries, test results, and case notes.

It uses NLP to detect Protected Health Information (PHI) – DetectPHI API

Amazon SageMaker

It is a fully managed service for ML/AI engineers/data scientists to build ML models.

It helps solve some pain points of building ML models by putting all the processes in one place, such as provisioning servers, preparing, building, training, tuning, and deploying high-quality machine learning models. In other words, Amazon SageMaker puts all ML processes in one place. This helps provide a faster turnaround time to build ML pipelines.

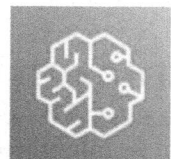

Amazon SageMaker JumpStart provides a collection of solutions for the most common use cases that can be deployed readily with just a few clicks.

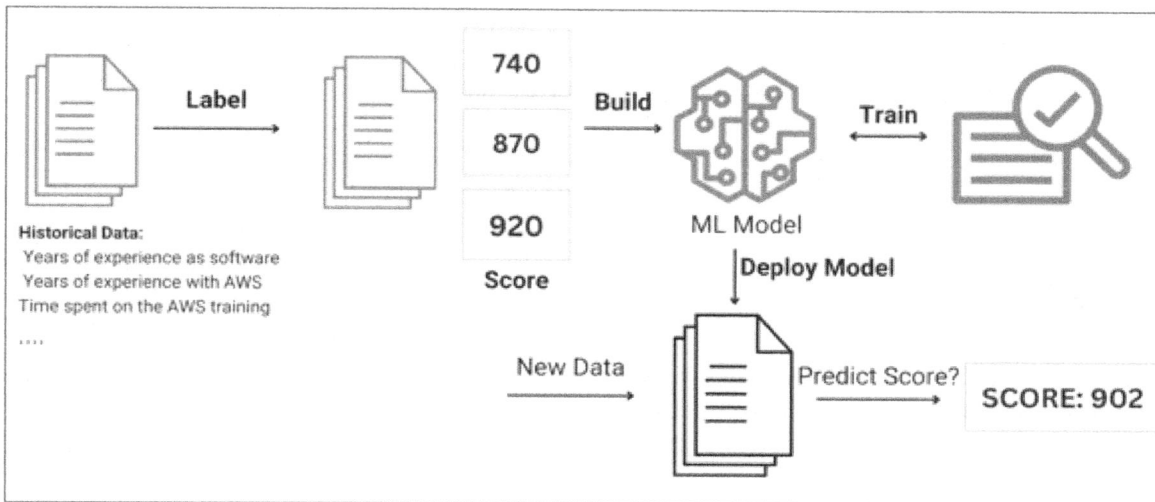

For example, as you can see in the diagram, how Amazon SageMaker ML Model predicts the exam's score by learning (train) from historical data.

Amazon Forecast

Amazon Forecast uses statistical and machine learning algorithms to deliver highly accurate time-series forecasts – without any machine learning experience.

It is a fully managed service. Amazon Forecast provides automation by finding the optimal combination of machine learning algorithms for your datasets. In addition, it offers several filling methods to automatically handle missing values in your datasets.

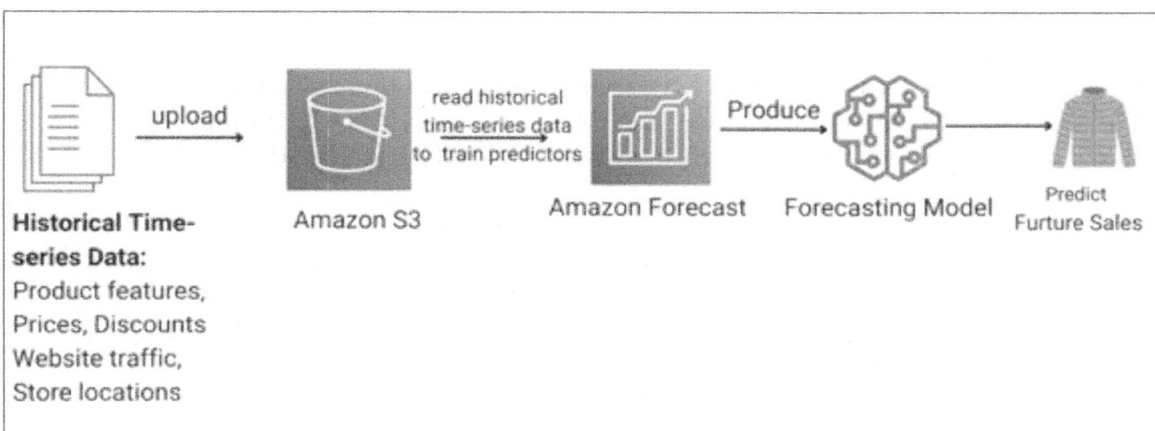

You can use this service for use cases such as retail demand planning to predict product demand, allowing you to vary inventory and pricing more accurately at different store locations. It can also be used in supply chain planning to forecast the quantity of raw goods, services, or other inputs required by manufacturing.

Another use case is a resource planning to predict staffing, advertising, energy consumption, and server capacity requirements. And finally, Amazon Forecast can be used in operational planning to predict levels of web traffic, AWS usage, and IoT sensor usage.

You can use the APIs, AWS Command Line Interface (AWS CLI), Python Software Development Kit (SDK), and Amazon Forecast Console to import time-series datasets, train predictors, and generate forecasts.

Amazon Kendra

Amazon Kendra is fully managed intelligent search service that adds natural language search capabilities. Amazon Kendra reimagines enterprise search for websites and applications so that employees and customers can easily find the right answers to questions when that they need them.

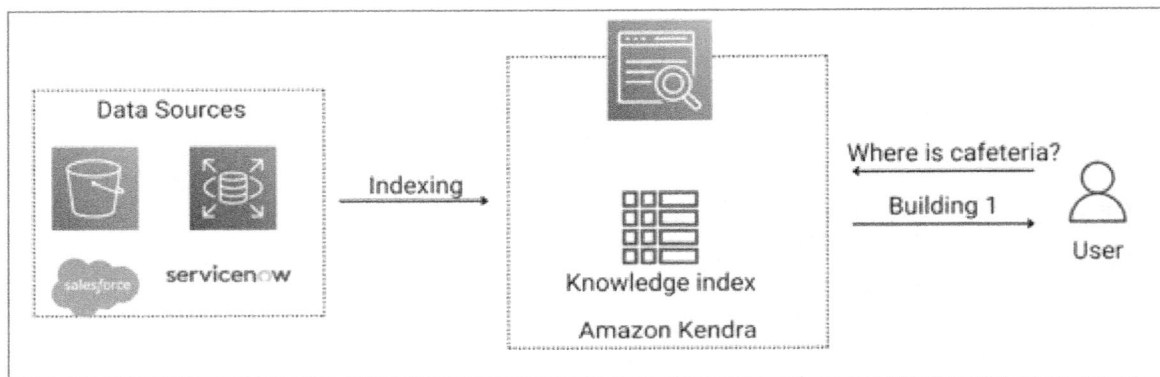

How Kendra does it -- Kendra does it by searching through troves of unstructured data to provide the right answer.

Amazon Personalize

Amazon Personalize is a fully managed ML service to build real-time personalized recommendations. For example, you can use this service for product recommendations, personalized product re-ranking, and customized direct marketing.

Amazon Personalize provisions the infrastructure and manages the entire ML pipeline, including pre-processing, features extraction, applying the best algorithm. It also trains, optimize, and deploy the model. You just need to call API endpoints for the deployed model. All data is encrypted, private, and secure, and is only used to create recommendations for your users.

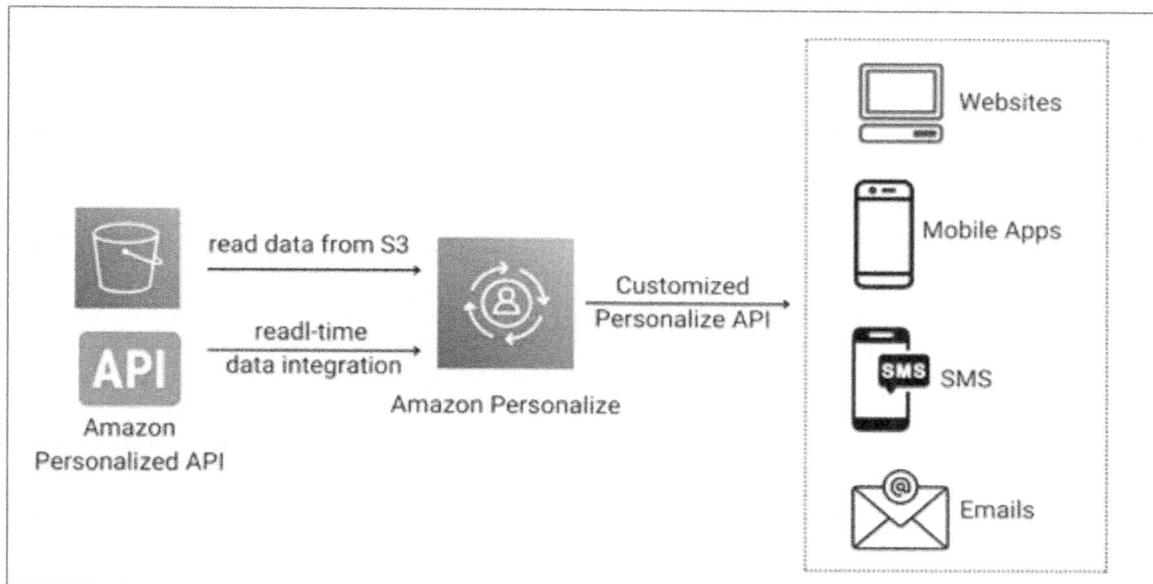

The same technology is used by Amazon.com. It can be integrated into existing websites, applications, SMS, email marketing systems.

It can be implemented in days, not months -- you don't need to build, train, and deploy ML solutions.

Amazon Personalize supports the following key use cases:
- Personalized recommendations
- Similar items
- Personalized reranking i.e. rerank a list of items for a user
- Personalized promotions/notifications
- To recommend personalized products for users based on their previous purchases

Amazon Textract

Amazon Textract service enables you to add document text detection and analysis to your applications easily. Using Amazon Textract, customers can automatically extract text and data from millions of scanned documents in just hours. It can read and process any type of document such as PDFs, images.

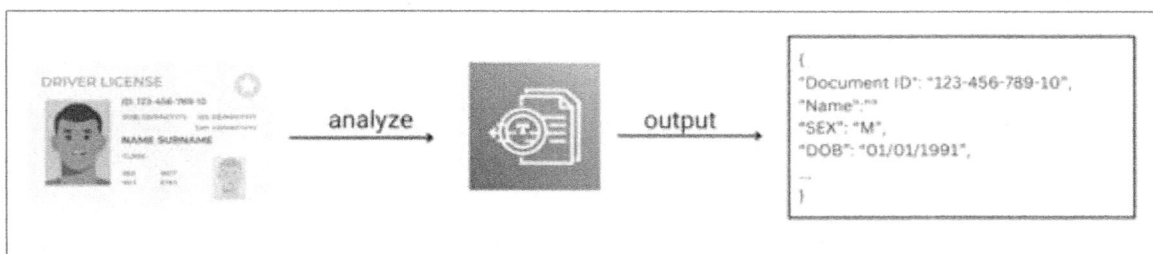

Amazon Textract has many use cases.
- Using the Amazon Textract Document Analysis API, you can extract text, forms, and tables from structured data documents.
- By using AnalyzeExpense API you can process invoices and receipts.

- By using the AnalyzeID API, you can process ID documents such as driver's licenses and passports issued by the U.S. government.

Amazon Fraud Detector

Amazon Fraud Detector is a fully managed service enabling customers to identify potentially fraudulent activities. For example, you can flag suspicious online payment transactions before processing payments and fulfilling orders.

In another example, you can detect new account fraud. You can accurately distinguish between legitimate and high-risk account registrations, so that you can selectively introduce additional checks — such as phone or email verification.

Amazon Sumerian

Amazon Sumerian is a managed service that lets you create and run 3D, Augmented Reality (AR) and Virtual Reality (VR) applications.

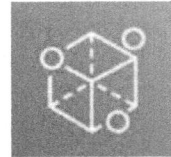

You can build immersive and interactive scenes that run on AR and VR, mobile devices, and your web browser. Whether you are non-technical, a web or mobile developer, or have years of 3D development experience, getting started with Sumerian is easy.

You can design scenes directly from your browser and, because Sumerian is a web-based application, you can quickly add connections in your scenes to existing AWS services.

Amazon Sumerian leverages the power of AWS to create smarter and more engaging front-end experiences. Easily embed conversational interfaces into scenes using Amazon Lex and embed scenes in a web application using AWS Amplify.

Amazon Sumerian embraces the latest WebGL and WebXR standards to create immersive experiences directly in a web browser, accessible via a simple URL in seconds, and able to run on major hardware platforms for AR/VR. Build your scene once and deploy it anywhere.

AWS ML Summary
- Amazon Rekognition: face detection, labeling, celebrity recognition
- Amazon Transcribe: speech to text
- Amazon Polly: text to speech
- Amazon Translate: translations
- Amazon Lex: build chatbots
- Amazon Connect: cloud contact center
- Amazon Comprehend: natural language processing (NLP)
- Amazon SageMaker: ML for developer/data scientist
- Amazon Forecast: build highly accurate forecasts
- Amazon Kendra: ML-powered search engine
- Amazon Personalize: real-time personalized recommendations
- Amazon Textract: detect text and data in documents

Section 9. Security

Chapter 30. AWS Security & Encryption

You will learn the following in this chapter:

- AWS Security & Compliance
- AWS Artifact
- What & Why Encryption?
- AWS Security Token Service (AWS STS)
- AWS KMS (Key Management Service)
- Master Key (KMS Keys) and Data Key
- Encryption in Transit (SSL)
- Server-Side Encryption
- Client-Side Encryption
- KMS Key Types
- KMS Key Policy
- Copy Snapshots Across Regions
- Copy Snapshots Across AWS Accounts
- Multi-Region KMS Keys
- S3 Replication with Encryption
- Sharing Encrypted AMI Across Accounts
- SSM Session Manager
- SSM Parameter Store
- AWS Secrets Manager
- AWS Certificate Manager (ACM)
- AWS WAF
- AWS Firewall Manager
- DDoS Attacks
- AWS Shield Standard
- AWS Shield Advanced
- Best Practices for DDoS Resiliency
- AWS Threat Detection and Monitoring
- Amazon Inspector
- Amazon Macie
- Amazon Detective

We live in a time when any enterprise application is like a castle that needs to be secured and protected. Security becomes even more crucial when the application is deployed on a cloud platform – not in your on-prem data center. In this chapter, we will discuss how the AWS cloud platform handles security and compliance at a high level.

AWS Security

AWS cloud security is much like security in an on-premises data center. It doesn't matter whether organizations have their applications on-premises or on the cloud. Security is crucial for the deployed applications.

Security, a core non-functional requirement in most enterprise systems. It deals with accidental leakage, theft, integrity compromise, or deletion of a valuable information asset.

How AWS Handles Security

Highly Secured Data Centers

To maintain trust and confidence in their customers, AWS has implemented comprehensive security mechanisms or safeguards to keep customers' data safe. All data are stored in highly secured AWS data centers.

To continue on how AWS approaches security to provide peace of mind to its customers. AWS has built its data centers and network architecture in such a way to meet the requirements of the most security-sensitive organizations. What it means is that organizations can get their security requirements with much lower operational costs. Organizations would also inherit best practices of AWS policies, architecture, and operational processes already built into the AWS core security infrastructure. That way, AWS satisfies the demand of most security-sensitive organizations.

Shared Security Model

AWS Infrastructure is designed from the cloud architectural perspective -- with the security best practices in mind. AWS shares security responsibilities with the organizations where AWS takes care of the security of the underlying infrastructure while organizations must take care of the applications' security.

Layered Security

AWS uses a layered approach to security. It makes sure that underlying systems are monitored from potential threats and protected round the clock. AWS environments are continuously audited, with certifications from accreditation bodies across geographies and verticals.

AWS Compliance

Another essential foundational concept to understand is how AWS approaches compliance. AWS helps organizations when it comes to compliance with applications deployed on its platform. Compliance requirements vary country or region-wise. When applications are deployed on AWS, organizations have complete control and ownership of their applications in that region to set up their secure, governance-focused applications. Additionally, they apply compliance and audit features.

Assurance Programs

The following is a partial list of assurance programs with which AWS complies. It complies with SOC1, SOC2, and SOC 3. It complies with Federal Information Security Management Act (FISMA),

Department of Defense Information Assurance Certification, Accreditation Process (DIACAP), and Federal Risk and Authorization Management Program (FedRAMP). It also complies with Payment Card Industry Data Security Standard (PCI DSS) Level 1. Finally, it complies with various ISO such as ISO 9001, 27001.

AWS Security Benefits

What benefits do AWS security, Identity, and Compliance related services provide to enterprise applications deployed on its platform?

Data Protection

The AWS infrastructure provides strong safeguards in place to help protect your privacy. All data are stored in highly secure AWS data centers. Furthermore, AWS also provides services that help protect your data, accounts, and workloads from unauthorized access. AWS has different data protection-related services that provide encryption and key management. In addition, AWS also provides threat detection-related services to continuously monitor and protect your accounts and workloads from unauthorized access.

The following services help in data protection:

AWS Service	Use Cases
Amazon Macie	Discover and protect your sensitive data at scale
AWS Key Management Service (KMS)	Key storage and management
AWS CloudHSM	Hardware based key storage for regulatory compliance
AWS Certificate Manager	Provision, manage, and deploy public and private SSL/TLS certificates
AWS Secrets Manager	Rotate, manage, and retrieve secrets

Threat detection & continuous monitoring

AWS continuously monitors the network activity and account behavior for any abnormality within your cloud environment and identifies threats.

The following services help in threat detection & continuous monitoring:

AWS Service	Use Cases
AWS Security Hub	Automate AWS security checks and centralize security alerts
Amazon GuardDuty	Protect AWS accounts with intelligent threat detection
Amazon Inspector	Automate vulnerability management
AWS Config	Record and evaluate configurations of your AWS resources
AWS CloudTrail	Track user activity and API usage
AWS IoT Device Defender	Security management for IoT devices
Amazon Detective	Investigate potential security issues
AWS Elastic Disaster Recovery	Scalable, cost-effective application recovery to AWS

Identity & Access Management

AWS Identity Services enable you to securely manage identities, resources, and permissions at scale.

The following services help in identity & access management:

AWS Service	Use Cases
AWS Identity & Access Management (IAM)	Securely manage access to services and resources
AWS Single Sign-On	Cloud single-sign-on (SSO) service
Amazon Cognito	Identity management for your apps
AWS Directory Service	Managed Microsoft Active Directory
AWS Resource Access Manager	Simple, secure service to share AWS resources
AWS Organizations	Central governance and management across AWS accounts

Compliance & data privacy

AWS manages dozens of compliance programs in its infrastructure. AWS provides a comprehensive view of your AWS IT environment with regard to compliance status. It does this by continuously monitoring your environment using automated compliance checks based on the AWS best practices and industry standards.

The following services help in compliance & data privacy:

AWS Service	Use Cases
AWS Artifact	No cost, self-service portal for on-demand access to AWS' compliance reports
AWS Audit Manager	Continuously audit your AWS usage to simplify how you assess risk and compliance

Network & Application Protection

Network and application protection services help you to manage fine-grained security policy at different network boundaries across your AWS IT environment. For example, AWS services help you inspect and filter traffic to prevent unauthorized resource access at the host, network, and application boundaries.

AWS Service	Use Cases
AWS Network Firewall	Network security
AWS Shield	DDoS protection
Amazon Route 53 Resolver DNS Firewall	Filter and control outbound DNS traffic for your VPCs
AWS Web Application Firewall (WAF)	Filter malicious web traffic
AWS Firewall Manager	Central management of firewall rules

Saves Cost

Customers save in cost as they would not have to manage on-premises security. The region is the security would be addressed in AWS data centers.

Scale Quickly

Security scales based on the AWS cloud usage. No matter the size of your business, the AWS infrastructure is designed to keep your data safe.

AWS Artifact

AWS Artifact is a central place for compliance-related information that matters to you. It provides on-demand access to AWS' security and compliance reports and select online agreements. AWS Artifact is a portal using which an enterprise can access security and compliance reports related to the AWS public cloud.

The following reports are available in AWS Artifact: SOC (Service Organization Control) reports, PCI (Payment Card Industry) reports, and certifications from accreditation bodies across geographies and compliance verticals that validate the implementation and operating effectiveness of AWS security controls. Agreements available in AWS Artifact include the Business Associate Addendum (BAA) and the Nondisclosure Agreement (NDA).

These reports can also guide team members, such as developers, to ensure that they adhere to these standards. Additionally, a user can download reports and other internal AWS documents via Artifact to ensure and demonstrate to auditors or regulators that the AWS offerings meet security and compliance standards.

Benefits

COMPREHENSIVE RESOURCE

Access all of AWS' auditor issued reports, certifications, accreditations and other third-party attestations.

AGREEMENT GOVERNANCE

Review, accept, and manage your agreements with AWS. Apply your AWS agreements to all current and future accounts within your organization.

DEEP INSIGHTS

Perform due-diligence of AWS with enhanced transparency into our security control environment. Continuously monitor the security and compliance of AWS with immediate access to new reports.

AWS Artifact Reports

AWS Artifact Reports provides several compliance reports from third-party auditors who have tested and verified our compliance with a variety of global, regional, and industry specific security standards and regulations. When new reports are released, they are made available in AWS Artifact. For more information, go to the Compliance Reports FAQ page.

Screenshot Ref: https://aws.amazon.com/artifact/

What & Why Encryption?

Encryption is simply the process of encoding data **so only those with authorized access can read it**. In encryption, the information is "scrambled" so an unintended person cannot read it.

In other words, encryption involves transforming/scrambling data with a key into a format such that only the intended persons with a decryption key, also called a secret key, can read it.

Encrypting information is critical to secure confidential information during storage (at rest) or when transferred (in transit) from one computer system to another.

Encryption is essential as it enables privacy and security. Encryption is critical not only for an individual's privacy and security but also for cybersecurity. It protects national security.

Before encryption, the information is referred to as **plaintext**; after encryption, the information is termed **ciphertext**.

Where to Encrypt Data?

Now that we know what encryption is and why it is essential, we can encrypt data in three places.

In Transit -- This is about encrypting data while data is moving to different locations, for example, from server to server.

At Rest -- This is about storing the data on storage devices in encrypted form.

In Use -- This new approach ensures sensitive data is never left unsecured, regardless of the lifecycle stage. (Reference: https://www.soterosoft.com/blog/data-in-use-encryption-data-in-motion-encryption/)

AWS Encryption SDK

The AWS Encryption SDK is a client-side encryption library that you can use to encrypt and decrypt data using industry standards and best practices. AWS Encryption SDK is provided of charge by AWS under the Apache 2.0 license.

AWS Security Token Service (AWS STS)

AWS Security Token Service (STS) generates temporary security credentials. It is a web service that allows you to request temporary, limited-privilege credentials for AWS Identity and Access Management (IAM) users or federated users (users outside of AWS). AWS STS is a global service, and all AWS STS requests go to a single endpoint at https://sts.amazonaws.com. You can only access it programmatically.

An STS will return AccessKeyID, SecretAccessKey, SessionToken, Expiration, and AssumeRoleUser.

You can use this service to create and provide temporary security credentials to trusted users so that they can get access to AWS resources. Suppose you have a user that doesn't have access to upload a document in a particular S3 bucket. Then, using the concept of AssumeRole, you can generate temporary AccessKeyID and SecretAccessKey by the STS service. Using this temporary SecretAccessID, SecretAccessKey can upload the document in the S3 bucket. Since STS credentials are temporary, it expires based on the expiration time.

Temporary security credentials are short-term credentials, as the name implies. They can be configured to last for a few minutes to several hours. After that, AWS no longer recognizes the credentials or allows access from API requests after the credentials expire.

AWS KMS (Key Management Service)

- AWS Key Management Service (KMS) enables an easy way to control access to your data. It gives you centralized control over the cryptographic keys used to protect your data.

- You create KMS keys in AWS KMS.

- It can also generate data keys that you can use outside AWS KMS.

- An AWS KMS key is a logical representation of a cryptographic key. It contains metadata, such as the key ID, key spec, key usage, creation date, description, and key state. More importantly, it references the key material used in cryptographic operations with the KMS key. By default, AWS KMS creates the key material for a KMS key. You cannot extract, export, view, or manage this key material.
(Ref: https://docs.aws.amazon.com/kms/latest/developerguide/concepts.html

- It is fully integrated with IAM and other AWS services (EBS, S3, RDS, SSM...), making it easy to encrypt data you store in these services and control access to the keys that decrypt it.

- KMS Key encryption/decryption is also available through API calls (SDK, CLI).

- You can audit KMS key usage using CloudTrail.

- You should never store your secrets in plaintext, particularly in your code!

Master Key (KMS Keys) and Data Key

You will encounter both of these terms in encryption on AWS quite often. So let's understand these two keys as it relates to KMS.

A master key, also called a Customer Master Key (CMK), needs to be created to generate a data key. The CMK is used to generate a data key.

KMS Keys is the new name for Customer Master Key (CMK).

The data key is used to encrypt a file. The encrypted data key is stored along with the encrypted file. The data key is decrypted first, and then the decrypted data is used to decrypt the file. This process of encrypting with a data key and then encrypting it and storing it with the encrypted object is called envelope encryption.

Generating a data key returns a symmetric data key that can be used outside of AWS KMS. The operation returns a data key and an encrypted data key under a symmetric encryption KMS key that you specify.
(Ref: https://docs.aws.amazon.com/kms/latest/APIReference/API_GenerateDataKey.html)

The generated data keys are free -- except for API calls. However, AWS KMS keys are not free ($1/month, prorated hourly).

Encryption in Transit (SSL)

One of the places where we need to encrypt data to ensure protection and privacy is when data is in transit. To maintain the security and privacy of information, data is encrypted during transit and decrypted after receiving. SSL certificate helps encrypt/decrypt information.

Encryption in flight ensures that information is secured and protected from source to target – no MITM (man-in-the-middle attack).

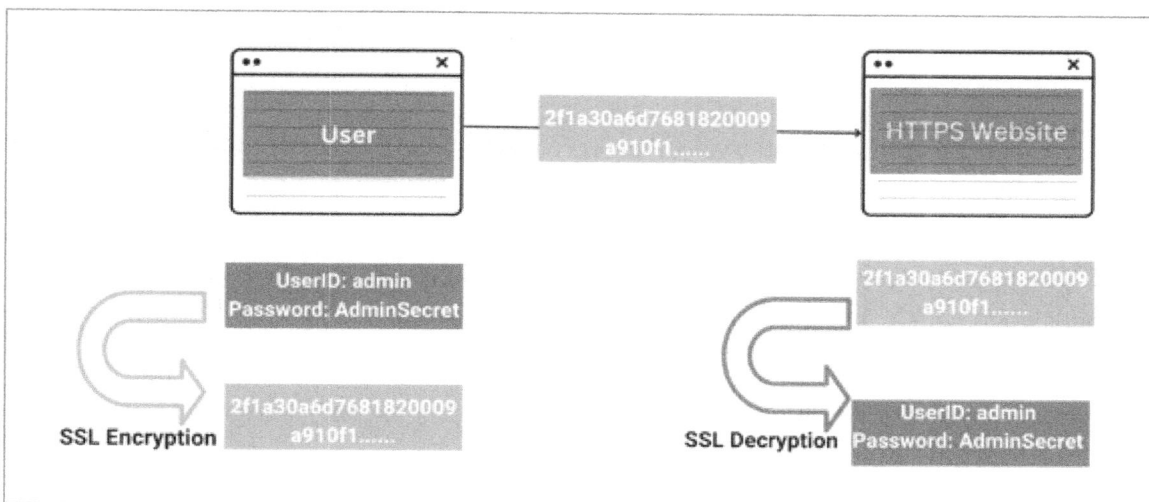

Let's try to understand the basics with this diagram. An admin user logs into a website (https://...) that is SSL enabled. Since the website uses SSL, the user enters UserID and the Password is encrypted when it leaves the user's computer. When the information reaches the website, it is decrypted, and the user can log in.

Here, the website provides its public key to anyone -- who would like to communicate with the website – to encrypt the information before sending it to the website.   And the website decrypts the received encrypted information using its private key, which only the website knows. This is the basic concept in SSL communication using public/private keys.

Server-Side Encryption

In server-side encryption (encryption at rest), the server encrypts data after receiving it. The data can be stored in permanent storage. The server decrypts the data before sending it to the client.

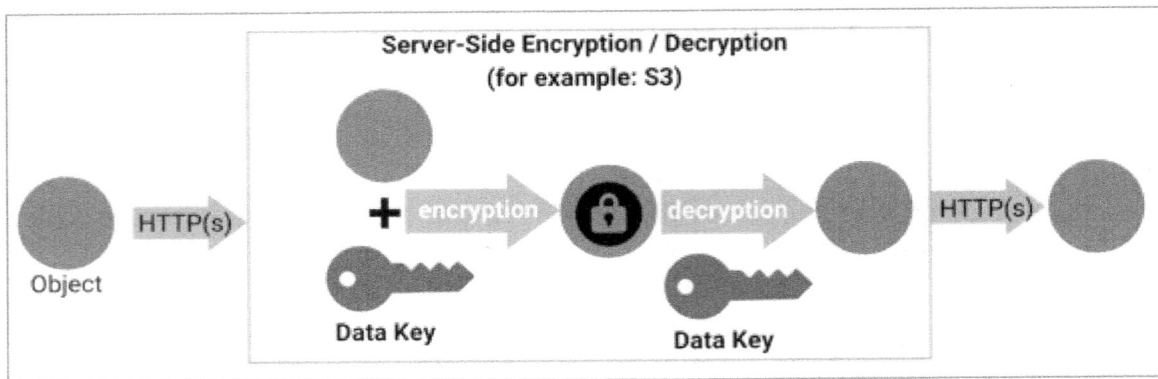

Server-Side Encryption / Decryption (for example: S3)

This is called server-side encryption, as the server holds the key, and encryption/decryption is performed at the server end.

Server-side encryption encrypts data at rest. For example, when encryption is enabled, Amazon S3 encrypts an S3 object with a key and decrypts it when clients access it. In another example, on the same token, when data is stored on an encrypted EBS volume, it is encrypted with a key before storing it in EBS and is decrypted before sending it to a client.

Server-side encryption: encryption/decryption is done by the server/backend application/service using a key -> used for encrypting data at rest.

Client-Side Encryption

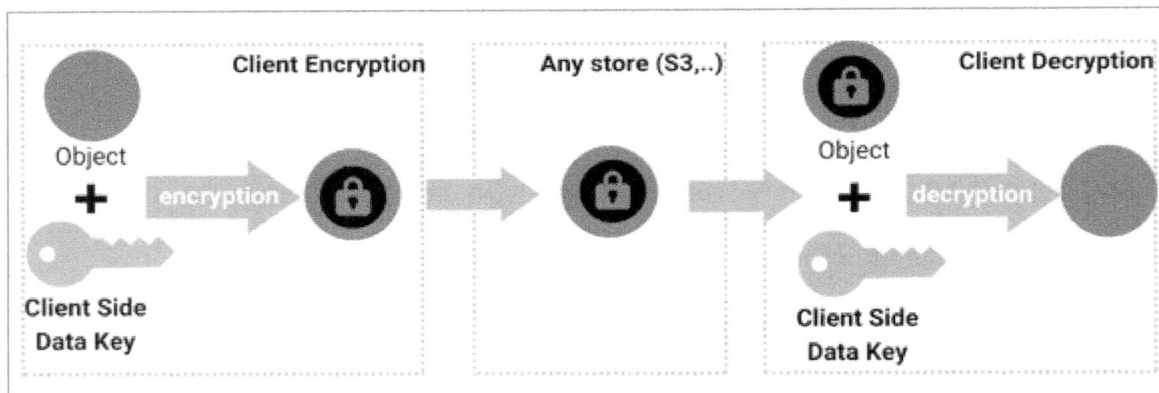

In Client-side encryption, the client encrypts data locally, ensuring its security as AWS receives data. The Amazon service receives your encrypted data but does not get involved in encrypting or decrypting it. Instead, the client decrypts data when receiving it.

By remaining encrypted through each intermediary server, client-side encryption ensures that data retains privacy from the origin to the destination server. This prevents data loss and unauthorized disclosure of any type, providing increased peace of mind for its users.

Reference: https://www.freecodecamp.org/news/envelope-encryption/

KMS Key Types

Symmetric (AES-256 keys)
- Typically, you will use symmetric KMS Keys. They use the AES-256 symmetric key algorithm.
- Since this is a symmetric key, in symmetric key encryption, the same key is used for decryption as well.
- AWS services that are integrated with KMS use Symmetric KMS Keys.
- You can never get access to KMS Keys unencrypted. -- must use KMS API to use KMS Keys.

Asymmetric (RSA & ECC key pairs)
- It is based on public/private key cryptography.
- It is used for encryption/decryption or sign/verify operations.
- You can download the public key, but you can't access the private key unencrypted.
- They are used out of AWS by users who can't access the KMS API.

HMAC KMS keys
An HMAC KMS key, which is a symmetric key of varying length, is used to generate and verify hash-based message authentication codes (HMAC).

Customer keys and AWS keys

There are three types of KMS Keys: Customer Managed Keys, AWS Managed Keys, and AWS Owned Keys.

AWS Managed Keys
AWS services that use KMS keys to encrypt your service resources often create keys for you. KMS keys that AWS services create in your AWS account are AWS-managed keys. Therefore, they are free (free (aws/service-name, example: aws/rds or aws/ebs).

AWS Managed keys are rotated automatically every year.

AWS managed keys (7)			
Aliases	Key ID		Status
aws/cloud9	171a7797-2283-4d5a-a035-d1ca0cbc235d		Enabled
aws/sqs	4e2f13ae-9b5a-4fbc-ba65-a9c63fa6c2cf		Enabled
aws/ebs	7c4b0722-7301-4b0e-8651-e5297216cc69		Enabled
aws/rds	ced5a071-a00c-4b57-a7db-9d2aaa485366		Enabled
aws/lightsail	dcada3b5-78b8-48ce-8f66-7d92298c9e74		Enabled
aws/acm	e886468b-17b5-400c-a170-7d10463a6117		Enabled
aws/fsx	ec62d13d-8da9-43aa-b7f7-703e7374f024		Enabled

Customer-Managed Keys

The KMS keys that you create are customer-managed. They are charged $1/month. Customer Managed Keys that are imported must be a 256-bit symmetric key. They are also charged at the rate of $1/month.

Aliases		Key ID		Status	Key spec ⓘ	Key usage
	▽	5c99ea22-ac14-4dbd-b5da-26f6d422c64e	▽	Pending deletion	SYMMETRIC_DEFAULT	Encrypt and decrypt
Test-RSA2048		912cb158-4911-4816-8520-56278ba0c0d7		Enabled	RSA_2048	Encrypt and decrypt
Test-HMAC		644e1074-ee33-4347-a856-f3a400c4a1e3		Enabled	HMAC_224	Generate and verify MAC

KMS > Customer managed keys

Customer managed keys (3)

Key actions ▼   Create key

You can create both Symmetric and Asymmetric customer-managed keys with single-region key and multi-region key options.

Customer Managed keys are rotated automatically every year -- rotation must be enabled.
For imported Customer Managed keys, you need to rotate them manually using an alias.

AWS CloudHSM / Custom Key Store
You also have the option to store your keys in a custom key store instead of a standard KMS key store. Custom key stores are created using the AWS CloudHSM cluster you own and manage.

AWS CloudHSM, a cloud-based hardware security module (HSM), enables you to generate, use, and manage cryptographic keys, including storing them securely. AWS CloudHSM words as custom key store -- keys are accessible only by you. The service uses dedicated Hardware Security Module (HSM) instances in the AWS cloud. The service can also help you meet data security requirements related to corporate, contractual, and regulatory compliance.

KMS Key Policy

```
{
    "Sid":"Allow use of the key",
    "Effect":"Allow",
        "Principal":{
            "AWS":"arn:aws:iam::ACCOUNT-ID/user"
        },
        "Action":[
            "kms:Encrypt",
            "kms:Decrypt"
        ],
        "Resource":"*"
}
```

- KMS Policies are used to control access to KMS keys. A key policy is a resource policy for an AWS KMS key. The concept is similar to S3 bucket policies.
- You can create and manage key policies in the AWS KMS console by using AWS KMS API operations, such as CreateKey, ReplicateKey, and PutKeyPolicy, or by using an AWS CloudFormation template.

Default KMS Key Policy:
- It is created by default if you don't provide a specific KMS Key Policy. The default KMS Key policy provides the root user complete access to KMS keys.
- The default key policy allows you to choose IAM users and roles and external AWS accounts and make them key users.

Custom Key Policy:
- Besides the default KMS Key policy, you can also use a custom key policy.
- You can define users and roles that can access the KMS key. For example, you can define who can administer the key.
- it is useful for cross-account access of your KMS key.

Copy Snapshots Across Regions

Let's take a use case of copying snapshots across AWS Regions to understand encryption/decryption using a KMS key.

For example, in the example, we are copying a snapshot from AWS Region us-east-1 to AWS Region us-west-2.

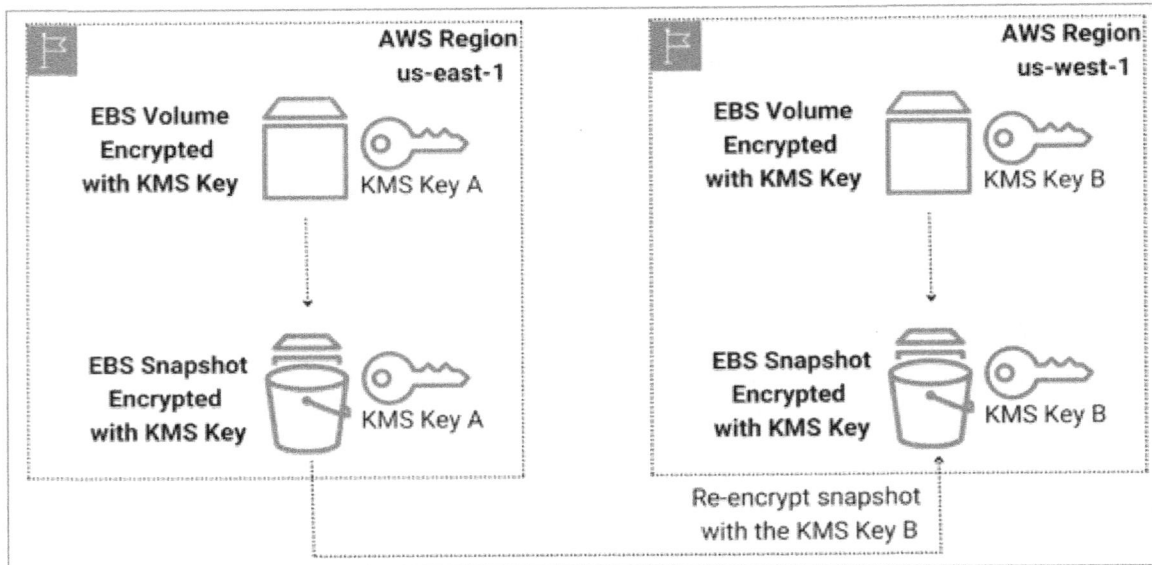

First, we create a snapshot in the us-east-1 region, encrypted with the same KMS key by which the EBS volume is encrypted.

Next, when we copy the snapshot to the us-west-1 region since keys are region scoped, we need to re-encrypt the snapshot with the KMS key B from the us-west-1 region.

When we copy an encrypted snapshot, the copy of the snapshot must also be encrypted. If we copy an encrypted snapshot across regions, we can't use the same AWS KMS key for the copy used for the source snapshot because AWS KMS keys are Region-specific. Instead, we must specify a valid AWS KMS key in the destination AWS Region. The source snapshot remains encrypted throughout the copy process.

Then in the us-west-1 region, when we create volume from the snapshot, it will be encrypted by KMS key B.

Copy Snapshots Across AWS Accounts

Let's take another use case of copying snapshots across AWS accounts to understand encryption/decryption using a KMS key and KMS key policy more practically.

- Create a snapshot encrypted with your own KMS Key.
- Attach a KMS Key Policy to authorize cross-account access.
- In the target account, create a copy of the snapshot, and encrypt it with a KMS key from your account.
- Create a volume from the snapshot.

```
{
    "Sid":"Allow use of the key with a destination account",
    "Effect":"Allow",
        "Principal":{
            "AWS": "arn:aws:iam::TARGET-ACCOUNT-ID:role/ROLENAME"
        },
        "Action":[
            "kms:Encrypt",
            "kms:CreateGrant"
        ],
        "Resource":"*"
        "Condition": {
            "StringEquals": {
                "kms:ViaService":"ec2.REGION.amazonaws.com",
                "kms:CallerAccount":"TARGET-ACCOUNT-ID"
            }
        }
}
```

Multi-Region KMS Keys

- AWS KMS multi-Region keys let you replicate a KMS key in different AWS Regions that can be used interchangeably.

- Since we now with multi-Region keys, we can have the exact same key replicated in multiple AWS Regions, and we can more easily move encrypted data between Regions -- no need to decrypt and re-encrypt with different keys in each Region. The replicated keys get the same key ID, key material, and automatic rotation.

- Multi-Region keys are NOT global -- you have primary and replica keys.

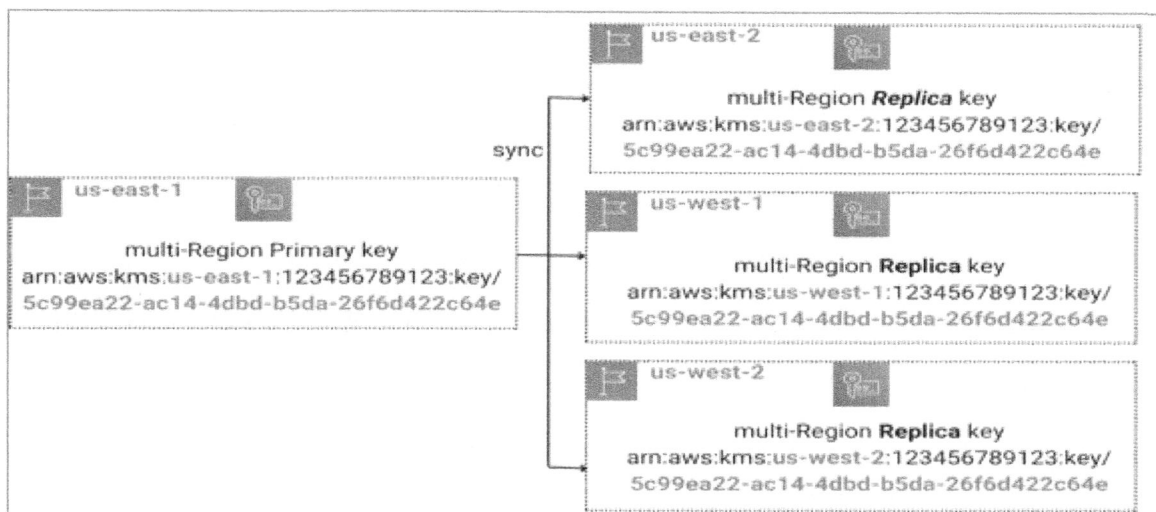

- Each Multi-Region key is managed independently.

- Multi-Region keys are supported for client-side encryption in the AWS Encryption SDK, AWS S3 Encryption Client, and AWS DynamoDB Encryption Client.

- **Use cases:** multi-Region KMS keys can be used in use cases such as taking backups for disaster recovery, DynamoDB global tables, or for digital signature applications that require the same signing key to be available in multiple Regions.

S3 Replication with Encryption

- In S3, there is default replication for unencrypted objects or any object encrypted with SSE-S3.
- Objects that are encrypted with SSE-C (customer-provided key) are never replicated.
- For objects encrypted with SSE-KMS, you need to enable it.

Sharing Encrypted AMI Across Accounts

You have a use case where you need to share your AMI, encrypted with a KMS key, with another account.

For another account to share your AMI, you will need to share the KMS key, which was used to encrypt the snapshot with the target account / IAM Role. In addition, the IAM Role / User in the target account must have the permissions to DescribeKey, ReEncrypted, GreateGrant, and Decrypt.

The other account can launch the AMI. Or, they can copy the snapshot while re-encrypting it with their own key. Then, the other account can register it as a new AMI as they own the copied snapshot.

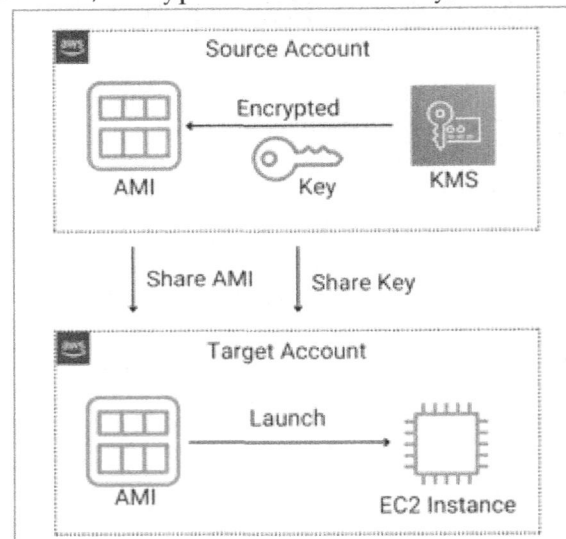

AWS Systems Manager

AWS Systems Manager is a set of fully managed services and capabilities that simplify the management of your Windows and Linux instances regardless of whether they are running on EC2 or on-premises.

AWS Systems Manager allows performing tasks such as collecting system inventory, applying operating system patches, automation of creating Amazon Machine Images (AMIs), and configuring operating systems and applications at scale.

This helps accelerate the cloud journey by addressing the shortcomings of the traditional system management approach. It provides a flexible and easy-to-use automation-focused approach for both traditional and cloud-based workloads.

The benefits of AWS Systems Manager

- It provides a consistent experience and set of tools to manage both cloud-based and on-premises workloads to configure and manage your infrastructure irrespective of where your infrastructure resides.
- The same tool is used for both AWS and on-premises, windows, or Linux platforms.
- It is scalable
- You get integration with AWS services; for example, AWS Systems Manager is integrated with AWS CloudTrail, and AWS CloudWatch.
- AWS Systems Manager comes with no additional charge.

Reference:
https://aws.amazon.com/systems-manager/faq/

SSM Session Manager

AWS SSM Session Manager is a fully-managed service that provides an interactive browser-based shell and CLI experience. It helps provide secure and auditable instance management without opening inbound ports, maintaining bastion hosts, and managing SSH keys. Session Manager helps to enable compliance with corporate policies that require controlled access to instances and increase security and suitability of access to the cases while providing simplicity and cross-platform instance access to end-users.

Reference:
https://docs.aws.amazon.com/systems-manager/latest/userguide/session-manager.html

SSM Parameter Store

- AWS Systems Manager Parameter Store (SSM) provides an easy and secure way to store config variables (configurations/secrets) for your applications --secure storage for configuration and secrets. SSM can store plaintext parameters or KMS-encrypted secure strings.

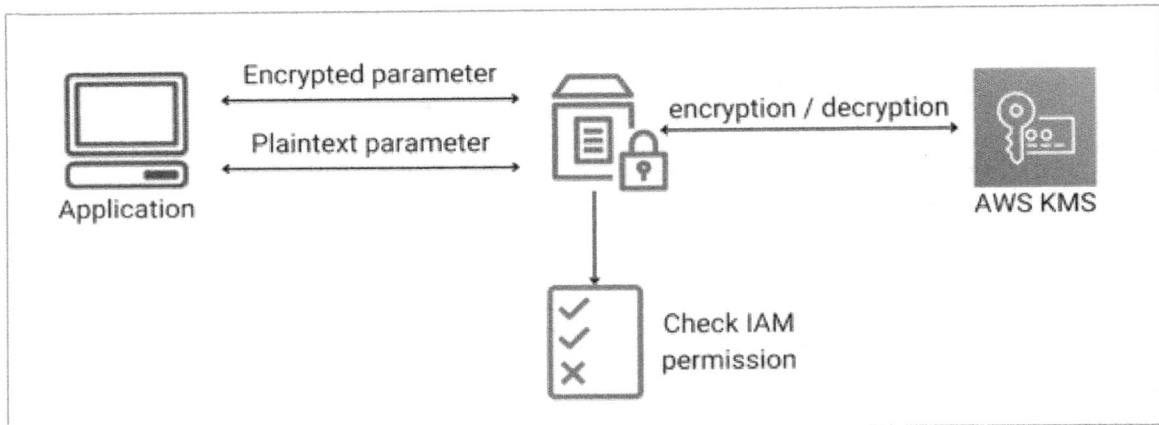

- Since parameters in the SSM parameter store can be identified by ARNs, you can set up fine-grain access control on them with IAM.

- It is serverless, scalable, and easily accessed from SDK, CLI, or AWS console.

For example:

```
aws ssm put-paramater --name "DB_NAME" --value "myDb"
```

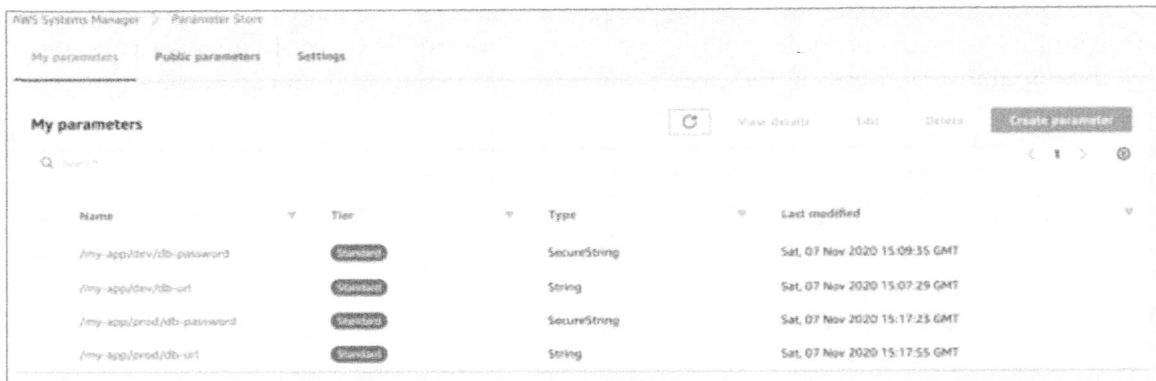

- You can also do version tracking of parameters.

- You can set up notifications with CloudWatch events.

Use Cases:

You can use SSM Parameter Store for storing configuration for Docker containers, secrets for Lambda functions, and parameters for your custom applications, such as ETL data pipelines that you developed to run on the AWS cloud. You can also use SSM Parameters in CloudFormation.

SSM Parameter Store Hierarchy

Parameter Store has hierarchy support. The hierarchical feature of Parameter Store lets you organize parameters based on your deployments, such as Dev, Test, and Prod. It provides powerful tools for parameter organization, querying, and permission control.

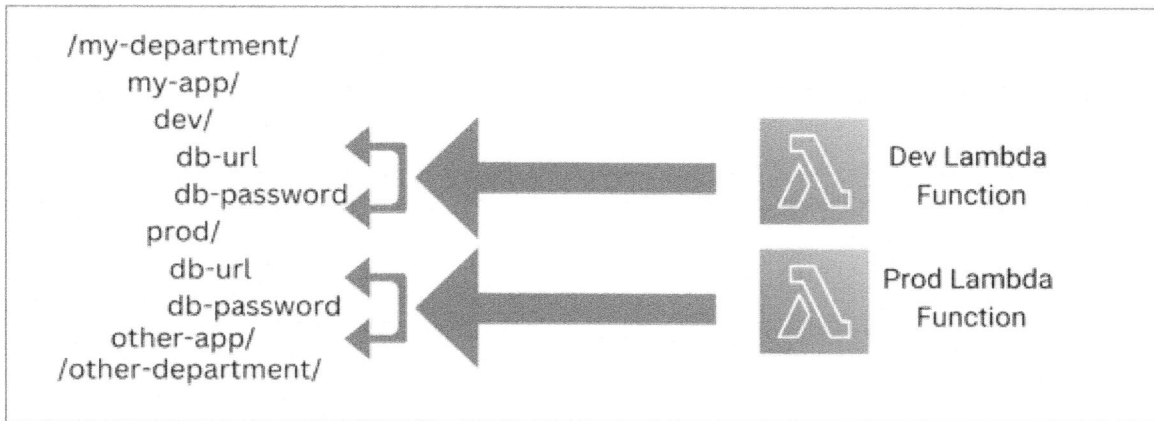

```
/my-department/
    my-app/
        dev/
            db-url
            db-password
        prod/
            db-url
            db-password
        other-app/
/other-department/
```

As you can notice in the diagram above shows how parameters are stored in a hierarchical fashion for Dev and Prod environments. The Lambda functions for Dev and Prod environments can retrieve the db-url, db-password from the Parameter Store easily as they are organized in a hierarchy.

When you create a deployment configuration, particularly in DevOps, you can use Parameter Store to save your settings and use them with different values for each environment, e.g., Dev, Test, and Prod.

SSM Standard and Advanced Parameter tiers

The SSM Parameter Store includes standard (the default tier) parameters and advanced parameters.

You can change parameters from standard to advanced at any time, but you can't change an advanced parameter to a standard parameter. The reasons we can't revert from advanced to standard:

- It would cause the system to truncate the parameter size (8 KB to 4 KB), resulting in data loss.
- Reverting also removes any policies attached to the parameter.
- Advanced parameters use a different form of encryption.

The following table describes the differences between the tiers.

	Standard	Advanced
Total number of parameters allowed (per AWS account and AWS Region)	10,000	100,000
Maximum size of a parameter value	4 KB	8 KB
Parameter policies available	No	Yes For more information, see Assigning parameter policies.
Cost	No additional charge	Charges apply For more information, see AWS Systems Manager Pricing ⃗.

Screenshot ref: https://docs.aws.amazon.com/systems-manager/latest/userguide/parameter-store-advanced-parameters.html

Parameters Policies for Advanced Parameters

- It allows assigning a TTL to a parameter (expiration date) to force updating or deleting sensitive data such as passwords.
- We can assign multiple policies at a time.

Expiration (to delete parameters)

```
{
  "Type": "Expiration",
  "Version": "1.0",
  "Attributes": {
    "Timestamp": "2022-11-23T11:3124.12.001"
  }
}
```

Expiration Notification (CW Events)

```
{
  "Type": "ExpirationNotification",
  "Version": "1.0",
  "Attributes": {
    "Before": "10",
    "Days": "Days"
  }
}
```

AWS Secrets Manager

- AWS Secrets Manager service enables you to store secrets.
- It also adds the capability to force secret rotation every X days.
- Secrets are encrypted using KMS.
- You can automate the generation of secrets on rotation (uses Lambda)
- The service helps you easily rotate, manage, and retrieve database credentials, API keys, and other secrets throughout their lifecycle.
- Users and applications retrieve secrets with a call to Secrets Manager APIs. This call eliminates the need to hardcode sensitive information in plain text.
- It has built-in integration for Amazon RDS, MySQL, PostgreSQL, Aurora Redshift, and Amazon DocumentDB.
- It is mostly meant for RDS integration.

AWS Certificate Manager (ACM)

- AWS Certificate Manager enables you easily provision, manage, and deploy SSL/ TLS Certificates.
- It provides in-flight encryption for websites (HTTPS).
- It supports both public and private SSL/TLS certificates.

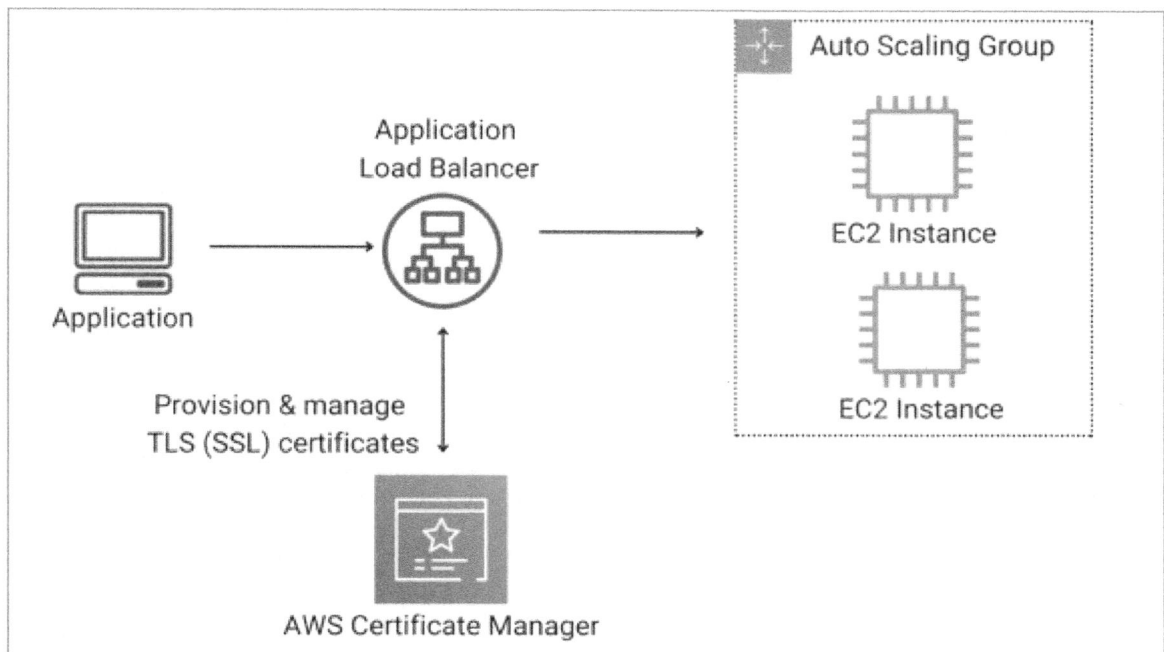

- You can provision and manage SSL/TLS certificates with AWS services and connected resources.
- There is no cost to using ACM with its integrated services. For example, ACM has integrations with Elastic Load Balancers (CLB, ALB, NLB), CloudFront Distributions, and APIs on API Gateway.
- ACM public certificates are free when used exclusively on AWS infrastructure.
- It simplifies the process of obtaining certificates. It performs Automatic SSL/TLS certificate renewal.

Use Cases:
- Protect and secure your website by provisioning and managing SSL/TLS certificates
- Protect your internal resources by enabling secure communication between connected resources on private networks
- Improve uptime through automatic certificate renewals and automated certificate management.

Requesting Public Certificate

1. Provide domain names to be included in the certificate:
   - You can provide a fully qualified domain Name (FQDN): corp.example.com.
   - Or wildcard domain: *.example.com
2. Select the Validation method: DNS validation(recommended) or Email validation.
   - DNS Validation is preferred for automation purposes.
   - DNS Validation will leverage a CNAME record to DNS config (ex: Route 53)
   - Email validation will send emails to contact addresses in the WHOIS database.
3. Verification takes a few hours.

4. The certificate will be enrolled for automatic renewal - ACM automatically renews ACM-generated certificates 60 days before expiry.

Importing Public Certificate

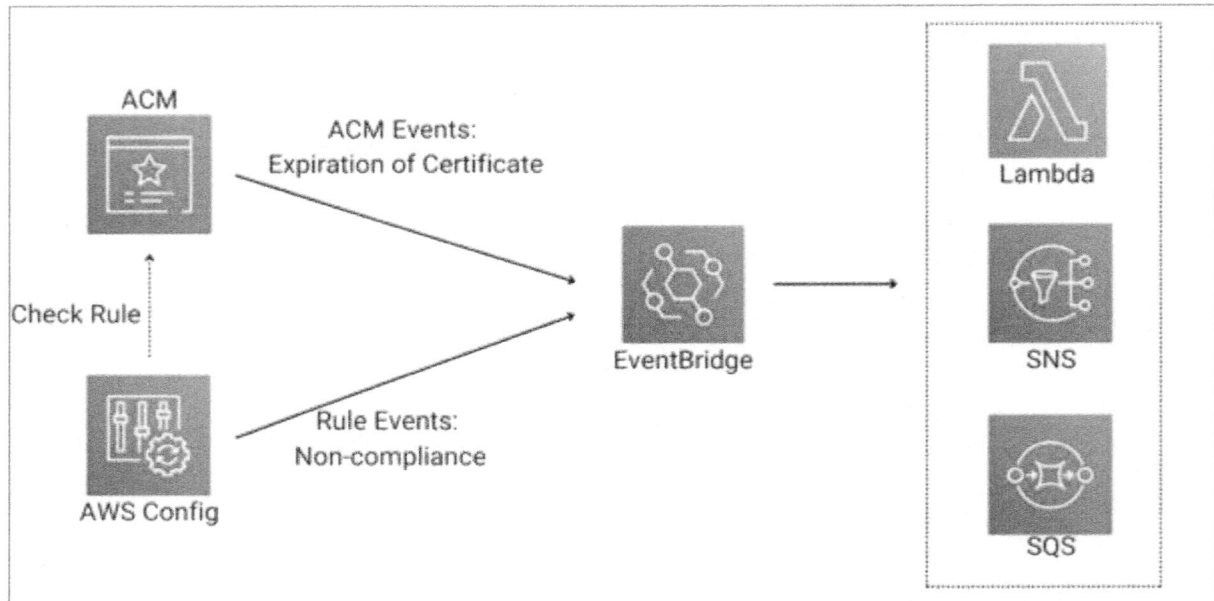

- You can generate the certificate outside of ACM and then import it. However, you will not get an automatic renewal. You must import a new certificate before expiry. Certificates provided by ACM are automatically renewed. ACM does not automatically renew the certificates that you import.

- ACM sends daily expiration events starting 45 days before expiration for all active certificates (public, private, and imported)

- The number of days can be configured by using the PutAccountConfiguration action of the ACM API. Customers can listen to this event to alert them if an ACM-issued public or private certificate in their account expires.

- AWS Config has a managed rule named ACM-certificate-expiration-check to check for expiring certificates – the number of days is configurable. The event can be sent to EventBridge to manage the renewal of the certificate.

- You can integrate ACM with EventBridge. with EventBridge, you can use events to trigger targets, including AWS Lambda functions, Amazon SNS topics, and Amazon SQS to manage certificate renewal.

Integration with ALB

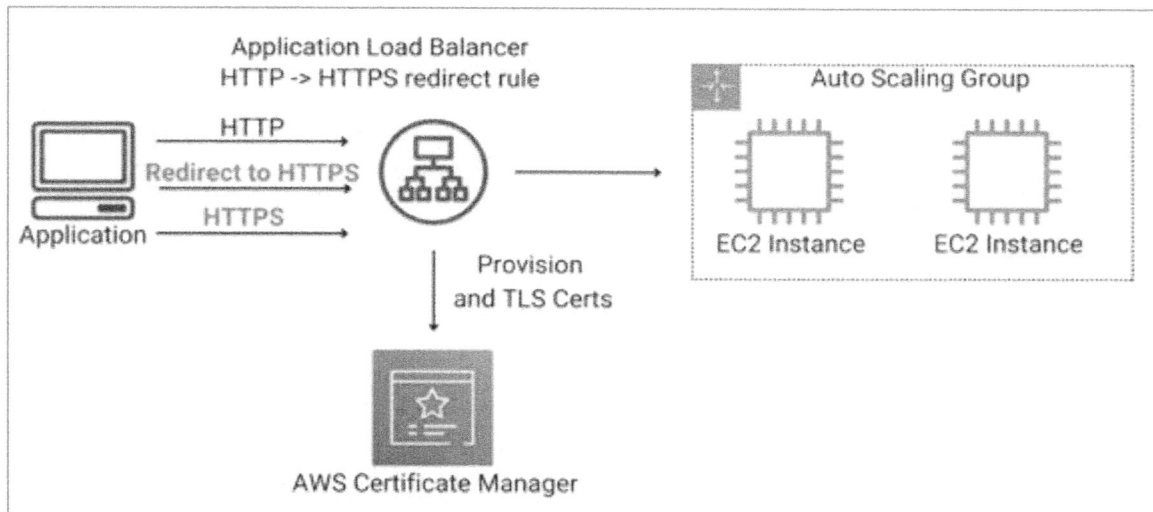

ACM is integrated with Elastic Load Balancing (ELB). You can request a public certificate using ACM or import a certificate from outside into ACM. After you have created a public certificate or imported your certificate, you can associate the certificate with CLB, NLB, or ALB (Classic, Network, or Application Load Balancer).

Integration with API Gateway

API Gateway - Endpoint Types

Edge-Optimized (default): (Uses for global clients)
- In this Endpoint type, requests are routed through the CloudFront Edge locations, improving latency. The API Gateway still lives in **only one region**.

Regional:
- This Endpoint type is used for clients within the same region. It could manually be combined with CloudFront for more control over the caching strategies and the distribution.

Private:
- This type of Endpoint can only be accessed from your VPC using an interface VPC endpoint (ENI). You need to use a resource policy to define access.

Now we got the idea of different types of API Gateway Endpoint types. In order to integrate ACM with API Gateway, you will need to create a Custom Domain Name in API Gateway.

Integrating Edge-Optimized (default) Endpoint Type API Gateway with ACM (for Global clients)

Requests are routed through the CloudFront Edge locations, improving latency.

The API Gateway still lives in only one region. The SSL/TLS Certificate must be in the same region as CloudFront.

Setup CNAME / or(better) an Alias record in Route53.

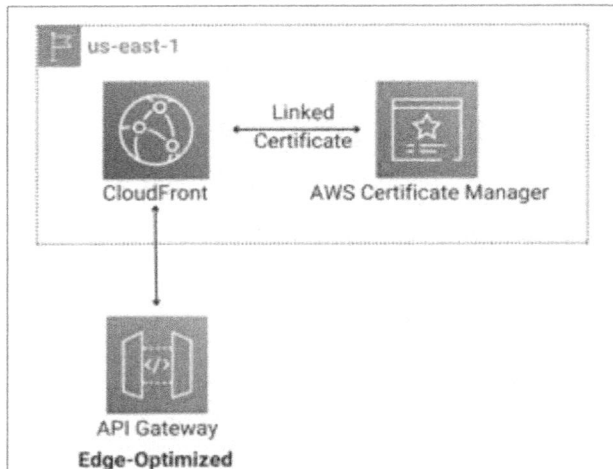

Integrating Regional Endpoint Type API Gateway with ACM (for clients within the same region)

The TLS Certificate must be imported into API Gateway in the same region as the API Gateway.

Setup CNAME / or an Alias record in Route53.

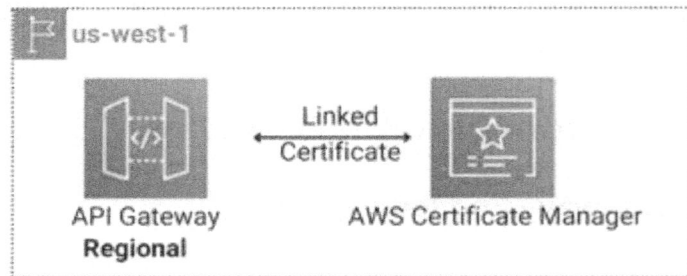

AWS WAF

There is a general understanding that web applications and APIs have security risks that can cause application availability issues or can consume access resources in case of security attacks such as DDoS.

AWS WAF is an AWS web application firewall that is used to help protect web applications and web APIs from Layer 7 attacks which are common web exploits, bots, and application layer attacks. These Lay 7 attacks may affect applications' availability, compromise security, and sometimes consume excessive resources to impact the overall system's performance.

AWS WAF helps protect web applications from attacks by allowing you to configure rules that will enable, block, or monitor web requests based on conditions that you define. These conditions include IP addresses, HTTP headers, HTTP body, URI strings, SQL injection, and cross-site scripting. In addition, you can use the IP address-based match rule to block specific geographies.

AWS WAF includes pre-configured rules for the OWASP top 10 security risks and protection against common bot traffic. You can edit the pre-configured rules to configure them, or you can add your custom rule to filter out unwanted traffic patterns.

You can deploy AWS WAF with a few clicks on Amazon CloudFront, Amazon API Gateway, Application Load Balancer, and AWS AppSync GraphQL to protect your applications against common web exploits and bots, whether applications run in the cloud or on-premises.

Amazon API Gateway, Application Load Balancer, and AWS AppSync GraphQL are regional resources. However, Amazon CloudFront is a global resource.

AWS WAF includes Web ACLs, IP Sets, Regex pattern sets, Rule groups, and AWS Marketplace. Web ACLs consist of a set of rules that are used to protect web applications.

AWS WAF lets you monitor and control HTTP and HTTPS traffic that is forwarded to Amazon CloudFront, Amazon API Gateway, an Application Load Balancer, or an AWS AppSync GraphQL. AWS WAF controls access to content based on different rules, such as whether requests from particular IP or CIDR are allowed or blocked or if the particular URL pattern can be accessed. AWS can apply the rate limit rule to protect URLs against brute force attacks; for example, you can protect login URLs by applying the rate limit rule.

AWS WAF also provides monitoring by offering near real-time traffic visibility by CloudWatch metrics. In addition, you can log the header data of each inspected request for security automation, analytics, or auditing purposes.

Using AWS Firewall Manager and AWS WAF fast rule propagation, you quickly and easily deploy protection across your organizations to keep your applications and APIs protected and available. You can set up Web ACLs for regional resources or for global resources. You can add blacklist or whitelist IPs and CIDR block. You can add a regex (regular expression) pattern. You can also buy WAF Rule from AWS Marketplace.

How it Works

The first step in configuring WAF is to create Web ACLs. In configuring Web ACLs, you need to choose to decide where you are going to apply the Web ACLs. Is it going to be applied to Regional resources such as Application Load Balancer, Amazon API Gateway, or global resources such as AWS CloudFront, Rount53?

Using IP Sets, you can add blacklist or whitelist IPs and CIDR block and set up where this blocklist or whitelist IP list will be deployed. You can have 10000 IP addresses or a CIDR block in one IP Set.

You can add a regex (regular expression) pattern. In the Rule group, you can create your own set of rules. You can also buy WAF Rule from AWS Marketplace.

AWS WAF also creates CloudWatch metrics for each Web ACL. You add which resource you are trying to protect using each Web ACL. You can select add pre-configured managed rules. For example, managed rules protect against OWASP's top 10 security risks, WordPress rules, or you can add custom rules.

You can create a rule to protect admin URLs. Or you can create a rate limit-based rule to protect brute force login; for example, 100 requests are allowed in a five-minute rolling window.

Managed rules also have many subrules. You can enable or disable subrules. You can also change the mode: block to count or count to block.

When you add rules, rules can enable in block mode, or they can be enabled in count mode. The rule is allowed, triggered, logged, and monitored in count mode. But in block mode, the request is blocked.

In the beginning, when the rule is new, it is safer to be enabled in count mode, and later based on the impact, you can change to the block mode.

Web ACLs rule from top to bottom. If the first rule is matched, then the rest are ignored. CloudWatch metrics log can only log sampled requests – not all requests.

Main Points:
- Protects your web applications from common web exploits at Layer 7.
- WAF is Deployed on, Application Load Balance, API Gateway, CloudFront, AppSync GraphQL API, Cognito User Pool
- Web ACLs are Regional except for CloudFront
- A rule group is a reusable set of rules that you can add to a web ACL
- Define Web ACL (Web Access Control List) Rules:
  - IP Set: up to 10,000 IP addresses – use multiple Rules for more Ips
  - Using IP Sets, you can add blacklist or whitelist IPs and CIDR blocks.
  - HTTP headers, HTTP body, or URI strings protect from common attacks: SQL injection and Cross-Site Scripting (XSS)
  - Rate-based rules (to count occurrences of events) – for brute force, DDoS protection
- WAF does not support the Network Load Balancer (Layer 4)
- We can use Global Accelerator with Fixed IP in front of ALB with WAF. Global Accelerator improves the performance and availability of applications for users all over the world. It provides static IP addresses that act as fixed entry points for single or multiple AWS regions' application endpoints, such as Application Load Balancer, Network Load Balancer, and Amazon EC2.

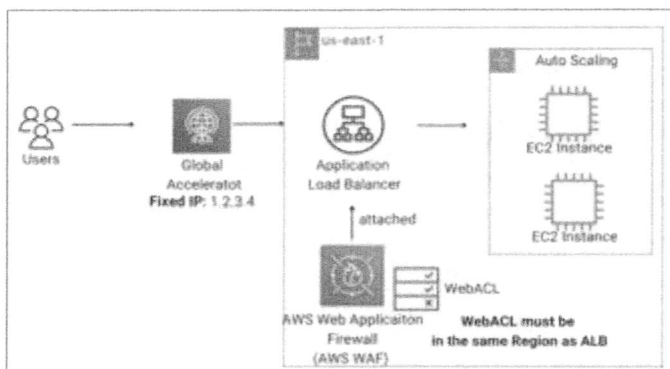

AWS Firewall Manager

AWS Firewall Manager, a security management service, allows you to configure and manage firewall rules -- centrally -- across your accounts and applications in AWS Organizations. Using AWS Firewall Manager, you can build firewall rules, create security policies, and enforce them consistently across your AWS infrastructure from a central administrator account.

When new applications are created, AWS Firewall Manager makes it easy to bring new applications and resources into compliance by enforcing a common set of security rules.

Using AWS Firewall Manager, you can easily implement AWS WAF rules for your application load balancers, API Gateways, and Amazon CloudFront distributions. You can create AWS Shield Advanced protection for your Application Load Balancers, ELB Classic Load Balancers, Elastic IP Addresses, and CloudFront distributions. You can deploy AWS Network Firewalls across accounts and VPCs in your organization.

Regarding its benefits, AWS Firewall Manager helps simplify the management of firewall rules across your accounts, quickly deploys managed rules across accounts, ensures compliance with existing and new applications, and centrally deploy protections for your VPCs.

Main Points:

- Manage rules in all accounts of an AWS Organization
- A common set of security rules, such as:
    o AWS WAF rules for your application load balancers, API Gateways, and Amazon CloudFront distributions.
    o AWS Shield Advanced protection for your Application Load Balancers, ELB Classic Load Balancers, Elastic IP Addresses, and CloudFront distributions.
    o AWS Network Firewalls across accounts and VPCs in your organization.
- Rules are applied to new resources as they are created across all and future accounts in your organization. This feature is very helpful for compliance.

DDoS Attacks

What is DDoS? Let's first understand what it is DoS? DoS stands for Denial of Service. Essentially in DoS, the target compute is flooded with useless traffic to choke all the network bandwidth. In other words, it is a malicious attempt to flood the website with a large number of fake traffic, which as a result, disrupts regular traffic to the website.

The number of DDoS attacks, attack volume and sophistication of attacks are growing every year.

Types of DDoS Attacks

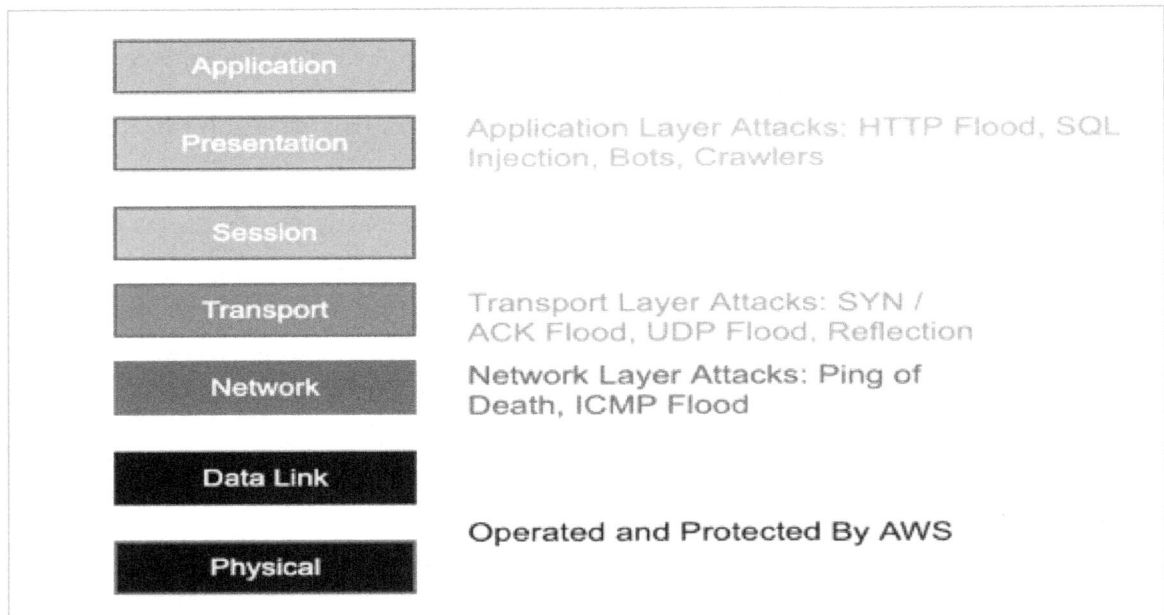

DDoS attacks are mainly of three types depending on what layer of OSI they attack. The physical and data link layer is protected by AWS; AWS customers need not be concerned at that level.

Volumetric DDoS

When we move to the Network layer, in this layer, we can get attacks such as Ping of Death and ICMP Flood. For example, if the target computer is sent a million ping requests per second to test the network connection to the target computer. There is a possibility that network bandwidth will be flooded and will not be available for other legitimate requests to succeed.

Volumetric DDoS is the most common type of DDoS attack. In this attack, the attacker floods the target's computer to consume all network bandwidth. This is Layer 3 – Network Layer -- type DDoS attack.

Protocol DDoS

In the Transport layer, we can get attack such as SYN/ACK flood, UDP Flood, and Reflection attacks. In this layer, the transport will be flooded such that they will not be able to send the packet to the target computer because the connection tables within the firewalls or routers will be filled.

In this type of attack, the attacker fills up connection tables within firewalls or routers so that even the network bandwidth is available, but the networking infrastructure can handle packets sent to them. This is layer 4 – Transport Layer – type DDoS attack.

Application DDoS

Then as you move at the stack, you will start seeing application-level DDoS attacks. You will see HTTP flood, SQL injection, SSL abuse, malformed SSL, crawlers, and app exploit types of attacks.

These attacks aim to consume the server's resources, whether it be web, DNS, or some other kind of application forcing the application to deal with illegitimate requests instead of genuine requests. This is an application layer-type DDoS attack.

As you can see, since DDoS attacks can come on many layers, it's important to protect them.

Problems caused by DDoS attacks

The question here is, why do we need to be concerned about DDoS attacks? DDoS attacks cause three types of issues: impact the availability of applications, impact financially, and impact security.

With respect to the availability of applications, these attacks sometimes last for hours and days. This causes the application to be not unavailable for regular users, which leads to financial loss such as loss in revenue. For example, if your application is e-commerce, you cannot take orders. This also impacts reputation if this becomes public. It also causes increased infrastructure expenses. Because to mitigate attacks, you will need to scale your resources to make your application available – this will cost you extra. Sometimes attackers seek extortion. You also possibly could have an impact on your business reputation. If your application is down or if the application going down becomes a pattern, your customers might go somewhere else, or they might think that your business is not reliable. So, it takes a hit on the reputation.

Also, you might have data loss in case of an application layer attack. If someone's attack vector is SQL injection, They might steal data if they successfully attack the application's data. There could also be an issue where scrapers can steal contents.

Traditional Challenges with DDoS Protection

The first important mitigation technique is the availability of bandwidth. You need lots of it depending on the attack size and speed. Your network infrastructure will start becoming constrained very fast. So, it would be best if you scaled bandwidth. Scaling of resources becomes expensive as well because you need to scale resources to maintain availability. You need to detect DDoS attacks to stop them – you need to find out bad actors from among all the traffics. Lastly, DDoS experts who can mitigate and manage DDoS attacks are in short supply. At the bottom, you should focus on your main business instead of building an army of DDoS experts to mitigate or fix the issue if an attack happens.

AWS Shield

AWS Shield prevents DDoS (Distributed Denial of Service) attacks on AWS resources for both global and regional resources. AWS Shield is available in two levels: AWS Shield Standard and AWS Shield Advanced. AWS Shield Standard is free and open to all customers. AWS Shield Standard protects all AWS customers against common and most frequently occurring infrastructure (layer 3 and 4) attacks like SYN/UDP floods, reflection attacks, and others to support the high availability of your applications on AWS. AWS Shield Advanced is a paid service. Being a paid service, it provides every feature that AWS Shield Standard. Additionally, it offers additional protection such as visibility and monitoring of DDoS attacks, 24x7 support from the AWS DDoS support team, and AWS WAF subscription at no cost.

AWS Shield Standard

All AWS customers get the default AWS Shield protection for most common DDoS attacks, by default with no additional charge. It protects from Layer 3 and Layer 4 DDoS attacks for any AWS resource in any AWS Region.

It protects against common network attacks such as SYN floods, UDP floods, Reflection attacks, etc., at layer three and layer 4 for any Resources in any AWS Region.

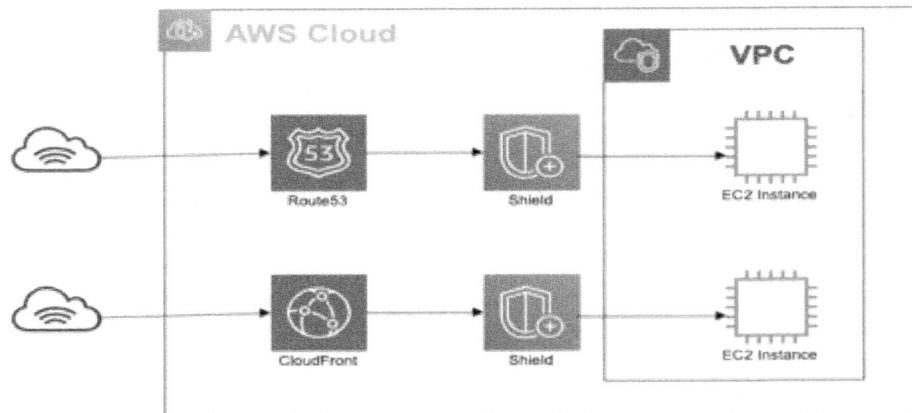

It provides comprehensive defense on layer 3 (Network) and layer 4 (Transport) for the most common DDoS network attacks for CloudFront and Route 53. In other words, if you have your EC2 instance fronted with CloudFront or if you have a DNS request hitting Route 53, you are protected at Layer 3 and Layer 4 of DDoS attacks.

If you have a concern about layer seven attacks, you can subscribe to AWS WAF. AWS WAF is a paid self-service with a pay-as-you model. AWS WAF protects layer 7 – the application layer – from DDoS attacks.

AWS Shield Advanced

AWS Shield Advanced is a paid service. Being a paid service, it provides additional protection and a number of benefits. It also provides WAF.

With AWS Shield Advanced, **AWS does additional detection and monitoring**. In particular, AWS looks into network flows and data streams more at a customer level, which helps in anomaly detection at a little more granular level. This helps in providing visibility to AWS Shield Advanced customers, which is not available for AWS Shield Standard customers.

AWS Shield Advanced also provides enhanced protection against large and complex DDoS attacks. This is particularly important for customers who cannot run their workloads or application using CloudFront – they can run only out of an AWS Region. Because when traffic is not directly sent to CloudFront, there is a chance of a little constraint on resources, which needs some engineering effort to scale the resources to mitigate DDoS attacks in order to protect availability.

AWS Shield Advanced also provides visibility into DDoS attacks that is not available in AWS Shield Standard. This visibility is helpful to customers who are interested to know about the bad actors that are impacting their applications' availability. You get visibility at the console, and the ability to create CloudWatch metrics creates alarms.

AWS Shield Advanced customers gets AWS WAF without any additional cost. Since advanced protection needs to protect all layers, AWS WAF is included in the AWS Shield Advanced subscription. For example, suppose you have protected AWS Load Balancer with AWS Shield

Advanced. In that case, you can also enable AWS WAF to provide application-level protection (layer seven attacks) of that resource with no additional charge.

AWS Shield Advanced customers also have access to a DDoS response team – a team of DDoS experts. The team is available 24x7 to help solve customers' DDoS-related issues. They are also engaged in monitoring and mitigating attacks on amazon.com. They can help set up an alarm for DDoS events and can review your architecture for resiliency. The DDoS Response team can look up attack signatures and appropriate put-up rules to block that event. The team can advise you about DDoS mitigations, can help implement WAF mitigations, and help in re-architecture.

AWS Shield Advanced also gives you cost protections. Sometimes, the simplest thing to do is scale resources to absorb traffic to mitigate attacks. If you didn't have AWS Shield Advanced subscription, and if you decided to scale resources, you will have to pay for those resources. With DDoS, if AWS finds that the resources are spiked due to DDoS attacks, then those extra costs are taken off.

Main Points:
- DDoS: Distributed Denial of Service – many-many concurrent requests simultaneously.
- AWS Shield Standard:
  - Free service that is available for every AWS customer
  - Protects from attacks such as SYN/UDP Floods, Reflection attacks, and other layers 3/4 attacks
- AWS Shield Advanced:
  - Optional DDoS mitigation service – it is not FREE.
  - Protect against more sophisticated attacks on EC2, ELB, CloudFront, Global Accelerator, and Route 53
  - 24/7 access to AWS DDoS response team
  - Protect against higher fees during usage spikes due to DDoS
  - Shield Advanced automatic application layer DDoS mitigation automatically creates, evaluates, and deploys AWS WAF rules to mitigate layer seven attacks

WAF vs. Shield vs. Firewall Manager
- WAF, Shield, and Firewall Manager are used together for comprehensive protection as they complement one another with some overlap.
- For the granular protection of your resources, WAF alone is sufficient. Use WAF to define your Web ACL.
- Use Firewall Manager with AWS WAF -- if you want to use AWS WAF across accounts, accelerate WAF configuration, and automate the protection of new resources,
- Use Shield Advanced if you need dedicated support from the Shield Response Team (SRT) and advanced reporting. In Shield, Advanced adds, extra features are added on top of AWS WAF. (Shield Advanced = AWS WAF + 24 /7 SRT support + advance reporting + some other extra feature)
- Consider using Shield Advanced if there are more chances of frequent DDoS attacks– it is not free, however.

AWS Threat Detection and Monitoring

Amazon GuardDuty

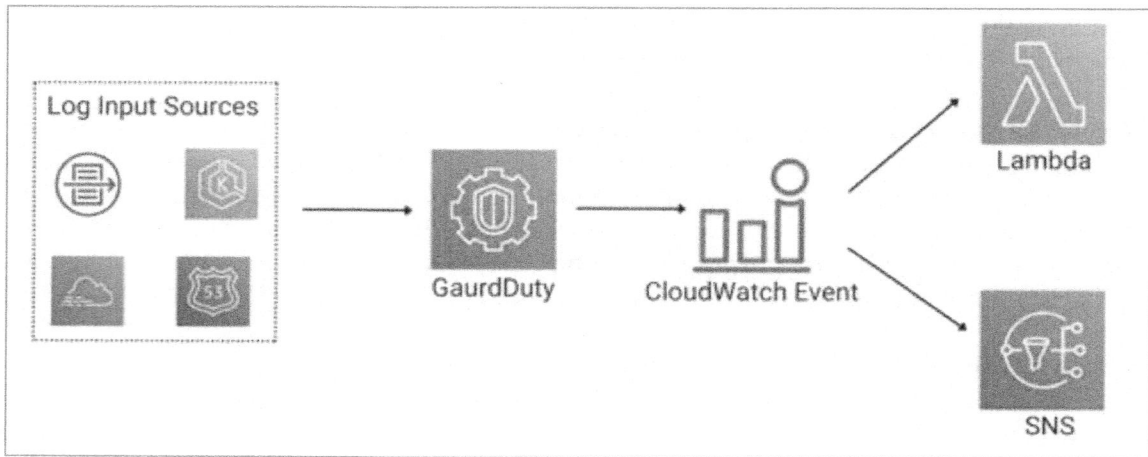

Amazon GuardDuty service, to identify and prioritize potential threats, uses services related to machine learning, anomaly detection techniques, and other various threat intelligence techniques.

- Amazon GaurdDuty is an intelligent threat discovery service to protect your AWS account. It is used to identify and prioritize potential threats.
- It uses machine learning algorithms, anomaly detection techniques, and other threat intelligence techniques.
- You can enable it with a single click. You get a 30-day free trial.

- It can use the following input data:
  - CloudTrail Events Logs – look for unusual API calls, unauthorized deployments
  - VPC Flow Logs – look for unusual internal traffic, unusual IP address
  - DNS Logs – look for compromised EC2 instances
- You can set up CloudWatch Event rules to be notified in case of findings. CloudWatch Events rules can target AWS Lambda or Amazon SNS.

Amazon Inspector

- Amazon Inspector is an automated vulnerability management service or Automated Security Assessments service. With Amazon Inspector, you can stay secure by detecting and remediating security issues early. Amazon Inspector assesses your operating system, virtual machines, network, and application configurations and compares them with a detailed knowledge base of common security standards, vulnerabilities, and best practices.

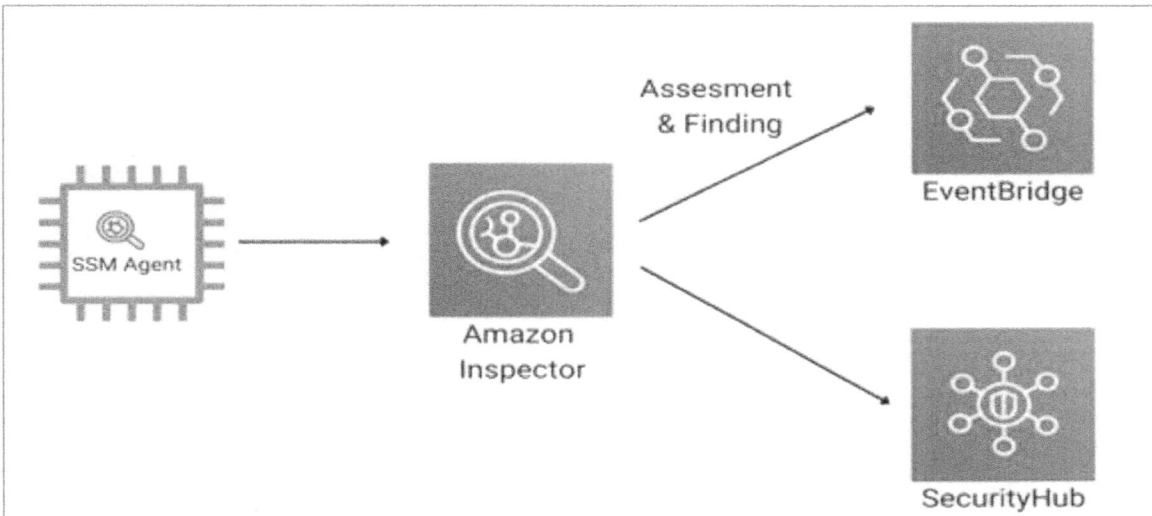

- You can use Amazon Inspector to continuously scan your environment for vulnerabilities and network exposure, assess vulnerabilities accurately with the Amazon Inspector Risk score, identify high-impact findings with the Amazon Inspector dashboard, manage your findings using customizable views, and monitor and process findings with other services and systems.

- it continually scans EC2 instances leveraging SSM AWS Systems Manager) agent to analyze unintended network accessibility and the running OS against known vulnerabilities.

- It analyzes container workloads for software vulnerabilities and unintended network exposure. Amazon Inspector generates a detailed report and dashboard of your security assessment, and it tracks what tests are performed and the results in the CloudTrail.
    - It has Reporting & integration with AWS Security Hub
    - It can send findings to Amazon Event Bridge.

What does AWS Inspector evaluate?
- Remember: only for EC2 instances and container infrastructure
- Continuous scanning of the infrastructure, only when needed
- Package vulnerabilities (EC2 & ECR) – database of CVE
- Network reachability (EC2)
- A risk score is associated with all vulnerabilities for prioritization

Amazon Macie
- Amazon Macie, a fully-managed data security and data privacy service, uses machine learning and pattern matching to discover, classify, monitor, protect and report your sensitive data in AWS S3 buckets.
- Macie helps identify and alert you to sensitive data, such as personally identifiable information (PII)

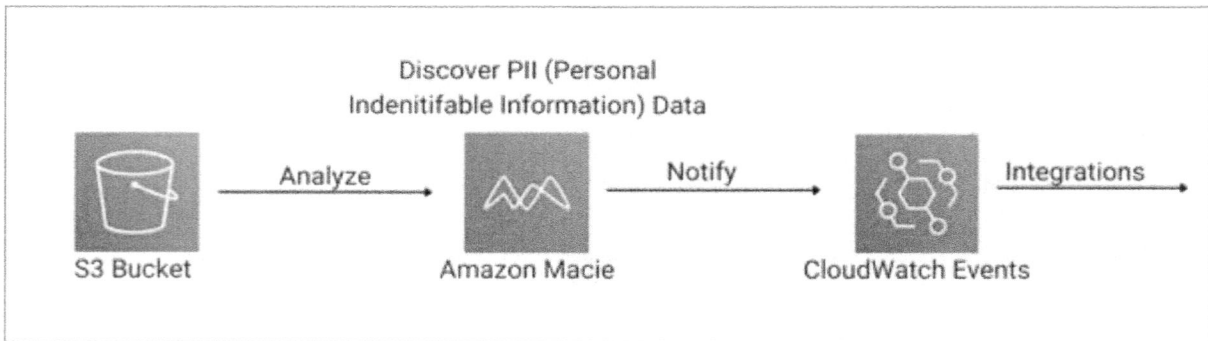

Discover PII (Personal Indenitifable Information) Data

S3 Bucket → Analyze → Amazon Macie → Notify → CloudWatch Events → Integrations

- Managing volumes of data as it grows can be challenging, complex, and expensive, particularly at scale, particularly in industries that have strong regulations such as HIPPA and GDPR. Amazon Macie helps automate the discovery of sensitive data at scale, thus lowering the cost of protecting your data.

- Amazon Macie automatically offers a list of unencrypted buckets, publicly accessible buckets, and buckets shared with AWS accounts outside of AWS Organizations. Macie then alerts you about personally identifiable information (PII), such as personal, financial, and health-related data, by applying machine learning techniques, including pattern matching to the buckets you select.

- Amazon Macie's alerts, or findings, can be searched and filtered in the AWS Management Console and sent to Amazon EventBridge for easy integration with existing workflow or event management systems. The alerts or findings can also be combined with AWS services, such as AWS Step Functions, to take automated remediation actions.

Amazon Detective

Security is extremely important when you move your on-premises applications to the cloud or develop, test, and deploy your applications in a cloud environment. Some services can alert you if a potential issue arises. But sometimes, digging deeper is needed to find out the root cause. That being said – looking further into a problem can be expensive. Uncovering the root cause requires you to collect various logs and convert all the data into information that you can then use for an investigation.

Amazon Detective simplifies investigating security findings and identifying the root cause. Amazon Detective collects the log data from AWS resources of your account. This collection helps Amazon Detective quickly analyze, investigate, and identify the root cause of potential security issues or suspicious activities. Amazon Detective can analyze trillions of events from multiple data sources such as Virtual Private Cloud (VPC) Flow Logs, AWS CloudTrail, and Amazon GuardDuty. Based on this analysis, it automatically creates a unified, interactive view of your resources, users, and their interactions over time. Amazon Detective applies machine learning, statistical analysis, and graph theory to build a linked data set. This linked data set enables you to conduct faster and more efficient security investigations.

When you enable Amazon Detective, the service automatically collects and analyzes trillions of events from multiple data sources. It uses graph analytics to build a unified interactive view of your resources, users, and interactions between them over a configurable timeline. As a result, you can visualize the details surrounding an issue in one place and get an answer to your security questions without manually inspecting raw logs, fine-tuning queries, or developing algorithms.

Amazon Detective's easy-to-use visualizations are continuously updated as terabytes of event data -- such as network traffic, AWS account activities, and security-related detections -- become available. This means you can focus on fixing potential problems instead of managing constantly changing data.

Amazon Detective helps you analyze and visualize security data in one place, which can help you conduct faster and more effective investigations.

Amazon Detective use cases are triage security findings, incident investigations, threat hunting.

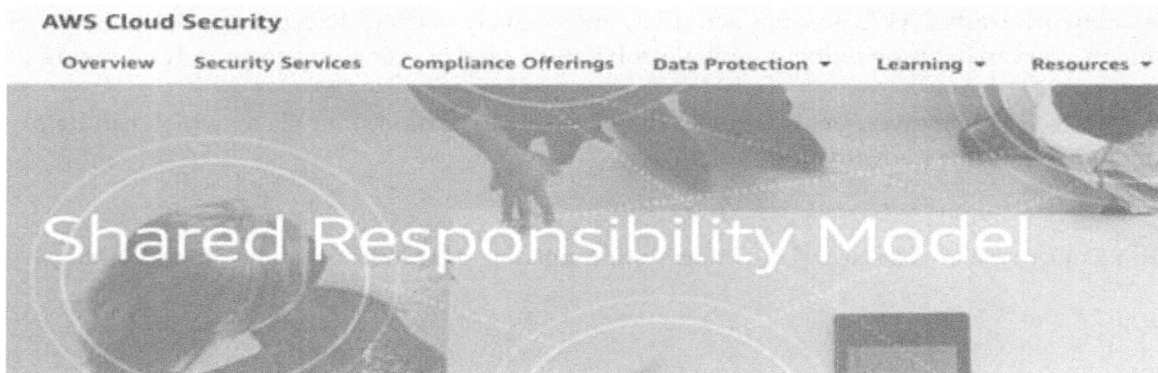

Chapter 31. AWS Shared Responsibility Model

You will learn the following in this chapter:
- AWS Shared Responsibility Model

Security and Compliance are a shared responsibility between AWS and the customer. This shared responsibility model can help reduce the customer's responsibility on the AWS Cloud. What it means is that AWS operates, manages, and controls the components in the host operating system, in the virtualization layer, and in the physical security of data centers. The customer assumes management responsibility of the guest operating system, including updates, security patches, and other associated application software; however, AWS provides a security group firewall. It is essential for AWS customers to carefully consider the services they choose as their responsibilities vary depending on the services used and applicable laws and regulations. This differentiation of responsibility between AWS and AWS Customers is commonly referred to as Security "of" the Cloud versus Security "in" the Cloud.

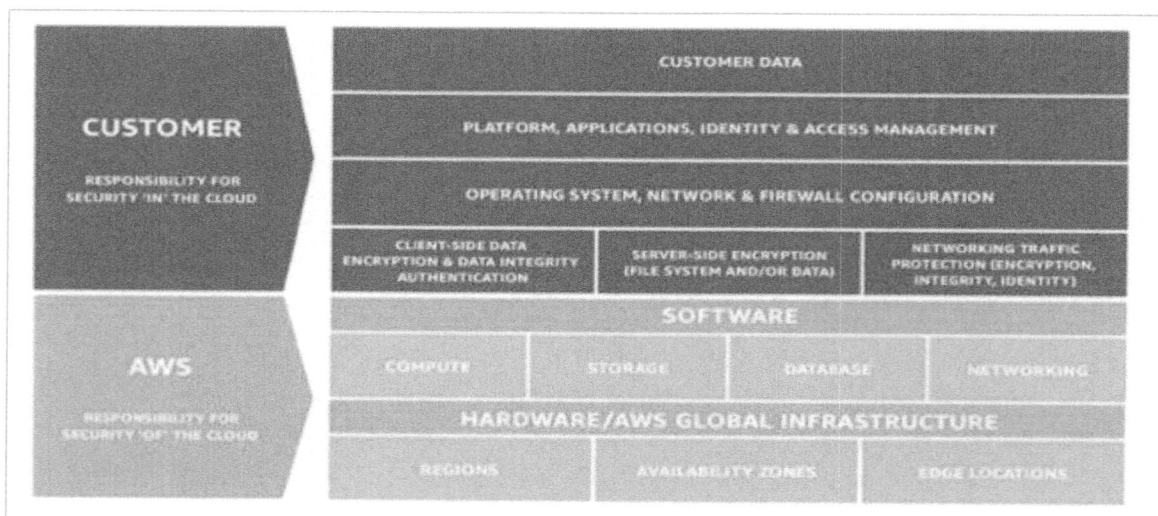

Reference: https://aws.amazon.com/compliance/shared-responsibility-model/

Security of the Cloud

AWS is responsible for "Security of the cloud." What it means is that AWS is responsible for the infrastructure that runs the Cloud. The infrastructure includes physical hardware, software, network, and physical facilities that host infrastructure and run Cloud services. Based on the AWS Responsibility Model, AWS is responsible for AWS's global infrastructure, which means the hardware and software of AWS Regions, AWS Availability Zones, and Edge Locations. AWS is responsible for computing, storage, databases, and networking infrastructure along with physical facilities hosting data centers for the AWS global infrastructure.

Security in the Cloud

"Security in the Cloud" is the responsibility of the customer. AWS Customer responsibilities depend on the AWS services. For example, the customer has more responsibility and control when the customer is using EC2. In the case of EC2, the customer is responsible for securing the instance by configuring Security Groups and Network ACLs, along with applying updates and security patches.

"For abstracted services like Amazon S3, AWS operates the infrastructure layer, the operating system, and platforms" - For abstracted services, such as Amazon S3 and Amazon DynamoDB, AWS operates the infrastructure layer, the operating system, and platforms, and customers access the endpoints to store and retrieve data. It includes the disposal and the replacement of disk drives as well as data center security.

Inherited Controls

Physical and Environmental controls

Physical and Environmental controls are part of the inherited controls, and hence these are the responsibility of AWS. AWS is responsible for protecting its infrastructure, which is composed of the hardware, software, networking, and facilities that run AWS Cloud services. For example, replacing faulty hardware of Amazon EC2 instances comes under the infrastructure maintenance "of" the cloud. This is the responsibility of AWS.

Shared Controls

As we have discussed above, how AWS operations in an IT environment are shared between AWS and its customers. Likewise, management and verification of IT control on AWS are handled between AWS and the AWS customers. I have added a screenshot that shows examples of controls that are managed by AWS, AWS Customers, and/or both.

Screenshot reference: https://aws.amazon.com/compliance/shared-responsibility-model/

Patch Management

The customers must provide their own control implementation within their use of AWS services. The customers are responsible for patching their guest OS as well as for configuring their applications. AWS is responsible for fixing flaws within the infrastructure.

Configuration Management

Configuration Management forms a part of shared controls - AWS maintains the configuration of its infrastructure devices. However, AWS customer is responsible for configuring their own guest operating systems, databases, and applications. Customers are responsible for the management of the guest operating system, which includes updates and security patches, any application software or utilities installed by the customer on the instances, and the configuration of the AWS-provided firewall (which is called Security Group) on each instance. For example, AWS services such as Amazon EC2 are categorized as IaaS, and as such, it requires that the customer performs all of the necessary security configuration and management tasks.

Training AWS And Customer Employees

Awareness & Training is also a shared responsibility. For example, AWS trains AWS employees, but a customer must train their employees.

OS Configuration

OS configuration as a whole is a shared responsibility but be careful: the host OS configuration is the responsibility of AWS, and the guest OS configuration is the customer's responsibility.

Data Security and Encryption

Under the shared model, customers are responsible for managing their data, including data encryption. AWS is responsible for keeping data on AWS Cloud Secure, Durable, Available, and Reliable. AWS is responsible for keeping the data safe from hardware and software failure.

Enabling Multi-Factor Authentication for AWS accounts in your organization is the AWS customer's responsibility. On the other hand, AWS is responsible for making sure that the user data created and their relationships and policies are stored on fail-proof infrastructure.

Creating bucket policies for Amazon S3 data access is the responsibility of the customer. The customer decides who gets access to the data he stores on S3 and will use AWS tools to implement these requirements. Creating user roles and policies is the responsibility of the customer. Customers will decide "which" resources get "what" access. In the Shared Responsibility Model, customers are responsible for managing their data (including encryption options), classifying their assets, and using IAM tools to apply for the appropriate permissions.

Customer Specific Responsibility

Customers are responsible for Service and Communications Protection or Zone Security which may require the customers to route or zone data within specific security environments.

- Customer is responsible for maintaining versions of a lambda function.
- Under the AWS Shared Responsibility Model, customers are responsible for enabling MFA on all accounts, analyzing access patterns, and reviewing permissions.

Reference:

https://aws.amazon.com/compliance/shared-responsibility-model/

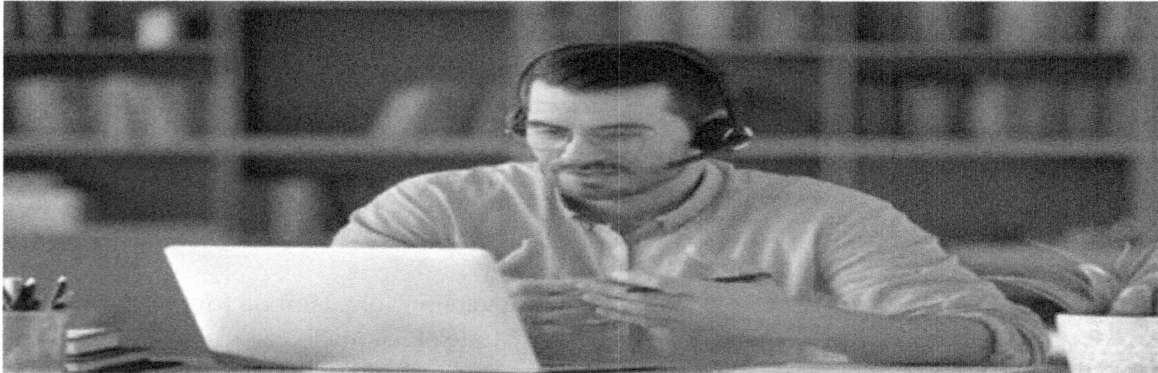

Chapter 32. How to Get Support on AWS

You will learn the following in this chapter:
- AWS Support Plans
- Basic Support Plan
- Developer Support Plan
- Enterprise Support Plan
- Technical Account Manager (TAM)
- AWS Concierge
- AWS Marketplace
- AWS Service Health Dashboard
- AWS Personal Health Dashboard
- Contact AWS for Resource Abuse
- AWS Acceptable Use Policy

AWS Support Plans

AWS offers three different support plans to cater to its customers - Developer, Business, and Enterprise Support plans.

Basic Support Plan

A Basic Support plan is included for all AWS customers, which includes 24x7 access to customer service, documentation, whitepapers, and guidance to provision your resources following AWS best practices to increase performance and improve security. A Basic Support plan also includes access to core Trusted Advisor checks. Additionally, using AWS Personal Health Dashboard, you get a personalized view of the health of AWS services and alerts when your resources are impacted.

Developer Support

The Developer Support plan only supports general architectural guidance. For example, if you are testing or doing early development on AWS and want the ability to get email-based technical support during business hours as well as general architectural guidance as you build and test, you can leverage the Developer Support plan option. AWS Developer Support plan allows one primary contact to open unlimited cases.

Developer Support Plan Overview

We recommend AWS Developer Support if you are testing or doing early development on AWS and want the ability to get technical support during business hours as well as general architectural guidance as you build and test.

In addition to enhanced technical support and architectural guidance, Developer Support provides access to documentation and forums, AWS Trusted Advisor, and AWS Personal Health Dashboard.

Technical and billing support

Enhanced technical support

Business hours email access to Cloud Support engineers. You can have one primary contact that can open an unlimited amount of cases. Response times for general guidance is less than 24 business hours* and system impaired is less than 12 business hours*.

Architectural support

General guidance on how to use AWS products, features, and services together. AWS Solutions Architects leverage the AWS Well-Architected framework when providing recommendations.

Customer service and communities

24x7 access to customer service, documentation, whitepapers, and support forums.

Self-service support

AWS Trusted Advisor

AWS Trusted Advisor provides you real time guidance to help you provision your resources following AWS best practices. Trusted Advisor checks help optimize your AWS infrastructure, increase security and performance, reduce your overall costs, and monitor service limits. Seven core checks are included with Developer Support.

AWS Personal Health Dashboard

AWS Personal Health Dashboard provides a personalized view of the health of AWS services, and alerts when your resources are impacted. Also includes the AWS Health API for integration with your existing management systems.

AWS Support Automation Workflows

AWS Support Automation Workflows enable you to diagnose and resolve common Support issues following AWS best practices. Access to Support Automation Workflows with prefix **AWSSupport** is included with Developer Support.

Screenshot Reference: https://aws.amazon.com/premiumsupport/plans/developers/

Business Support

The AWS Business Support plan provides you access to guidance, configuration, and troubleshooting of AWS interoperability issues with many common operating systems, platforms, and application stack components. You also get access to Infrastructure Event Management for an additional fee. The Business support plan provides contextual guidance on how services fit together to meet your specific use case, workload, or application. You also get full access to AWS Trusted Advisor Best Practice Checks in a Business Support plan.

AWS recommends a Business Support plan if you have production workloads on AWS and want 24x7 technical support or architectural guidance in the context of your specific use-cases by phone, email, and chat access.

Enterprise Support

Technical and billing support

Enhanced technical support

24x7 access to Cloud Support Engineers via phone, chat, and email. You can have an unlimited number of contacts that can open an unlimited amount of cases. Response times for general guidance is less than 24 hours, system impaired is less than 12 hours, production system impaired is less than 4 hours, production system down is less than an hour, and business critical system down is less than 15 minutes.

Billing and account management

AWS billing and account experts specialize in working with enterprise accounts. They will quickly and efficiently assist you with your billing and account inquiries, and work with you to implement billing and account best practices so that you can focus on what matters: running your business.

Third-party software support

Guidance, configuration, and troubleshooting of AWS interoperability with many common operating systems, platforms, and application stack components.

Screenshot Reference: https://aws.amazon.com/premiumsupport/plans/enterprise/

With Enterprise Support, AWS customers get access to online training with self-paced labs, 24x7 technical support, tools, and technology to automatically manage the health of your environment, consultative architectural guidance, a designated Technical Account Manager (TAM) to coordinate access to proactive/preventative programs and AWS subject matter experts. The Enterprise Support plan supports architectural guidance contextual to your application. AWS Enterprise Support provides customers with a concierge-like service where the main focus is on helping the customer achieve their outcomes and find success in the cloud.

Technical Account Manager (TAM)

AWS Technical Account Manager (TAM) who helps you onboard and provides advocacy and guidance to help plan and build solutions using best practices is your designated technical point of contact. TAM coordinates access to subject matter experts and assists with case management. In addition, TAM presents insights and recommendations on your AWS spend, workload optimization, and event management. It proactively keeps your AWS environment healthy. With Enterprise Support, you get technical support from high-quality engineers, 24x7. You will also get tools and technology to automatically manage the health of your AWS environment and consultative architectural guidance delivered in the context of your applications and use-cases.

Technical account management

Designated point of contact

A Technical Account Manager (TAM) is your designated technical point of contact who helps you onboard, provides advocacy and guidance to help plan and build solutions using best practices, coordinates access to subject matter experts, assists with case management, presents insights and recommendations on your AWS spend, workload optimization, and event management, and proactively keeps your AWS environment healthy.

Access to subject matter experts

Cloud Support Engineers, Solutions Architects, Technical Account Managers, and product teams are available to provide guidance and help as needed. The AWS Trust & Safety team assists you when your AWS resources are used to engage in abusive behaviors, such as spam, port scanning, denial-of-service (DoS) attacks, or malware.

Screenshot Reference: https://aws.amazon.com/premiumsupport/plans/enterprise/

AWS Concierge

AWS Concierge is a senior customer service agent assigned to your AWS account when you subscribe to an Enterprise Support plan or qualified Reseller Support plan. The Concierge agent is your primary point of contact for billing or account-related inquiries. When you don't know whom to call, The Concierge agent will find the right people to help you. The AWS Concierge, in most cases, is available during regular business hours in your headquarters' geography.

The Concierge teams are AWS billing and account experts working with enterprise accounts. The Concierge Support Team is only available for the Enterprise Support plan -- they assist you with your billing and account inquiries. The enterprise Support plan provides fewer than 15 minutes of response time for business-critical systems. Additionally, it gives a response time of less than an hour for production systems-related outages.

AWS Infrastructure Event Management

Proactive reviews

Launch and event planning

Infrastructure Event Management (IEM), included with Enterprise Support, offers architecture and scaling guidance and operational support during the preparation and execution of planned events such as shopping holidays, product launches, or migrations.

Architectural reviews

Evaluate your architecture and implement designs that can scale over time through architectural reviews with AWS Solutions Architects and TAMs and leveraging the AWS Well-Architected framework.

Proactive guidance

Proactive services delivered by AWS Support experts are included with Enterprise Support. These services help you review the health of your cloud operations, optimize costs, and scale workloads efficiently through workload reviews, best practices workshops, and deep dives.

Screenshot Reference:
https://aws.amazon.com/premiumsupport/plans/enterprise/

AWS Infrastructure Event Management, which is a short-term engagement with AWS Support, is available as part of the Enterprise-level Support product offering. It is also available for additional purchase for Business-level Support subscribers. AWS Infrastructure Event Management partners with your technical and project resources to gain a deep understanding of your use case and provide architecturally and scaling guidance for an event. AWS Event Management common use cases include advertising launches, new product launches, and infrastructure migrations to AWS.

Self-service support

Self-service support

AWS Trusted Advisor

AWS Trusted Advisor provides you real time guidance to help you provision your resources following AWS best practices. Trusted Advisor checks, with full set of checks included with Enterprise Support, helps optimize your AWS infrastructure, increase security and performance, reduce your overall costs, and monitor service limits.

AWS Personal Health Dashboard

AWS Personal Health Dashboard provides a personalized view of the health of AWS services, and alerts when your resources are impacted. Also includes the AWS Health API for integration with your existing management systems.

AWS Support API

AWS Support API provides programmatic access to AWS Support Center features to create, manage, and close your Support cases, and operationally manage your Trusted Advisor check requests and status.

AWS Support Automation Workflows

AWS Support Automation Workflows enable you to diagnose and resolve common Support issues following AWS best practices. Access to Support Automation Workflows with prefixes **AWSSupport** and **AWSPremiumSupport** is included with Enterprise Support.

Your TAM and other AWS experts can provide reporting and insights across customer accounts subscribed to Enterprise Support leveraging these Support tools.

This plan provides Enhanced Technical Support as follows:
- 24x7 access to Cloud Support Engineers via phone, chat, and email. You can have an unlimited number of contacts that can open an unlimited number of cases. Response times are as follows:
- General Guidance - < 24 hours
- System Impaired - < 12 hours
- Production System Impaired - < 4 hours
- Production System Down - < 1 hour
- Business Critical System Down - <15 min

- Customers with a Developer, Business or Enterprise support plan have access to best practice guidance.
- Customers with a Business or Enterprise support plan have access to use-case guidance.
- Customers with an Enterprise support plan have access to infrastructure event management which is a short-term engagement with AWS Support to get a deep understanding of customer use-cases. After analysis, AWS provides architectural and scaling guidance for an event.

AWS Support Center

AWS Support Center is the hub for managing your Support cases. The Support Center is accessible through the AWS Management Console, providing federated access support. All Developer-level and higher Support customers can open a Technical Support case online through the Support Center. Business and Enterprise-level customers can ask for Support by calling them or can open a chat session with one of the Support engineers. Enterprise-level customers can have direct access to their dedicated Technical Account Manager.

AWS Knowledge Center

AWS Knowledge Center provides the most frequent & common questions and requests, and AWS provides solutions. AWS Knowledge Center is a distinct resource compared with the AWS Documentation, the AWS Discussion Forums, and the AWS Support Center. It covers questions from across every AWS service. This should be the starting point for checking for a solution or troubleshooting an issue with AWS services.

The URL for Knowledge Center is:
https://aws.amazon.com/premiumsupport/knowledge-center/

AWS Marketplace

AWS Marketplace, which is an online software store, helps customers find, buy, and immediately start using software and services that run on AWS. The AWS Marketplace enables qualified AWS partners to market and sells their software to AWS Customers.

AWS Marketplace consists of thousands of software listings from popular categories such as security, networking, storage, machine learning, IoT, business intelligence, database, and DevOps.
AWS Marketplace is designed for ISVs (Independent Software Vendors), Value-Added Resellers, and Systems Integrators who have software products they want to provide to customers in the AWS Cloud.

You can use AWS Marketplace as a buyer, a seller, or both. In addition, anyone with an AWS account can use AWS Marketplace as a consumer and register to become a seller.

Contact AWS for Resource Abuse

AWS Support can't assist with reports of abuse or questions. AWS Abuse team is the right contact point for raising voice on abusive behavior using AWS resources.

The AWS Abuse team can assist you when AWS resources are used to engage in the following types of abusive behavior: spam from AWS-owned IP addresses or AWS resources, port scanning, Denial-of-service (DoS) or DDoS from AWS-owned IP addresses, intrusion attempts, hosting objectionable or copyrighted content, distributing malware.

I suspect that AWS resources are used for abusive or illegal purposes. How do I let AWS know?

Resolution

The AWS Trust & Safety team can assist you when AWS resources are used to engage in the following types of abusive behavior:

- **Spam:** You are receiving unwanted emails from an AWS-owned IP address, or AWS resources are used to spam websites or forums.
- **Port scanning:** Your logs show that one or more AWS-owned IP addresses are sending packets to multiple ports on your server. You also believe this is an attempt to discover unsecured ports.
- **Denial-of-service (DoS) attacks:** Your logs show that one or more AWS-owned IP addresses are used to flood ports on your resources with packets. You also believe that this is an attempt to overwhelm or crash your server or the software running on your server.
- **Intrusion attempts:** Your logs show that one or more AWS-owned IP addresses are used to attempt to log in to your resources.
- **Hosting prohibited content:** You have evidence that AWS resources are used to host or distribute prohibited content, such as illegal content or copyrighted content without the consent of the copyright holder.
- **Distributing malware:** You have evidence that AWS resources are used to distribute software that was knowingly created to compromise or cause harm to computers or machines that it's installed on.

If you suspect that AWS resources are used for abusive purposes, contact the AWS Trust & Safety team using the Report Amazon AWS abuse form, or by contacting abuse@amazonaws.com. Provide all the necessary information, including logs in plaintext, email headers, and so on, when you submit your request.

The AWS Trust & Safety team will use the information that you provide in this form to investigate and attempt to resolve the incident you have reported. We might share your information, if it is necessary for the investigation of your report.

Note: AWS Support can't assist with reports of abuse or questions about notifications from the AWS Trust & Safety team. If you have questions for the AWS Trust & Safety team, reply directly to their email.

Screenshot from:
https://aws.amazon.com/premiumsupport/knowledge-center/report-aws-abuse/

If you suspect that AWS resources are being used for abusive purposes, you need to contact the AWS Abuse team for prohibited use of AWS services using the Report Amazon AWS abuse form or by contacting abuse@amazonaws.com.

AWS Acceptable Use Policy

AWS Acceptable Use Policy

Last Updated: July 1, 2021

This Acceptable Use Policy ("**Policy**") governs your use of the services offered by Amazon Web Services, Inc. and its affiliates ("**Services**") and our website(s) including http://aws.amazon.com ("**AWS Site**"). We may modify this Policy by posting a revised version on the AWS Site. By using the Services or accessing the AWS Site, you agree to the latest version of this Policy.

You may not use, or facilitate or allow others to use, the Services or the AWS Site:

- for any illegal or fraudulent activity;
- to violate the rights of others;
- to threaten, incite, promote, or actively encourage violence, terrorism, or other serious harm;
- for any content or activity that promotes child sexual exploitation or abuse;
- to violate the security, integrity, or availability of any user, network, computer or communications system, software application, or network or computing device;
- to distribute, publish, send, or facilitate the sending of unsolicited mass email or other messages, promotions, advertising, or solicitations (or "spam").

Investigation and Enforcement

We may investigate any suspected violation of this Policy, and remove or disable access to any content or resource that violates this Policy. You agree to cooperate with us to remedy any violation.

When determining whether there has been a violation of this Policy, we may consider your ability and willingness to comply with this Policy, including the policies and processes you have in place to prevent or identify and remove any prohibited content or activity.

Reporting of Violations

To report any violation of this Policy, please follow our abuse reporting process.

Screenshot Reference: https://aws.amazon.com/aup/

Chapter 33. Advanced Identity

You will learn the following in this chapter:
- AWS Organizations
- AWS Service Control Policy
- IAM Conditions
- IAM Roles vs. Resource-Based Policies
- IAM Permission Boundaries
- IAM Policy Evaluation Logic
- Amazon Cognito
- AWS Control Tower
- AWS Single Sign-On (AWS SSO)
- AWS Security Hub
- Amazon Cloud Directory

AWS Organizations

AWS Organizations is a management service that consolidates multiple AWS accounts. The consolidation helps in the central management of accounts. As a result, AWS Organizations can help simplify account management – particularly for organizations with multiple AWS accounts.

For example, AWS Organizations can help create automated account creation, apply policies to the group of accounts, and consolidate billing. Thus, AWS Organizations provides centralized account and billing management control for organizations and companies with multiple AWS accounts.

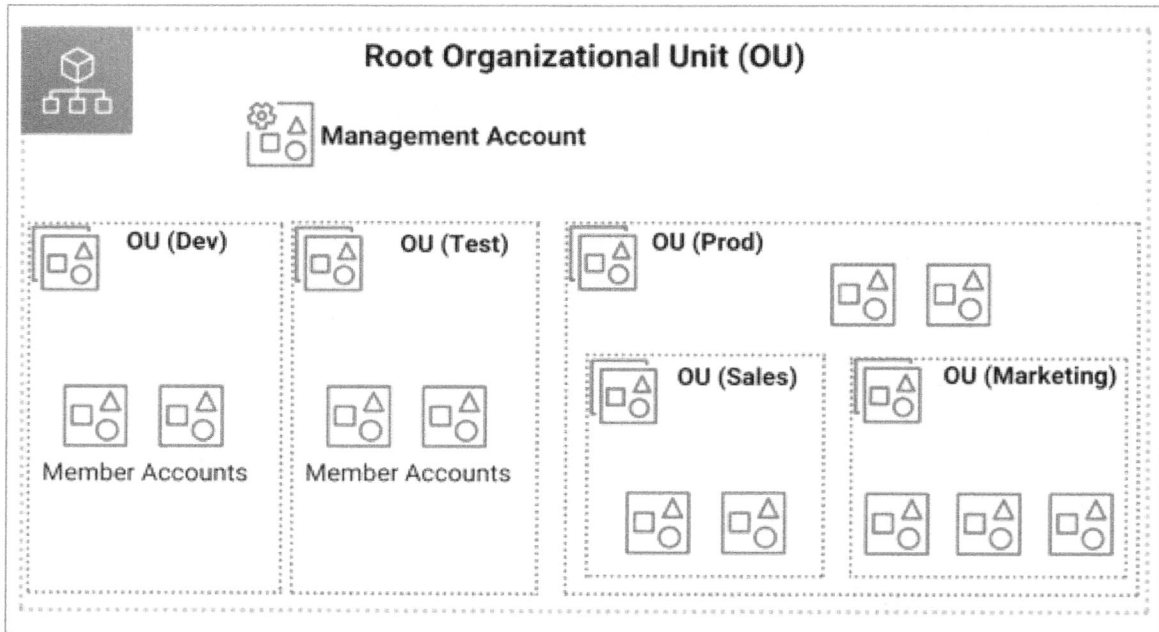

Many organizations have used multiple AWS accounts as they have scaled up their AWS usage for various reasons. For example, some customers have added AWS accounts incrementally as more users or departments started using AWS. Other customers have created separate AWS accounts for Dev, Test, and Prod environments to meet strict guidelines such as HIPPA, PCI, or other compliance.

As these AWS accounts grow, these customers would like to add policies and manage billing across their accounts in a simple and more scalable way – without requiring manual processes or custom scripts. And they also would like to add or create new accounts with the policies applied.

AWS Organizations can help with account management. Organizations want policy-based management for multiple AWS accounts.

You can create a group of accounts and then add policies to those accounts that centrally control the use of AWS services down to the API level across multiple accounts. For example, you can create a collection of production accounts and then apply policies about which AWS services, resources, and API calls those accounts can use.

You can also use AWS Organizations API to help automate the creation of AWS accounts. With simple API calls, you can create new accounts programmatically and then apply policies to these new accounts automatically.

With AWS Organizations, you can set up a single payment to all AWS accounts to get consolidated billing.

AWS Organizations is free and available to all AWS customers at no additional charge.

Organization Units (OU) Examples

Example 1:

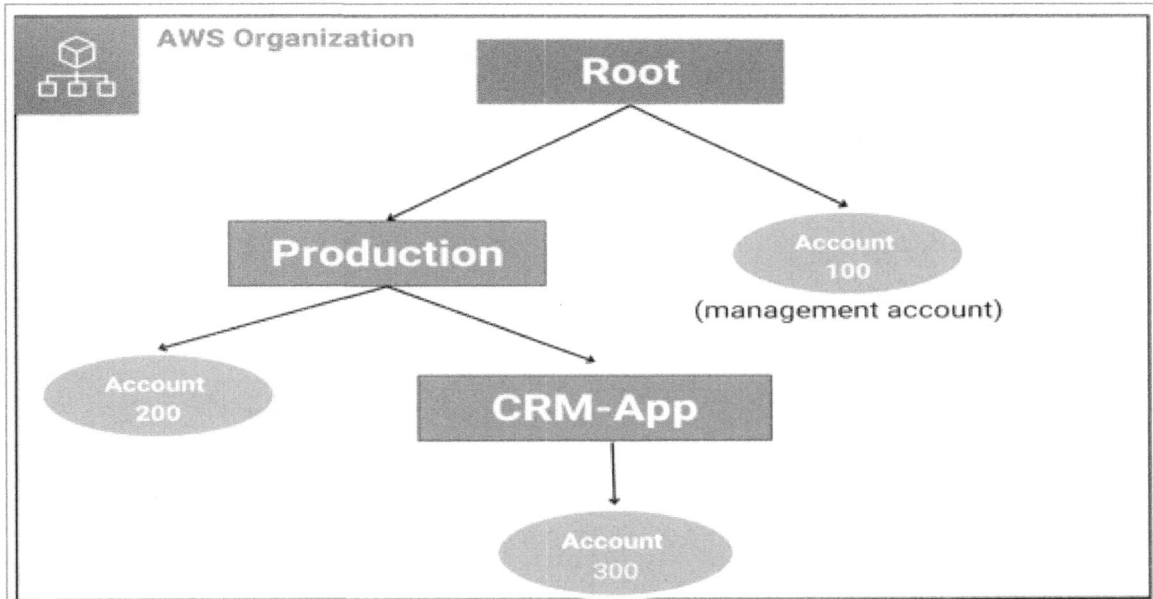

Example 2:

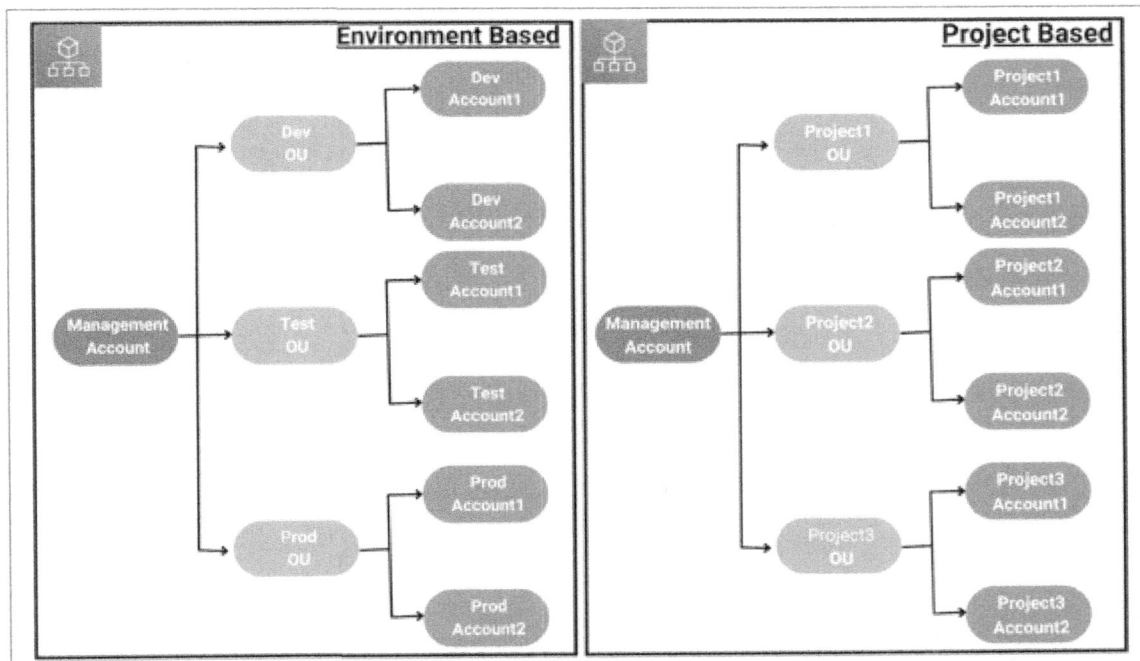

As you can see in the diagram, we can organize AWS Organizations in different ways. For example, one is environment based, and the other is project-based. We could have AWS Organizations based on business functions (sales, HR, finance, etc.).

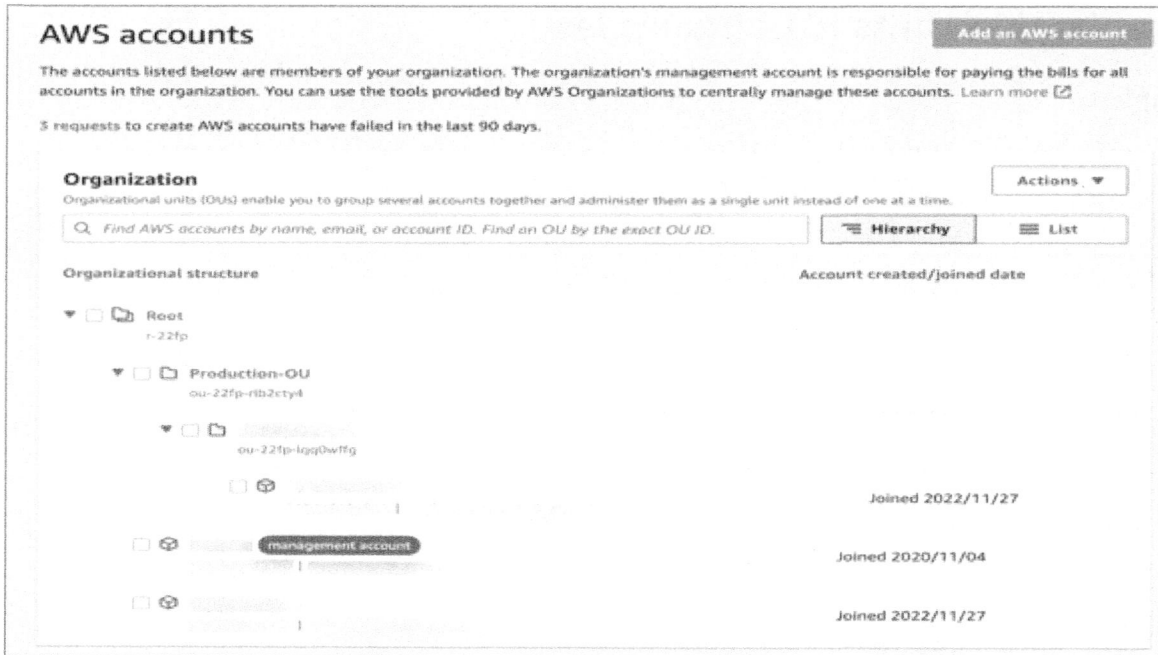

Screenshot of an AWS Organization

KEY POINTS

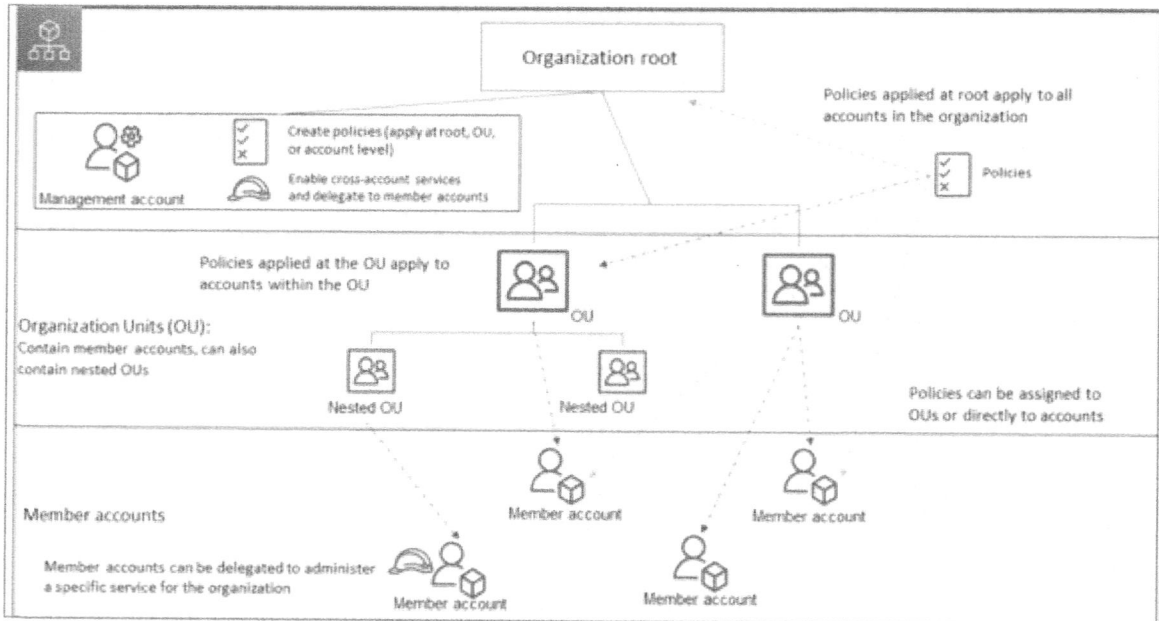

Screenshot for AWS Organizations Concepts and Terminologies
Reference: https://docs.aws.amazon.com/organizations/latest/userguide/orgs_getting-started_concepts.html

- It is a global service.

- It allows the managing of multiple AWS accounts, Multi VPC.
- The default maximum number of accounts allowed in an organization is **10.**

Management Account
- The main account is the management account.
- Management account has full admin power.

Member Accounts
- An AWS account can be a member of only one organization at a time.
- Other accounts are member accounts.
- Member accounts can only be part of one organization.
- AWS account creation can be automated with API.

Security
- Establish Cross Account Roles for Admin purposes
- IAM policies applied to OU or accounts to restrict users and roles
- It must have an explicit allow -- it does not allow anything by default – like IAM.
- SCP can be assigned to OUs or directly to accounts. In other words, you can apply SCPs to OUs and only member accounts in an organization. They do not affect users or roles in the management account.

Logging
- Enable CloudTrail on all accounts
- Send CloudWatch Logs to the central logging account.

Billing & Pricing
- Consolidated Billing across all accounts.
- Use tags for billing purposes.
- Pricing benefits from aggregated usage (such as volume discount for EC2, S3, etc.)
- Shared reserved instances and Savings Plans discounts across accounts.

AWS Service Control Policy

AWS Service Control Policy is a tool if you would like to control policies organization-wide centrally. It is a type of organizational policy you can use to manage permissions in your organization. Service control policies (SCPs) offer central control over the maximum available permissions for all accounts in your organization.

SCPs help you ensure your accounts stay within your organization's access control guidelines. SCPs are available only in an organization that has all features enabled. For example, SCPs aren't available if your organization only enabled consolidated billing features.

SCP can be assigned to OUs or directly to accounts. In other words, you can apply SCPs to OUs and only member accounts in an organization. They do not affect users or roles in the management account.

SCPs alone are insufficient to grant permissions to the accounts in your organization. An SCP grants no permissions. Instead, an SCP defines a guardrail or sets limits on the actions that the account's administrator can delegate to the IAM users and roles in the affected accounts.

To grant permissions, the administrator must still attach identity-based or resource-based policies to IAM users, roles, or the resources in your accounts. Effective permissions are the logical intersection between what is allowed by the SCP and what is allowed by the IAM and resource-based policies.

SCP Hierarchy

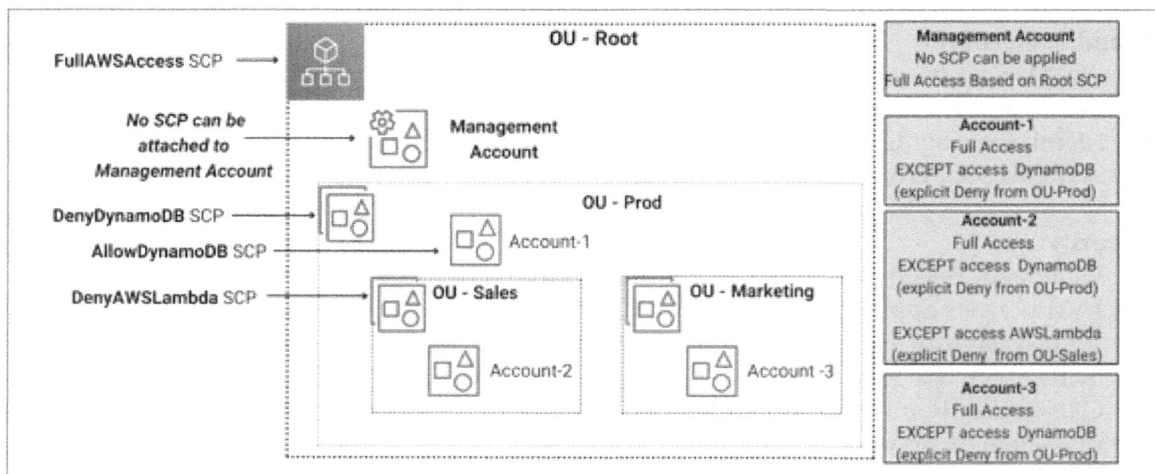

Strategies for Using SCP

To configure SCPs in an AWS Organization, you have two options: deny list and allow list.

deny list: by default, **actions are allowed**, and you specify the services and actions you want to restrict.

allow list – by default, **actions are not allowed**, and you specify what services and actions you want to allow.

Using SCPs as a deny list

This is the default configuration of AWS Organizations.

To support this, AWS Organizations attaches an AWS-managed SCP named FullAWSAccess to every root and OU when it's created. This policy allows all services and actions.

```
{
  "Version": "2012-10-17",
  "Statement": [
    {
      "Effect": "Allow",
      "Action": "*",
      "Resource": "*"
    }
  ]
}
```

You can attach an SCP that explicitly restricts actions that you don't want users and roles in certain accounts to perform.

```
{
  "Version": "2012-10-17",
  "Statement": [
    {
      "Sid": "AllowsAllActions",
      "Effect": "Allow",
      "Action": "*",
      "Resource": "*"
    },
    {
      "Sid": "DenyDynamoDB",
      "Effect": "Deny",
      "Action": "dynamodb:*",
      "Resource": "*"
    }
  ]
}
```

The users in the affected accounts can't perform DynamoDB actions because the explicit "Deny" element in the second statement that overrides the explicit "Allow" in the first.

You could also configure this by leaving the FullAWSAccess policy in place and then attaching a second policy with only the Deny statement, as shown here.

```
{
  "Version": "2012-10-17",
  "Statement": [
    {
      "Effect": "Deny",
      "Action": "dynamodb:*",
      "Resource": "*"
    }
  ]
}
```

The combination of the FullAWSAccess policy and the Deny statement has the same effect as the single policy that contains both statements.

Using SCPs as an allow list

To use SCPs as an allow list, you must replace the AWS-managed FullAWSAccess SCP with an SCP that explicitly permits only those services and actions that you want to allow.

Your custom SCP then overrides the implicit Deny with an explicit Allow for only those actions that you want to allow.

An allow list policy might look like the following example, which enables account users to perform operations for Amazon EC2 and Amazon CloudWatch, but no other service.

```
{
  "Version": "2012-10-17",
```

```
    "Statement": [
      {
        "Effect": "Allow",
        "Action": [
          "ec2:*",
          "cloudwatch:*"
        ],
        "Resource": "*"
      }
    ]
}
```

Reference:
https://docs.aws.amazon.com/organizations/latest/userguide/orgs_manage_policies_scps_strategies.html

IAM Conditions

With IAM Conditions, you can grant principals access only if specified conditions are met. For example, you could grant temporary access to users so they can resolve a critical production issue, or you could grant access only if an API call is requested from a certain IP address.

The Condition element (or Condition *block*) lets you specify conditions for when a policy is in effect. The Condition element is optional.

Let's see some examples of IAM Policy having a Condition block.

Restrict Based on Source IP
Condition block with aws:SourceIp

The example restricts the client IP **from** which the API calls are being made.

```
{
    "Version": "2012-10-17",
    "Statement": {
        "Effect": "Deny",
        "Action" "*",
        "Resource": "*",
        "Condition": {
            "NotIpAddress": {
                "aws:SourceIp": [
                    "192.0.2.2/24",
                    "204.0.113.1/24"
                ]
            }
        }
    }
}
```

Reference:
https://aws.amazon.com/premiumsupport/knowledge-center/iam-restrict-calls-ip-addresses/

Restrict Based on Region

Condition block with
aws:RequestedRegion

The example restricts the Region the API
calls are made **to**.

```
{
    "Version": "2012-10-17",
    "Statement": {
        "Sid": "AllowFromOnlyInsideUS",
        "Effect": "Allow",
        "Action": [
            "ec2: *",
            "rds: *",
            "s3: *"
        ] ,
        "Resource": "*",
        "Condition": {
            "StringEquals": {
                "aws:RequestedRegion": [
                    "us-east-1",
                    "us-west-1"
                ]
            }
        }
    }
}
```

Restrict Based on Tags

The example IAM policy restricts
based on tags.

```
{
    "Version": "2012-10-17",
    "Statement": {
        "Sid": "StartStopInstanceIfTag",
        "Effect": "Allow",
        "Action": [
            "ec2: StartInstances",
            "ec2: StopInstances",
            "ec2: DescribeTags"
        ],
        "Resource": "arn:aws:ec2:region:account-id:instance/*",
        "Condition": {
            "StringEquals": {
                "ec2:ResourceTag/Project": "ETL-Pipeline",
                "aws:PrincipalTag/Department": "Analytics"
            }
        }
    }
}
```

Restrict Based on MFA (Force MFA)

The example IAM forces MFA to stop and terminate EC2 instances.

```json
{
    "Version": "2012-10-17",
    "Statement": [
        {
            "Sid": "AllActionsOnEC2",
            "Effect": "Allow",
            "Action": "ec2.*",
            "Resource": "*"
        },
        {
            "Sid": "DenyStopAndTerminateActionsIfNoMFA",
            "Effect": "Deny",
            "Action": [
                "ec2:StopInstances",
                "ec2:TerminateInstances"
            ],
            "Resource": "*",
            "Condition": {
                "StringEquals": {"aws:MultiFactorAuthPresent": false}
            }
        }
    ]
}
```

Reference:
https://docs.aws.amazon.com/IAM/latest/UserGuide/reference_policies_elements_condition.html
https://docs.aws.amazon.com/eventbridge/latest/userguide/eb-use-conditions.html

IAM for S3

The example IAM policy shows two IAM statements:

- Allowed ListBucket action on the bucket.
- Allowed GetObject, PutObject action on the bucket. This is object-level permission.

```
{
    "Version": "2012-10-17",
    "Statement": [
        {
            "Sid": "S3ListBucket",
            "Effect": "Allow",
            "Action": ["s3:ListBucket"],
            "Resource":["arn:aws:s3:::test"]
        },
        {
            "Sid": "GetPutObjectOnS3",
            "Effect": "Allow",
            "Action": [
                "s3:PutObject",
                "s3:GetObject"
            ],
            "Resource":["arn:aws:s3:::test/*"]
        }
    ]
}
```

IAM Roles vs. Resource-Based Policies

Often, an IAM user may not have sufficient permissions to perform some operations, such as accessing a bucket in another account or accessing some resources in the same account on which the IAM user doesn't have the required permission.

In these scenarios, instead of modifying the IAM policy associated with the IAM user, the IAM user can be assigned (or assumed) a role as a proxy to perform the operation, or a resource-based policy can also be used.

The question is when to use IAM Roles and when to use Resource-Based Policies.

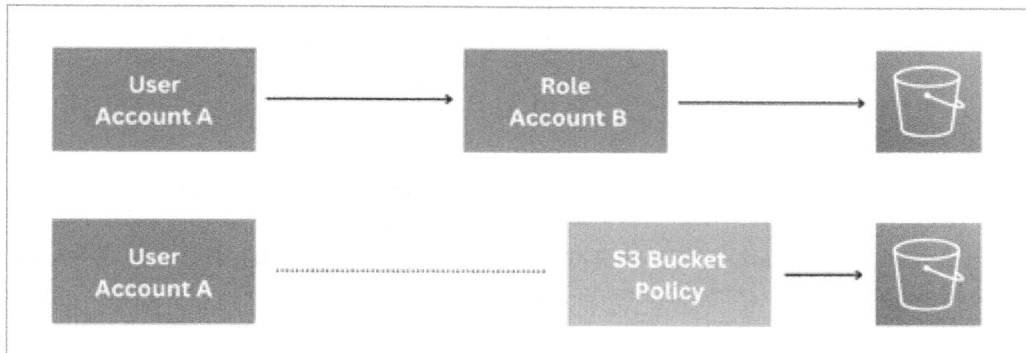

- **Roles are the common way to grant cross-account access**. However, for some AWS services, you can attach a policy directly to a resource (instead of using a role as a proxy). These policies are called resource-based policies, and you can use them to grant principals in another AWS account access to the resource. Some of these resources are S3 buckets, S3 Glacier vaults, SNS topics, and SQS queues.

- IAM roles and resource-based policies delegate access to accounts within a single partition. For example, assume that you have an account in us-west-1 in the standard aws partition. And, say you also have an account in China (Beijing) in the aws-cn partition. You can't use an Amazon S3 resource-based policy in your account in China (Beijing) to allow access for users in your standard aws accoun

- When you assume a role (user, application, or service), you give up your original permissions and take the permissions assigned to the role.

- When using a resource-based policy, the principal doesn't have to give up his permission. That way, cross-account access with a resource-based policy has some advantages over cross-account access with a role.

    As the principal doesn't have to give up his permission, a resource-based policy is useful for tasks such as copying information to or from the shared resource in the other account.

Reference: https://docs.aws.amazon.com/IAM/latest/UserGuide/id_roles_compare-resource-policies.html

IAM Permission Boundaries

A permissions boundary is an advanced feature for using a managed policy to set the maximum permissions that an identity-based policy can grant to an IAM entity.

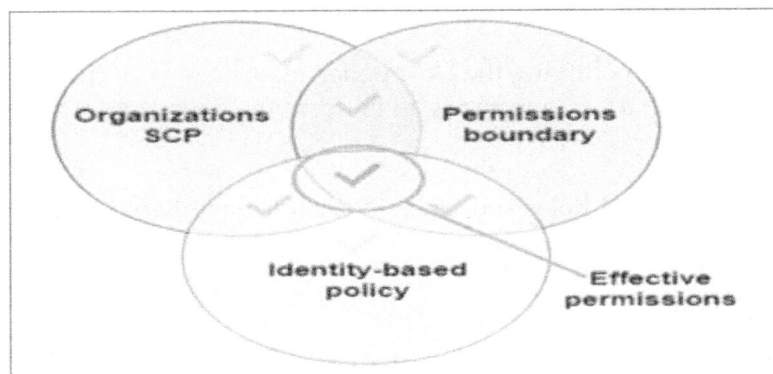

Reference: https://docs.aws.amazon.com/IAM/latest/UserGuide/access_policies_boundaries.html

An entity's permissions boundary allows it to perform only the actions that are allowed by both its identity-based policies and its permissions boundaries.

IAM Permission Boundaries are supported for users and roles -- not groups

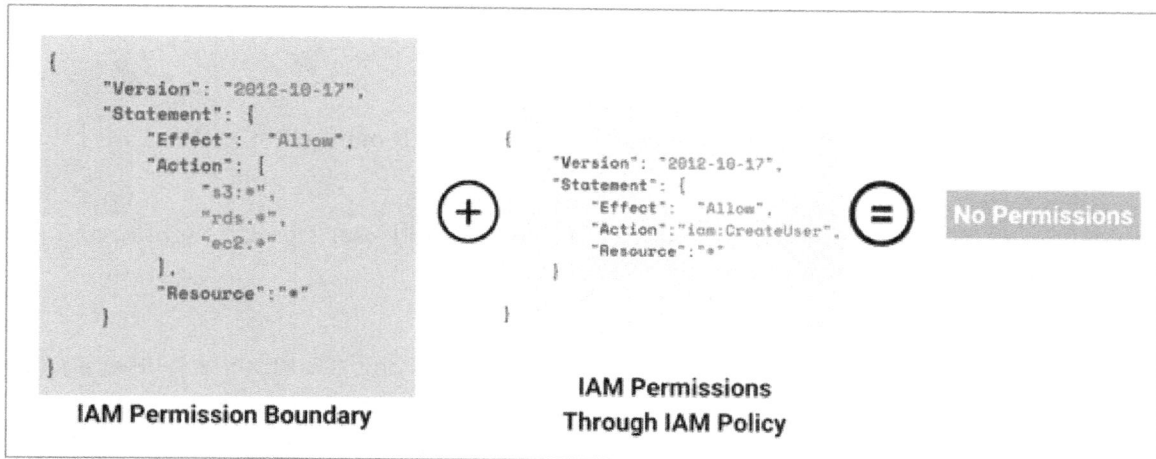

IAM Permission Boundaries can be used in combinations of AWS Organizations SCP

Use Cases
- o It can be used to delegate responsibilities to non-administrators within their permission boundaries, for example, to create new IAM users.
- o It allows developers to self-assign policies and manages their own permissions while making sure they can't "escalate" their privileges (in other words, make themselves admin)
- o It is useful to restrict one specific user -- instead of an entire account using Organizations & SCP.

IAM Policy Evaluation Logic

When a principal tries to use AWS, the principal sends a *request* to AWS. Before making the final decision about allowing or denying the request, AWS performs multiple steps: authentication, processing the request context, evaluating policies within a single account, and finally, determining whether a request is allowed or denied.

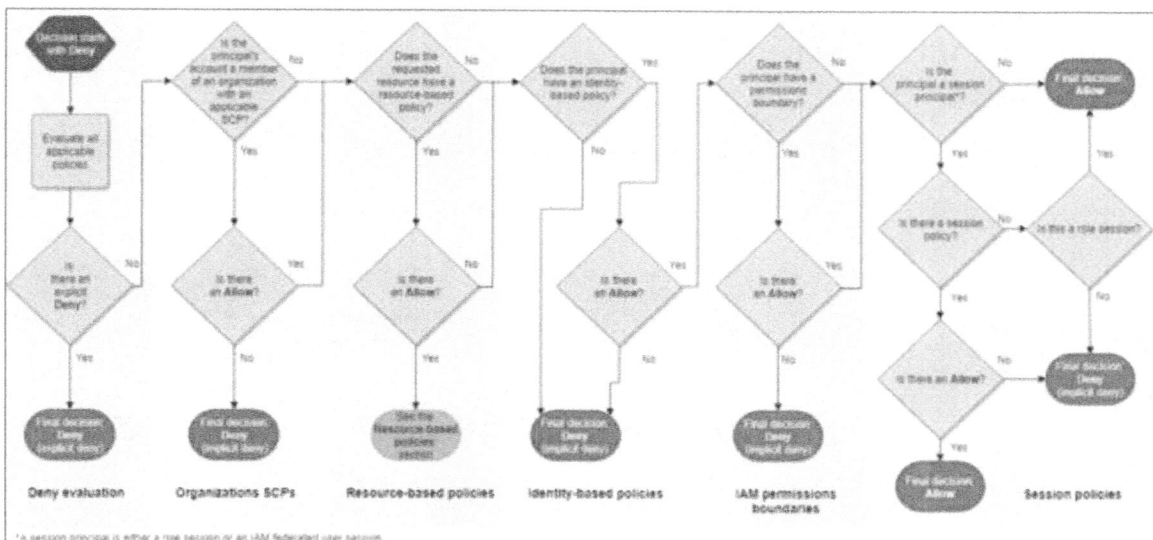

Reference: https://docs.aws.amazon.com/IAM/latest/UserGuide/reference_policies_evaluation-logic.html

Amazon Cognito

In more simple words, it provides users an identity to interact with our web or mobile application.

Amazon Cognito is a simple user identity service. It lets you add user sign-up, sign-in, and access control to your web and mobile apps quickly and easily.

It has two main features to authenticate users. One is Cognito User Pools (CUP), and the other is Cognito Identity Pools (Federated Identities).

Cognito User Pools is used for sign-in functionality for app users. It can be integrated with API Gateway and Application Load Balancer.

Cognito Identity Pools is a Federated Identity. It provides AWS credentials to users to access AWS resources directly. It is integrated with Cognito User Pools as an identity provider. You can authenticate users through social identity providers such as Facebook, Twitter, or Amazon, with SAML identity solutions or by using your identity system.

How Cognito differs from IAM? With IAM, you can scale with hundreds of users. Cognito is a simple, scalable solution when dealing with authenticating users for web and mobile applications on AWS. For example, you can scale your application for mobile users or authenticate with SAML.

Cognito User Pools creates a serverless database of the user for your web & mobile apps. It provides simple login: Username or email & password. It provides a password reset feature, email and phone number verification, also supports MFA. You can also use federated identities. For example, a user from Facebook, Google, and other federated identities can authenticate using Cognito.

Cognito User Pools (CUP) integrates with API Gateway and Application Load Balancer.

Integration with API Gateway

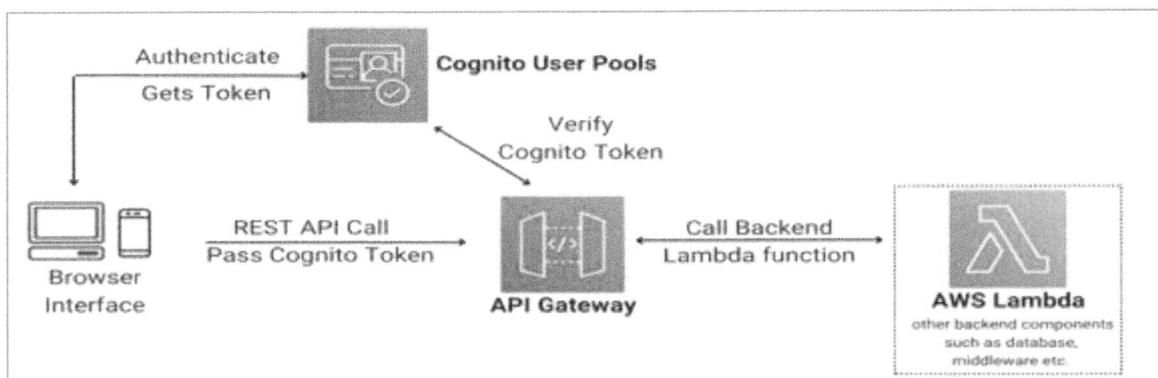

Integration with Application Load Balancer

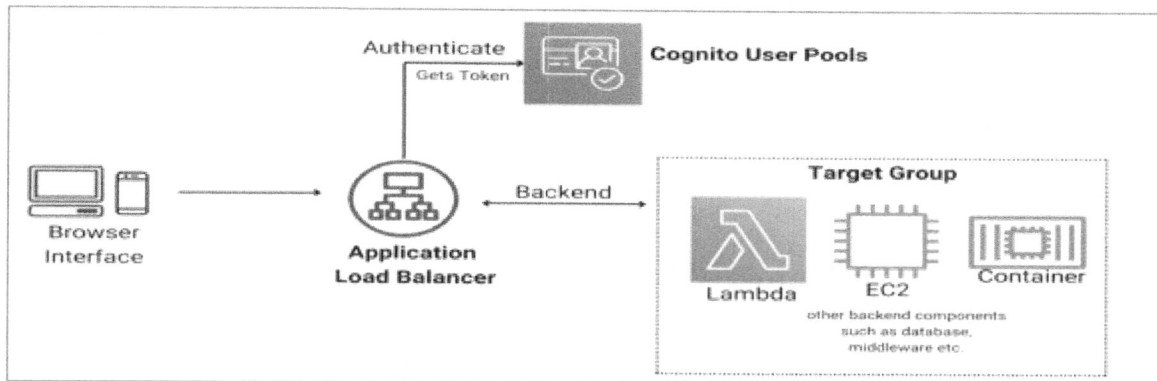

AWS Control Tower

If you have multiple AWS accounts and teams, cloud setup and governance can be complex and time-consuming -- it may slow down your AWS innovation, development, testing, or deployment. AWS Control Tower provides the easiest way to set up and govern a secure, multi-account AWS environment called a landing zone.

AWS Control Tower creates a landing zone by leveraging AWS Organizations. This brings ongoing account management and governance and implements best practices based on AWS's experience of working with thousands of customers as they move to the cloud.

Builders can provision new AWS accounts in a few clicks while you have peace of mind knowing that your accounts conform to company policies. You can extend governance into new or existing accounts and quickly gain visibility into their compliance status. Whether you are building a new AWS environment, starting on your journey to AWS, or starting a new cloud initiative, AWS Control Tower can help you quickly start with built-in governance and best practices.

Benefits

Quickly set up and configure a new AWS environment

Automate the setup of your multi-account AWS environment with just a few clicks. The setup employs blueprints that capture AWS best practices for configuring AWS security and management services to govern your environment. Blueprints are available to provide identity management, federate access to accounts, centralize logging, establish cross-account security audits, define workflows for provisioning accounts, and implement account baselines with network configurations.

Automate ongoing policy management

AWS Control Tower provides mandatory and strongly recommended high-level rules, called guardrails, that help enforce your policies using service control policies (SCPs), or detect policy violations using AWS Config rules. These rules remain in effect as you create new accounts or make changes to existing accounts, and AWS Control Tower provides a summary report of how each account conforms to your enabled policies. For example, you can enable data residency guardrails so that customer data, the personal data you upload to the AWS services under your AWS account, is not stored or processed outside a specific AWS Region or Regions.

View policy-level summaries of your AWS environment

AWS Control Tower provides an integrated dashboard so you can see a top-level summary of policies applied to your AWS environment. You can view details on the accounts provisioned, the guardrails enabled across your accounts, and account level status for compliance with your guardrails.

Screenshot from:
https://aws.amazon.com/controltower

AWS Single Sign-On (AWS SSO)

- AWS Single Sign-On allows you to grant users access to AWS resources across multiple AWS accounts.

- You can enable this highly available SSO service without upfront investment and ongoing maintenance costs -- just with a few clicks.

- With AWS SSO, you can easily manage SSO access and user permissions to all of your accounts in AWS Organizations centrally.

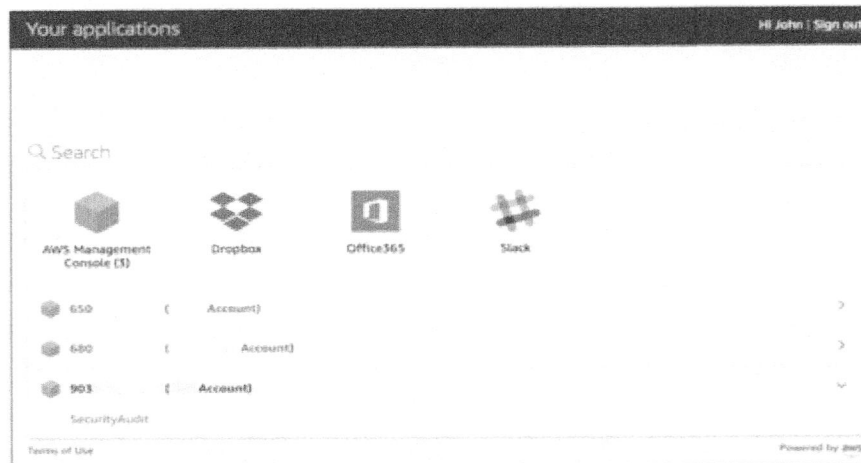

Reference: https://aws.amazon.com/blogs/security/introducing-aws-single-sign-on/

- You can create or connect your workforce identities in AWS once you are using AWS SSO. And then you can manage access centrally across your AWS organization.

- You can add user identities directly in AWS SSO or bring them from your Microsoft AD. You can also bring users from other identity providers, for example, Okta or Azure AD. AWS SSO helps you offer a unified administration experience to define, customize, and assign fine-grained access.

- In addition, your workforce users get a user portal to access all of their accounts, such as AWS accounts, EC2 instances, Windows instances, or deployed applications. AWS SSO can also be configured to run alongside or replace AWS account access management via AWS IAM.

KEY POINTS

- You can centrally manage Single Sign-On (SSO) to access multiple accounts and 3rd-party business applications.
- It can be integrated with the on-premises Active Directory
- It is integrated with AWS Organization.
- It supports SAML 2.0 markup.
- Centralized permission management and centralized auditing with CloudTrail

AWS Security Hub

AWS Security Hub provides a centralized and organizational-wide cloud security posture management of all your workloads. It performs security best practice checks, aggregates alerts, and enables automated remediation. You can run AWS Security Hub in standalone mode for a single account. Or you can run it in organization mode, where it aggregates data from all your AWS account.

AWS Security Hub provides you with a view of the comprehensive security state in your AWS account. Additionally, it helps you check your AWS environment against security industry standards and best practices.

The AWS Security Hub collects security data from AWS accounts, services, and supported third-party partner products. The data helps analyze security trends and identify the highest-priority security issues.

Once enabled, AWS Security Hub begins to consume, aggregate, organize and prioritize findings from AWS services you have enabled, such as Amazon GuardDuty, and Amazon Inspector. AWS Security Hub also generates its own findings by running continuous, automated security checks based on AWS best practices and supported industry standards. Security Hub then correlates and consolidates findings across providers to help you to prioritize the most significant results.

Service Quotas

Service Quotas enable you to view and manage your quotas for AWS services from a central location. Quotas, also referred to as limits in AWS, are the maximum values for the resources, actions, and items in your AWS account. Each AWS service defines its quotas and establishes default values for those quotas.

Amazon Cloud Directory

Amazon Cloud Directory is like Microsoft AD (Active Directory) or LDAP in terms of its core use case. However, Amazon Cloud Directory is a more advanced solution on the cloud for hierarchical data. For example, traditional directory solutions, such as Microsoft AD or LDAP, are limited to a single hierarchy, which is single. Cloud Directory, however, offers the flexibility to create directories with hierarchies that span multiple dimensions. For example, you can create an organizational chart that can be navigated through separate hierarchies for reporting structure, location, and cost center.

Amazon Cloud Directory has extensive scalability -- it can automatically scale to hundreds of millions of objects. It provides an extensible schema that can be shared with multiple applications. It is a fully-managed service – for example, it eliminates time-consuming and expensive administrative tasks, such as scaling infrastructure and managing servers.

Working with Amazon Cloud Directory is very easy -- first, you define the schema, then create a directory. After that, you can populate the directory by making calls to the Cloud Directory API. It is integrated with AWS CloudTrail. AWS CloudTrail can help you log the date, time, and identity of users who accesses your directory data. You can tag your directories and schemas with resource tagging to better track and manage resources.

With regards to its use cases, you can efficiently organize hierarchies of data across multiple dimensions and search your directory for objects and relationships.

Section 10. Networking

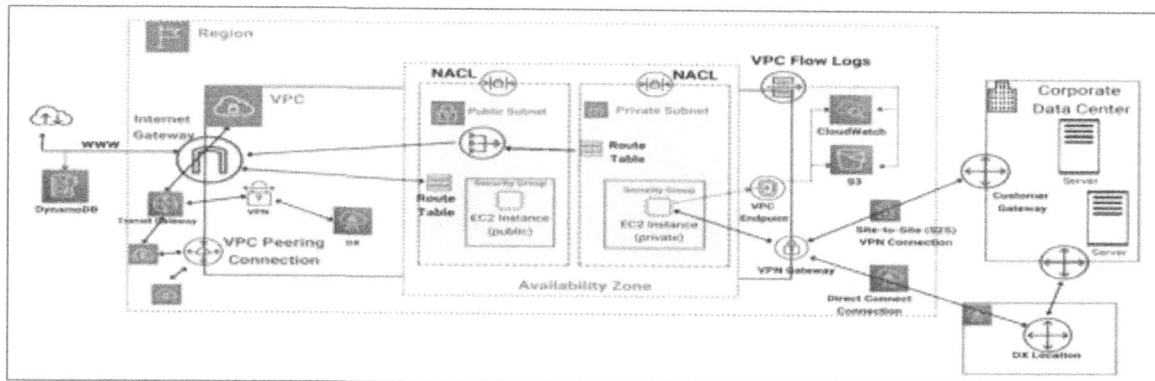

Chapter 34. AWS Networking

You will learn the following in this chapter:
- Understanding CIDR – IPv4, CIDR Components
- AWS VPC Concepts and Fundamentals: public and private subnets
- Internet Gateway (IGW)
- Bastion Hosts
- NAT Gateway
- Security Group
- Network Access Control List (NACLs)
- Ephemeral Ports
- VPC Peering
- VPC Endpoints
- AWS Transit Gateway
- VPC Flow Logs
- DNS in VPC
- AWS Site-to-Site VPN
- AWS VPN CloudHub
- AWS Direct Connect
- AWS Networking Components Architecture Diagram

Understanding CIDR – IPv4

CIDR (Classless Inter-Domain Routing) is a method for allocating IP addresses that improves the efficiency of address distribution in a network

The CIDR is used in Security Groups rules and AWS networking in general.

IP version ▽	Type ▽	Protocol ▽	Port range ▽	Source ▽	Description ▽
IPv4	HTTPS	TCP	443	0.0.0.0/0	-
IPv4	HTTP	TCP	80	0.0.0.0/0	-
IPv4	SSH	TCP	22	73.81.154.236/32	-

They help to define an IP address range.

- For example, in **XX.YY.ZZ.WW/32**. The CIDR XX.YY.ZZ.WW/32 has an IP address range for one IP.

- In **0.0.0.0/0.** the CIDR 0.0.0.0/0 has an IP address range for all IPs.

- We can also define, for example,**192.168.0.0/27**. The CIDR 192.168.0.0/27 has an IP address range from **192.168.0.0 – 192.168.0.31**(32 IP addresses). It means if you use this CIDR, you will be able to allocate 32 different IP addresses for different machines in your network.

CIDR Components

A CIDR has two components: base IP address and subnet mask.

Base IP: Base IP represents an IP address part in the range -- similar to what would be seen in a normal IP address, such as 192.168.0.0, 10.0.0.0, etc.

Subnet Mask: CIDR notation is just shorthand for the subnet mask and represents the number of bits available to the IP address. For instance, the /24 in 192.168.0.101/24 is equivalent to the IP address 192.168.0.101 and the subnet mask 255.255.255.0

Or we can also understand it in another way, as a subnet mask defines how many bits can be changed in the CIDR.

For example:
/8 ⇔ 255.0.0.0 [last three octets can change]
/16 ⇔ 255.255.0.0 [last two octets can change]
/24 ⇔ 255.255.255.0 [last octets can change]
/32 ⇔ 255.255.255.255 [no octet can change]

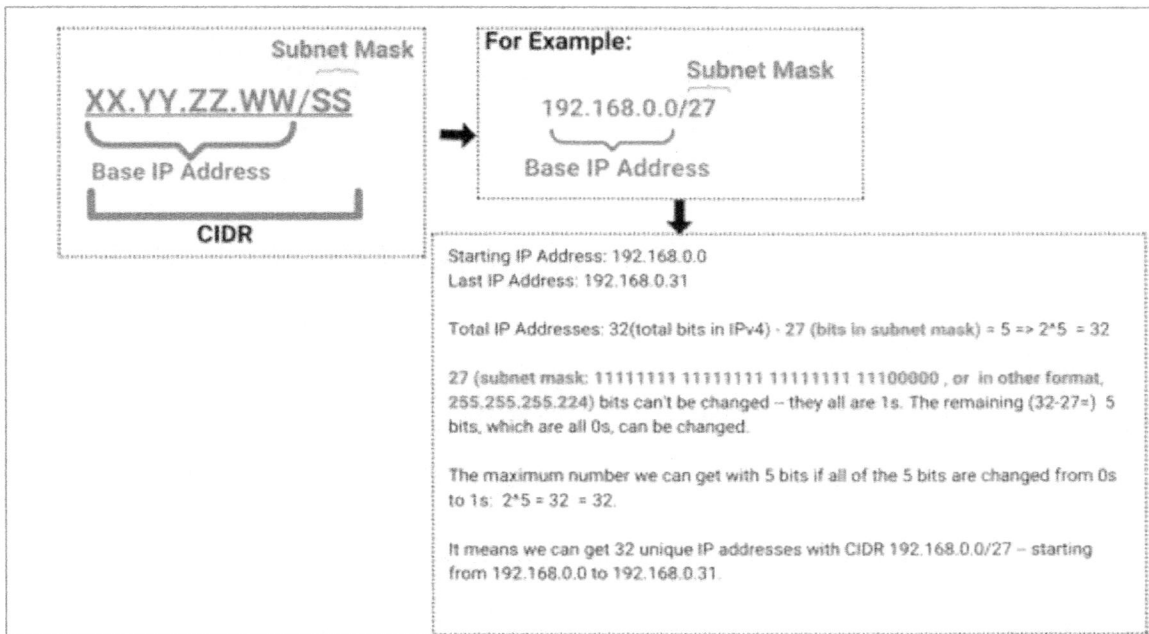

Starting IP Address: 192.168.0.0
Last IP Address: 192.168.0.31

Total IP Addresses: 32(total bits in IPv4) - 27 (bits in subnet mask) = 5 => 2^5 = 32

27 (subnet mask: 11111111 11111111 11111111 11100000 , or in other format, 255.255.255.224) bits can't be changed -- they all are 1s. The remaining (32-27=) 5 bits, which are all 0s, can be changed.

The maximum number we can get with 5 bits if all of the 5 bits are changed from 0s to 1s: 2^5 = 32 = 32.

It means we can get 32 unique IP addresses with CIDR 192.168.0.0/27 – starting from 192.168.0.0 to 192.168.0.31.

Subnet Mask

The Subnet mask allows to the allocation of a range of IP addresses starting from the base IP. The concept depends on changing bits that can be changed. For example, if the subnet mask is /27, we can change 32-27 = 5 bits from 0 to 1 to get different IP addresses. The one permutation is when all 5 bits are 1s. and that will be the last IP address for the CIDR having subnet mask /27.

Let's see in detail to get a better understanding.

CIDR – Review Exercise

- **192.168.0.0/24 =?** => 192.168.0.0 – 192.168.0.255 (256 IPs)

- **192.168.0.0/16 = ?** => 192.168.0.0 – 192.168.255.255 (65,536 IPs)

- **134.56.78.123/32 =?** => just 134.56.78.123

- **0.0.0.0/0** => All IPs!

When you need a quick look-up, you can use: https://www.ipaddressguide.com/cidr

Public vs. Private IP Address

Public IP Address

- A public IP address is a unique identifier assigned to your ISP (Internet Service Provider) by your internet connection (or router) by your ISP (Internet Service Provider). Your router uses its public IP address to communicate with the rest of the internet.

- A public IP address is unique -- other devices do not use it.

- A public IP address is used to communicate with sites and servers on the internet.

- Public IP addresses are traceable by ISPs, advertisers, governments, and hackers.

- You can find your public IP address by searching for "What is my IP address" on Google.

Private IP Address

- On the other hand, the private IP address identifies different devices connected to the same local network. Once your router has received information from the global network to send it to one of the devices on your network, it needs to know which device to send it to. The private IP address helps the router identify different devices on your network to forward the response.

- Private IP addresses are not unique – different routers can reuse them.

- Private IP addresses are used to communicate between devices on a local network.

- They are traceable by other devices on the local network.

- You can find a private IP address by using system settings and preferences.

IP Addresses for Public and Private IP

The Internet Assigned Numbers Authority (IANA) established certain blocks of IPv4 addresses for the use of private (LAN) and public (Internet) addresses.

Private IP can only allow specific values:
- 10.0.0.0 – 10.255.255.255 (10.0.0.0/8) [Used commonly in big networks which need lots of IP addresses]
- 172.16.0.0 – 172.31.255.255 (172.16.0.0/12) [AWS default VPC range]

- 192.168.0.0 – 192.168.255.255 (192.168.0.0/16) [Used commonly in home networks]

All the rest of the IP addresses on the internet are Public IP addresses.

AWS VPC

People tend to use AWS as if it were a virtual data center. As a result, they deploy the same kind of stuff in their on-premises data center. For example, they might launch EC2 instances, databases, EMR instances, etc. These instances need to live in some network and talk to the Internet.

AWS has VPC (Virtual Private Cloud), a private, isolated network to group AWS resources. You also think of VPC as a private virtual network on AWS Cloud.

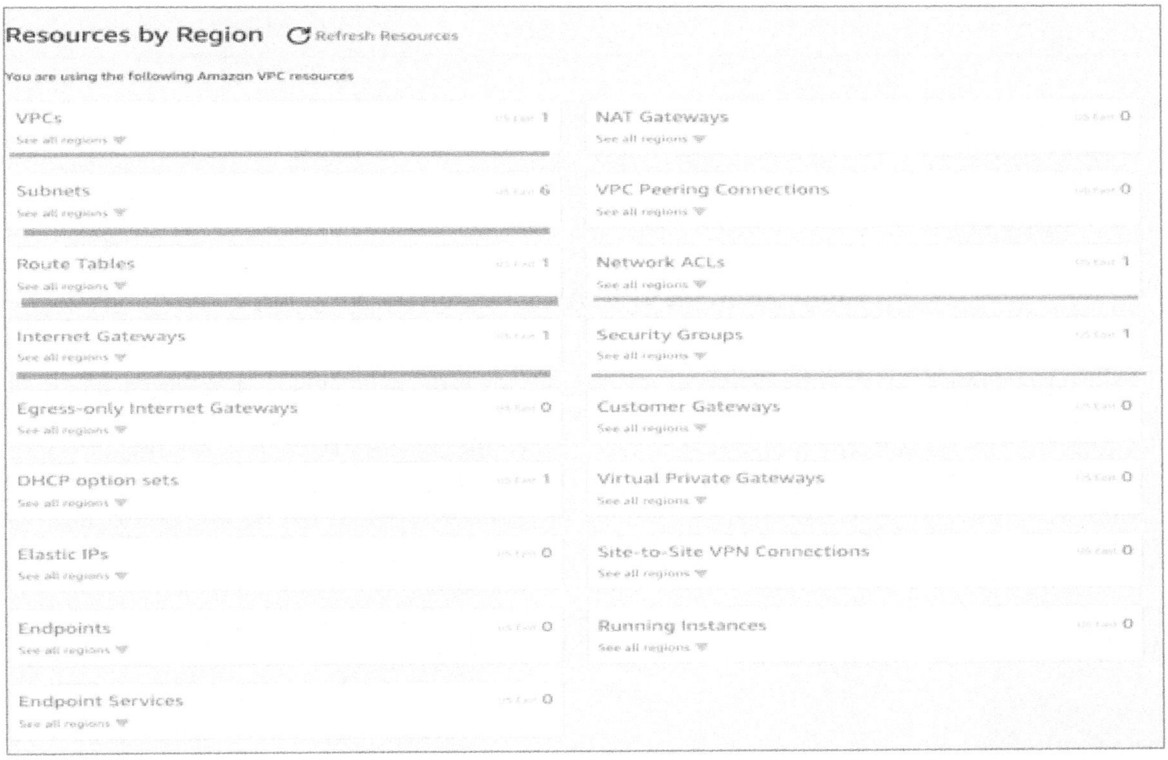

The above screenshot shows different defaults you get related to AWS VPC in your account.

When you create a new AWS account, AWS gives many things to help start with a network in your AWS account. It provides you with a default VPC with a CIDR range. It provides you with subnets for AZs for resiliency. It gives Route tables and Internet Gateway to connect AWS resources to the Internet. It also gives you security groups and Network ACLs to provide security.

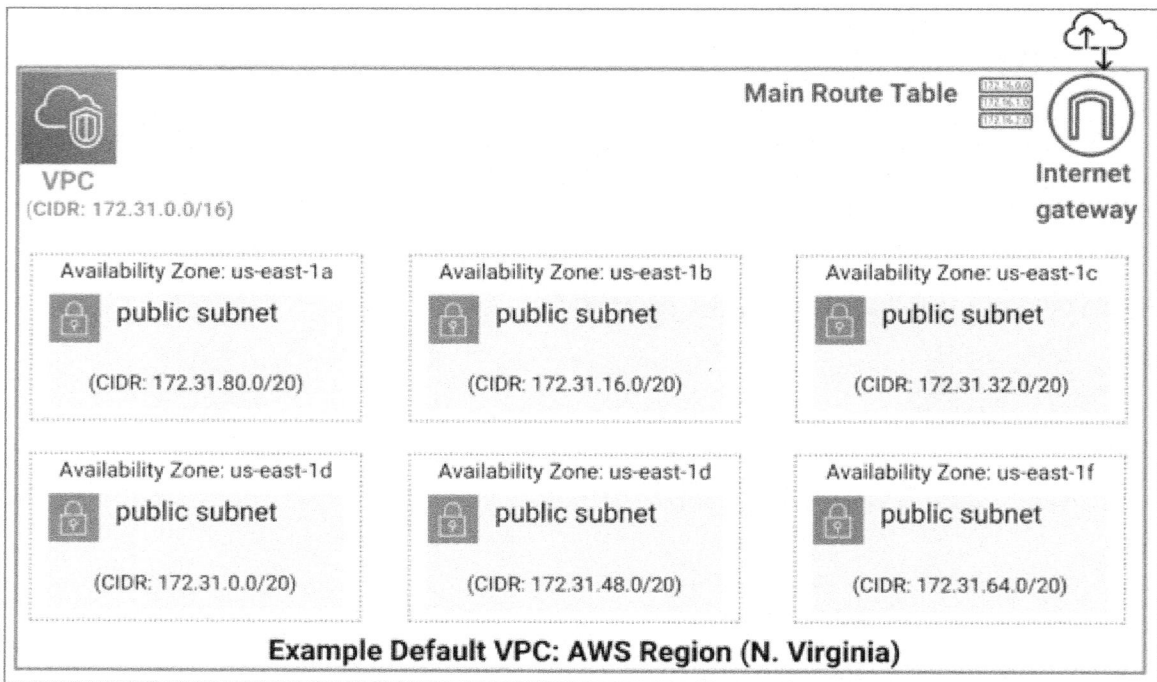

Example Default VPC: AWS Region (N. Virginia)

The above diagram is another way to get an idea about a default VPC that AWS gives you when creating a new account. In the diagram, the AWS Region is N. Virginia with 6 AZs. Each is associated with a subnet. The main Route table is related to each subnet in the VPC. An Internet Gateway is also connected to the VPC to manage Internet traffic. You can notice that the CIDR block is assigned to each subnet and the VPC. No hosts are shown in any subnet as this is the default setup, and no EC2 instance has been launched yet.

Default VPC is a good starting point. Next, we will understand different components of AWS networking to help build your VPC or modify the default VPC for your requirements.

KEY POINTS

- All new AWS accounts get default VPC. When you sign up for a new account, you will get a default VPC.
- New EC2 instances are launched into the default VPC if no subnet is specified.
- Default VPC has Internet connectivity, and all EC2 instances inside the default VPC have public IPv4 addresses.
- Each EC2 instance launched in a public subnet also gets public and private IPv4 DNS names.

AWS VPC Concepts and Fundamentals

What is VPC?

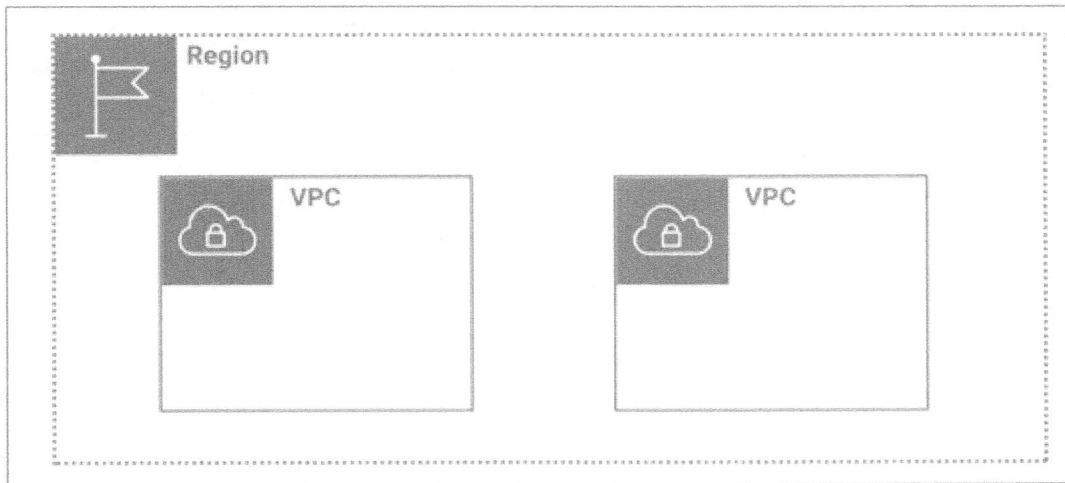

Virtual Private Cloud (VPC) is conceptually like a traditional network in a data center, with the additional benefits of leveraging the massively scalable infrastructure of AWS. Virtual Private Cloud (VPC) enables you to launch AWS resources into the network you have set up. A Virtual Private Cloud (VPC) allows selecting your IP address range, creating subnets, and configure route tables and network gateways. A Virtual Private Cloud (VPC) controls how the AWS resources inside your network are exposed to the Internet.

IP Address CIDR Block

Let's start with IP addresses. At the time of AWS account creation, you get a default VPC. So, for example, in my AWS account, with N. Virginia is the default AWS Region, and the CIDR range for the VPC is 172.31.0.0/16.

In the CIDR block (172.31.0.0/16.), the first half portion of the first two octets ("172.31") describes the network portion of the IP address, and the next two octets ("0.0") represent the host portion of the IP address. The "172.31.*" is a private IP range. If you use this IP range in your private VPC, you will not have overlapping or conflict with any other IP address on the Internet. We should not have overlapping IP addresses because overlapping IP addresses can't talk to each other.

Let's talk about the host portion of the CIDR block (172.31.0.0/16). In the host portion of the CIDR block, we have "0.0/16," -- which means we can get around 65536 IP addresses. There are many IP addresses to launch resources in a private network.

When defining your IP CIDR block, think about how many resources you will be launching and choose the IP address CIDR block accordingly.

VPC Subnets

What is a subnet? -- A subnet is a range of IP addresses in your VPC. You can launch AWS resources into a specific subnet, such as EC2 instances. When you create a subnet, you specify a subset of the VPC CIDR block for the subnet. Each subnet must reside entirely within one Availability Zone (AZ) and cannot span zones. Launching instances in separate Availability Zones can protect your applications from the failure of a single zone.

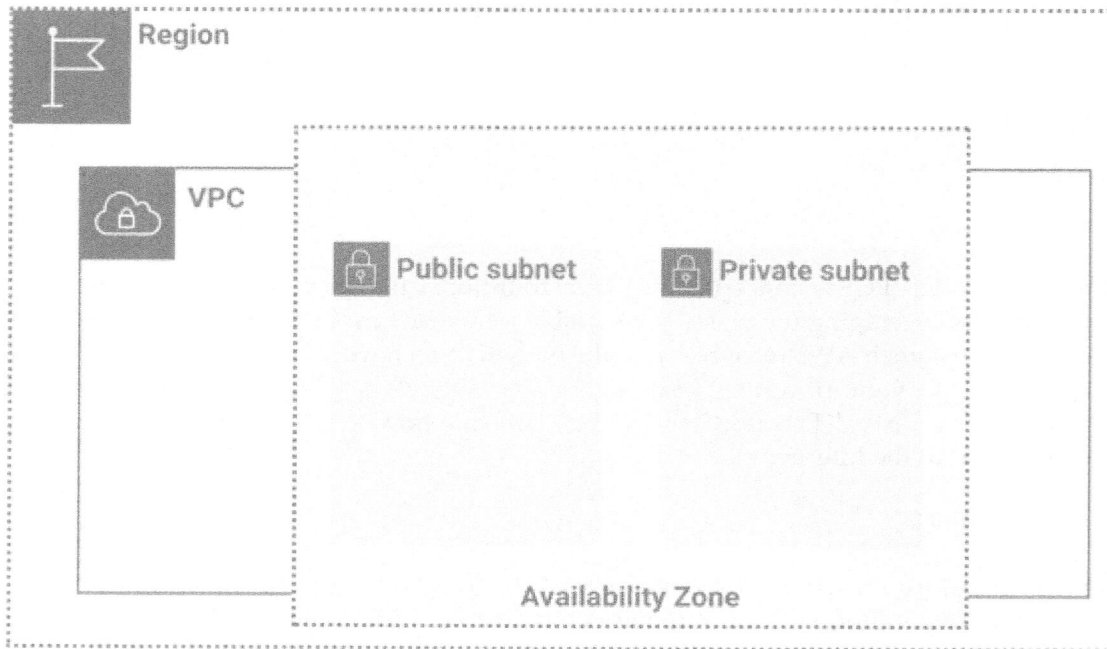

When a default VPC is created, AWS creates subnets based on the number of Availability Zones (AZs) and assigns a CIDR range to each subnet. It establishes one subnet for each AZ.

When creating yourself, assign IP address CIDR to each subnet of the VPC and make sure there are no overlapping IP addresses.

As you can see in the screenshot, in the default VPC with six subnets – there are six AZs in the us-east-1 (N. Virginia) Region. Each of them has been assigned a CIDR range. Each AZ has one or more data centers with a separate power grid, away from the city to avoid floods or other natural calamities.

Each AZ is associated with a subnet in a Region. This subnet association with an AZ helps resources in a subnet talk to resources in the other subnet using their private address yet having logical separation.

When defining your subnet, we need to put subnet in AZs so that they can talk to a subnet of other AZs in the same Region. To do that, we need to divide the CIDR range of VPC into different subnets. For example, from the screenshot of the subnets given above, in the case of subnet-2c9eb173, the IPv4 CIDR is 172.31.32.0/20. That means the network address for this subnet is 172.31.32.0 and starting IP address for the first host is 172.31.33.0, and the ending IP address is 172.31.46.255, with the max possible hosts in this subnet being 4094.

You can use the CIDR calculator https://codebeautify.org/cidr-calculator to get the ideal network address and max hosts about other subnets based on the CIDR block address.

As you can see in the default setting with VPC IP CIDR (172.31.0.0/16), the first two octets are used for the network portion of subnets.

Private Subnet
You need a private subnet when you want your AWS resources not reachable from the Internet. In the case of a private subnet, the Route table associated with the subnet doesn't have an association with the Internet Gateway. In other words, there will be no entry for the Internet Gateway in the Route table.

KEY POINTS

- You can have multiple VPCs in an AWS region -- the maximum of 5 VPCs per region, which is a soft limit.

- For each CIDR, the minimum size is /28 (16 IP addresses), and the maximum size is /16 (65536 IP addresses)

- Because VPC is private, only Private IPv4 ranges are allowed:
  - 10.0.0.0 – 10.255.255.255 (10.0.0.0/8)

-     o   172.16.0.0 – 172.31.255.255 (172.16.0.0/12)
-     o   192.168.0.0 – 192.168.255.255 (192.168.0.0/16

- VPC CIDRs should NOT overlap.

- AWS reserves 5 IP addresses in each subnet – the first four and the last one from the CIDR range. These 5 IP addresses are unavailable for use and can't be assigned to an EC2 instance.

- Example: if a subnet has CIDR block 10.0.0.0/24, then reserved IP addresses are:
  - 10.0.0.0 – network address
  - 10.0.0.1 – reserved by AWS for the VPC router
  - 10.0.0.2 – reserved by AWS for mapping to Amazon-provided DNS
  - 10.0.0.3 – reserved by AWS for future use
  - 10.0.0.255 – Network broadcast addresses AWS does not support broadcast in a VPC; therefore, the address is reserved.

  (Reference: https://docs.aws.amazon.com/vpc/latest/userguide/configure-subnets.html)

- For example: if you need 30 IP addresses for EC2 instances:
  You can't choose a subnet of size /27, which is 32 IP addresses (32 – 5 = 27 < 30)
  You need to choose a subnet of size /26, which is 64 IP addresses (64 – 5 = 59 > 30)

Internet Gateway (IGW)

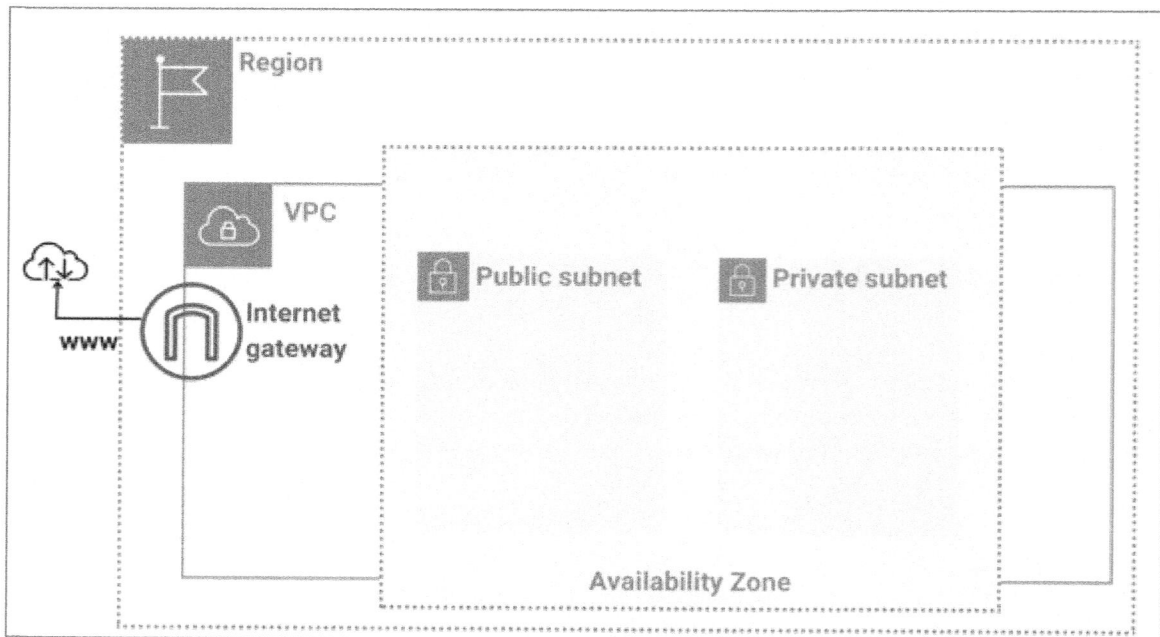

- Internet Gateway allows resources (such as EC2 Instances) in a VPC to connect to the Internet. It scales horizontally and is highly available.

- A default VPC comes with a public subnet in each AZ, an internet gateway, and the main route table. In other words, there is an Internet Gateway in your default VPC. But for other

VPCs, an internet gateway needs to be created separately because one internet gateway can be attached to only one VPC.

- Just creating an internet gateway will not default allow access to resources from VPC to the Internet. You will need to add/edit an entry in the Route table.

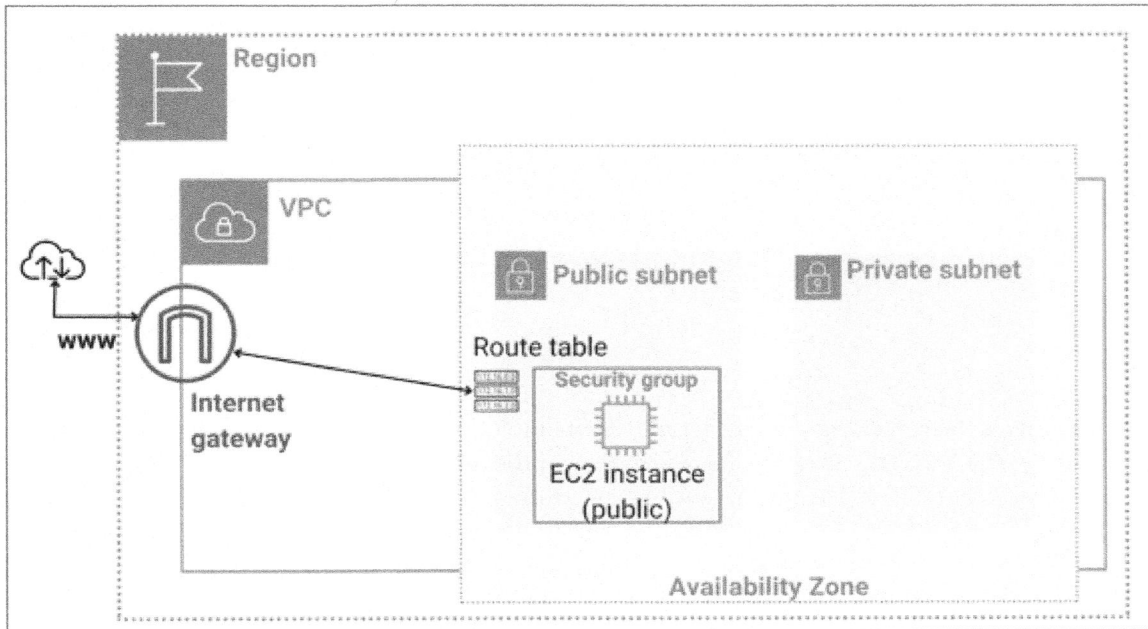

Routing in VPC

Routing is critical to talk to two addresses on a VPC. How two IP addresses talk to each other – the rules – are contained in a Route table. In other words, a Route table includes rules about how two IP addresses talk to each other on a VPC or where to send the next packet.

A routing table specifies how packets are forwarded between the subnets within your VPC, the internet, and your VPN connection.

Every VPC has a default Route table, in which a rule says a target for every request in CIDR range is inside the VPC.

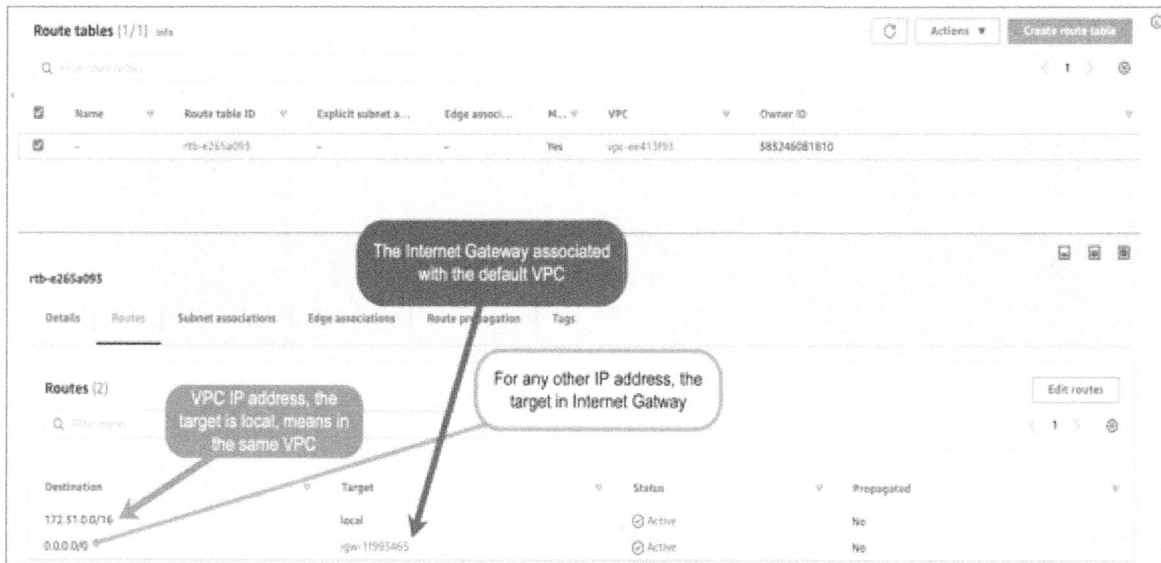

As you can see, this is the screenshot of the default Route table for the default VPC. When a destination is the IP address of the VPC, the target is local – means in the VPC. If the destination IP address is not from the VPC IP address CIDR, the target is Internet Gateway, associated with the default VPC.

You can also create a Route table and assign it to any subnet in your VPC. Then that Route table will replace the default route table of the VPC.

What About VPC Resources Talking to the Internet

For resources in VPC to connect to the Internet:
- Your VPC needs to have a connection to the Internet. You will get the default Internet Gateway when you get your AWS account.
- You need a route to the Internet Gateway from the Route table associated with the subnet. Next, you need to have a public IP address for the resource in the subnet trying to connect to the Internet.

The above screenshot shows all the subnets in the N. Virginia Region in my AWS account. Since there are six AZs in the N. Virginia, that's why if you notice in the screenshot, there are six subnets.

In the case of default subnets that AWS creates for the default VPC, each of them, by default, is associated with the default route table. As you saw earlier, that default Route table has an entry to the Internet Gateway. In other words, if we launch an EC2 instance in a subnet created by AWS for the default VPC, the EC2 instance will get a public IP address.

Please keep in mind that any subnet in which the Route table has an entry for the Internet Gateway means the subnet is public. Therefore, all subnets associated with default VPC is, by default, a public subnet unless we add a different Route table that doesn't have an entry for Internet Gateway.

Private Subnet

In many use cases, you need a private subnet where you want AWS resources not reachable from the Internet. In the case of a private subnet, the Route table associated with the subnet doesn't have association with the Internet Gateway. In other words, there will be no entry for the Internet Gateway in the Route table.

A typical use case for EC2 instances running in a private subnet is a scenario in which instances should not be accessible from the Internet. Still, they are, however, allowed to connect to the Internet to download any software or get an update about their installed software.

The question is how to allow a host inside a private subnet to access the Internet. The answer is NAT Gateway. Unfortunately, there is no default NAT Gateway created with the default VPC.

Bastion Hosts

If you have worked in complex big enterprise projects, particularly with many Unix servers, you have come across or used bastion hosts to SSH to Unix servers such as database / Hadoop servers. Because of their functions, these servers do not typically allow inbound connections from any machines on the network and are typically behind a company firewall. In other words, you cannot SSH to them directly -- you will have to use a Bastion host to SSH to them.

On AWS, you can set up bastion hosts inside a public subnet to connect to (SSH) EC2 instances running in a private subnet.

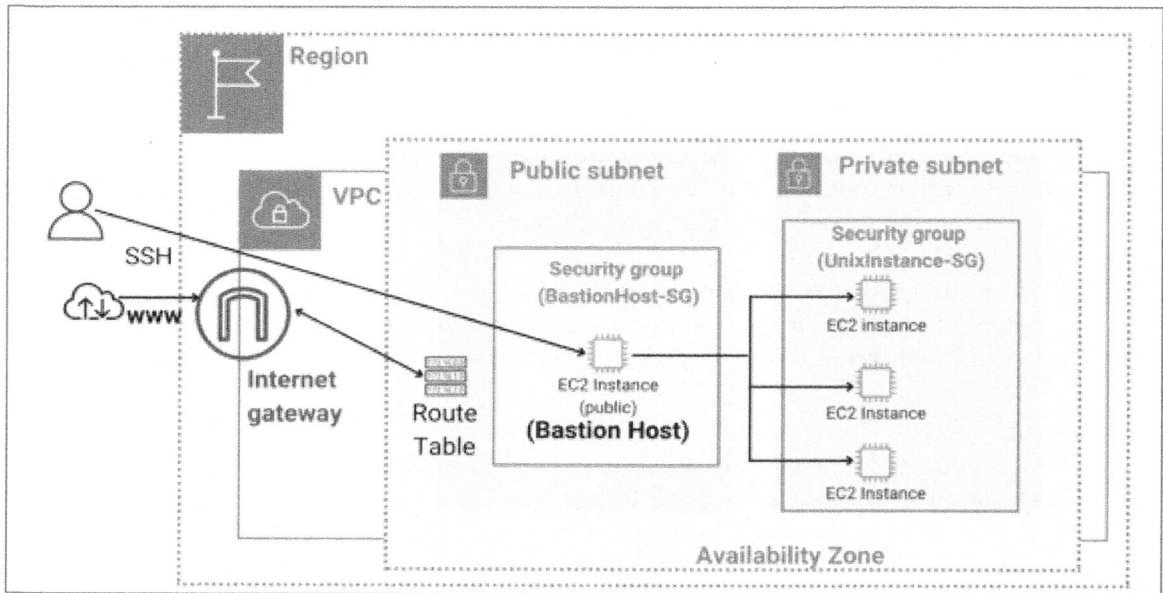

- The bastion host is in the public subnet, which then can be used to connect to all other EC2 instances running in a private subnet.

- Bastion Host security group must allow inbound connection from the internet on port 22 from restricted CIDR, for example, the public CIDR of your corporation.

- Security Group of the EC2 Instances must allow the Security Group of the Bastion Host or the private IP of the Bastion host.

NAT Gateway

What is NAT Gateway? A NAT gateway is a Network Address Translation (NAT) service. You can use a NAT gateway so that instances in a private subnet can connect to services outside of your VPC. However, the external services cannot initiate a connection with instances inside the private subnet.

When you create a NAT gateway, you specify one of the following connectivity types:

Public – (Default) Instances in private subnets can connect to the internet through a public NAT gateway but cannot receive unsolicited inbound connections from the internet. You create a public NAT gateway in a public subnet and must associate an elastic IP address with the NAT gateway at creation. Then, you route traffic from the NAT gateway to the internet gateway for the VPC. Alternatively, you can use a public NAT gateway to connect to other VPCs or your on-premises network. In this case, you route traffic from the NAT gateway through a transit gateway or a virtual private gateway.

Private – Instances in private subnets can connect to other VPCs or your on-premises network through a private NAT gateway. You can route traffic from the NAT gateway through a transit gateway or a virtual private gateway. You cannot associate an elastic IP address with a private NAT gateway. You can attach an internet gateway to a VPC with a private NAT gateway, but if you route traffic from the private NAT gateway to the internet gateway, the internet gateway drops the traffic.

Reference:
https://docs.aws.amazon.com/vpc/latest/userguide/vpc-nat-gateway.html

Suppose you would like hosts in the private subnet to connect to the Internet. You will need to create NAT Gateway and associate the NAT Gateway to the subnet.

Please note that the NAT Gateway is one way street to connect. What it means inbound traffic from the Internet to the NAT Gateway is not allowed.

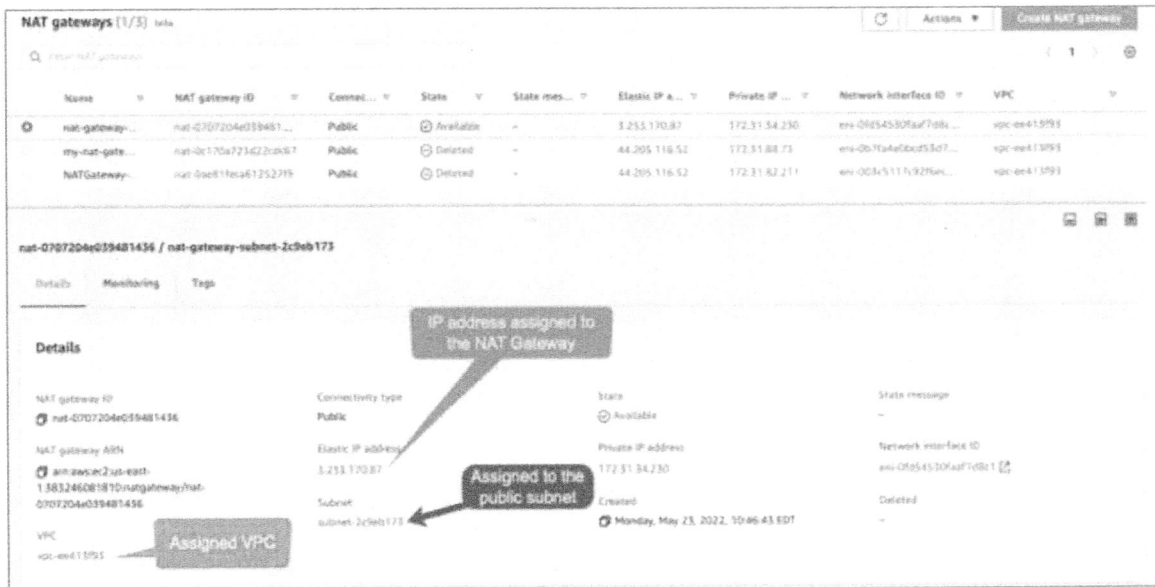

The above screenshot is related to a NAT Gateway. The NAT Gateway is assigned an Elastic IP address, which is a must. For devices to connect to the Internet and find and talk to other devices or machines on the Internet, a public IP address is necessary.

The next point to notice is that it is assigned to a VPC, and VPC is connected to the Internet Gateway.

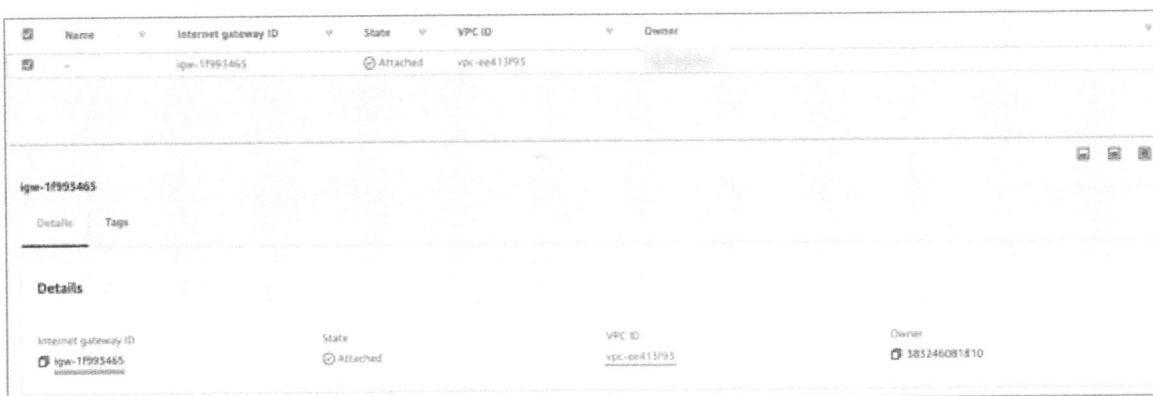

As you can notice in the above screenshot of an Internet Gateway, it is connected to a VPC.

Going back to the screenshot of the NAT Gateway, another vital point to notice is that it is assigned a public subnet. It is an important point – a NAT Gateway must be associated with a public subnet.

You have created a NAT Gateway in the public subnet. The NAT Gateway is associated with a VPC assigned Internet Gateway, which will take care of Internet traffic. Please keep in mind that NAT Gateway is a device for one-way traffic. In other words, a NAT Gateway allows making outbound calls to the Internet from resources in the private subnet -- not the inbound calls from the Internet to the subnet. The typical use case is to get patches or install software on the machines in a private subnet.

The next question is: how will a host in a private subnet connect to the NAT Gateway to go to the Internet, for example, download a patch or a software.

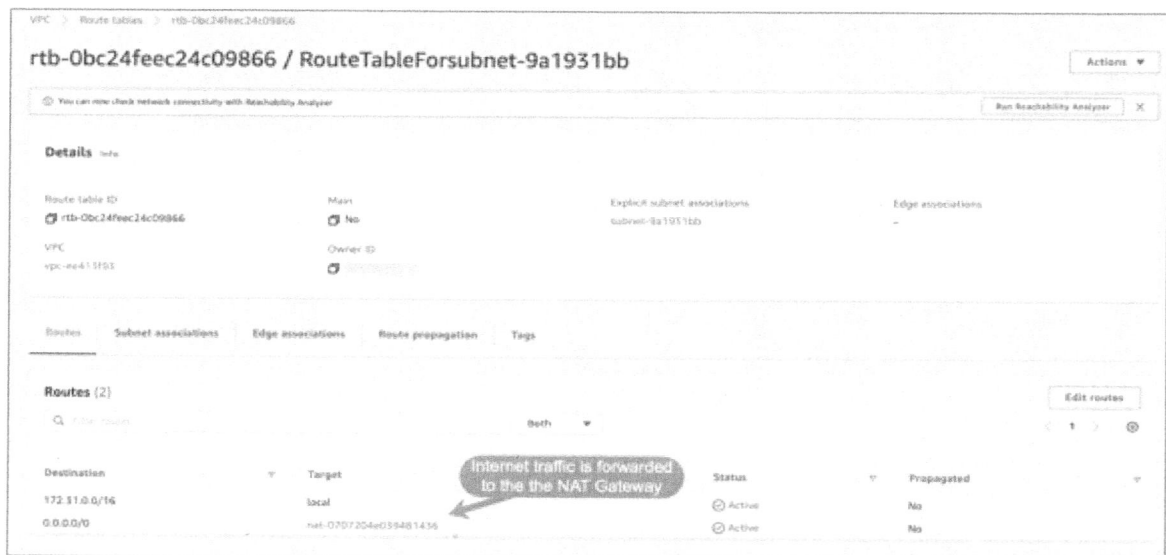

The answer in the Route Table of the private subnet is straightforward: add an entry for the Internet traffic to forward to the NAT Gateway, as you can see in the screenshot above.

For hosts in a private subnet to make outbound requests to the Internet, in the Route table associated with the private subnet, an entry will be added to direct Internet 0.0.0.0/0 traffic to the NAT Gateway, as you can notice in the screenshot above.

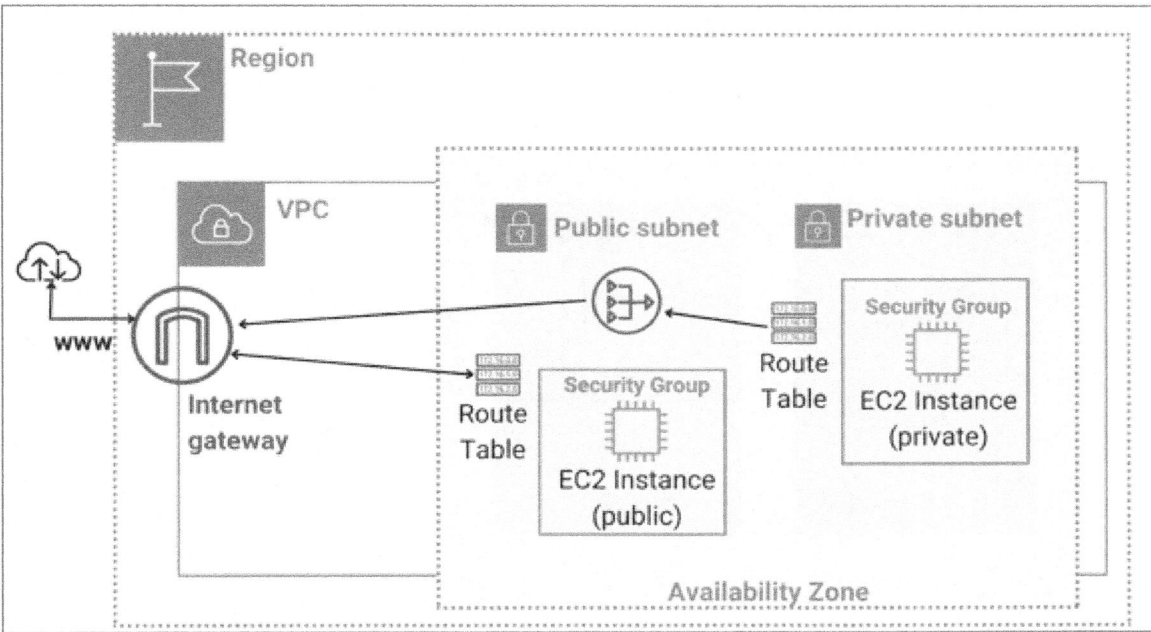

The above diagram shows setting up NAT Gateway in the public subnet to access the Internet from the hosts in the private subnet. If you notice, traffic from the private subnet goes to the NAT Gateway. And from there, then, it is sent to the Internet Gateway connected to the Internet.

KEY POINTS

- NAT Gateway (NATGW) is associated with a specific Availability Zone and uses an Elastic IP.
- NAT Gateway is created in a public subnet.
- NAT Gateway (NATGW) is connected to the Internet Gateway in the VPC. The connection order is Private Subnet => NATGW => IGW
- Provides 5 Gbps of bandwidth with automatic scaling up to 100 Gbps
- Typically used for connecting EC2 instances in a private subnet to the Internet. For example, if the instances in the private subnet want to download software from the Internet. They can use NAT Gateway connectivity to connect to the Internet.

NAT Gateway With High Availability

Though NAT Gateway is resilient within a single Availability Zone, you must create multiple NAT Gateways in multiple AZs for fault tolerance.

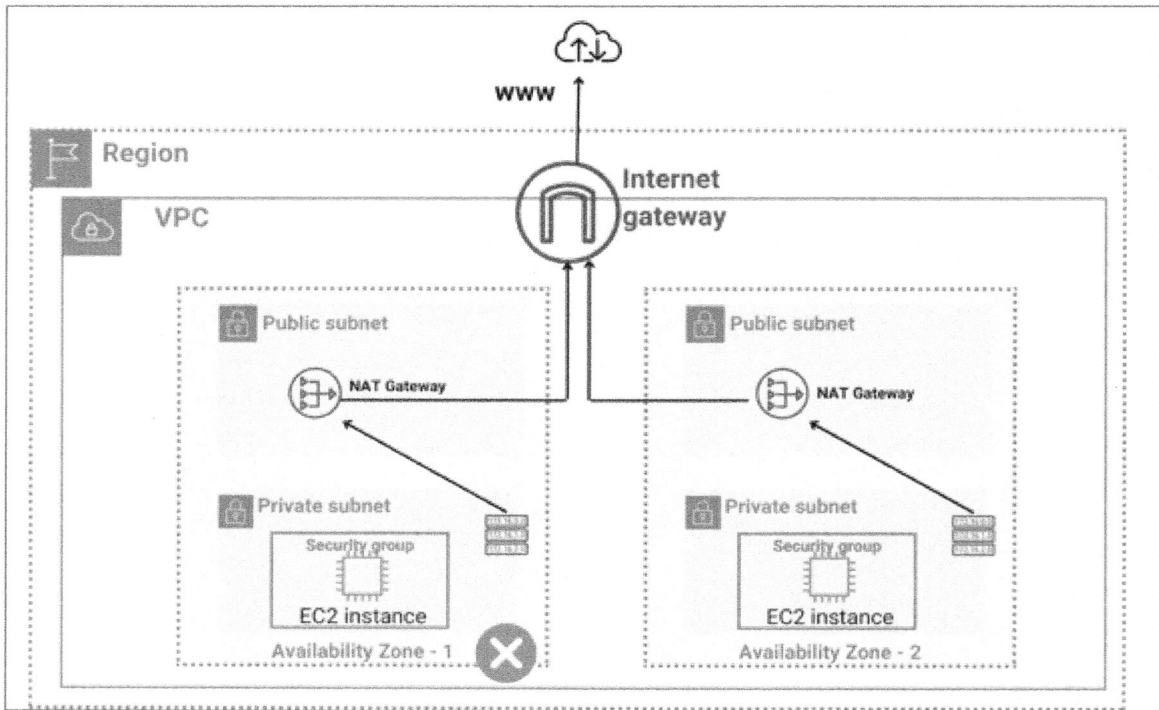

NAT Gateway and Internet Gateway

- Internet Gateway allows Internet access to public AWS resources -- within a VPC.
- NAT Gateway allows Internet access to AWS resources – that are in a private subnet.

In other works, Internet Gateway is way out to the Internet for your public AWS resources. However, NAT Gateway, which is connected to the Internet Gateway, allows your private AWS resources way out to the Internet.

☑	Name	▽	Internet gateway ID	▽	State	▽	VPC ID	▽	Owner		▽
☑	-		igw-1f993465		⊘ Attached		vpc-ee413f93				

Screenshot showing Internet Gateway in the default VPC.

AWS Network Security

When we talk about AWS network security, it is essential to understand security group, Network Access Control List (NACLs), and VPC Flow Logs.

Security Group

What is a security group? Security groups are AWS distributed firewalls. The important point to know about the AWS Security Group, or in general, about any firewall, is that they are stateful. So, for example, if a request is allowed, a response is automatically allowed.

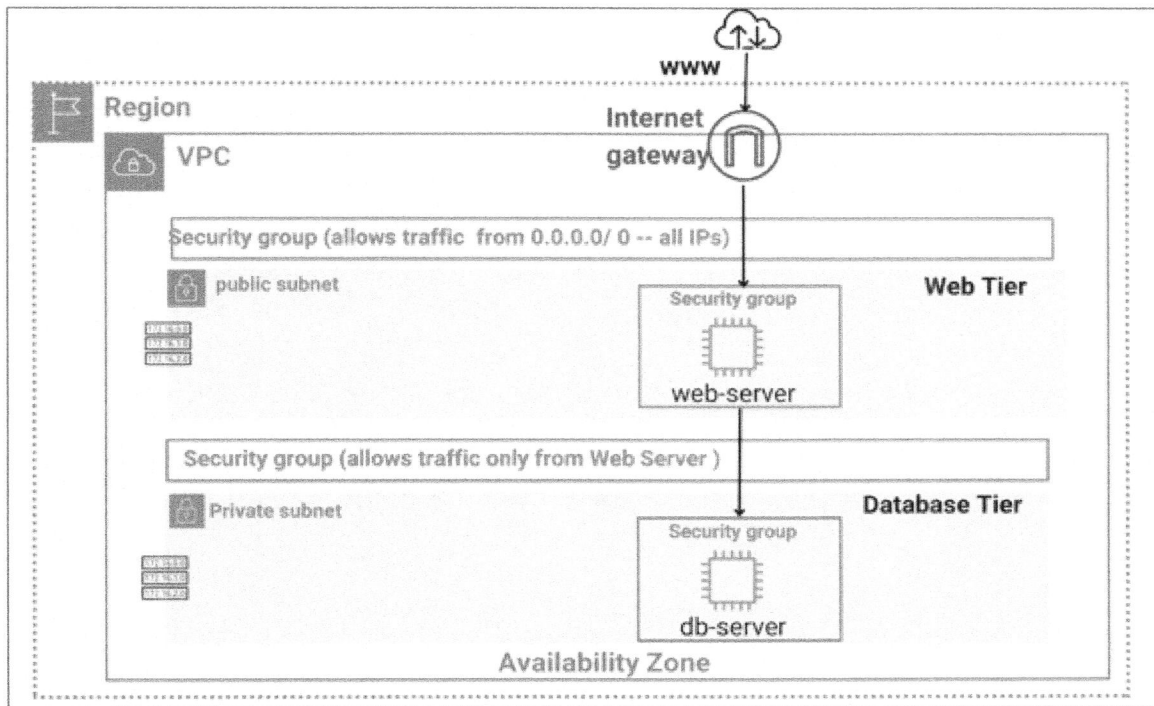

Let's try to understand Security Group with the diagram shown above. One EC2 instance runs a web server, and one EC2 instance is for the database. It's always a good practice to protect your databases. So EC2 instances running database servers are in a private subnet. And they only accept traffic from the web server. On the other hand, the EC2 instance running the web server is in a public subnet. The reason is that the web server needs to be accessed from the Internet.

Now that was the concept of the security group. How will you create it? You can create it by clicking on the Security Group link on VPC or EC2 instance. Also, when you launch an EC2 instance, you can assign a default security group, create a new one, or choose from the existing ones.

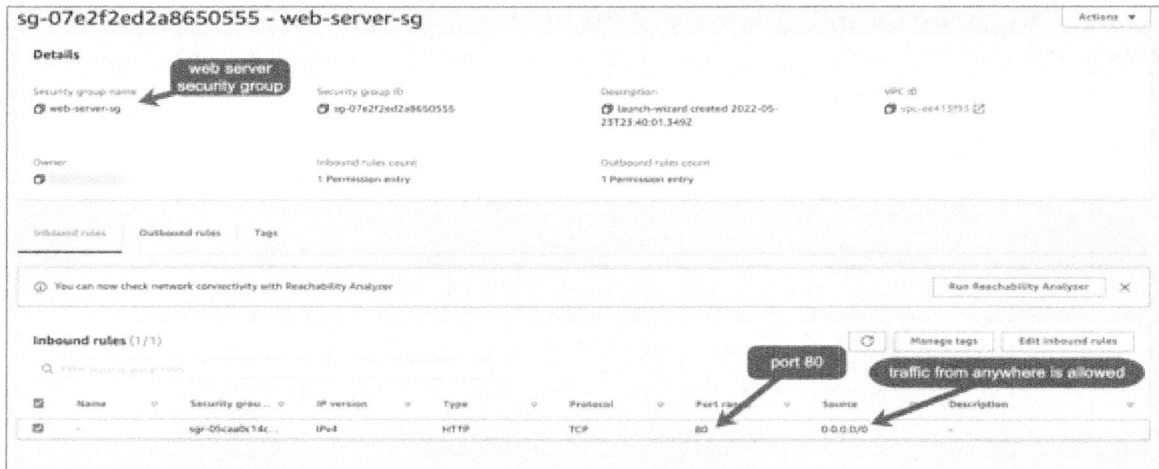

This is the screenshot of the security group of the web tier. If you notice, inbound traffic from anywhere is allowed at port 80.

The screenshot below is another view of the web server security group.

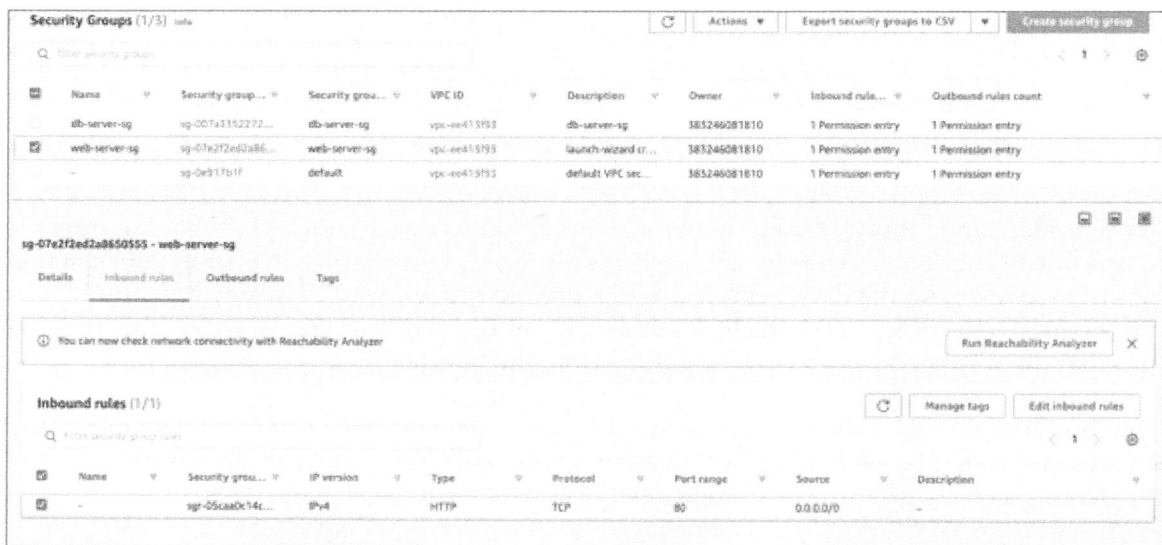

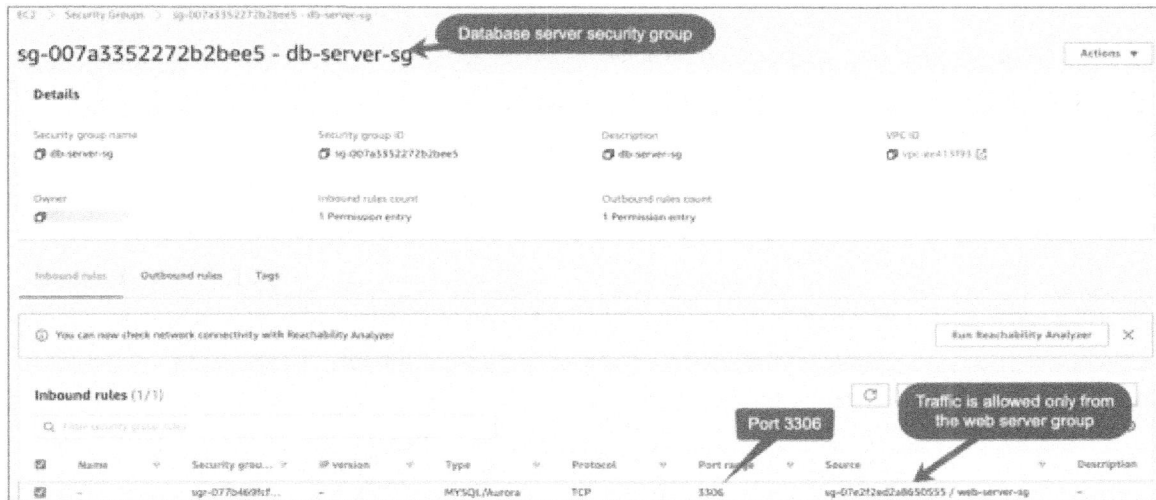

The above screenshot is for the security group of the database server. This security group allows traffic only from the web server security group- an excellent concept. First, providing a security group as a source protects the input traffic by ensuring that the input is allowed from the machines that have that security group (for example, web-server-sg in this case) traffic. And secondly, if more web servers are added to the webserver group, you will not have to change the database security group – imagine a scenario where you have to provide the IP address of each web server machine.

(Note: the example is for explaining security groups. Standard implementations have an application load balancer that forwards web traffic to web server instances in an auto-scaling group.)

Adding a security group as a source is a scalable solution.
The screenshot below is another view of the database server security group.

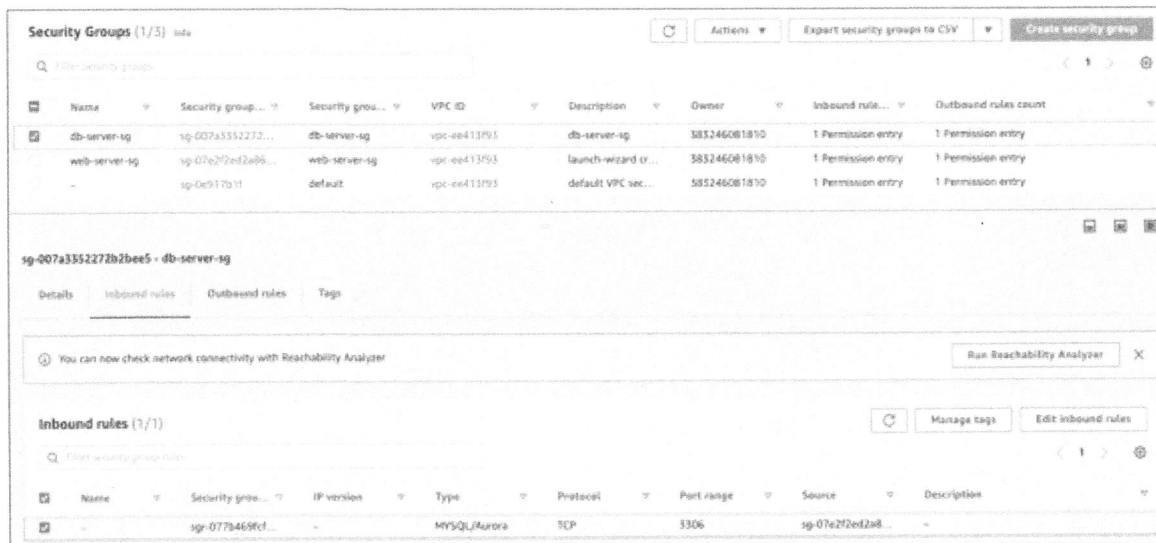

Another critical point is that though more than one security group can be assigned to one EC2 instance, at least, one security group must be assigned to an EC2 instance.

A security group can be modified, changed, and deleted.

Default Inbound Rule

When you create a security group, it has no inbound rules. Therefore, no inbound traffic originating from another host to your instance is allowed until you add inbound rules to the security group.

Default Outbound Rule

A security group includes an outbound rule that allows all outbound traffic by default. It is best to remove this default rule and add outbound rules that would enable specific outbound traffic only.

KEY POINTS

- Security Group acts as a virtual firewall controlling inbound and outbound traffic on an EC2 instance. When you create VPC, it comes with a default security group. You can modify the default security group or create an additional security group. The default security group has no inbound rules until you add inbound rules. You only add Allow rules – not Deny rules. For each security group, you add rules that control the traffic based on protocols and port numbers. There are a separate set of rules for inbound and outbound traffic.

- There are quotas about how many security groups can be created in a VPC, how many rules can be added to a security group, and how many security groups can be associated with a network interface. A security group can only be assigned to the resources in the security group's VPC.

- Security groups are stateful. What it means for each allowed inbound request, the response is also allowed.

- You can assign multiple security groups. Based on the aggregation of rules, it is decided whether particular traffic is allowed or not on a resource.

Network Access Control List (NACLs)

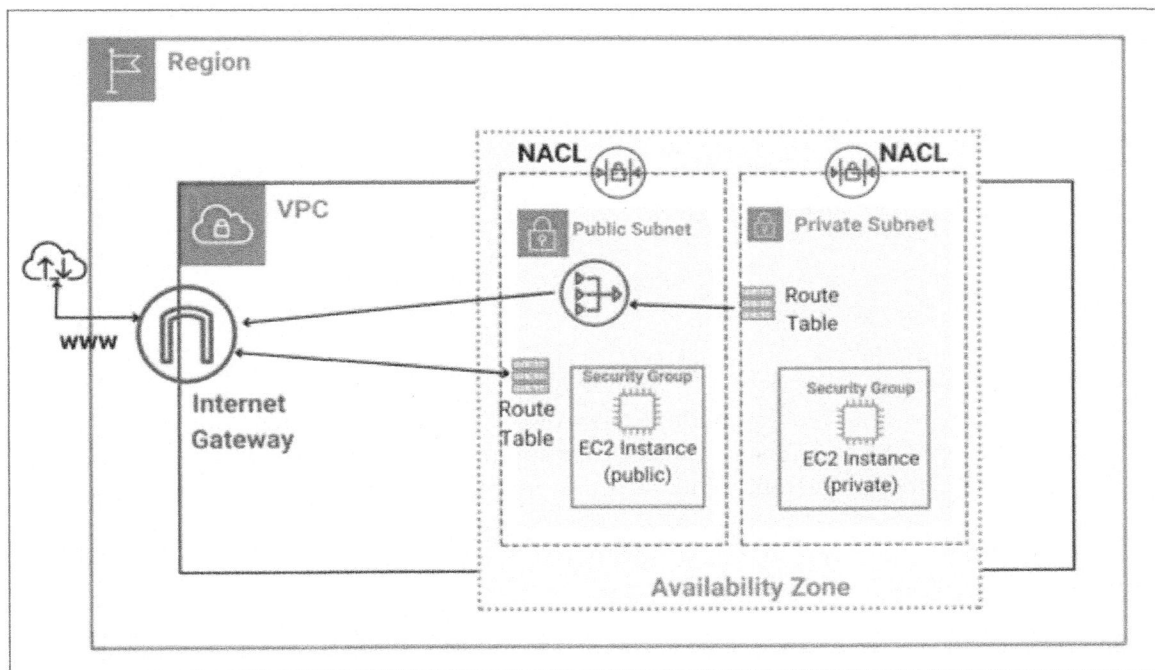

To understand the Network Access Control List, it would be better if we go through the differences between security group and Network ACL.

Security Group	Network ACL
Security groups operate at *instance level*	Network ACLs operate at *subnet level*
Security groups support *allow rules* only	Network ACLs support *allow and deny rules*
Security groups are *stateful* – the return traffic is automatically allowed regardless of any rules	Network ACLs are *stateless* – the return traffic must be allowed by rules.

All rules are evaluated before deciding if the traffic is allowed	Rules are evaluated in order (low to high) in deciding whether to allow traffic
Applies only to instances explicitly associated with the security group	Automatically applies all instances launched into associated subnet

Network Access Control List are coarse-grained controls, and they should be allowed to work at the edges of the network. However, suppose you have too many complex sets of rules configured in NACLs. It could be highly likely that you are using NACLs as a security group. If this is the case, it is better to review them to ensure that you are not configuring security groups in the NACLs. To understand the Network Access Control List (NACLs), it would be better if we go through the differences between a security group and NACLs.

NACLs should be coarse grained.

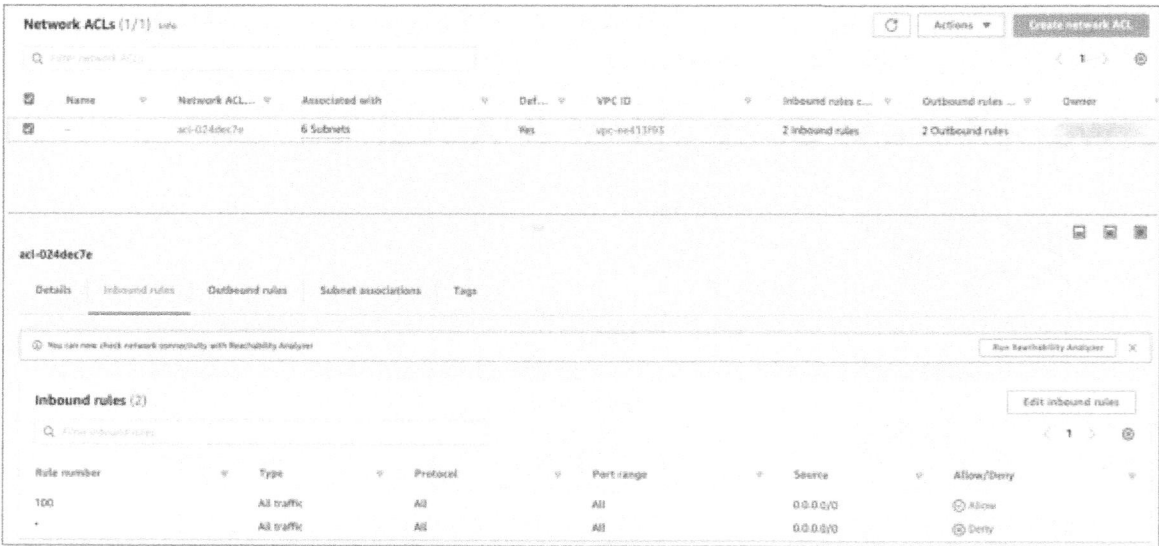

The above is the Screenshot showing default Network ACLs inbound rules. You can notice that the NACLs are associated with six subnets. There are six subnets because my default Region is N. Virginia which has 6 AZs. Another important to notice is that inbound traffic is allowed from anywhere.

Below is the Screenshot showing NACLs outbound rules -- this is the default setup. In the Screenshot, the outbound traffic is allowed from anywhere.

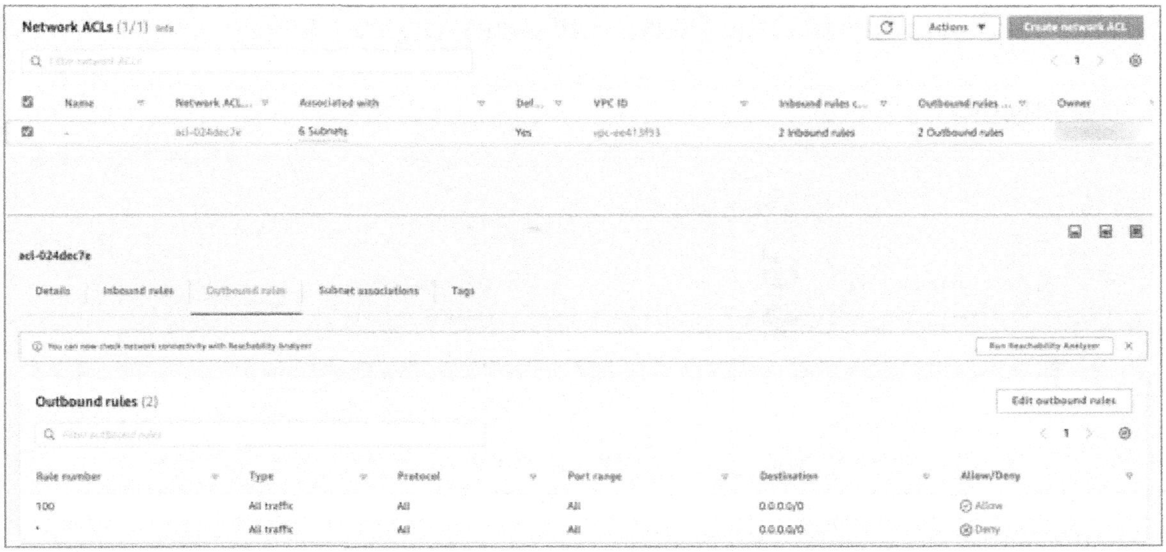
Network ACLs (1/1)
Actions
Create network ACL
Name
Network ACL...
Associated with
Def...
VPC ID
Inbound rules c...
Outbound rules ...
Owner
acl-024dec7e
6 Subnets
Yes
2 Inbound rules
2 Outbound rules
acl-024dec7e
Details
Inbound rules
Outbound rules
Subnet associations
Tags
Outbound rules (2)
Edit outbound rules
Rule number
Type
Protocol
Port range
Destination
Allow/Deny
100
All traffic
All
All
0.0.0.0/0
Allow
*
All traffic
All
All
0.0.0.0/0
Deny

Security Groups & NACLs Request Response Flow

Incoming Request

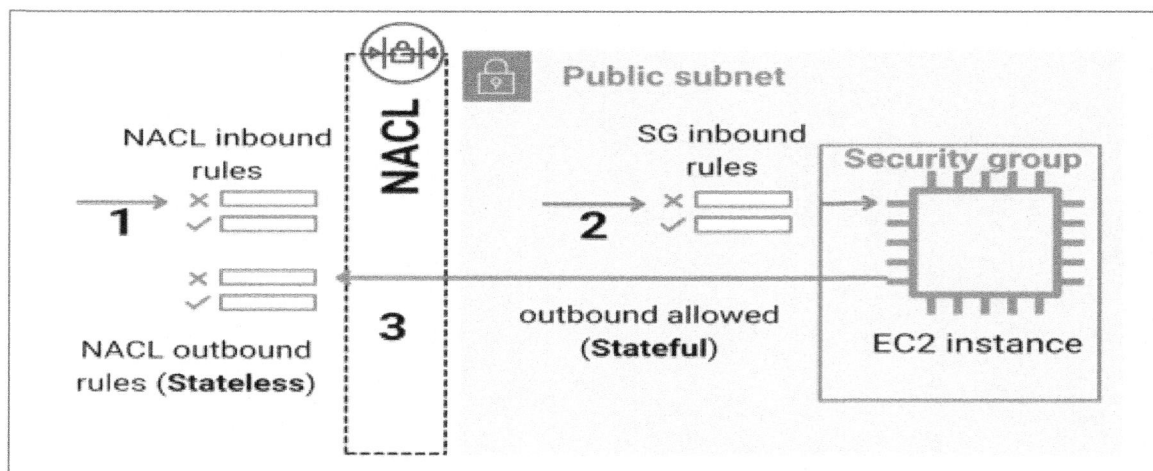

Let's understand how an incoming request is handled with NACL and Security Group. In the diagram, the request (1) is first checked by NACL rules whether the request is allowed.

Then the request (2) is checked at the instance level security group rules whether the request is allowed.

Then the outgoing response (3) is not checked by the security group as the **security groups are stateful** (if a request is allowed, its outgoing response is allowed). However, the outgoing response is evaluated at the NACL whether the outgoing response is allowed as the **NACLs are stateless** (which means both a request and its response are checked against the NACL rules).

Outgoing Request

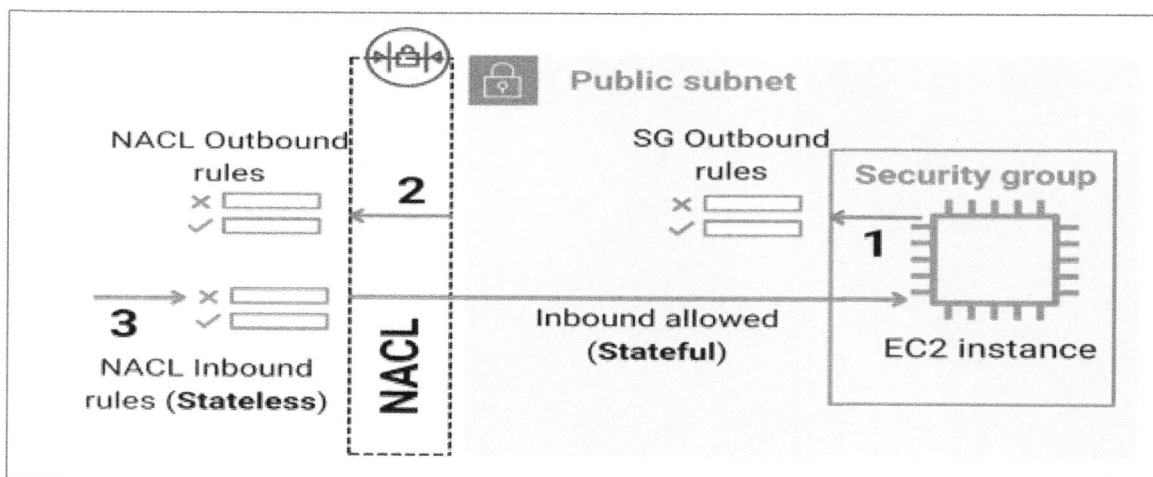

Handling of the outgoing request by Security Group and NACLs are conceptually the same – it's just the reverse of how an incoming request is handled.

From the diagram above, request (1) is first handled by the security group rules. Then the request is checked at the NACL (2). Regarding response, since NACLs are stateless, response (3) is checked against NACL rules. However, when the response goes through the security group, it is allowed as Security Groups are stateful.

Default NACL

By default, your VPC has default Network ACLs that allow all inbound and outbound traffic.

Inbound Rules

Rule#	Type	Protocol	Port Range	Source	Allow / Deny
100	All IPv4 Traffic	ALL	ALL	0.0.0.0/0	ALLOW
*	All IPv4 Traffic	ALL	ALL	0.0.0.0/0	Deny

Outboud Rules

Rule#	Type	Protocol	Port Range	Source	Allow / Deny
100	All IPv4 Traffic	ALL	ALL	0.0.0.0/0	ALLOW
*	All IPv4 Traffic	ALL	ALL	0.0.0.0/0	Deny

Though the default Network ACL can be modified, Do NOT modify the Default NACL. Instead, create custom NACLs.

KEY POINTS

- Network ACLs provide an optional layer of security for your VPC. It acts as a firewall controlling inbound and outbound traffic for one or more subnets.

- One NACL per subnet. New subnets are assigned the Default NACL.

- You can create a custom Network ACL and assign it to a subnet. By default, each custom Network denies all inbound and outbound rules until you add rules.

- Each subnet in a VPC must be assigned to a Network ACL. If the subnet is not assigned to a Network ACL, the subnet is automatically assigned to a default Network ACL.

- Network ACLs have separate inbound and outbound rules -- each rule can deny or allow traffic.

- Network ACLs are stateless, which means the response to inbound traffic is only allowed if outbound traffic is permitted and vice-versa.

- NACL rules:

  - Network ACL contains numbered rules (1 – 32766) highest number can be 32766. The order is evaluated for the lowest numbers; as soon as the lowest number rule matches, it is applied, and higher number rules are ignored.

  - Example: if you define #100 ALLOW 10.0.0.10/32 and #200 DENY 10.0.0.10/32, the IP address will be allowed because 100 has higher precedence over 200.

  - The last rule is an asterisk (*) and denies a request in case of no rule match.

  - AWS recommends adding rules by increments of 100.

- Network ACLs are different from security groups – security groups are applied at the instance level, while Network ACLs are used at the subnet level.

- NACLs are an excellent way of blocking a specific IP address at the subnet level.

Troubleshoot SG & NACL Related Issues

Analyze the "Action" field in flow logs.

Incoming Requests	Outgoing Requests
Inbound REJECT => NACL or SG	Outbound REJECT => NACL or SG
Inbound ACCEPT, Outbound REJECT=> NACL	Outbound ACCEPT, Inbound REJECT=> NACL

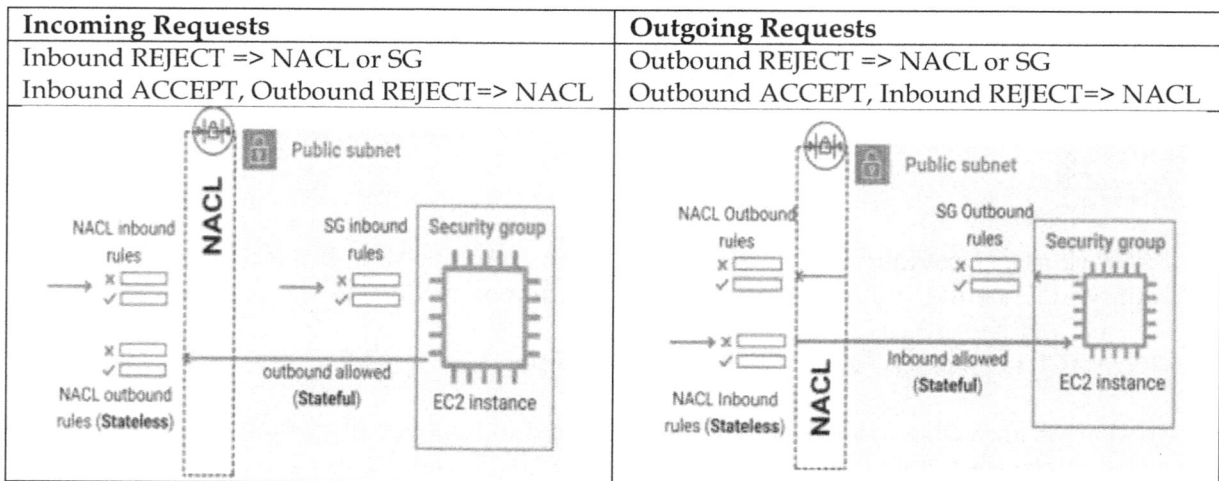

Ephemeral Ports

In networking, two devices must establish a connection to communicate on an endpoint and use ports.

Client devices connect to a defined fixed destination port and expect a response on an ephemeral port.

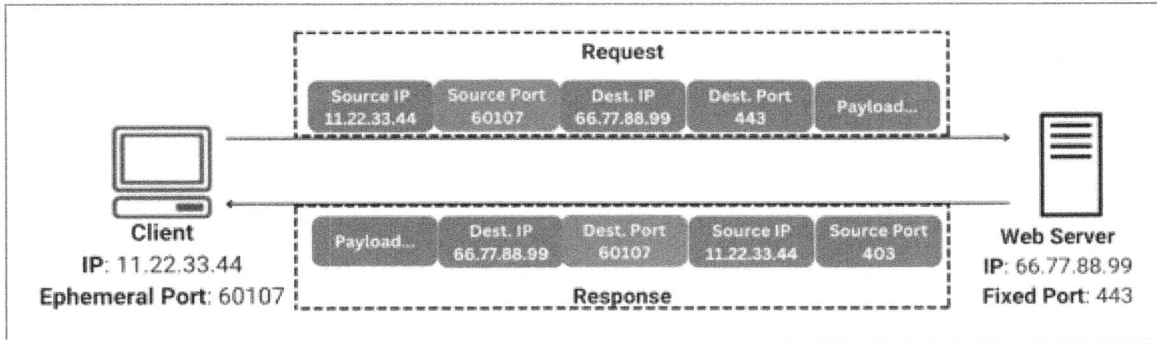

As you can see in the diagram, the client machine uses its port 60107 (ephemeral port) to connect to the web server at 443 and expects a response on its port 60107.

Different operating systems use different port ranges as ephemeral ports. For example, MS Windows uses ports between 49152 and 65535, and many Linux kernels use between 32768 and 60999.

Ephemeral Ports with NACL Example Diagram

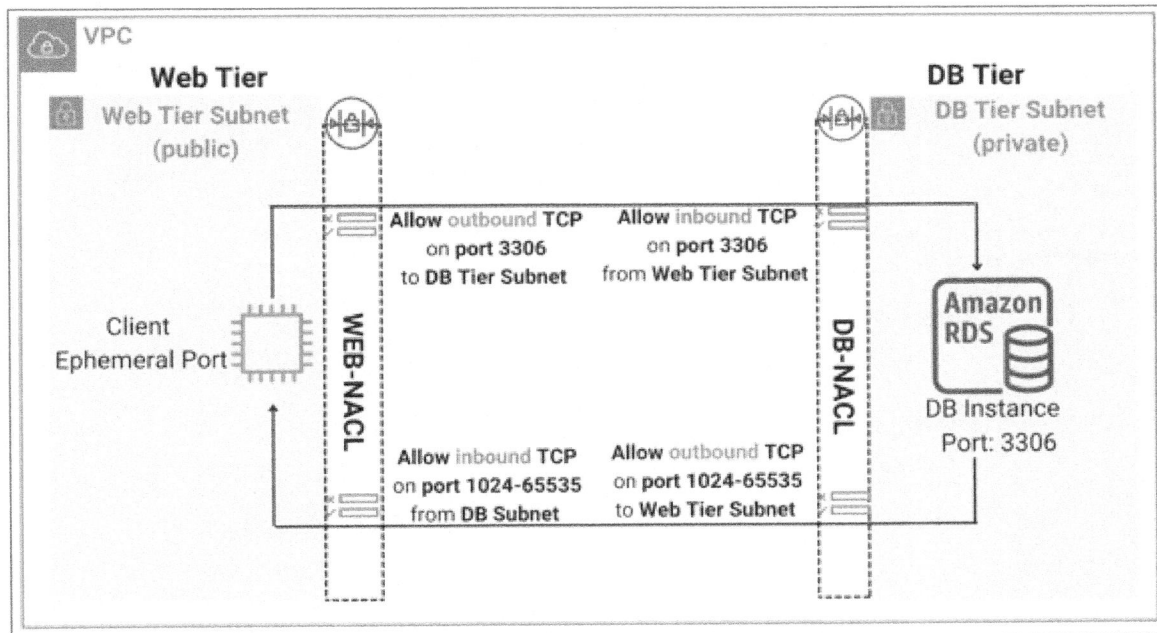

Security Groups vs. NACLs

Security Group	NACL
Operates at the instance level	Operates at the subnet level
Supports "allow" rules only	Supports both "allow" and "deny" rules
All rules are evaluated before deciding whether to allow traffic	Rules are evaluated in order from lowest to highest when deciding whether to allow traffic, the first match is used.
Stateful: response traffic is automatically allowed regardless of any rules.	**Stateless**: response traffic must be explicitly allowed by rules – think of ephemeral ports
Applies to an EC2 instance when specified	Automatically applies to all EC2 instances in the subnet

Reference: https://docs.aws.amazon.com/vpc/latest/userguide/vpc-network-acls.html

VPC Peering

VPC Peering is one of the connectivity options for connecting one VPC to another VPC.

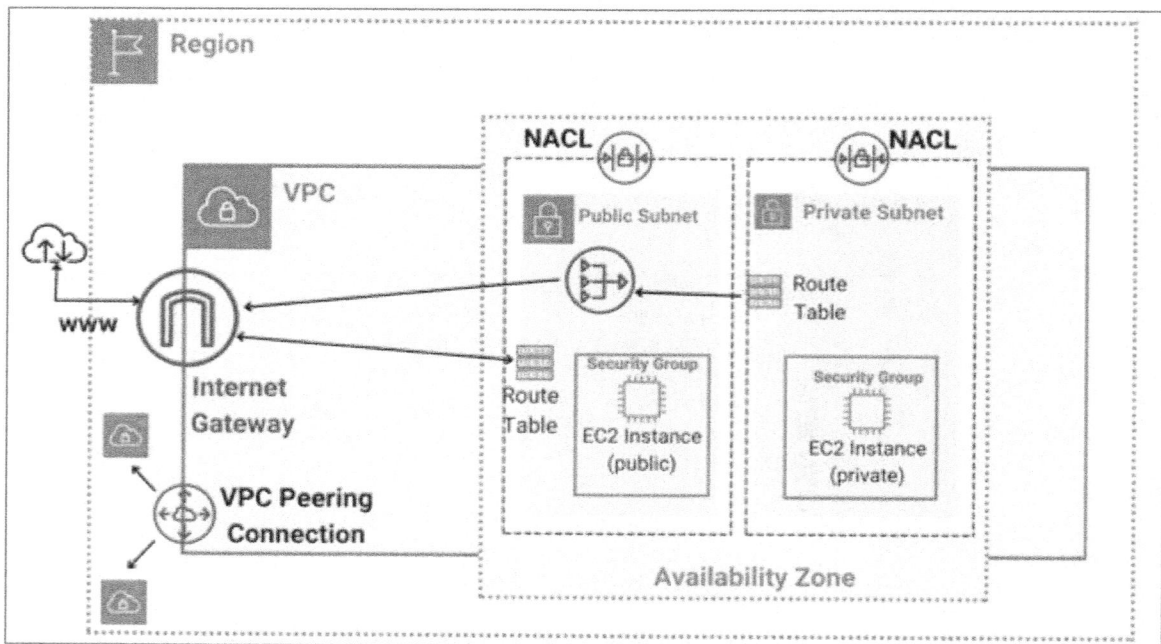

A VPC can be understood as a data center within an on-premises environment. Since VPC is a cloud construct, it can be considered a virtual data center in a cloud. VPC Peering can be understood as a leased line or fiber cable connectivity between two data centers.

Suppose you have two VPCs. You can set up VPC Peering between two VPCs, and they can start communicating with each other.

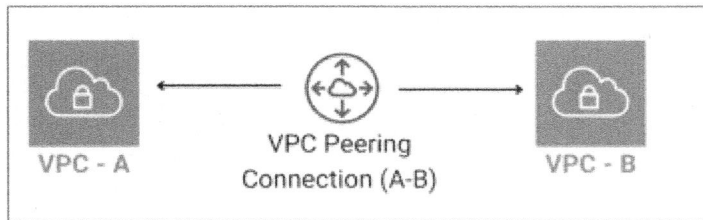

If you have another VPC, you can add one more VPC Peering to communicate with each other.

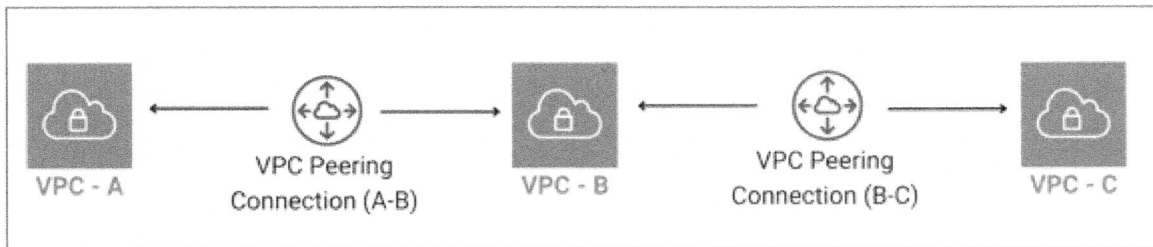

But an important point to note is that VPC Peering is a one-to-one association. So, traffic from VPC-C cannot traverse into VPC-A via VPC-B without adding VPC Peering between VPC-C and VPC-A.

If you need to set up a connection between VPC-C and VPC-A, you will have to set up another VPC Peering.

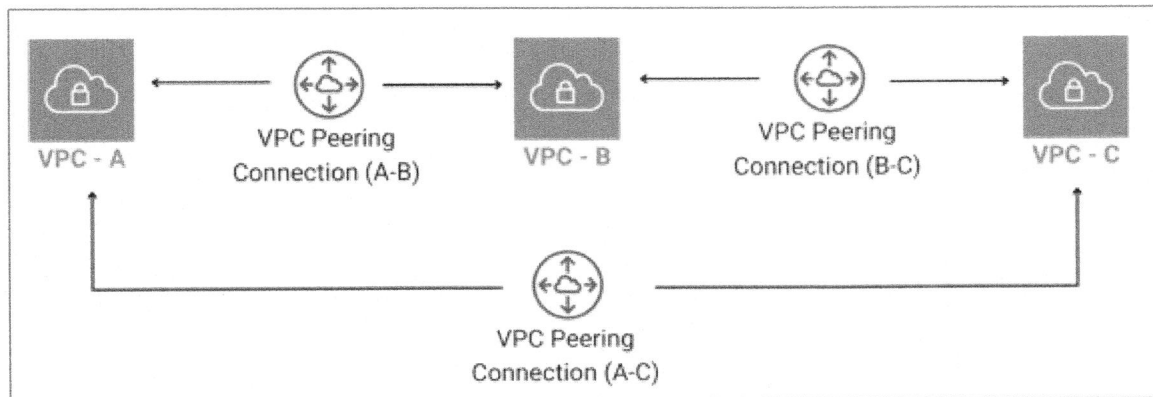

How to establish VPC Peering

Establishing VPC Peering is a decentralized process.

In the first step, a peering request is sent. Then in the second step, the request is accepted. And then, in the final step, Routing tables are modified to establish the VPC Peering.

Note: If you are testing using ping from the EC2 instance in one VPC to another VPC, make sure you have modified the security group settings to allow inbound connection for ICMP to the other VPC CIDR, and vice-versa.

Security group rul...	Port range	Protocol	Source	Security groups
sgr-04fe976de29e...	22	TCP	69.253.60.121/32	vpc-dev-1-sg
sgr-0ecfdc2e8362...	All	ICMP	10.1.0.0/16	vpc-dev-1-sg

CIDR block of the other VPC

Modify the route table of the subnet to allow peering connection in which you have the launched EC2 instances.

rtb-0a25a4ca305638995 / dev-vpc-2-rtb-public

This is the screenshot for the Route table of the subnet in which the EC2 instance is launched.

KEY POINTS

- Connectivity is performed using private IP. In other words, it privately connects two VPCs using AWS' network -- behaves as if both VPCs are in the same network.
- You can peer VPCs across two regions – connect VPCs on the US East Coast to the VPCs on the US West Coast.
- VPC Peering connection is NOT transitive. You must be established for each VPC that needs to communicate with one another.
- You must update route tables in each VPC's subnets to ensure EC2 instances can communicate with each other.

- VPC CIDR range must not overlap.
- You can create VPC Peering connections between VPCs in different AWS accounts/regions.
- You can reference a security group in a peered VPC -- works across accounts in the same region.

VPC Endpoints

Many AWS services live outside VPC in the public address space, such as DynamoDB, S3, CloudWatch, AWS Lambda, etc. We can access them using AWS Direct Connect from the on-premises data center – but what about accessing them within your VPC.

You can do that using an Internet Gateway. But maybe you don't want to deploy an Internet Gateway in your VPC. So for this use case, there are different types of endpoints.

*A VPC endpoint enables you to **privately** connect your VPC to **supported AWS services** and **VPC endpoint services** powered by AWS PrivateLink without requiring an internet gateway, NAT device, VPN connection, or AWS Direct Connect connection. Instances in your VPC **do not require public IP addresses** to communicate with resources in the service. Traffic between your VPC and the other service does not leave the Amazon network. (Reference : https://docs.aws.amazon.com/whitepapers/latest/aws-privatelink/what-are-vpc-endpoints.html)*

As you can see in the architecture diagram, we have VPC endpoints for CloudWatch and S3. However, there is no VPC Endpoint for DynamoDB, so the traffic travels through the Internet.

VPC endpoints are virtual devices -- strictly networking constructs. They allow communication between instances in an Amazon VPC and services that don't reside in VPC, such as S3, DynamoDB, and CloudWatch, without imposing availability risks or bandwidth constraints.

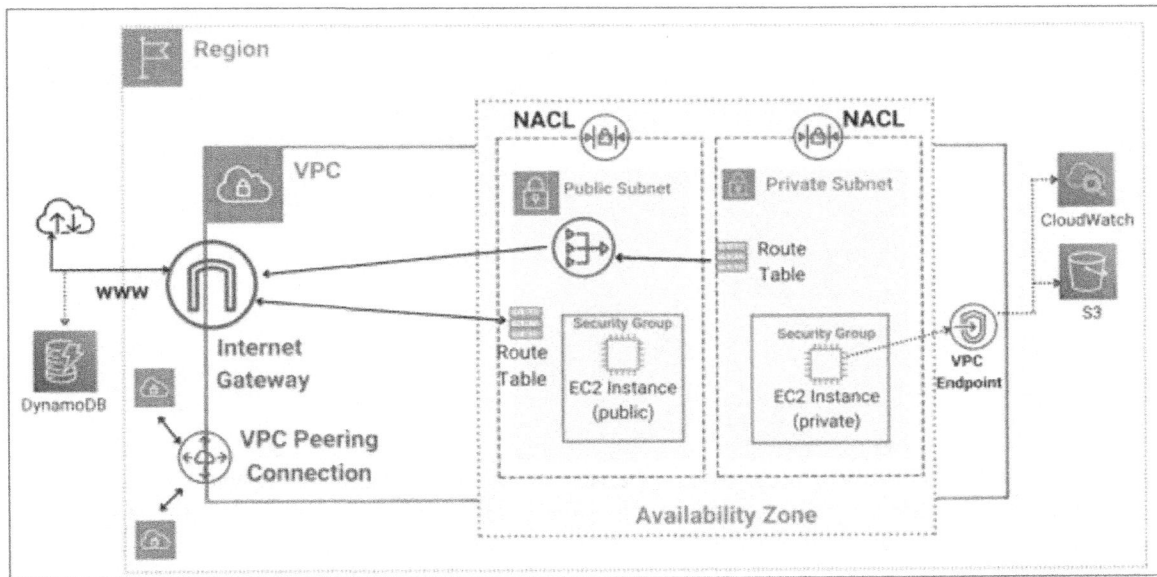

VPC endpoint allows you to connect your VPC to supported AWS services privately. It doesn't require deploying an internet gateway, network address translation (NAT) device, Virtual Private Network (VPN) connection, or AWS Direct Connect connection.

VPC endpoints are horizontally scaled, redundant, and highly available Amazon VPC components.

If you don't have a VPC endpoint for services, you can still make the connection to them, but then the connection will use a public endpoint – which means traffic will have to travel through the Internet.

Connecting to AWS services, e.g., S3, DynamoDB over the internet – and not through VPC Endpoint -- has the following issues:

Outbound Firewall Rules: You will have to set up outbound firewall rules, e.g., IP allow-lists and domain allows-lists, which can get cumbersome. Furthermore, you have to know these domains and IP addresses beforehand to allow them out. Debugging and properly implementing this is also time-consuming and can be very involved.

Not Free: If you use a managed NAT Gateway, AWS charges your data processing on egress traffic.

Latency: public Internet will almost always be slower by the nature of it than traffic taking a private connection.

Types of VPC Endpoints

Interface Endpoints (powered by PrivateLink)

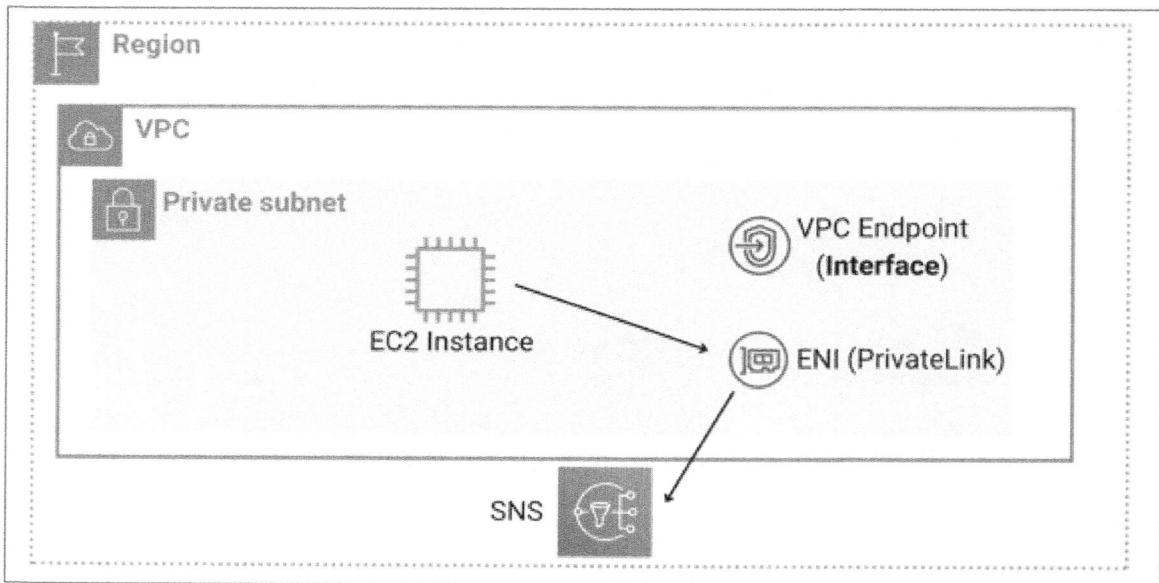

An interface endpoint is an ENI that allows VPC resources having private IP inside a subnet to connect to a number of AWS services, such as CloudFormation, Elastic Load Balancers (ELBs), SNS, and more. Interface endpoints are powered by AWS PrivateLink, and use an elastic network interface (ENI) as an entry point for traffic destined for the service.
(Reference: https://docs.aws.amazon.com/vpc/latest/privatelink/aws-services-privatelink-support.html)

VPC Interface Endpoints are used by all the other available services inside your VPC. So, for example, if you would like to connect to AWS Services API, you can use an Interface Endpoint, and instead of doing any routing, it will look as if the service lives inside your VPC. And it will use IP addresses from within your VPC range. So if your EC2 instances are connecting to that service, they would be connecting to a local IP address and, behind the scene, privately transported to the service they want to communicate with.

This mechanism also allows you to override the public domain name for the service publicly. Only inside your VPC will it resolve to your private IP address.

The technology behind the VPC Interface Endpoint is AWS PrivateLink. With this technology, you can share your services with other consumers in many VPCs., also consumers can call your web services.

AWS PrivateLink provides private connectivity between virtual private clouds (VPCs), supported AWS services, and your on-premises networks without exposing your traffic to the public internet.

For example, you have an HTTPS service that you would like to share with others; many other VPCs may be some third parties. You can put that service behind a network load balancer and make it available as a VPC Endpoint service. It helps other VPCs subscribe to that service and create Endpoints representing your service in their VPCs.

They will be connecting to a local IP address, representing your service, and transporting your service hosted in the other VPC. Using PrivateLink allows only exposing a specific service port that the service is connecting. So if it is HTTPS, then it will be only port 443. Connectivity is allowed in only one direction. Only consumers can connect to the service; service provider VPC cannot connect to service consumer VPC. And finally, you don't need to care about IP addresses in this scenario.

It provisions an ENIs (private IP address), which will act as an entry point. You need to attach the ENI to the Security Group.

An elastic network interface (ENI) is a virtual network card in a VPC. It has a primary private IPv4 address from the address range of your VPC.

Cost wise: $ per hour + $ per GB of data processed.

Gateway Endpoints

A gateway endpoint is a gateway that targets a specified route in your route table for traffic destined for a supported AWS service.

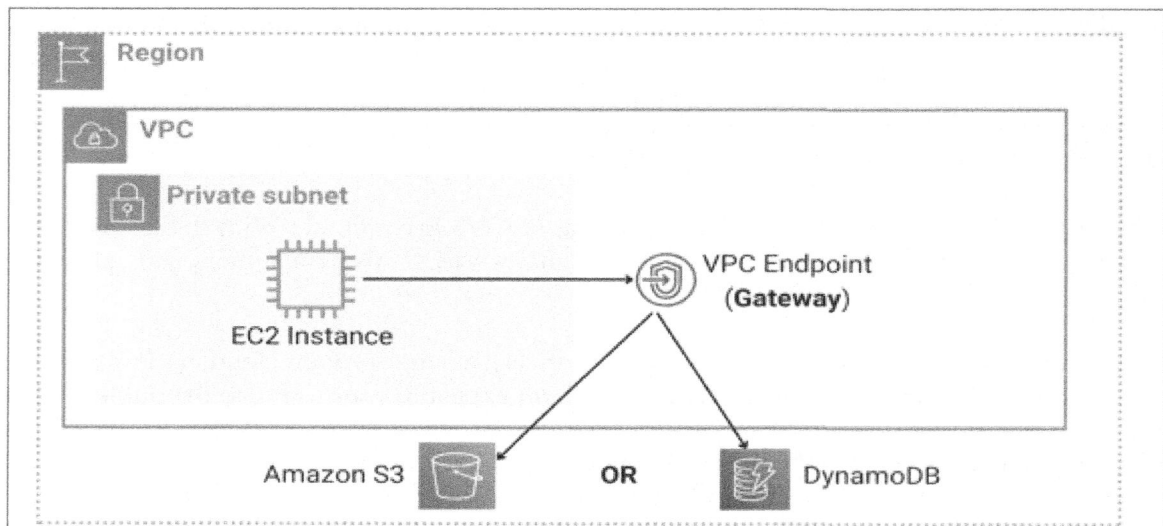

- It provisions a gateway and must be used as a target in a Route table, as it does not use security groups.
- **It supports only S3 and DynamoDB**, providing reliable connectivity without any need for an internet gateway or a NAT device for your VPC.
- Gateway endpoints do not enable AWS PrivateLink.
- It's free -- there is no additional charge for using gateway endpoints.

Gateway or Interface Endpoint for S3?

An interface endpoint is preferred when connecting from on-premises (Site to Site VPN or Direct Connect), from a different VPC, or an AWS region.

Cost: Gateway Endpoint is free; however, Interface Endpoint is not free.

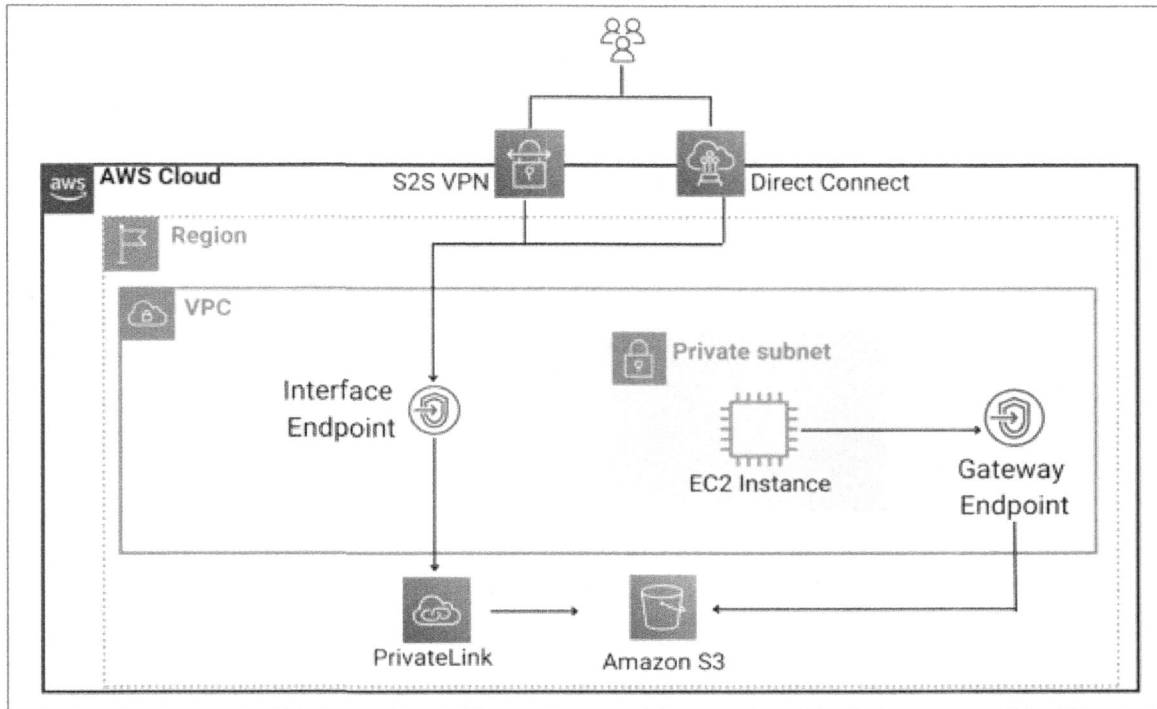

AWS Transit Gateway

One of the challenges of VPC Peering is if you start to have more than VPCs, say around 10, 12, 20 VPCs, and so on, it will become complete to manage one-one peering between one VPC to the other. The other limitation you will face is the maximum limitation of 125 peering connections per VPC.

That's where AWS Transit Gateway becomes helpful in establishing connections between VPCs.

So, how does the Transit Gateway help us? Transit Gateway is distributed managed routing service that you deploy into a Region. So, you can connect and attach VPCs in the same Region to your Transit Gateway. And then, you can allow any-to-any connection from a routing perspective. Or, you can isolate some VPCs to talk to each other.

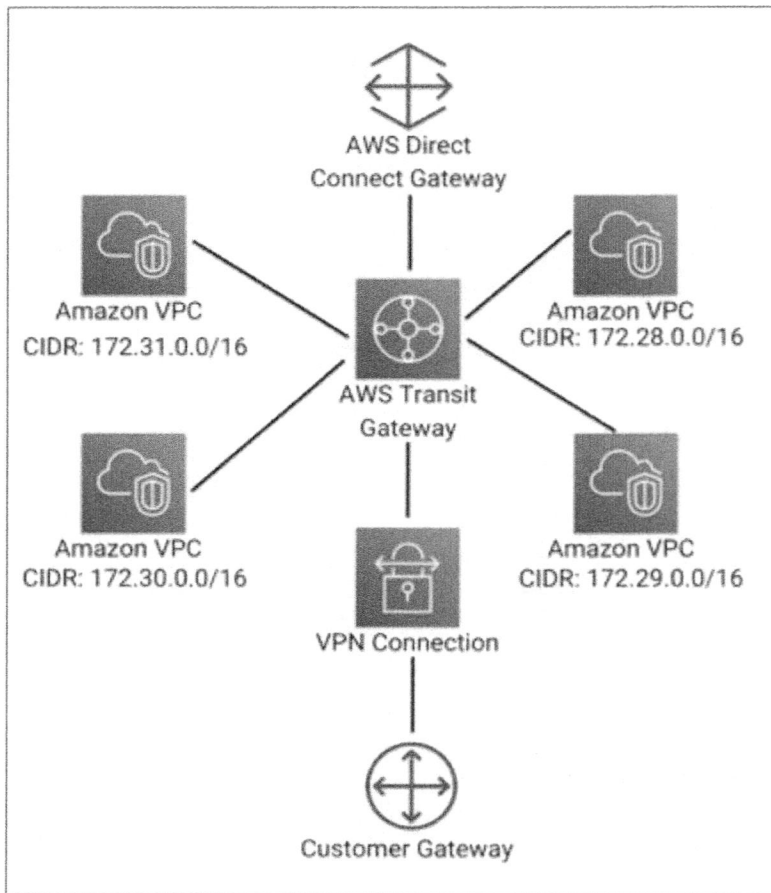

In the diagram, all the VPCs are in the same Region with 172.*/16 block, and the Transit Gateway is connected with all of the VPCs.

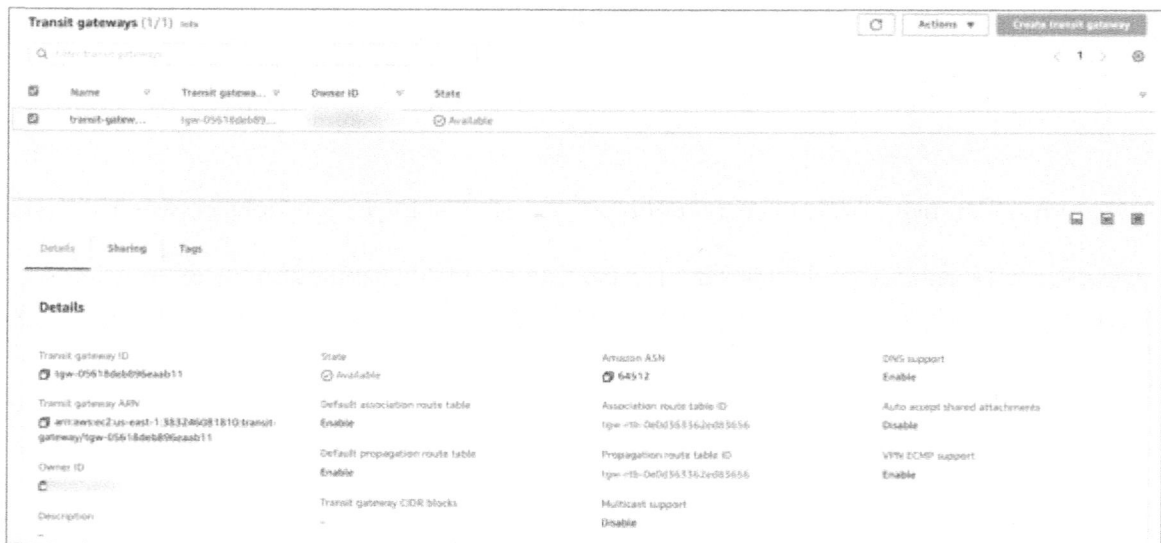

The above screenshot is of a Transit Gateway.

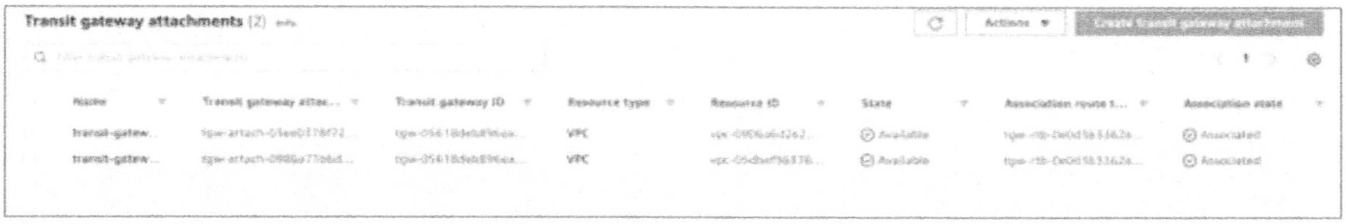

The screenshot in which the Transit Gateway is connected to two VPCs in the same AWS Region.

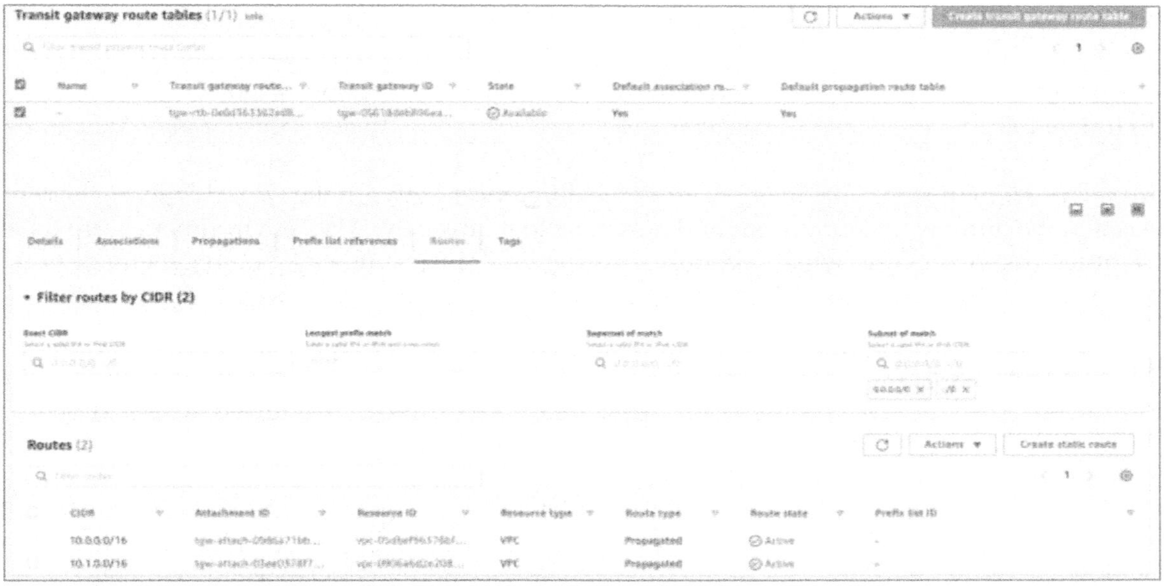

The above screenshot shows the routes of the Transit Gateway route table.

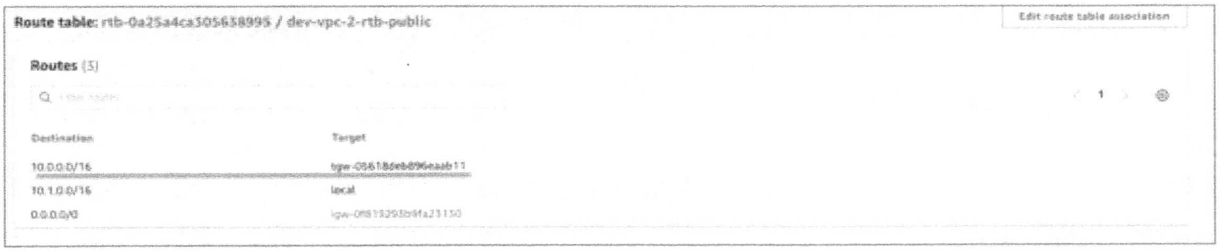

The above screenshot is of the Route table of one of the subnets. Notice how the destination of other VPCs and the Transit Gateway is added. In the Security Group of the EC2 instance, make sure you have added to allow ICMP protocol if you are using "ping" to test Transit Gateway connectivity using EC2 instances between two VPCs.

KEY POINTS

- Centralized private IP connectivity between multiple VPCs
- VPCs can be in different Regions.
- VPCs can be in separate accounts.
- Used for having transitive peering between thousands of VPC and on-premises, hub-and-spoke (star) connection.

- It's a regional resource -- can work cross-region.
- You can share cross-account using Resource Access Manager (RAM)
- Using Route Table, you can limit which VPC can talk with other VPCs.
- It works with Direct Connect Gateway and VPN connections.
- It supports IP Multicast -- not supported by any other AWS service.

Difference between VPC Peering and Transit Gateway

	VPC Peering	Transit Gateway
Bandwidth Limit	125 max peering	5,000 attachments
Management	Decentralized	Centralized
Cost Dimension	Data Transfer	Date Transfer and Attachment

As you can see from the table above, there are some differences between the two. However, the central theme is that the number of connections and how easy to manage the AWS environment -- are the two important factors in deciding what to choose, Peering or Transit Gateway. So, in general, if you are configuring more than ten or more VPCs, it's better to go for a Transit Gateway.

VPC Flow Logs

In the previous sections, we discussed ensuring that correct traffic is allowed to the subnet (via NACLs) and instances (via Security Groups).

But the question is how to look into traffic: the question is Flow Logs. We can create Flow Logs at the VPC and the Subnet levels. When we create Flow Logs at a VPC, it applies to all subnets in the VPC. However, when we create Flow Logs at the subnet, it applies only to the associated subnet.

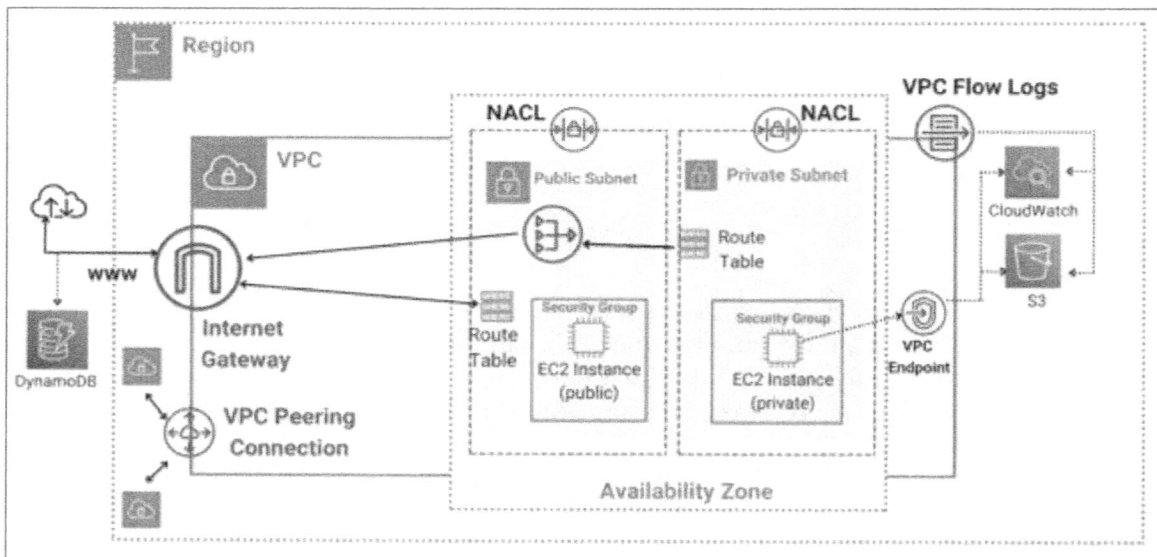

The VPC Flow Logs can be written either to a CloudWatch group or an S3 bucket. It provides visibility about what's going on in your VPC, such as troubleshooting if wrong rules are set up or analyzing traffic flows. One important point is that Flow Logs do not contain the payload of a request and response. Instead, the Flow Logs only include a packet description, such as a source and destination address, port, payload size, and whether the request is denied or accepted.

How to Create VPC Flow Logs

Go to VPC, click on the Flow Logs tab and then click on Create flow Log button. You can notice in the screenshot above that the Flow Log is associated with the VPC, and the destination is CloudWatch logs.

How to Create Subnet Flow Logs

You can also create flow logs for the subnet as well. Go to VPC and select subnets. Select the subnet to which you would like to add a flow log. Then click on the Flow Logs tab and the Create flow log button. You can notice in the screenshot above shows a flow log associated with the subnet subnet-3af17877, and the destination is CloudWatch logs.

Analyzing Flow Log Record

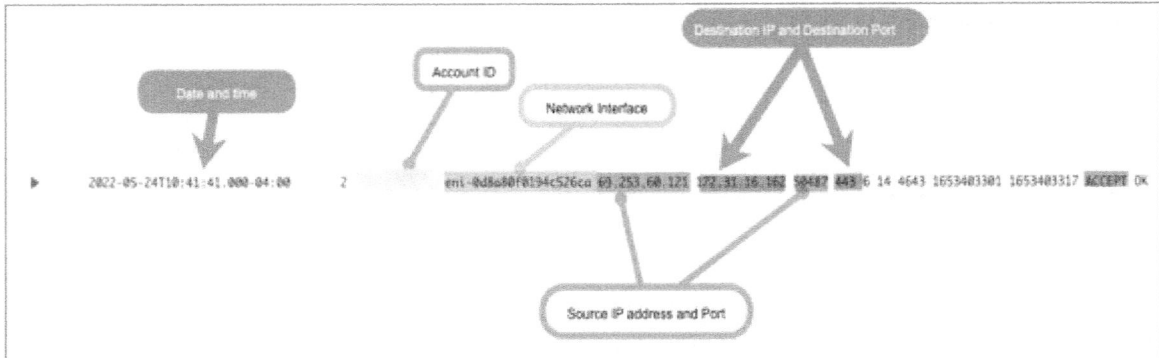

The above screenshot is for one sample Flow Log record. You can notice different parts of a request in the Flow Log.

- Source IP address and Port – help identify the problematic source
- Destination IP and Destination Port - help identify the problematic destination
- **Action** – success or failure of the request due to Security Group / NACL. It can be used for analytics on usage patterns or malicious behavior.
- You can query VPC flow logs using Athena on S3 or CloudWatch Logs Insights.

Reference: https://docs.aws.amazon.com/vpc/latest/userguide/flow-logs- records-examples.html

KEY POINTS

- It enables you to capture information about the IP traffic going to and from network interfaces (VPC Flow Logs, Subnet Flow Logs, Elastic Network Interface (ENI) Flow Logs) in your VPC.
- VPC Flow Logs help to monitor & troubleshoot connectivity issues, such as diagnosing security group rules, and monitoring the traffic.
- Flow log data can be sent to Amazon CloudWatch Logs, Amazon S3, or Amazon Kinesis Data Firehose.
- Flow log data does not affect network throughput or latency as the logs are collected outside the path of your network traffic.
- You can create or delete flow logs without any risk of impact on network performance.

DNS in VPC

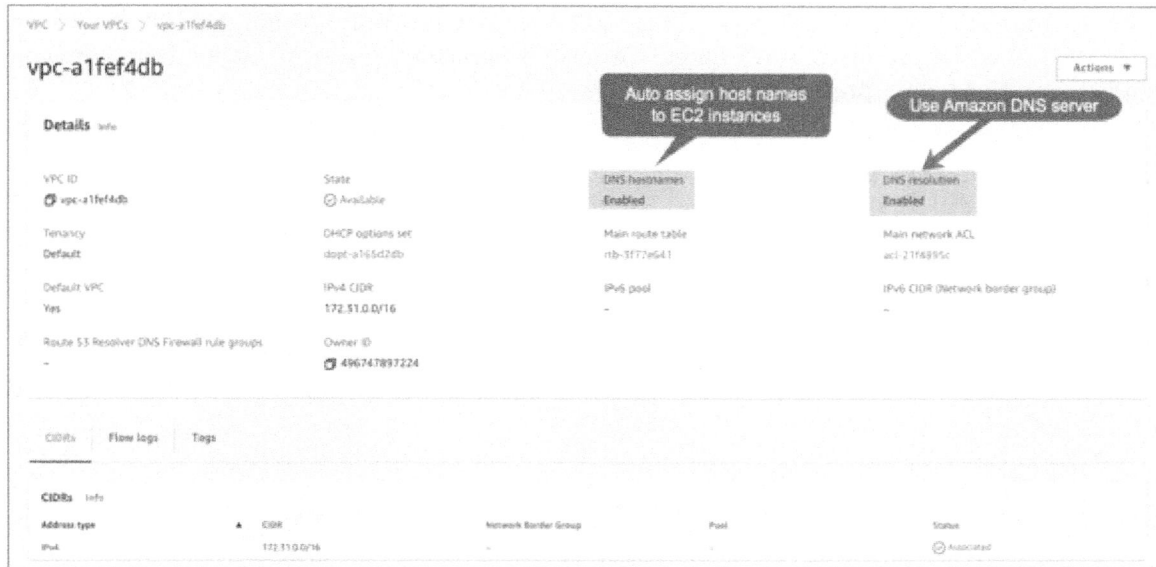

As you can see in the screenshot, AWS provides options for DNS hostnames and DNS hostname resolutions – by default, these options are enabled. However, you can disable them if you would like for your use case.

DNS hostname resolutions help resolve the public hostname of your EC2 instance. DNS hostnames option adds the ability to add a hostname to an EC2 instance. This helps to avoid using IP addresses.

For details about managing DNS for your servers, please look into the Route53 service.

Connecting on-premises network to VPC

When connecting an on-premises network to VPC to extend the connectivity to AWS, we have two options: AWS site-to-site VPN and AWS Direct Connect.

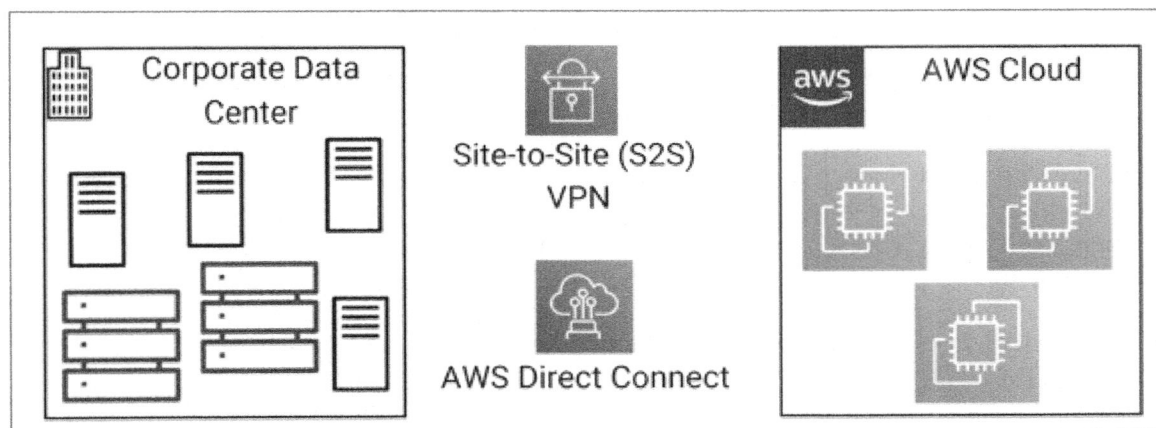

AWS site-to-site VPN is essentially an IPSec VPN tunnel typically running over the Internet, connecting a VPC to on-premises. AWS Direct Connect is dedicated physical connectivity between an on-premises and the AWS infrastructure.

AWS Site-to-Site VPN

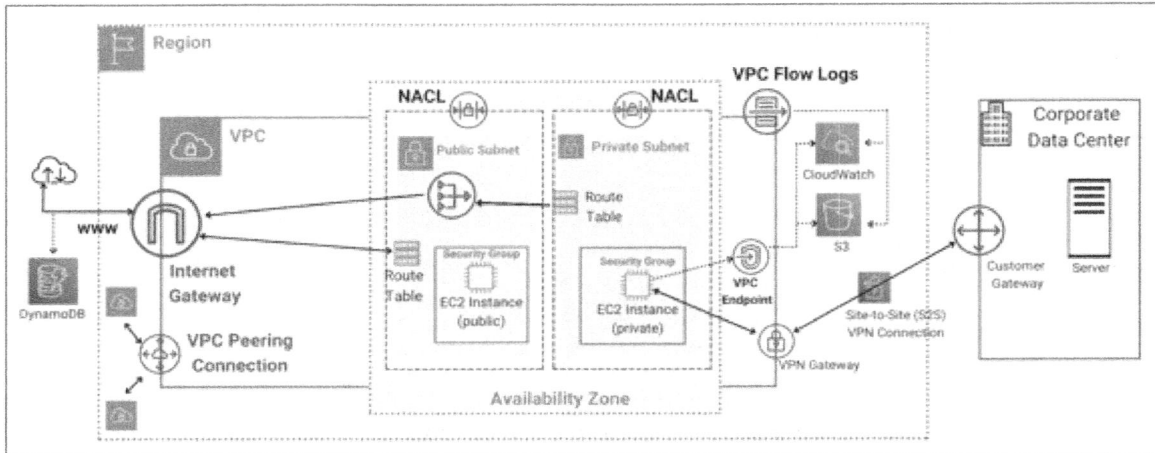

When extending an on-premises environment to the AWS Cloud, VPN is generally fast and easy to set up for many AWS customers.

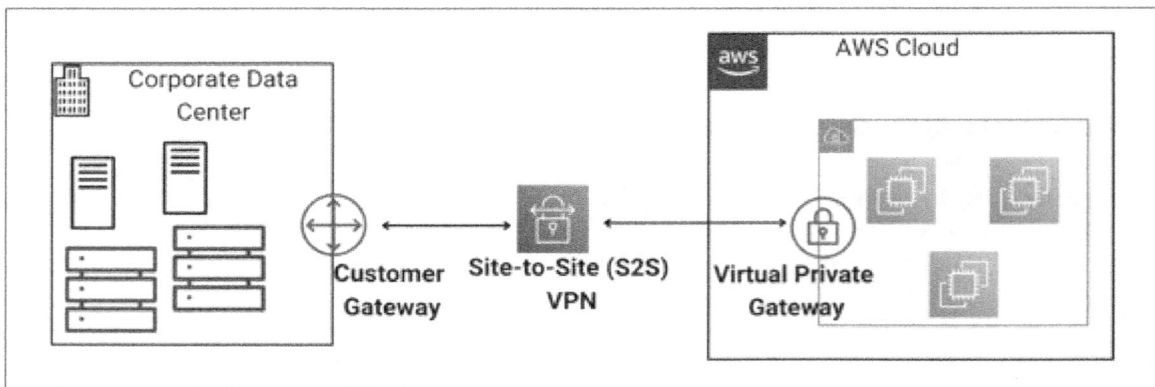

You need two things: Customer Gateway and Virtual Private Gateway. The Customer Gateway could be your Router, firewall, software application, or other things that support IPSec in your on-premises environment. The Customer Gateway resides at the on-premises end, and it is used in AWS Site-to-Site VPN connection.

The next is Virtual Private Gateway which you create on AWS and associate that Virtual Private Gateway to a VPC.

Virtual Private Gateway

A virtual private gateway (VGW) is part of a VPC that provides edge routing for AWS managed VPN connections and AWS Direct Connect connections. You associate an AWS Direct Connect gateway with the virtual private gateway for the VPC. A virtual gateway allows resources that are outside of your VPC to communicate to resources that are inside of your VPC.

Once you have the Customer Gateway, Virtual Private Gateway, and Site-to-Site VPC connection, you create a VPN connection. Each VPC connection consists of two separate IPSec tunnels. Having two VPN endpoints in two different Availability Zones (AZs) allows for high availability. If you were not using a dynamic routing protocol, PGP, for example, you would have to update the routing table of VPC to define how to reach the on-premises range.

- **Enable Route Propagation for the Virtual Private Gateway in the Route table associated with your subnets.**
- **If you need to ping your EC2 instances from on-premises, make sure you add the ICMP protocol on the inbound of your security groups.**

Site-to-Site VPN connection is easy to set up, and it is secure. However, since it runs over the Internet, you may have some unpredictable experiences because of the inherent nature of the Internet.

If you would like to get a more predictable and consistent experience for on-premises connectivity to AWS, that's where you would consider looking at AWS Direct Connect.

AWS VPN CloudHub

- Provide secure communication between multiple sites.

- Use this approach if you have multiple branch offices and existing internet connections and would like to implement a convenient, potentially low-cost hub-and-spoke model for primary or backup connectivity between these remote offices.

- To set it up, connect multiple VPN connections on the same virtual private gateway, set up dynamic routing, and configure route tables.

- The following figure shows the AWS VPN CloudHub architecture, with dashed lines indicating network traffic between remote sites being routed over their AWS VPN connections.

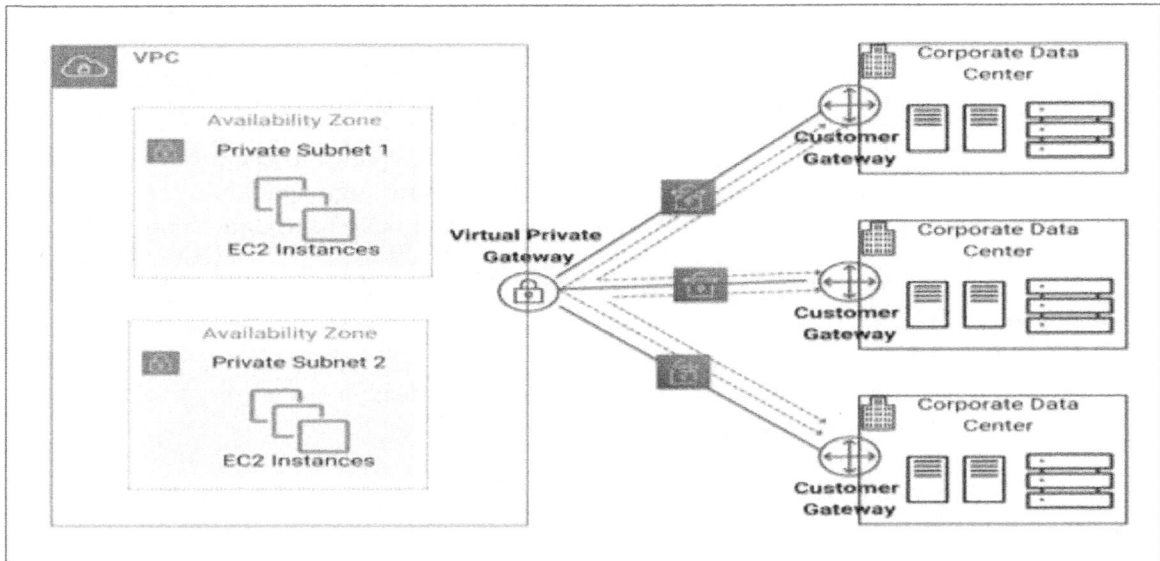

AWS Direct Connect

If we look at AWS, by default, VPCs are provided by AWS. And we can also create our own VPCs. In VPC, we launch EC2 and services which needs EC2, such as Elastic Load Balancer, NAT Gateway, Amazon RDS, Amazon EMR, Amazon Redshift, Amazon Elasticsearch, and AWS Elastic Beanstalk.

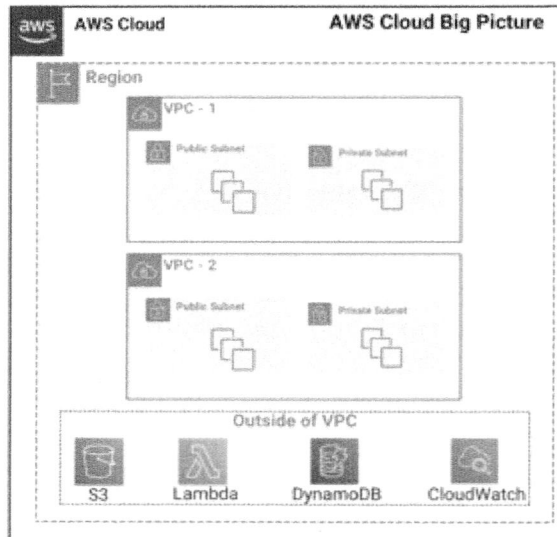

But outside of VPC, the private environment, AWS also provides managed services such as Amazon S3, Amazon DynamoDB, AWS Lambda, CloudWatch, and many other managed services. These services live outside of VPC – in the AWS public address space.

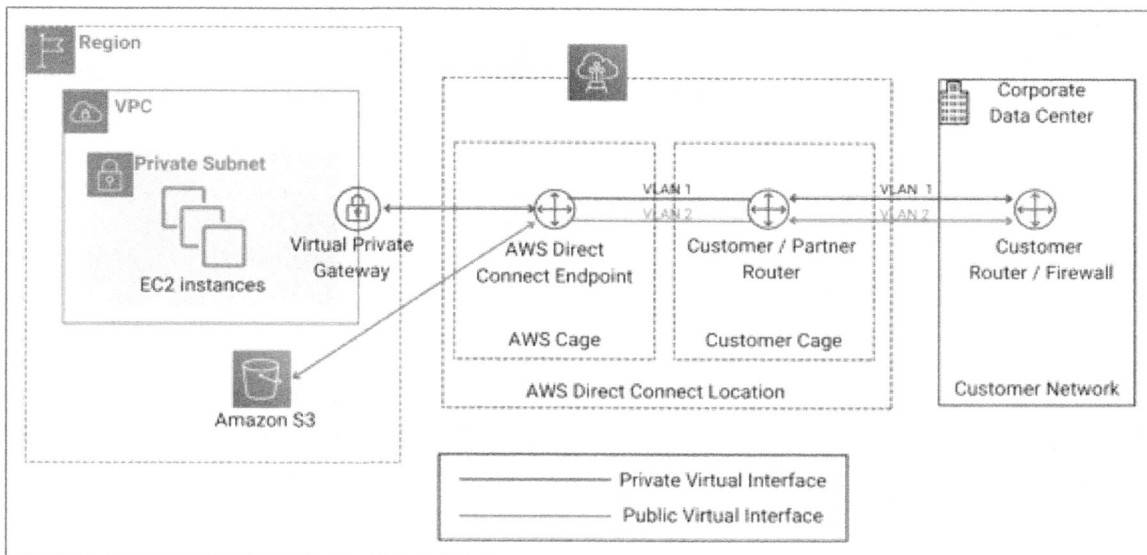

Now using AWS Direct Connect, we want to connect to a VPC (a private network) and AWS services in a public address space.

To use AWS Direct Connect, you can use the AWS Direct Connect location near your data center location. AWS has many Direct Connection locations; each of these locations has Routers managed by AWS. Then you request port on one of these Routers – maybe 1G/sec or 10 G/sec. And then, you can set up AWS connectivity either by yourself or by taking the help of an AWS Connectivity partner.

The AWS Direct Connect is a physical connection. The AWS Direct Connect provides more predictable and consistent experience for on-premises connectivity to the AWS.

KEY POINTS

- It provides a dedicated private connection from a remote network, such as an on-premises data center, to your VPC.
- A dedicated connection between your data center and AWS Direct Connect locations must be set up.
- You need to set up a Virtual Private Gateway on your VPC.
- Access public resources (S3) and private instances (EC2) on the same connection.
- Use Cases:
  - Increased bandwidth throughput helps work with large data sets at a lower cost.
  - More consistent network experience when applications using real-time data feeds
  - Hybrid Environments (on-prem + AWS Cloud)

AWS Direct Connect Gateway for Multiple VPCs

If you connect more than one VPC from your on-premises environment, you can use AWS Direct Connect Gateway. That way, you can connect up to 10 VPCs that reside in the same Region or in the different AWS Regions across the world (except China).

If we needed to connect multiple VPCs before we have Transit Gateway, we would have to create AWS site-to-site VPN for each VPC. So each VPC would have its VPC connection. So if you have 10 VPCs, we would have 20 VPN connections (one VPN has two tunnels).

virtual private gateway
A virtual private gateway (VGW) is part of a VPC that provides edge routing for AWS managed VPN connections and AWS Direct Connect connections. You associate an AWS Direct Connect gateway with the virtual private gateway for the VPC. A virtual gateway allows resources that are outside of your VPC to communicate to resources that are inside of your VPC.

Transit Gateway Associations
Using Direct Connect, you can connect all VPCs using one logical connection. So, for example, if we add Transit Gateway with Direct Connect Gateway, just by using one physical link from on-premises to AWS, we can reach up to 5000 VPC using Transit Gateway. Transit gateway allows VPCs to intercommunicate as long as they are connected to the same transit gateway.

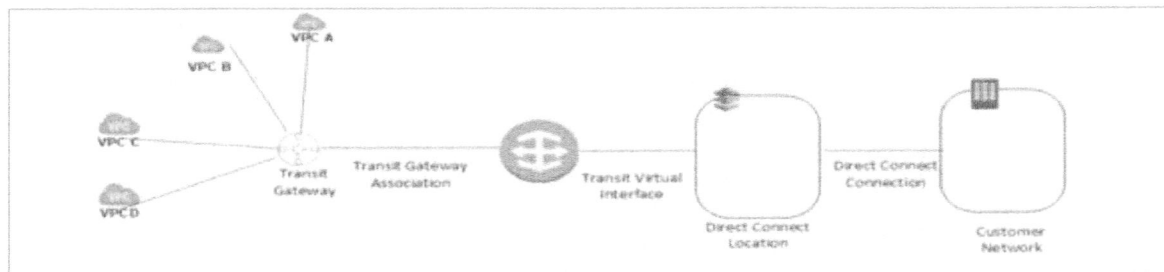

The above screenshot is from:
https://docs.aws.amazon.com/directconnect/latest/UserGuide/direct-connect-gateways-intro.html

It shows that how the Direct Connect gateway using Transit Gateway enables you to create a single connection to your Direct Connect connection that all of your VPCs can use, and provides connectivity to on-premises as well.

https://blog.opstree.com/2020/09/01/why-we-should-use-transit-direct-connect-gateways/

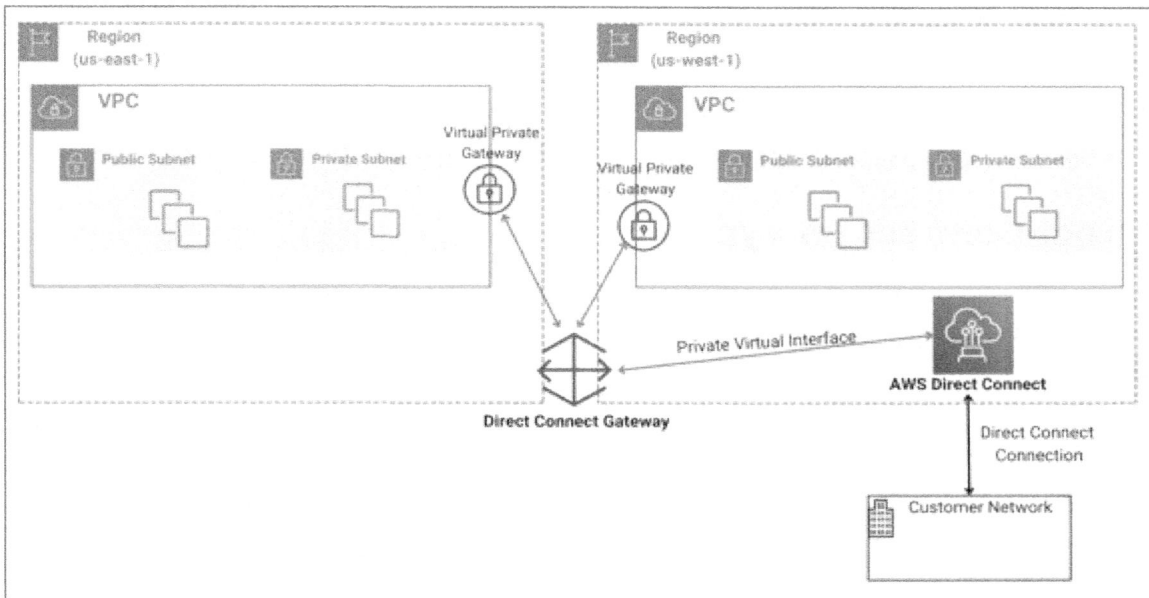

Use a Direct Connect Gateway if you want to set up a Direct Connect to one or more VPCs in many different AWS Regions -- in the same AWS account.

You can associate an AWS Direct Connect gateway with either a transit gateway (when you have multiple VPCs in the same Region) or a virtual private gateway.

The Direct Connect gateway has a connection to a Direct Connect location in a Region. The on-premises data center has a Direct Connect connection to the Direct Connect location.

A Direct Connect gateway is a global resource. You can create the Direct Connect gateway in any Region and access it from different Regions.

Direct Connect Connection Types

Dedicated Connections
- Port Speed: The possible values are 1 Gbps, 10 Gbps, and 100 Gbps.
- It's a physical ethernet port dedicated to a customer. You need to request AWS first.
- AWS Direct Connect Partners complete the request.
- The port speed cannot be changed after you create the connection request. You must create and configure a new connection to change the port speed.

Hosted Connections
- Port Speed: the possible values are 50 Mbps, 100 Mbps, 200 Mbps, 300 Mbps, 400 Mbps, 500 Mbps, 1 Gbps, 2 Gbps, 5 Gbps, or 10 Gbps
- Connection requests are made via AWS Direct Connect Partners.
- Only those AWS Direct Connect partners who have met specific requirements may create a 1 Gbps, 2 Gbps, 5 Gbps, or 10 Gbps hosted connection.

- The port speed cannot be changed after you create the connection request. You must create and configure a new connection to change the port speed.

Lead times are often longer than one month to establish a new Direct connection.

AWS Direct Connect Encryption

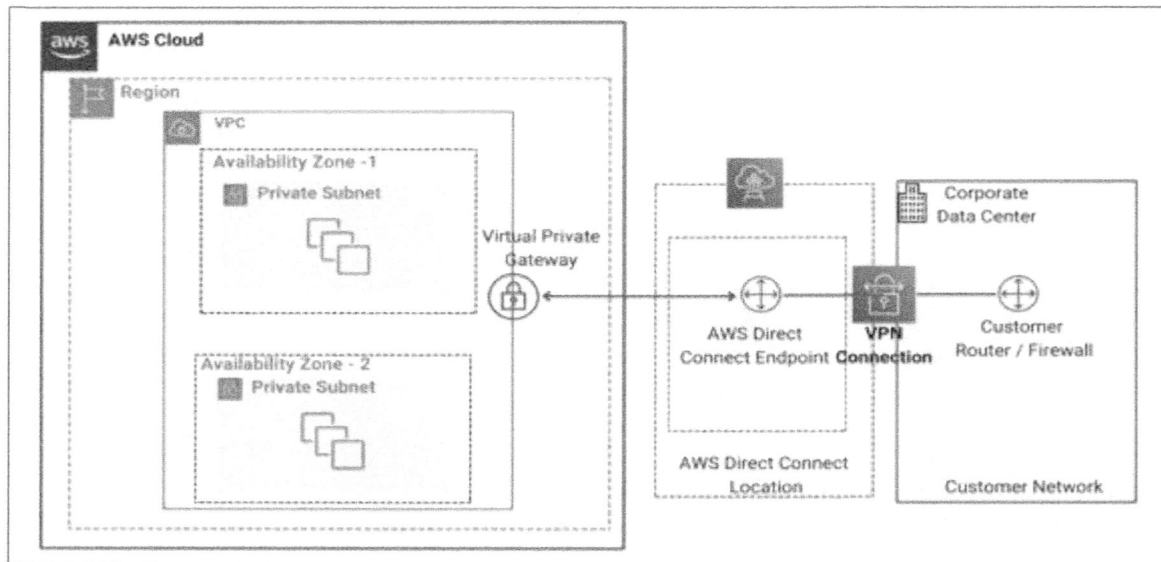

- In AWS Direct Connection, connection, data in transit is private – but not encrypted.

- To encrypt data, which is good for an extra level of security (though slightly more complex to put in place), add a VPN connection with AWS Direct Connect.

- The VPN connection provides an IPsec-encrypted private connection.

Amazon Direct Connect Resiliency

The failure might happen in the Amazon Direct Connect connection -- the Amazon Direct Connect Resiliency Toolkit provides multiple resiliency model choices to help you achieve resiliency in Amazon Direct Connect connections to achieve your SLA objective.

There are three resiliency models in the Amazon Direct Connect Resiliency Toolkit:

High Resiliency: This model provides high resiliency for critical workloads by using two single connections to multiple locations. It can be used for use cases for resiliency against connectivity failures caused by a fiber cut or a device failure and helps prevent a complete location failure.

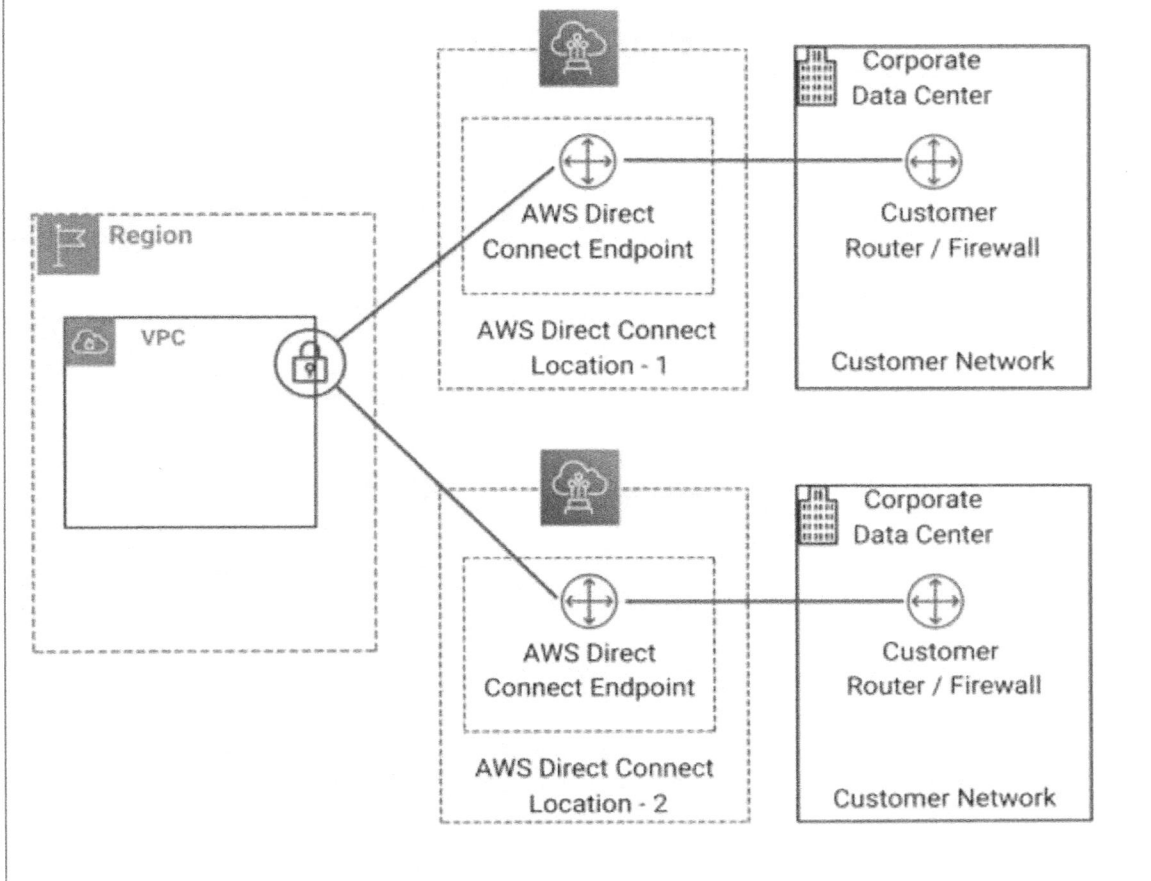

High Resiliency for Critical Workloads

Maximum Resiliency: This model provides maximum resiliency for critical workloads by using separate connections that terminate on separate devices in more than one location. It can be used for use cases for maximum resiliency against connectivity and complete location failures.

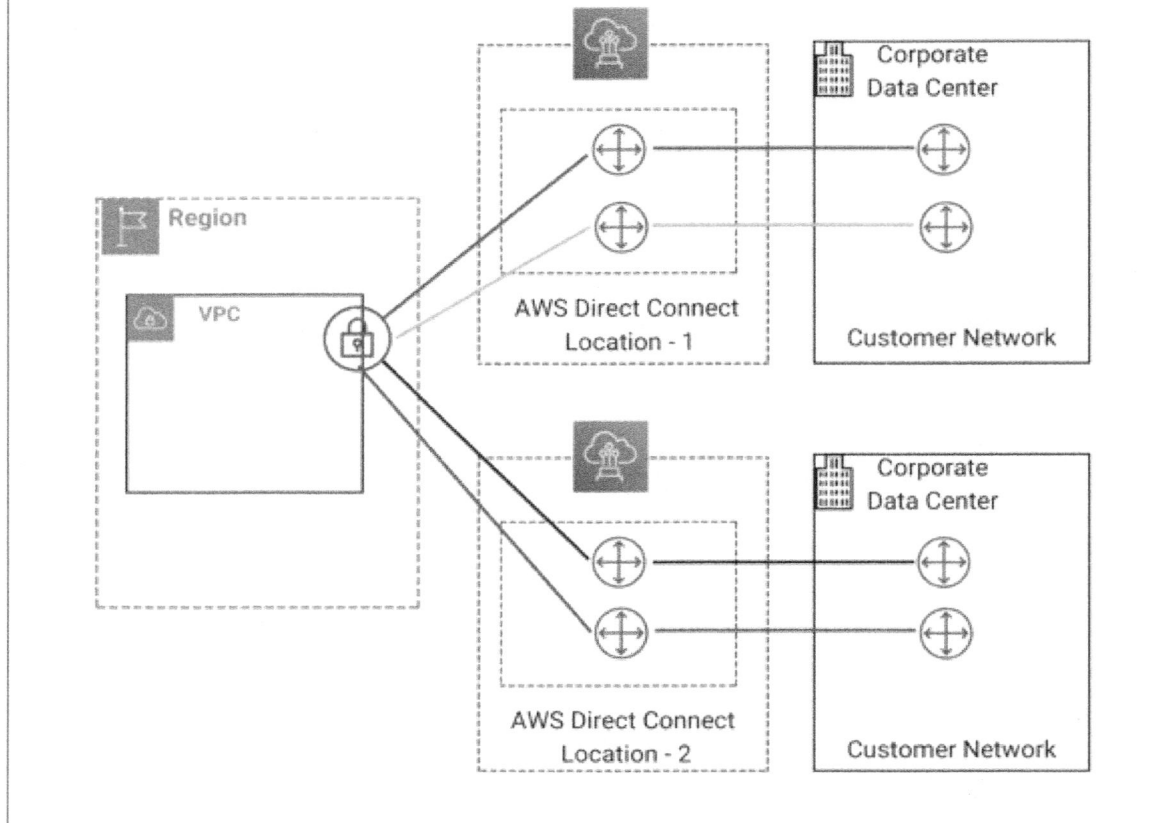

Maximum Resiliency for Critical Workloads
-- by having separate connections terminating on separate devices in more than one location.

Development and Test: This model provides development and test resiliency for non-critical workloads by using separate connections that terminate on separate devices in one location. It can be used for use cases for resiliency against device failure but **does not provide resiliency against location failure.**

Reference:
https://docs.aws.amazon.com/directconnect/latest/UserGuide/WorkingWithConnections.html

Site-to-Site VPN Connection as a Backup

You can set up a backup Direct Connect connection or a Site-to-Site VPN connection to handle a scenario where a Direct Connect connection fails.

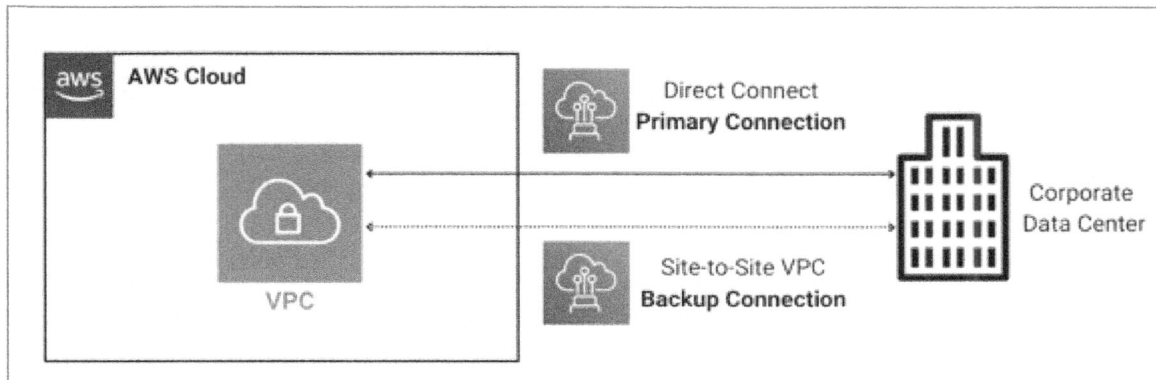

Route 53 Resolver

We have a hybrid environment and an on-premises environment connected to AWS. What about DNS? AWS customers deploy their resources in the private domain in an on-premises environment or on VPCs on the AWS cloud. However, they would like to resolve domains no matter where they are.

So, for that purpose, AWS has Route 53 Resolver service. AWS Route 53 is a managed DNS resolver service offered by Route 53. It allows you to create conditional forwarding rules to redirect query traffic between your on-premises data center and your AWS VPC. In addition, it enables you to use DNS over AWS Direct Connect or Managed VPN.

Route53 Resolver allows you to create Endpoint Resolvers in one of the VPCs connected to on-premises. This Endpoint is used for DNS forwarding. You can make resolutions from on-premises to AWS or vice-versa. For example, you can create your own forwarding rules. The rules will help decide which should be resolved in an on-premises environment and which should be forwarded to the AWS or vise-versa.

VPC Sharing (Sharing VPC Resources)

VPC Sharing is changing the model of how you organize VPCs. Before VPC sharing, when you create a VPC, it has to belong to an AWS account, and all the services you deploy in that VPC would have to belong to the same account. With VPC Sharing, that model is changing.

AWS has a concept of an owner account. Maybe this is an AWS account owned by your networking team, infrastructure, or DevOps team. They would build all the networking constructs. They would create the VPC, create the CIDR range, create subnets, set up all the route tables, set NACLs, and set up all the route tables and connectivity to the other environments.

In other words, they would set up the VPC exactly, in the same way you would set up a regular VPC, but the other teams would use the VPC -- they would not be owners or would not control the VPC. They can use it, however.

The big difference is that in VPC sharing, subnets can be shared with the other AWS accounts. In other words, the other team, let's say the engineering team, can deploy their EC2 instances in the subnet(shared) and configure security groups for the EC2 instances.

However, they cannot change the configuration or setup done by the owner of the subnet. On the same token, they cannot modify or change resources deployed by the other team. For example, they cannot change the routing table or the NACLs.

You can share the subnet with multiple accounts. For example, one account may manage databases or create an RDS service. However, the teams cannot modify other resources they do not own; they can only manage their resources.

One interesting point is from the networking perspective, if the owner of the resource modifies their security group, they can access the other resources, provided the owner of the other resource changes their security group to allow the access.

Why would you use VPC Sharing?
- *VPC Sharing helps in preserving IP space.* If you run out of IPv4 addresses, you can create VPC sharing to utilize the resources more efficiently.

- *No VPC Peering is required.* If you have fewer VPCs, you have little connectivity between different VPCs.

- *Separation of duties.* A central team can create and manage VPCs. You will have separation of duties where owner creates the VPCs and users cannot change it.

- *Billing and Security.* Please continue to have separation of accounts and billed for the resources they create.

AWS Networking Components Architecture Diagram

Section 11. Cloud Architecture

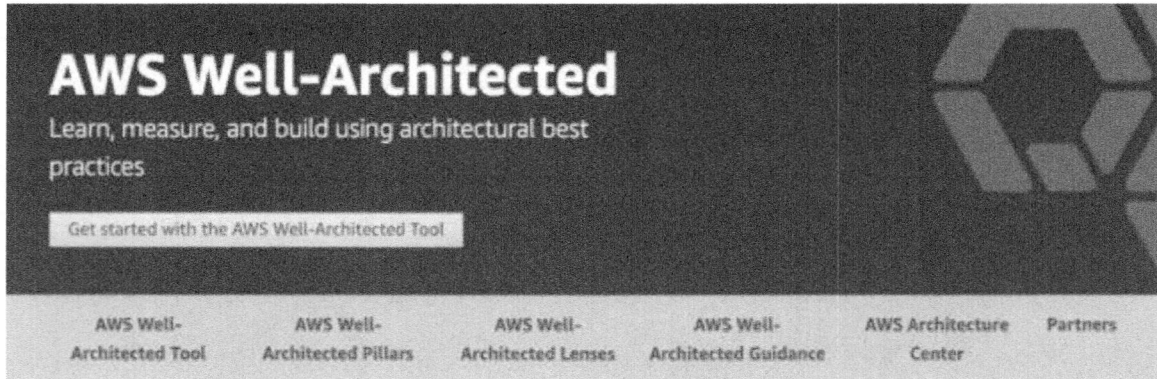

Chapter 35. AWS Well-Architected Framework

You will learn the following in this chapter:
- Pillars of AWS Well-Architected Framework
- Well-Architected Framework General Design Principles
- AWS Well-Architected Tool

Software design is one level below software architecture. Before discussing the design principles, let's briefly discuss software architecture — engineering enterprise software solutions in many ways building civil engineering systems such as building bridges. If the foundation is not architected, designed, and built-in a proper engineering way, the structural building problem may undermine the integrity and function of the building. Or it may cause extension, modification, and repair to be expensive. Building software systems have two types of requirements: functional and non-functional. The software architecture addresses non-functional requirements, for example, performance, reliability, scalability, security, etc.

Cloud systems also have functional and non-functional requirements. What it means is that when building software systems on the cloud, we need to consider quality attributes to build well-architected software solutions. Now the question is what those quality attributes are that we need to consider when building software solutions on the cloud platform.

Architecting Software Solutions on the AWS Cloud

AWS Well-Architected and the Six Pillars

Framework Overview

The AWS Well-Architected Framework describes key concepts, design principles, and architectural best practices for designing and running workloads in the cloud. By answering a few foundational questions, learn how well your architecture aligns with cloud best practices and gain guidance for making improvements.

HTML | Kindle | Labs

Operational Excellence Pillar

The operational excellence pillar focuses on running and monitoring systems, and continually improving processes and procedures. Key topics include automating changes, responding to events, and defining standards to manage daily operations.

HTML | Kindle | Labs

Security Pillar

The security pillar focuses on protecting information and systems. Key topics include confidentiality and integrity of data, managing user permissions, and establishing controls to detect security events.

HTML | Kindle | Labs

Reliability Pillar

The reliability pillar focuses on workloads performing their intended functions and how to recover quickly from failure to meet demands. Key topics include distributed system design, recovery planning, and adapting to changing requirements.

HTML | Kindle | Labs

Performance Efficiency Pillar

The performance efficiency pillar focuses on structured and streamlined allocation of IT and computing resources. Key topics include selecting resource types and sizes optimized for workload requirements, monitoring performance, and maintaining efficiency as business needs evolve.

HTML | Kindle | Labs

Cost Optimization Pillar

The cost optimization pillar focuses on avoiding unnecessary costs. Key topics include understanding spending over time and controlling fund allocation, selecting resources of the right type and quantity, and scaling to meet business needs without overspending.

HTML | Kindle | Labs

Sustainability Pillar

The sustainability pillar focuses on minimizing the environmental impacts of running cloud workloads. Key topics include a shared responsibility model for sustainability, understanding impact, and maximizing utilization to minimize required resources and reduce downstream impacts.

HTML | Kindle | Labs

Screenshot from: https://aws.amazon.com/architecture/well-architected/

According to a blog on the AWS Partner Network (https://aws.amazon.com/blogs/apn/the-6-pillars-of-the-aws-well-architected-framework/), there are six pillars of the well-architected framework. These are operational excellence, security, reliability, performance efficiency, cost optimization, and sustainability. Therefore, architecting systems by focusing on these six pillars help produce efficient and stable systems. So, let's discuss these quality attributes for building well-architected solutions on the AWS cloud platform.

Operational Excellence

The Operational Excellence pillar of the AWS Well-Architected framework includes supporting the development team and effectively running workloads most efficiently. The support to the development team and effectively running workloads are critical to a successful cloud platform. The reason is that your engineers will be using the AWS cloud platform to do all their development work. In addition, depending on your business area, you will be running different workloads such as analytic jobs, machine learning-related models, and many other operations. The important points are you need to continuously gain insights to improve the processes and procedures to deliver business value.

There is a saying from the Greek philosopher Heraclitus: "The only constant in life changes." Things change: your customers' requirements and business context may change. Therefore, it is essential to design operations in such a way as they can evolve quickly with the change and incorporate changes from the insights.

Key design principles to consider for the Operational Excellence pillar:
- Perform operations as code:
- Make frequent, small, reversible changes

- Refine operations procedures frequently
- Anticipate failure
- Learn from all operational failures

Security

Security is another essential pillar to consider for well-architected solutions on the AWS platform. The Security pillar includes the ability to protect data and IT assets. You can leverage various AWS security-related services such as IAM, KMS, and other related services to provide security to your solutions. It would be best if you had proper procedures to manage any security incidents. Strong security and operations to handle security incidents help mitigate financial loss and help comply with regulatory obligations.

AWS has a concept of the Shared Responsibility Model. What it means is that the AWS platform protects your physical infrastructure. As a result, this helps you focus on using AWS services to achieve your business goals and not being concerned or responsible for the security of the physical infrastructure, such as servers and other components of a data center.

Key design principles to consider for the Security pillar:

- Implement a strong identity foundation
- Enable traceability
- Apply security at all layers
- Automate security best practices
- Protect data in transit and at rest
- Keep people away from data
- Prepare for security events

Reliability

Reliability is another pillar of well-architected solutions on the cloud. Reliability emphasizes the ability of a system to operate without any failure. Before running your workloads, testing what resources are required for compute, storage, and network helps run the workloads reliably in production. Cloud by design has theoretically unlimited resources. That means you should easily find the resources and services you need to build reliable solutions, for example, AWS Auto-Scaling service, to run workloads without any failure or outage.

To build a reliable system, you will need to anticipate changes such as a spike in workload or changes in the environment – what if the server running workload fails, and other related demands of resources such as extra resources needed when deploying new feature releases. And you will need to take steps such as fault isolation, automated failover to healthy resources, and a disaster recovery strategy to implement resiliency.

Keep these in mind to help you increase reliability:
- Automatically recover from failure
- Test recovery procedures
- Scale horizontally to increase aggregate workload availability
- Stop guessing capacity
- Manage change in automation

Performance Efficiency

The Performance Efficiency pillar includes the ability to use computing resources efficiently to manage the current demand of resources, including when there is a change in requirements – essentially maintaining SLA (Service Level Agreements) by utilizing compute resources efficiently.

The question is how we can ensure we are using resources efficiently. First, we can review our AWS solution to find out if we are using resources efficiently – logs and monitoring will be a good help. We can also review if there is any alternate way to use the system more efficiently. For example, we can tradeoff such as compression or caching to improve managing resources efficiently.

The following design principles can help you achieve and maintain efficient workloads in the cloud.

- Democratize advanced technologies
- Go global in minutes
- Use serverless architectures
- Experiment more often
- Consider mechanical sympathy

Cost Optimization

Cost Optimization pillars deal with the system's ability to deliver business value at the lowest cost. The point here is not to concede service level agreements to save costs. Instead, we must review our choices and if there are alternate ways where we can provide the same business value – go for it. That's the essence of the cost optimization pillar.

Some key design principles to manage cost optimization:

- Implement cloud financial management
- Adopt a consumption model
- Measure overall efficiency
- Stop spending money on undifferentiated heavy lifting
- Analyze and attribute expenditure

Sustainability

The Sustainability pillar addresses how in the long-term, architecture manages the change in business requirements, environment, or economic change.

The following are the key design principles when architecting your cloud workloads to maximize sustainability and minimize impact.
- Understand your impact
- Establish sustainability goals
- Maximize utilization
- Anticipate and adopt new, more efficient hardware and software offerings
- Use managed services
- Reduce the downstream impact of your cloud workloads

Please review key design principles of each of the pillar – there may be question(s) in the exam related to the key design principles of the AWS Well-Architected Framework pillars.

Well-Architected Framework General Design Principles

The Well-Architected Framework identifies a set of general design principles to facilitate good design in the cloud:

- **Stop guessing your capacity needs**: Before deploying an application, you often buy expensive idle resources or deal with limited capacity when you plan to make a capacity decision. With cloud computing, you can use and access the suitable capacity -- as much or as little capacity as you need. In addition, you can scale up and down very quickly as required. Cloud computing helps you stop guessing capacity.

- **Test systems at production scale**: In the cloud, you can create a production-scale test environment on-demand to help set up and perform the complete testing of your application. And then, you can release the resources. Simulating a live production environment is much cheaper because you only pay for what resources you used for the testing.

- **Automate to make architectural experimentation easier**: Automation saves time and money on repetitious tasks and avoids the expense of manual effort when you have to do the same thing next time. In addition, automation helps you track changes, audit the impact, and revert to previous parameters when necessary.

- **Allow for evolutionary architectures**: In traditional classic enterprise architecture, architectural decisions are often slow and implemented as static, one-time events, with a few major versions of a system during its lifetime -- again, a slow and sometimes a bureaucratic process. However, as a business and its context continue to evolve, these initial decisions might hinder the system's ability to deliver changing business requirements. The capability to automate and test on-demand lowers the risk of impact from design changes in the cloud. This allows systems to evolve so that businesses can take advantage of innovations as a standard practice.

- **Drive architectures using data**: In the cloud, you can log and collect data about how your architectural choices affect the behavior of your workload --cost, performance, etc. This helps you make more fact-based decisions on how to improve your architecture. Your cloud infrastructure is code, so you can use that data to inform your architecture choices and improvements over time.

- **Improve through game days**: Try simulating events in production by regularly scheduling game days. This will help you understand where improvements can be made and can also help develop organizational experience in dealing with different types of events.

AWS Well-Architected Tool
The AWS Well-Architected Tool guides reviewing the workloads state and compares them to the architectural best practices of AWS. The AWS Well-Architected Tool using the AWS Well-Architected Framework is developed to help cloud architects build secure, high-performing, resilient, and efficient application infrastructure.

To use the AWS Well-Architected Tool, which is available in the AWS Management Console, first define your workload and then answer a set of questions regarding operational excellence, security, reliability, performance efficiency, and cost optimization. The AWS Well-Architected Tool then provides a plan on how to architect for the cloud using established best practices.

The AWS Well-Architected Tool gives you access to knowledge and best practices used by AWS architects whenever you need it. You answer a series of questions about your workload, and the tool delivers an action plan with step-by-step guidance on how to build better workloads for the cloud.

Chapter 36. Cloud Architecture Key Design Principles

You will learn the following in this chapter:
 Different cloud architecture design principles

In the previous chapter, we discussed six pillars of a well-architected AWS framework: operational excellence, security, reliability, performance efficiency, cost optimization, and sustainability. The idea behind a well-architected framework's pillars is to help cloud architects build operationally excellent, most secure, resilient, high-performance, and cost-effective IT infrastructure possible for their applications. The Well-architected AWS Framework provides a consistent approach for customers and partners to evaluate architectures. In addition, it guides to help implement design principles that will help scale your cloud applications as they need to grow over time.

Key Design Principles in Building Cloud Architecture

We mentioned design principles that help implement a well-architected AWS Framework. Now, look into crucial design principles that help build well-architected cloud solutions. The design principles are scalability and elasticity, automation, loose coupling, security, caching, cost optimization, think parallel, and design for failure. First, we will start with scalability and elasticity, as these two are one of the most compelling reasons for cloud adoption besides cost and other features.

Scalability

Scalability is the ability of a system to scale without changing the design as input or workload increases. Cloud infrastructure and applications are designed with the premise that the load on the application can grow. In this scenario, if proper mechanisms are not in place in the design, the system will suffer – either the system will stop functioning or underperform. We need to design the system to allow components to be added when demand increases on the system – without changing the design.

Additional components can be added to manage the extra load to drive seasonal traffic. However, automatic scalability is considered a much better design, where the additional system components are added automatically based on the runtime metrics such as CPU, memory, or storage utilization. Design horizontally scalable cloud applications. There are two ways to manage scalability: horizontal and vertical.

A "vertical scalable" system is considered constrained on resources such as CPU, RAM, and storage, negatively impacting the overall system's performance. Therefore, to improve this system's implementation by the "vertical scalable" mechanism means adding more resources such as CPU, RAM, and storage. However, since there is still no addition of a machine or node, making the system vertical scalable doesn't improve the fault tolerance of the overall design.

A "horizontally scalable" system increases its resource capacity by adding more nodes or machines to the system. If we compare a horizontally scalable system with a scalable vertical design, the horizontally scalable system is preferred over vertically scalable systems. The reason is that a horizontally scalable system helps increase the degree of fault tolerance of the overall strategy and helps improve performance by enabling parallel execution of the workload and distributing that workload across multiple machines. Horizontal scalability helps increase in making the system horizontally scalable. In a horizontally scalable system, since more machines are added to increase the pool of resources, thus if one machine goes down, the other machine is allocated to process the workload of the failed machine. Thus, helping to increase the degree of fault tolerance of fault the overall system.

Vertical Scalability is an old style in which the application is ported to a new server with more CPU, memory, or storage. It could lead to some downtime. The other one, horizontal Scalability, is more modern and a common approach to handling Scalability. In horizontally scalable systems, additional resources such as servers are added automatically to maintain the same performance as the load increases—design horizontally scalable cloud applications.

To summarize, scalable architecture is critical to take advantage of a scalable infrastructure. Increasing resources results in a proportional increase in the system's performance. A scalable service is capable of handling heterogeneity, operationally efficient, and resilient, and it becomes more cost-effective when it grows.

Elasticity

Let's talk about elasticity as a design principle in architecting cloud applications. Elasticity and scalability are generally considered together when architecting solutions on the cloud application. Elasticity is the ability of a system to use resources in a dynamic and efficient way to maintain the SLA as the workload on the system increases and release them as the workload on the system decreases. The deallocation or release of the resources dynamically when they are not needed is the key aspect of elasticity as it avoids the cost of over-provisioned resources such as server, power, space, and maintenance.

Don't assume that components will always be in good health. Don't assume the fixed location of components. Use designs to re-launch and bootstrap your instances. Enable dynamic configuration to help answer instances on boot question: Who am I & what is my role?

Automation

DevOps, in which automation is one of the key features, has become an essential role in many software engineering organizations. Automation is one of the key design principles for architecting applications on a cloud platform. The reason is it avoids human intervention – particularly if it relates to repetitive tasks, integrating systems, or batch jobs. Thus, many operations become more automated and efficient, and organizations save time on staff – particularly maintenance staff. This frees up some staff time. Time saved from the automation could be utilized on some other high-priority tasks in line with the organization's business objectives. Moreover, with automation with thoroughly tested scripts, we not only automate start, stop, and terminate operations, but we also minimize failures by handling failures in codes. As the system throws an error, we look up the error and fix the script so that next time we don't need to handle it manually. These automated processes overtime make the system resilient -- running with very less human intervention.

AWS has an extensive set of APIs to automate its services. For example, you can easily write a Python script (AWS Python SDK is called boto 3) to automate launching EC2.

Loose Coupling

Enterprise systems have many modules or services (term used in modern micro-services architecture) encapsulating unique business features such as shopping cart service, checkout service, billing service, warehouse service, and support service. These modules are loosely coupled in well-architected systems – typically using web services or messaging frameworks (for example, JMS in Java).

Design everything as a Black Box.

Loose coupling is a key design principle in building any kind of system – even in monolith systems. Loose coupling becomes critically important in building distributed and cloud applications. The reasons are many. We can replace, modify, maintain, or test part of the application in isolation as a separate module or as a separate component by not taking down the entire application, as the price of taking down the entire system could be huge. Imagine if Google, CNN, BBC, Amazon, or any critical applications are going down even for a few seconds for maintenance, to add a new release feature, or fix some bugs.

Security

Security is paramount for any organization, startup, small, medium-sized, or large enterprise. It is even critical for organizations that are handling data related to public health and money. These organizations are also bound to many security and compliance regulations.

Design security in mind. Design security in every layer.

When designing systems, security must be thought of from the very beginning as opposed to thinking and implementing security in bits and pieces when the application is deployed on production. It could be catastrophic if any security-related incident happens.

Broadly speaking, we can divide security into three aspects: physical security, platform security on which application runs, such as operating system and web server, and application security. When it comes to designing the security of data, data should be secured at transit and at rest. In other words, data should be stored in encrypted form both at rest and at transit.

With the cloud, you lose some part of physical control but not your own. A few guidelines related to cloud security. Restrict external access to specified IP ranges. Encrypt data "at-rest" and encrypt data "at-transit" (SSL). Consider an encrypted file system. Rotate your credentials. When passing arguments, pass the arguments as encrypted. Use Multi-factor factor authentication.

Caching

Cloud computing's architecture basis is distributed computing. Distributed computing, on the one hand, by using the basic computing science technique divide-and-conquer, helps to improve processing workload and loose coupling improves modifiability, maintainability, and scalability. There are extremely important features for enterprise systems. However, distributed computing adds in some challenges, for example, more indirection and more layer to communicate to get the final result. This increases latency and thus impacts how fact an output will be retrieved by the end-user

Not all information in the system needs to fetch or calculated each time to process a request. There is any information that changes almost very less, for example, country names, city names, persons' demographic, and such – in fact, master data, or look up values in database terms. On the same token, many contents such as images, videos, or documents in general, don't frequently change in production systems.

Since this information is of mostly static nature, we can leverage caching design principle of cloud architecture to not only improve request processing time but also help reduce operational cost. Data movement from the bottom layer to the top layer is reduced by a few layers reducing data transfer cost. Also, computing resource usage is also reduced due to caching.

As we discussed above that, caching improves request processing time, saves cost on data transfer, and saves cost on computing resource utilization. Let's understand the type of caching. There are two types of caching: application data caching and edge caching.

In application data caching, essentially, data that is mostly of static nature, such as master data, are cached in the in-memory cache. There are many products you can leverage to manage application data caching, such as Amazon ElasticCache (managed Memcache), Redis (in-memory database), and Hibernate Ehcache. You can also implement your custom application data caching for problems smaller in scope.

The other type of caching mechanism which is, by and large, very common in cloud architecture is edge caching. Essentially, for content management, the common caching solution is edge caching. In cache caching, content is served by the infrastructure's edge node server's (AWS Edge Locations) which is closer to the user, thus improving latency and overall system performance. Amazon CloudFront is a typical example of edge caching.

Cost Optimization

Cost optimization is the most important design principle. The reason is cloud costs, to a large part – particularly in the public cloud -- are based on OpEx (operating expenditure) model. Cost optimization essentially becomes an extremely important consideration.

Some principles are common: utilizing the right services for the right duration. For example, if an EC2 medium size instance provides the required performance, then utilizing large or z-large will cost more. If services are being utilized, terminate them or stop them if you are using on-demand instances.

You can also consider reserved instances and spot instances as opposed to on-demand instances for EC2 instances to optimize costs.

Auto-scaling is also a very good feature to optimize the cost. Using Auto-scaling, you can not only scale by adding more instances horizontally to maintain performance if the workload increases, but you can also scale down to terminate the resources if they are needed automatically by adding some configuration using the CloudWatch service.

The main points here are: right service for the right job, and do not use more resources and for more time if you don't need it. Look into various cost options and their pros and cons (for example, on-demand instances, reserved instances, and spot instances) provided by the cloud provider, and select the best option for your use case to optimize the cost.

Think Parallel

Many software engineering problems can be solved in less time if the concept of parallel processing is used. For example, a data processing job can be divided into many parts, and each part can be processed parallel. Map-Reduce job is a good example of parallel processing. Extending on the parallel processing, when you are designing applications to run an on a cloud platform, parallel thinking becomes even more important and valuable as the cloud has massive resources. Parallel processing helps solve large problems in less time.

There are two main reasons for using parallel computing. Parallel computing saves time (wall clock time) and it helps solve large problems. Some guidelines for parallel thinking: experiment different architectures for multi-threading and concurrent requests. Run parallel MapReduce jobs. Use Elastic Load Balancing with Auto-Scaling to distribute loads across multiple machines.

Design for Failure

"Everything fails, all the time," Werner Vogels, CTO, Amazon.com. Design for failure, and nothing will really fail!

A few guidelines: *Avoid single points of failure -- assume everything fails*. Design with a backward goal as applications should continue to function even if the underlying physical hardware fails, is removed, or replaced.

Practice Tests

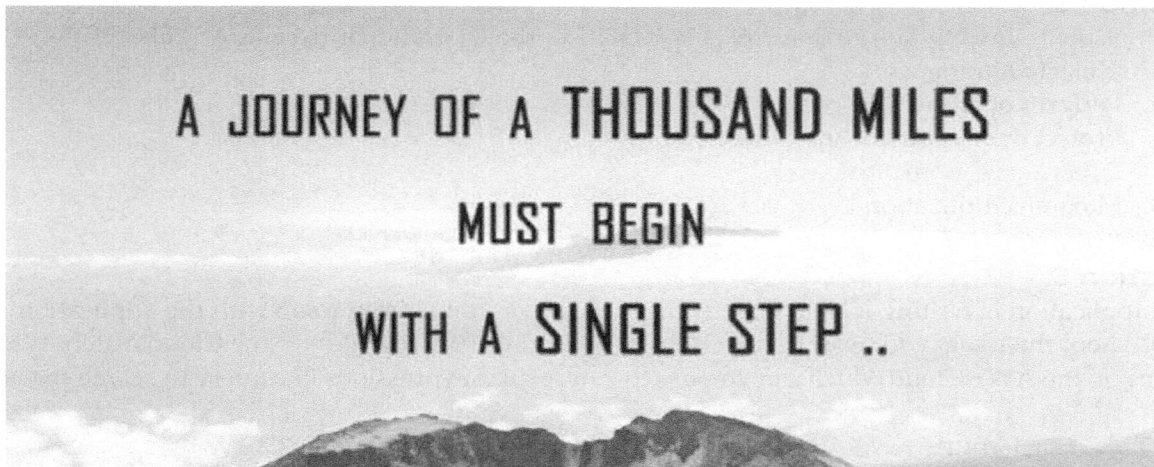

Test Set 1 - Practice Questions Only

Question 1:
Which of the following is not a pillar of AWS Well-Architected Framework?
- A. Security
- B. Reliability
- C. Scalability
- D. Sustainability

Question 2:
Which of the following AWS services can perform multiple builds concurrently?
- A. AWS CodeStar
- B. AWS Code Build
- C. Amazon CodeGuru
- D. AWS CodeCommit

Question 3:
Which of the following AWS services can you use to find trends related to your AWS cost and usage?
- A. AWS CloudWatch Dashboard
- B. AWS Cost Explorer
- C. AWS Organizations
- D. AWS Budgets

Question 4:
You have deployed a web application on an EC2 instance which allows users to upload images into S3 buckets. You have users all over the world for this application. Which of the following services would you use to make the experience as good as possible for worldwide users?
- A. Amazon CloudFront
- B. AWS S3 Accelerator
- C. AWS Global Accelerator
- D. Edge Locations

Question 5:
Which of the following design principles is related to the Operational Excellence Pillar of the AWS Well-Architected Framework?
- A. Perform operations as code
- B. Protect data in transit and at rest
- C. Experiment more often
- D. Maximize utilization

Question 6:
Your application is writing logs to CloudWatch. However, there is an issue with the application. To troubleshoot the issue, you need to search through around 1000 log files on the CloudWatch. Which options on the AWS CloudWatch can you use to run regular expressions like query to search through 1000 logs?
- A. Log Groups
- B. Insights
- C. Rules
- **D.** Event Buses

Question 7:
Which of the following is the most efficient way to access DynamoDB from an application running on an EC2 instance?
- A. Internet Gateway Endpoint
- B. VPC Gateway Endpoint
- C. VPC Interface Endpoint
- D. Virtual Private Endpoint

Question 8:
Which AWS services should you use to detect customer sentiment and analyze customer interactions to categorize inbound support requests automatically?
- A. Amazon Kendra
- B. Amazon Textract
- C. Amazon Transcribe
- D. Amazon Comprehend

Question 9:
Which of the following is a persistent block storage service?
- A. Amazon EFS
- B. Amazon EBS
- C. Amazon S3
- D. Amazon EC2 Instance Store

Question 10:
You have been planning to deploy an event-driven microservices applications to the AWS cloud. You have around 200 microservices in the application. Which of the following services of AWS you can use to help troubleshoot performance issues of a particular microservice?
- A. Amazon Macie
- B. AWS Lambda

C. AWS CodeStar

D. AWS X-Ray

Question 11:

Which of the following services can you use get recommendations about what Reserved Instances to purchase based on your historical AWS usage?

A. AWS CloudWatch Dashboard

B. AWS Cost Explorer

C. AWS Organizations

D. AWS Budgets

Question 12:

Which of the following statements is not true about Security Group?

A. EC2 Security Groups are stateless.

B. You can assign multiple Security Groups to an EC2 instance.

C. There are quotas about how many rules per Security Groups allowed.

D. When you create VPC, it comes with a default Security Group.

Question 13:

You have a use case where you need to use on-premises data to build machine learning models using AWS SageMaker. Which of the following AWS Storage Gateway types can you use to copy on-premises files to S3 cost-effectively?

A. Tape Gateway

B. File Gateway

C. Volume Gateway

D. AWS Direct Connect

Question 14:

You have many developers in your organization who are busy architecting, designing, and developing the code using Java as the main programming language. Your senior developers who are involved in the code review process complain about not having enough bandwidth for quality code review. In addition, there are many critical pull requests which are pending to be reviewed. Which of the following AWS tools can you use to help speed the code review process?

A. AWS CodeStar

B. AWS CodeBuild

C. Amazon CodeGuru

D. AWS CodeCommit

Question 15:

Which of the following services is FREE?

A. AWS WAF

B. AWS Shield Advanced

C. AWS Shield Standard

D. Amazon S3

Question 16:

You are working as a DevOps lead in your company. The software engineering team is deploying a new application in the test environment. However, the developer who is deploying the application doesn't have access to the EC2 instance of the test environment. Which features or services can you use to provide temporary credentials to the developer so that the developer can deploy the application in the test environment?

- A. AWS Security Token Service
- B. AWS Secrets Manager
- C. AWS Web Application Firewall
- D. Amazon Cognito

Question 17:
You are looking for the most cost-effective option to run around 1000 ETL jobs for about 1 month. Each of them runs hourly every day. You are ok if these jobs are interrupted as you have added a hook to handle the interruption to save the state of a job so that next time the job gets the instance, the job resumes from the state it was interrupted. Which of the following EC2 Instance types would be the most cost-effective option?

- A. On-Demand Instance
- B. Reserved Instance
- C. Spot Instance
- D. Dedicated Host

Question 18:
The AWS team in your organization is involved in automating many processes such as account creation and applying policies to the group of accounts. Which AWS services can you use to create AWS accounts programmatically?

- A. AWS IAM
- B. AWS Roles
- C. AWS Management Console
- D. AWS Organizations

Question 19:
What is the time limit of an AWS Lambda function per execution?

- A. 5 min
- B. 10 min
- C. 15 min
- D. 20 min

Question 20:
You are working as VP of software engineering. You have been asked to find out the organization-wide security posture of the AWS environment in your organization by automated checks based on a security best practice. Which of the following AWS services can you use for this use case?

- A. AWS Security Hub
- B. AWS Encryption SDK
- C. AWS Secrets Manager
- D. AWS Artifact

Question 21:
Which of the following statements is NOT correct?

- A. AWS WAF can be deployed on Amazon CloudFront.
- B. AWS WAF can be deployed on Amazon API Gateway

C. AWS WAF can be deployed on Amazon S3

D. AWS WAF can be deployed on Application Load Balancer

Question 22:

You would like to bring your Windows license, which is based on number of cores, to AWS Cloud. Which of the following instance types can you use for your Windows license?

A. On-Demand

B. Spot Instance

C. Reserved Instance

D. Dedicated Host

Question 23:

You are executing an AWS Lambda function to process a file when it is uploaded to an S3 bucket. Which of the following options is correct about how an AWS Lambda function's execution is charged?

A. The number of times the function is executed and the time taken to execute the function.

B. The time is taken to execute the function.

C. The number of times the function is executed.

D. The number of times the function is executed, the time taken to execute the function, and the memory consumed by the function during the execution.

Question 24:

Which of the following AWS service uses machine learning, anomaly detection techniques, threat intelligence techniques to identify traffic having potential threats?

A. AWS Shield Advanced

B. Amazon GaurdDuty

C. AWS WAF

D. AWS Shield Standard

Question 25:

Which of the following AWS services can you use to secure documents by identifying and redacting Personally Identifiable Information (PII)?

A. Amazon Kendra

B. Amazon Textract

C. Amazon Transcribe

D. Amazon Comprehend

Question 26:

Which programming language cannot be used to write an AWS Lambda function?

A. Java

B. Python

C. C++

D. Ruby

Question 27:

You are looking for an EC2 instance for 1 month for doing integration testing of the application that your team has recently worked on. You don't want the testing EC2 instances to be interrupted. Which of the following instance types will be the best fit for this use case?

A. On-Demand Instance

B. Reserved Instance
C. Spot Instance
D. Dedicated Host

Question 28:
Which of the following statements is true related to AWS Shield Standard?
    A. AWS Shield Standard cannot protect the Network layer from DDoS attacks.
    B. AWS Shield Standard cannot protect the Transport layer from DDoS attacks.
    C. AWS Shield Standard cannot protect the Application layer from DDoS attacks.
    D. AWS Shield Standard cannot protect CloudFront from layer 3 and layer 4 DDoS attacks.

Question 29:
You have a use case where you need to use cloud storage for your current tape backup without making any change in the existing backup and archive workflow. Which of the following AWS Storage features can you use to replace the current on-premises tape backup solution with the AWS cloud backup solution cost-effectively?
    A. Tape Gateway
    B. File Gateway
    C. Volume Gateway
    D. AWS Direct Connect

Question 30:
You are having an availability issue with one of AWS services. Which of the following can help you find out if a particular service is available or not?
    A. AWS CloudWatch
    B. AWS CloudTrail
    C. AWS Service Health Dashboard
    D. AWS Systems Manager

Question 31:
Which of the following statements is not true with regards to EC2 instance data transfer?
    A. There is no charge for inbound data transfer across all services in all Regions.
    B. Data transfer from AWS to the internet is charged per service,
    C. If the internet gateway is used to access the public endpoint of the AWS services in the same Region, there are no data transfer charges.
    D. If a NAT gateway is used to access the same services, there is a data no processing charge.

Question 32:
You have deployed a microservices application on three EC2 instances. You have fronted this with Application Load Balancer. You would like to protect the login URL from brute force attacks. Which of the following services can you provide protection and monitoring?
    A. AWS Shield Standard
    B. AWS Web Application Firewall (WAF)
    C. AWS Firewall Manager
    D. AWS CloudWatch

Question 33:

You are working as an AWS consultant for a company that is involved in a cloud migration project. The company would like to extend its on-premises IT infrastructure to connect to the AWS VPC to speed up some of its projects. The company would like to have a consistent high-bandwidth connection set up between on-premises and the AWS VPC. Which of the following options would you recommend for this use case?

A. AWS Direct Connect
B. AWS Site-to-Site VPN
C. Virtual Private Gateway
D. Customer Gateway

Question 34:

You are looking for a large number of computing resources immediately. Which of the following instance types will be the best fit for this use case?

A. On-Demand Instance
B. Reserved Instance
C. Spot Instance
D. Dedicated Host

Question 35:

Your company has many departments and each of these departments has many AWS accounts. There are budget issues, and your finance controller needs to see consolidated AWS billing to centralize the cost. You being the DevOps lead, which of the following AWS services /features will you use to consolidate AWS bills of multiple AWS accounts?

A. AWS Budgets
B. AWS Organizations
C. Amazon CloudWatch
D. AWS Cost and Usage

Question 36:

You deployed a static web application on S3 and used CloudFront to handle global traffic efficiently. You want to protect an application from common web exploits against OWASP's top 10 security risks. Which of the following services can you use to protect an application from common web exploits?

A. AWS Shield Standard
B. AWS WAF
C. AWS Firewall Manager
D. AWS CloudWatch

Question 37:

Which of the following AWS services don't require a VPC to run? (Select Two)

A. Amazon EC2
B. Amazon RDS
C. Amazon S3
D. Amazon DynamoDB
E. Elastic Load Balancer

Question 38:

You have a fleet of 10 EC2 instances running in one AWS Region. You need to apply a patch script, which is stored on GitHub, to all of the EC2 instances, but you are only allowed to apply patch remotely. Which of the following services can you use to apply the patch script on the fleet of all EC2 instances remotely?

    A. AWS Config

    B. Use Run command of AWS Systems Manager

    C. AWS Web Application Firewall (WAF)

    D. Amazon CloudWatch

Question 39:

You have an application that stores information in DynamoDB. The application also uses S3 to store files and images. You are designing a feature for this application where if a user uploads an image, the image thumbnail should be displayed quickly. Which of the following AWS services will you help you implement this feature cost-effectively?

    A. Amazon EFS

    B. Amazon SageMaker

    C. AWS Elastic Beanstalk

    D. AWS Lambda

Question 40:

You have two database servers on EC2 instances in a private subnet. You would like these instances to connect to the Internet so that they can download the latest patches. Which of the following can you use to allow EC2 instances in the private subnet to connect to the Internet?

    A. AWS Direct Connect

    B. NAT Gateway

    C. Customer Gateway

    D. Transit Gateway

Question 41:

You have a use case where you need to connect your on-premises IT infrastructure to the multiple VPC using a consistent high bandwidth connection. Which of the following options would you recommend?

    A. AWS Site-to-Site VPN

    B. AWS Direct Connect with Direct Connect Gateway

    C. Virtual Private Gateway

    D. Customer Gateway

Question 42:

You are planning to run a build job. The job is of predictable nature in terms of compute resource requirements. You have a Reserved EC2 Instance available. Which of the following is a cost-effective to run the job using the Docker container on AWS?

    A. ECS on EC2

    B. AWS Fargate

    C. AWS Lambda

    D. AWS Lambda or AWS Fargate

Question 43:

Your company is involved in modernization projects for many applications to migrate them to the AWS cloud. You have been asked to build a design solution for one of the applications in such a way as to use AWS services wherever possible so that the application can be more cloud-native. The application that you have been assigned to modernize uses LDAP for authentication. Your use case is to replace the LDAP with an AWS service in your new design. Which of the following services can you use for this use case?

A. Amazon DynamoDB
B. Amazon Cognito
C. Amazon Cloud Directory
D. AWS Secrets Manager

Question 44:

You have concerns about a possible DDoS attack on your application and are interested to find out bad actors if that happens. Which of the following AWS services can you use to address the issue?

A. AWS Shield Advanced
B. AWS Shield Standard
C. Amazon CloudWatch
D. Amazon Cognito

Question 45:

You have a fleet of 10 EC2 instances running in one AWS Region. You need to turn off SSH on all the instances, but you are only allowed to do it remotely. Which of the following services can you use to turn off SSH on all the EC2 instances remotely?

A. AWS Config
B. Use State Manager of AWS Systems Manager
C. AWS Web Application Firewall (WAF)
D. Amazon CloudWatch

Question 46:

Which of the following options is true related to the protection provided by AWS Shield Standard?

A. It defends against the most common, frequently occurring Network, Transport, and Application layer DDoS attacks.
B. It defends against the most common, frequently occurring Network, Transport layer DDoS attacks.
C. It defends against the most common, frequently occurring DDoS attacks only at the Network layer.
D. It defends against the most common, frequently occurring DDoS attacks only at the Application layer.

Question 47:

You have a use case where you need to connect your on-premises IT infrastructure to the multiple 250 VPCs using a consistent high bandwidth connection. Which of the following options would you recommend?

A. AWS Site-to-Site VPN
B. AWS Direct Connect with Transit Gateway
C. Virtual Private Gateway
D. Customer Gateway

Question 48:
You are working as a lead software engineer. You have been asked to translate large volumes of text for analysis quickly. Which of the following AWS service can you use for this use case?
    A. Amazon Rekognition
    B. Amazon Transcribe
    C. Amazon Polly
    D. Amazon Translate

Question 49:
Your company is required to maintain a history of all changes to EC2 to maintain compliance. Which of the following services will you use to record the history of changes?
    A. Amazon CloudWatch
    B. AWS CloudTrail
    C. AWS Config
    D. AWS Logs

Question 50:
Which of the following is not true about VPC Sharing?
    A. If you run out of IPv4 addresses, you can create VPC sharing to utilize the resources more efficiently.
    B. The only owner of the VPC can change the configuration or setup, such as creating subnets, setting up all the route tables, setting up NACLs, etc.
    C. The owner of the VPC can share the subnet with multiple accounts.
    D. There will be one billing account for all the resources created in a shared subnet.

Question 51:
You are working as a lead software engineer for a media company. You have been asked to quickly document clinical conversations into electronic health record (EHR) systems for analysis.
Which of the following AWS service can you use for this use case?
    A. Amazon Rekognition
    B. Amazon Transcribe
    C. Amazon Personalize
    D. Amazon Kendra

Question 52:
You are working in a DevOps group of your company. There are concerns about AWS cost, and your group has been asked to make sure all Elastic IP Addresses must be used otherwise released. Which of the following services will you use to find out if each Elastic IP Address is associated with an EC2 instance or not?
    A. Amazon CloudWatch
    B. AWS CloudTrail
    C. AWS Config
    D. AWS X-Ray

Question 53:
You are working as a lead software engineer. You have been asked to implement a feature in an existing application to flag suspicious online payment transactions before processing payments and fulfilling orders. Which of the following AWS service can you use for this use case?
A. Amazon Rekognition
B. Amazon Fraud Detector
C. Amazon Kendra
D. Amazon Textract

Question 54:
You are working as a lead software engineer. You have been asked to implement features in an existing application to add product recommendations, personalized product re-ranking, and customized direct marketing. Which of the following AWS service can you use for this use case?
A. Amazon Rekognition
B. Amazon Fraud Detector
C. Amazon Personalize
D. Amazon Kendra

Question 55:
Which AWS service can you use make SSH connection to an EC2 instance without opening inbound port?
A. AWS Systems Manager
B. AWS Systems Manager Session Manager
C. AWS CloudTrail
D. AWS Config

Question 56:
You are working as a lead software engineer. You have been asked to redesign a search feature of an existing application to add natural language search capabilities so that employees and customers can easily find the right answers to questions when they need them instead of searching through troves of unstructured data. Which of the following AWS service can you use for this use case?
A. Amazon Polly
B. Amazon Kendra
C. Amazon Rekognition
D. Amazon Textract

Question 57:
Which of the following AWS service can you use to eliminate the need to hardcode database credentials in getting a connection from the MySQL database?
A. AWS Shield
B. Amazon IAM
C. AWS Secrets Manager
D. AWS Config

Question 58:
Which of the following AWS service/feature can you use to scan your AWS infrastructure, compare it with AWS best practices, and provides recommended action?
A. AWS Trusted Advisor

B.   AWS Systems Manager
C.   AWS Shield Advanced
D.   AWS Config

Question 59:

Which AWS service can quickly process ID documents such as driver's licenses and passports issued by the U.S. government?
A.   Amazon Polly
B.   Amazon Kendra
C.   Amazon Rekognition
D.   Amazon Textract

Question 60:

You have been designing a real-time analytic application, in which if a user submits an order, the order information is sent to the DynamoDB database. Which of the following AWS services can you use to implement this highly available application cost-effectively? (Select Two)
A.   Amazon Kinesis
B.   Amazon SageMaker
C.   AWS Elastic Beanstalk
D.   AWS Lambda
E.   Amazon EFS

Question 61:

You are working as an AWS consultant for a client. The client would like to do operational planning to predict levels of web traffic, AWS usage, and IoT sensor usage. Which of the following AWS services is the best fit for this use case if you need to implement this use quickly?
A.   Amazon Lex
B.   Amazon Kendra
C.   Amazon Rekognition
D.   Amazon Forecast

Question 62:

Which of the following can you use to connect Window File Server from an EC2 Linux instance?
A.   AWS Systems Manager
B.   Amazon FSx for Windows
C.   Amazon API Gateway
D.   AWS Direct Connect

Question 63:

Which of the following storage service is transient?
A.   Amazon EFS
B.   Amazon EBS
C.   Amazon S3
D.   Amazon EC2 Instance Store

Question 64:

You need to access a file from two EC2 instances running in two separate AZs. Which of the following storage service can you use for this use case?

A. Amazon EBS
B. Amazon S3
C. Amazon EFS
D. Amazon EC2 Instance Store

Question 65:

Which of the following AWS services can you use to enrich events from SaaS applications using AWS AI/ML services to gain valuable insights?
A. Amazon SageMaker
B. Amazon EventBridge
C. AWS Glue
D. Amazon SNS

Test Set 1 – Answers

1. C	2. B	3. B	4. B	5. A	6. B	7. B	8. D	9. B	10. D
11. B	12. A	13. B	14. C	15. C	16. A	17. B	18. D	19. C	20. A
21. C	22. D	23. A	24. B	25. D	26. C	27. A	28. C	29. A	30. C
31. D	32. B	33. D	34. C	35. B	36. B	37. C, D	38. B	39. D	40. B
41. B	42. A	43. C	44. A	45. B	46. B	47. B	48. D	49. C	50. D
51. B	52. C	53. B	54. C	55. B	56. B	57. C	58. A	59. D	60. A, D
61. D	62. B	63. D	64. C	65. B					

One, who makes no mistakes, makes nothing at all

Test Set 2 - Practice Questions Only

Question 1:
Which of the following statements is not correct?
- A. Cloud computing can be a good choice for applications having high scalability requirements.
- B. Cloud computing can be a good choice for applications needing to reduce costs on their IT infrastructure.
- C. Applications including strong low-latency, security, audit, and regulatory SLA can be the right fit for cloud computing.
- D. Cloud computing can be a good choice for applications having high availability requirements.

Question 2:
Which of the following options can automate build, deployment, and save time using AWS best practices?
- A. AWS OpsWorks
- B. AWS Auto Deploy
- C. AWS Quick Starts
- D. AWS Elastic Beanstalk

Question 3:
Which of the following AWS services is free of cost?
- A. AWS IAM
- B. Amazon RedShift
- C. Amazon GaurdDuty
- D. Amazon Cloud Directory

Question 4:
To improve the security of the subnet, which of the following options would you recommend?
- A. Security Group
- B. Network ACLs
- C. AWS Shield

D. Virtual Private Cloud (VPC)

Question 5:
Which of the following architectures is not related to Cloud Computing?
A. Micro-Services
B. Service-Oriented Architecture (SOA)
C. Monolith
D. Client-Server

Question 6:
Which of the following AWS services can host Git-based repositories securely?
A. AWS CodePipeline
B. Amazon CodeGuru
C. AWS CodeStar
D. AWS CodeCommit

Question 7:
Which of the following AWS services provides a visual representation to help make a better decision about the utilization of AWS resources?
A. AWS CloudWatch Dashboard
B. AWS Organizations
C. AWS Budget
D. AWS Cost Explorer

Question 8:
One of your teammates, who is new to AWS, needs your help protecting an EC2 instance. He has deployed a Web application on that EC2 instance. The teammate wants to ensure that only HTTP and HTTPS traffic are allowed to the EC2 instance. Which of the following options would you recommend to your teammate to ensure that only HTTP and HTTPS traffic are allowed to the EC2 instance?
A. Network ACLs
B. AWS Shield
C. Virtual Private Cloud (VPC)
D. Security Group

Question 9:
Which of the following statements is INCORRECT with respect to Scalability, one of the design principles of the Reliability Pillar of AWS Well-Architected Framework?
A. Horizontal Scalability implies adding more machines to the existing machines.
B. Vertical Scalability implies adding more power, for example, RAM, to the machine.
C. Vertical Scalability helps in increasing the fault tolerance of the machine.
D. Horizontal Scalability helps in increasing the fault tolerance of the machine.

Question 10:
You have developed a microservice, which generally executes in a few seconds. However, the load on the microservice is inconsistent. Some days, there will be only a few calls to this microservice; however, there will be too many hits to this service on some other days. Which of the following is your best option for running the application cost-effectively?
A. EC2 Spot Instance

B. AWS Lambda
C. EC2 Reserved Instance
D. On-demand EC2 Instance

Question 11:
You are working as an AWS consultant for an organization and helping the organization in its cloud migration project. The organization plans to migrate some of its applications to the AWS cloud platform. Your client has some questions about AWS costs. For example, which of the following operations doesn't have a charge associated with it?
A. Outbound data transfer to the Internet from an EC2 instance
B. EBS snapshot
C. Inbound data transfer within the same region and same availability zone using private IP address
D. Outbound data transfer to the Internet from an S3 bucket

Question 12:
You have been asked to protect an EC2 instance from DDoS attacks with no additional cost. Which of the following AWS services or features provides basic protection against DDoS attacks?
A. Network ACLs
B. AWS Shield
C. Virtual Private Cloud (VPC)
D. Security Group

Question 13:
Which of the following defines the ability of a system to perform even upon the occurrence of unexpected events?
A. Durability
B. Resiliency
C. Consistency
D. Latency

Question 14:
You are planning to run a build job. The job is of predictable nature in terms of compute resource requirement. You have Reserved EC2 Instance available. Which of the following is a cost-effective to run the job using Docker container on AWS?
A. ECS on EC2
B. AWS Fargate
C. AWS Lambda
D. Either AWS Fargate or AWS Lambda as both of them serverless and cost effective

Question 15:
A late-stage startup uses AWS for all its development and production needs. The company would like to get separate invoices for both of its environments. Which of the following options would you recommend for this use case?
A. Create separate AWS accounts for the development and production environments to get the individual invoices.
B. Tag all resources in the AWS account as either "Dev" or "Prod." Then, use the tags to create separate invoices.

C. Use AWS Organizations to get separate invoices for the development and production environments.

D. Use AWS Cost Explorer to create separate invoices for the development and production environments.

Question 16:

You have been asked to set up a secure network like VPN. You will create subnets and assign your IP address range. Then, you will configure route tables and network gateways to manage how the Amazon EC2 resources inside your network are exposed to the Internet. Which of the following options will help you achieve this objective?

A. Network ACLs

B. AWS Shield

C. Virtual Private Cloud (VPC)

D. Security Group

Question 17:

Which of the following providers is of software-as-a-service (SaaS) cloud computing type?

A. Data Service Provider

B. Application Service Provider

C. Internet Service Provider

D. Infrastructure Service Provider

Question 18:

Which of the following options is one of the main advantages of deploying an RDS database with a Multi-AZ configuration?

A. Increases database availability

B. Improves database read performance

C. Keeps database available in case of a AWS Region failure

D. Reduces RDS cost

Question 19:

A fintech startup has formed an innovative group. The group has a limited budget; they can get more funding in the next quarter as more funds become available. In the meantime, they need to continue working on their various small POC (proofs-of-concept) types of projects by launching EC2 instances that can be interrupted. Which of the following options would be the most cost-effective for the group?

A. On-Demand Instance

B. Dedicated Host

C. Reserved Instance

D. Spot Instance

Question 20:

According to the AWS Shared Responsibility Model, which of the following options is the responsibility of an AWS customer?

A. Physical security of AWS data centers

B. Maintaining AWS global infrastructure servers' hardware

C. Encryption of objects on S3 buckets

D. Applying patches on RDS OS instances

Question 21:
To save costs to avoid buying and maintaining expensive servers, a start-up software organization would like to test and deploy its software solutions on the cloud platform. Therefore, the company is looking for a cloud provider which offers virtual server provisioning and on-demand storage services. Which of the following cloud computing delivery models is the start-up company looking for?
  A. Software-as-a-Service
  B. Platform-as-a-Service
  C. Application-as-a-Service
  D. Infrastructure-as-a-Service

Question 22:
Which of the following AWS Route 53 routing policies is the best alternative to improve the performance --related to latency -- by routing the requests to the AWS endpoint?
  A. Weighted routing policy
  B. Simple routing policy
  C. Failover routing policy
  D. Latency routing policy

Question 23:
You have joined an organization in their DevOps group. You are the first person in this group. You have been assigned some tasks to which you think you can find a better answer in the AWS forum, where the most frequent questions and requests from AWS customers are listed along with AWS-provided solutions. Which of the following options is the best fit for this use case?
  A. AWS Support Center
  B. AWS Marketplace
  C. AWS Knowledge Center
  D. AWS Service Health Dashboard

Question 24:
AWS platform can be accessed in many ways. For example, programmatic access is possible using AWS Access Key ID and AWS Secret Access Key. An AWS developer working in a DevOps team has been provided AWS Access Key ID and AWS Secret Access Key. However, the developer has lost the Access Key ID and Secret Access Key. How can the developer get the Access Key ID and Secret Access Key?

  A. Use the "Forgot Password"
  B. Request AWS admin to generate a new Access Key ID and Secret Access Key
  C. Credentials can only be generated once
  D. Raise a support ticket with the AWS Support

Question 25:
In which distribution model of cloud computing a software application is hosted on the cloud platform, and users can access the software using a web browser?
  A. Software-as-a-Service
  B. Platform-as-a-Service
  C. Infrastructure-as-a-Service
  D. Function-as-a-Service

Question 26:
Which of the following AWS services enables users to search and buy different types of software to use in their AWS environment?
- A. AWS Systems Manager
- B. AWS OpsWorks
- C. AWS Marketplace
- D. AWS Config

Question 27:
The AWS Trusted Advisor can analyze the AWS environment and provide recommendations about AWS best practices. In which of the following categories AWS Trusted Advisor provides recommendations about AWS best practices? (Select TWO)
- A. Service Limits
- B. Documentation
- C. Change Management
- D. Cost Optimization
- E. Elasticity

Question 28:
Which of the following AWS services can be used to generate, use, and manage encryption keys on the AWS Cloud platform?
- A. AWS GuardDuty
- B. AWS CloudHSM
- C. AWS Secrets Manager
- D. AWS Systems Manager

Question 29:
Which of the following design principles are related to Operation Excellence pillar of the AWS Well-Architected framework? (Select Two)
- A. Perform operations as code
- B. Enable traceability
- C. Anticipate failure
- D. Implement a strong identity foundation
- E. Test recover procedures

Question 30:
You have joined a small size company as an AWS consultant which is more of a Windows shop. The company is looking for a scalable storage system with low latency for many of its Windows-based applications. Which of the following AWS services would you recommend to the company?
- A. Amazon EBS
- B. Amazon FSx for Windows File Server
- C. Amazon FSx for Lustre
- D. Amazon EFS

Question 31:
Which of the following AWS services can provide data-driven business cases to help make sound planning and migration decisions when transitioning your business' on-premises IT infrastructure and applications to AWS Cloud?

A. AWS Billing and Cost Management
B. AWS Migration Evaluator
C. AWS Trusted Advisor
D. AWS Budgets

Question 32:
A small community bank has a hybrid deployment model: on-premises and AWS Cloud. The bank IT leadership team needs to be notified in case of any configuration change for security and compliance reasons. Which of the following AWS services can be used for this use case?
A. AWS Secrets Manager
B. AWS Config
C. AWS Trusted Advisor
D. Amazon Inspector

Question 33:
As a Cloud Practitioner, you have been asked to build a solution in such a way as the system's components should not negatively impact other components of the system. Based on the Well-Architected Framework which of the following options would you recommend?
A. stateless services
B. loosely coupled system
C. automatic data backup
D. request throttling

Question 34:
A large organization's IT infrastructure deployment includes a combination of on-premises deployment and AWS deployment. Which of the following deployment models does this deployment represent?
A. Private deployment
B. Hybrid deployment
C. Mixed deployment
D. Cloud deployment

Question 35:
A physical store sells gift items for various occasions such as Thanksgiving, Christmas, New Year, and Valentine's Day. Usually, during the holiday season, from October to January, there is more demand for gift items, and thus it drives the overall sale of the store. To increase its sale of gift items further and reach customers in other parts of the country, the store is planning to use an online store. However, they plan to run the online store only from November to February. Given the scenario, which EC2 instance would be best fit?
A. On-Demand Instances
B. Reserved Instances
C. Spot Instances
D. Dedicated Instances

Question 36:
You have developed a web chat application and deployed it on AWS. You would like to extend the application by adding a user management feature. Which of the following AWS services will you use to easily add user sign-up, sign-in, and access control for users?

A. Amazon Cognito
B. AWS Organizations
C. AWS Identity and Access Management (IAM)
D. AWS Single Sign-On (SSO)

Question 37:

You have been asked to migrate an application, which runs 24x7 in the on-premises data center, to the AWS Cloud. The application has a consistent load pattern. When migrating to the AWS Cloud, which of the following economic features will benefit you the most?

A. pay less by using more
B. pay-as-you-go
C. save by reserving resources
D. pay-per-compute-time

Question 38:

An online casino company's engineering team has completed the project and deployed the application on the AWS cloud platform. The company would like to block users from certain geographies from accessing the application. Which of the following AWS services can be used for this use case? (Select two)

A. Route 53 Geolocation Routing Policy
B. AWS Protect
C. CloudWatch
D. AWS WAF
E. AWS Shield

Question 39:

Which of the following statements are true about Cost Allocation Tags in AWS Billing? (Select two)

A. Each tag key must be unique but can have multiple values.
B. Only user-defined tags need to be activated before they can appear in reports.
C. Each tag key must be unique, and it can only have one value.
D. Tags are a mandatory configuration item to run reports; they help in organizing resources.
E. Both user-defined tags and AWS generated tags need to be activated before they can appear in Cost Explorer or in Cost Allocation report.

Question 40:

You have deployed a Web application, which is an online clothing retail store. From the web server access logs, you find the access pattern of one particular IP address a bit suspicious based on the IP address' access patterns. You would like to stop this IP address from accessing your web application. Which of the following security control mechanisms can be used to deny traffic from a specific IP address?

A. AWS GuardDuty
B. Security Group
C. VPC Flow Logs
D. Network ACL

Question 41:

A company's on-premises data center and its applications are connected to AWS using Direct Connect (Dedicated) Service. What type of Cloud Deployment Model is the company utilizing?
- A. Public Cloud
- B. Private Cloud
- C. Hybrid Cloud
- D. Multi-Cloud

Question 42:

AWS Storage Gateway service supports many types of storage gateways. Which of the following options are correct with regards to different storage gateway types supported by the AWS Storage Gateway service?
- A. Object Gateway, Tape Gateway, and Volume Gateway
- B. Object Storage Gateway, File Gateway, and Block Gateway
- C. Tape Gateway, File Gateway, and Volume Gateway
- D. Tape Gateway, File Gateway, and Block Gateway

Question 43:

John and Mary work for a startup company. Each of them has an AWS account in AWS Organizations. Mary has six Reserved Instances (RIs) of the same type; however, John has no Reserved Instances. Both of them are working on AWS-related projects. One day both of them launch some instances during one particular hour -- Mary launches three instances, and John launches six for nine instances. Which of the following statements are correct about consolidated billing in AWS Organizations? (Select two)

- A. John receives the cost benefits from Mary's Reserved Instances only if John launches the instances in the same Region where Mary has purchased the Reserved Instances.
- B. John doesn't get any credit for RIs as John hasn't purchased any Reserved Instances.
- C. AWS bills three instances as Reserved Instances (RIs) while six instances as Regular Instances.
- D. John gets credit for using Mary's RIs only if John launches the instances in the same Region for which Mary has purchased RIs.
- E. AWS bills three instances as regular instances while six instances as Reserved Instances.

Question 44:

Which of the following services/tools can you use to provide temporary security credentials to trusted users to control access to AWS resources?
- A. AWS Security Token Service
- B. AWS Single Sign-On
- C. AWS Web Application Firewall
- D. Amazon Cognito

Question 45:

Which of the following statements are correct with regards to AWS Lambda? (Select two)
- A. AWS Lambda lets you run code without managing or provisioning servers.
- B. AWS Lambda provides access to the underlying operating system.
- C. AWS Lambda allows you to install databases on the underlying operating system.
- D. When using AWS Lambda, you pay for the compute time used by a workload.

E. AWS Lambda allows you to orchestrate and manage Docker containers to facilitate complex containerized applications on AWS.

Question 46:
Which of the following statements is NOT true for KMS encryption on S3?
- A. The KMS key can be rotated automatically.
- B. The KMS key is integrated with CloudTrail for auditing purposes.
- C. The KMS key cannot be deleted.
- D. The KMS key cannot be rotated manually

Question 47:
A company wants to migrate its IT infrastructure and applications to the AWS Cloud so that it can release new features in quick iterations using different AWS services. When the company is making this argument, which of the following features of cloud computing the company would like to leverage?
- A. Elasticity
- B. Scalability
- C. Reliability
- D. Agility

Question 48:
A photo-sharing web application wants to store thumbnails of user-uploaded images on Amazon S3. The thumbnails are not used regularly but need to be accessed immediately if needed from the web application. Furthermore, the thumbnails can be regenerated easily if they are lost. Which of the following options is the most cost-effective way to store these thumbnails on S3?
- A. Use S3 Standard Infrequent Access (Standard-IA) to store the thumbnails
- B. Use S3 Glacier to store the thumbnails
- C. Use S3 Standard to store the thumbnails
- D. Use S3 One-Zone Infrequent Access (One-Zone IA) to store the thumbnails

Question 49:
An AWS developer has deployed an application on an EC2 instance. In order for the application to run successfully, the application needs access to a few AWS resources such as S3, and DynamoDB. First, the developer added their credentials to the EC2 instance so that the EC2 instance can have access to the resources that the application needs. However, in review, the idea of AWS developer using its credential is not allowed by the DevOps team lead as the developer's AWS credential (access key id and secret access key id) is considered a long-term credential and there is a risk of compromise when using an IAM user's access key on EC2 instances. Which one is the other alternative to provide access to the AWS resources to the application running on the EC2 instance?
- A. User IAM tag
- B. Use IAM group
- C. Use IAM role
- D. There is no alternate way except using an IAM user's credential

Question 50:
An AWS Customer is using AWS services in many scenarios. In which scenario, the customer may not get an economic benefit of using the AWS cloud platform?
- A. The customer is using S3 Glacier Storage service.

B. The customer is using Spot instances to run ETL batch jobs.

C. The customer is using AWS Reserved instances for a relatively predictable and consistent resource demand.

D. The customer is running a dedicated MySQL Database server on AWS using its own CPU bound license (BYOL).

Question 51:

Which of the following statements is INCORRECT about AWS Auto Scaling?

A. New instances can automatically be registered to a Load Balancer.

B. Unhealthy instances can be removed automatically.

C. More EC2 instances can be added to scale out to match an increase in demand; conversely, EC2 instances can be removed to scale in to match reduced demand.

D. AWS Shield is automatically deployed to handle DDoS attacks when the attack is detected.

Question 52:

Which of the following options can you use to control the incoming HTTP traffic to an Amazon EC2 instance?

A. Route Table

B. Security Group

C. NACL (Network ACL)

D. AWS Resource Group

Question 53:

Which of the following options is the advantage of AWS Cloud over traditional on-premises data centers?

A. Trade capital expense for variable expense

B. No guesstimate of infrastructure capacity needs

C. Provides lower latency because of on-premises servers

D. Increase in speed and agility by keeping servers ready before go-live to save costs

E. Make a capacity estimate before go-live to save costs

Question 54:

Several Amazon EC2 instances are deployed in different Availability Zones of an AWS Region. These EC2 instances need to access a file stored centrally on a system. Which of the following services can be used for this use case?

A. Elastic Block Store (EBS) Volume

B. Elastic File System (EFS)

C. EC2 Instance Store

D. Amazon S3

Question 55:

Which of the following security best practices does AWS suggest for Identity and Access Management (IAM)? (Select two)

A. When creating IAM policies, follow the least privileges principles – grant minimal permissions which are required to perform a task.

B. Enable AWS multi-factor authentication (MFA) only on AWS root user account.

C. Don't share security credentials between accounts -- use IAM roles, instead.

D. Do not change passwords and access keys once created as changing credentials will break the deployed applications.

E. Share your AWS account root user credentials only if troubleshooting a complex EC2 instance issue.

Question 56:

Which statement is correct about AWS Region?

A. All AWS services have a Region scope.

B. All AWS services have global scope.

C. Most AWS services are specific to a Region; however, some have global scope.

D. An AWS service is specific to an AWS Availability Zone.

Question 57:

Which of the following statements is correct about different AWS Storage services?

A. S3 is file-based storage. EBS is block-based storage, and EFS is object-based storage.

B. S3 is object-based storage. EBS is file-based storage, and EFS is block-based storage.

C. S3 is block-based storage. EBS is object-based storage, and EFS is file-based storage.

D. S3 is object-based storage. EBS is block-based storage, and EFS is file-based storage.

Question 58:

You are working as an AWS cloud engineer for a startup company. After a security review, it was found that there is a need to enhance security at the subnet level. What would be your best choice to improve security at the subnet level, given the choices below?

A. Network Access Control List (NACL)

B. Virtual Private Cloud (VPC)

C. Security Group

D. VPC Peering

Question 59:

Which of the following statements is INCORRECT concerning Scalability, a design principle of Reliability Pillar of AWS Well-Architected Framework?

A. Horizontal scalability implies adding more resources to the existing pool of resources

B. Vertical scalability implies adding more power (CPU, RAM) to the machine or node

C. Vertical scalability helps in increasing fault tolerance of the machine or node

D. Horizontal scalability helps in increasing fault tolerance of the cluster

Question 60:

A company's flagship product runs on several Amazon EC2 instances. As per the new policies, the cloud team is looking for the best way to provide secure shell access to AWS EC2 instances without opening new ports or using public IP addresses. Which of the following AWS services can be used for this scenario?

A. Amazon EC2 Instance Connect

B. Amazon Route 53

C. AWS Systems Manager Session Manager

D. Amazon Inspector

Question 61:
A mid-size e-commerce company planning to move to the AWS Cloud. Which of the following statement is correct with respect to the cost savings when it moves to the AWS Cloud?

    A. Cost savings on the physical security of data centers
    B. Cost savings on SaaS applications license fee
    C. Cost savings on buying computer hardware
    D. Cost savings on project manager salary
    E. Cost savings on developer salary

Question 62:
Which of the following AWS services helps in improving the availability and performance of applications with local or global users using the AWS global network?
    A. Amazon CloudFront
    B. Elastic Load Balancer
    C. Global Accelerator
    D. Amazon Route 53

Question 63:
Which of the following AWS services publishes up-to-the-minute information on the general status and availability of all AWS services in all the AWS Regions of the AWS Cloud platform?
    A. Amazon CloudWatch
    B. AWS CloudFormation
    C. AWS Service Health Dashboard
    D. AWS Personal Health Dashboard

Question 64:
A company has an application that delivers objects from S3 to users. Of late, some users spread across the globe have complained of slow response times. Which of the following additional steps would help build a cost-effective solution and help ensure that the users get an optimal response to objects from S3?
    A. Use S3 Replication to replicate the objects to AWS Regions closest to the users.
    B. Ensure S3 Transfer Acceleration is enabled to ensure all users get the desired response times.
    C. Place an Elastic Load Balancer in front of S3 to distribute the load across S3.
    D. Use CloudFront with S3

Question 65:
Which of the following options can be used to access AWS services? (Select Three)
    A. AWS Management Console
    B. AWS Secrets Manager
    C. AWS Command Line Interface (AWS CLI)
    D. Amazon API Gateway
    E. AWS Systems Manager
    F. AWS Software Developer Kit (AWS SDK)

Test Set 2 – Answers

1. C	2. C	3. A	4. B	5. C	6. D	7. A	8. D	9. C	10. B
11. C	12. B	13. A	14. A	15. A	16. C	17. B	18. A	19. D	20. C
21. C	22. D	23. C	24. B	25. A	26. C	27. A, D	28. B	29. A, C	30. B
31. B	32. B	33. B	34. B	35. A	36. A	37. C	38. A, D	39. C, E	40. D
41. C	42. C	43. A, E	44. A	45. A, D	46. D	47. D	48. D	49. C	50. D
51. D	52. B	53. A, B	54. B	55. A, C	56. C	57. D	58. A	59. C	60. C
61. A, C	62. C	63. C	64. D	65. A, C, F					

References

- https://docs.aws.amazon.com/AWSEC2/latest/UserGuide/concepts.html
- https://aws.amazon.com/autoscaling/
- https://aws.amazon.com/s3/
- https://aws.amazon.com/ebs/
- https://aws.amazon.com/iam/
- https://docs.aws.amazon.com/vpc/latest/userguide/VPC_Internet_Gateway.html
- https://aws.amazon.com/directconnect/
- https://aws.amazon.com/rds/
- https://aws.amazon.com/elasticache/
- https://aws.amazon.com/redis/
- https://aws.amazon.com/emr/
- https://aws.amazon.com/kinesis/
- https://aws.amazon.com/ses/
- https://aws.amazon.com/sns
- https://aws.amazon.com/ecs/
- https://aws.amazon.com/location/
- https://aws.amazon.com/api-gateway/
- https://aws.amazon.com/amplify/
- https://aws.amazon.com/sagemaker/
- https://aws.amazon.com/workspaces/
- https://aws.amazon.com/workmail/
- https://aws.amazon.com/workdocs/
- https://aws.amazon.com/about-aws/global-infrastructure/regions_az/
- https://en.wikipedia.org/wiki/Cloud_computing
- https://www.backblaze.com/blog/vm-vs-containers/
- https://www.ibm.com/cloud/blog/containers-vs-vms
- https://www.vxchnge.com/blog/different-types-of-cloud-computing
- https://www.cloudflare.com/learning/serverless/what-is-serverless/
- https://aws.amazon.com/serverless/
- https://www.ibm.com/cloud/learn/serverless
- https://dzone.com/articles/serverless-services-on-aws-an-overview
- https://docs.docker.com/desktop/mac/install/
- https://docs.docker.com/desktop/windows/install/
- https://www.zdnet.com/article/using-google-authenticator-heres-why-you-should-get-rid-of-it/
- https://hub.docker.com/
- https://docs.docker.com/engine/reference/commandline/docker/
- https://en.wikipedia.org/wiki/Multi-factor_authentication
- https://www.aboutamazon.com/news/aws/partnering-with-the-nfl-to-transform-player-health-and-safety
- https://www.contino.io/insights/whos-using-aws
- https://press.aboutamazon.com/news-releases/news-release-details/twitter-selects-aws-strategic-provider-serve-timelines
- https://docs.aws.amazon.com/whitepapers/latest/aws-overview/security-and-compliance.html
- https://www.zdnet.com/article/using-google-authenticator-heres-why-you-should-get-rid-of-it/
- https://www.youtube.com/watch?v=0R23JRR671I

- https://www.reddit.com/r/askscience/comments/5imnis/how_do_gemalto_tokens_work_curious_how_the_system/

- https://www.youtube.com/watch?v=hiKPPy584Mg
- https://docs.aws.amazon.com/vpc/latest/userguide/flow-logs.html
- https://docs.aws.amazon.com/AWSEC2/latest/UserGuide/security-group-rules.html
- https://docs.aws.amazon.com/vpc/latest/userguide/vpc-network-acls.html
- https://docs.aws.amazon.com/AWSEC2/latest/UserGuide/ec2-security-groups.html
- https://docs.aws.amazon.com/vpc/latest/userguide/working-with-vpcs.html
- https://docs.aws.amazon.com/vpc/latest/userguide/vpc-nat-gateway.html
- https://aws.amazon.com/directconnect/
- https://docs.aws.amazon.com/vpc/latest/tgw/what-is-transit-gateway.html
- https://docs.aws.amazon.com/vpc/latest/peering/what-is-vpc-peering.html
- https://docs.aws.amazon.com/vpn/latest/s2svpn/VPC_VPN.html
- https://docs.aws.amazon.com/vpc/latest/userguide/flow-logs.html
- https://docs.aws.amazon.com/vpn/latest/s2svpn/your-cgw.html
- https://www.youtube.com/watch?v=UANm3DC_IxE
- https://aws.amazon.com/cloud-directory/
- https://aws.amazon.com/organizations
- https://aws.amazon.com/blogs/apn/the-6-pillars-of-the-aws-well-architected-framework/
- https://docs.aws.amazon.com/wellarchitected/latest/framework/sec-design.html
- https://docs.aws.amazon.com/wellarchitected/latest/operational-excellence-pillar/design-principles.html
- https://docs.aws.amazon.com/wellarchitected/latest/performance-efficiency-pillar/design-principles.html
- https://docs.aws.amazon.com/wellarchitected/latest/reliability-pillar/design-principles.html
- https://docs.aws.amazon.com/wellarchitected/latest/cost-optimization-pillar/design-principles.html
- https://aws.amazon.com/blogs/apn/the-6-pillars-of-the-aws-well-architected-framework/
- https://www.botmetric.com/blog/aws-cloud-architecture-desig n-principles/
- https://aws-certified-cloud-practitioner.fandom.com/wiki/1.3_List_the_different_cloud_architecture_design_principles
- https://aws.amazon.com/premiumsupport/plans/enterprise/
- https://aws.amazon.com/premiumsupport/plans/developers/
- https://aws.amazon.com/premiumsupport/plans
- https://aws.amazon.com/premiumsupport/knowledge-center/report-aws-abuse/
- https://aws.amazon.com/premiumsupport/knowledge-center/
- https://status.aws.amazon.com/
- https://aws.amazon.com/aup/
- https://aws.amazon.com/premiumsupport/knowledge-center/
- https://docs.aws.amazon.com/rekognition/latest/dg/recommendations-camera-streaming-video.html
- https://github.com/aws-samples
- https://www.youtube.com/watch?v=v662kWVBmdc
- https://docs.aws.amazon.com/codecommit/latest/userguide/welcome.html
- https://aws.amazon.com/codestar/
- https://aws.amazon.com/codeguru/
- https://aws.amazon.com/codebuild/
- https://aws.amazon.com/codeartifact/
- https://aws.amazon.com/quickstart
- https://docs.aws.amazon.com/AWSCloudFormation/latest/UserGuide/Welcome.html

- https://aws.amazon.com/rds/instance-types/
- https://www.amazonaws.cn/en/rds/features/multi-az/
- https://aws.amazon.com/rds/
- https://aws.amazon.com/rds/features/read-replicas/
- https://aws.amazon.com/dms/
- https://docs.aws.amazon.com/whitepapers/latest/disaster-recovery-workloads-on-aws/disaster-recovery-options-in-the-cloud.html
- https://aws.amazon.com/blogs/architecture/disaster-recovery-dr-architecture-on-aws-part-iii-pilot-light-and-warm-standby/
- https://jayendrapatil.com/aws-classic-load-balancer-vs-application-load-balancer/
- https://docs.aws.amazon.com/elasticloadbalancing/latest/userguide/what-is-load-balancing.html
- https://docs.aws.amazon.com/elasticloadbalancing/latest/gateway/introduction.html
- https://aws.amazon.com/blogs/aws/new-predictive-scaling-for-ec2-powered-by-machine-learning/
- https://www.datadoghq.com/blog/why-do-aws-cloudwatch-and-datadog-seem-to-disagree/
- https://docs.aws.amazon.com/AWSEC2/latest/UserGuide/viewing_metrics_with_cloudwatch.html
- https://docs.aws.amazon.com/AWSEC2/latest/UserGuide/dedicated-hosts-overview.html
- https://aws.amazon.com/ec2/spot/
- https://docs.aws.amazon.com/whitepapers/latest/cost-optimization-reservation-models/standard-vs.-convertible-offering-classes.html
- https://docs.aws.amazon.com/AWSEC2/latest/UserGuide/concepts.html
- https://docs.aws.amazon.com/AWSEC2/latest/UserGuide/accelerated-computing-instances.html
- https://docs.aws.amazon.com/AWSEC2/latest/UserGuide/placement-groups.html
- https://aws.amazon.com/ec2/instance-types/
- https://aws.amazon.com/iam/
- https://docs.aws.amazon.com/IAM/latest/UserGuide/best-practices.html
- https://docs.aws.amazon.com/IAM/latest/UserGuide/id_credentials_access-keys.html
- https://docs.aws.amazon.com/IAM/latest/UserGuide/access_policies.html#access_policies-json
- https://aws.amazon.com/types-of-cloud-computing/
- https://www.10thmagnitude.com/opex-vs-capex-the-real-cloud-computing-cost-advantage/
- https://ieeexplore.ieee.org/document/6149074
- https://www.cloudzero.com/blog/cloud-tco
- https://www.wired.com/insights/2012/03/licensing-cloud/
- https://aws.amazon.com/blogs/enterprise-strategy/rightsizing-infrastructure-can-cut-costs-36/
- https://voleer.com/blog/2019/9/17/reduce-your-cloud-costs-with-these-5-strategies
- http://tsologic.com/resources/economics-of-cloud-migration-2017/
- https://docs.aws.amazon.com/IAM/latest/UserGuide/id_credentials_mfa.html
- https://aws.amazon.com/iam/features/mfa/
- https://fidoalliance.org/
- https://docs.aws.amazon.com/IAM/latest/UserGuide/id_credentials_mfa_enable_fido.html

thank you!

Congratulations on completing this book! I hope you found this book helpful.

If you enjoyed this book and felt that the book was helpful to add value to your life, we ask you to please take the time to review it. Your honest feedback is highly appreciated. If you noticed any problem, please let us know by emailing us at support@knodax.com before writing any review online. It will be beneficial for us to improve the quality of our books.

Made in the USA
Middletown, DE
04 September 2023